Wisdom & Creation

The Theology of Wisdom Literature

LEO G. PERDUE

ABINGDON PRESS
Nashville

WISDOM AND CREATION

Copyright © 1994 by Abingdon Press

This book is printed on recycled, acid-free paper.

Library of Congress Cataloging-in-Publication Data

Perdue, Leo G.
  Wisdom and creation: the theology of wisdom & literature/Leo G. Perdue.
    p. cm.
  Includes bibliographical references.
  ISBN 0-687-45626-6 (alk. paper)
  1. Wisdom literature—Criticism. interpretation, etc.
2. Creation—History of doctrines.   I. Title.
BS1455.P39 1994
223'.06—dc20
                                         94-17507
                                       CIP

All Scripture quotations are the author's own translation.

94 95 96 97 98 99 00 01 02 03 — 10 9 8 7 6 5 4 3 2 1

MANUFACTURED IN THE UNITED STATES OF AMERICA

In memory of
Professor Walther Zimmerli
(January 20, 1907–December 4, 1983)

CONTENTS

PART I. WISDOM AND OLD TESTAMENT THEOLOGY: ISSUES AND APPROACHES

PART II. THE THEOLOGY OF WISDOM LITERATURE

CONTENTS

ABBREVIATIONS

AB	Anchor Bible
ABRL	Anchor Bible Reference Library
AJSL	*American Journal of Semitic Languages and Literature*
AnBib	Analecta biblica
ANET	J. B. Pritchard (ed.), *Ancient Near Eastern Texts*
ATD	Das Alte Testament Deutsch
ATR	*Anglican Theological Review*
BA	*Biblical Archaeologist*
BASOR	*Bulletin of the American Schools of Oriental Research*
BBB	Bonner biblische Beiträge
BETL	Bibliotheca ephemeridum theologicarum lovaniensium
BHT	Beiträge zur historischen Theologie
Bib	*Biblica*
BKAT	Biblischer Kommentar: Altes Testament
BN	*Biblische Notizen*
BO	*Bibliotheca orientalis*
BT	*The Bible Translator*
BWANT	Beiträge zur Wissenschaft vom Alten und Neuen Testament
BWL	*Babylonian Wisdom Literature*

11

ABBREVIATIONS

BZAW	Beihefte zur *ZAW*
CBC	Cambridge Bible Commentary
CBQ	*Catholic Biblical Quarterly*
CBQMS	Catholic Biblical Quarterly—Monograph Series
ETL	*Ephemerides theologicae lovanienses*
EvT	*Evangelische Theologie*
FOTL	Forms of Old Testament Literature
FRLANT	Forschungen zur Religion und Literatur des Alten und Neuen Testaments
HAR	*Hebrew Annual Review*
HAT	Handbuch zum Alten Testament
HBT	*Horizons in Biblical Theology*
HdO	Handbuch der Orientalistik
HR	*History of Religions*
HSM	Harvard Semitic Monographs
HSS	Harvard Semitic Studies
HUCA	*Hebrew Union College Annual*
IB	*Interpreter's Bible*
ICC	International Critical Commentary
IDB	G. A. Buttrick (ed.), *Interpreter's Dictionary of the Bible*
Int	*Interpretation*
JAAR	*Journal of the American Academy of Religion*
JAOS	*Journal of the American Oriental Society*
JBL	*Journal of Biblical Literature*
JCS	*Journal of Cuneiform Studies*
JEOL	*Jaarbericht . . . ex oriente lux*
JNES	*Journal of Near Eastern Studies*
JNSL	*Journal of Northwest Semitic Languages*
JQR	*Jewish Quarterly Review*
JSOTSup	Journal for the Study of the Old Testament—Supplemental Series
JSS	*Journal of Semitic Studies*

ABBREVIATIONS

JTS	*Journal of Theological Studies*
KAT	Kommentar zum Alten Testament
KD	*Kerygma und Dogma*
MT	Masoretic Text
MVAG	Mitteilungen der vorderasiatisch-ägyptischen Gesellschaft
NEB	New English Bible
OBO	Orbis biblicus et orientalis
OrAnt	*Oriens antiquus*
OTL	Old Testament Library
OTS	*Oudtestamentisch Studiën*
PTMS	Pittsburgh Theological Monograph Series
RB	*Revue biblique*
RevExp	*Review and Expositor*
RHPR	Revue d'histoire et de philosophie religieuses
RHR	Revue de l'histoire des religions
RSR	*Recherches de science religieuse*
SBLDS	SBL Dissertation Series
SBLMS	SBL Monograph Series
SBS	Stuttgarter Bibelstudien
SBT	Studies in Biblical Theology
SAIW	James L. Crenshaw, ed. *Studies in Ancient Israelite Wisdom*
SJT	*Scottish Journal of Theology*
SPOA	*Les sagesse du Proche-Orient Ancien*
SUNT	Studien zur Umwelt des Neuen Testaments
TDOT	*Theological Dictionary of the Old Testament*
TQ	*Theologische Quartalschrift*
TS	*Theological Studies*
TLZ	*Theologische Literaturzeitung*
TWAT	G. J. Botterweck and H. Ringgren (eds.), *Theologisches Wörterbuch zum Alten Testament*
UF	*Ugarit-Forschungen*

ABBREVIATIONS

VT	*Vetus Testamentum*
VTSup	Vetus Testamentum, Supplements
WMANT	Wissenschaftliche Mongraphien zum Alten und Neuen Testament
WO	Die Welt des Orients
ZÄS	*Zeitschrift für ägyptische Sprache und Altertumskunde*
ZAW	*Zeitschrift für die alttestamentliche Wissenschaft*
ZTK	*Zeitschrift für Theologie und Kirche*

PREFACE

This volume began to take shape during my sabbatical year in Göttingen in 1982–83. I spent that year as a Fulbright senior research scholar in the theological faculty of the Georg-August Universität. My *Gastgeber* for that most stimulating time was Professor Doctor Walther Zimmerli, who, while *emeritiert*, continued to lecture at the Theologicum and to write at a prodigious pace. At the time Herr Zimmerli was working on a commentary on Genesis and a larger, more ambitious project—a theology of the prophets. I remember him speaking of his hope to write one day a comprehensive theology of the Old Testament, but he wished first to complete his work on the prophets. Herr Zimmerli was interested in my own work on wisdom theology, even though my thoughts and ways of proceeding were still in an embryonic, clumsy form. He was the one who convinced me of the thesis that the sages worked out of a theology of creation and providence. Many other insights that have been incorporated into this present volume came from conversations with him over the course of that wonderful year.

Herr Zimmerli was more than a splendid lecturer and prolific scholar whose theological writings, interpretations of wisdom literature, and commentary on Ezekiel led to his much deserved reputation as one of the twentieth century's truly great biblical scholars. He was also a humane, kind, and unpretentious man who bore the many honors bestowed upon him with sincere humility. His deep faith and piety were obvious to all. I recall how he would open each class with a well-known German hymn, with his theological students joining in the singing. He would then move into his lecture, always rigorously scientific and carefully argued, but afterward, as was his custom, he would conclude with a

15

hermeneutical application for contemporary faith. Praise, learning, and faith—carefully delineated and yet made one.

Herr Zimmerli suffered a stroke toward the end of that academic year, shortly before I returned to the United States in the summer of 1983. He died a short time later. During a subsequent sabbatical in Chicago in 1987–88, I was to learn much about metaphor and imagination. While the methodological formulation of the theology of the sages in this volume draws a great deal from what I learned that year in Hyde Park, the stimulus for what follows I owe to Herr Zimmerli. I dedicate this volume to that brilliant and kind man, for my memories of him are among my most cherished.

PART I

Wisdom and Old Testament Theology: Issues and Approaches

Where Shall Wisdom Be Found?

OLD TESTAMENT THEOLOGY AND WISDOM LITERATURE

INTRODUCTION

The setting forth of the theology of wisdom literature is a difficult challenge for three reasons. First, most Old Testament theologies written since the Second World War have given little consideration to the concept of wisdom and to wisdom literature.[1] This benign neglect may be attributed to the view that the themes of salvation history and Sinai (covenant and law) are primary to biblical faith, while creation is secondary. Since the theological grounding of wisdom literature is creation and not redemptive history, covenant, and law—at least until Ben Sira in the early part of the second century B.C.E.—biblical theologians' lack of serious interest in the writings of the sages is not particularly surprising.

Second, there are few comprehensive articulations of the theology of wisdom literature. Most studies to date have limited their ambitions to setting forth prolegomena—that is, descriptions of what a fully developed wisdom theology would look like. While these prolegomena are helpful, their arguments cannot be sustained without a thorough treatment of the literature itself.

Third, with the recent fragmentation of method for doing biblical research, including the various approaches to Old Testament theology, dominant paradigms for interpretation no longer elicit the same confidence they once did. In many ways, we are back to the task of articulating methodologies that enable the task of interpretation to move forward. While great excitement is occasioned by these new ventures into methodology, there is also considerable risk. The persuasiveness of any interpretation depends to a large extent on how compelling the procedure for getting at the meaning of texts may or may not be.

In any event, this book undertakes the task of rendering the theology of the sages by interpreting through a paradigm of metaphor and imagination the five major wisdom books: Proverbs, Job, Qoheleth (Ecclesiastes), Ben Sira, and the Wisdom of Solomon. The thesis is that creation theology and its correlative affirmation, providence, were at the center of the sages' understanding of God, the world, and humanity.

THE PLACE OF WISDOM IN OLD TESTAMENT THEOLOGY

While the dominant trend in Old Testament theology has been either to neglect wisdom literature or to consider it to be outside the mainstream of Israelite faith, some scholars have offered important insights into both the theology of the sages and how it relates to the larger biblical theology. We begin with the place of wisdom in several of the leading presentations of Old Testament theology since the Second World War and then move to the different approaches to understanding the theology of the sages by contemporary wisdom scholars.

Wisdom and the Paradigm of History[2]

A leading member of the Biblical Theology movement, G. Ernest Wright provided perhaps the most formidable synthesis of historical-critical research, biblical theology, and field archaeology to appear in America in the post World War II period.[3] According to Brevard Childs, the Biblical Theology movement that dominated North American understanding of the Bible for a generation (ca. 1950 to 1970) had several distinguishing features and interests: the recovery of the theological character of the Bible, especially redemptive history; the unity of the Bible; revelation in history; a distinctive biblical mentality that was verbal, personal, and dynamic; and the contrast of Israel's society and religion with its pagan environment (e.g., a historical consciousness over against myth and nature). These features were at the heart of Wright's work.

As an Old Testament scholar, Wright's historical-critical research sought to reconstruct Israelite history and to place the interpretation of biblical books within that narrative scheme.[4] As a field archaeologist, Wright helped to shape biblical archaeology that attempted to locate biblical texts and Israelite religion within their proper historical and cultural settings of the ancient Near East. As a theologian, he looked to history, specifically the history of God's events of the election and redemption of Israel, to fill the content of Israelite faith.

Wright sought to define and delineate what the original writers and editors of the Bible thought about God, Israel, creation, and humanity, ideas he saw to be an integral part of Israelite religion and Judaism. However, history shaped both the method and the content of Old Testament theology for Wright. He concluded that Israelite faith centered on salvation history—that is, God acted in great redemptive events to determine Israel's destiny and, through Israel, that of the larger world. These "mighty acts" of God in Israel's early faith included the promise to the patriarchs, the exodus from Egypt, the wilderness wandering, covenant and law at Sinai, the entrance into the land of Canaan, and the covenant with David. Creation was important, although Wright thought its affirmations were construed primarily through Israel's covenant relationship with God (i.e., the God who met Israel in its history and entered into a covenant was at the same time the creator and sustainer of heaven and earth).[5] Even so, creation for Wright took a backseat to history. This was due not only to Wright's insistence on the importance of the themes of salvation history in the Old Testament, but also to what he considered to be distinctive for Israelite religion among the religions of the ancient Near East. Wright contrasted the Israelite emphasis on salvation history with the mythical understandings of reality that focused on nature. Fertility gods of ancient Near Eastern myths were the personifications of natural forces who through the origination and sustaining of creation brought their worshipers life, while Israel's God was a God of history. Wright thought Israel's presentation of mighty acts of God in history was unique among the cultures of the ancient Near East.[6]

As a theologian and hermeneut seeking to engage the Old Testament with contemporary faith, Wright's major premise, understandably so, given what has been said, was that history was the avenue for divine revelation and redemption. "Faith was communicated . . . through the forms of history, and unless history is taken seriously one cannot comprehend biblical faith which triumphantly affirms the meaning of history."[7] For Wright, contemporary hermeneutics involves the same dialectic that one finds in the Old Testament: proclamation and response. The faithful community proclaimed and then confessed the acts of divine salvation. Wright defined and shaped his own hermeneutical appropriation of Scripture within the major categories of neo-orthodoxy: the sovereignty and providence of God, the eschatological act of divine redemption in Jesus Christ, salvation through encounter with the Word, the centrality of Christ as Lord and Redeemer, the corruption of human nature, justification by faith, and the authority of Scripture.

When it came to wisdom literature, Wright found writings with a theological locus in creation, not history. He struggled to answer the fundamental question of how to bring this corpus of canonical texts within his under-

21

standing of the Old Testament. Wright wrote: "In any attempt to outline a discussion of Biblical faith it is the wisdom literature which offers the chief difficulty because it does not fit into the type of faith exhibited in the historical and prophetic literatures. In it there is no explicit reference to or development of the doctrine of history, election, or covenant."[8]

Wisdom's international origin and character also troubled Wright. If one is searching for the distinctive character of Israelite faith, how is it possible to give a significant place to texts that admittedly reflect religious and moral views that are common to many ancient Near Eastern cultures? Israel's distinctiveness resided in its predilection for history, while pagans believed their gods were cosmic powers who were revealed in the order of the cosmos.[9] Furthermore, wisdom's epistemological approach to revelation and moral instruction combined the powers of observation of nature and social life with critical reflection on human experience. This approach was open as well to pagan nations. There was no place in wisdom literature for special revelation through either history or law. According to Wright, wisdom articulates a clear view of natural revelation, but it does not set forth a theology of the Word that proclaims and interprets the meaning of history.

The theological implications of wisdom's rather one-sided reliance on reason and experience also bothered Wright. What of the doctrine of the fall, which led to the corruption of human nature and placed severe restraints on the capacity of reason and experience to come to a knowledge of God? Wisdom has no place for the transformation of life and reconciliation through the salvific actions of God. What of eschatology, which points to the final consummation of creation and history through divine action?[10] Hebrew wisdom, prior to Ben Sira, has no place for eschatology. (salvation theory)

Wright understood creation as both the prologue to history and its eschatological climax in the new heaven and new earth. Creation stands at both the beginning and the end of the divine-human drama, but it has very limited importance for what occurs in between. Wisdom could provide guidance for the moral life, but it did not articulate a distinctive faith centered in the salvific actions of God.

While giving a more important role to creation and wisdom in Old Testament theology than did Wright, Gerhard von Rad continued to place greater theological weight on the category of salvation event.[11] Approaching Old Testament theology through the method of tradition history, von Rad also argued that "the Old Testament is a history book."[12] In his two-volume theology, von Rad attempted to combine a history of Israelite religion, placed at the beginning of volume one, with the developing traditions of Old Testament theology. He sought to trace the history of the different traditions of Old Testament faith, recognizing the difficulty and at times the impossibility of reconstructing the actual events that these traditions celebrated. Subsequently, von Rad searched out the history of developing traditions that embodied Israelite faith, and not the history of events in the life of Israel.

Central to von Rad's understanding of Old Testament theology was the presence of an ancient creed, embedded within a larger narrative context. Von Rad argued that Israel confessed this "little creed" within a liturgical context of festival. This confession contained the following list of redemptive acts of God: the promise to the fathers, the exodus from Egypt, the wandering in the wilderness, and the gift of the promised land. Sinai covenant and law were absent in the earliest formulations of this creed, meaning that they did not become central to faith until the postexilic period (see Neh. 9:6).

Von Rad argued that Israelite faith was dynamic, not only in calling for new interpretations of these redemptive acts, but also by allowing for the continuing formulation of new themes. He pointed to a second complex of faith that developed in Jerusalem and Judah during the time of the monarchy: the David-Zion tradition, which included God's covenant with the House of David (i.e., his dynasty, which ruled in Judah until 587 B.C.E.), and Jerusalem as the city of God, signified particularly by the presence of the Temple. The notion of Jerusalem as the center of the cosmos where the God of creation and history took up residence opened the door to creation theology. However, even creation theology did not achieve a prominent place in Israelite faith until the period of the exile, as seen in the formative work of Second Isaiah. Von Rad argued that creation did not achieve a central and normative role as an independent tradition of faith, save in wisdom literature. Rather, creation served as a prolegomenon to salvation history. Von Rad suggested that Israel viewed creation with suspicion because of its association with fertility religion and natural revelation.

In structuring his Old Testament theology, von Rad placed the wisdom literature, together with the psalms, in the section "Israel Before Jahweh (Israel's Answer)"—i.e., Israel's response to the proclamation of the great acts of God, embodied in the Hexateuch's traditions of faith. This is rather curious, since the canonical wisdom literature that von Rad treats makes no response at all to the events of redemptive history, but only to creation.

Von Rad pursues his analysis of the book of Job in association with the laments of the Psalter ("Israel's Trials and the Consolation of the Individual"). He understands Job in terms of the character's being torn between the caring, righteous, saving God of tradition and the God he experiences as a destructive enemy. The resolution of this conflict comes through Job's experience of theophany in which "God turns a smiling face to his creation. . . . Accordingly, the purpose of the divine answer in the Book of Job is to glorify God's justice towards his creatures, and the fact that he is turned towards them to do them

23

good and bless them. . . . This justice of God cannot be comprehended by man; it can only be adored."[13] Thus humans are to glorify the God who providentially maintains creation, even though they may not understand the whys and hows of divine justice. Von Rad thought that the book of Job was written during the time of the exile, when the monarchy had ended, Jerusalem was destroyed, and, therefore, saving history was not theologically relevant.

Von Rad traced the development of wisdom through two stages. He characterized the first stage largely as "wisdom deriving from experience."[14] This early wisdom represented "practical knowledge of the laws of life and of the world, based upon experience."[15] The goal of the wise person was to master life by the adherence to maxims that were "an art for living," or a "technique for life."[16] According to von Rad, early wisdom sought to discern a hidden order in reality, but did not operate with an idea of "nature" or of a Greek "cosmos." Rather, reality was unstable, at times imponderable. However, for the early sages Yahweh sustained the world; thus its "orders [were to be] apprehended by faith."[17] Even so, God was largely mysterious, residing outside the domain of immediate human perception.

Still in its first stage, early wisdom moved into the court and schools to provide education. These sages were people of higher social standing.[18] The starting point for wisdom in the court and the schools is the "fear of God," meaning that sapiential instruction began with faith and recognized the validity and authority of divine commandments. The counsel of sages did not command the same authority as the law. However, the sages were concerned with the commandments as they related to everyday life, and not to the sphere of the cultus. Retribution was not a forensic means of regulating the world by God or fate, but rather grew out of the sapiential sense of disregard or awareness of "orders" for life. The sages stressed obedience to the will of God, though considering God to be mysterious and beyond the limits of human comprehension. While the sages in this first stage recognized that there were imponderables, the spirit exuded in their teachings was one of optimism, untouched by a deep sense of the tragic.

Von Rad argues that the second stage is theological wisdom, which develops during the postexilic period.[19] Now wisdom is God's call to people, the mediator of revelation, the teacher of nations, and a divine principle permeating the world since creation. Wisdom was a divine gift to humans and revealed to them the will and nature of God. Personified, wisdom drew symbols and images from fertility goddesses. Eventually Ben Sira identified wisdom with Torah.

Theological wisdom seeks to explore and understand the secrets of the mystery of reality and God (see esp. Job 28; Prov. 8:22-31; Sirach 24). Now wisdom becomes a part of the saving revelation of God. In wisdom "interest in the traditions of the saving history had grown weak. It was all the more turned towards the miracle of creation, its systematic arrangement, its technical riddles and its rules."[20] Now wisdom sought to make a theological statement apart from the saving history, and it did so in articulating an understanding of creation. The call to wisdom, thus to salvation and life, is identified with the same call issued by God at creation (Genesis 1).

Von Rad treats Qoheleth under the category of skepticism.[21] Now there is a sage who doubts God is involved in human history and individual life. Indeed, Qoheleth represents the loss or negation of history: "But Ecclesiastes thinks entirely without any reference to history—with him the Wisdom literature lost its last contact with Israel's old way of thinking in terms of saving history and, quite consistently, fell back on the cyclical way of thinking common to the East."[22] God is mysterious, not known, yet determines what happens. Life is insecure, and there is a breakdown between human deed and moral consequence. Since the only certainty is death, humanity's "portion" in life is to eat, drink, and experience enjoyment. Von Rad concludes that wisdom's theological efforts to find an authentic place for creation ended in skepticism. The sages could not discover God. Subsequently, the failure of wisdom led to the emergence of apocalyptic.

While offering many important insights into creation and wisdom, von Rad does not give either of them a significant place in his theology. Creation, for him, is still a secondary theme, while wisdom's ignoring of salvation history presented him with a distinctive corpus of literature that largely resisted his theological presentation.

The Dialectic of History and Creation

In his theological writings, Claus Westermann has given a more significant and constructive place to creation and wisdom than have either Wright or von Rad.[23] Westermann's theological construction consists of two interactive poles: soteriology (history) and blessing (creation).[24] His presentation of history follows essentially von Rad in setting forth an ancient historical credo that becomes the basis for the themes or traditions developed in the Exodus-Sinai complex that later join with the covenant of Deuteronomy. Westermann sees the Old Testament as eschatological in its basic movement: The goal of history is the salvation of the world. Within this driving thrust of history, Yahweh saves his chosen people through means of great acts of redemption.

The second pole, blessing, incorporates the divine power that preserves and enhances life and undergirds the continuing order of creation. Divine blessing includes the gift and continuation of the power of procreation, the provision of sustenance, and support for the structures of life. According to Westermann's view of the Old Testament, creation is beyond history, meaning that it does not exist within a temporal movement. While creation is the presupposition of faith, it is not a historical saving act and thus not the object of confession. Creation was not a part of the ancient credo, for the Old Testament could not conceive of an alternative to God's creation of the world. Furthermore, in Westermann's view, creation is not associated with revelation; it does not testify to God.

However, creation theology does seek to secure the present by linking the order of reality to the wellsprings of primal origins. Creation theology embraces universalism; Israel points to God as the creator of humankind and the world. Westermann argued that Israel inherited its understanding of divine creation from the ancient Near East, and, like its sources, developed two separate traditions: the creation of humanity, the older of the two, and the creation of the world.

Subsumed under the pole of blessing (creation), wisdom is given an important place in Westermann's Old Testament theology. Wisdom's gifts are maturity, longevity, reproduction, and the general enhancement of life; but these come as a result of divine blessing. God's power of blessing is encapsulated within wisdom sayings. Like the larger theme of creation, wisdom is not specifically limited to the chosen people; rather, it is universal in scope. Wisdom and creation share this universalism, for God creates, sustains, and blesses all of life. Wisdom is the power, design, and life-enhancing gift of God that shapes and undergirds reality.[25]

Westermann used his bipartite division of the two traditions of creation (anthropology and cosmology) to speak of the development of wisdom theology. The early sayings in Proverbs understand humans to be creatures made by God with possibilities and limits that are indigenous to their creatureliness. Humanity is a creature of the earth, gifted with organs of sense to know and perceive. The place of the human creatures is among other creatures, a part of a whole, bound to creation, and blessed by the creator of the land with nourishment, sustenance, and well-being. This is the older tradition. Later wisdom takes up the tradition of the creation of the world with Yahweh through wisdom's establishing, designing, and ordering the cosmos.[26]

It is clear that Westermann offers an approach to Old Testament theology that gives an important place to creation and wisdom. However, while regarded as an important pole of the dialectic with history, creation is still not for Westermann an object of confession, but rather only a given that provides a prologue to an Israelite faith still centered in salvation history.

Wisdom and Canonical Theology

In 1970 Brevard Childs announced that the Biblical Theology movement in America had fallen into crisis, largely because historical criticism did not yield theological results for modern communities of faith.[27] Childs proposed a canonical approach to biblical studies that he thought would lead directly to Old Testament theology and contemporary hermeneutics.

Childs begins with two fundamental assumptions. First, the canon, not the history of Israel or of Israelite religion, is the primary context for interpreting the Old Testament. Second, the Old Testament is normative scripture intentionally shaped by communities of faith to address the Word of God to future generations.

Building upon this foundation, Childs articulates the following features of the canonical approach. First, the primary task of interpretation is to understand the shape and function of canonical books. This means that the task is not to uncover the various layers of tradition that comprise a book, but rather to concentrate on the final form of the book that entered into the canon. Second, the canonical approach takes seriously the community of faith that not only shaped the canonical books, but also was shaped by them. Third, by means of "intertextuality" the interpreter uses scripture to interpret scripture, for texts in the canon are meant to be read and understood in reference to each other. And fourth, the canonical shape of books actualizes their meaning—a meaning that transcends the limitations of historical time and space to address a Word of God to future generations.

In his *Introduction to the Old Testament as Scripture*, Childs concentrates on interpreting individual books in the Old Testament, including wisdom texts, and offers a number of insights into their canonical meaning.

In his treatment of Job, Childs begins by noting the impasse reached by traditional historical criticism in attempting to address the problems of the literary composition of the book.[28] These problems include the relation of the prose narrative to the poetic dialogues, the literary integrity of the divine speeches in 38:1–41:26, the issue of whether the Elihu speeches (32–37) are secondary, the question of the order and location of speeches in the third cycle of debate, and the problem of the apparently intrusive character of the poem on wisdom in chapter 28. Also problematic have been the dating of the book and its literary form.

Growing out of these literary questions has been the larger issue of the purpose or meaning of the entire book. Is the book designed to present Job as a paradigm of the suffering righteous man? Is the book written to undermine the traditional theory of retribution? Is the answer to the problem of suffering found in Job's religious experience of encounter with Yahweh in the whirlwind speeches, or does it reside in the content of the book? These questions are complicated, of course, by the issues of literary integrity.

Childs argues that instead of attempting to resolve the issues of literary composition, one should recognize that they demonstrate that the book of Job has structured within it a diversity of functions. Thus, in the context of the entire book, including the prose epilogue, it is not incongruous for Yahweh to commend Job, while within the poetry the rebuke of Job in the divine speeches makes good sense. These are not in opposition, argues Childs, as long as one understands that diversity of purpose and literary composition is the major canonical feature of the book. For Childs, then, the key to understanding the book is to recognize that it presents a variety of different perspectives. While the poetic dialogues struggle with the question of innocent human suffering and attempt to enable the reader to identify with Job's dilemma if not necessarily to affirm his accusations, the narrative poses the question "Can a human love God for God's own sake?"[29] Read through the lens of the narrator, the book of Job directs one back to the nature of God to learn that divine wisdom is of a different order and kind than human wisdom, which is critically undermined.

The Elihu speeches offer a different perspective on the book by moving the issue from Job's assault on the justice of God to the question of omnipotence and the discipline of human suffering. In the poem on wisdom in chapter 28, Job comes to acquiesce to the limits imposed by God on human wisdom.

Thus the book of Job is structured in such a way that it seeks to provide various perspectives on a wide range of theological questions. This means it is legitimate to search out the meaning of only a particular part—say, for example, the Elihu speeches—all the while not ignoring the holistic reading of the entire book.

Childs's assessment of Proverbs proceeds in a similar fashion. The long-standing interpretive problems are outlined, including literary composition, the questions of forms and redaction, historical background, and the theology of wisdom.[30] The major theological questions have to do with the extent that divine order serves as a constitutive element in older wisdom, the issue of retribution, the understanding of wisdom in the wisdom poems (Job 28; Proverbs 8; Sirach 24), and, perhaps most problematic, the relation of Israel's wisdom literature to the rest of Old Testament theology. What these studies lack, argues Childs, is a clear description of the canonical function of Proverbs for an ongoing community of faith.

Childs provides this description by pointing out what he considers to be several indications of canonical shaping. First, the superscription's attribution of the book to Solomon preserves its identity and keeps it from being subsumed under or merged with other types of biblical literature, including the Law and the Prophets. At the same time, the superscription represents the view that wisdom was associated with the royal court in its early beginnings. This opposes efforts to place wisdom and the book entirely in the postexilic period. In Childs's reading, Proverbs 1–9 serves as a hermeneutical introduction to the meaning and theology of the entire book. The focus on the "fear of Yahweh" underscores the religious character of the book of Proverbs and opposes the notion of an early, secular wisdom that was eventually brought within the realm of Yahwistic religion. This means that a dialectic of wisdom as a gift of God and wisdom as an object for human striving is set up within the book and serves as a creative tension. And, perhaps most important, the role of wisdom in creation in 3:19 and chapter 8 establishes creation, not salvation history, as the theological context for reading Proverbs.

One other important example of canonical shaping, according to Childs, is found in Proverbs 30:1-6. According to him, this text describes the despair of finding wisdom and the knowledge of God and then presents the response in vv. 5-6a, which cites two other passages: 2 Samuel 22:31 (Ps. 18:31) and Deuteronomy 4:2. The response indicates, in Childs's reading, that God is revealed in the written word. This suggests that the proverbs that derived from critical reflection on reality now are understood as divine words—that is, as scripture. Childs draws the salient conclusion that a canonical reading accepts the full integrity of the theology and authority of wisdom literature as scripture. Wisdom is not legitimized by reference either to law or to salvation history.

In Childs's canonical assessment of Ecclesiastes (Qoheleth), he sets out the complicated literary, historical, and theological questions that the book raises and the variety of responses to these by the scholarly world. Childs takes his own direction by examining the canonical shape of Ecclesiastes.[31] The conclusions he reached in applying this approach include the following. First, the superscription that identifies the book with the "son of David" (obviously Solomon) seeks to undergird the assault on wisdom with its most authoritative voice. Second, the epilogue legitimates the book as authoritative, divine wisdom and not as private fancy, while indicating in the final analysis that all human wisdom and behavior will come under divine judgment. The epilogue indicates that the book, then, is to serve as a guide for the community's critical reflection on wisdom. At the same time, the epilogue warns that the message of the book, limited to human wisdom and behavior in the present, is relativized ultimately by the eschatological judgment of God.

In his Old Testament theology, Childs moves from the description of the canonical shape and function of individual books to major theological themes. Here the canon functions primarily as a context for interpretation of these themes. His Old Testament theology is divided into twenty chapters; the first lays out the interpretative features of the canonical approach, and the remaining nineteen are thematic. Childs does not set forth a systematic theology for the Old Testament with a center that integrates a variety of several areas (e.g., God, Israel, humanity, cosmos), but rather each of his thematic chapters is largely self-contained: "The Old Testament as Revelation," "The Law of God," and "Male and Female as a Theological Problem." Childs does not contribute a chapter to either creation or wisdom as an individual theme, though the topics are broached from time to time.

Childs's treatment of wisdom is an important element in three of his chapters: "How God Is Known," "The Shape of the Obedient Life," and "Life Under Threat." The first of these chapters deals with the important topic of revelation, and, among other points, speaks to the relationship between creation and wisdom. For Childs, the canonical approach emphasizes both the horizontal (the believing community) and the vertical (the Word of God conveyed in human words) dimensions of revelation. God's revelation, the Word of God, is expressed in a variety of written forms, including narrative, psalm, and prophetic oracle. Yet God is also known through creation that witnesses to divine reality in acts of origination, providential support, and eschatological future; divine acts in history; the name of God that testifies to divine identity and will; and wisdom. Childs understands wisdom as involving, at least partially, divine mystery at work in creation. This cosmological wisdom is "concealed within the divine purpose and planted within his creative works."[32]

Yet, this wisdom is also the active voice of God, which calls people to true life, establishes thrones and kingdoms, speaks through the decisions and actions of leaders to rule justly, and witnesses to the creator. This revelatory voice of God also assumes the providential role of directing human life in the areas of moral behavior and discourse. "As an essential witness to God's purpose in his creation, wisdom is built into the very structure of reality, and in this role seeks to guide humanity to the way of truth."[33] This wisdom is found, not through reason, but through the "fear of God."

Similar to von Rad, Childs regards an obedient life as a response to God's acts of salvation, initiation of covenant, and creation.[34] The canonical shape of the Psalter emphasizes the importance of Psalm 1, a Torah psalm that designates Israel's psalms or prayers as a medium through which the people respond to God's address in word and deed. These psalms also become understood as fresh words of God to the congregation. The response of human wisdom to God's address is not limited to ethics, though certainly this is an important dimension to the divine imperatives. Wisdom's response is larger, for it encompasses the totality of human experience. Like the Torah, wisdom requires a faithful response in commitment to God and the divine order, to engage in acts of justice, to care for the poor and needy, and to regard life as a good gift from God.

Childs also examines wisdom in his chapter on "Life Under Threat." The posing of threat and the response of wisdom in the book of Job is similar to that of the psalms of lament. The reality of suffering and death is ever present, and God's role as just redeemer to whom the righteous may appeal becomes critical in both. However, in Ecclesiastes one encounters skepticism that doubts, not that God acts dramatically and decisively in ruling the world, but that anyone can know what God is doing. As a result, humans are encased in dark despair, living in an alien world that moves forward in divinely determined, but unrevealed, ways.[35]

Finally, Childs also addresses both creation theology and the wisdom tradition in his biblical theology.[36] Building on his major assumptions outlined in his introduction to *Biblical Theology of the Old and New Testaments,* Childs indicates that the canonical approach focuses on the theological forces that were at work in shaping the composition and development of biblical literature. He argues that tradents who formed and transmitted the biblical materials worked with hermeneutical concerns that would enable the traditions to speak to later generations in an authoritative manner. These hermeneutical concerns may be identified, at least in part, by the biblical theologian.

In doing biblical theology, Childs argues that the witness of each testament needs to be heard. While the Old Testament is largely promise, its own witness should not be silenced by the fulfillment of the New Testament. The tension between the two testaments, while not to be overplayed, should not be ignored or removed. There is theological continuity between the two, but there is also discontinuity. This means that the witness of the Old Testament and its various voices need to be heard.

Childs emphasizes that the Old Testament essentially witnesses to God's encounter with Israel in "great revelatory events in Israel's history and their subsequent appropriation by the tradition."[37] While this view is quite similar to von Rad's, Childs distinguishes his approach by stressing, not the streams of developing tradition as the vehicle of Israel's witness, but the canonically shaped literature. In getting at the "discrete witness" of the Old Testament, Childs sets forth three goals: determining the initial settings of the distinct witnesses, the tracing of the trajectories of these witnesses, and hearing both their unity and diversity in articulating Israel's faith.[38]

In his assessment of creation theology in the Old Testament, Childs isolates the historical locations for the texts and traditions that articulate the theme and notes the variety of ways it is understood. Childs argues that Israel understood creation not only as the beginning of God's creative activity, but also as the beginning of history. Israel did not view history as beginning with its own origins, but rather with creation, thus making history a universal category. Nevertheless, for Childs, Israel's faith developed primarily from encounters with the God of redemptive history, beginning with the exodus, and only secondarily from a theology of creation.[39]

In approaching creation theology in the wisdom tradition, Childs largely summarizes the work of Gerhard von Rad's *Wisdom in Israel*.[40] Childs notes that wisdom is not a late tradition in the Old Testament, but rather belongs to the earliest layer of tradition. While rejecting the characterization of early wisdom as secular, Childs still contrasts old wisdom's moorings in human experience with late wisdom's propensity for theological reflection. Childs emphasizes that wisdom looks to nature and not history as the basis for its theological reflections. Wisdom, not history, is the voice of divine revelation in creation that testifies to a divine order that provides the basis for faith and life. At least this is true until Ben Sira finally includes salvation history within his theology. Childs argues that wisdom offers an important witness, for it demonstrates how divine revelation and human experience "could be brought into a profound harmony without destroying either testimony."[41]

Wisdom, Rhetoric, and Feminist Theology

While no comprehensive feminist biblical theology has yet been written, Phyllis Trible has made some important suggestions about what such a biblical theology would look like.[42] In so doing, she offers some interesting insights about the role and place of wisdom and creation in this theological approach. She begins with three preliminary assumptions. First, her feminist theology might well be informed by the traditional disciplines of biblical theology and exegesis, but the approach would move beyond description to be consciously constructive and hermeneutical in addressing contemporary issues. Second, a feminist biblical theology would not regard the Bible as the property of any one group, but would belong to both Jew and Christian, academy and church, and indeed the world. Third, this approach would not work out of a single methodological paradigm, but would be eclectic, embracing many methods.

Moving from assumptions to description, Trible characterizes her approach in the following terms. First, familiar and neglected biblical texts would be approached with the recognition of the reality of biblical androcentricity and patriarchy. Second, important would be texts that depict God in feminine images as well as those that focus on women. Third, a particular focus would be gender and sex in the Bible, beginning with an articulation of the theology of male and female in the image of God in Genesis 1–3. Fourth, this approach would move outside the Bible to include other ancient resources: ancient Near Eastern literature and especially Israelite "folk religion," which may have included women in important roles that were denied them in traditional Yahwism. Fifth, the design of a feminist biblical theology would be to demonstrate not only the multiplicity of images and metaphors used to portray God, but also to show that no one view of the Bible is normative. Sixth, this theology would encounter and subvert patriarchy. Seventh, authority would center more in the reader than in the text. The Bible might be regarded as authoritative, but not necessarily as prescriptive.

In a variety of publications, Trible also has contributed some insightful readings of certain Old Testament texts that combine a feminist hermeneutic with rhetorical criticism.[43] Trible's *God and the Rhetoric of Sexuality* includes feminist readings of texts relating to creation (especially Genesis 1–3) and wisdom (particularly Job). Her reading of Genesis 1 focuses on verse 27. Combining rhetorical analysis with a compelling interpretative argument, Trible demonstrates that male and female together comprise the image of God. This metaphor for God is incomplete, unless both male and female are included. Indeed, this fundamental metaphor provides the impetus for examining other metaphors, including feminine ones for God.

Trible then proceeds to examine texts that deal with the "womb" or "uterus" *(rehem)*. She notes that the word in the plural expands to the abstraction of compassion, mercy, and love. The plural, as related to God, intimates, she suggests, that the deity is the one who creates humanity in the womb, prepares the uterus for birth, participates in the birthing of the child, receives the infant from the mother, and then nurtures the new life from birth to death. God's compassion, then, is understood in terms of the imagery associated with that of the mother, who conceives, bears, gives birth to, and nurtures a child. In examining one wisdom text, she notes that Job presents the theology of the womb as the place of divine creativity (Job 31:13-15), although earlier he had castigated God for having formed him in the womb, only to seek out his life to destroy him after birth (Job 3; 10:18-19). The womb is the place in the Hebrew Bible, including wisdom texts, where God creates and predestines human life.[44]

While not exhaustive, Trible's work finds an important place for wisdom and creation in the presentation of a feminist biblical theology. Particularly important are the feminine images for God associated with birth and the creation of the individual. To these could be added the role of Woman Wisdom in the shaping of the cosmos and as the mediator between God and humanity.[45]

Summary and Evaluation

These Old Testament theologians have offered some important understandings of wisdom theology and its place in Israelite faith and contemporary hermeneutics. First, they have noted that wisdom literature is theologically grounded in the creation of the cosmos and of humanity. Whether creation is viewed as an important witness of Old Testament faith depends on the theological judgment of the scholar working out of his or her own confessional and methodological orientation. Creation is certainly a pervasive theme through every area of the Hebrew canon. The judgment that creation is less theologically important than salvation history, covenant, and law is not based primarily on exegetical analysis, but on the theological traditions out of which the interpreter operates. The view that redemptive history, including the events of Sinai, takes theological priority over creation cannot be defended by reference to the Hebrew Bible itself.

A second insight of theological importance is the recognition that wisdom literature affirms a universal orientation to faith and ethics. This has several implications. While the Israelite sages may point to the superiority of their achievements and insights, they nevertheless admit the legitimacy and authority of non-Israelite wisdom. This means, then, that God is a universal deity who speaks to all people through the voice of creation and gives to everyone organs of perception and understanding that make wisdom accessible. Further, the wisdom tradition affirms the importance of the role of reason and human experience in the analysis and critique of faith. The use of reason and empirical analysis moves the objects of faith out of the realm of credulity into tested beliefs that correlate to human understanding and experience. This is especially important for hearing the witnesses of the critical books of Job and Qoheleth.

Finally, the witness of wisdom literature allows for the exposing of patriarchy's one-sided emphasis on male metaphors for God. The roles of Woman Wisdom in creation, providence, and revelation and the feminine images associated with God's involvement in the conception and nurture of humanity are iconoclastic texts that subvert the idols of patriarchy.

APPROACHES TO WISDOM THEOLOGY

Introduction

New developments in approaches to Old Testament theology, giving a greater role to creation, hold significant promise for incorporating wisdom literature within the larger parameters of Old Testament faith.[46] At the same time, important work has already been done in articulating the theology of wisdom literature, though rarely in a comprehensive way.[47]

In his ground-breaking article published in 1964, Walther Zimmerli argued that wisdom theology is grounded in creation.[48] Noting the absence of salvation history in the writings of the wise that made their way into the Jewish canon, Zimmerli contended that wisdom has its own structure for theological expression. While such divine names as "Maker" and "Creator" occasionally occur in wisdom texts (Prov. 14:31; 17:5; Qoh. 12:1), Zimmerli notes that in Proverbs and Qoheleth God is never addressed as the "God of Israel," the "God of the ancestors," Yahweh Sabaoth, or any other name or title specially associated with the election traditions of Israel. Even in Job, while God is occasionally called "Yahweh" (see the prose tale in Job 1–2; 42:7-17; and the speeches from the whirlwind in 38:1–42:6), the book does not bring up the themes of election and salvation history. Jesus ben Sira, writing in the early second century B.C.E, is the first sage to integrate redemptive history and creation.

What Zimmerli has noted in his 1964 article has been expressed in many different ways by various scholars of the wisdom tradition. The issue is generally not the theme of creation, though this is not always affirmed to be of major importance in wisdom, but rather how best to capture the richness of the expression of this theme. I would go a step further by suggesting that creation is truly at the "center" of wisdom theology, meaning that creation integrates all other dimensions of God-talk as well as anthropology, community, ethics, epistemology (both reason and revelation), and society. Earlier examinations of wisdom theology have approached the task through four major organizing principles: anthropology, cosmology, theodicy, and the dialectic of anthropology and cosmology.[49]

Anthropology

Many scholars have contended that wisdom literature is largely a human enterprise with its focus on human nature and function.[50] They have argued that at least this is true of early wisdom, if not also for the entire corpus of canonical literature. Thus they submit that wisdom is either largely concerned with the individual person or with humanity, but not with God and the general themes of Israelite faith. Walther Zimmerli, early in his study of the literature of the sages, contended that wisdom was in essence the quest to master life. For Zimmerli, "wisdom is radically anthropocentric."[51] A more mature Zimmerli later brought the notion of wisdom as a human enterprise under the theological rubric of creation, stressing the nature and role of humanity under the idea of *creatio continua*. Referring to wisdom as the "art of steering," Zimmerli submitted that the objective of the wise person is "to master life" by means of coming to a knowledge of the world (expressed in the literary form of the proverb that apprehends the data of reality) and in applying that knowledge to any and all circumstances in life (captured by the form of the admonition).[52] This means that humans are active creatures who seek out their place in God's world, order reality, and master life. For Zimmerli in his later theological reflection, the "fear of God" in wisdom refers, not to an unthinking and passive bowing of the knee to divine sovereignty, but to the "comprehensive ability to direct the whole of life."[53] This does not necessarily place the sage in opposition to God, but establishes a creative tension in which people are free to think and to act while at the same time God continues to create and direct both the cosmos and human life.[54]

In similar fashion, O. S. Rankin referred to Israel's wisdom corpus as "the documents of Hebrew humanism." These texts did not reject or ignore God's place in creation and history; instead, they recognized both "God's interest in the individual life"[55] and human responsibility based on freedom. This dual emphasis is found, for example, in the ethical imperative to care for the poor. An extension of the creator's concern for humanity (Prov. 14:31; 17:5; 19:17), human caring was not limited to nation or race, but became a universal duty embracing all people. This universal obligation to love the neighbor resided at the center of wisdom's social ethics framed within creation theology. For the sages, creation was not limited to primordial beginnings, but also included a strongly developed faith in providence with a distinctive focus on divine compassion for and nurture of the individual person. The sages' own formulation of retribution based on a universal moral order governing creation and society issued from the "belief that the natural forces and the moral purposes of the Creator are complementary powers."[56] Indeed, for Rankin this consciously espoused humanism eventually led to the crisis of theodicy, for even the creator was expected to act with justice tempered by compassion.

In his address to the American Academy of Religion in 1968, John Priest lamented the noticeable absence of humanism in most Old Testament theologies, since scholarship has falsely assumed that Israel was preoccupied with God. Defining humanism as "a fundamental perspective that focuses its interest upon man in his individual and collective life," Priest submitted that much of the Old Testament, and especially wisdom literature, affirmed the value of life and placed primary concern on humanity's well-being.[57] Indeed, biblical humanism is characterized by confidence in the human ability to encounter life and address its challenges. Following Zimmerli, Priest contended that wisdom's earliest expression set forth a "belief in man's innate ability to get along in the world in which he finds himself, a confidence in reliance upon purely human abilities and instruments." In the latter stages of wisdom's development, skepticism led to the radical questioning of the theological and social principles espoused by wisdom, and culminated in Qoheleth's radical pessimism, denying any legitimate affirmation of divine retribution in human history. This skepticism resulted in an even greater passion for the essentially human in some wisdom circles.

Finally, in an influential collection of essays appearing in 1972, Walter Brueggemann stressed that wisdom is primarily a human enterprise, a thesis contained in the title of the corpus: *In Man We Trust*. Brueggemann wrote that the previous neglect of wisdom texts was due in part to significant features of sapiential theology, contradicting many of the major tenets of Christian faith. These include wisdom's major affirmation that the goal and meaning of existence is a this-worldly life full of joy, well-being, and wholeness. This contrasts with Protestant other-worldliness, which looks toward the culmination of history as the ultimate reference for human existence. Wisdom legitimates social knowledge as the authoritative ground for ethics and values the human capacity to discern the true and the good, while Protestantism tends to devalue the human capacity to know and to act properly in favor of church and Scripture as sources of revelation. Brueggemann further contended that wisdom stresses human freedom and the requisite responsibility to forge social and individual destiny under the impress of divine direction, while many Protestants tend to disdain human nature as fallen and crippled in the ability to discern and choose the good. This contrast is continued in wisdom's belief that humans are created to live an orderly existence in an ongoing world that is beneficent and good, while Protestant Christianity places emphasis on interruptions of mighty acts of God in history, discontinuous with a fallen world and, therefore, redemptive. Finally, wisdom celebrates humanity as the "king" of God's good creation, being given sovereignty over the world by God and regarded as an essentially good and trusted creature. By contrast, Protestants see humans as sinful creatures in desperate need of salvation. For Brueggemann, any comprehensive presentation of Old Testament theology should not ignore this "neglected side of biblical faith."

Cosmology

A second understanding of creation in wisdom focuses on the cosmos or world order.[58] This approach argues that in the wisdom traditions of the ancient Near East creation was thought to be permeated by cosmic order that integrated into a harmonious whole the various components of reality. Hartmut Gese identified this world order in the Egyptian understanding of *ma'at*, "truth, justice, and order," which at times was personified as the daughter of Re, the sun god. In Egyptian theology, this order was a divine attribute of the creator that enabled him both to structure and to maintain creation. At the same time, Gese noted that *ma'at* was the power and guiding principle for the organization

37

of humans by means of social institutions. Through the just and orderly functioning of human society, harmony with the cosmos was achieved and sustained. Creation was not perfect, as demonstrated by the lame and the blind (Amenemopet 24:8-20; *ANET*, 421-25). And creation was not held together by a static principle, but rather was dynamic, being actualized in the divine reign of the enthroned ruler of Egypt.[59]

Gese argued that this understanding of cosmic and social order entered into Israelite thought especially through the sages and provided the organizing center for their teachings. Yet Gese recognized that they did not develop a mechanical theory of retribution in which the wise righteous were rewarded and the foolish sinners punished. This was due to their emphasis on divine freedom, which enabled Yahweh to transcend the restrictions of moral legalism to govern the world with divine grace.

A more detailed treatment of order in Israelite and ancient Near Eastern thought appeared in the form of Hans Heinrich Schmid's *Gerechtigkeit als Weltordnung* in 1968. Although not limited to wisdom texts, Schmid systematically analyzed the major spheres of order in Egyptian, Sumero-Akkadian, and Israelite cultures: law, wisdom, nature/fertility, war/victory, cult/sacrifice, and kingship. And he observed that it was especially the royal tradition that encompassed all other spheres. In Egypt, where a more pronounced doctrine of order was developed, the creator was believed to have brought *ma'at* into existence to replace chaos. Thus, for example, Re was the "Lord of *ma'at*," and *ma'at* was his divine daughter. As the son and devotee of Re, the king had responsibility for maintaining and actualizing both the order of creation and human society. Wisdom was the attribute of the king that gave him the capacity for orderly, beneficent rule. The sages, particularly Egyptian officials (e.g., Ptah-hotep), worked in the service of the king, thereby bringing social structures into harmony with creation. The sages issued "instructions of ma'at" that, when taken into the heart, enabled one to live in concert with the world and the human community. Wise acts constituted and realized both world and social order. In Schmid's judgment, a similar, though less pronounced, understanding of world order developed in Mesopotamian cultures. In the Sumerian myth of Inanna and Enki, for example, one hundred laws (*me*) were thought to govern all reality to provide the collective structure that maintained the continuation of life. Here, too, the king as sage was responsible for the support and realization of order.

In turning to Israel, Schmid contended that while ancient Near Eastern conceptions of order were appropriated through a Canaanite medium, the unity of reality characterizing the major areas of order in Egypt and Mesopotamia was fragmented. While law, wisdom, and kingship were the spheres in which *sĕdāqâ* ("justice, righteousness, order") functions, it is especially rare in the traditions of cult, war, and to a certain extent nature. The Hebrew term for "order" ("justice"), according to Schmid, is expressed in the root *sdq*, though one should differentiate between *sdq* ("justice"), which originally designated cosmic order made concrete in wisdom and law and maintained in the social realm by the king, and *sdqh* ("righteousness"), which embraced behavior and thought, creating a just and beneficent order in creation and society.[60] The one who engaged in order creating behavior is the *saddîq* ("righteous one"), who lives in harmony with God and society and experiences well-being in life. Yet Schmid qualified this conception by stressing that the understanding of order in Israel was historically nuanced, at least until the exile. This implies that prior to the end of the state of Judah, the freedom of God and human limitations meant order was not a static, mechanistic principle operating in and through a system of retribution, but rather was historically conditioned. However, after the exile certain circles developed a mechanical theory of retribution and an ahistorical conception of order in which human actions led inevitably to certain consequences. This distortion of the conception of order led to the radical protestation of Job.[61]

In several publications, Horst Dietrich Preuss also characterized wisdom theology as "thoughts about order" (*Ordnungsdenken*), established through observation, experience, and tradition.[62] However, he emphasized that older wisdom was quite secular and became theological only at a much later stage of its history. For Preuss, retribution was a continuous component of this way of thought, and the causal relation between deed and consequence was so inflexible it tended to negate the possibility of divine freedom, even when the tradition became more theologically aware. Crisis developed in wisdom thought because of two factors: Collective experience came to realize that a moral order was not universally and unquestionably in operation in the world, and increasing emphasis was placed on the freedom of God. After the failed attempt to bring older wisdom within the sphere of Israelite faith as witnessed by Job and Qoheleth, the remnant of continuing tradition was radically transformed. Then wisdom became the "fear of God," a successful, though somewhat misguided, attempt, according to Preuss, to place the tradition within the parameters of Yahwistic faith. Indeed, the seriously altered character of later wisdom demonstrated how much Israel had to transform the originally pagan, order-thinking wisdom to alleviate the erupting exilic and postexilic crisis that would have led inevitably to the total disintegration of its tradition.[63]

A final example of approaching wisdom theology through cosmology appears in the work of Hans-Jürgen Hermisson. In his important study of the wisdom saying, Hermisson detected what he considered to be constitutive for sapiential thought: The saying is a form connecting deed and result, thereby recognizing, transmitting, and creating an order of life.[64] In a later article, he extended his argument about the basic form of Israelite wisdom to a comprehensive statement about sapiential theology.[65] In Hermisson's view, wisdom sought regularity in the multiplicity of phenomena, a regularity observable in both nature and human society. This regularity led to a unified construction of reality that established a correspondence between what was observed and its perception. The developing sapiential epistemology led to the articulation of a creation theology in which order in the world was consistent with the process of human perception and the knowledge it acquired. The regularity, purposefulness, and beauty of wisdom as human perception were part of the essential nature of creation itself. This insight provided human life its *raison d'être*, for it implied that existence had purpose: to live so as to actualize and experience the beneficent order of creation. Sapiential teachings provided guidance for the proper way of existing in the world.

Theodicy

A third approach is represented by those who point to theodicy as the major theme in wisdom.[66] Perhaps the leading advocate for this approach has been James Crenshaw, who has examined wisdom's questioning of divine justice in many different publications.[67]

Recognizing that creation is at the heart of wisdom thought, Crenshaw noted that any discussion of the distinctiveness of the sapiential formulation of this tradition had to take seriously the element of chaos, which posed enormous difficulties for the sages. Indeed, Crenshaw argued that the experience of chaos and its ongoing threat in all areas of life (cosmic as well as social) led to the development of creation theology in the wisdom tradition. The appearance and purpose of creation theology was to articulate a defensible doctrine of theodicy.[68] In presenting their understanding of creation, the question of the relationship of God to chaos in its natural, social, and moral forms prompted the sages to defend divine justice.[69]

According to Crenshaw, the threat of chaos appeared in three fundamental areas: human perversion, human ignorance, and human consciousness of divine presence. In commenting on Qoheleth 7:29, he says concerning human perversion that this text "asserts that mankind alone is responsible for the corruption of the order of the created world."[70]

The second area, ignorance, is underscored in Qoheleth's observation that the lack of human knowledge and the ability to perceive and ascertain divine activity means that the traditional correlation of event and time leading to a successful conclusion cannot be known (see Qoh. 3:11; 7:13-14). Finally, the third area, consciousness of divine presence, is explained by Crenshaw in terms of the tension between the mystery of God expressed in the notion of transcendence and the immanence of God in creation. To overcome this tension, the sages, argues Crenshaw, introduced the idea of Woman Wisdom, who mediated the polarity of transcendence and immanence.

According to Crenshaw, creation theology for the wise assures them that the world is comprehensible and open to human investigation. Further, creation affirms the principle of order, which holds together the components of reality. Even when chaos threatens and gains the upper hand, creation theology assures the sage that wholeness still remains a possibility.[71]

Burton Mack's essay on the wisdom poems also underscored the importance of theodicy in sapiential theology.[72] According to Mack, the poems on Woman Wisdom clearly demonstrate the use of mythological traditions involving ancient Near Eastern goddesses of fertility and wisdom. However, the sages did not attempt to fashion an Israelite goddess in the shape of Isis or Maat, but used the language of myth to transform linguistically their tradition into a formidable construct that successfully engaged the historical and cultural crisis that engulfed Judah following the fall of Jerusalem. Wisdom, personified as a goddess, became the intermediary between a transcendent creator and the human world. It was in response to the crisis precipitating challenges to the rule and justice of God that the sages used the theologoumena of myth to place their tradition in the foundation and continuing structure of creation.

Anthropology and Cosmology

The fourth approach to creation theology in wisdom literature brings together in creative tension two of the above approaches: anthropology and cosmology. One of the most formidable presentations of this dialectic is found in the work of Gerhard von Rad.

Early wisdom, according to von Rad, represented practical insight gained from individual experience of life.[73] Thus older wisdom, centered in human experience, presented the goal of humans going into the world to master life. While there were connections and relationships to which the early sages pointed, von Rad denied they posited a world order in the fashion of a Greek cosmos. Von Rad thought that even the early stage of wisdom pointed to both contingencies beyond human control and prediction as well as limitations to the human capacity to know. Mystery continued to cloak and to veil divine activities as well as occurrences within the world, denying to early wisdom the capacity to know and thus control the realities the sages faced. The task of the wise was to perceive what regularities and patterns they could and to forge a teaching that enabled one to live as best one could a life of well-being and to avoid threats that brought failure and even destruction.

41

Most important for von Rad was the contention that this early wisdom, while not atheological, did not engage in serious theological reflection. Early wisdom was concerned only with the everyday life of human beings. Creation theology and the revelation of God to the wise entered into wisdom reflection only in a later stage (Job 28; Proverbs 9; Sirach 24).[74] Von Rad argued that wisdom's developing theological capacity, moving from human experience to cosmology and from anthropology to theology, paralleled the development of creation theology in Israel, which, in his judgment, did not gain full acceptance and mature formulation until the time of the exile in the sixth century B.C.E.

Von Rad qualified this developmental analysis of wisdom in his important book on wisdom.[75] Faith and reason for the sages were not opposing polarities, for they believed that the knowledge of God was not radically different from their experience and knowledge of the world. One came to encounter God in human experience.

Rejecting the view that the sages developed and adhered to a simple theory of retribution, von Rad still contended that the sages recognized that there were regularities and structures to be observed. However, there was no direct, unbreakable link between cause and event. Knowing the "times" was important, for the sages recognized that the successful outcome of events and behavior often was tied to the proper time. Even a wise and righteous act, if performed at the wrong time, could fail.[76] Instead of a mechanical theory of retribution restricting even divine action, von Rad spoke of the idea of the "good." The "good" was not a virtue, but a "social phenomenon" that produced a sphere of well-being. In other words, this "good" was identified with blessing that brought success and good fortune to both the righteous sages and the society in which they functioned.[77] This good consisted of "life-giving forces" that enhanced the existence of both individuals and communities. Evil, too, was a power that brought destruction. Wisdom was not utilitarian in either its character or its intention. Still, the sages were to integrate themselves into a divine order of goodness where blessing may be experienced. Nevertheless, the freedom of God could not be contained by any system of retributive justice. The God of the sages transcended human knowledge and efforts to impose even ideological constraints on divine activity.[78]

Even so, while there were contingencies that denied the guarantee of human success, even when actions were wise and just, the sages affirmed that both creation and life were good and to be affirmed. They continued to trust in the goodness of God, even when under threat. This is true eventually of Job, whose encounter with the whirlwind taught him that God had turned toward him in grace. Thus, for von Rad, Job is one who returns the guidance of the world and his own life to the hand of God.

As noted earlier, Claus Westermann divides texts that address creation theology into two major groups: the creation of the cosmos and the creation of humanity.[79] The lament and its response in the oracle of salvation is the form-critical setting for the creation of humanity, the oldest of the two traditions. In the lament, individuals remind the creator that he has shaped them in the womb, given them life, and promised to nurture and sustain their existence. This is the basis upon which their appeal is made for salvation from present distress. The thanksgiving is their expression of praise and grateful thanks for their deliverance and the restoration of their relationship with God. The tradition begins with the general accounting of the creation of humanity and develops eventually into God's creating of humans. Creation and divine providence for human life entwine in the theology of the lament and thanksgiving. The later tradition, the creation of the world, finds its form-critical setting in the hymn that praises God for creating the cosmos and sustaining it with power and care.

Rainer Albertz and Peter Doll have used Westermann's analysis of the two major creation traditions to assess the wisdom corpus.[80] Albertz argues that the two traditions are important in understanding the theology of the book of Job and of its different literary segments.[81] In the dialogues, Job does not use the tradition of the creation of the world to praise the majesty and sovereignty of the creator, but to indict him for his abuse of creation and failure to demonstrate caring concern for its creatures, including even righteous mortals. God does not turn a smiling face toward his creation. Rather, a great gulf separates the creator from frail humanity. Job uses the theme of God's care for human creatures in the anthropological tradition to accuse the creator of failure to respond to human crisis and need. Instead of moving in the direction of reconciliation, intended by the theology of the lament and thanksgiving, Job uses the creation of humanity tradition as an indictment against the lack of divine compassion.

In the speeches of Job's opponents, both traditions of creation are brought into play, though their meaning and use are significantly different from his. The tradition of the creation of the cosmos, argue the friends, points to God's providential care for humans in distress who may turn to him for salvation. In contrast, God punishes the arrogant wicked who do not repent. However, by the end of the debate the friends also use the cosmological tradition of creation to humiliate Job by contrasting the radical difference between a weak and insignificant Job, daring to challenge the Almighty, and the powerful creator who rules heaven and earth. Therefore, how can a weak mortal like Job dare to call God into question? The friends also use the anthropological tradition of creation to speak of the distance between the creator and insignificant humanity. The tradition is not used to speak of divine compassion.

43

It is important to note, argues Albertz, that in the speeches from the whirlwind God uses only the cosmological tradition and not the anthropological one. The God speeches use the creation of the world tradition as a form of divine self-praise, instruction, and debate. In addition to the praise of the wondrous and mysterious nature of creation, God speaks of his compassion and care for even wild and fearsome creatures. While a great gulf separates the sovereign Lord from insignificant humanity, God demonstrates loving concern for the creation.

Peter Doll examines the two creation traditions (cosmology and anthropology) in the book of Proverbs. According to Doll, the tradition of the creation of humanity is reflected in Proverbs 10–29, while the tradition of the creation of the world is the theological basis for Proverbs 1–9. Doll argues that the social setting that is at the basis of the early strata of Proverbs 10–29, reflecting the first stage of wisdom thought, is that of peasant farmers in the village and the criticism directed against their exploitation by landed nobility (cf. Amos). The form that dominates the material is the proverb. Two motifs are especially important: the polarity of the rich and the poor, and the common humanity shared even by people who exist in different social groups. Furthermore, Doll notes that the emphasis on the creation of human organs of speech and perception (eyes, ears, and mouths) reflects early wisdom's teaching about the ability to know and understand the world and its orders for life as well as the commission to go forth into the world to master life. This tradition originates in preexilic times and continues into the postexile period.

The middle stage of wisdom is prominent in Proverbs 1–9. Here, according to Doll, the social location moves to the education of officials, and the dominant form is the instruction. This middle stage of wisdom thinking places in antithesis the wise and fools (the royal period) and the righteous and the wicked (prominent in the postexilic age). Most important for Doll, however, is the late stage of wisdom, marked by the appearance of wisdom poems in the postexilic period. Now wisdom is located in the temple school. In these poems (1:20-35; 3:13-26; 8; 9:1-6, 13-18), education and faith are closely linked. Now what is of theological importance is the tradition of the creation of the world. These wisdom poems are similar to the psalms that praise God for creating and sustaining the cosmos and its structures for life. The desire is to locate wisdom at the very origins of reality in order to undergird the quest to come to a knowledge of nature and its orders.

Roland Murphy also points to the bipolar features of anthropology and cosmology in wisdom theology.[82] He rejects the argument that wisdom is an alien corpus of literature within the Bible or that creation resided outside Israelite faith. Indeed, Israel embraced creation and wisdom traditions from the ancient Near East and made them their own. Thus creation and wisdom are a genuine expression "of the faith of the Israelites as they encountered the Lord in the created world."[83]

Murphy speaks of two types of creation traditions in wisdom: creation as "beginnings" and creation as the arena of human existence. Creation as "beginnings" is expressed in such wisdom texts as Proverbs 3:19; 8:30; Wisdom of Solomon 7:22; 8:6; 14:2; and Sirach 24. In these texts, the concern is to place wisdom at the origins of creation in order to present its tradition as the means of understanding the nature of reality. Subsequently, Woman Wisdom becomes the voice of God, which reveals, not simply creation, but indeed the creator to those who listen to her instruction. However, Murphy rejects the notion that wisdom is identified with or reveals an overarching cosmic order.

The second tradition expresses the notion of creation as continuous and represents the totality of the world in which humans live. Experience of the world is in some measure also seen as an experience of God, for faith and reason were not dichotomized into two opposing types of knowing. Wisdom is not a group of rules or a teaching; rather, says Murphy, it is "a dialogue with the created world."[84] Indeed, God was beyond wisdom, but this did not mean that revelation was not captured in the teachings of the sages who listened for and on occasion heard the voice of God.

Finally, one should mention the work of Ronald E. Clements, who has approached the theology of wisdom literature under several topics: "Wisdom and the World," "Wisdom and Health" (i.e., the theme of suffering and healing), "Wisdom and Politics" (i.e., the role of wisdom at the court), "Wisdom and the Household," and "Wisdom and the Divine Realm."[85] According to Clements, wisdom did not present an integrated philosophy, though the tradition did inherit "certain fundamental insights and assumptions which came gradually to be co-ordinated into a more coherent and established form."[86]

According to Clements, the sages' views of the world were grounded in their "confidence concerning human ability to perceive and grasp the nature of reality."[87] The sages viewed reality as a composite of human behavior, society, and nature, that might best be regarded as a "sustaining order of wisdom" originating at creation. The order in nature could be seen in the areas of human life and social organization. Wisdom thinking did move in the directions of humanizing and demythologizing sacred times and space, thus differentiating it from priestly theology.[88] The sages proposed the existence of a pattern of time, observable to human beings, that provided the context for human behavior. And space was viewed as a cosmos, "a realm of designed order and beneficence," though its operations and wonders cannot be fully perceived and understood (Job 38–41).[89] Yet there is no dichotomy of space in the categories of sacred and profane or clean and unclean, as in priestly literature. The personification of wisdom played an important role in the theologizing of the sages, notes Clements, for this revelatory figure came to represent the inalienable bond that unites the creative intention of God with the experienced working of the world. Through wisdom the world can "know" God and discover the purpose and grandeur of God.[90] This figure combines the transcendence and immanence of God in a creative way.

Clements also acknowledges the importance of human life, both social and individual, in the teachings of wisdom. He notes the importance of the teaching of retribution, for the sages argued that God was at work in the moral operations of the world while they still recognized the tensions between affirmations and observations. Nevertheless, the sages acknowledge the sovereignty and providence of the creator, who established an order of life for humans to follow.[91]

Summary and Evaluation

Each of these approaches to wisdom theology has something of value to offer. The tradition of the sages certainly is directed to human beings, who are invited to take up wisdom's call. This call is issued to those who would live in harmony with God, creation, and human society and hope to experience well-being. However, it is incorrect to regard even the earliest stage of wisdom as largely anthropocentric and secular. Wisdom, even from its earliest stages, is a teaching grounded in the "fear of God," an expression that points both to worshipful piety and faithful affirmation that God is the creator and sustainer of life.[92] And the social, even communal, character of wisdom is prominent throughout the teachings of the sages. Subsequently, efforts to regard the tradition as fundamentally individualistic are wrongheaded.[93] Finally, creation theology in both its anthropological and cosmological expressions is assumed as the basis for the entire sapiential tradition. This means that the affirmation of the providence of God, the order of the cosmos, the divine gift of life, the nurturing of human beings throughout life, and the goal of living in harmony with creation are fundamental themes throughout the wisdom corpus.

The stress on cosmology as central to wisdom theology provides an important corrective to reading the tradition through primarily a human lens. The affirmation of a cosmic order seems essential to the world view of wisdom throughout its history. God is the creator of heaven and earth and the one who continues to sustain the order of reality, making life in its various manifestations not only possible, but indeed vital and blessed as well.

Even so, cosmology understood through the single lens of order may pose certain problems, including some possible distortion. Too much emphasis on order may lead to an understanding of wisdom as a legalistic tradition in which retribution operates automatically. This would deny to God the freedom to act or not act according to divine will, justice, or grace, while the sages' recognition of the contingencies of life would have no real meaning. Further, the sages often admitted to serious limits to their understanding, a confession that yielded to the reality of both divine mystery and chaos. Divine freedom and mystery led the sages to acknowledge that God's intentions and actions could not be easily calculated and that trust in God's care, goodness, and justice were to be affirmed even when a beneficent order could not be easily discerned. Further, the sages understood that history as well as creation contained dimensions of chaos. Folly, evil, suffering, and death were a daily part of human experience, and mitigated against the notion of a perfected cosmic order. Finally, there is the element of cosmology that is often ignored: that of beauty, esthesis, and delight.[94] The sages responded to the goodness and glories of creation with joyous praise of the creator of heaven and earth. In many ways, the sages developed a philosophy of esthetics in capturing the beauty of reality in the sounds, tones, and images of sapiential language.

Theodicy offers another option for approaching wisdom theology, and no doubt a number of important texts express this important theme. Proverbs (perhaps the "Sayings of Agur," 30:1-9), Job, Qoheleth, several wisdom psalms (e.g., Psalm 73), Ben Sira, and the Wisdom of Solomon all take up the question of the justice of God and offer various understandings. Indeed, divine justice was perhaps the most important attribute of God for the theology of the sages. In this respect, the sages largely agreed with other shapers of Israelite religion and theology. However, the defense of divine justice develops as a response to its denial, or at least to its questioning, and not as an a priori consideration. In other words, the affirmation of divine justice was the norm for Israelite faith, a justice that came to expression in the operation and sustaining of creation and in the providential guidance of the world. One may make a case that theodicy was more openly addressed by the sages,[95] though certainly Jeremiah, Habakkuk, and apocalyptic texts were fundamentally involved in the issue. The traditional sages believed that justice not only was the most important divine attribute, but also that this attribute permeated creation and was to provide the basis for human communal existence. It is more logical to argue that theodicy became an issue of pressing concern during those occasions in the development of the wisdom tradition when both the justice of God and its observation in creation and providence came under serious question. Indeed, this is the argument made by H.-H. Schmid, who contends that wisdom does respond to historical developments within the life of the community that bears the tradition.[96] Theodicy is an important, but

47

subsidiary, theological theme that derives from questions about or a lack of trust in basic affirmations about the nature of God and reality.

In my view, the dialectic of anthropology and cosmology represents the best approach to expressing the theology of wisdom literature. In my estimation, it should be regarded as a true dialectic, and not as a development from one (anthropology) to another (cosmology) or from an emphasis on one to a greater stress on the other. Indeed, certain wisdom texts may present either an anthropological or a cosmological theme. But it is difficult to argue that the anthropological tradition of creation was present in the early stages of wisdom and that cosmology came into play in an important way only within later stages.

But perhaps the fundamental question is how one attempts to interpret and then capture the theology of creation in wisdom literature. Elsewhere, I have used the image of the Dionysian dance and the Apollonian vision to speak of the theology and language of the wise.[97] By this I mean that the sages were concerned to create and maintain an order of justice within reality, an order that was not static, but dynamic in its character. Order as justice was not once and for all attained, but it continued to come into existence through divine and human actions and behavior. At the same time, the sages were also concerned with beauty, emotion, passion, and delight. The "love" of wisdom, the passion to possess it, and the elegance of deed and expression, both oral and written, were of equal concern to the sages.

On the whole, previous soundings, then, have primarily conceptualized and presented in discursive, largely rational language the theology of the sages. However, in so doing, the imagistic and esthetic dimensions of sapiential language have been slighted. It is important to set forth clearly and coherently in discursive language the conceptions of the sages about creation. But it is also equally vital to point out the importance of the imagistic qualities of the language itself, especially organizing metaphors that shape a linguistic esthesis—that is, a coherence of beauty and justice that expresses sapiential faith and ethics. Once a description of wisdom's own way of speaking about the realities of faith and ethics is presented, then a discursive presentation of the conceptual features of this faith and moral philosophy would be in order.

One way to capture the duality within the wisdom tradition that speaks of and expresses both order and beauty is to pay particular attention to the nature and character of sapiential imagination and in particular the images or, better put, the metaphors for God, humanity, and the world in the literature. It is also important to pay attention to the rhetoric of sapiential language, for this rhetoric is designed, not simply to enhance the elegance of linguistic expression, but to stimulate the imagination by creating a world of beauty, justice, and meaning.

"Come to Me, Those Who Are Unlearned, and Lodge in My School"

IMAGINATION, RHETORIC, AND SOCIAL LOCATION IN WISDOM LITERATURE

INTRODUCTION

In Sirach 51:23, Ben Sira issues a paraenetic invitation to the unlearned to take up residence in his "school" (or "house of learning"). The second-century sage uses the term *school* literally and metaphorically to refer both to a residential setting where learning was cultivated and to a world view, a *Weltanschauung*, in which students and would-be sages took up habitation and lived out their lives. Through their language, the sages shaped a view of reality that made sense of life and guided human existence, and they did so within instructional settings in the larger society of ancient Israel and early Judaism.

Before moving inside the wisdom texts to describe the specific content of their theology, four methodological considerations should be examined. The first consideration is the nature and role of sapiential imagination in shaping and understanding reality (i.e., in their world building). The second consideration, related to the first, is to determine how the sages used language, in particular metaphor, to construe and hold together their affirmations about creation. The third consideration is to describe the rhetoric of sapiential language, recognizing that content and the manner of expression are intrinsically related. One cannot discard the rhetoric as only external trappings in order to get at the content. The fourth, and final, consideration, is to locate sapiential imagination and language within specific social locations that gave rise to and carried forth the teachings and rhetoric of the sages. Or to use Ben Sira's language: "Come to me, those who are unlearned, and lodge in my school."

49

THEOLOGICAL IMAGINATION IN WISDOM LITERATURE[1]

Defining and Describing Imagination

Broadly speaking, imagination is the capacity of the human mind to form images, organize them into a coherent whole, and provide them meaning.[2] Imagination may be broken down into two types: common and creative. Common imagination, in contrast to sense perception, projects to exist in the mind and then seeks to interpret or explain something that is not subject to the immediate experience of the senses. This type of imagination may involve a spatial dimension in that it completes the fragmentary data of the senses, since one cannot perceive the whole of an object at once. The act of completion also involves classifying an object in a general category and then assuming that it has certain existing characteristics or features. Through memory, this projection also may be connected to past experience, as the imagination calls to mind objects and perceptions from the past. Or through projection, imagination may move into the future by positing the continued existence of an object perceived in the present. This activity of common imagination gives coherence to experiences, combines perceptions into integrated wholes, and places into relationships and categories things that are sensed and perceived.

Israel's sages made their way in the world, at least in part, by using common imagination to form, classify, organize, combine, and synthesize the images indirectly derived from their sense experience to articulate in the artful presentation of language their character and substance. These images were placed into the variety of literary forms created by the sages: sayings, instructions, poems, dialogues, and narratives. While the literary forms possessed general characteristics, the sages shaped these by rhetorical structures and images designed to create a literary esthesis that brought together form, structure, and content into an elegant, compelling, and insightful teaching. The teachings of the sages evoked the imagination, provided insight into faith and morality, stimulated critical reflection, and became the basis for rational decision making and moral action. For example, the sages observed such things as the drunken behavior of the fool, the soothing effect of the calming word, and the admirable industry of the ant, classified them into common categories, sought out their relationships with other objects and their characteristics, and then used them as the substance of wisdom teaching. Sayings and instructions of various kinds were especially used to incorporate into moral discourse what was learned from reflecting on the images of sense perception. Comparisons, even between objects and experiences that did not seem to be related, were made that contributed to a body of knowledge that made sense of the world.

50

Yet, there is also another type of imagination that moves beyond filling in the unobservable features of fragmentary data, classification, reflection, and artful presentation that combines content and form. This is creative imagination, which involves what is commonly designated as the construction of a world view. One level of creative imagination is at work in placing the various objects of reality into a meaning system that makes sense of human experience and provides a context for making one's way in the world. However, what about things that exist beyond human experience or perception, either past or present? A second level of creative imagination moves from more conventional portrayals of images to unconventional ones by associating with objects and segments of reality new features or by putting them into unusual configurations and combinations. A third level of creative imagination allows the mind to transcend the present world to shape realities that reside beyond the immediacy of experience and perception. This type of creative imagination may involve envisioning new possibilities that do not yet exist, save in the mind's eye. A future is envisioned that may be grounded in the past and the present or even represents a radical break from either of these two temporal spheres. This type of creative imagination may move totally outside the boundaries of space and time to speak of transcendence. Indeed, the images that are used to describe this transcendent reality are taken from the everyday world of human life. There is no other way for humans to speak about God. But the referent of these images exists outside the normal realm of human experience and sense perception. Subsequently, while transcendence may be conveyed through the lenses of these images, their specific identification with God becomes idolatrous. This is both the challenge and the danger of God language—to convey transcendence in ways that make sense, but always to recognize the severe limitations of such renderings. Theological imagination attempts to create and then interpret divine character and the world of the holy through skillful presentation.[3] The substance and mode of theological imagination is not rational discourse that presents through discursive language a systematic rendering of God, humanity, and the world. Rather, through images available indirectly through sense experiences, views of God are presented that are intelligible, that make some sense to human reason and emotions. To move into rational and systematic presentation is a second order of theological discourse that is critically important. But in so doing, the theologian has taken, but then moved beyond, the imaginative renderings of God.

A fresh or transformed image may shatter existing meaning structures and lead to the creation of a new world view. Creative imagination may subvert orthodox conventions in order to usher into existence a new life-defining and life-orienting reality. This is the type of imagination that Ricoeur describes in his important work on metaphor. As we shall see momentarily, metaphor has the ability to redefine reality and transform those who live within its world. While all levels of creative imagination may have disclosive power, i.e., they enable an object under consideration to signify or mean something as a result of interpretation, creative imagination at its highest level possesses transforming power by disclosing new possibilities of meaning for existence and self and their attainment in the world of the not-yet-actual.

The sages used their creative imagination in the shaping of a world view that provided the context of wise living and being.[4] I suggest that this structure of sapiential imagination involves six components: tradition and memory, critical engagement and reformulation of understanding, envisioning the world, imagining God as central to and yet outside of that world, imagining human existence within that world, and acknowledging the limits and restrictions of mystery.

Tradition and Memory

In their presentation of a world in which to take up human dwelling, an effort that builds on the linguisticality and historicality of human existence, the sages drew on the cultural traditions they inherited from their predecessors. These materials provided much of the substance and language for what the sages had to say about their own views of reality and human existence. These cultural traditions included ancient Near Eastern wisdom literatures and myths. Wisdom was, after all, both an international affair of royal courts and a folk tradition indigenous to native cultures. Certainly much later, by the time of Ben Sira, the sages as scribes, tradents, and redactors were the preservers of the wide variety of Israelite and Jewish cultural traditions, including the law, history, and the prophets. For example, Ben Sira uses this wider sweep of cultural traditions to inform his own articulation of wisdom.

Every time sapiential imagination was put to work in the formation of sayings, narratives, and poems, the sages did not create the world *de nouveau*, because they lived in a world constructed at least in part from inherited tradition. They did, of course, reshape these traditions through their creative freedom, but inherited images still pressed themselves into their imaginations.

One example of an inherited metaphor is the "tree of life" used to describe Woman Wisdom. In Proverbs 3:13-20, the poem on the value and desirability of wisdom, the poet-sage writes of wisdom:

> She is a tree of life to those who possess her;
> those who embrace her are called blessed.
> (Prov. 3:18)

The metaphor of the tree of life derives from the mythic traditions of the ancient Near East and perhaps was mediated through the Yahwist narrative in Genesis 2–3, but not necessarily so.[5] In the mythic traditions, the metaphor is linked at times to immortality, which humans are denied, or to fertility, which humans cannot obtain except as the gift of the gods. The sages in Israel used this metaphor to speak of the gift of wisdom, which enabled humans to experience well-being.

Traditions are by nature at least partly linguistic—that is, they are conveyed by means of language (spoken and written) as well as by visual representation and dramatic performance. Thus humans are not only ontologically creatures of language, but they also shape and transmit spoken and written traditions that reflect and form a culture. This means that individual imagination is not an autonomous activity; rather, it occurs within a linguistic field informed by existing tradition. By means of participation in the collective memory of their culture, the sages drew from tradition images to shape their linguistic world. Through memory, faith and moral teachings were brought into human consciousness to be actualized in sapiential existence.

Engagement and the Reformulation of Images of Faith and the Moral Life

The reflection on theological images conveyed within traditions of faith is not simply an act of human reason. Images and their meaning worlds of story and poem push their way into the mind through both the activation of memory and the senses that hear and see them yet again. The world of story and poem is reborn in the mind of the one who hears and sees. The receptor of these narrative worlds enters into their structure either as active participant or as observant bystander. Through entrance into these worlds, their reality, construed through language, is experienced or reexperienced. However, while the memory of these worlds is fresh and vital, the human participant then tests their validity according to existing cultural and personal norms. In retelling  these narratives and representing these poems, the sages often reshaped them in new ways to convey their meaning in a changing culture. Of course, in their retelling their authenticity may be denied, calling for new literary constructions to convey faith and understanding. But even in denying authenticity, it is rare for traditions to be completely abandoned, for they have shaped culture and community often for many generations. Thus, in the efforts at shaping new linguistic renderings, even the fragments of tradition are used to reconstruct the world. The act of engagement leading to representation or transformation is as much a process of imagination as an act of rational inquiry. In engagement, imagination and reason combine to take the images and content

53

of faith and the moral life, assess their power for conveying meaning in the present, and reshape them into new forms consistent with the cultural norms of a contemporary community. The representation or transformation of the images of faith and moral discourse involves an act of imagination, for the substance of past teaching is reshaped into a new esthesis that combines content and form.

In their reflection on inherited traditions and teachings that convey a world view and way of life, the Israelite and Jewish sages did not regard them as inflexible in either form or content.[6] Indeed, each generation of sages assumed the responsibility to reshape their understanding of reality in the present. Tradition, of course, was important and to be regarded with great seriousness and respect. Yet it was not simply to be transmitted without critical engagement, reformulation, and then new affirmation. The validity of critical engagement was contested, of course, in the Joban dialogues. The friends of Job, sages all, claimed to base their teachings on the traditions of the ancestors. Eliphaz, for example, contends:

> I will demonstrate to you, pay attention;
> what I have experienced I shall set forth.
> What the sages have transmitted,
> and their ancestors have not withheld,
> to whom alone the land was given,
> and no stranger passed among them.
> (Job 15:17-19)

Eliphaz argues that his teaching, in this case a dogmatic understanding of retribution, correlates with traditional sapiential teaching and his own experience. Job does not deny that tradition has an important place in sapiential reflection. But what he does deny is that the teaching of retribution is as inflexible as his opponents make it to be and that it correlates with either human experience in general or his own specific situation at present. Job, of course, is far more willing to take on tradition in a critical fashion than are his contestants in the dialogues, for he seeks to redescribe reality in new and unconventional ways.

This means, then, that Israel's sages moved beyond the merely representational by reconfiguring traditional images in new ways, and at times they even rejected them for fresh ones. Certainly this is true of Qoheleth and Job, and possibly the "sayings of Agur" in Proverbs 30. It is common for scholars to regard the writings of some sages (Job, Qoheleth, and perhaps Agur) as representing a crisis of such immense intellectual and religious proportions that their teachings threatened the dissolution of the wisdom tradition. While this crisis has been exaggerated, these unconventional sages, nevertheless, were still operating within the framework of sapiential imagination when they engaged in a critique of traditional teaching to test and determine its adequacy and ability to correlate with their own human experience in the cultural and historical reality in which they lived. This traditioning process, requiring critical engagement, is both historical and linguistic and continues forward in space and time, because it occurs within the context of a community of teachers.

Envisioning the World

The sages of Israel and Judah, then, were not simply content to engage past tradition through acts of memory and sense perception that recreate the world of story and poem in their imagination and then to test it in terms of their own experiences and understandings. They also used their imagination to redescribe reality by seeing an altered world similar to or even radically different from the one presented them through tradition. They set forth the contours and substance of this world, articulating in artful form its characteristic features, and then sought to live it into being through teaching and wise behavior. For example, Ben Sira uses creative imagination to produce a theological synthesis that combines creation, wisdom, history, and Torah into a fresh world view; all of creation and history have been divinely guided toward their culmination in the priestly-scribal community in Jerusalem. For Ben Sira, the reality toward which creation has been divinely guided is coming into realization in his own Jewish community of the early second century B.C.E. This view, articulated especially in the "Praise of the Ancestors" (chaps. 44–50), is the best example of a largely realized eschatology in wisdom literature. Of course, the form of this artful synthesis takes its shape within literary categories of wisdom poetry and storytelling. In the Wisdom of Solomon, creative imagination is used to shape a reality within the form of a homily of persuasion that is in some measure still future. Combining wisdom with eschatology, this sage envisions a world in which Israel's typological journey will reach its climax in a future time of God's redemption. The task of faithful Jews who follow the teachings of the wise is to help to live that new reality into existence.

Imagining God at the Center of Reality

Sapiential imagination is especially at work in envisioning God, for the sages locate God at the center of their historical and linguistic world of space, time, and action. At the same time, God stands outside this world and brings it into judgment. The wise believed that regardless of how compelling and meaningful their constructed world may be, God is still a transcendent, often mysterious deity whose freedom cannot be constrained by the boundaries of a sapiential world view. In traditional teachings (Proverbs, Ben Sira, and the Wisdom of Solomon), there were consistent features of God's character and activities. God was the just and loving creator who originated and sustained both the living cosmos and human creatures. Just how these activities of the origination and sustaining of life were carried out may reside beyond human knowledge, but the sages trusted God to engage in these activities with justice and compassion. The critical sages, the poet of Job and the teacher who composed Qoheleth, brought these traditional depictions of God under assessment. The speeches of Job come close to a rejection of these teachings about God, before finally reaffirming their validity. Qoheleth does cast aside some of the inherited portrayals, especially divine justice and compassion, because of his own human experience and his avowal of the severe limits placed on the ability even of the sage to know much about "the God."

God, for the sages, is not directly experienced by the senses, but is known through the revelation of creation, the traditions of the past, and, at least for Job, religious experience ("I have heard of you by the hearing of the ear [that is, through tradition], but now my eye sees you"). Conceptions of God require the constructive and continuing use of sapiential imagination. Descriptions of God even in past traditions represent what earlier generations had believed about God, while the view that creation reveals something of the nature and activity of God requires certain conceptual moves possible only to the imagination.

However one wishes to explain religious experience as represented by Job's "seeing" of God, it is an image that occurs only within the imagination, and not through the senses. The wisdom tradition sets forth a variety of representations of God, but each is the product of creative imagination. It is doubtful that early wisdom was secular and then only later was baptized into Yahwistic faith by religious scribes who developed more acutely their theological expertise. Religious imagination about God is a part of the wisdom tradition from its earliest beginnings.

The sages imagined God by the use of metaphors that are usually implied and not directly stated. This simply means that the sages imagined God by reference to common objects that are attainable to perception. The sages did not often name God through specific metaphors, but in their description of divine character and especially activity they alluded to specific roles common to Israelite and Jewish society as ways of shaping their theological discourse. These metaphors, even if not directly stated, served as the lenses through which to imagine the nature, character, and activity of God. For example, in wisdom various images of divine activity derive from common social life: father, king, judge, architect, sage, warrior, mother, midwife, and so on. While acting in terms of these images, God is rarely specifically named father, king, judge, and so on. This may have been due to the sages' reluctance to move too far in theological imaginings that would strip away the layers of divine mystery. Perhaps this was the way they attempted to avoid the dangers of idolatry that would render too precisely the nature and activity of God. The rendering of God in specifically human terms would have led to a theological anthropomorphism that would lessen the sovereignty and otherness of the creator and sustainer of reality. Even so, their descriptions of divine activity, roles, and character point rather clearly to these metaphorical descriptions. Their rendering of God is a constructive, nonreferential enterprise. This simply means that God is active in the world of sapiential imagination, but at the same time remains outside this world, bringing it into judgment.

The sapiential allusions to metaphors for God were not often new creations, for many were borrowed from other traditions, including myth. However, positioned within the context of sapiential teaching they became fresh and provocative representations that shaped theological understanding, at least to a degree. The sages certainly had the capacity to render God in more precise terms, but to venture too far in this direction would have resulted in the idolatry of linguistic images.

Certainly, Job's portrayal of God as a divine warrior draws on long-standing tradition from Israel and the ancient Near East. However, his description of the divine warrior who attacks the righteous reshapes this traditional image in provocative and even startling terms. Likewise, Qoheleth's portrayal of "the God" behaving like an enigmatic tyrant suggests the image of God as king, but the teacher shapes it into one of despotism, instead of the traditional beneficent ruler who embodies *noblesse oblige*.

Imagining the Nature and Destiny of Human Beings: Historicality and Linguisticality

Another feature of sapiential imagination addresses human nature and destiny. Underlying the efforts of Israel's sages to describe or redescribe reality is their recognition of the historicality and linguisticality of human existence. With imagination, the sages constructed a world in which to live (historicality), and their tools for this world construction were metaphors that were embodied in both poetry and narrative (linguisticality). Important metaphors were used to construe human nature and actions. Humans were the children of God, works of art, kings, slaves, and lovers of wisdom. These metaphors are at times directly stated and at other times inferred from the descriptions of human nature and behavior. The sages were more comfortable in naming human beings in terms of specific roles and activities than they were in speaking of God. Whether stated or implied, these metaphors for humanity became the means for setting forth the sages' theological anthropology.

Discursive language that places into conceptualities the theology of wisdom is not a step the sages took. Rather, their rhetoric included root metaphors, literary forms, linguistic structure, repetition of words and images, sounds (assonance and alliteration), parallelism, and inclusions. The rhetoric of the wise, combined with the content of their teachings to shape an esthesis of beauty and order that stimulated the imagination, led to understanding, and offered a compelling invitation to enter the world of sapiential making.

Mystery

The sages recognized contingencies in life that were not under human control or that could not be anticipated. And they also recognized that there were mysteries in both the reality they experienced and the world they imagined, residing beyond their capacity to know or to explain. God, of course, was the greatest mystery, whose nature could not be directly known and whose actions were beyond human awareness.

> A human mind plans the way,
> but the Lord directs the steps.
> (Prov. 16:9)

The reality of contingencies and mystery did not, however, absolve the sage from the quest for knowledge, regardless of how little might be learned. And the ultimate object of this quest was the knowledge of God, revealed especially in the order of creation.[7] Neither were they released from the responsibility to develop ways for existing in the world. While it may be an overstatement to argue that the sages were seeking to master life, they did articulate the manner of prudent behavior that in general was designed to offset as much as possible disasters that overcame the unthinking fool. Thus they knew that preparations for storing food during periods of scarcity could preclude famine and starvation, though unforeseen disasters could negate success for even the best-laid plans. God, of course, resided beyond human perceptions. Even so, the sages assumed that God was good, caring, and just. And they generally assumed, save for the Job of the dialogues and Qoheleth, that God could be trusted to support and bless with life those who lived wisely and justly. They imagined God in roles that were known from their own experience: the king, the potter, the judge, the parent, and so forth. Even so, the sages' insistence on divine mystery usually precluded their specific naming of God by these roles. When Yahweh speaks to Job, it is as the voice from the whirlwind (Job 38–41), but the language suggests that God comes as the divine warrior.

However, whatever Job sees with his eyes in this theophany (42:5) is not clearly stated. The sages could speak of God in ways that made sense by using familiar images and roles, but at the same time protected the elusiveness of divine nature and activity.

METAPHORS AND THEOLOGICAL IMAGINATION[8]

Introduction

In their observations, which they deposited in sapiential teachings, then, the wise men and women of Israel used their imagination to create a world for human habitation, to engage in moral discourse with a tradition that invited participants to righteous living in harmony with cosmos and society and to shape a poetic esthesis that formed a reality of both beauty and delight. For the wise, the theology of creation, moral discourse that imagined and then compelled the pursuit of justice, and the ascertaining and crafting of what was pleasing as well as good came to reside in the power of words, particularly metaphors of creation. While not always specifically stated in naming God, the world, and humanity, they are present at least inferentially in the descriptions of these three areas. Imagination is the place where metaphors functioned to posit the nature and identity of reality—that is, to create a world view.

The Nature of Metaphor[9]

Creation in wisdom literature requires, then, an understanding of both metaphor and the metaphorical process—a phenomenological activity that requires the engagement of root metaphor, the literary tradition (narrative or poetry) in which it is found, the "voice" that is heard within the tradition, and the audience that enters into the linguistic world created by the tradition.

To begin with, metaphor is "as ultimate as speech itself, and speech as ultimate as thought," being "the instinctive and necessary act of the mind exploring reality and ordering experience."[10] Metaphors are part of the linguistic essence of all human speech, which, in turn, is grounded in human thinking and, as we have seen, imagination. Language is the distinctive and, therefore, primary feature of what it means to be human.[11] With the ability to imagine and to think rationally and conceptually, and with the capacity to express images and thoughts in words, humans have the singular ability to construct meaning systems that define and interpret their world in all of its aspects. And at the heart of this world building capacity is metaphor.[12]

Communities use root metaphors to be the linguistic, organizing center of traditions that carry the most important and cherished understandings of their faith and religious affirmations.[13] Since language, through the power of imagination, both describes and shapes reality, metaphor moves beyond the merely factual description to participate in the very process of world building. Metaphors become the semantic building blocks in the linguistic construction of reality.

Metaphor is far more than simple literary enhancement of declarative, straightforward language, whether spoken or written. Neither is a metaphor simply a comparison of one thing to another. An interactional model defines a metaphor as the interfacing of two distinct subjects within a sentence. These two subjects are sometimes called the tenor and its vehicle.[14] The tenor is the principal subject that is conveyed by a vehicle, or secondary subject.[15] In bringing the tenor and vehicle into a relationship, new insight into the meaning and nature of the principal subject is given. The vehicle becomes a means by which the tenor is described, understood, and given meaning. And yet at the same time, the vehicle also is given a meaning context and signifies as a result of its combination with the tenor. In the interaction of tenor and vehicle, meaning for the sentence is constructed. Vehicles not only convey meaning but also are the receptors of meaning. Further, the vehicle suggests that the tenor is but also is not something. The vehicle provides insight into the tenor, but there is no literal identity to the point that the individual identity and meaning of the two subjects are lost so that they merge into each other and become inseparable.

Metaphors are the cornerstones of meaning systems and participate in the construction of reality, but at the same time they are themselves constructed by the very worlds they build; they signify only by reference to the sentence and the larger linguistic world in which they dwell. When removed from the reality systems they produce, they as well as the semantic world they create disintegrate. Subsequently, metaphors, regardless of how important they are in conveying even the most cherished values and beliefs of a community, remain finite and limited. They are not immortal. To deny them the characteristics of finitude and limitation results potentially in the worst kind of cultural and, in the arena of religion, theological idolatry.

Theological language is metaphorical, and, in a sense, it has to be, for it attempts to capture within words the nature and character of God, who is not directly accessible to human perception. Subsequently, things that are familiar and that are directly perceived are used to give expression to the portrait of God conceived by the imagination. With the creation of central metaphors, a community conveys the important features of its religious understandings, derived from its imagination.[16]

The Metaphorical Process

Living metaphors defy isolation, for they must exist in relationship with other words that make up the linguistic worlds of sentence, story, and life. Metaphors are not static creatures frozen eternally in time; rather, like living creatures, they are active and subject to new insights, interpretations, and significations. Metaphors, to continue living, are fluid in meaning, since their signification depends, at least in part, on the hermeneutical process in which change and difference are endemic.

The reservoirs of past tradition provide a cadre of what might be regarded as traditional metaphors, not in the sense that they are static and one dimensional, but that they are open to new insights and understanding. Unless radically redefined, traditional metaphors do not lead to a dramatically new transformation of reality. In other words, they support the meaning system in which they provide the center. Some alteration of this meaning system is always a possibility, since metaphors and the traditions they help to convey are open to new understandings. However, the radical redefinition of old metaphors or the creation of new and compelling ones does have the power to reshape reality, to construct a world view that requires an altered way of existing for a community and those who are its constituents. This radical redefinition or creation of new metaphors may also involve an assault on the integrity of older, traditional ones. In other words, the traditional metaphors may be maintained, but only by significantly altering the meanings they convey and hence the traditions they help to preserve. Or they may be the objects of direct attack, for the creation and vitality of new ones require the death of the old.

Subsequently, a radically redefined metaphor or a new one invites an audience to move through a process that involves the deconstruction of previous meaning systems and the construction of new and compelling ones. The stages in this process include the following.

The first stage on the way to world building is destabilization. Metaphors pose a meaning that, if taken literally, is nonsense.[17] Nelson Goodman remarks: "The oddity is that metaphorical truth is compatible with literal falsity; a sentence false when taken literally may be true when taken metaphorically, as in the case of 'The joint is jumping' or 'The lake is a sapphire.' "[18]

Common, ordinary understanding is challenged and by means of powerful metaphors disintegrates, at least for the moment of new revelation. Absurdity is a "strategy of discourse" that both deconstructs the literal meaning of a statement and at the same time poses a meaningful contradiction that provides for the possibility of new insight.[19] For example, to personify the wisdom tradition as a woman of wealth, intelligence, and beauty or reality as an

61

elegant, spacious manse in which the wise take up their dwelling is nonsense on a rational level. But effective metaphors have the ability to engage the attention and move the audience out of a normal, everyday frame of rational thought and logical discourse to awaken the imagination in order to consider new possibilities of meaning and insight. The movement to this possibility occurs only when the audience is willing and able to move beyond the obstacle of absurdity to consider new possibilities. This initial engagement with metaphor, then, results in a disorienting shock.

The second stage in this process is the correlation of the absurd contention of the metaphor with the possibility of truth. Theologically conceived, revelation becomes a possibility. This stage is sometimes called mimesis, for it is here that the audience recognizes, at least for a moment, that something in the relationship between the tenor and the vehicle is true. Imposing a different, unusual set of features on the tenor by means of its association with the vehicle may lead to the recognition that something in the relationship between tenor and vehicle is true.[20] This stage involves a second shock, this time the "shock of recognition."[21] At least for the creative moment of meaning that opens up the possibility of reflection, the tenor and its vehicle have united as one. Particularly compelling metaphors that lead to the conviction that what they propose contains at least some element of truth may lead the audience to the third stage: transformation. The word *metaphor* derives from the term *metamorphosis*, "change, alteration, transformation." This stage leads to a new understanding of the subject, an understanding that is so important that the world view of an audience is changed or even newly created.

The final stage of the process, then, is restabilization. This altered or new reality is reshaped, the meaning system is restabilized, and a new way of living in the world takes place.[22] Disorientation is now replaced by a nomos for life, a world view that provides coherence and direction.

Metaphors not only alter the way an object is understood, but, if they are particularly engaging and compelling ones, they may also become the center of a new reality that combines beliefs and values into a coherent whole.[23] This means, of course, that this type of metaphor is potentially dangerous, for within its reality system, conveyed by tradition, it contains the capacity to transform one's vision of the world, a vision that commands obedience and summons one into the future. It reconstructs and refashions reality into new and powerful symbolic worlds that are evocative of significant commitment.[24] And when a metaphor becomes the organizing symbol of a community, it provides sustaining vitality for a people through memory, rite, and tradition.

Even when transformation brought on by the reshaping of reality occurs, a tensive relationship continues between what is affirmed by the metaphor and what is considered both true and false.[25] Metaphors, after all, do not loose themselves from the element of the absurd, although when they become an accepted part of tradition, and at times even its organizing center, they are generally accepted as true without producing the intensity of shocks described above. And there is the inevitable clash of significations with competing metaphors and their linguistic contexts.[26] Ironically, however, these tensive qualities provide metaphors and the worlds they build the energy they need to continue to exist.[27] When tensions are removed by literal and factual definitions, the reality shaped by metaphors has the tendency to become either uncritical assertion or even inflexible dogma that demands assent. The removal of tensions eventually leads to the dissolution of the linguistic traditions in which metaphors existed. And the meaning systems articulated by these traditions collapse.

Living metaphors also continue to be ambiguous, for they contain a surplus of meaning that defies one-dimensional definition.[28] Metaphors, by their very nature, defy "steno-meanings" that are universally acknowledged. Inevitably, metaphors include a range of possible understandings, grounded, at least in part, in individual experience and the fact that traditions and the tradition bearers, the culture-producing community, change.[29]

Finally, it should be recognized that metaphors, even those that are central to traditions of cherished beliefs and important values, are not immortal. When they lose their power to shape identity and summon into the future, they become impotent and eventually perish. No longer capable of sustaining the world they have created, they die, and through their passing threaten the world that depends on their sustaining power to exist. This means that communities are required to create new root metaphors that alter tradition and transform meaning. Otherwise, these communities stagnate and lose their capacity to organize and sustain their common life.[30]

THE RHETORIC OF SAPIENTIAL IMAGINATION AND MORAL DISCOURSE

Introduction

Metaphors, stated or implied, were central to the nature and content of sapiential imagination. But also important is the rhetoric of moral discourse in which metaphors played such a key role for conveying and provoking meaning. The teachings of the sages combined elegance of form with moral content to shape a world of imagination for human dwelling. Subsequently, to understand the sages is to appreciate the esthetic dimensions of their teachings. To cast aside and then ignore the rhetoric in the effort to discover the content often leaves the interpreter with little more than a list of moralisms and pious platitudes.[31] An important key to understanding the writings of the sages is to allow the elegance and content of their teachings to provoke the readers' imagination, to allow, at least in the moment of interpretation, entrance into their sapiential world of beauty and order.

Literary Forms

The literary character of sapiential teaching includes several forms: sayings, instructions, narratives, dialogues, and poems.[32] These forms are present throughout the history of the wisdom tradition and are used to shape its distinctive discourse.

In a wisdom context, *mašal* is the general term for any sapiential form (1 Sam. 10:12; 24:14; Prov. 1:6; 26:7, 9), while the plural, *mešalîm*, refers to a collection of wisdom sayings and other forms (Prov. 1:1; 10:1; 25:1). The most common form was the "saying," or proverb (*mašal*), although the word also covers a wide variety of other literary forms, including didactic psalms (Pss. 49:5; 78:2), poems (Isa. 14:4-11), and parables (Ezek. 17:2). The etymology of the word suggests two understandings: "rule" and "comparison." In the first instance, the term points to wisdom's desire to master life. Through the embodiment of wisdom teaching, the sage has the ability to rule or control the vicissitudes of life and to be successful. Language in itself has power, and wise teaching, guiding proper behavior, enabled the sage to master a situation and to be successful. The second understanding suggests that endemic to wisdom thinking was the view that there was an underlying connection between the things subject to human experience. The comparative efforts by the sages suggest that they saw within reality an order that enabled them to make sense of the world.

The specific types of "sayings" in wisdom literature include proverbs, comparative sayings, better sayings, happy sayings (or beatitudes), numerical sayings, questions, and riddles. These are usually artistic sayings in that many of the features of Hebrew poetry are present.

The proverb, the most common form of saying, is normally a sentence of two parallel lines (synonymous, antithetical, and synthetic) in the indicative mood that registers a conclusion drawn from experience (e.g., Prov. 20:1, 3, 4, 8).

> The sluggard does not plow in the autumn;
> he will seek at harvest and have nothing.
> (Prov. 20:4)

At times proverbs use metaphors, when the statement is made that one thing is (but also is not) another. Thus in Proverbs 14:27, the "fear of the Lord is a fountain of life."

In synonymous proverbs, the second line, while restating the thought of the first, usually adds something new. The addition is usually not dramatic, but adds a different twist or nuance. Thus Proverbs 21:12 comments:

> The righteous observe the house of the wicked;
>   the wicked are cast down to ruin.

In the second line, "the wicked" is repeated, though what the righteous observe in the first line is extended to include, not just "the wicked," but also the fate that awaits them; they "are cast down to ruin." (See also Prov. 22:7, 8, 14.)

Antithetical proverbs contrast two things. Thus Prov. 14:3 contrasts the subjects of the two lines:

> The talk of a fool is a rod for his back,
>   but the lips of the wise will preserve them.

Also see Proverbs 14:5, 6, 8, 9; 21:31. Synthetic proverbs are sayings where the thought of the first line is developed in a continuing movement in the second. For example, Proverbs 15:3 states:

> The eyes of the Lord are in every place,
>   keeping watch on the evil and the good.

Also see Proverbs 21:6, 7, 21-22, 25.

Comparative or like sayings share the same features of proverbs, but they seek to find points held in common between two different objects to give insight into one or the other. In this way, they are quite similar to metaphors (e.g., Prov. 10:26; 11:22; 19:12; 20:2; 25:3, 13-14; 26:7-11). Thus:

> Like vinegar to the teeth and smoke to the eyes,
>   so is the sluggard to those who send him.
>   (Prov. 10:26)

A particular type of comparative saying uses the principle of "if this, then how much more or less this." For example:

> Sheol and Abaddon lie open before the Lord,
>   how much more people's hearts.
>   (Prov. 15:11)

65

The better saying compares one thing to another, though with the judgment that something is to be preferred or is of more value than that with which the comparison is made. It should be noted, however, that the two things compared are always qualified by modifiers or circumstances. Thus Proverbs 15:16 reads:

> Better is a little with the fear of the Lord
> than great treasure and trouble with it.

See Proverbs 15:17; 16:8; 19:1, 22; 21:9, 19.

"Happy sayings" typically begin with the Hebrew word ʾašrê ("happy") and pronounce people "happy" who, because of wise and righteous behavior, have entered into a state of well-being and joy. For example, Proverbs 14:21 states:

> He who despises his neighbor is a sinner,
> but happy is he who is kind to the poor.

Also see Proverbs 8:32, 34; 16:20; and 29:18.

The pattern of numerical sayings consists of a title line and a list of things that have in common the feature or features of the title line. The list contains two, three, four, or even seven things that share one or more features in common. Thus Proverbs 30:21-23 reads:

> Under three things the earth trembles;
> under four it cannot bear up:
> a slave when he becomes king,
> and a fool when he is filled with food;
> an unloved woman when she gets a husband,
> and a maid when she succeeds her mistress.

Also see Proverbs 30:15-16, 18-19, 24-31.

The question in wisdom literature is most often rhetorical—that is, it has an obvious answer. For example, Proverbs 20:9 reads:

> Who can say, "I have made my heart clean;
> I am pure from my sin?"

See also Proverbs 20:24; 22:27. However, some interrogatives pose "impossible questions," questions that have no answers or at least no conceivable answers (see Job 38–41).

Riddles ("dark or hard sayings") may at one time also have been a type of wisdom saying used by the sages; unfortunately, few have survived in the Bible and deuterocanonical literature. A riddle makes an enigmatic statement that obscurely or even paradoxically describes something in terms of one or more of its characteristic features. The referent of the description is to be guessed. The purpose of the riddle is to confuse and dumbfound the hearer. The sages, skilled in the art of formulating and answering "hard sayings," demonstrated their wisdom by proposing riddles that confounded their hearers and by answering the riddles of others (see 1 Kings 10:1-3). There is within the riddle as stated a clue or key to its answer. The classic riddle in the Old Testament is the one posed by Samson to his Philistine wedding guests in Judges 14:14:

> From the eater comes forth food;
> from the strong comes forth sweetness.

The answer is given in v. 18:

> What is sweeter than honey?
> What is stronger than a lion?

This riddle draws on the double meaning of the Hebrew word '*ārî,* meaning "lion" and "honey."[33] For whatever reason, complete riddles have not survived in the wisdom corpus.

In addition to a variety of sayings, wisdom literature also contains a second major form: the "instruction" or "discipline" (*mûsār*; Prov. 1:3; 8:10, 33; 24:32). *Mûsār* includes instruction in values and piety, the incorporation of virtue and religion in life, and the use of the imagination to construct a world within which sapiential behavior makes sense. In regard to form, the instruction sets forth values and guidance for behavior within the following structure:

1. Introduction: The teacher addresses the students and calls upon them to listen, i.e., give heed to the teaching that follows;
2. The Teaching: A list of admonitions (imperatives) and prohibitions, with or without motive or result clauses, that exhort the students to follow certain sapiential values and to avoid various types of foolish behavior.
3. The Conclusion: Some instructions end with a conclusion that consists of either a statement of the results of wise or unwise behavior, a saying that summarizes the teaching, or a return back to the introduction.

Instructions in Proverbs 1–9 include 1:8-19; 2:1-22; 3:1-12, 21-35; 4:1-9, 10-19, 20-27; 5:1-23; 6:20-35; and 7:1-27.[34]

The main section of instructions contains two related forms: the admonition and its opposite, the prohibition.[35] Admonitions are imperatives that attempt to persuade the hearer to engage in a course of action or to embody a particular virtue. Prohibitions are imperatives plus a negative ("no," "not"), designed to dissuade the hearer from taking a course of action or from embodying some sort of vice or foolishness. Both may be followed by the attachment of motive or result clauses stressing respectively either the reasons behind the command or prohibition or the results of a course of action or type of behavior. Many admonitions and prohibitions occur within the larger structure of instructions, though others are preserved independently in proverbial collections (see Prov. 3:3-12).

The wise also composed didactic narratives of two types: first-person narratives in which the teacher recounts an experience and then registers a conclusion, and third-person narratives in which the narrator, presumably a sage, tells a story of a wise person. First-person narratives include Proverbs 7:6-27, where the sage (or perhaps Woman Wisdom herself) recounts observing the seduction of a simpleton by a harlot. The conclusion is that succumbing to the wiles of the "strange woman" leads to death. Subsequently, the teacher issues a warning at the end of the poetic narrative, advising youths to avoid her advances. Other examples include Psalm 37:35-36 and, of course, the first part of Qoheleth (see esp. 1:12–2:26). The prologue and epilogue of the book of Job contain a third-person narrative in which the hero or protagonist, in this case Job, embodies a virtue (piety and morality for their own sake) that is contested by an antagonist. Finally, after going through a series of difficult challenges, the hero is vindicated and his opponents are shamed.

Dialogues, or debates, also had an important place among the literary forms of the wise. Two or more sages debate the superiority of a value, an ethical position, or an element of reality. This form comprises the heart of the poetic book of Job, in which Job and his three opponents—Eliphaz, Bildad, and Zophar—debate the issues of theodicy and human suffering.

Finally, the wise wrote poems of various kinds, including those imitating at times some of the more common types of psalms used in worship (Pss. 1; 34; 37; 49; 73; 127; 128). Among the best-known poems are those that speak of Woman Wisdom (Job 28; Prov. 1:20-33; 8:1-31).

Sapiential Rhetoric[36]

The origins of rhetorical criticism are usually traced to James Muilenburg, though he himself acknowledged important predecessors, including especially Hermann Gunkel, Robert Lowth, and J. G. Herder. The major tasks of rhetorical criticism are to define the limits of a literary unit (prose or poetry), uncover the component parts and structural patterns at work in its shape, and point out the literary techniques used in ordering its artistic composition. The focus is the literary work itself, and not the mind of the author or the understanding of the original audience. The artistry of the text renders its meaning. This means that the artistic composition and the meaning of the text are inseparable.

The literary techniques that enable a unit to cohere and engage the imagination include anaphora (the repetition of an initial word or words of several clauses, lines, or strophes); refrains (repeated words or phrases at the end of strophes or other subunits); interweaving words or phrases (*mots crochets*) that blend the entire unit or major subunit; inclusions (the repetition of the opening word or words at the close of the unit, thus marking the unit's literary boundaries); and parallelism of members (strophes or lines within a poem that parallel in some fashion, though there is also a "seconding sequence" in the second part that extends, differs from, or in some fashion changes the idea in the first part).[37] Among the different kinds are especially synonymous, antithetical, and synthetic parallelism. Other features of artistic composition include onomatopoeia (words imitating sounds), alliteration (the correspondence of sounds at the beginning of words), assonance (the correspondence of the sounds of accented vowels), and a variety of different structures for lines, paragraphs (narrative), and strophes (subunits of a poem that express normally one central idea), including chiasms (literally, an "x" formed by a pattern of lines: e.g., a, b, c, c1, b1, a1) and acrostics (particularly alphabetic ones).[38]

These literary features of Hebrew poetry and narrative are used by the sages in the esthetic shaping of their teaching. Form, metaphor, and rhetoric combine with content to transmit the values and beliefs of the sages in ways that will provoke the imagination and open the mind to learn about and reflect on God, the world, and human existence.

SOCIAL LOCATIONS AND MORAL DISCIPLINE

The Social Settings of Sapiential Discourse

One social location for the wisdom tradition was the Israelite and Jewish family.[39] The ethos and social structure of the Israelite family has been the object of research, although a comprehensive overview has yet to be written.[40] Throughout much of its history, the Israelite family was largely patriarchal, patrilineal, and patrilocal. This means that the dominant authority in the family was the father, that identity and inheritance passed from the father to the sons (with the firstborn son succeeding his father as the head of the family), and that normally the wife left her own household to join that of her husband. The "house of the father" (*bēt 'ab*) was the nuclear family that consisted of a husband (father), wife or wives (mother[s]), unmarried children, married sons and their families, and widowed daughters. Older and/or poor family members might also be included, along with slaves and "foreigners" (sojourners who had alien status). Several families related by blood and living in close proximity to each other comprised the extended family, or clan (mišpāḥâ).[41] Several clans comprised the tribe (šēbet or maṭṭeh), while the tribes of Israel ("sons of Israel") were the largest sociopolitical unit (šibtê-yisrāēl or běnē-yisrāēl). The social unit of the tribe began to fragment after the establishment of the Israelite monarchy.

Within the family, the head of the household, the father, was the sage or teacher responsible for socializing the sons in the traditions of the family and larger social units, for teaching them their responsibilities as future heads of families, and for educating them in occupations for a future livelihood. Mothers presumably taught young children (sons and daughters) and older daughters in the Israelite households in the areas of socialization and social roles within the family. The teaching of the mother is also authoritative (see Prov. 1:8; 6:20; 10:1; 15:20; 20:20; 23:22, 25; 28:24; 31:10-31), and indeed her role as teacher was a central role in the Israelite family.[42] This instruction (mûsār, "discipline," "teaching") of children by parents may be reflected in a variety of wisdom texts (Prov. 1:8, 10, 15; etc.). However, familial titles also were used in wisdom schools to refer to teachers and students in wisdom schools.

Distinguished heads of families played more public roles in the villages (largely populated by clans), tribes, and leagues of tribes. These "elders" (zĕqēnîm), endowed with wisdom, provided both the legal and the moral authority in a tribal society in the far-ranging areas of economics (e.g., the settling of boundary disputes among families, clans, and tribes), social legislation, military decisions, and religious traditions. After the rise of the Israelite monarchy, elders served as counselors to kings (see Num. 11:16-30; Josh. 9:11; 2 Sam. 17:4; 1 Kings 12:6-11; 21:8; 2 Kings 10:1, 5; 23:1; and Ps. 105:21-22). How much of this familial, clan, and tribal wisdom made its way into sapiential literature preserved in the canon and apocrypha is open to debate, but it seems likely that family and tribal wisdom would have been reshaped by sages active in a variety of schools associated with the court and temple.

A second social location for wisdom was the royal court. With the formation of the Israelite state, the institution most responsible for nurturing the wisdom tradition was the monarchy.[43] This is suggested by a variety of sources, including the Solomonic narrative in 1 Kings 3–11 and the headings given to several collections of wisdom teachings in Proverbs. Solomon is presented as the wise king whose divine endowment with "an understanding mind" (1 Kings 3:1-15) enabled him to rule justly and well (1 Kings 3:16-28) the Davidic empire. His administrative reorganization of the Israelite state

(1 Kings 4:1-28), involvement in the creating of sapiential forms (1 Kings 4:29-34 = MT 5:9-14), building of the Temple and palace (1 Kings 5–9), and great prosperity are attributed to his wisdom (1 Kings 10:1-13).[44] This connection of Solomon with the wisdom tradition is also represented by three superscriptions in the book of Proverbs (1:1; 10:1; and 25:1[45]) as well as by the attribution to him of the books of Qoheleth, the Song of Solomon (Canticles), and the Wisdom of Solomon. Historically speaking, there is no basis for assuming any direct association of Solomon with these books, and the superscriptions that attributed three collections to Solomon may be no more than an indication of royal patronage of the tradition by the House of David, rather than any direct Solomonic authorship. It may be the case that the editors of 1 Kings 3–11 were more interested in shaping a tradition of royal propaganda designed to legitimate the Davidic monarchy than in reflecting social history. Nevertheless, the association of Solomon and the House of David with wisdom suggests that sages, some of whom would have been active as officials and scribes within the royal state, sought to legitimate this dynasty through its writings. At the same time, it seems likely that the power and wealth of the royal house sanctioned and supported through a patronage system the work and activity of the sages.

The emergence of the royal state required not only the introduction of a new administrative structure, but also a new social, religious, and intellectual tradition that would sanction and undergird royal claims.[46] The sages may have been active in the efforts to create an intellectual climate in which the state and its social organization could carry on its work.[47] These sages served in a variety of capacities in the administration, including courtier, scribe, recorder of annals, counselor, secretary, herald, architect and builder, lawyer, author, and quite probably redactor.[48] These sages grounded the sociopolitical and religious institutions in Israel and Judah (government, religion, law, military, and economics) in the order of creation.[49] This means they believed that God originated and sustains a righteous order of life. The king and the royal court were responsible for the administration of justice through a system of laws, judicial processes, and punishments. The rituals of the royal cult were designed to secure divine blessing and to renew the forces of well-being that enabled the state to continue.[50]

The danger of this type of world view is that it attempts to control reality and its human inhabitants by the power of ideology that has a propensity for being uncritical. When the king and other leaders in the state are corrupt and unjust, wisdom in Proverbs, designed in part to legitimate and socialize members into the larger society, cannot easily step into a critical mode as did some of the prophets critical of kings and court politics.[51] Wisdom could be corrupted into an instrument motivated by the desire to obtain power and wealth (see the oracle against the prince of Tyre in Ezekiel 28). Thus Proverbs is cautious at times about those who hold power (especially the king) and condemns behavior that places self-interest above integrity.

A third social location for the development and transmission of wisdom was the school. The wisdom tradition, more than likely, was developed to a large extent within schools designed to educate administrators, scribes, lawyers, and teachers. The evidence for the existence of schools and specific information about their structure and programs unfortunately is rather sparse. Several sources of information include canonical and deuterocanonical texts that explicitly and implicitly point to schools, archaeological and epigraphic data, and comparative analogies from the ancient Near East.[52]

In a text often cited to point to the existence of schools, Jesus ben Sira, around 200 B.C.E., issues an invitation to potential students who would take up a course of study with him:

> Come to me those who are unlearned,
> and lodge in my school.
>
> (Sir. 51:23)

Ben Sira's school (*bĕtmidrāš*; "house of study") is probably a residential academy where well-to-do youth in Jerusalem and perhaps areas outside the sacred city studied in order to enter into leading positions in Jewish society during the reign of the Seleucids. The epilogue to Qoheleth (Qoh. 12:9-14) also suggests that the author of this text was a Jewish teacher who lived in Jerusalem in the late fourth and/or early third centuries B.C.E. He may have taught in a wisdom school for youths seeking an education to prepare for careers in Jewish society. (Royal schools are hinted at in 1 Kings 12:8, 10; 2 Kings 10:1, 5-6; 2 Chron. 17:7-9; as are Temple schools in 2 Kings 12:3; 2 Chron. 22:11; and Isa. 28:7-13.)

There is no explicit archaeological evidence for school buildings in ancient Israel. However, schools may have existed in private houses, public buildings (especially associated with governmental buildings and sanctuaries), and other civic locations that included gates and courtyards.[53] Furthermore, the question of the existence of schools involves far more than physical space. Teachers, students, courses of study (subjects and texts), and times for instruction are also considerations.

Parents instructed children in social and religious traditions, social roles in the family, and familial careers and livelihoods. Officials, priests, lawyers, and scribes, among others, may well have educated their children and other aspiring youths in their professions. And, more than likely, schools were established at a national level to educate officials and administrators to carry on governmental work. Increasing literacy and hence the expansion of education is indicated by the growing number of Hebrew inscriptions from the eighth to the sixth centuries B.C.E.[54] These materials indicate literacy beyond the narrow circles of professional scribes working in the state bureaucracies.

Finally, the existence of schools from surrounding ancient Near Eastern societies suggests by analogy that Israel may have had similar institutions responsible for the creation and transmission of culture and for education in the various professions necessary for social life at a national level. It is obvious that education was necessary for Israel and, later on, for early Judaism to carry out a rather sophisticated socioreligious life. The wisdom texts themselves, including Proverbs and Ben Sira, may have been part of a much larger curriculum that would have included mathematics, foreign languages, geography, architecture, reading, writing, and law. Wisdom texts would have been used to teach ethics and social decorum to students pursuing an education.[55]

Based on comparative evidence, schools in Israel may have been associated with sanctuaries in ancient Israel. Certainly, in the ancient Near East, libraries and schools were at times associated with temples.[56] Moshe Weinfeld has submitted the thesis that the authors and editors of Deuteronomy and the Deuteronomic traditions in the Bible were the *sōferîm-ḥăkāmîm,* wise scribes who also produced the wisdom texts.[57] They may have been active in a school, or at least occupied rooms associated with the reading of books located near the Temple (see Jeremiah 36). Certainly, in the postexilic period, the place of the Temple in Jewish society continued to grow in significance, and the association of scribes with the religious teachings of the Torah seems to have grown even closer than before the fall of Jerusalem to the Babylonians. Indeed, Ezra, the Jewish sage-scribe who also served in the Persian government as minister for Jewish affairs, was a student of the Torah who came to Jerusalem and led a major religious reform. Whether Ben Sira's school had an affiliation with the Temple is unclear, though his positive views of and teachings about Temple worship, Torah, and the high priesthood suggest a close relationship between education and the priestly system.[58]

Wisdom as Discipline[59]

Moral discourse between teacher and student in wisdom literature, whether in the social contexts of family or school, involves "discipline" (*mûsār*)—that is, education or training through a course of study and a process of correction (Prov. 1:2-3, 7-8; 15:33; 23:23). Through conversation and reflection, the objective of "discipline" is to inculcate within the individual a moral order in which knowledge, character, and righteous conduct would achieve integration. The process of correction involved many aspects, from the repetitions required for memorization and learning to write, to the efforts to apply to concrete situations what has been learned. Correction involved a teacher's use of a variety of techniques to motivate a student's efforts to learn and to improve, from gentle persuasion, to harsh rebuke, to corporal punishment.

Yet "discipline" did not stop after leaving the settings of formal instruction and the direct influence and guidance of teachers. It continued on through life as self-discipline in a continuing quest to accumulate knowledge, acquire understanding, enhance character, and act wisely. Becoming wise is a way of life, a process that continues for a lifetime, as the wise person seeks to live in harmony with God, the cosmos, the social order, and a human nature, which requires the discipline and structure of teaching.

PART II

The Theology of Wisdom Literature

CHAPTER THREE

"The Lord Created Me at the Beginning of His Work"

CREATION AND MORAL DISCOURSE IN PROVERBS

INTRODUCTION

The Literary Structure of Proverbs

The book of Proverbs consists of eight separate collections of varying forms of wisdom language, including instructions, wisdom poems, and sayings. Each collection, save for the last one, is introduced by a title or superscription:

1:1.	"The Proverbs of Solomon" (1–9 and the entire book as well)
10:1.	"The Proverbs of Solomon" (10:1–22:16)
22:17.	"The Sayings of the Wise" (22:17–24:22)
24:23.	"These also belong to the Wise" (24:23-34)
25:1.	"These also are the Proverbs of Solomon that the Men of Hezekiah, King of Judah, copied" (25–29)
30:1.	"The words of Agur" (30)
31:1.	"The words of Lemuel" (31:1-9)
31:10-31.	No title. Acrostic poem on the ideal Wise Woman (31:10-31).

These collections (*mĕšālîm*) consist of a variety of wisdom forms that were often placed together in smaller literary units shaped by different rhetorical devices and themes. Each level of the book points to evidence of literary artistry that combines content with rhetoric in the didactic process. Sapiential genres, small literary units, and larger collections were designed to teach and persuade, doing so by shaping an esthesis—a poetic world of beauty, harmony, order, and balance that is to be actualized in the life of the one seeking wisdom, for this same esthesis describes the nature of the external world of God's creation.[1] Through sapience—that is, a way of being and acting that actualizes moral discourse—the sages learned not only to live in harmony with the various components of reality, but also to shape and strengthen the structures of goodness and life that, taken together, comprise the righteous and just order of the cosmos, society, and human nature.

COSMOLOGY AND ANTHROPOLOGY IN PROVERBS 1–9[2]

Literary Structure

Proverbs 1–9 is an elegantly crafted collection consisting of a general introduction, ten instructions, five related poems on Woman Wisdom, and a variety of short wisdom sayings scattered throughout the collection.[3] The instructions are found in 1:8-19; 2:1-22; 3:1-12, 21-35; 4:1-9, 10-19, 20-27; 5:1-23; 6:20-35; and 7:1-27.[4] Poems on Woman Wisdom are strategically placed at the beginning and end of the collection (1:20-33; 8:1-11, 12-21, 22-31; and 9:1-18) to form a literary inclusio. The literary positioning of the poems on wisdom underscores the importance and role of Woman Wisdom in creation, providence, and instruction in the moral life.[5] This rhetorical structure stimulates the imagination to find behind the voice of the teacher in Proverbs 1–9 a second, even more authoritative and revelatory voice, that of Woman Wisdom, who is teacher, sage, Queen of Heaven, the child of God, and the mediator between heaven and earth. And behind her, more distant, but still audible, is the voice of God, who addresses through the teacher and Woman Wisdom those who take up sapiential instruction.[6]

Purpose of the Collection

The introduction in 1:2-7 sets forth the purpose of Proverbs 1–9, and, for that matter, the entire book of Proverbs. The purpose of the collection and the larger book is instruction in wisdom, or *mûsār*—that is, knowledge about God, the world, and human life; the embodiment of sapiential piety and virtue; and the construction of a world for human dwelling.[7] The introduction serves as an invitation to pursue the study of wisdom.[8]

Sapiential teaching is directed to three groups: humanity in general, the "simple" or unlearned, and the "sage" who seeks to enhance the understanding and embodiment of wisdom. This teaching exhorts humans in general "to know wisdom [*hokmâ*] and discipline [*mûsār*]" and "to understand sayings of insight [*bînâ*]." But not all answer wisdom's universal invitation. Thus the teaching is directed especially to two groups of people who take up residence in a wisdom school: the "simple," or unlearned, who are beginning their course of study, and the sage, already advanced in insight, who seeks to increase in knowledge and skill. Thus the sapiential teaching in Proverbs 1–9 seeks "to provide the unlearned with shrewdness [`ormâ`]" and "youths with knowledge [*da`at*] and planning [*mezimmâ*]." At the same time "the sage will hear and increase in learning [*leqaḥ*]," and the person of insight will "receive guidance [*taḥbūlôt*]."

The pursuit of wisdom begins with "the fear of the Lord." Fear (*yirâ*ʾ) of the Lord, which provides the major inclusio for the entire book of Proverbs (1:7 = 31:30), is not terror of divine power or what Rudolf Otto calls the religious experience of awe occasioned by standing in the presence of the Holy (*mysterium tremendum*).[9] Rather, it is a religious piety characterized by faith in God as the creator and sustainer of life (see 9:10; 15:33; 31:30; Job 28:28; Ps. 111:10).[10] The life of the spirit for the sages is not a mystical quest for divine knowledge aided by prayer and meditation, leading to religious encounters with the Holy. Rather, the pursuit of wisdom that leads to the understanding of God and the embodiment of the moral life is grounded in religious piety. Study, on one hand, and meditation and prayer, on the other, are not placed in opposition as fundamentally different activities and orientations to life. The intellectual quest to know God and to act on the basis of that knowledge and the spiritual disciplines of prayer, meditation, and worship designed to lead to the presence of God and the development of personal piety are not different pursuits. They are related activities that comprise sapiential discipline (*mûsār*). To trace the development of wisdom from an early, secular tradition to a late, pietistic tradition that comes to include faith in Yahweh is simply wrongheaded and makes modern distinctions that cannot be sustained by the literary evidence.[11] Wisdom, then, begins with a faith in God that seeks understanding.

Theology

The faith of the sages in Proverbs 1–9 is expressed in a theology of creation.[12] Drawing on a rich variety of creation myths and their root metaphors, the sages depicted God as the creator of heaven and earth, who used wisdom to create and then to continue to sustain the world. Creation was not a once-for-all event locked in the primordial past, but rather a continuous action. The sages in Proverbs used four metaphors to describe world origins and maintenance: word, artistry, fertility, and battle or struggle. Thus God issues an edict to the primordial deep, keeping it from overwhelming the created order (Prov. 8:29). Or the creator is the divine architect who designs and constructs the cosmos in the form of an elegant and well-planned building or city (Prov. 3:19-20; 8:26-29). In Proverbs 1 and 8, the world is a city where Woman Wisdom enters the gates, walks along the walls, and issues in the marketplace her invitation to life. In 9:1-6 Woman Wisdom constructs her seven-pillared house, initiating her worship by an invitation to the unlearned to come and partake of her festival of life. And in her hymn of self-praise (Prov. 8:22-31), Woman Wisdom speaks of being "fathered" by God (*qānâ*) and "begotten" (*ḥûl*) as the first of the divine acts of creation.[13]

For the sages, creation is a process of ordering by which pre-existent chaos is fashioned and contained by spoken word and skillful act. Creation is not *ex nihilo*, but is a continuous process by which God shapes chaos into an enduring cosmos and sustains a world that is intelligible, orderly, and good. No chaos threatens this order or seeks to bring it to an end, though there may be a faint echo of a long-ago battle when God defeated the powers of chaos prior to the creation of the world. However, in the present world in which the sages resided, God is the sovereign ruler of heaven and earth and whose power continues to create and sustain a living cosmos that offers its bounty to the wise righteous, whose words and deeds enable them both to live in harmony with the world, human society, and themselves and to shape the structures of existence. As teacher, Woman Wisdom invites the unlearned to take up their course of study with her and to experience the fullness of life.[14]

PROVERBS 3:13-20

Introduction

Proverbs 3:13-20 is a wisdom poem of three strophes: The first speaks of the joy of the one who finds wisdom; the second describes wisdom as a goddess of life; and the third depicts wisdom's role in creation (cf. the poems in Prov. 8:1-11, 12-21; Psalm 19). Possessing both hymnic and didactic features, the poem is an *'asrê* ("happy") psalm, which, like Psalms 32 and 119, begins with an extended "happy" saying (vv. 13-15), providing the theme and helping to shape the poem's rhetorical structure.[15] The adulation of wisdom in this poem is similar to hymns in the Psalter that praise God as the creator and sustainer of the world and as the redeemer who delivers Israel and individuals from their distress (e.g., Psalms 8; 78; 104; 105; and 139).[16] Hymns extol the majesty and greatness of God, demonstrated in these acts of creation and redemption. However, in this wisdom poem, drawing on the hymn, the praise of the sage is directed toward Woman Wisdom both as the giver of life, riches, honor, and joy, and as the attribute of God used in the creation and ordering of the cosmos.

> Strophe I: The Joy of Finding Wisdom (3:13-15)
> 13. Happy is the person who has found wisdom,
>   and the one who continues to obtain insight.
> 14. For her gain is better than silver,
>   and her yield than fine gold.
> 15. She is more costly than corals,
>   and all of your delights cannot compare with her.

Strophe II: Wisdom as Goddess (3:16-18)

16. Long life is in her right hand,
    in her left are wealth and honor.
17. Her ways are pleasant ways,
    and all her paths are peaceful.
18. She is a tree of life to those who lay hold of her,
    and all who embrace her are happy.

Strophe III. Wisdom's Role in Creation (3:19-20)

19. The Lord by means of wisdom established the earth,
    the heavens were secured through understanding.
20. By means of his knowledge the primeval deep was divided,
    And the skies continue to drip their dew.

The Joy of Finding Wisdom (3:13-15)

The initial strophe begins with a "happy" saying in verse 13, describing the state of well-being and joy entered by the one who discovers wisdom and obtains understanding. The saying is extended by the addition of two "better" sayings that follow the traditional formula of "x is better or of more value than y." In this case, the gain derived from wisdom is of more value than the profit offered by silver, gold, and coral jewelry (cf. Ps. 19:11; Prov. 8:18). The value of wisdom reaches its climax in the last line of the strophe (v. 15*b*), which asserts that nothing that is the object of the heart's "desire" is comparable to wisdom.

Wisdom as a Goddess of Life (3:16-18)

In the second strophe, wisdom is personified as a goddess. For the sages, the fruits of the attainment of Wisdom are long life (Prov. 3:2; 22:4), riches (Prov. 14:24), and honor (Prov. 8:18). These fruits were not earned or grasped, but were divine gifts bestowed upon the wise by God (1 Kings 3:3-14). By means of poetic imagination, the sages gave wisdom, a feminine noun (*ḥokmâ*), the form and characteristics of a goddess who dispenses these gifts to those who love her.[17] As a goddess she offers to her devotees life in her right hand and riches and honor in her left.[18] Thus those who find and "embrace" Wisdom are "happy" (3:13, 18).

A narrative illustration of the incomparable value of wisdom is Solomon's prayer for a "wise and understanding heart [mind]" to govern Israel and to know how to "discern between right and wrong" (1 Kings 3:3-14). Pleased by the request, God not only endows the young king with wisdom, but also gives him honor and riches so that no other king will compare with him during his lifetime. In addition, if Solomon is obedient to the divine statutes and

81

commandments, God promises to lengthen his days. Only in Proverbs 3:16-18 does Woman Wisdom offer these gifts to those who possess her.

The pursuit of wisdom is not only an intellectual quest that leads to the attainment of virtue and piety and their embodiment in life, but is also one of the heart that desires to find and then possess Wisdom as the supreme object of human affection and love. Seeking and finding Wisdom is compared on a human level to finding and embracing a lovely and graceful woman who is the object of the heart's desire. On a mythical level, operating in the world of fertility religion, affections of the heart were directed toward goddesses (e.g., Asherah) whose possession and adulation led to life and well-being. In the imagination of the sage, Wisdom, the embodiment of the sapiential tradition and an attribute of God, is metaphorically presented, not simply as a desirable woman, but as a goddess of love whose possession leads to life and well-being.

Images of paradise (cf. Gen. 2:4b-25) are used in the portrayal of Wisdom and her gifts.[19] Metaphorically conceived, Wisdom becomes in the sage's imagination the tree of life (cf. Prov. 11:30; 13:12; 15:4), a common symbol for goddesses of fertility in the ancient Near East.[20] For instance, Asherah was often presented as a living and sprouting tree, giving emphasis to her powers of fecundity in producing new life. In Genesis 2–3 (the J narrative), the tree of life (2:9; 3:22-24) and the tree of knowledge of good and evil (wisdom) are two separate trees. Perhaps in a polemic against the wisdom tradition, the Yahwist identifies the primeval pair's grasping for the "fruit" of the tree of wisdom as a violation of God's prohibition, resulting in their expulsion from the garden and divine presence, the denial of access to the tree of life, and the punishment of death. For the Yahwist, wisdom is a divine attribute separating human creatures from God; therefore, it cannot be grasped without the penalty of alienation and death. But for the sage in this poem, those who "embrace" Woman Wisdom, standing in the midst of the garden and offering her fruit to those who seek her, are called "happy." In using the word *happy* in verse 18, the sage refers to the initial line of the poem and provides a literary connection between the first and second strophes.

Wisdom's Role in Creation (3:19-20)

The final strophe then describes wisdom's role in the creation of the cosmos, emphasizing that the tradition that leads to life, well-being, riches, and honor is grounded in the structures of the cosmos itself.[21] God uses wisdom in creating and ordering the world and in governing its life-producing activities (cf. Pss. 104:24; 136:5; Jer. 10:12; 51:15).[22] The verbs of divine creation, translated "established" (*yāsad* = Isa. 24:18; 48:13; 51:13; Amos 9:6; Zech. 12:1; cf. Prov. 8:29) and "secured" (*kûn* = Job 28:25, 27; Pss. 93:1; 119:90;

Prov. 24:3; cf. Prov. 8:27), derive from the metaphor of God as the builder/architect who lays the stable and secure foundations of a building prior to the erection of the columns and the walls (cf. Job 38:4-7; Ps. 104:5). In this image of the divine architect, wisdom is the skill, plan, and knowledge God uses to secure and order the cosmos, depicted as a great building with pillars (mountains, Job 26:11; Ps. 18:7) to support the sky and with a foundation constructed over the cosmic ocean.[23] Subsequently, divine wisdom continues to bring stability to the ongoing cosmic order. In the embrace of Wisdom (i.e., in the knowledge and actualization of sapiential teaching), the student embodies the same cosmic power of life and knowledge that God used in creating and governing reality. The same power that originates and sustains life in the world is offered to those who incorporate within their lives the teachings of the sage.

Verse 20 uses a third verb for creation, "divide" (*bāqā*ʾ): "by means of his knowledge the primeval deep (*tĕhômôt*) was divided."[24] This verb has its origins in the mythological image of the divine warrior Marduk, "splitting open" the chaos monster, who threatened the divine world of the Babylonian gods (see "The Creation Epic," *ANET,* 67).[25] *Tĕhôm* in Hebrew, the deep or cosmic ocean (Gen. 1:2, 7:11; Job 38:16, 30; Prov. 8:24, 27-28), may be linguistically related to the Akkadian name for the chaos monster, Tiamat. Indeed, Marduk, having slain her in combat, splits her in half (*ANET,* 67) and uses her carcass in creating the universe. Prior to the battle, the power of magical incantation and the curse, forms of ancient wisdom especially in Mesopotamia, was used in his mastery of the dragon (*ANET,* 64). *Tĕhôm* or *tĕhômôt* (a plural of *majesty*) as the chaos monster is reflected in several poetic texts in the Hebrew Bible, including the well-known depiction of the creator's defeat of the dragon in Psalm 74 (especially vv. 12-15; cf. Gen. 49:25; Deut. 33:13; Ps. 77:17; and Hab. 3:8-10). Yahweh's dividing of the sea following the liberation of the Israelites from Egyptian slavery (Exod. 14:16; Neh. 9:11; Ps. 78:13) alludes to this mythological battle. Prince Yam, the Canaanite god of the sea and the personification of chaos, was identified with the sea that is crossed in Isaiah 51:9-11. Yet there is only a faint echo of this battle between the creator and the chaos monster in Proverbs 3:19-20.

Finally, one act of the governance of creation is mentioned in Proverbs 3:19-20: "The skies continue to drip their dew." God is the one who, by means of divine wisdom, provides the cosmos with life-sustaining moisture (cf. Job 28:25-26; 36:27-28; 38:28, 37; Ps. 78:23). In the Yahwist narrative, the first act of creation is a "mist," arising from the earth to moisten the dry land (Gen. 2:6).

Metaphor and the Rhetorical Structure of Imagination

For the sages, divine wisdom, used by God in originating and sustaining the cosmos, dwells within the elegance of a poem and is offered to those who would enter its world.[26] Through the study of and love for wisdom, the life-sustaining, ordering power of creation is made accessible to humans. Indeed, the wisdom tradition in its continuing and dynamic formulation is grounded in the life-giving order of the cosmos.[27] Wisdom comes to humans as both a divine gift (i.e., as a charisma bestowed upon the sage by God) and the result of human study and desire. Wisdom must be given by God; it cannot be grasped. Yet wisdom cannot be attained, unless it is desired.

By means of the rhetorical structure of this three-strophe poem and the metaphors for wisdom and creation, the teacher opens up to students a world of sapiential imagination in which God through Wisdom continues to dwell and sustain life. In the elegance and content of a poem, reality becomes an esthesis in which order and beauty cohere. Through God's original and continuing acts of creation, expressed in a variety of metaphors, reality is providentially sustained and guided toward the future. Through the appropriation of and entrance into the world constructed by the teacher's instructions, the one in the process of becoming wise experiences the joys of knowing and embracing Wisdom. Life in its fullness is made vital and then experienced. Those who find and possess Wisdom are called "happy." They have entered into Wisdom's linguistic world construed by the rhetoric of a poem, and within that world they experience the joy of life.

PROVERBS 8:1-36

Introduction

Proverbs 8 is a well-crafted section on Woman Wisdom, consisting of five related parts: 8:1-3 ("The Sage's Introduction to Woman Wisdom"), 8:4-11 ("Wisdom's Call"), 8:12-21 ("Wisdom's Providential Rule"), 8:22-31 ("Wisdom's Place in Creation"), and 8:32-36 ("Wisdom's Instruction of Life").[28] Once again the wisdom tradition is personified as a woman. Wisdom as a teacher begins (8:1-11) and concludes (8:32-36) the section, providing an inclusio that enfolds two poems on Wisdom's roles in providence (8:12-21) and creation (8:22-31). In 8:1-3 the voice of the sage introduces Woman Wisdom as a teacher who journeys to a city to find students. In the protrepsis ("invitation to a course of study") in 8:4-11, Wisdom herself speaks as the peripatetic teacher who attempts to persuade prospective students to learn from her. A hymnic poem of self-adulation follows (8:12-21) in which Wisdom is the enthroned Queen of Heaven, providentially directing human history, enabling kings to rule justly, and enriching those who love her with wealth. In the following poem, also a hymn of self-praise (8:22-31), Wisdom describes her origins as the child of God present at creation and her position as the mediator between heaven and earth. Finally, she returns to the role of teacher and in a first-person instruction offers her students a teaching of life (8:32-36).[29]

The Sage's Introduction to Wisdom (8:1-3)

Once again Wisdom is personified as a peripatetic teacher who goes in search of students, inviting them to take up her course of study and learn from her (cf. 1:20-33).[30] More than likely, this protrepsis, or invitation to study, reflects a school setting where a teacher offers to impart to the untutored the ways of wisdom.

> Part I: The Sage's Introduction to Woman Wisdom (8:1-3)
>
> 1. Does not Wisdom call,
>   and Insight lift up her voice?
> 2. On the summit of the acropolis,
>   on the street[31] to the temple,
>   standing by the pathways.[32]
> 3. Besides the gates, at the entrance to the city,
>   by the entry of the portals, she summons forth.

In the ancient Greek and Hellenistic world, the tradition of peripatetic teachers is well known. These teachers would travel throughout cities and towns to find students who would accept their invitation (protrepsis) to study under them. Teachers in the philosophical schools attempted to persuade youngsters to study under them, usually for tuition. Protrepsis ("persuasion") was a rhetorical form in the Greek schools used by teachers to induce students to study under them. Paraenesis was both "exhortation" and "affirmation"— teaching that admonished and shaped the moral life of students seeking wisdom and that undergirded the validity of what was taught. Whether Israelite teachers also traveled to find students is not clear, though Ben Sira's statement that the sage travels to foreign countries to study wisdom suggests that sages made journeys to find knowledge outside of Israel (cf. 2 Chron. 17:7-9).

It is significant to note the social locations of wisdom as the peripatetic teacher who searches for students from all humanity. Yet, the text also points beyond these social spheres to evoke the imagination by presenting creation as a city where Woman Wisdom dwells and offers her teaching of life. Once again, as was the case in 1:20-33, Wisdom is present at the entrance (the "gate") to a city (*qāret*),[33] and she is on the heights, presumably the acropolis of the urban center (cf. Prov. 9:3, 14).[34] The city points to Wisdom's (and thus God's) presence in the world of human beings. In ancient Near Eastern mythology, the cosmos on occasion is depicted as a city.[35] Indeed, sacred cities, dedicated to particular deities, and political capitals were seen as the microcosm of the larger cosmos as well as the center of the earth that maintains the order of heaven and earth. In some cities, the creator deity had his dwelling, and through his power the forces of chaos were kept at bay (see Psalms 46; 48; 76). Sacred and royal cities, like Jerusalem, played an important role in mediating between sacred (heaven) and cosmic (earth) space.

In many ancient cities, the temple was located on the highest point, emphasizing the imagery of transcendence and proximity to the heavenly world, which was the abode of the gods. Israelite and Canaanite sanctuaries were traditionally referred to as "high places," though a different word (*bāmâ*) is used than the one for "acropolis" (*rō'š mĕrōmîm*) in Proverbs 8 (see 1 Sam. 9:12-25; 10:5-13; 1 Kings 3:2-4; Jer. 19:5; 32:35).

Palaces also were often positioned on the high points of a city, making them defensible against attack as well as reflecting the symbols of power and authority. In Solomon's Jerusalem and later, palace and Temple (see 1 Kings 5–9) were within a close distance of each other, and may have been located within the same sacred wall. This was true, of course, of Jerusalem, for the Temple was on the heights (see Jer. 17:12; 31:12; Ezek. 20:40), as was the probable location of Solomon's palace. David's palace was partially down the mountain.[36] Only in the metaphorical world of the city is wisdom the link between heaven and earth, directing the well-being of the cosmos.

Finally, wisdom is also at the gates of the city (see 1:21), a common place for a variety of public activities. In Israelite cities, the major gate was a large complex with rooms that were used for a variety of public functions, including legal proceedings and commerce (e.g., see 2 Sam. 18:24; 19:1). Here judges sat to settle disputes and render legal decisions (2 Sam. 15:2; Job 29:7) while prophets approached to speak of justice and to utter oracles of judgment and salvation (Amos 5:12, 15). It was in the chambers of the gate that the sages taught their students and at the gates that they issued their invitations to come and learn from them. The central idea of the images involving gates in the Hebrew Bible is judgment. The imagery of Wisdom teaching in the gates may link the sapiential tradition to justice and the administration of law that secured harmony and well-being in Israelite society.[37] Yahweh was, of course, the divine judge whose decrees originated creation and continued the course of the world in justice.[38] Wisdom's presence at the gate points to her involvement in the life-giving and life-sustaining justice that is at the center of social and even cosmic life.

The world to which Wisdom comes is thus a city teeming and bustling with the traffic of human life. Wisdom does not withdraw from everyday life in order to offer the quiet repose of meditation or rare encounters with God through mystical or cultic rituals that distinguished between the sacred and the profane (i.e., between the world of divine dwelling protected by cultic regulations ensuring the holiness of God and the world of everyday life inhabited by human beings). Rather, like the tradition she embodies, Wisdom goes in search of people in their customary pursuits and offers them an instruction for life, so that in their various activities, from marriage to business dealings to the advising of kings, they possess the means by which to live in harmony with the world and to experience success. In other words, they may become a sage (ḥākām) and a righteous person (ṣaddîq) who achieves well-being.

Wisdom's Call (8:4-11)

Calling to humanity, as she did in chapter 1 (see 1:21, 24, 28) and will do again in chapter 9 (9:3), Wisdom invites people to pursue their course of study with her and to take up the path of the moral life that she offers.[39] This is a universal call to all who would learn from her. Woman Wisdom raises her voice and offers an instruction (see Job 34:16; Prov. 5:13; Isa. 28:23), only here she is the "voice" of God (Isa. 40:3, 9), embodying the wisdom tradition and urging its actualization in human life through discipline.[40] Her invitation, both urgent and important, is expressed by the word *summons forth* (*rnn*) in verse 3. Elsewhere, this word may be either a shout of exultation (Job 38:7; Jer. 31:7) or a lament of great distress (Lam. 2:19). However, in 1:20-33 the word is one of exhortation, coupled with warning, for those who resist or ignore wisdom's invitation will experience great distress and calamity and will turn too late to seek the life-giving counsel that she no longer offers (see Prov. 8:3).

Wisdom as teacher issues to those she meets in the city and on the streets a poetic invitation to come and learn of her in the first two strophes:

> Strophe I: Wisdom's Appeal for Attention (8:4-7)
> 4. "It is to you, O people, I call,
>   and my voice addresses humankind.
> 5. Discern prudence, O simple ones,
>   and pay attention,[41] O dullards.
> 6. Listen, because I address princes,[42]
>   and my lips open up with uprightness.
> 7. Because my mouth utters truth,
>   for wickedness is the abomination of my lips.

Strophe II: The Value of Wisdom's Teachings (8:8-11)
8. All the sayings of my mouth are righteous,
 none of them is twisted or perverted.
9. All of them are straightforward to the perceptive,
 and upright to those who discover knowledge.
10. Take my instruction instead of silver,
 and knowledge in place of choice gold.
11. For wisdom is better than coral,
 and no earthly delight may compare with her." [43]

The fruits (i.e., words) of her lips are truth, correctness, and fairness, features of her teaching, but also characteristics that those who learn of her may come to embody through discipline. She compares the worth of her teachings to great treasures, exceeding in value even precious metals and jewels (see 3:13-18 and the following poem). No "earthly delight" can match what Wisdom offers.

Wisdom as Goddess (8:12-21)

Now Wisdom speaks as a royal goddess, the Queen of Heaven, who possesses both fertility and wisdom.

Strophe I: Wisdom's Providential Rule (8:12-17)
12. I, Wisdom, dwell in prudence, [44]
 and I discover the knowledge of plans.
13. The fear of the Lord is the hatred of evil,
 I despise pride, self-exaltation, and a perverse mouth.
14. I possess counsel and sound wisdom;
 I have both insight and might.
15. By me kings rule,
 and potentates decree righteousness.
16. By me officials govern,
 and nobles, all who judge with righteousness. [45]
17. I love those who love me,
 and those who seek me shall find me.

Strophe II: Wisdom's Inestimable Worth (8:18-21)
18. Riches and honor are with me,
 enduring wealth and righteousness.
19. My fruit is better than gold, even refined gold,
 and my yield than choice silver.
20. I walk in the path of righteousness,
 in the midst of the ways of justice.
21. Giving existence as an inheritance to my lovers,
 and filling their storehouses.

Like God in 1 Kings 3:1-15, Woman Wisdom dispenses to kings and princes both the power of legitimate governance and the justice they need to rule and issue righteous decrees.[46] She gives rulers life-giving counsel ($\bar{e}$ṣâ) that enables them to carry out well-conceived plans that succeed.[47] Wise and righteous rule brought nations into concert with the larger cosmic order and enabled them to experience well-being and success (Job 12:18; 36:7).

Wisdom also bestows upon her lovers life and wealth. Among the images used to describe Woman Wisdom are those that portray her as a fertility goddess whose lovers include monarchs. Ancient Near Eastern myth is replete with stories of female goddesses who take on human lovers and either bestow upon them great blessings and long life or, tiring of their embrace, bring them to destruction. In these two strophes, Wisdom invites humans to become her lovers and to experience the intimacies of her embrace.[48] She gives those who search her out and finally discover her not only the joys of intimacy, but also wealth and prosperity.

Wisdom's Place in Creation (8:22-31)[49]

This hymn of self-praise by Woman Wisdom consists of two strophes that describe the origins of the cosmos and the place of wisdom in creation.

> Strophe I. The Procreation of Wisdom (8:22-26)
> 22. Yahweh fathered me as the first of his creative activity,
>   before all other things made in primeval times.
> 23. From of old I was poured out,
>   from the beginning, before the origins of the earth.
> 24. When there were no depths, I was brought forth,
>   When there were no streams coursing with water.
> 25. Before the mountains were set deeply in their shafts,
>   before the hills I was brought forth.
> 26. Before he made the land and fields,
>   and the first of the dust of the earth,
>
> Strophe II: Creation and the Place of Wisdom (8:27-31)
> 27. When he established the heavens, I was there,
>   when he inscribed a circle upon the face of the deep,
> 28. When he made firm the skies above,
>   when the springs of the deep grew strong,
> 29. When he set forth his decree concerning Yam,
>   that the waters would not transgress his command.
>   When he issued a decree that shaped the foundations of the earth,
>   I was beside him like a little child,
> 30. And I was the one in whom day by day he took delight,[50]
>   making merry before him in every moment,
> 31. Making merry over his inhabited world,
>   and taking delight in the human creatures.

Leaving the world of the present presided over by Woman Wisdom as the Queen of Heaven, this poem returns to the ancient past to portray the origins of creation and the birth of Goddess Wisdom, who now serves as mediator between Yahweh and the inhabited world.[51]

One of the important theological metaphors in this first-person hymn of self-praise presents Yahweh as the divine parent. In this case, Yahweh's offspring is Woman Wisdom, at first a newborn infant and then a small child. Yahweh fathers (qnh)[52] and gives birth ($h\hat{u}l$) to Wisdom.[53] As the father and mother of wisdom, Yahweh "procreated" her as the firstborn of creation. The term for "firstborn" in 8:22 ($r\bar{e}$ '$\check{s}\hat{i}t$) echoes Genesis 1:1 ($b\check{e}r\bar{e}$ '$\check{s}\hat{i}t$), a temporal adverb meaning "when" that opens the priestly creation text in Genesis 1:1–2:4a. In the first creation narrative in Genesis, a cosmological portrayal of origins, God creates the heavens and the earth primarily by means of the divine word that orders and structures the cosmos and brings into being the various types of living creatures. In Proverbs 8:22, the term $r\bar{e}$ '$\check{s}\hat{i}t$ points to wisdom as the firstborn of creation (see Job 40:19; Pss. 78:51; 105:36).[54] The firstborn in Israelite society, normally a son, held a privileged rank (Gen. 43:33), receiving a double portion of the inheritance (Deut. 21:17) and at his father's death replacing him as the head of the family.[55] The first of the harvest was considered the choicest and best of what was to follow and thus was given to Yahweh as the "first fruits" (Lev. 2:12; 23:10). In the present context, Wisdom is the firstborn, the first and best, of all the things formed and brought into existence by the potency of God's "creative activity" (drk).[56] And Wisdom, a female, holds this high position, shattering social convention.

Wisdom's origins in hoary antiquity are described in verse 23 in images of either birth ("poured out") or the inauguration of royal rule ("installed"). The verb nsk may mean both. "Poured out" (Gen. 35:14; Exod. 25:29) would allude to either the pouring out of semen or the breaking of the water in the mother's womb during the birthing process. "Installed" (Ps. 2:6) would suggest the inauguration of royal rule. Either meaning would fit the context of Wisdom's portrayal as the child of Yahweh or as the Queen of Heaven (see the preceding poem in 8:12-21). In either case, Wisdom's origins precede all else created by God.

In a typical formula found in ancient Near Eastern creation texts, the individual lines of the three couplets in verses 24-26 are, with one exception (v. 26b), introduced by "when there were no" or its parallel "before." This negative way of describing reality prior to creation suggests, not *creatio ex nihilo* ("creation out of nothing"), but that the present order of life was shaped out of an unformed, lifeless chaos. These lines, and the antithetical ones that follow in verses 27-29 that are introduced by "when," portray reality as tripartite: earth, the deep, and the heavens (skies). This three-dimensional cosmos is secured by the mountains, serving as the great pillars that keep the earth from sinking into the cosmic oceans, and by a heavenly vault (see Gen.

1:6-8) that restrains the waters of chaos (cf. Genesis 1). This well-structured creation is portrayed as the work of a master craftsman or architect who carefully orders, secures, makes stable, and arranges the three components of reality.

Then Yahweh becomes the royal judge who issues two decrees: one restrains Prince Yam,[57] the embodiment of chaos, keeping him from inundating the cosmos; the other legislates into existence the "foundations of the earth." Both decrees secure the stability and continuation of the new creation.

The final section of the poem then returns to Wisdom's self-description of her activity. Verse 30a has long been a *crux interpretatum,* especially due to the ambiguity of the meaning of the noun 'amôn. A variety of translations have been proposed, but two are most probable. One is represented by the NRSV: "Then I was beside him, like a master worker."

This translation portrays Wisdom as a pre-existent architect who designs and builds the cosmos.[58] This is possible, since the imagery in verses 27-29 presents the metaphor of Yahweh as architect. The Greek word *technitis* ("artisan") used of Wisdom in the Wisdom of Solomon 7:22 supports this view.

The other meaning is the one given in my own translation: "I was beside him like a little child." Here, 'amôn is understood as a child, a metaphor appropriate for this context, since Wisdom is "fathered" and "begotten" earlier in the poem. If "little child" is taken to be the meaning, then the "delight" of the proud parent in the offspring and her own playful "delight" in the world of humanity provide the intimate link between the creator and the created.[59] Making merry or rejoicing over both creation and the inhabited world points to both the wisdom tradition's celebration of life (cf. Qoh. 2:24-26) and the joy that derives from beholding the wonder and elegance of the cosmos and the place of humanity. Wisdom as a young girl is a precious delight to the eyes of the parent creator, even as the cosmos and its human creatures are wondrous in the sight of the divine child.[60]

Wisdom's Exhortation to Life (8:32-36)

The final section, an instruction, returns to the initial part of the unit: protrepsis—the invitation to take up the study of wisdom to experience well-being. Wisdom, the firstborn of creation, perhaps active in the shaping of the cosmos, and the providential ruler of history, now issues once more the call to life that she had offered in the first section of the poem (8:1-11). This closure, where the end returns to the beginning, gives the invitation of Woman Wisdom even greater authority.[61]

The instruction of life exhorts humans to embody the teaching that encompasses the life-giving order of the cosmos and that guides human history providentially into the future. The time for decision is at hand. Through accepting the invitation and through study and action (knowing and doing), humans may receive and learn to actualize in both word and deed the wisdom that orders the cosmos and guides human history.[62] Through their words and deeds, they participate in shaping the structures of life necessary for reality to endure. By taking up Wisdom's invitation, they begin to travel the path to sagehood.

> 32. And now, O children, pay me heed,
>   for happy are those who keep to my paths.
> 33. Listen to instruction and become wise,
>   and do not turn away.
> 34. Happy is the one who pays heed to me,
>   watching day by day at my gates,
>   waiting by the posts of my doors.
> 35. Because the one who finds me finds life,
>   and obtains well-being from Yahweh.
> 36. But the one who misses me does violence to himself;
>   all those who hate me love death.

It is important to note that twice (8:32, 34) Woman Wisdom uses the term *happy* (*ašrê*), a reference to the state of well-being into which one enters after taking up the study of wisdom (see 3:13-20). The goal of instruction is the cultivation of that personal wisdom in which piety, reflection, and character form the identity and being of the sage (*hăkāmû*, "to become wise," v. 33).

Once again, Woman Wisdom issues her protrepsis (i.e., an invitation to follow and learn of her). Indeed, the imagery suggests those who each day stand at the door to her house, perhaps a wisdom school, and wait for her to give them entrance. What Wisdom offers to those who enter her dwelling is life and the avoidance of death. Here, the often-found contrast between life and death in sapiential literature sets up the bipolarity of human experience and destiny. Life refers to a wide range of values and desired experiences, from longevity to prosperity to good health to family to love to outer and inner harmony and to "success" in one's deeds. The state of well-being is another way of expressing wisdom's view of life. Death, of course, also encompasses a wide range of experiences as well as the state of worthlessness or meaninglessness.[63] These experiences include brevity of existence, psychological states of anxiety and anger, conflict, dishonor, unhappiness, poor health, and failure in one's pursuits. A state of wretchedness or turmoil in life, and not simply nonexistence, is a general way of capturing the meaning of the term. Mythically conceived Goddess Wisdom, like her counterparts, ancient Near

Eastern goddesses of fertility and wisdom, is the dispenser of life to those she chooses to embrace. Now in another dress, Sage Wisdom offers life to those who come and learn of her.

Woman Wisdom and Sapiential Imagination

Drawing on important metaphors from cosmological and anthropological traditions, Proverbs 8 provokes the imagination to conceive of reality as the well-designed world of a divine architect who, by means of wisdom, proportions its components into a harmonious, elegant whole: The heavens are established, a vault is made to keep back the waters of the deep, the skies are strengthened to serve as the cosmic roof also protecting the earth from the downpour of rain, and the foundations of the cosmos are laid giving stability to the structure of reality. As divine judge, Yahweh issues the restraining decree that keeps Yam at bay. Chaos, indeed, has its place in the depths of the waters, but it is not allowed to overrun and destroy God's beautiful earth. Outside the command to Yam, no hint of a cosmic battle remains. Reality is a dynamic order that continues in its cosmological and historical forms by means of the power of God and the guiding presence of Woman Wisdom. Reality is both a well-constructed and proportioned cosmos, with strength to continue to stand, and a kingdom ordered by the power of divine decree that limits Yam (chaos) to the cosmic depths.

Yet the chapter also draws on the anthropological tradition, not in speaking of the origins of humanity, but in offering humanity the opportunity to participate in the beneficent life that wisdom offers. The nurturing feature of God now resides within Woman Wisdom, who addresses humans as her "children" (8:32). The values of intimacy link the would-be students to their wise mistress and lover. Indeed, dwelling within the midst of this poetic world of imagination is Woman Wisdom, and her personification in a variety of roles is the most striking of all. As peripatetic teacher, she goes in search of the simple, who are invited to learn of her and thus to achieve well-being that results from the implementation of her teachings. As the Queen of Heaven, she sits enthroned over creation, chooses and nurtures with her instruction and bounty kings and princes to govern their nations, and offers the blessings of prosperity, life, and honor to her lovers. As the offspring of Yahweh, Wisdom is the firstborn of creation and thus was present when the creator-architect shaped the beauty and order of the cosmos. Through the delight Yahweh has for this child, Wisdom serves as the mediator between heaven and earth. Because playful Wisdom rejoices in the world of human habitation and the human race, and because Yahweh delights in the firstborn, the world becomes the recipient of divine blessing that enables life and its abundance to continue.

93

Finally, in the movement of this chapter, Wisdom reappears as the sage who now, because of her identity as the Queen of Heaven and the firstborn of Yahweh, commands attention. Those who eagerly watch for the wise teacher and follow her instruction have the possibility of finding and actualizing well-being in their lives. But those who fail to find and follow wisdom may expect to experience only death.

WISDOM AND FOLLY IN PROVERBS 9

Introduction

The personification of wisdom as teacher, goddess, and offspring of God continues in this poem, only now Wisdom is contrasted with her nemesis, Woman Folly. The literary transition to this new poem on Wisdom and Folly is provided by the reference to life and death in the protrepsis of Sage Wisdom in her concluding instruction in 8:35-36.

The Rhetoric of Proverbs 9:1-18

The rhetorical structure of 9:1-18 consists of an antithetical wisdom poem that envelops an instruction. The poem contains two contrasting strophes: 9:1-6 (Woman Wisdom) and 9:13-18 (Woman Folly). The formal structures of the two strophes of the poem are quite similar. Following a third-person description of the personified subjects (Wisdom, then Folly), they issue an invitation (protrepsis) that attempts to persuade the unlearned to come and learn of them. The second strophe, however, adds an element not in the first. Verse 18 returns to third-person description, only in this case it is the surprise that awaits the simpleton who accepts Folly's invitation. He discovers, too late, that those who accept Folly's invitation and participate in her banquet are the dead. Enfolded within this poem is the teaching of Wisdom, the sage, who offers to those who accept her invitation an instruction of life. This teaching offers to the unlearned the chance to escape the deadly embrace of Woman Folly.[64]

Wisdom's Invitation to Her Feast (9:1-6)

Once again Wisdom is personified as a goddess of wisdom and fertility who, in this text, builds her temple (or palace) and inaugurates her reign.[65]

Strophe I: Woman Wisdom Builds Her House (9:1-6)

1. Woman Wisdom has built her temple,
     she has hewn out her seven pillars.
2. She has slaughtered her animals,
     she has mixed her wine,
     she also has set her table.
3. She has sent out her maidens,
     she calls from the elevated heights of the city.
4. "Whoever is unlearned, let him turn aside here."
     She speaks to him who lacks sense.
5. "Come, eat of my bread,
     and drink of the wine I have mixed.
6. Abandon simpleness and live,
     and walk in the way of insight."

The metaphorical depiction of Wisdom's "hewing out her seven pillars" refers to the stonecutter preparing dressed columns taken from the quarry (cf. 1 Chron. 22:2).[66] Her pillars suggest those used to support the roof of a large building, perhaps a temple, though Solomon's Temple also had two free-standing ones (Yakin and Boaz) positioned in front of the vestibule (*ûlām*; 1 Kings 7:15-22; 41-42). These two pillars may have represented either stelae (*maṣṣēbôt*; in Canaanite sanctuaries, they represented deities) or the columns founded upon the earth (i.e., the mountains) to hold up the cosmic sky (Job 9:6; 26:10-11; Ps. 75:4). The number seven has many possible explanations, ranging from an indication of the large size of the house to a temple to the planets to the pillars that support the heavens and the entire cosmos, keeping it from collapse. However, the images may be seen best as cultic.

The World as Wisdom's Dwelling

The cosmological symbolism of temples in the ancient world has been suggested by many scholars. For example, the theology and symbolism of the Solomonic Temple (1 Kings 5–7) includes the divine presence of the creator in Jerusalem, mythically understood as the center of the cosmos where God created the world and continues to sustain its existence (Psalms 46; 48; 76); the molten sea supported by twelve oxen representing the control of chaos (sea = Yam); the two pillars (Yachin and Boaz) standing for the pillars of the earth; and the roof of the Temple pointing to the skies and the firmament.[67] The theology and symbolism of Wisdom's temple may indicate similar connotations that are especially suggestive of her association with creation and maintenance of the world.

The construction of temples also points to the beginning of the reign of gods and their royal devotees (1 Kings 8).[68] The inauguration of Wisdom's reign, symbolized by the construction of her temple or palace, is followed by a great festival. She slaughters animals, mixes wine, and arranges a table. Then she sends out her maidens from the high places to invite the unlearned to participate in her meal, to leave behind their ignorance, and to walk in the path of insight. The metaphorical construction of reality, made possible by this poem, suggests a cultic meal, not a private banquet, in Wisdom's domicile. In the world of imagination that this poem evokes, the festive celebration of the inauguration of a new reign, accompanied by the building of a palace or temple, has cultic overtones. To the imagination, the food prepared by Goddess Wisdom, evoking images of sacrifices in celebration of a deity's new reign, is the feast of knowledge offered to those who take up the path of learning. Sacrifices of food and drink in major festivals were consumed, in part, by the celebrants, and this seems to be the suggested symbolism here. The sending out of Wisdom's maidens points to her royal retinue of attendants, inviting the simple to come to Wisdom's table. Indeed, this invitation may even be one of marriage, where Woman Wisdom, exalted Queen of Heaven and the Goddess of Life, offers the intimacy of spiritual marriage to those who join her in sapiential discipline.[69] In the symbolic presentation of Wisdom as a goddess of insight and fertility, her maidens were imagined as priestesses sent out to attract devotees to her worship. But they invite them, not to the delights of feasting and sexual intimacy, but to the insights of Wisdom, which lead to life.[70]

This text offers several possible meanings. First of all, verses 1-6 may reflect the creative activity of wisdom in the construction of the cosmos. The world metaphorically presented as a building, even a sacred one, is not an uncommon idea in ancient Near Eastern religions. In the poem in 8:22-31, Yahweh's activity of architect is outlined, and it could be that Wisdom is depicted as a "master builder" in 8:30. In any case, Wisdom is clearly portrayed as an architect/craftswoman in the Wisdom of Solomon 7:22. Second, this first strophe points to the enthronement of Wisdom as the Queen of Heaven, who, having built her cosmic temple, sends out her votaries, or priestesses, to invite people to come and worship her. Now Wisdom's reign is inaugurated, and those who seek life are invited to participate in her life-giving cultus.

Third, Wisdom's house and its inauguration point to the placement of wisdom within the ontological character of reality. Divine wisdom permeates all of reality and continues to sustain the structures of the life that originated at creation. Those who wish to partake of the abundant life are invited to take up Wisdom's invitation to come and learn of her. The wisdom tradition does not consist merely of learned insights by intelligent people or practical advice about how to get on in life, but is a teaching that is grounded in the fundamental structures of the cosmos and the nature and character of God. The study of wisdom leads to the knowledge of creation and ultimately to the knowledge of God.

Fourth, Wisdom's house may also reflect the building of a magnificent house with seven columns.[71] Perhaps the house is a wisdom school. Wisdom's "house" is a tradition, certainly, but it may also reflect a building in which a library was placed and students studied and lived. It is a space where learning and discourse occurred, learning that led to the shaping and continuation of the tradition, educated generations of young men and women for professions in Israelite and Judean society, and shaped a symbolic world that undergirded and legitimated social reality.

Finally, Wisdom's house may be the poem itself (9:1-18), which by means of the imagination constructs a reality in which wisdom and folly struggle for domination and rule, where an instruction offers life to those who enter this world, and where the followers of folly enter into the world of the dead.[72]

The images of women votaries of Woman Wisdom reflect the cultic personnel of fertility goddesses in the ancient Near East. Their priests and priestesses served as sacred prostitutes who enticed devotees to participate in fertility rituals. These sexual images, of course, are in concert with those of seduction, beauty, and lovemaking throughout the wisdom corpus.[73] But their more explicitly cultic character are also found, particularly in the portrayal of the "strange woman," a devotee of fertility deities, in chapter 7[74] and in the description of Woman Folly as a fertility goddess in the second strophe of the poem.

Wisdom's Instruction of Life (9:7-12)

Located between the two strophes contrasting Wisdom and Folly is a teaching from Woman Wisdom.[75] Having built her temple and inaugurated her reign, she now offers an instruction of life.

> Strophe II: Woman Wisdom's Teaching (9:7-12)
> 7. The one who instructs a scorner
>   receives for himself disgrace;
>   And the one who reproves a wicked person,
>   (receives) unto himself moral shame.
> 8. Do not set straight a scorner, lest he hate you;
>   Set straight the righteous one, for he will love you.
> 9. Give to the sage, and he will increase in wisdom,
>   give knowledge to the righteous one and he will add to his learning.
> 10. The beginning of wisdom is the fear of the Lord,
>   and knowledge of holy things is insight.
> 11. For by me your days will increase,
>   and years will be added unto your life.

12. If you become wise, become wise for your own sake,
    If you become a scoffer, you alone will bear the responsibility.

The teaching opens with Woman Wisdom's proverbial observation, which also serves as a warning: The "teacher" should not instruct a "scorner." The Hebrew word for "teacher," "teaching," "instruction" is used for the discipline of study and piety, the form and content of instruction, and the guidance of correction (Job 4:3; 5:17; Prov. 1:2-3, 7; 19:18; 23:23; 29:17). "Scorners" (*lṣ*) are those who, because of their arrogance and contentiousness (Prov. 21:24; 22:10), are incapable of discipline (Prov. 13:1; 15:22). The term for "correcting" *(ykḥ;* Job 5:17; 13:10; Prov. 3:12) also refers to judging (Job 9:33; 16:21), arguing (Job 19:5), convincing (Prov. 30:6), and reproving (Prov. 28:23). These are various aspects of inquiry, learning, and discipline that, in the case of those who are "disorderly" *(rs⁵)*, are wasted. The "disorderly" are those who, because of moral corruption, carry on lives not in concert with righteousness. In the context of the larger poem, the emphasis is placed on not accepting into the course of study those for whom the teaching will be wasted. Indeed, in the accepting of "scoffers" and "disorderly persons" into the wisdom school, teachers will bring disgrace and shame to themselves and will experience much personal torment.

By contrast, in teaching the sages and "orderly" persons (i.e., righteous ones), they will continue to grow in the gifts and graces of wisdom. Becoming wise is a lifelong quest, not a destination point or a state of perfection that one finally reaches. The student of wisdom continues the quest to find, embody, and grow in wisdom as long as life endures.

The teaching of Woman Wisdom then moves from the issue of the admission of those who should or should not be accepted into the wisdom school to the fundamental basis and beginning point of the study of wisdom and the pervasive motivation for taking up residence in wisdom's school; "the fear of the Lord" refers, not to terror of divine power, but to piety and faith in the creator as the maker and sustainer of heaven and earth and as the giver and nurturer of life. Wisdom is never a secular teaching that depends solely or even primarily on human insight and experience or that is motivated by goals of self-enhancement. The quest for wisdom is in a real sense the quest for the knowledge of God, a quest that begins in faith.

Woman Folly's Deadly Seduction (9:13-18)

In contrast to Woman Wisdom, who brings life, Woman Folly, in the world of sapiential imagination, seduces her naive devotees into following the pathway to death.[76] While she is the exact opposite of Wisdom—indeed is her

98

nemesis (see Prov. 14:1)—the identity of Woman Folly is open to a number of nuances.

> Strophe III. Woman Folly's Invitation to Death (9:13-18)
> 13. Woman Folly is noisy, a simpleton
>   who knows nothing.
> 14. She sits at the door of her temple,
>   upon a throne at the heights of the city.
> 15. To call to those who pass by the way,
>   those who walk straight ahead.
> 16. "Whoever is simple, let him turn aside here,"
>   she says to him who lacks sense.
> 17. "Stolen waters are sweet,
>   and bread obtained in secret is pleasant."
> 18. But he does not know that the Rephaim are there,
>   in the depths of Sheol are her guests.

This description of "Woman Folly" is the last in a series of texts dealing with the "strange woman" (see 2:1-22; 5:1-23; 6:24-35; and 7:1-27). She is portrayed in each case as one who seduces the unlearned and leads them to death. To avoid this fatal attraction, students are exhorted to devote themselves to Woman Wisdom, who offers the alternative of life. The identities of the "strange woman"[77] are varied and seem to include prostitute, fertility priestess, adulteress, worshiper of a fertility goddess, and a literary personification of foolishness. In each description of the strange woman in Proverbs, her sexual promiscuity represents the epitome of folly. It is likely that the imagery of the strange woman suggests, at least in part, fertility religion and goddesses who were competing with Yahwistic religion for the devotion of potential followers. Since normative Israelite religion did not provide a divine consort for Yahweh, the personification of Wisdom as a goddess was, to the imagination, a metaphorical alternative. Now two goddesses compete for the loyalty of the Israelite faithful.[78]

In 9:13-18, "folly" (kĕsîlût) is a feminine noun that indicates stupidity, foolishness, and even stubbornness. In wisdom literature, the "dullard" is one who lacks sense, is often incapable of receiving instruction, speaks and acts foolishly, and violates either unknowingly or contemptuously the just norms that create and sustain life. Thus the behavior of the fool leads to destruction (Ps. 49:11; Prov. 1:22; 10:23; 12:23; 15:2, 14; 18:2).

Yet there are also specific features of the literary presentation of folly that attract attention. While she is like the lazy dullard, sitting instead of standing when she invites unwitting passersby to enter her abode, she still positions herself on a "throne" at the door of her "temple" (see 5:8; 7:8), located at "the heights of the city," and she offers a proverbial invitation intended to seduce the passerby: "Stolen waters are sweet, and bread obtained in secret is pleasant."

The word for "throne" (*kissē'*) is a general term for "seat" or "chair," though in certain contexts it refers to a royal throne (Gen. 41:40; Exod. 11:5; Isa. 6:1; Ezek. 1:26). "Temple" (*bēt*) may only be a house or building, but its location on the "heights" of the city (the acropolis) likely points to either a palace (1 Kings 9:1, 10) or a temple (1 Kings 7:12, 40, 45, 51). Of course, Wisdom was also found "on the heights" (see Prov. 8:2). In the case of deities, of course, there is no real distinction between a god's palace and a temple.

Folly is portrayed as an ancient Near Eastern fertility goddess, an Ishtar, Asherah, or Anat who offers wisdom and life to her followers.[79] She engages in an invitation to passersby, perhaps in the form of a cultic summons to engage in fertility rites presumably leading to life and well-being. The poet points out, however, that Folly's house is the portal to the underworld where the "shades" (*rĕpā'îm*) dwell.[80] Entrance into her house is the beginning of the descent into the underworld where the "shades," or the dead, dwell.[81]

Conclusion

The opposing of two deities who engage in mortal combat for sovereignty over the cosmos is common to ancient Near Eastern myth. In Egypt, Horus, the divine ruler, battles Seth, the god of chaos and death, while in Babylonia the god of creation, Marduk, slays Tiamat to gain kingship over the gods. Of course, Baal and Lotan, the god of the sea, duel for rulership of the earth, and in the same mythic cycle of texts Baal and his consort contest Mot, the god of death and ruler of the underworld, for lordship over the world of human habitation. In the use of mythic imagery, the poets of Israel present similar struggles between Yahweh and various incarnations of chaos and death. In Proverbs 9, Wisdom and Folly, personified as rival goddesses, struggle for rulership over human lives and the world constructed by imagination.

Two forces, then, contend for the rulership of the earth: life and death, Yahweh and Mot, and Wisdom and Folly (see Prov. 14:1). Having mythically conceived it by the power of the imagination, the sages portray a world in which Wisdom is enthroned as Queen of Heaven offering through her cultic meal of insight life to those who accept her invitation to study. Her nemesis, Folly, is a rival goddess, also competing for devotees. A collage of images shapes her identity: native stupidity, the turning away from sapiential instruction, open disregard for the orders of life, and the active participation in the fertility cults that entered into popular Yahwistic religion and on occasion even the sacred confines of the Temple cult (2 Kings 21:7). However, her promises of life are lies. Those who pass through her portals enter the realm of darkness, where only the dead dwell.

COSMOLOGY AND ANTHROPOLOGY
IN PROVERBS 10:1–22:16

Introduction

The second collection in the book of Proverbs is largely a list of sayings (some 375 of them) of various types and many topics.[82] The larger collection breaks down thematically and formally into two parts: chapters 10–15 and 16:1–22:16. The contrast between the righteous sage and the wicked fool is a major theme in chapters 10–15. The second division (16:1–22:16) is characterized formally by the predominance of synonymous and synthetic sayings, while "Yahweh sayings" and sayings dealing with kingship and the court are especially important thematically. Both parts of the larger collection are particularly interested in wise and foolish speech.[83]

Creation and Justice for All (Prov. 14:31)

Several sayings in this second collection approach the issue of rich and poor/wealth and poverty from the theological perspective of creation.[84] One of these is the antithetical saying in 14:31:

> He who oppresses a helpless person insults his creator,
> but he who is kind to the needy honors him.

The topic of rich and poor/wealth and poverty receives significant attention in the Old Testament. Social networks for the sustenance of the poor are found in many types of biblical texts, from legal codes to prophetic oracles to historical narratives to wisdom literature. Especially important were the principle of family solidarity (kinsmanship), the law of the levirate, and the sharing of provisions for the poor.

Originating within the intimacy of family life in premonarchic, tribal Israel of the Iron I period, kinsmanship was a significant social principle that continued within village agrarian society during the preexilic period of the royal state and the postexilic state of the Judean theocracy, whose local center was the Temple and its priesthood. Kinsmanship, or family solidarity, emphasized the social responsibility of the family to care for the fundamental needs of those members experiencing the deprivation of poverty. At the heart of this social network of care was the gō 'ēl ("redeemer"), who redeemed, protected, and defended the weaker members of the extended family.[85] Family members who had to sell their land, other property, and perhaps themselves into slavery to meet debts were to be redeemed by the *gō 'ēl,* most often the next of kin to whom this responsibility fell (Leviticus 25; Ruth; Jeremiah 32). A corollary to this social responsibility was the law of the levirate: The male next of kin was to marry the widow of his deceased relative in order to conceive and raise up for the dead man children who would carry on his name and inherit his property (Deut. 25:5-10).[86] The next of kin could renounce this responsibility through legal action, though in a society of honor and shame the disgrace from such an action would have led to his humiliation and loss of status in the family and larger community (cf. Ruth).

In a number of Old Testament texts, including especially the Covenant Code (Exod. 20:22–23:33), the book of Deuteronomy, and prophetic literature (e.g., Amos), the principle of kinsmanship was broadened into a general social principle that governed the responsibilities of all Israelites toward impoverished members of society and even resident aliens. Widows, orphans, and resident aliens, having no family to support them, particularly enjoyed the protection of social legislation designed to alleviate their poverty (Exod. 22:21-27; Deut. 10:18; 24:17-21; 26:12-13; 27:19). The giving of alms to the poor (Deut. 15:7-11), the return of the poor's property, left in pledge when borrowing tools and implements from their more affluent neighbors (Exod. 22:25-26; Deut. 24:12-13), the prohibition against charging interest (Exod. 22:24), and the payment of day laborers (Deut. 24:14-15) were legal statutes that protected the poor.[87] Gleanings from the harvest were to be left in the fields so that the poor could gather food for themselves (Ruth 2), and the tithe of the third year was collected to benefit the destitute (Deut. 14:28-29). Laws were even put into place in order to eliminate poverty, though whether they were actually implemented is an interesting question. The sabbatical year, for example, required that the harvest be left for the poor and wild animals (Exod. 23:11), debts be rescinded (Deut. 15:1, 4), and slaves offered their freedom (Exod. 21:2-6; Deut. 15:12-18), while the year of Jubilee (the fiftieth year in a cycle of seven times seven years) required the returning of ancestral land to the original landowning families (Lev. 25:10).

In addition to social legislation and prophetic oracles, social responsibility for the poor was associated with the major institutions of kingship and temple cultus. The kings were especially given the responsibility for protecting the weaker members of society (see Pss. 22:26; 72:4), while the temple cult made provisions to allow them to offer less expensive gifts (Lev. 12:8; 14:21; 27:8). Poverty was not to keep the poor from participating in the celebration of festivals (Deut. 16:11-12). This did not mean that the poor were not abused by the powerful in Israelite society, but such abuse was condemned by the law and the prophets.

The theology of care and protection for the poor in Israelite religion normally was grounded in a view of God as redeemer (*gō 'ēl*) who delivered Israel from bondage in Egypt (Exod. 15:13; Ps. 74:2; 77:16; 78:35). This same redeemer is the special protector of the poor who acts to alleviate their suffering and oppression (Exod. 22:21-27; Jer. 50:34). Indeed, as protector of the poor, God required Israelites to extend them the charity necessary for their sustenance and punished those who ignored this responsibility. It was Israel's encounter with the God of the poor in its historical experiences, especially the exodus, that provided the theological grounding for social legislation and action to address poverty.

The sages also speak often about the topic of rich and poor/wealth and poverty, but with some degree of ambiguity.[88] On one hand, wealth is highly valued for its many benefits (Prov. 10:15; 13:8; 14:20; 18:16, 23; 19:4-7). Indeed, wealth is even regarded as a divine gift (Prov. 10:22) and the reward for righteous living (Prov. 13:22) and hard work (Prov. 10:4-5). On the other hand, poverty is generally regarded in negative ways with many limitations and dreadful consequences (Prov. 14:20; 18:23; 22:7). Poverty is not a state of existence that enhances the discipline of spirituality and ethical maturity, but an undesirable and wretched condition of helplessness to be avoided (Prov. 10:15). The wise in Proverbs do not suggest that those with resources should divest themselves of life's goods in order to enter a voluntary state of poverty that will allow them to concentrate on developing a life of the spirit. Poverty is at times considered to be the consequence of sloth (6:6-11; 10:4-5; 24:30-34; 26:13-16) and evil behavior (Prov. 12:3; 13:25). Yet there are also important qualifications to these general associations. The sages recognized that the wicked at times did achieve positions of wealth and power through evil behavior (Prov. 11:16; 28:15-16; 30:14), while counted among the poor were some who were righteous and God-fearing (Prov. 15:16-17; 16:8, 16, 19; 17:1; 28:6). If forced to choose between wealth and wisdom, riches and righteousness, the wise selected the moral virtues. Finally, it is clear that the sages in Proverbs recognized that poverty was not always the result of wicked behavior or sloth, even as riches could be obtained in dishonest and unjust ways. But they did envision a future in which, somehow and in some fashion, the wicked rich would eventually come to ruin while the righteous poor would be redeemed. It is the capacity of sapiential imagination to see a world of justice, a reality of the not-yet-actual to be lived into being by wise existence in the present and faith in a God who protected the poor and one day would bring vindication and judgment (Prov. 2:21-22; 10:30; 21:13; 22:16; 24:20; 28:20).[89]

Given this ambiguity, it is all the more remarkable that the saying in Proverbs 14:31 admonishes unqualified support for the poor, whoever they may be. While they may be comprised of widows, orphans, resident aliens, sojourners, and day laborers, the classes of those in constant states of destitution, the poor may also be those who lost their land due to misfortunes that included famine, war, and oppressive treatment. In other words, the poor may well be those who have no control over the circumstances that led to their poverty and helplessness. In addition, the poor included some who were in poverty because of sloth or folly or wickedness. Nevertheless, they, too, are to receive the charity of the sage.

While the sages appear to accept and even legitimate a social system in which there are significant inequities regarding access to goods and power, they did believe that they have an unqualified responsibility to sustain the poor. Wealth and poverty were viewed as social realities, and there is no idealistic program that attempts to eliminate poverty or to raise the poor from the depths of their poverty. The sages articulate an understanding of justice in which each person has the God-given right to the necessities of life. This right to exist, as it were, is grounded, not in a theology of exodus liberation, but rather in a sapiential understanding of creation and providence: God is the creator of both the rich and the poor as well as the powerful and the weak.

However, the sages did not argue that the social classes of rich and poor were grounded in the order of the cosmos. Nor did they argue that God is the one who has predestined some to poverty and low status and others to wealth and significant position. At most they interpreted sinking into poverty at times as divine testing and discipline that, successfully endured, could enhance their faithfulness and improve their character. Wealth at times was viewed as a divine gift, but God is also the special protector of the poor and underprivileged who will plead their case at court and rise up as their redeemer to save them and to punish their oppressors (Prov. 22:23; 23:10-11). More important is the social imperative of the sages to actualize justice (the right to exist) by moral behavior so that even the poor and socially vulnerable may exist.[90] This is in line with the justice that permeates the cosmos—that life-giving and enhancing force that sustains the structures of existence for God's good creation and his creatures. And behind this life-giving force of justice is God, who continues to shape and sustain creation and those creatures who inhabit its world.[91]

To return to the saying in 14:31, two interchangeable terms are used to name the poor: *dal* and *'ebyôn* ("poor, lowly, weak, and helpless").[92] These terms designate the destitute, who depend on others to provide them with the bare necessities of life (Lev. 14:21; Ruth 3:10; Job 31:16; 34:19; Pss. 82:3; 109:16; Prov. 22:9; and Deut. 15:7, 9; 24:14). They are often contrasted with the rich and powerful, who have more than they need to survive and thus have resources to share (Exod. 30:15; Prov. 10:15; 22:16; 28:11). Social categories of people specifically mentioned as belonging to the poor include in particular families devastated by war or other catastrophes (2 Sam. 3:1), orphans (Prov. 22:22), and widows (Job 31:16). Because of low status, the poor required the support of those in positions of influence to receive justice, understood at its fundamental basic level as access to the goods necessary to survive (Job 29:16; 30:25; Prov. 29:14; 31:9). Without the support of those with more resources than they need, the poor often will not survive. Yet at the same time, the weakest of society's members are those whose mistreatment may lead to increased resources for the unscrupulous (Ps. 37:14; Prov. 28:8; Amos 2:6; 5:12). Thus the poor enjoy the special protection of the wise and the God of wisdom.

Like the law and the prophets, wisdom portrays God as one who is on the side of the poor and is active on their behalf (Job 5:15; Prov. 19:17). The theological undergirding of social responsibility for the poor, then, is clear. The rich and poor and the haves and the have nots possess the same common origins: God is the creator of life, the Lord of the womb, who is responsible for conception, nurturing the fetus, giving birth to or attending to the birth of the newborn child, and like a parent sustaining the life of the individual. The imperative for the sage is to care for the poor, for they have the same origins and share a common humanity. They both are creatures of God. Subsequently, God requires the sages and other members of Israelite society to provide for the poor (Job 29:16; 30:25; 31:16-23; Ps. 112:9; Prov. 31:9).

In the antithetical saying of 14:31, two types of treatment of the poor are contrasted. "Oppress" ($\bar{o}\check{s}\bar{e}q$) refers to wronging the poor by various means: extortion, exploitation, defrauding them of their goods and rights, unremunerated labor, enslavement for debts, and the general neglect of their needs (Deut. 24:14; Jer. 7:6; Ezek. 22:29; and Amos 4:1). The oppression of the poor in this saying "insults" ($\hbar\bar{e}r\bar{e}p$) the creator. The term points to reproachful language that mocks, derides, and even taunts (Prov. 17:5; see Judg. 8:15; 1 Sam. 17:10, 25-26, 36, 45; 2 Kings 19:4, 16, 22-23; Isa. 65:7). The saying asserts that in the act of speaking reproachfully or mockingly to the poor, whether it is blaming them for their own misery or refusing to provide resources necessary for their survival, one is reproaching and mocking God. This is due to the strong identification of the creator with the poor.

The second type of action, to be "kind" ($\hbar\bar{a}nan$) to the poor, points to generosity and liberal giving. It is an important term for the concept of grace, because the recipient does not necessarily merit the generosity and may not be able to return the favor. Thus to show kindness is a free act of charity that characterizes the caring and loving righteous person (see Pss. 37:21, 26; 112:5; Prov. 19:17; 28:8). To be "kind" in this saying is an act of mercy extended to the poor that is more than a smiling face or a warm embrace. Rather, it is a gift of substance that enables the helpless to survive.

This act of charity also "honors" (*kibbēd*) the creator. The term for "honor" refers to many types of actions that bring glory and show respect to others, including God (1 Sam. 2:30; Pss. 22:24; 50:15, 23; Isa. 24:15; 25:3; 43:20). It is a term that on occasion refers to the worship of God, including offering sacrifices (Isa. 43:23). For the wise, even as sacrifices "honor" the creator, so do acts of kindness and mercy extended to the poor (cf. Mic. 6:6-8).

Creation and Theodicy (Prov. 16:4)[93]

One of the most difficult questions raised by creation theology is theodicy ("the justice of God"). Simply put, if a good and just God created and rules providentially over the world, then why is there evil in both its moral and natural dimensions? Many other subsidiary questions found their grounding in this most fundamental, underlying question. These include the origins of evil, the relationship between behavior and result (the so-called doctrine of retribution), the prosperity of the wicked, and the suffering of the righteous. The issue becomes a very critical one for Job and later on Jesus ben Sira, as we shall see in subsequent chapters.

Near the beginning of the second subsection of the collection in 16:1–22:16 a wisdom saying offers the following explanation of evil: "Yahweh has made everything with its counterpart, / even the wicked for the day of trouble" (16:4).

Occurring within a series of four proverbs that deal with human plans and their correspondence to divine purposes (16:1-4), this proverb broaches the topic of theodicy. The verb translated "has made" (*pā'al*), when God is the subject doing the acting, is used for creation, providence, and retribution (Job 36:3; Ps. 74:12; Isa. 41:4). The word translated "counterpart" (*ma'aneh*) literally means "answer, response" (Prov. 15:1; 29:19; Job 32:3, 5). It conveys the notion of an action that is accompanied by its response or result, or a subject that has its corresponding object. In this case, the creation of the wicked person is accompanied by an appropriate response or correspondence: the "day of trouble." The expression "day of trouble" picks up the sapiential understanding of the divine determination of time, not in the sense of God's predestining every event, but in the understanding that the successful, righteous, or wise action is inseparable from its appropriate, corresponding time, while the failing, wicked, or foolish action corresponds to or is associated with its time of trouble. Qoheleth is the best example of a sage who speaks of the effort (though ultimately impossible) of the wise to know the times—that is, when to act so as to be successful and when not to act so that failure may be avoided (7:14; 9:12; 12:1).[94] The more traditional sages articulated the view of a bipolar reality in which good and evil were opposites, though each had its corresponding time to exist (see Ben Sira).

This saying does not appear to intimate that Yahweh has created people to be wicked or is responsible for their evil deeds. Rather, he is the creator of all people, some of whom choose to engage in wickedness and then embody those acts in their manner of life. Yahweh is also the creator of the "day of trouble," a time of judgment and punishment as well as a period when misfortune occurs. Subsequently, the wicked are those who in times of judgment and misfortune will pay for their evil deeds. The sages were not naive in thinking that only the wicked suffered during times of trouble, while the righteous escaped any difficulty. But they did attempt to explain that behind the reason for times of trouble was the punishment of evildoers.

While not a sophisticated answer to theodicy free of its own problems, the saying touches on an approach that will be developed at length by Ben Sira in his theory of opposites.[95]

Creation and Economic Justice (Prov. 16:11)

For the sages, God establishes and oversees the social order and requires it to operate according to the principles of justice. Institutions of Israelite society, including especially the monarchy, are based on the order of righteousness that permeates the cosmos. The creator established kingship in order to implement and maintain justice in every arena of social life.[96] One image of this responsibility is that of justice, or righteousness, as the foundation or pedestal of the ruler's throne (Prov. 16:12; 20:28 [LXX]; 25:5). Hellmut Brunner has argued that these proverbs reflect the Egyptian view that the pedestal of the royal throne is identified with the primeval hill upon which the creator stood when he brought reality into existence and established *ma'at* ("justice," "truth") as the order of creation. Brunner bases his argument on the fact that the hieroglyph for the royal pedestal and *ma'at* is the same.[97]

For the Israelite sages, one important area that is regulated by divine justice is economics. Law codes, of course, regulated all phases of social life, but it is the king who, in the monarchic period, is especially responsible for economic justice. And it is God who created and maintains economic justice. This is the point of Prov. 16:11:

> A just balance and scales belong to the Lord,
> all the weights in the bag are his work.

This saying occurs within a short list of kingship sayings (16:10-15) that deal with royal decrees, the requirement for a king to act justly, the king's need of those who speak the truth, the danger of royal anger, and the blessing that derives from the king's favor. While this saying does not specifically mention the king, its location in the midst of this small section of royal sayings suggests that the monarchy is principally responsible for economic justice.

Even so, God establishes and oversees the workings of justice, in this case the accurate weighing of products to ensure that a proper measure and fair price are given in the buying and selling of goods. Israel apparently operated some system of standards to ensure that balances and measures were fair and accurate. This is implied in texts that point to the requirements of just weights and measures (Lev. 19:35-36; Ezek. 45:10) and that condemn those who cheat and steal by shorting those with whom they do business (Deut. 25:13; Prov. 11:1; 20:10, 23; Amos 8:5; Mic. 6:10-11).[98]

Worthy of note is the statement in the second line of the saying: "weights in the bag are his [God's] work [ma'aseh]." The word translated "work" is often used to refer to either the whole of creation or to the things that God has created, including the cosmos, various elements of the created order, and human beings (Job 14:15; 34:19; Pss. 8:4; 19:2; 103:22; 104:24; 111:2, 7). At the same time, the term is used to refer to divine activity in history and human life (Josh. 24:31; Judg. 2:7, 10; Qoh. 8:17). The theological basis for just measurements varies. It is interesting to note that the requirements for "just balances and weights" in Lev. 19:36 are theologically based in God's deliverance of Israel from Egyptian slavery. However, the wisdom saying in Prov. 16:11 indicates that God is the one who creates and oversees the accuracy and fairness of scales, measurements, and the use of weights in the process of buying and selling. Thus creation theology, not exodus liberation, is the basis of the social theory of the sages.

Creation and the Integrity of the Poor (Prov. 17:5)

Once again the topic of the poor is broached within the theological framework of creation theology:

> He who mocks the poor insults his creator,
> he who is glad at calamity will not be held innocent.
> (Prov. 17:5)

The crimes against the poor in this saying include mocking (lō 'ēg) them and being glad or rejoicing (sāmēah) over their calamity ('ēd). Mocking involves deriding the poor, shaming them, presumably when they approach a person of some means to request help. Instead of offering charity and aid, a duty required by morality and regulated by law, the poor person is verbally abused and his or her request is spurned (see Job 21:3). To add insult to injury, the one who turns aside the poor person's request rejoices over her or his calamity (see Ps. 35:26).

Punishment for those who fail to extend charity and care to the poor and instead choose both to deride them and to rejoice over their misfortune is the general statement that they will not be held innocent (*yinnāqeh*). The term for "innocent" may be taken in the sense of exemption—that is, mockers will not be exempt from their social responsibility or obligation toward the destitute (Gen. 24:8, 41; Num. 32:22). The same term may take on a more juridical understanding in the sense of being found guilty of a particular sin or crime in a court of law (Num. 5:28, 31). In other words, the one who mocks the poor and rejoices over their misfortune will be found guilty of failing to perform required social obligations designed to protect and preserve the impoverished (Deut. 15:7-11; 24:12-15).

Similar to Proverbs 14:31, the theological undergirding is that these actions against the poor or failures to give them their due "insults" or "taunts" (*ḥērēp*) their "creator" (*ʿōśēh*). As noted earlier, God strongly identifies with the poor (see Deut. 10:18; Prov. 22:22-23; Isa. 3:13-15; Sir. 4:1-10). In the legal and prophetic traditions, the theological basis for the responsibility to care for the poor is the exodus from Egypt. In wisdom, the theological basis of responsibility for the poor is creation.[99] The creator will not hold guiltless the person who rejoices over the calamity of the destitute, ignores their pleas for help, and exploits them. As both public defender and judge in a civil case, it is the creator of both the well to do and the impoverished who will bring to ruin those who are irresponsible to and oppressive of the poor. In this saying, there is no hint of the idea that providence has assigned the poor to destitution or that they are responsible for their own misery. Rather, the creator is their defender and punishes those who mock and oppress them. To "mock" the poor is to "mock" Yahweh (cf. Prov. 14:31).

Organs of Knowing and Perceiving (20:12)

Knowledge of the world and knowledge of God were not sharply differentiated in wisdom's epistemology. For the wise, all knowledge, including knowledge of God, is revealed through the order of creation, the tradition of the ancestors, and sapiential imagination, which begins with the perception of creation and the memories of tradition, but then moves into other areas: critical reflection, redescribing reality, and imagining God and human existence. These three avenues of knowing, along with the content of what is known, are, taken together, one way of defining wisdom as epistemology. The sages believed that wisdom, while ultimately a divine gift, was developed by the sharpening of their ability to observe, reason, experience, reflect, and imagine.

> The hearing ear and the seeing eye,
> the Lord has made them both. (20:12)

In this saying, the organs of perception that receive, transmit, and shape knowledge are created by God. For the sages of Proverbs, knowledge or insight, including the revelation of God, is not normally derived by means of charismatic endowment or inspired dreams, as was the case with the prophets. Knowledge, including revelation, does not come typically by means of religious experience or theophanic vision, one source, in addition to torah, claimed by the priests. Rather, the capacity to learn, perceive, and imagine is at the essence of human nature, a nature that is created by God. God endows humans, not with special knowledge known only by a few, but with the common ability to know and experience. Through seeing and hearing— through the use of the God-given organs of perception—humans have the innate capacity to know God, the world, society, and themselves. Wisdom is needed, along with piety and learning, but the means to come to a knowledge of God and reality belongs to all.

In late wisdom, at least some sages began to claim for themselves and their teaching various kinds of inspiration that went beyond the illumination and insight offered by the gift of wisdom. Eliphaz, in attempting to legitimate his views of a corrupt human nature that leads people to sin, tells Job of a "spirit" who appeared and spoke to him in his "visions of the night" (Job 4:12-21). Eliphaz indicates that while he could not clearly "recognize its appearance," his eyes could make out its form, and his ears could hear its voice. And, of course, there is the dramatic appearance of Yahweh to Job in the whirlwind in 38:1–42:6. In the second response of Job to the speeches from the whirl-wind, he notes:

> I had heard of you by the hearing of the ear,
> but now my eye sees you. (42:5)

Here Job confesses that his former knowledge of God was based largely on what he had been taught through tradition. Now, his knowledge of God comes directly from a theophanic encounter. This type of revelation goes far beyond what most sages, even Eliphaz, would claim as the source of their under-standing.

It is also the case that Ben Sira and the wise author of the Wisdom of Solomon claim that wisdom is their source of knowledge, insight, and even revelation of the mysteries of the divine reality. Ben Sira, while pointing to the usual means of obtaining knowledge and insight from the study of tradition and experience, indicates that the sage may receive the "spirit of intelligence," which enables him to create wisdom teachings that are insightful and authoritative (39:1-11).[100] In the following poem, he likens his state of insight or inspiration that issues forth in hymnic praise to a full moon (39:12). In the Wisdom of Solomon, the narrator prays for wisdom that gives insight and understanding of all things, including the knowledge of God (Wis. 7–9). Qoheleth, of course, is skeptical of such claims, for he places severe limits on the ability to know and understand the observable world as well as human existence. Indeed, for Qoheleth God is beyond knowing.

Rich and Poor (22:2)

The topos of rich/poor and wealth/poverty dominates the thematic interests of 22:1-16. A better saying (v. 1) values a "good name" (honor) more than wealth, and "favor" (or "elegance," or "grace"; $h\bar{e}n$) more than silver and gold. Humility and piety ("the fear of the Lord") are rewarded by wealth, honor, and life (v. 4). In verse 7 a descriptive, antithetical saying contrasts the power of the rich to rule over the poor with the latter's being forced into slavery because of their inability to take care of their indebtedness to the wealthy. No judgment is rendered in this saying; rather, it is simply an observation of a sometimes harsh, oppressive social reality. Verse 9, however, indicates that the generous person who shares bread with the poor is blessed—that is, experiences well-being in one or more of its features: contentment, sufficiency of life's necessities, happiness, health, longevity, a good relationship with God and other people, and so on. The last saying (v. 16) concludes that the person who becomes rich by oppressing the poor or who gives only to the wealthy will one day experience destitution.

The saying that deals with the rich and poor in the context of creation theology is found in verse 2:

> The rich and the poor meet together;
> Yahweh is the maker of them all.

The expression that complicates the interpretation of this saying is "meet together" (*nifgāšû*; see 29:13). "To meet" means normally an encounter between two or more persons, including at times God as one of the "persons" (see Gen. 32:18; 33:8; Exod. 4:24, 27; 1 Sam. 25:20; 2 Sam. 2:13). Usually the meeting has a reason and is not simply a chance encounter. And the reason often involves either intercession, negotiation, or even litigation in order to avoid or bring to an end mistreatment (Gen. 32:18; 33:8; Exod. 4:24-26). If this is the intimation here of the meeting between the rich and the poor, then one may well imagine that the saying refers to meetings in which the destitute ask for resources from the wealthy to sustain their lives.[101]

The reference to creation theology would then make sense. In encounters between the rich and the poor, each is to remember that the same God has created them both. This appears to have nothing to do with either the notion of predestination[102] or the suggestion that the rich and the poor merit their economic status. Rather, the rich person is to remember when approached by the poor that God is the creator of all people. And if indeed righteousness permeates the creation and the creator of all is a God of justice, two fundamental affirmations of sapiential faith, then the wealthy are to remember that they have the responsibility to share their resources with the poor. At the same time, the poor, who come to request from the rich something needed to sustain life, may remember that their creator also created the wealthy. They all have a common origin. And the poor also should remember that the creator is their protector and has a special stake in their survival. All people, as God's creatures, have inherent rights, including the rights to justice, respect, and charity.[103]

CREATION, RICH, AND POOR IN PROVERBS 25–29

Introduction

This collection, attributed to the literary activity of the "Men of Hezekiah," who are said to have copied Solomonic proverbs, points to sapiential activity at the court of this Judahite king who ruled from 715 to 687/86 B.C.E. If the superscription is given credibility, it may be that the collection was put together for the education of courtiers or youths who were being educated for a variety of positions in the royal state. The references to kingship (see esp. 25:2-7, 15) and the concern for justice found in this collection support the argument for the court and possibly the royal school as the social location.[104]

In regard to structure, it may be that this collection has two parts because of rather different literary features. Chapters 25–27 are dominated by comparative sayings and metaphors, while 28–29 consist primarily of antithetical sayings, with a significant emphasis once again on the contrast between the just and the wicked (cf. chaps. 10–15).[105] Among these antithetical sayings is one more that deals with rich and poor.

The Poor and the Oppressor (29:13)

Very similar to 22:2 is the saying found in 29:13:

> The poor person and the oppressor meet together,
> Yahweh gives light to the eyes of both.

If we follow the interpretation given to "meet together" in the preceding discussion, the situation envisioned by the saying would once again be that of a typical encounter, this time between the poor and their oppressors. The occasions for these meetings would be those times when the poor informally petition their oppressors to cease their harmful activities or more formally even to enter into litigation to redress their grievances. The term for "oppressor" (literally, "person of oppressions" or "injuries"), *tôk*, refers to one who causes harm, in this case, to the poor (see Pss. 10:7; 55:12; 72:14). Psalm 10 offers an important depiction of those who oppress the destitute and helpless. In this lament, structured as an alphabetic acrostic, the psalmist calls upon Yahweh to hear the oppressed in their cries for deliverance from the wicked and to rise up in judgment and bring the oppressors to a sure and swift destruction. In their pleas for justice, the poor make supplication to their oppressors, whose direct action or irresponsible refusal to help causes injury.

The second line of the saying of 29:13 points to creation as the theological tradition that should inform such encounters between the oppressors and the poor: Yahweh "gives light to the eyes of both." "To give light" (*mē 'îr*) refers to several possibilities. It may suggest "enlighten" in the sense of imparting understanding that especially comes through study of the law (Pss. 19:9; 119:130). The priests use a similar expression, "to cause the face to shine," to point to divine blessing (Num. 6:25). Qoheleth, referring to this priestly expression, speaks to the capacity of the sage to make a gracious response to others (8:1).[106] Finally, "to enlighten the eyes" points to the gift of life or reviving from death (Ps. 13:4; Ezra 9:8).

The last meaning seems the most appropriate one for the present context. As creator, Yahweh gives life to both the poor and their oppressors. Thus in this context of meeting in which the poor seek justice from those who cause them injury, both need to remember the commonality of their origins. And both should remember that Yahweh is the special defender of the poor who are treated uncharitably. Yet, the intimation may also be that Yahweh is the one who "revives" from death, a note of hope for the poor in this effort to redress their grievances against their oppressors, but also a warning to those guilty of harming the weak overtly or through neglect that their own hope to escape future confrontations with death is grounded in their just and kind treatment of the poor. Yahweh is the creator and sustainer, the one who gives life, but also revives from death.[107]

Conclusion: The Rich and the Poor (Wealth and Poverty)

In Proverbs the topos of wealth and poverty/rich and poor is presented with a measure of ambiguity. We are not given a clear definition of what the sages considered wealth to be or who belongs to the category of the rich. This lack of explanation also clouds the effort to determine their understanding of both poverty and the poor. It may be argued, however, that for the sages the poor are specifically those who lack the means to sustain their existence (food, drink, clothing, perhaps shelter). Deuteronomy offers the social categories of widow, orphan, Levite, and stranger (resident alien) as a way of defining the poor. One may also argue that the wealthy are not simply those with great riches, but may include those who have not only the basic necessities and means by which to support themselves and their dependents, but in addition a surplus of goods that may be shared with the destitute.

At times, there is simply a descriptive observation of the social reality of rich and poor, wealth and poverty. This descriptive saying offers no explanation, renders no judgment, and presents no exhortation. Wealth and poverty, rich and poor are simply a part of the social reality. Elsewhere wealth is greatly valued and much to be desired. It provides one with not only necessities, but also surplus commodities that offer some security against the contingencies of life and even luxuries. In the list of values, however, certain intangibles that are a part of the character and behavior of the righteous, wise person are more valued and desirable than wealth (e.g., "a good name"). The wealthy, however they are specifically understood, have responsibilities to share their excess resources with the poor. No specific limits or amounts are articulated by the sages, though generosity is an important virtue in wisdom texts. The rich also are subject to critical scrutiny. Those wealthy who do not share their goods with the poor or who gain their wealth by oppression or other dishonest means receive the judgment of the sages, and in their view, the punishment of God. Indeed, at times retributive justice is thought to operate in social reality: The wealthy who are unjust and/or refuse to share their resources with the destitute will one day come to ruin. This ruination of the wicked rich is probably understood more literally than metaphorically, though certainly destitution could also be understood in terms of a poverty of spirit, unhappiness, broken relationships, and so forth.

Poverty in itself is never valued by the sages of Proverbs. It is never a state of existence that is thought to enhance one's wisdom and piety, though the poor are often presented as enjoying divine protection. The ill effects of poverty are legion. Never does one find the sages admonishing their disciples to give all that they have to the poor in order to enter into a state of voluntary poverty. However, God not only requires the wealthy to share their goods with the destitute, but also will rise up in judgment against those who oppress or ignore the poor.

The reflections of the sages of Proverbs indicate at times that wealth is a reward for righteous, ethical behavior and even private initiative and hard work. And at times they regard poverty as a punishment for the wicked and/or lazy. Yet the sages also realized that wealth and poverty may come to those who have no personal responsibility for either. War, drought, unjust actions by the powerful, and the death of a provider may rob people of their resources and livelihoods. On the other hand, wealth may be inherited or even result from an unexpected stroke of good fortune. The sages do not suggest that God has predestined certain ones to wealth and others to poverty, regardless of their merits and failures. The sages will speak of a retributive understanding of justice, at least in general terms, thereby affirming their strong belief that righteousness is the order of creation and society as well as an integral feature of God's character. God is understood as the one who rewards and punishes, at times with wealth and poverty. Yet, God also is the defender of the destitute who rises up in judgment as their advocate and at the same time the judge who decrees and carries out punishment against those who abuse the poor or ignore their responsibilities to them. And the sages have an uncommon belief in justice. One day, God's justice will prevail and things will be set right and grievances addressed.

CREATION AND WORLD ORDER IN THE WORDS OF AGUR (PROV. 30:1-33)

Introduction

The wisdom teachings of Agur may include all of chapter 30, although the extent of this collection is debated.[108] The superscription (30:1*a*) is difficult to translate, but the following is suggested:

> The words of Agur, son of Yakeh, a revelation [*maśśā*];
> the oracle of the man.

The word *maśśā* may be either a geographical location, Massa (cf. Prov. 31:1), or a noun used to designate the collection as a "revelation." Massa may have been a place in Arabia (see Gen. 25:14). If this is the reference of the word, then Agur is a sage from the East whose wisdom has been preserved by the editors of Proverbs. However, the word *maśśā* ("burden," "utterance," "revelation") also may refer to prophetic speech given in the state of revelation (2 Kings 9:25; 2 Chron. 24:27; Isa. 14:28; Jer. 23:33-38; Zech. 9:1; 12:1). The term is found in the superscription of Habakkuk to refer to the vision he saw concerning the destruction by the Babylonians (1:1). Indeed, the entire collection of Habakkuk's materials is designated by this term.

In addition, the "words"[109] of Agur appear to be called a *nĕʾ ūm*—an "oracle." "Oracle" is also generally a term that refers to a prophetic word of God ("says the Lord"; Gen. 22:16; Isa. 14:22; 30:1; 31:9; Ezek. 13:6-7). Indeed, in several places it is the ecstatic speech of a prophet or utterance of an inspired psalmist (Num. 24:3, 15; 2 Sam. 23:1).[110] Thus Agur's wisdom may have been considered inspired in some sense. It may well be that the "wisdom" claimed by Agur is ecstatic or charismatic wisdom. That is, he has not been schooled in traditional wisdom and lacks the education and credentials of those who went through sapiential education in a royal or Temple school (see vv. 2-3). Even so, he claims to possess a type of mantic wisdom,[111] given him in inspired states by God (see Job 4:12-21).[112]

If the entire chapter comprises the collection of Agur, its structure would consist of a variety of literary and thematic materials:

Verses	Form(s)	Theme
30:1b-4	Rhetorical Questions	Enigma of Creation
30:5-6	Saying and Admonition	Divine Truth
30:7-9	Numerical Saying	Deceit and Contentment
30:10	Admonition	Dangerous Speech
30:11-14	Four Sayings	The Wicked
30:15-16	Numerical Saying	Insatiable Desire
30:17	Saying	Dishonoring Parents
30:18-19	Numerical Saying	Mystery
30:20	Saying	The Adulteress
30:21-23	Numerical Saying	World Upside Down
30:24-28	Numerical Saying	Wisdom of Little Creatures
30:29-31	Numerical Saying	Arrogance
30:32-33	Admonition	Arrogance

It is interesting to note that this small collection contains most of the numerical sayings in Proverbs. But more important is the observation that a major theme in this collection is the arrogance or self-exaltation that leads to rejection of divine sovereignty and rebellion against or upsetting of the social order. This is the theme in 30:1b-4, 7-10, 13, 17, 21-23, 29-33. Arrogance leading to rebellion may suggest that this collection is issued during a time of significant turmoil when the traditional social order has been subverted and insatiable greed and the grasping for wealth and power are unrestrained. The normal order of society is being subverted. Perhaps the traditional teachings of wisdom and justice are being largely ignored, due to the collapse or near collapse of traditional society. Thus the usual authority of wisdom, grounded in the prestige of the sage, and the respect for what the ancestors have taught no longer suffice to claim the people's allegiance. An "inspired" wisdom, emanating, not from the schools, but from a mantic teacher, is called for.

Creation and Rebellion

Verses 1b-4 appear to contain enigmatic, perhaps even impossible, questions about creation:

> 1b. I am weary, O God,
>   I am weary, O God, and I have become exhausted;[113]
> 2. Because I am more stupid than anyone else,
>   and I lack human insight.
> 3. While I have not studied wisdom,
>   I possess nevertheless the knowledge of the holy ones.[114]
> 4. Who has ascended to heaven and come down,
>   who has gathered the wind in the fold of his hands?
>   Who has wrapped the waters in a garment,
>   who has established all the ends of the earth?
>   What is name and what is his son's name?
>   Surely you know!

Enormous difficulties confront the translator of this truly enigmatic section in the "Words of Agur." And the proposed translation suggests only one way of reading a very troubled text. However, if indeed the entire collection of the "Words of Agur" is primarily concerned with the sin of arrogance, then it may well be that this first section presents in the form of either impossible questions or rhetorical questions the theme of rebellion against creation, a mythic theme that, in the ancient Near East, is grounded in hubris (the arrogant pride that leads human beings to reject the rule of heaven).[115] If so, this means, then, that the questions of Agur are probably not asking for information that is beyond human knowledge, but more likely are rhetorical questions with obvious answers.[116] The teacher, Agur, would be saying: God, not human beings, has the wisdom and power to rule the cosmos.

Of particular interest is the expression of ascending (ʿlh) and descending (yrd) in the first question. In Genesis 28:12, Jacob dreams that he sees "angels" ascending and "descending" a ladder that reaches to heaven. He awakens and names the place Bethel. This language of "ascending" and "descending" has to do in part with the obtaining of divine knowledge and perhaps other things possible only for the gods. Thus the establishment of a sanctuary points to a place where divine revelation may occur. In Isaiah 14:12-21, the fall of the king of Babylon is told in the language of the myth of "Day Star," the lower deity whose hubris leads him to attempt to ascend (ʿlh) to the heavens in order to sit on the throne of the high god, only to be "brought down" (*yrd*) to Sheol when the sun appears and burns out the weakening light of the ascending star. While Ezekiel (chap. 28) uses similar mythical language to describe the king of Tyre's sitting on the throne of gods, claiming to be divine, and his fall (or being cast down, *yrd*), he does not use the term 'lh ("ascend"). Here, the prophet historicizes the myth of rebellion against divine rule by the first man to condemn the king of Tyre. Ascending to heaven is used at times metaphorically to refer to hubris, the arrogant pride that pushes people to believe that they can reject divine rule to follow unrelentingly their own selfish ambitions, while descending (or being cast down) is used to describe on occasion the fall of the arrogant (Job 20:6; Ps. 73; Isa. 14:14-15; Amos 9:2).[117]

The question "Who has ascended to heaven and come down?" is found in a variant form in Mesopotamian wisdom of a cynical bent. In the "Dialogue of Pessimism,"[118] a text dating perhaps from the early Iron Age (1200 B.C.E.), the master, a rich nobleman who despairs of life and meaningful human activities, asks his wise slave: "What, then, is good?" To this query, the slave, obviously a sage and the more clever of the two, responds: "To have my neck and your neck broken and to be thrown into the river is good." To support this rather shocking counsel, the wise slave appends two questions:

> Who is so tall as to ascend to the heavens?
> Who is so broad as to compass the underworld?

These related questions in their present context suggest that human wisdom is incapable of discerning the good in human existence, since the sources of the comprehensive knowledge needed to determine the answer to the nobleman's quest for the good, the gods, are in heaven and beyond human reach. A similar question occurs in the *Gilgamesh Epic,* in which the semidivine hero eagerly pursues his quest for immortality.[119] Gilgamesh says to Enkidu, prior to their battle with Huwawa, the monster guarding the cedar forest: "Who, my friend, can scale heaven?" The question is rhetorical, expecting at this point in the story "no one" for an answer. The context is that of the gods' limiting immortality to themselves and ordaining death for humanity. No human may ascend to the heavens and live forever as a god, but humans may obtain a "name" for themselves and live through their fame. Or so Gilgamesh thinks. These texts point to the notion that humans, of themselves, cannot obtain divine wisdom or immortality. They may attempt to obtain these attributes for themselves, and they may even try to rule in the place of God. But they inevitably fail.

In returning to Proverbs 30, Agur emphasizes that, while he is himself not reared in the wisdom schools of Israel and Judah, he still possesses charismatic knowledge—that is, insight given to him by God, much like that of the prophets who stood in the council of Yahweh and were given a revelation encapsulating divine knowledge and action. Using the language of ascent (ʿlh) and descent (yrd), it may be that Agur is alluding to those lower gods, humans, and semidivine heroes, who, spurred on by their hubris, tried, without success, to ascend (ʿlh) to heaven to obtain divine knowledge, power, or immortality but were cast down (yrd). The answer to the question "Who has ascended to heaven and come down?" is that cadre of mythic and legendary beings who have attempted to usurp the rule of heaven or to obtain a divine attribute (wisdom or immortality), but have in the end failed. Either that, or the question is rhetorical, expecting as an answer "no human."

If this is the meaning of "ascending" and "descending" in the first question in verse 4, then it would follow that the next three point to divine activities associated with the creative power of God to control the forces of chaos:

> Who has gathered the wind in the fold of his hands?
> Who has wrapped the waters in a garment?
> Who has established all the ends of the earth?

The expression "gathering the wind [ʾasap-rûaḥ]" occurs two other times in the Hebrew Bible: Job 34:14-15 and Psalm 104:29. In both of these cases, the image is that of God's power to take back ("gather") his divine, life-giving spirit, an action that leads to the expiration of living creatures. In Proverbs 30 the image is similar, though it shifts slightly from that of breathing out and breathing in the life-giving spirit to enfolding it within the hands. The creator gives life by means of his divine spirit or wind and takes life back again, an act possible only for God and not for humans.[120] One may note that the great disappointment of Qoheleth is that no human is able to retain the breath of life (Qoh. 4:6; 8:8; 12:7). The second question centers on the activity of wrapping the waters (ṣārar-mayim) in a garment, a creation image that occurs elsewhere in Job 26:8: "He [God] wraps the waters in his thick clouds." Both of Agur's latter two questions appear to have the answer "God and no mortal."

The fourth question has a similar answer. The "ends of the earth" may refer to the outermost boundaries of the cosmos (Deut. 33:17; Ps. 59:14), including even those regions that stand in opposition to divine rule (1 Sam. 2:10; Ps. 2:8-9). "To establish" may mean in this context "to set up" the orderly limits of creation, differentiating between chaos and cosmos. Once again the answer to this question is God alone and no human.

The fifth and final question, "What is his name and what is his son's name?" drives home the point: Only God, not humans, has the strength and wisdom to create and sustain the cosmos. Agur has learned this, so he claims, not from the wisdom schools or from the observation of the orderly workings of the cosmos, but from an inspired state in which God has given him insight and understanding. This mantic wisdom underscores Agur's teaching here and later that arrogance leads to rebellion against the creator and ruler of the universe and threatens the divine order of cosmos and history. This arrogance, with mythic intimations in this text, is also at the center of a numerical saying (30:21-23) in the "Words of Agur."

The World Upside Down (30:21-23)[121]

A second reference to creation theology in the "Sayings of Agur" occurs in the series of numerical sayings that dominate this collection.

> Under three things the earth quakes,
> yea under four it is unable to endure:
> A servant when he becomes a king,
> A fool[122] when he has sufficient bread,
> A spurned woman when she marries,
> And a maid when she supplants her mistress.

The numerical saying compares several things, usually in groups of three, four, or seven, that have something in common. In this example, the common element is that people of low standing, should they reach a higher position, become arrogant and destructive to social order.[123] Four examples of turning the social order upside down threaten creation: a slave becoming a king, a fool having enough to eat, a despised woman obtaining a husband, and a maid replacing her mistress. In the conservative social world of traditional wisdom, it was unthinkable that a slave, often a foreigner taken in war or an indebted Hebrew, could become a king. If a slave were to become a king, the entire social order would collapse. A fool, in wisdom thinking, usually did not have enough to satiate his appetite. But a fool who disregarded wisdom's teachings and the rule of law, given a full stomach, posed a threat to the regularity of social law and sapiential custom through the folly of his or her actions. A woman, despised or perhaps "spurned" by suitors for unstated reasons (which could include divorce, sexual defilement, abuse, or homeliness; see Deut. 22:13-14; 24:3; 2 Sam. 13:15), would drive to ruin any man foolish enough to marry her.[124] And a maiden, usually a lowly servant who performs only menial tasks (Exod. 11:5; 1 Sam. 25:41; 2 Sam. 17:17), supplants her mistress, say by catching the eye of her mistress's husband, only to cause him great duress even as she made life difficult for the one whom formerly she had served (see the rivalry between Sarah and Hagar in Genesis 16 and 21).

What is particularly intriguing about this numerical saying is the argument that the upheaval of the social order leads to the "quaking" (*rgz*) of the earth.

"Quaking" is a term for earthquakes in theophanic texts, describing the reaction of the created order to the Divine Warrior who comes to do battle against chaos, either in mythic form or historical incarnation (Job 9:6; Ps. 77:16-20; Isa. 13:13; Joel 2:10; Amos 8:8-10). Social upheaval, warns this saying, leads to cosmic disorder. What happens in Israelite society affects creation, for both are grounded in a just and proper order.

Following this line of interpretation, Agur is not a skeptic who denies either the existence of God or the possibility of discovering true wisdom. Rather, he, an unlearned man, claims charismatic endowment in knowing that God alone is the creator and sustainer of the earth and in pinpointing hubris as the sin that leads to the human quest to obtain sovereignty over creation and to the unwillingness of humans to accept their place in the cosmic and social order.

CONCLUSION: CREATION AND MORAL DISCOURSE IN PROVERBS

Through the activation of imagination, the sages in Proverbs portray the cosmos as the creation of a God who established and now oversees the structures of life. In their descriptions of divine activity in the creation and guidance of the cosmos, the sages allude to metaphors of creation that become the major vehicles for conveying their teachings, while the rhetorical structure of poetic units, from sayings to instructions to poems, shape an elegant esthesis of order and beauty that engages the imagination to envision the world of sapiential existence and persuades the hearer to enter and take up residence. God is not specifically named warrior or king or judge or parent or teacher, but the sages' depiction of divine activity opens up a metaphorical description of reality in which God has these roles and functions.

Permeated by justice, the cosmos is a reality of beauty and life. Drawing on the memories of mythic traditions about fertility goddesses, the sages speak especially of the role of Woman Wisdom, who, incarnate in the instruction of the wisdom tradition, assumes the role of teacher and offers her moral discourse of life to those who would accept her invitation to come and learn of her. She is the voice of God who gives understanding and insight into the nature and character of God, reality, and human existence. This teacher of life is also the Queen of Heaven, who dispenses wisdom and life to her devotees and chooses kings to rule in justice. The first of God's creation, Wisdom is the child of the divine parent who rejoices over the wonders of the inhabited world and the humans who dwell therein. The cosmos is an object of art, a city, a kingdom, even a household in which God, Wisdom, and humans dwell in harmony and joy. The explicit use of metaphors for Wisdom, humanity, and reality is rare, but the descriptions of each often move within these imaginative construals.

The sages of Proverbs imagine God as the one who dwells within and yet also outside this world, creating it but also bringing it into judgment. God creates and sustains life through the words of wisdom that reside within the teachings of the sages. God is the architect who, through wisdom, crafts a well-ordered cosmos that sustains and enhances life and the ruler whose edicts and judgments provide a sapiential and legal structure for the governance of the world and human life. Through divine edicts, chaos is kept at bay and cannot overwhelm the good earth. The purpose of instruction and laws is to provide an order of life that guides humans to experience well-being. God is the father and mother of Woman Wisdom, God's divine child in whom God takes delight. Only a dim echo of the Divine Warrior's primordial struggle with chaos is heard in Proverbs. Finally, while creation and the voice of Wisdom testify to the nature of God, God is not fully known.

The sages also use their imagination to reflect on and envision the nature and character of human existence. As their creator, God has provided humans the gifts of organs of perception that enable them to receive sapiential instruction and to become wise. And as the protector of the poor, God demands justice for the weakest members of society. All people, rich and poor, have the same origins: They are the creatures of God and deserve both respect and sustenance necessary for survival. Through sapiential teaching and legal codes, the poor enjoy the special protection of God. He will rise up in judgment against their oppressors and bring the wealthy who ignore their pleas to destitution.

Finally, through Woman Wisdom, God offers a world of justice and blessing that students who take up her invitation may have as their dwelling place. Humans are Wisdom's students, lovers, and children who may embody the fruits of her discourse in their lives. Through their actions and speech, guided by sapiential teaching, they shape their own character, actualizing the wisdom tradition within their lives. And through their actions and speech, they shape a reality of history and language that supports and enhances social and cosmic justice.

"You Have Not Spoken Rightly About Me"

THE BOOK OF JOB AND THE IMAGINING OF GOD IN HUMAN TORMENT[1]

INTRODUCTION

Date

The book of Job contains no specific indication of its date. Subsequently, placing the book within the continuing wisdom tradition and the sociohistorical setting of ancient Israel and early Judaism depends on how one assesses rather indirect evidence. Most scholars agree that the book of Job developed over a period of many years and use tradition history or redaction criticism to trace the composition of its stages. However, in dating the book in its present form, two periods are frequently mentioned: the time of the Babylonian exile (587–539 B.C.E.)[2] and the Persian period (539 B.C.E. to 332 B.C.E.).[3] Favoring the exilic date are Ezekiel's reference to Job (14:14-20); specific linguistic features, including the presence of many Aramaisms; the references to "the satan" as an office and not as a personal name; the possible literary dependency of Job 3 on the lament of Jeremiah in 20:14-18; a literary style that is closest to the exilic prophet Second Isaiah; and the general argument that the crisis of the exile would have precipitated the composition of a book like Job. The Persian period is supported by the following arguments: Job's probable identity as an Edomite would oppose the exclusivity of Ezra's reform; the mentioning of "kings, counselors, and princes" may reflect the political hierarchy of the Persian Empire (see Ezra 7:28, 8:25; Esth. 1:3-4); and the absence of polygamy may indicate a post-exilic social development.

The best piece of evidence, although inferential in character, is Ezekiel 14:14-20, where the prophet points to Noah, Daniel (Dan'el), and Job as three well-known paragons of righteousness.[4] This text from Ezekiel may be dated to the critical period shortly before the fall of Jerusalem to the Babylonians in 587 B.C.E. It is important to note that Ezekiel's reference to Job is made during the most critical period in the history of Judah. Not only is the survival of the nation and its culture at stake, but also the fall of Jerusalem and the subsequent exile produced a profound religious crisis that demanded a compelling theological explanation. Various explanations were produced that enabled at least the transition to a colonial nation and the eventual development of early Judaism to occur. The book of Job, at least the poetic dialogues, may well represent one theological response to the crisis of the fall of Jerusalem and the Babylonian exile.

My own general dating of the book offers the following scenario: the didactic story of the prose narrative emerged in preexilic times and represented one traditional response to the relationship between suffering and human behavior; the composition of the poetic dialogues occurred during the exile to address the resulting crisis in Israelite wisdom theology; and the poem on wisdom (chap. 28) and the Elihu speeches (32–37) were added sometime after the exile as further responses to the theological issues raised by the earlier materials.

Literary Form[5]

A variety of literary forms, associated with different social contexts, have been suggested for the book of Job as a whole. These include a dramatized lament,[6] a "paradigm of the answered lament,"[7] a process of litigation,[8] and a sapiential disputation.[9] Other readings of Job move from form criticism and tradition history into more recent expressions of literary criticism. These readings attempt to interpret the book as a literary unit, and not as a compilation of sources. For example, one scholar has suggested that Job is a comedy comprising two features: "a vision of incongruity" and the reconciliation of the hero with society and God.[10] Marvin Pope has concluded that there is no single literary form for classifying the book of Job.[11] Instead, he sees the book as *sui generis,* for it brings together a variety of different literary forms. Thus it defies one single classification.

In my own judgment, the book of Job represents the culmination of a rather lengthy compositional history that brings together three major literary forms: didactic narrative, lament, and disputation. At the same time, these various components have been fashioned into a largely unified presentation. This does not mean that the book does not represent some significant interruptions in thought and movement. However, the poet who composed the dialogues in chapters 3–27, 29–31, and 38:1–42:6 is responsible for providing the major literary structure of the existing book, taking an existing prose narrative and using it as the framework for the poetic disputations. Sometime later, after the work of the poetic author of the dialogues, at least two additions were inserted that proposed different understandings of the theological questions raised by the book: the poem on wisdom in chapter 28 and the Elihu speeches in chapters 32–37.

The narrative frame of the book (1–2; 42:7-17) is a didactic narrative that parallels the Joseph story, the tale of Ahiqar, the Egyptian "Protests of the Eloquent Peasant," the Akkadian "Poor Man of Nippur," and the Hittite "Tale of Appu."[12] What is common to these stories is a virtuous hero who encounters misfortune at the hands of an antagonist. After conflict between the two, the hero is exonerated and restored to a position of prominence, while the antagonist is punished. The virtue or set of virtues of wisdom is embodied in the hero. Based on form-critical criteria, the narrative frame of Job—along with the later expansions in the Septuagint, Targums, and the pseudepigraphic Testament of Job—belongs to the classification of a "didactic narrative," a type of story that originated and continued to circulate within wisdom circles.

The lament is a second literary genre in the book of Job. Originating within the setting of public worship, this literary form was adapted for use by the sages in the ancient Near East. Examples of wisdom texts that make significant use of the lament include the Sumerian "A Man and His God," the Akkadian Ludlul bel nemeqi, two Akkadian texts from Ugarit (R.S. 25.460 and Louvre AO 4462), a Middle Kingdom Egyptian text ("The Lamentation of Khakheperre-sonbe") and Job's two soliloquies in chapters 3 and 29–31.[13] These sapiential texts have in common a suffering, righteous sage who at times speaks in the first person and the formal features of the individual lament (invocation, complaint or description of suffering, questions of reproach, a petition for help, condemnation of enemies or imprecations against evil persecutors, affirmation of confidence, confession of sins or assertion of innocence, acknowledgment of divine response, vow or pledge, and hymnic praise and blessings).

The third literary form significant for the structure of the book of Job is the sapiential disputation, paralleled especially by "The Babylonian Theodicy"[14] and the Egyptian "Dialogue Between a Man and His Ba."[15] As is the case with Job, these two examples portray a righteous, wise man who enters into debate with a wise antagonist. The goal of the disputation is to attempt to debate an issue and reach some major conclusions or insights into the issue or issues under consideration. Other examples of disputations, though they lack the righteous sufferer theme, include the Letter of Hori to Amenemope,[16] several Edubba essays,[17] various fables,[18] and the judicial rîb.[19] The four components of the disputation are the address of the opponent, accusation, argument, and concluding summary or counsel given to the opponent. This form, the disputation, dominates most of the book of Job.

Other wisdom texts that combine two of these forms include the Sumerian "A Man and His God" (narrative and lament), the "Protests of the Eloquent Peasant" (narrative and disputation), and the "Dialogue between a Man and his Soul" (disputation and lament). However, the book of Job brings together all three genres: didactic narrative in 1–2 and 42:7-17; lament in 3 and 29–31; and disputation in 4–27 and 38:1–42:6. Two later insertions occur in second and third editions: the Elihu intrusion in 32–37 and the poem on the inaccessibility of wisdom in 28. The fact that the book of Job brings together several wisdom forms does not mitigate against reading it as a literary whole. Yet recognizing these formal features adds to the interpretative enterprise in two important ways. First, Job belongs to wisdom literature and should be interpreted within its literary, social, theological, and ethical features. Second, the dominance of the sapiential disputation indicates that while the book engages the wisdom tradition in a critical fashion, it still belongs to this trajectory of religion and culture. After all, an important feature of sapiential imagination is critical reflection and engagement that leads to the reshaping of the tradition and even offers the possibility of the redescription of reality.

Literary Integrity

A careful reading of the book of Job points to questions about the literary integrity of the following parts: the present arrangement of the third cycle of dialogue (esp. chaps. 24–27), the wisdom hymn (28), the Elihu speeches (32–37), and the Yahweh speeches and Job's responses (38:1–42:6). An even more significant question involves the relation of the prose narrative (1–2, 42:7-17) to the dialogues (3–27; 29–31; and 38:1–42:6).

One of the more obvious literary problems is the disarray of speeches in the third cycle.[20] The pattern of alternating speeches is broken when Zophar has no final speech at all and Bildad has only a truncated statement in 25:1-6. Further, in the material attributed to Job, he occasionally presents arguments that are characteristic of his opponents (especially 27:13-23, and probably 26:5-14). While there are a variety of suggestions as to how to deal with this problem, the simplest rearrangement that provides a comprehensible text is

21—Job
22—Eliphaz
23—Job
24—Zophar (?)
25:1-6; 26:5-14—Bildad
26:1-4; 27:1-12—Job
27:13-23—Zophar.[21]

A second problem is the poem on wisdom in chapter 28. Its content does not make sense in the mouth of Job, at least in its current location, unless one wishes to argue that Job entertains, at least for a brief moment, the possibility that wisdom is beyond human comprehension and that the proper course of action is to return to the traditional sapiential piety of the prologue in chapters 1–2: "fear God and turn from evil." The poem's contention that wisdom (save for sapiential piety) is beyond human comprehension and thus belongs to the domain of divine understanding simply does not fit either the preceding arguments of Job, those of the friends, or Job's following soliloquy in chapters 29–31.

Job and his three opponents all claim at least some knowledge of wisdom, though the opponents admitted that divine understanding transcended human comprehension. However, this poem negates the possibility of obtaining any form of wisdom, save for a sapiential piety that essentially abandons the quest for knowledge of God and the larger reality. This view of wisdom as piety and morality returns us to the wisdom of chapters 1 and 2. Furthermore, Yahweh's assault on Job's limited wisdom in the speeches from the whirlwind (38:1–42:6) would make little sense, if Job has already conceded the issue of human comprehension of divine wisdom in an earlier chapter.

The poem is best understood as a later insertion by a pious sage who objects to the quest to discover wisdom. As we shall see, this parallels the addition of the epilogue to Qoheleth (12:9-14). The attribution of the poem to Job results in his own self-condemnation. For the pious sage who inserts and possibly wrote the poem, Job's quest to obtain divine wisdom is foolish, for it is doomed to failure.

The sudden appearance of Elihu for the first time in chapter 32 raises doubts about the appropriate location of his unanswered monologues, which extend for six chapters (32–37). In addition, Yahweh opens his initial speech in chapter 38 with a rebuke of the person who last spoke, thus fitting Job but not Elihu. Further, some of the language and content of Elihu's speeches parallel those of Yahweh (e.g., 37:14-20), thus preempting some of Yahweh's thunder. And in terms of content, Elihu's speeches tend to restate the positions of the three opponents, failing to advance the argumentation or to provide new insight. Recent efforts to include these speeches within the literary flow of the book do not appear particularly convincing.[22]

The present structure and content of the speeches of God and the responses of Job have been subjected to critical scrutiny, with the attempt by some to compress the two speeches of Yahweh and the two responses of Job into a single speech and one response.[23] However, the persuasiveness of this approach is not particularly compelling. Indeed, the elimination or major truncating of the Leviathan description seems questionable in view of the

127

importance of the chaos monster throughout the dialogues and the literary role it plays as a rather splendid inclusio (see 3:8). While the issues remain complex, I am inclined to accept the present arrangement and content of the two speeches and two responses.

Finally, the most often posed literary question concerns the relationship between the prose narrative and the poetic dialogues. Three major positions have been taken: An early narrative story is taken by the poet who uses it as a foil to reject the teaching that suffering is divine discipline;[24] the poet takes the earlier narrative tale and intends either to have the entire text read as a continuous story or chooses to juxtapose two contrasting compositions; and the narrative and dialogues were both written by the same author and intended to be read together.[25]

The differences between the narrative and the poetic dialogues are rather striking, ranging from literary style to content. For example, "the satan" plays a prominent role in chapters 1–2, but then disappears altogether in the poetry. Job suffers patiently and with unquestioning piety in the narrative tale, while he becomes the angry blasphemer in the poetic dialogues. The theme of retribution, nuanced by divine discipline, is supported by the narrative, but subverted by the poetic dialogues. It would seem that the poet has taken a well-known didactic narrative and replaced part of its content with the poetic dialogues. The connection of the narrative with the poetic dialogues results in a new reading of the narrative story. Retribution, suffering as divine discipline, and a capricious God who kills in response to unwarranted suspicion are no longer possible in a world of enormous pain that requires an intelligent response to this age-old dilemma.

To argue that the present book of Job has developed over several centuries and in many stages does not mean that the result is an incoherent piece of literary nonsense. The redactors have done an excellent job of adding new materials to the book that reconstitute at each step of the way the meaning of the story. Yet, at the same time, these stages may be reconstructed with some success. The following interpretation concentrates particularly on the meaning of the book prior to the later additions of the wisdom poem in chapter 28 and the Elihu speeches in chapters 32–37.

Sapiential Imagination and Narrative Enactment

The book of Job is a narrative redescription of reality, occasioned by dramatic crisis, most likely the Babylonian holocaust of the late sixth century B.C.E. It proceeds by means of presenting a legendary sage, known for his piety, wealth, and wisdom, who encounters a God who has thrown even innocent children into the whirlwind of inexplicable agony and death. Indeed, the book explores, not the question of innocent suffering, but the nature and character of God as creator and sustainer of the world. The suffering of the righteous leads to this larger question of God's nature and character. And the book explores, not moral virtue exemplified in the behavior of one who at first is unbelievably pious, but the nature and function of being human in a narrative world of the struggle with evil. The story of Job presents a new view of the world, the redescription of which is occasioned by Babylonian holocaust. Key to the presentation of this new reality is the role played by metaphors for creation that largely construe the meaning of the narrative world constructed by the story of Job.

THE NARRATIVE EPILOGUE AND DIVINE JUDGMENT (JOB 1–2)

Introduction: The Telling of the Tale

The prologue (chaps. 1–2) is a didactic tale told by an omniscient narrator who knows even more than the divine head of the assembly of the gods. The six scenes alternate between heaven and earth, with the hero of the story, Job, unaware of what transpires in the heavenly conversations between Yahweh and "the satan." The hero is a legendary sage of great wealth, moral virtue, faithfulness to God, and piety. He embodies the piety and virtue at the heart of traditional wisdom, for Job "fears God and turns away from evil (1:1-5)."[26]

The antagonist, introduced in the first heavenly scene (1:6-12), is "the satan," who, as a member of the divine council, has the responsibility to search out and discover evil on the face of the earth and to make a report to the divine judge.[27] He contends that Job's piety and loyalty to God are the payment Yahweh has purchased by special favor. If disaster strikes, he argues, Job would curse God and die. A suspicious ruler of the divine counsel falls prey to the temptation of "the satan" and turns over to him the hero. In two different assaults, Job loses his possessions and his children and then is afflicted with great physical torment. He is left with a wife who, assuming the role of the antagonist, attempts to shame her husband into cursing God. Yet Job responds with words of blessing, not cursing, and he maintains his loyalty to God. To drive home the truthfulness and authenticity of the hero's pious response, the narrator maintains that, in response to the first assault of "the satan," Job "did not sin or charge God with wrong" (1:22). At the end of the second assault, the narrator adds: "In all this Job did not sin with his lips" (2:10). The prologue ends with the visit of the three friends who come to console Job, but are silenced by the horror of his condition.

129

Metaphors for God: King

The controlling metaphor for God in this opening tale is the ruler who stands at the head of the divine assembly. One may assume that Yahweh has won this position through the defeat of chaos and now, as divine judge, convenes the gods presumably on New Year's Day ("the day"[28]) to issue the edicts that will determine the destiny of nations and individuals for the coming year.[29] This is the day when creation is reconstituted and order is maintained by divine decree.

The divine council in Israelite religion (Pss. 82; 89:8; Isa. 14:13; Amos 8:14) consisted of Yahweh, the divine king and judge, and lower gods (Deut. 33:2-3; Job 5:1; Ps. 82:6) who convened on Mt. Zion, the place of Yahweh's habitation and the center of the cosmos (Pss. 46; 48; 76). In the issuance of edicts, the order of creation is maintained (Job 38:11, 33) against the forces of chaos, the wicked are condemned (Psalm 82), and the destiny of nations and people is determined (Deut. 32:8; 1 Kings 22:19-23; Psalm 82; Isaiah 40). Prophets were called to the assembly to learn the fate of God's people (Jer. 23:18).

In the Joban prologue, the assembly meets twice, presumably during two successive New Year's days, and the divine edicts that elicit attention in the narrative are the ones that determine Job's fate. The first edict is in response to "the satan's" insinuation that Job's loyalty to God is self-serving. Without the reward of divine blessing, the antagonist contends that Job would curse God. Yahweh turns Job over to the affliction of "the satan," with the one restriction that he should not harm Job. The second edict is issued in response to "the satan's" contention that Job's piety and virtue would disappear, should he suffer physical torment. Yahweh again turns Job over to "the satan," with the command that he may not take the hero's life. Yahweh, much like El in the Baal Cycle, holds the power of the divine decree that he wields in order to maintain his own position at any cost. The paranoid suspicion incited in Yahweh by "the satan" leads to the unjust death of Job's children, the loss of wealth and position, and excruciating physical suffering. Job's piety and loyalty may have passed muster, but now the interest shifts from the character of Job to the integrity of God.

Metaphors for Humanity: Slave and Child of God

The prologue uses two metaphors for describing the place and function of humanity in the world: slave and child of God. Even the most exemplary person embodying virtue and piety, the legendary Job, is Yahweh's devoted slave. His scrupulous attention to cultic devotion and his pious responses to the two assaults of "the satan" point to one whose integrity and loyalty to

130

Yahweh should have been unquestioned. Job is unaware of the divine edicts that have made him destitute and brought him great suffering (cf. Ps. 139:17). Instead of uttering a curse against his personal god, Job blesses Yahweh's name, language designed to support divine sovereignty and to praise the creator who determines the fates. The "fear of God" is exemplified by the righteous Job's humble acceptance of God as creator and determiner of individual destinies.

The second metaphor, child of God, is mentioned in Job's response to the first text: "Naked I came from my mother's womb and naked shall I return; Yahweh has given and Yahweh has taken away; blessed be Yahweh's name" (1:21). The womb in this pious response may contain an allusion to the birth imagery associated with an earth mother goddess (e.g., Asherah, who personifies the fertile earth), but that is not the important point. Rather, in Job's world of piety and integrity, Yahweh is the sovereign lord of the womb who nurtures and blesses his children, but also takes away when he so chooses. Unquestioning piety, not curse or wrongful accusation, represents this slave's response to his master.

Metaphors for World: Kingdom

The implicit metaphor for the world of the narrator is that of a cosmic kingdom ruled over by a suspicious tyrant who determines the destiny of nations and persons on judgment day. The divine edict secures the stability of reality, but at great cost. It is a nightmare world of divine tyranny in which unsubstantiated suspicions of disloyalty may lead to the death of the innocents and to unbelievable personal suffering even by those renowned for their wisdom, devotion, and moral virtue. Humans are to respond, perhaps unbelievably, not in defiant rebellion, but in accepting acquiescence as the "slaves" of the divine master.

THE OPENING SOLILOQUY: THE ASSAULT ON CREATION (JOB 3)[30]

Introduction: The Cursing of Existence

Beginning with chapter 3, the poetic dialogues present a radically different Job, who, having experienced the drudgery and pain of creaturely existence comprised of slavery and toil, revolts against divine tyranny and injustice. Instead of compliant acceptance of his destiny, Job engages in wholesale revolt. Instead of blessing and praising God as creator and sovereign Lord, Job begins by cursing existence—not simply his own, but all creation as well.

WISDOM AND CREATION

Introduction (vv. 1-2)

1. Afterwards, Job opened his mouth and cursed his Day.
2. And Job responded and said:

Strophe I (vv. 2-11)

3. "Let the Day perish on which I was born,
    And the Night which said, 'A man child is conceived.'
4. Let that Day be darkness,
    Let not Eloah above divine for it,
    Let not light break forth upon it.
5. Let primordial darkness and deep blackness defile[31] it,
    Let a thick cloud settle upon it,
    Let the priests[32] of Yam[33] fill it with terror.
6. Let the darkness of the underworld seize that Night,
    Let it not rejoice among the days of the year,
    Let it not enter the number of the months.
7. Behold, let that Night be barren,
    Let no ecstatic cry occur in it,
8. Let the cursers of Yam[34] damn it,
    The skilled ones who awaken Leviathan,
9. Let the stars of its dawn become dark,
    Let it wait in hope for light but find only nothingness,
    Let it not look upon the eyelids of Dawn,
10. Because it did not close the doors of my womb
    And conceal sorrow from my eyes."

Strophe II (vv. 12-19)

11. "Why did I not die at birth,
    Expire at the time I came forth from the womb?
12. Why did the knees receive me,
    Or the breasts that I should suck?
13. For now I would be at rest and silent,
    I would sleep, then I would have rest,
14. With kings and counselors of the earth,
    Those who rebuild ruins for themselves;
15. Or with princes who have gold,
    Who fill their houses with silver.
16. Or why was I not like an aborted fetus,
    Like infants who did not see light?
17. There the wicked cease their raging,
    And there those whose strength has expired are at rest.
18. There the prisoners together are in repose,
    They do not hear the voice of the taskmaster.
19. The small and the great are there,
    The slave is free from his lord."

Strophe III (vv. 20-26)

20. "Why is light given to the weary,
    And life to the bitter in soul?
21. Those who wait for Death (Mot), but he does not come,
    And dig for him like hidden treasures.

22. Those who rejoice greatly,
    And exult when they find the tomb.
23. Why is light given to a man whose way is hidden,
    Whom Eloah has hedged in?
24. For my sighing comes before my bread,
    And my groanings are poured out like water.
25. For what I exceedingly fear comes upon me,
    And what I abhor approaches me.
26. I am not at ease, and I am not quiet,
    I do not rest for wrath comes."

This opening soliloquy, a beautifully crafted poem of three well-defined strophes, echoes the major features of an individual lament: verses 3-10—the cursing of Day and Night; verses 11-19—the wish for premature death; and verses 20-26—the desire to understand the enigma of human torment. Within the temporal reality of poetic reflection, Job moves from birth (past) to death (future) and then to human suffering (present), reaching finally the point where the desire to understand is stronger than the wish for oblivion.

Images of creation abound in this poem, particularly the binary pair of light and darkness, which evokes others: day and night, life and death, birth and tomb, order and chaos, and knowledge and mystery.[35] And by means of the mood occasioned by the content of Job's speech and the blackness of his situation, what Job desires is a return to oblivion, not only for himself, but indeed for the entire creation. Job seeks by the power of his spoken word, formulated in lament and curse, to obliterate all existence.[36] The "rest" (*nūaḥ*) for which Job longs (v. 17) is the end of all existence, and not the divine repose (*šabbāt*) on the sabbath that unleashed through means of divine blessing the creative forces that ordered and maintained the newly formed cosmos (cf. Gen. 2:1-3). Job's "rest" is also an ironic reversal of that associated with repose (*nūaḥ*) in the promised land (Deut. 5:14). Job seeks to subvert not only creation and blessing, but all life-giving traditions of salvation in Israelite faith. By destabilizing the language of faith, Job attempts to negate all of reality.

Metaphors of God

The dominant metaphor for creation in this poem is word, making God the divine sovereign whose language speaks reality into being.[37] In its typical mythic context, it is the creative power of the royal Lord ruling over the divine assembly (see Gen. 1:26-28; Ps. 82; and the *Enuma elish*). The word originates and then sustains the created order. However, instead of acts of creation enhanced by the sustaining power of blessing (see Gen. 1:22, 28; 2:3), Job begins in the first strophe with seven curses. Curses are powerful language designed to bring destruction to that against which they are directed. They are especially uttered against enemies, both personal and communal, as well as the forces of destruction[38]—only in this case, Job utters them against the day of his birth and the night of his conception. Job seeks to enlist magicians or pagan priests to awaken the dark powers of chaos (Yam and Leviathan) to destroy not only his own existence, but the very temporal order of creation as well.[39] The uttering of seven incantations in the first strophe brings to mind the seven days of creation in 1:1–2:4a, as does the period of seven days and seven nights of silence intervening between the arrival of Job's comforters and his soliloquy of negation (Job 2:13).

The negation of the creation of the world in Genesis 1:1–2:4a is also accomplished by Job's use of sixteen jussives and prohibitions in his formulation of the seven curses to counteract the fifteen jussives and prohibitions in the Priestly tradition and by the formulation of Job's first curse, "let that day be darkness," (3:4) to counteract the first act of divine creation, "let there be light" (Gen. 1:3).

The initial soliloquy also introduces the dominating mythic metaphor in Job: the battle with the monster of chaos. This metaphor, so important to many mythic traditions of the ancient Near East, portrays the creator as a warrior who struggles with chaos, usually personified as a monster or warrior, for mastery of the cosmos. Winning this struggle, the creator is proclaimed king and then forms the cosmos (at least in myths of origins) and sets up its structures for continuation or issues edicts (in myths of maintenance) that sustain the order of reality and limit the destructive powers of chaos (Job 7:12; 38:10-11). The power of chaos, while subdued, is never completely vanquished, save in eschatological myths of a new age. Normally chaos is a continuing threat that must be defeated daily (in the battle of the sun with the forces of the deep) or yearly (in a New Year's setting) (see Gen. 49:25; Deut. 33:13).

In contrast to the traditional use of this metaphor of battle in creation traditions of origins and maintenance, Job attempts to subvert this image by redescribing its content. His incantation in verse 8 implores the "cursers of Yam,"[40] priests or magicians skilled in the power of curse, "to awaken, stir up Leviathan,"[41] the slumbering dragon, in order to devour Night and thereby collapse the temporal order of creation. These "skilled ones" also employ magic to destroy (see Isa. 51:9-11). In the *Enuma elish*, Anshar instructs Marduk prior to battle, "Calm [Tiamat] with thy holy spell."[42]

The stars (v. 9) in mythological understanding are divine armies, the heavenly hosts, who establish and extend divine power throughout the cosmos. They are among those in heavenly regions who respond in joyous praise to Yahweh's magnificent creation (Job 38:4-7).[43] The magicians and priests who practice the black arts, a forbidden craft in normative Israelite religion

(2 Kings 23:5; Zeph. 1:4), are solicited to destroy creation. More is at stake here than empty words or vain hopes. In Yahweh's hymn to Leviathan at the conclusion of the poetic drama (Job 40:24–41:26), shortly before the battle begins, it is clear that Job has succeeded in arousing the monster to do battle once again with the divine warrior.

Metaphors of Anthropology

The poet uses the metaphor of birth and nurture to describe both Job's origins (Strophe I) and his desire to have died at birth (Strophe II). The image of the gift of light in Strophe III could point to the initial sensual experience of the newborn at birth. God as father and/or mother, the Lord of the womb who forms the fetus, the midwife who delivers the infant, and the parent who then nurtures the offspring through life are specific images that belong to the cluster of images associated with this metaphor of individual creation (see Job 10:8-13; Ps. 139:13-18; Jer. 1:4-10). Normally, a newborn's birth is the cause for rejoicing (see 1 Samuel 1–2; Luke 1:46-55), but for the language of reversal in Job, his own birth is a time for cursing, not for celebration. Blessing is the divine power that enhances fertility and life (see Genesis 1), but now blessing is replaced by its opposite, cursing. Day and Night, personified as the objects of Job's cursing, are to become sterile, incapable of producing life. Indeed, they are to be overwhelmed by darkness, even devoured by Leviathan, the monster of the deep.[44] The priests of Yam are called on by Job to curse Night with sterility and to arouse a sleeping Leviathan, monster of the Deep, to devour her.[45]

The second strophe (vv. 11-19) continues the imagery of fertility and birth, only now the language is that of accusatory lament: Job agonizes over why he was born and suckled at his mother's breast instead of dying immediately or being stillborn (cf. Qoh. 6:4-5). Job's language is at the very least an indirect indictment of God as the Lord of the womb (see Pss. 22:9-11; 139:13-16). For the sages, creation by God in the womb also meant common origins for all, both rich and poor. This meant that the prosperous were ethically required to care for the needy (see Job 31:13-15; Prov. 22:2). Instead, for Job, the tomb is the place where social differentiations are eliminated. It is only in the womb of Sheol, not that of the mother, that the rich and poor find that brotherhood and sisterhood of equality.

In traditional wisdom, the dominant metaphor for human existence in the world is king or ruler. As was the case with the cosmological tradition, Job destabilizes the language of this tradition, with its emphasis on divine conception, providential care, rulership over God's creation, and active participation in ordering cosmos and society.

Job utters his curses of sterility against Day and Night, personified as the gods of conception and birth. Instead of using the metaphor of birth to call on Yahweh to rise up and protect his son, who is in distress, Job curses existence, his and that of the cosmos, and attempts to bring all reality to an end by fragmenting its linguistic infrastructure.

Intimations of royal imagery associated with human existence appear in the second strophe (vv. 11-19). In Sheol, Job would join as an equal both "kings and counselors of the earth who built ruins for themselves" and princes who had filled their "houses" with treasure. The construction of "houses," especially palaces and temples, assumed the stature of a world-building enterprise, sanctioned by deities of creation and order and assigned to kings. Temples were a microcosmic reflection of creation and the place where ritual maintained the vital forces of state and cosmos. Now Job, a tormented underling, would join the mighty in Sheol, no longer separated from them because of differences in power, wealth, and position.

While Albertz may be correct in his argument that Job was a former ruler, displaced by a new political order,[46] Job becomes here and throughout the discourse of the dialogues a slave whose only hope of escape from a tyrannical deity resides in the liberation of death. Job's faith language, having destabilized, no longer supports the social organizations important for the ancient world, including family, kingship, and religion. Indeed, they, too, collapse under the weight of curse. Like the foreign slave who must serve the master for a lifetime, Job and humankind find no escape from the dreaded lot of human existence, save in death. Job has experienced creation as slavery and begins, at least in the final strophe, to raise the questions that would lead, not to capitulation, but to all-out revolt.

Metaphors for the World

The reality of Job's present world is no longer that of a household in which the divine parent or parents give birth to and nurture their human children. It is a nightmare world of agony, torment, and alienation, which Job wishes to bring to an end. The dominating image for the reality Job seeks to shape is darkness, signifying oblivion and actualized in the kingdom of Sheol, that world of gloom and darkness, ruled over by the princes of death (see 18:13), where at least there is rest from the torment of present existence.

It is clear from this opening soliloquy that Job's own metaphors of faith have collapsed. While death is an appealing consummation of a life in torment, Job engages in an assault on creation that is designed not only to destroy the entire cosmos, but also to force Yahweh, creator of heaven and earth, from his throne. Indeed, Yahweh would have no world or human creatures for his dominion. Job's earlier, enduring faith has crumbled, and now in angry rage he seeks to collapse all traditional theological meaning that creates and sustains the world.

ELIPHAZ: THE DEFENSE OF DIVINE JUSTICE (JOB 4–5)

Introduction

In his initial response, Eliphaz attempts to counter Job's destabilizing curses by sapiential instruction and pious praise of Yahweh as creator and sustainer of a just world order. The dominant metaphor for God is that of divine ruler or judge whose edicts establish and carry out a retributive system of justice in which the wicked are punished and the righteous are rewarded. Even the righteous may at times receive divine rebuke, argues Eliphaz, but they should endure patiently, repent of their sins, and expect a merciful God to deliver them from evil. What is surprising is that Eliphaz grounds his teaching, not simply in sapiential modes of authority (experience, analogy from nature, and the appeal to tradition),[47] but also in prophetic revelation (4:12-17) and the doxology of confession (5:8-16). The "fear of God" for this defender of the faith disallows sapiential debate and critical reflection. Creative metaphor has been reshaped into inflexible dogma formulated in the language of retributive justice.

In verses 7-9, Eliphaz abuses metaphors of creation faith in two ways. First, "memory" (*zākār*) in the tradition of the laments calls on the Divine Warrior to subdue chaos and redeem the chosen (cf. Ps. 77:11-20). But Eliphaz does not allow for the suffering of the righteous community, which is at the basis of this liturgical tradition. Second, the life-giving breath (*nĕšāmâ* and *rûaḥ*) of God, one of the metaphors in the cluster of those associated with divine word that gives life to the cosmos and human creatures (Gen. 2:7; Ps. 104:27-30; Qoh. 12:7), now becomes the divine instrument of retributive justice, not the force at work in the cycle of life and death (cf. 2 Sam. 22:16; Ps. 18:16).

Another argument of Eliphaz in favor of the dogma of retributive justice uses the world of nature to bolster the notion that the wicked are eventually punished (4:10-11):

> 10. The roar of the lion and the voice of the hunted lion,
>   the teeth of young lions are broken.
> 11. The fierce lion perishes from lack of prey,
>   and the whelps of the lioness are scattered.

God is not the "Lord of the Creatures" who beneficently rules over the animal kingdom (Psalm 104); rather, God is the destructive tyrant who overpowers and even brings to their end animals who do not yield to the divine will (contrast the first Yahweh speech in chaps. 38–39).

The doxology in 5:9-16 is a word of praise sung either by the falsely accused, who await a declaration of innocence by the judge, or by the guilty, who confess their guilt and declare the judgment just.[48] For Eliphaz, the metaphor of word expresses God's rule, in this case, as the divine judge.

> 9. The one who creates great things[49] beyond comprehension,
>   wonderful things without limit.
> 10. The one who gives rain upon the face of the land,
>   and sends water upon the countryside.
> 11. Exalting the lowly to a high place,
>   and raising to safety those who mourn.
> 12. The one who frustrates the machinations of the calculating,
>   allowing their hands no abiding success.
> 13. The one who captures the wise in their own deceit,
>   and the counsel of the shrewd becomes hastily contrived.
> 14. They shall confront darkness by day,
>   and grope for their way at noontime as at night.
> 15. But the desolated[50] shall be saved from their mouth,
>   and from the hand of the strong.
> 16. And the poor shall have hope,
>   for injustice has shut her mouth.

Eliphaz' doxology involves three themes: creation (v. 9), nature (v. 10), and society (vv. 11-16). The "making/doing of great things" and "wonders" allude to God's defeat of chaos, divine creation, and providential rule over nature (7:5, 14; 9:9-10; 42:3; cf. Pss. 96:3; 98:1). For Eliphaz, retributive justice is grounded in the moral character of God.

The second theme speaks of God's providential rule of the natural order: the sending of rain to renew life. In Genesis 2:4b-6 (cf. Deut. 11:14, 17; 28:12; 1 Kings 8:35-36; Job 36:27; Ps. 147:8; Isa. 41:18-19; 43:19; 44:3-4.; 55:10; Jer. 14:22; Matt. 5:45), the first act of creation is Yahweh's sending a mist to moisten a dry desert, turning it into arable soil conducive for fertility. In this doxology, rain is a divine "gift" that renews the earth and makes the fields fertile.

The third theme speaks of God's providential guidance of history, in particular the punishment meted out to the arrogant self-righteous (Prov. 26:27; 28:10; Pss. 7:15; 9:16; 35:8; 57:7). This doxology opposes the self-sufficiency of politicians who ignore providence in human affairs.[51] Their hubris leads ultimately to alienation from God (cf. Genesis 2–11; Ezekiel 28).[52] In opposition to these rulers, filled with self-importance, God exalts the needy and poor and acts to establish justice. Job, argues Eliphaz, should abandon hubris and sing this ready-made doxology as a confession of guilt in order to receive divine mercy.

Metaphors in the Anthropological Tradition

What is particularly striking in this first speech by Eliphaz is his dark view of a universally perverse human nature, a view common to the slave metaphor (4:17-21):

> 17. Can humanity be righteous before God?
>   Can a man be pure before his creator?
> 18. He does not even trust his servants,
>   And he imputes error in his messengers.
> 19. How much more the inhabitants of houses of clay,
>   whose foundation is in the dust,
>   who are crushed before the moth.
> 20. From morning until evening they are destroyed,
>   they perish forever without name.[53]
> 21. Is not their tent-cord plucked up within them?
>   They die, and without wisdom.

This universal depravity opposes the more traditional Israelite view that humans are made in the image of God to rule creation as God's surrogate (cf. Gen. 1:26-28; Psalm 8). For Eliphaz, God is the divine craftsman who, in making humans, builds "houses of clay" with "foundations in the dust." Mortals die quickly like the moth and "without name"—that is, without honor and remembrance (Gen. 12:2; 2 Sam. 7:9; Qoh. 7:1).

In 5:1-7, Eliphaz draws on the image of the power of the curse in Genesis 3, indicating that the wicked are destroyed by the power-laden language of the righteous (see Prov. 24:24-25). Eliphaz' curse attempts to actualize the potency of curse to destroy the wicked:

> 3. I saw an evil man taking root,
>   and I suddenly cursed his land.
> 4. "Let his sons be far from salvation,
>   and let them be crushed in the gate with no one to deliver.
> 5. As for his harvest let the hungry devour it,
>   let him take it from thorns,
>   and the thirsty[54] trample upon their produce."
> 6. For surely[55] evil comes forth from the dust ('āphār),
>   and trouble sprouts up from the soil ('ădāmâ);
> 7. For humanity is born to trouble.
>   and the Sons of Reshef fly upward (5:3-7).

Using traditional language of sapiential first-person observation, Eliphaz mentions that he, having seen fools who had "taken root," uttered a curse against their "habitation" (*nāwe*)—their land and their children. What is of particular importance is Eliphaz' contention that people are born to experience trouble, just as surely as the Sons of Reshef (the god of pestilence and death; see Deut. 32:24; Hab. 3:5[56]) are responsible for disease and plague. Eliphaz contends that the dust of the earth and the arable soil that provide the substance used by God as craftsman in shaping humans are the source of human wickedness (Gen. 2:7; 3:19; 8:21). The potency of the earth yields crops, but cursed by God, it also produces thorns, weeds, and disease (Gen. 3:19; Job 7:21; 10:9; Ps. 104:29; Qoh. 3:20).

Metaphors for Reality

Reality for Eliphaz is like a kingdom ruled by a just but stern tyrant who uses the power of divine edict to bring destruction to the wicked and crafty and to deliver the righteous and humble of heart. This kingdom is not a complex and ambiguous reality, but a place of retributive justice in which the divine warrior, having conquered chaos, rules with unchallenged supremacy. The wicked may prosper for a time, even as the righteous may be disciplined, but ultimately God will set things right. However, the world of human habitation as well as its people are corrupt by nature and deserve any punishment God may choose. As an obedient and compliant subject, Job's hope is to utter a confession of guilt, turn to God for healing, and wait confidently for divine deliverance. Ultimately, Job's redemption will lead to his living in harmony with creation, the coveted future of old age, and the joy of many offspring who will continue his good name into the ages.

JOB: THE DESTINY OF SLAVERY (JOB 6–7)

Introduction

There is a point of agreement between Job and his opponents: Humanity are slaves, predestined to divine service. Job's second speech, in response to Eliphaz, is a disputation that parodies the view of humans as kings ruling over God's good creation. At the heart of the two acrostic poems that form the poetic structure of his disputation are the metaphors of the battle with chaos and creation and rule by word. In the first two strophes of Job's first poem (6:2-23), he complains of being assaulted by the Divine Warrior.

Strophe I (vv. 2-7)
2. If only my vexation were weighed,
and my misfortune were placed upon a scale.

3. They would then be heavier than the sands of the sea.
    Is this why my words have been wild talk?
4. Because the arrows of Shaddai are with me,
    My breath drinks their wrath.
5. Does the wild ass bray when he has fodder,
    or does the ox low over his feed?
6. Can something tasteless be eaten without salt,
    is there taste to the slime of purslain?
7. My appetite refuses even to touch them;
    it loathes my bread.[57]

Strophe II (vv. 8-13)

8. Oh that my petition might be granted,
    and God would concede to permit my hope.
9. Then God would be pleased to crush me,
    he would release his hand and sever me in two.
10. Yet I would be consoled,
    I would spring forth in joy.
  Although I have not denied the words of the Holy One,
    he has no mercy.
11. What strength do I have that I should wait,
    And what is my end that I should make myself patient?
12. Is my strength the strength of stones,
    or is my flesh bronze?
13. Indeed no help remains in me,
    and insight is driven from me.

As the Divine Warrior (cf. Marduk and Baal), God attacks Job with fierce wrath as though he were now the chaos monster threatening divine rule (cf. Pss. 74:13; 88:13-18; 89:11). The arrows in the arsenal of the warrior God (Ps. 18:15 = 2 Sam. 22:15; Pss. 77:18; 144:6; Hab. 3:11; Zech. 9:14) commonly convey in poetic imagery the theology of divine justice (Deut. 32:23, 42; Pss. 7:14; 38:3; 64:8; 120:4). In theophanic hymns, Yahweh marches forth in battle to slaughter and crush his fearsome enemy.[58] The "terrors" are the cohorts of divine or supernatural soldiers who follow the Divine Warrior into battle (cf. Habakkuk 3, "pestilence" and "plague").

An echo of Marduk's defeat of Tiamat appears to occur in the second poem:

Am I Yam or the Dragon,[59]
    that you have set up a guard against me? (7:12)

The establishing of a "guard" (*mišmār*) reflects the action taken by Marduk following his dividing of Tiamat into two parts to keep the waters of her corpse from escaping into the newly created order to inundate it.

Metaphors of Anthropology

In an accusatory lament (7:1-21), Job, finding himself alone and abandoned by his three false friends, questions the divine judge and wonders why he has been so savagely attacked. What makes the assault even more vicious and cruel is the view that God has ignored Job's human weakness and his condition of finite mortality.

Strophe I (vv. 1-6)

1. Is it not humanity's lot to endure hard service on earth?
   Are not their days like those of the hireling?
2. Like a slave who gasps for the shade,
   and like a hireling waiting expectantly for his wage?
3. Thus, I am allotted empty months,
   and nights of weariness are apportioned to me.
4. If I lie down then I say, "When shall I arise?"
   But the evening continues on and I am surfeited
   with restless tossings until the dawn.
5. My flesh is clothed with worms and clods of dust,
   my skin hardens and then oozes once again.
6. My days pass more swiftly than a weaver's comb,
   and they come to an end without hope.

Strophe II (vv. 7-16)

7. Remember that my life is but a breath,
   my eyes will never again see good.
8. The eye of the one who sees me will not behold me,
   your eyes are upon me, but I am no more.
9. As a cloud fades and disappears,
   thus the one who descends into Sheol shall not come up.
10. He will not return again to his house,
    and his dwelling place shall recognize him no more.
11. Therefore I will not restrain my mouth,
    I will speak in the distress of my spirit,
    I will complain in the bitterness of my being.
12. Am I Yam or Tannin,
    that you should place a guard against me?
13. If I say, "My couch will comfort me,
    my bed will ease my complaint,"
14. You frighten me with dreams,
    and you terrify me with visions.
15. So that I would choose strangling,
    death rather than my bones.
16. I protest! I shall not live forever.
    Leave me be, for my days are but a breath.

Strophe III (vv. 17-21)

17. What are humans, that you make them great,
    or that you consider them?
18. That you examine them each morning.

142

that you test them every moment?
19. How long will you not look away from me?
How long will you not leave me alone,
until I swallow my spittle?
20. I have sinned. What do I do to you,
O watcher of humanity?
Why have you made me your target?
Why am I a burden to you?[60]
21. Why do you not pardon my transgression,
and pass over my iniquity?
For now I shall lie down in the dust,
and you shall seek me but I shall not be.

In 7:1-6, Job compares human life to that of slave labor, which leads finally to an early death (7:1-6). He describes the lot of humanity with three expressions: *'ebed* ("slave"), *ṣābā* ("harsh labor"), and *śākîr* ("hired laborer"). In Israel, slaves were either foreign captives and their descendants (Exod. 12:44; Lev. 25:44-46) who were slaves for life and served the palace and temple as property of the state, or Hebrews who were allowed to serve another Hebrew for only six years. At the end of that period, the male Hebrew slave exercised his option of freedom or becoming a slave for life (Exod. 21:2-11; Deut. 15:12-18). Female Hebrew slaves had no other recourse but to be concubines for their male owners.[61]

Job also uses the term *ṣābā* to refer to human existence. The term refers to military service (Num. 1:3, 20; 1 Chron. 5:18; 7:11), cultic action performed by the Levites in the sanctuaries (Num. 4:3, 23, 30, 39, 43), and compulsory service that is imposed on a slave by a lord (Isa. 40:2; cf. Job 14:14). It is this last sense that Job intends. *Śākîr,* the third term, translates as "hired laborer" (Exod. 12:45; Lev. 19:13; 22:10; 25:6, 40, 50; Deut. 15:18; 24:24). These workers, because of economic circumstances, must work for very little wage just to survive, and were often victims of mistreatment (Mal. 3:5; see the protective legislation in Lev. 19:13; Deut. 24:14-15).

Then Job, the slave and hired laborer, asks God to remember (*zākar*) that Job's life is but "breath" (*rûaḥ*), the vital, though quickly departing, force that enters humans at birth and returns to its divine source at death (Job 10:12; 12:10; 27:3; cf. Gen. 2:7; Qoh. 12:7).[62] In drawing on this traditional creation imagery, Job reminds God of both the mortality of human creatures and the brevity of their existence (cf. Pss. 78:39; 103:14-18; 144:3-4). What is so different, however, is that the usual plea for deliverance is replaced by Job's reproach. He only wishes to be left alone to die peaceably.

Returning to active protest and accusation (7:11-21), Job again speaks of life as "breath," only this time the words are reminiscent of Qoheleth, whose recurring term *hebel* portrays life as quickly passing, worthless, and vain (Pss.

39:6, 12; 62:10; 94:11; 144:4; Qoh. 2:1, 14-15). Now Job rejects the tradition of providence: God does not charmingly shape the fetus in the womb, breathe life into the new creature, and providentially watch over this child. Rather, life is a vapor or breath that quickly vanishes (see Qoheleth).

Royal anthropology is directly subverted in 7:17-21 in an obvious parody of Psalm 8 (Ps. 8:5-6 = Ps. 144:3-4). Psalm 8 extols God for exalting humanity to kingship over creation.[63] Job, by contrast, speaks of God's exaltation of humanity in order to single them out for merciless judgment and destruction. *Pāqad* ("visit, examine") belongs to the language of salvation history and expresses God's gracious deliverance of his people (Exod. 3:16; 4:31; Ps. 80:15). The term also occurs in texts that speak of God's searching out the wicked for divine punishment (Ps. 17:3; Jer. 6:15). In Job, God's unrelenting surveillance is to bring judgment and swift destruction even for those, like Job, who confess their sins and plead for divine mercy.

Metaphors for Reality

Job's world is a nightmare kingdom governed by a divine tyrant who attacks even the righteous, should they be suspected of disloyalty. Human creatures are not exalted rulers in God's empire who reign on behalf of a kindly creator, but are humiliated slaves and mortals experiencing the oppression of cruel treatment. Job longs for death, pleading with his divine tormentor to allow him to die in peace, for his life is but a breath that soon departs.

JOB: THE PLEA FOR JUSTICE AND MERCY (JOB 9–10)

Introduction

While Bildad's disputation simply repeats the content of the earlier one of Eliphaz, Job in chapters 9–10 moves from accusatory lament to pursue litigation; he desires to haul God into court for trial.

Strophe I (9:2-12)
2. Truly I know that this is so,
    but how may a person be righteous before God?
3. If one desires to file suit against him,
    he could not answer him once in a thousand times.
4. He (God) is wise of heart and mighty in strength,
    who can harden himself against him and prevail?
5. Who moves mountains and they do not know,
    when he overturns them in his anger.
6. Who shakes the earth from its place,
    and its columns tremble.
7. Who commands the sun not to rise,
    and seals up the stars.

8. Who alone stretches out the heavens,
   and treads upon the back of Sea.
9. Who makes Aldebaran and Orion,
   Pleiades and the Chambers of the South (Wind).
10. Who does great, inscrutable things,
   marvelous things without number.
11. Behold he passes by me, but I see him not.
   He moves on, but I perceive him not.
12. Behold he seizes, who can restrain him?
   Who dares to ask him, "What are you doing?"

The Metaphor of Cosmology

Job imitates Eliphaz in setting forth a doxology that reflects the battle of the Divine Warrior, who conquered chaos and now rules and orders the world by royal decree. However, Job's reshaping of the doxology is intended to subvert, not undergird, the traditional theology of this confession of guilt and articulation of praise.[64] His doxology becomes instead an indictment of a God turned cruel who has abused and even turned against his own creation with malicious brutality.

The three themes of the doxology describe the coming of the Divine Warrior to engage in warfare with Prince Yam (vv. 5-8), God's subsequent creation of constellations and cosmos with an incomprehensible wisdom (vv. 9-10), and, what is Job's own unique contribution, the oppressive rule of the unjust tyrant (vv. 11-12).

The first two themes, then, are common to doxologies. The upheaval of creation (cf. Judg. 5:4-5; Pss. 68:8-9; 114:3-7; Hag. 2:21), including an earthquake, is due to the coming of the Divine Warrior to do battle with the dragon (Judg. 5:5; Ps. 77:19; Isa. 41:15; Jer. 4:24; Joel 2:10; Amos 8:8; Nah. 1:5; Hab. 3:5).[65] While God's approach brings darkness and not light, his victory as the Divine Warrior is signaled by his walking upon the back of the defeated Prince Yam (cf. Pss. 18:8-16; 77:17-20; Hab. 3:15). However, what is different in Job's doxology is that God's wrath is directed against creation, including Job. Destruction, not redemption and the ordering of creation by justice, is the result.

The second theme is the one that traditionally follows the defeat of chaos by the Divine Warrior: the creating of the cosmos. In this case, "stretching out the heavens" (Gen. 12:8; 26:25; 35:21) and the making of the constellations describe the ordering of the heavenly regions. The creation of the constellations is for the temporal order, which marks seasons, indicates times for travels, and aids in determining the calendar (cf. Gen. 1:14; 8:22).

The third theme is the unusual one, added by Job to underscore the enigmatic character of divine presence and the unlimited power of a deity who

145

takes what he wants (cf. Qoheleth). Two questions point to the unquestioned sovereignty of God, grounded in sheer power: "who will restrain him" and "who will say to him, 'What are you doing?'" Zophar uses the first question to point to God's ability to enforce his edicts to imprison (11:10), while Job uses it to refer to the inability to restrain God's will (cf. 23:13). The second is a question whispered by ordinary mortals about their sovereign lords (Qoh. 8:4; Dan. 4:35).

The strophe in 9:13-24 continues to combine two metaphors: the struggle with the Divine Warrior, in this case Job's own battle, and the divine word reflected in Job's pondering of whether to pursue litigation against God as a corrupt judge who should be issuing judgments to establish and maintain a just order in the universe. For Job, Yahweh has abused the standards of justice and should be brought to trial for egregious perversions of justice.

Strophe II (9:13-24)

13. A god could not restrain his (God's) anger;
    even the helpers of Rahab bowed beneath him.
14. How much less could I possibly answer him,
    or even choose my words with him?
15. Although I am innocent, I could not answer him;
    I must implore my judge for mercy.
16. If I called and he answered me,
    I would not believe that he was hearing my voice.
17. For he crushes me with a whirlwind,
    and he multiplies my wounds without cause.
18. He does not allow my breath to return,
    but rather fills me with bitterness.
19. If it is a matter of strength,
    behold he is mightier.
20. But if it is a matter of justice,
    who will arraign me?
21. Though I am righteous, my own mouth would condemn me.
    I am pure, but he would hold me perverse.
21. I am innocent, I do not care for myself,
    I despise my life.
22. It is all the same, therefore I say:
    he brings both the pure and the wicked to their end.
23. If a lash kills suddenly,
    he laughs at the calamity of the innocent.
24. The earth is given over to the wicked;
    he covers the face of its judges.
    If it is not he, then who is it?

If a god could not "turn back the anger" of God, how could a mere mortal like Job hope to contend with the Almighty? If the "helpers of Rahab" (a chaos monster; Job 26:12-13; Ps. 89:10-11; Isa. 51:9) were bowed into submission, how could Job stand against God? Wars between the gods, including especially those of order and of chaos who contend for sovereignty over the cosmos, are common in mythological lore in the ancient Near East. Now the Divine Warrior attacks Job without mercy and without cause—that is, without just reason (see 2:3), and he withholds the divine, life-giving breath, an important metaphor from the anthropological tradition.

Verse 19 indicates that Job intends to pursue litigation against the divine judge. If Job could assure himself that the case would be decided on the basis of justice, then he knows he could win. But his fear is that the issue would be settled in God's favor because of the intimidation of divine power (9:25-35). Even so, Job is convinced that God has become a wicked, corrupt judge who violates the rules of law (see Exod. 18:13-26; 23:8; Deut. 1:9-17; 16:18-20). God has turned over the rulership of the earth to wicked and corrupt rulers and judges. In verse 33, Job wonders whether there might be in the divine counsel an arbiter who could be empowered to adjudicate fairly the conflict between the two warring parties and would not be intimidated by the threat of divine violence (cf. 16:18-21; 19:23-27).[66]

The Anthropological Tradition

Job 10:1-17 is patterned after the form of an accusatory lament.[67] The two metaphorical clusters are those of the divine craftsman and the lord of the womb responsible for conception, birth, and nurture. The goal of the lament is to turn God's face toward the sufferer for the purpose of redemption (cf. Ps. 139:13-18), but in what is now standard fashion, Job destabilizes these metaphors of artistry and birth by indicating that the intent of God in the creation of Job was to destroy, not to nurture.

> 1. I loathe my life;
>   I will vent my complaint;
>   I will speak out in my bitterness.
> 2. I shall say to God, Do not condemn me;
>   make known to me why you are contending with me.
> 3. Is it good for you to oppress,
>   to despise the labor of your hands,
>   while you shine your light upon the plan of the wicked?
> 4. Do you have eyes of flesh,
>   or do you see as a human sees?
> 5. Are your days as the days of a human,
>   or are your years as the days of a man?
> 6. That you seek out my iniquity,
>   and search for my sin?
> 7. Although you know I am not guilty.
>   There is none to save from your hand.
> 8. Your hands have fashioned and made me,
>   but afterwards you turn around[68] to swallow me up.

147

9. Remember that you shaped me like clay,
   but now you are returning me to dust.
10. Did you not pour me out like milk,
    and curdle me like cheese?
11. You clothed me with skin and flesh,
    you knitted me with bones and sinews.
12. You created for me life and love,
    and your providence guarded my spirit.
13. But these things you hid in your heart;
    I know this was your intent.
14. If I sin then you watch me,
    You do not acquit me of my iniquity.
15. If I am guilty woe unto me;
    if I am righteous I could not lift up my head.
    Have your fill of dishonor and look upon my affliction.
16. If it (my head) rises up, you hunt me like the lion;
    once more you work your wonders against me.
17. You renew your witnesses against me,
    and you increase your vexation against me.
    Fresh troops are arrayed against me.

Job is perplexed in considering why the creator would now destroy what he has labored to produce. He also charges God once again with forgetting and, therefore, being unsympathetic with the limits of mortality. Job reminds God of human weakness and the shortness of life:

> Do you have eyes of flesh,
>   or do you see as a human sees?
> Are your days as the days of a human,
>   or are your years as the days of a man?
> That you seek out my iniquity,
>   and search for my sin? (10:4-6)

The word for "flesh" (*bāśār*) often connotes human mortality as well as the dependence of the human creature on God to breathe into the body the breath of life (cf. Job 34:14-15; Ps. 78:38-39).[69] "Eyes of flesh" and "seeing as a human sees" convey the notions of the limitations placed on human knowledge. The brevity of human life is often compared to a breath, cloud, flower (7:7; 14:2).

A series of contrasts designed to subvert the anthropological tradition of faith follows in verses 8-11. The first bicolon (v. 8) depicts God in the role of the divine craftsman shaping Job in the womb, and the expectation would be that some statement of divine nurture of the new life would follow. Instead, God is the cannibalistic god of death, Prince Mot, whose gullet swallows Baal[70] (see the appetite of Sheol in Prov. 1:12).

The second negation occurs in verse 9. God is at first the potter working with the clay to create a human vessel, and one would expect the gift of divine breath to follow (Gen. 2:7). Instead, in the second bicolon, Job is turned back into dust (Genesis 3; Ps. 104:29; Qoh. 12:7).

The third contrast is made in verses 10-17. Once again, God is the creator who like a cheese maker conceives and fashions Job or like a weaver who clothes him with flesh, bones, and sinews (cf. Ezek. 37:5-8). Then comes the expected comment about providence, in this instance rooted in "steadfast love" (*ḥesed*),[71] which is extended to Job after the gift of the sustaining breath of God. However, Job abruptly accuses God of becoming the suspicious tyrant who bides his time and waits for the right occasion to destroy him on the basis of trumped-up charges. While convinced of his "innocence," Job still knows he will not regain his honor. Even in his attempt to defend himself, the Divine Warrior hunts him down and sends his armies to destroy him.

It is interesting to note the reference to the divine hunt, a topic that will be developed in a critically important way in the Yahweh speeches later on. The hunting of lions in the ancient Near East was more than sport, for it was a ritual act designed to bring order to the kingdom. Wild beasts, such as lions, were considered the incarnations of chaos that threatened creation and society.[72] Now God is the hunter pursuing a helpless Job. The remark about "working his wonders against him" is a parody on the divine acts of creating the world, maintaining the order of the cosmos, and redeeming people from distress and even death (cf. Judg. 6:13).

Finally, in 10:18-22 Job returns to the metaphor of birth in language strongly reminiscent of chapter 3:

> 18. Why did you bring me forth from the womb?
>   Would that I had expired and no eye had beheld me.
> 19. It would be as though I had never lived;
>   I would have been carried from the womb to the grave.
> 20. Are now my days few? Let him cease.
>   Let him withdraw from me so that I may be cheerful.
> 21. Before I go where I shall not return,
>   To the land of darkness and deep darkness.
> 22. A land where light is like the darkness,
>   deep darkness and chaos,
>   where light is like darkness.

Instead of nurture and providential care, God brings forth human creatures in order to torment them until they perish.[73]

The World of Job

Job's metaphorical world continues to be that of a kingdom ruled by a tyrant who seeks to destroy anyone who comes under suspicion. Job becomes the innocent victim of assaults from the Divine Warrior. His reality is not that of a family in which he, an honored and cherished offspring, is cared for by the divine parent. Indeed, these images are used, but now to speak of a berserk parent who seeks to devour, torment, and destroy his own offspring. Job's hope for justice emerges in reference to an arbiter who might ensure that a trial or pretrial complaint would proceed fairly. Yet, even this appears to be more a wish than a possibility. God is the unjust judge who in Kafkaesque fashion assaults his servant for no known reason.

JOB: THE ILLUSION OF REDEMPTIVE HISTORY (JOB 12–14)

Introduction

In chapters 12–14, Job despairs over his chances of either being reconciled to God or removing this powerful, destructive tyrant from the throne of heaven and earth.

Metaphors of Cosmology

Chapters 12–14 are a disputation that incorporates sections that imitate both a hymn (12:13-25) and a lament (chap. 14). The hymnlike text and the preceding strophe include important features of creation theology.

Strophe II (12:7-12)

7. But ask the beasts and they will instruct you,
   and the birds of the heavens and they will tell you.
8. Or speak to the earth and it will teach you,
   and the fish of the sea will inform you.
9. Which among all these does not know
   that the hand of Yahweh has done this?
10. He who has the life of every living thing in his hand,
    and the breath of all human flesh.
11. Does not the ear test words,
    or the palate taste its food?
12. Among the aged is wisdom,
    and insight in the length of days.

In this disputation, Job refers to the common source of revelation in wisdom circles—creation, whose voice speaks of God and reality. To experience and understand the world was in some measure to experience and understand God, though the sages usually admitted that divine mystery and unforeseen contingencies denied them the ability to come to a complete knowledge of God and divine rule. Nevertheless, trust in God—that is, the belief that God had the well-being of creation and its human creatures in mind—was fundamental to the faith of the wise.

As is typical to this point, Job attempts to subvert this understanding of sapiential revelation centered in the metaphor of word—the instruction of the creatures and the earth. They reject the teaching of Job's wise opponents that God is just and that divine wisdom transcends all human understanding. Job tells his opponents to inquire of creation as to the true nature of God.[74] What creation reveals is that God is a cruel oppressor who supports the wicked and treads down the righteous. It is this destructive, unjust tyrant who has the power over the life and breath of all creatures (see Ps. 104:29-30). The image of being in the "hand (= power) of God" is not particularly comforting to Job (see 10:3, 7, 8; 13:21; 19:21; Qoh. 9:1).

A Doxology of Terror

Job continues to destabilize word theology in his second use of the language of doxology by describing the destructive power of divine providence in directing human history (12:13-25).

> 13. With him (God) is wisdom and might,
>   he has counsel and insight.
> 14. Behold he tears down, and there is no rebuilding;
>   he imprisons a person, and there is no release.
> 15. Behold he withholds the waters, and the lands dry up;
>   when he sends waters forth, they engulf the land.
> 16. With him are strength and sound wisdom,
>   the deceived and the deceiver belong to him.
> 17. He makes counselors walk naked,
>   and transforms judges into fools.
> 18. He loosens the instruction of kings,
>   and ties a waist cloth on their loins.
> 19. He makes priests walk about barefoot,
>   and ruins wise officials.
> 20. He takes away the speech of those who are trusted,
>   and deprives the aged of discernment.
> 21. He pours contempt upon princes,
>   and loosens the girdle of the strong.
> 22. He reveals deep mysteries from darkness,
>   and brings to light deep darkness.
> 23. He exalts nations and destroys them,
>   he expands them and then leads them away.
> 24. He removes reason from the leaders of the people of the earth,
>   and makes them wander in a pathless waste.

25. They grope about in the darkness with no light,
   causing them to stagger like one who is drunk.

Job concedes that God is wise and mighty, but what he denies is divine justice, so intrinsic to the nature and purpose of the doxology. God uses his wisdom and power, not to create and sustain life and nations, but to bring them to destruction. God arbitrarily withholds life-giving rain to create famine and death or sends floods to inundate the land. God denies to human leaders wisdom and brings mighty nations to their end.

In traditional wisdom, God imparts insight and understanding to human leaders (cf. 1 Kings 3—"Solomon's Wisdom"; Wisdom of Solomon 7–9). Yet a divine maniac denies to them the discernment necessary to lead with justice and success their nations (Job 12:21a, 24b = Ps. 107:40). The result, therefore, is historical chaos, not peace, well-being, and reconciliation among the nations (contrast the vision of J in Gen. 12:1-3). Wisdom literature contains no reference to the themes of salvation history until Ben Sira at the beginning of the second century B.C.E. However, for the sages, God does providentially guide human history, both collective and individual (Prov. 10:3, 29; 15:3, 29), doing so at least in part by bestowing upon leaders divine wisdom (e.g., Prov. 8:15-16). Sages believed that divine insight allowed them to give to kings and rulers "counsel" (*'ēṣâ*) that was life-producing and led to success in affairs of state. All this Job attempts to negate by his radical reformulation of traditional doxology.

The Anthropological Tradition: The Metaphor of Slave and the Death of the King

Job utters another complaint in chapter 14, in which he describes both the hopelessness of the destiny of human slavery (cf. chap. 7) and the unavoidable fate of death, which awaits all.

Strophe I (14:1-6)
1. A human being, born of woman, is of few days,
   and sated only with drudgery.
2. One sprouts like a flower that then withers,
   and one passes like a shadow that cannot remain.
3. Upon such a one you fix your stare,
   and bring him[75] into judgment before you.
4. Who can produce something clean from what is unclean?
   No one.
5. Indeed one's days are numbered,
   the number of one's months are fixed by you,
   one cannot surpass the prescribed limit you have ordained.
6. Turn your gaze from this one and desist,
   until like the hireling he may finish his day.

In this speech, the metaphor cluster of words used to describe the creation and direction of reality reemerges in the edict of the divine judge, whose decree is without appeal.[76] God sentences humans to lifelong slavery from which there is no reprieve. Realizing that slavery is inescapable and that survival beyond the grave or resurrection from death is impossible, Job hopes only for the cessation of God's attack until the release of death.

Strophe II (14:7-12)

7. For there is hope for a tree;
   if it is cut down it could sprout again,
   and its shoots might not fail.
8. If its root grows old in the soil,
   and its stump dies in the dust.
9. At the scent of water it will sprout up,
   and put forth branches like a young plant.
10. But a person dies and is brought low,
    one expires and then where is he?
11. Waters fail from a lake,
    a river parches and dries up.
12. So a human lies down and does not rise up,
    until the heavens are no more he will not awaken,
    he will not be roused from his sleep.

This strophe draws on the common metaphor of fertility. Trees and water are common symbols of fertility, longevity, death and rebirth, and immortality.[77] The Sumerian myth of Dumuzi the shepherd king and the goddess Inanna (who become Tammuz and Ishtar in Akkadian mythology)[78] presents the human ruler as the mortal consort of the goddess. Dumuzi dies, but comes back to life in the form of tree sap. The tree of life in Genesis 2–3, planted in the garden watered by the four rivers, symbolizes the immortality offered to Adam and Eve. In Mesopotamia the first man is a king who tends the garden and guards the tree of life. This mythical imagery is incorporated into the wisdom tradition in the form of wisdom as a fertility goddess who, as the tree of life (cf. Asherah in Canaanite religion), dispenses well-being and insight to the wise (Prov. 3:18; cf. Prov. 11:30; 13:12; 15:4, where the deeds and virtues of the wise are a "tree of life").

The first psalm, belonging to the literature of the wise, compares the wise and righteous person to a fruitful tree planted by an ever-flowing stream, while Job describes his former life in the image of a well-watered tree (29:19). Even so, in both Mesopotamia and Israel, immortality and resurrection were typically denied mortals, including kings.

Job's reference to the symbolism of the tree incorporates some of these images, though in his own mind, death is the inescapable fate of all human beings. Dumuzi and Baal may wait expectantly for resurrection from the dead that is occasioned by their deliverance from the underworld by their divine consorts, but mortal Job, like all human beings, concludes that there is no escape from the grave.

Strophe III (14:13-17)

13. O that you would place me in Sheol to conceal me,
    that you would hide me till your anger is past.
    that you would issue me a decree and remember me.
14. If a human dies, will he live again?
    Through all my days of harsh service I would
    expectantly wait, until my release should come.
15. You would call out, and I would answer,
    you would long for the work of your hands.
16. For then you would number my steps,
    and would not keep vigil over my sin.
17. My transgressions would be sealed in a bag,
    and you would plaster over my iniquity.

For Job, the many days of imprisonment in Sheol could be endured, if only God would one day long for the "work of his hands" (10:3, 8-12) and eventually release his slave from death. Yet this momentary hope is dashed by Job's realization that ultimately there is deliverance from the tomb.

Strophe IV (14:18-22)

18. However, as the mountain falls and crumbles,
    and the rock moves from its place,
19. As water wears away stones,
    and torrents wash away the soil of the land,
    thus you destroy the hope of a person.
20. You overpower him forever, and he passes away,
    changing his countenance, you dispatch him.
21. His sons come to honor, but he does not know it;
    they are brought low and he does not realize it.
22. He is pained only by his own flesh,
    and he weeps only for himself.

Job compares the hopelessness of a dying human to the steady deterioration of the cosmos. Death robs one even of the knowledge of descendants and their fate.

ELIPHAZ: THE FALL OF THE PRIMAL KING (JOB 15)

Introduction

Eliphaz uses the myth of the primal man to warn Job of the fate of those who rebel against God. In this new cycle of debate, the friends cast diplomacy to the wind as they enter into a direct indictment of Job. Images of words dominate this speech.

Strophe I (vv. 2-6)
2. Shall a sage answer with knowledge of wind,
    and fill his belly with the east wind?
3. Shall he argue with speech which does not profit,
    with words which do not benefit?
4. But you are destroying piety,
    and restrain meditation before God.
5. For evil teaches your mouth,
    and you choose the tongue of the crafty.
6. Your own mouth has pronounced you guilty, not I,
    and your lips have condemned you.

Metaphors for Creation and Cosmos

Eliphaz recognizes the power of language to create, but also to destroy, as he compares Job's words to the power of chaos (cf. the "mighty wind" in Gen. 1:2, and the desiccating desert storm in Gen. 41:6, 23, 27). In the view of Eliphaz, Job has changed from the wise man to the fool whose language brings destruction and undermines the traditions of faith and piety. For exilic and postexilic sapiential piety, meditation focuses its attention on two objects: creation and Torah (see Psalms 1; 19; 119). But Job's speech is a chaotic wind that threatens the order of the cosmos.

Anthropology: Royal Wisdom and the Primal Man

Eliphaz then speaks of the divine council ruled by God and the first man, who was present at creation:

Strophe II (vv. 7-16)
7. Were you born the Primal Man,
    and were you brought forth before the hills?
8. Did you listen in the council of God,
    and did you take wisdom for yourself?
9. What do you know that we do not,
    what do you perceive that is beyond us?
10. Both the hoary and venerable are among us,
    more advanced in age than your father.
11. Are God's consolations too slight for you,
    or the word that he gently spoke to you?
12. Why does your mind carry you away,
    and why do your eyes flash?
13. Because you turn your anger against God,
    and you bring forth words from your mouth?
14. What are humans that they should be clean,
    or those, born of woman, that they should be innocent?

15. Behold he places no trust in his holy ones,
    even the heavens are not clean in his sight.
16. How much less one who is abominable and corrupt,
    humanity who drinks iniquity like water!

The primal man is a royal figure who has divine wisdom and guards the tree of life in paradise. Ancient Near Eastern mythology uses this language to speak of the origins and nature of kingship. In the Bible, the tradition of the primal man takes on a negative connotation at times in depicting the hubris of the human creature who desires to become a god and rule over the divine council (see J in Genesis 3–11, and Ezekiel 28). In J the desire for wisdom was predicated on the serpent's deceitful promise that the human pair would "become like gods, knowing good and evil." This desire and grasping for divinity through the appropriation of wisdom ("knowledge of good and evil") is interpreted as revolt against divine rule, a rebellion that spreads throughout the primeval history in J, leading to the call of Abraham in Genesis 12. The curse that results from the rebellion of the first human pair is expulsion from the garden, including the presence of Yahweh, and death (they no longer have access to the tree of life).

Ezekiel also portrays the first man as the possessor of divine wisdom; only in this case he is identified with the king of Tyre, who in his hubris desired to sit on the throne of El, the head of the Canaanite assembly. Acquiring this position would have given him, in Canaanite mythology, the power of royal decree that determined the destiny of the world and sustained its continuation. The end of this king, according to the prophet, is similar to that of the first human pair in Genesis: He will be expelled from the sacred mountain of El and cast into the Pit.

This tradition of primeval rebellion is behind the question of Eliphaz, directed to what he perceives to be a Job filled with arrogance: "Were you born [*yālad*] the Primal Man [*ri 'š ôn 'ādām'*], and were you brought forth (*ḥûl*) before the hills?" As we have seen, the first human often representing collective humanity is fathered or given birth by the gods, and kings often traced their origins back to divine parents.[79] In addition, it is important to note that Eliphaz quotes Proverbs 8:25: "I was brought forth before the hills."[80] Proverbs 8:22-31 contains a hymn in which Wisdom, praising herself, describes her origins: She is the firstborn of creation, given birth prior to anything else that was created. As firstborn she was also the first and best of what followed, became the agent of divine creation, and mediated between heaven and earth.

Eliphaz also asks Job if he has stood in the divine council, that heavenly court where God rules and issues edicts that govern the divine world. The prophets refer to the heavenly assembly as the place to which they are called to receive divine judgments for human destiny, either redemption or destruction (see 1 Kings 22; Isaiah 6; Jer. 23:18). Indeed, for Eliphaz, the ancient tradition of wisdom does not belong only to Job. He claims that this tradition supports his views of divine retribution.

Eliphaz uses these references to creation tradition not only to warn Job of the fate that awaits those who in mythic tradition rebelled against the divine world (see 15:17-35), but also to humble Job by disputing he has the wisdom to know the workings of providence (chap. 12)[81] and to remind him of the corruption of human nature. Even the divine council ("holy ones," v. 15) God does not trust, presumably because of their rebellion (see Gen. 6:1-4) or misrule (Psalm 82). How much less could he trust sinful humans, corrupt to the core? In other words, God is well aware of human hubris and the propensity toward rebellion. Thus God is on the lookout for wickedness and controls sin, including rebellion, by meting out swift justice. The last part of the speech depicts, then, a battle in which a wicked man, portrayed as a foolish king, attempts to assault God in war, only to meet with destruction.

JOB: THE APPEAL TO A REDEEMER (JOB 16–17, 19)

Introduction

Job's two speeches in chapters 16–17 and 19 are replete with metaphorical clusters for creation and providence, including both the juridical features of the appeal to the earth and to a heavenly witness who would intercede with the divine judge (16:18-19) and a satirical presentation of reality as a family in 17:13-14. However, the dominating metaphor is once again the struggle with chaos in 16:6-17:

> 6. If I should speak, my pain would not be assuaged;
>   if I should forbear, what would go away?
> 7. Surely now he has wearied me,
>   you have devastated my community.
> 8. You have seized me, that is my witness.
>   My pain arises against me, it testifies against me.
> 9. His anger has torn and raged against me;
>   he has ground his teeth against me;
>   my enemy has sharpened his eyes against me.
> 10. They have opened wide their mouth against me;
>   they have struck my jaw;
>   together they have massed themselves against me.
> 11. God has delivered me up to the wicked,
>   he has cast me headlong into the hands of the wicked.
> 12. I was at ease, and he cut me asunder;
>   he seized the back of my neck, and he dashed me to pieces;
>   he raised me up to be his target.

13. His archers surround me;
      he cleaves open my kidneys showing no quarter;
      he pours out my gall upon the earth.
14. He opens in me breach upon breach,
      and he charges against me like a warrior.
15. I have sewn sackcloth upon my skin,
      and I have cast my strength into the dust.
16. My face is reddened from weeping,
      and the shadow of death is upon my eyes.
17. Although there is no violence in my hand,
      and my prayer is pure.

Earlier, Eliphaz had lampooned the wicked fool who attacked the Almighty (15:24-27). By contrast, now it is God who has become the warrior mercilessly slaughtering Job, a weak and defenseless warrior. Imprisoned, Job is taunted by his captors and beaten (cf. Ps. 3:8; Mic. 4:14). Job is then transformed into a besieged city assaulted by God's attacking army (cf. 1 Kings 11:27; Neh. 6:1; Job 19:11-12; Ps. 144:14; Amos 4:3). His defenses compromised, Job anticipates the final charge and has no recourse, save lamentation by which he hopes to receive mercy from his victorious enemy. He engages in mourning rites, hoping for mercy from the victor (cf. the lamentations of Jerusalem, Jer. 9:17-22; 14:19-22).

Now Job must appeal to two mediators to help him obtain mercy and justice. Using the language of the slain brother's blood crying out to God for revenge (Gen. 4:10), the earth is personified as a witness that is asked to support Job's case (Deut. 32:1; Isa. 1:2; Jer. 6:19; 22:29; Mic. 1:2). And Job once again hopes that a heavenly intercessor will argue his case before the divine assembly.

Creation and Anthropology: The Royal Creature

In 19:2-12 one discovers the destabilization not only of the battle metaphor, but also of humanity as an exalted king ruling over his creation. These are the two fundamental metaphors that Job seeks to subvert throughout his discourses, for they are at the center of wisdom theology's understanding of creation and providence. Their undermining takes on a particularly critical character at this point.

Strophe I (19:2-12)

2. How long will you cause me distress,
      and crush me with words?
3. Some ten times you have cast reproach upon me;
      are you not ashamed to treat me ill?
4. Even if it is true that I have gone astray,
      My error abides with me.

5. If it is true you exalt yourselves against me,
   and make my reproach a reproof against me,
6. Know that God has subverted me,
   he has closed his net around me.
7. Behold I cry out, "Violence!," but I am not answered.
   I shout aloud, but there is no justice.
8. He has walled up my way so that I may not pass by,
   he has placed darkness upon my paths.
9. He has stripped my glory from me,
   and taken the crown from my head.
10. He has torn me down from every side as I go forth,
    he has removed my hope like a tree.
11. He has kindled his anger against me,
    he considers me as his enemy.
12. His troops come together against me,
    they have besieged me with their power,
    they encamp around my tent.

Job becomes both the degraded king and the besieged city. Of course, the David-Zion (= Jerusalem) tradition brings both of these together in a significant fashioning of theological traditions in the Kingdom of Judah (see 1 Kings 8; Jer. 21:11–23:8; Amos 1:3–2:5). Witnessing the rape of his country, the royal Job cries out "violence" (ḥāmās), a term used on occasion to describe both a massacre by a ruthless army (Judg. 9:24; 2 Sam. 22:3; Hab. 2:8, 17; Obadiah 10) and the shedding of blood, which, polluting the earth, brings about the flood (Gen. 6:11). Even lamentation rituals on behalf of his people obtain no reprieve. The city under siege offers no opportunity to its inhabitants to escape.

The divestiture of the king by rituals of degradation, known from royal traditions in the ancient Near East, is reflected in this text.[82] But unlike the royal figure in the ancient world who may expect rituals of degradation to be followed by those of investiture and the resumption of rule, Job is simply degraded and humiliated. Like his city that may expect no last-minute reprieve, Job, the degraded king, has no hope for deliverance.

The Reality of Job

Job's redescription of reality is consistently portrayed throughout his speeches by means of the common image of a divine empire ruled over by a tyrannical despot who sends his armies to conquer or keep in control all subjects (even vassal kings and nations) by means of intimidation, physical restraint, and even ruthless slaughter.

159

BILDAD: THE SOVEREIGNTY OF GOD AND THE FOLLY OF REVOLT (JOB 25–26)

Introduction

The final cycle of debate in chapters 21–27 proceeds in similar fashion to the two earlier ones, although now the three opponents directly and with increased fervor bring charges against Job as a terrible criminal. But particularly intriguing is Bildad's description of God. This speech in its reconstructed form reads:

Strophe I (25:2-6)

2. Dominion and terror are his,
      he who establishes peace in his heights.
3. Is there any number to his troops?
      Upon whom does his light not shine?
4. How then may a person be righteous before God?
      And how may one born of woman be pure?
5. Behold he commands the moon, and it does not shine;
      even the stars are not pure in his eyes.
6. How much less then the human creature who is a maggot,
      And the son of humanity who is a worm?

Strophe II (26:5-10)

5. The Rephaim writhe below,
      the waters and their denizens.
6. Sheol is naked before him,
      and Abaddon has no covering.
7. He is the one who stretches Zaphon over the abyss, and
      hangs the earth over nothingness.
8. He gathers the water in his thick clouds,
      and the cloud beneath them is not split open.
9. He encloses the appearance of (his) throne,
      he spreads his cloud over it.
10. He has inscribed a circle over the face of the waters,
      at the boundary of light and darkness.

Strophe III (26:11-14)

11. The pillars of heaven tremble,
      stunned by his rebuke.
12. By his strength he has quieted the Sea,
      and by his perception he smote Rahab.
13. By his wind he ensnared Sea[83] in a net,[84]
      his hand pierced the fleeing serpent.
14. Behold these are only the traces of his power,
      and how small a whisper we hear of him.
      And the thunder of his strength who could perceive?

The Metaphors of Creation and Providence

Bildad's speech serves as a concluding and comprehensive summary of the world view of the three opponents of Job articulated throughout their preceding discourses. God is a tyrannical, unchallenged, and powerful king ruling over an empire that he has conquered in primeval times. Although hidden in mystery, God is able to see all that happens within his cosmic kingdom. While this awesome God is concealed in mystery, his all-seeing light penetrates even to the darkest regions of his empire, enabling him to know all that happens. Only a fool would dare to challenge divine rule or assume that God's knowledge of affairs is limited. The organizing metaphor for the speech is conflict, for God won and then holds on to his kingship by the real and threatened use of frightening power. Indeed, the opening line is the theme for the entire speech: "dominion and fear are his." Divine rule is based, not on justice, but on intimidation.

In the first strophe (25:2-6), Bildad limits kingship to God, undermining the traditional portrayal of humans as king in God's creation (Gen. 1:26-28; Psalm 8), ruling on God's behalf (Ps. 89:20-38). "Fear" for Bildad connotes, not piety, but "terror" or "dread" before the awesomeness of divine power (Exod. 15:16; Isa. 2:10, 19, 21).

In echoes of distant battles in primordial times, Bildad speaks of the "peace" (šālôm) resulting from God's struggle with rivals in the heavens.[85] Then Bildad moves from God's conquest in the heavens to the establishment of sovereignty over the underworld. Sheol is the region of death and the dead, often portrayed as hostile to God, devoid of divine comprehension and ungraced by Yahweh's presence. For Bildad, even Sheol has been brought into submission by God, along with its denizens, called the Rephaim.[86] Sheol and Abaddon, personified as both the spheres and rulers of the dead, stand naked before God's sight.[87] Finally, God's sovereignty is extended over the primordial ocean. Prince Sea and Rahab, cosmic incarnations of chaos, are defeated.

After describing the establishment through force of divine sovereignty over the heavens, the underworld, and the cosmic ocean, Bildad then speaks of God's setting up a sacred canopy over the abyss, assuming the judgment throne, and issuing decrees that govern the empire of heaven and earth.[88]

Images of light portray God as the sun god who in his daily rising, setting, and journeying across the sky watches over his creation, not, as does Shamash (the Babylonian sun god of justice), to establish and maintain justice, but to observe and be aware of all that happens. Certainly, this God would be aware of any revolutionary plot that a foolish man like Job might plan.

Metaphorical Portrayal of Human Nature

The rhetorical question "How shall a human creature be righteous before God, and how shall one born of woman be pure?" represents the friends' view of human nature (cf. 4:17). God has not chosen humans to rule over creation as kings; rather, humans are corrupt to the core, compared by Bildad to maggots and worms. In an obvious parody, the wording of verses 5-6 echoes Psalm 8 (esp. v. 5). Further, humans are not the children of God, conceived and nourished in the womb, given birth and then providentially sustained by divine care throughout their lives. Rather, humans are "maggots" and "worms," creatures who feed off the flesh of the dead (Job 7:5; 17:14; 21:26; 24:20; Isa. 14:11). When the brilliant lights of the heavens are impure in God's sight, how much more corrupt are human beings?

Conclusion

In his discourses with his three opponents, Job has undermined the traditional language of sapiential faith by subverting the metaphorical clusters that serve as linguistic foundations for creation (word, artistry, fertility, and struggle), God as creator of heaven and earth (king, judge, artisan, consort, and warrior), God as creator of humanity and the human person (parent, artisan, giver of the breath of life), human nature and being (child, king, and slave), and reality (kingdom, household, and life-sustaining world). Job has portrayed God as a divine warrior who has gained the throne by struggle, created the world of heaven and earth, and now rules as a corrupt tyrant who brings destruction to his own creation. Humanity is not the one chosen to rule over a life-sustaining creation, but is a slave who is predestined to a life of drudgery and ultimately death. Even the slightest suspicion of disloyalty brings down upon the helpless slave the cruel hand of the master.

To this point, Job has only contemplated seeking legal redress for his grievances. He has engaged in lamentation, but to no avail. He has asked God to cease and desist from his merciless attacks and wishes to die in peace. He has hoped wistfully for a God who would raise him from the dead, after the divine anger has passed away. And he has hoped for a trial in which justice would prevail, particularly if an intercessor would plead his case in the divine assembly. All the while Job has undermined traditional sapiential faith by debunking the metaphors that engage the imagination and provide the encounter with a meaning structure that gives orientation to a life of faith. Destabilization of the language and structure of faith—first for Job, and then for his audience—has occurred. A new and terrifying vision of a fascist reality governed by a tyrant has replaced a traditional world view of the wise. The time has come for action based on this emerging world view that has transformed Joban faith into outrage.

Now in the transitional chapters of renewed soliloquy (chaps. 29–31), Job seeks to dethrone the ruler of heaven and earth. He does so by changing his metaphor for human nature and function from that of passive slave to that of ruler opposing and rebelling against the divine tyrant. Job is the man who would be God.

JOB'S DECLARATION OF INNOCENCE AND REVOLT AGAINST GOD (JOB 29–31)

Introduction

This lengthy soliloquy consists of two parts: an accusatory lament addressed to God (chaps. 29–30) and a series of "oaths of innocence" (chap. 31) that represent Job's legal defense against the accusations of his wrongdoing by the friends.[89] The debate with the friends, ending without any apparent resolution, is over, and now Job moves directly to a confrontation with the Almighty.

Metaphors of Creation in the Anthropological Tradition

Job uses the metaphor of king to describe himself in two places: first in chapter 29 in speaking of his past, and then again in 31:35-37 when he presents his direct challenge to divine rule. Chapter 29 reminds one of a royal psalmist addressing his complaint to God.

Strophe I (29:2-6)
2. Oh, that I might return to the months that are past,
    to the days that God protected me.
3. When his light shone over my head,
    and I would walk by this light through the darkness.
4. When I was in my autumn days,
    and the council of God was over my tent.
5. When Shaddai was with me,
    and my children were about me.
6. When my steps were washed with curds,[90]
    and the rock poured out for me streams of oil.

Strophe II (vv. 7-13)
7. When I went to the gate of the city,
    in the square I set my judgment seat.
8. The youths saw me and hid themselves,
    and old men arose and stood.
9. Princes refrained from speaking,
    and placed their hand on their mouth.

10. The voice of the nobles grew quiet,
    and their tongue cleaved to the roof of their mouth.
11. When the ear heard, it called me "blessed,"
    and the eye that saw approved what I said.
12. For I would deliver the poor man who would cry out,
    and the fatherless who had no one to help him.
13. The blessing of the one about to perish came upon me,
    and the heart of the widow I made sing for joy.

Strophe III (vv. 14-20)

14. I wore righteousness, and it clothed me,
    my justice was like a robe and crown.
15. I was eyes to the blind,
    and feet to the lame.
16. I was father to the needy,
    and I searched out the case of one I did not know.
17. I broke the fangs of the wicked,
    and I cast forth the prey from their teeth.
18. And I said, "I shall expire in my nest,
    and like the sand I shall multiply my days."
19. My roots spread out to the waters,
    and the dew lodged on my branches.
20. My glory remained ever new,
    and my bow was renewed in my hand.

Strophe IV (vv. 21-25)

21. People listened to me and waited,
    they kept silent for my counsel.
22. After I spoke they would not speak again,
    and my word dripped like dew upon them.
23. They waited for me as for the rain,
    and they opened mouths as for the spring rain.
24. I smiled at them when they lacked confidence,
    and they did not reject the light of my countenance.
25. I chose their path, and I sat as their head,
    I dwelt like a king among his troops,
    even as one who comforted mourners.

These images may, of course, be understood as social description, indicating that Job was a royal figure.[91] More likely, they represent a metaphorical description of humanity, whom God commissioned to rule over creation (Genesis 1; and Psalm 8). In the halcyon days, Job experienced the blessing of a benign and caring God. The reference in the first strophe to the light and darkness remind one of creation, though here they point to a kindly providence caring for a royal son (Ps. 18:29 = 2 Sam. 22:29). Children and the abundance of curds and oil were symbols of Job's having curried the favor of God.

In the second strophe, Job recalls the adulation in which he was held by those who were amazed at the wisdom of his judgments (see 1 Kings 3). Job comes like a king to the gate of the city to sit in judgment (cf. 2 Sam. 18:24; 19:19; Psalm 72; Amos 5:12, 15). The recipients of his wise judgments called him "blessed" (cf. Psalm 17).

Job is dressed in a royal robe (1 Sam. 18:4; 24:5, 12) and a crown (Isa. 62:3) of justice and righteousness in Strophe III. Those often denied justice received the blessing of Job's judgments, while the wicked who preyed on the weak and oppressed were destroyed by his righteous procedures (cf. Ps. 72:14). Job even uses the mythical image of the well-watered tree (Psalm 1; Isa. 11:1) to describe his long and full life. The figures of royal glory and the living bow add to the royal description.[92]

The final strophe contains the description of Job's giving of wise counsel, defined as a plan for action that leads to success. Like a "king among his troops" Job gave counsel to those who sought his wisdom. Those who desired his succor would sit in the "light of Job's countenance," an image often associated with divine blessing. Indeed, the language of this entire chapter suggests that Job has come close to self-idolatry by using images suggestive of divine rule. But then this seems to be the point for one who momentarily is going to engage in all-out revolt.

Finally, in 31:35-37, the transition from self-defense to direct challenge, Job once more applies royal images to himself:

> 35. Oh, that I had someone to listen.
> Behold, here is my signature, let Shaddai answer me,
> Let my adversary write a document.
> 36. Surely I would wear it on my shoulder,
> I would fasten it to me like a crown.
> 37. I would provide him an accounting of my steps,
> like a prince I would approach him.

In this challenge to the divine judge, Job demands either a written indictment[93] or exoneration.[94] In either case, he plans to approach the judge's bench as a royal figure, not as a submissive slave. Job's signature, attached to the written series of oaths, adds legal weight to his plea that someone, most likely an arbiter, would "hear" the case,[95] and that God as "adversary" (see Judg. 12:2) would present his "indictment"[96] (vv. 35-37). This procedure is a legal challenge to God to appear with his charges, in effect a subpoena. If God does appear, then Job indicates he would place the indictment on his shoulder and wear it as a crown.

God's creation of humans is used in one of Job's attestations of innocence: 31:13-15 (Job's handling of his household slaves). Job's self-defense is placed within the form of a series of oaths consisting of one or more processes—that is, a condition introduced by "if" or "if not," and an apodosis or result. The general crime or sin is placed in the protasis, while the result clause, or apodosis, sets forth the punishment.[97] Four of Job's oaths follow this standard pattern (vv. 7-8, 9-12, 16-23, and 38-40), while the others contain only the protasis (vv. 24-25, 33-34)[98] or shape it into a declaration (vv. 26-28, 29-30, 31-32), an imperative (vv. 5-6), or a rhetorical question (vv. 1-2, 13-15). Oaths were commonly used in legal proceedings to determine by divine judgment a person's guilt or innocence, including the suspected thief (Exod. 22:6-12) or adulterer (Num. 5:5-28), especially in cases where there were no eyewitnesses of the crime or sin and no witnesses for the defense (see, e.g., 1 Kings 8:31-32). Since God was believed to oversee the process and because destructive power was attributed to the curse, the process was thought to possess a certain integrity.

In similar fashion to his opening soliloquy in chapter 3, the metaphor of birth, placed within the linguistic setting of curse, is used, only in this case to address, not humanity's place in the cosmos, but Job's own treatment of his slaves.

Treatment of Slaves (31:13-15)

13. If I have despised the justice of my slave and maidservant,
     when they contended with me,
14. Then what should I do when God rises up,
     and when he examines me, how shall I answer him?
15. Did not he who made me in the womb also make them,
     did not the same one fashion us[99] both in the womb?

Old Testament law codes contain a variety of laws that are designed to protect slaves from mistreatment and to dictate the conditions under which they may be released.[100] If their rights were denied, the courts were there to address their grievances. Job asserts that he has treated his slaves justly, including, it seems, those instances when he sat as judge to settle cases brought not only to him but also against him (e.g., 29:7-12).

Two theological affirmations provided the foundations for this legal situation: the righteousness of God and the common origins of all humans (cf. Prov. 14:31; 17:5; 22:2). Social justice, including that merited by slaves, was based on divine righteousness. What makes this protestation of Job's innocence most poignant is God's mistreatment of his own slave (cf. Job 7:1-2).

The second affirmation is the common wisdom teaching that all humans have the same origins and thus are entitled to justice, including fair treatment and the goods necessary for existence (Prov. 14:31; 17:5; 22:2). This affirmation is expressed through the metaphorical depiction of God as the lord of the womb and the divine parent who nurtures life, both before and after birth. Not only does Job defend his own just treatment of slaves, but he indirectly accuses God of violating those same standards of justice as well.

Reality as a Fertile Cosmos

Job's depiction of reality as a fertile cosmos draws on the traditional creation theology of the sages.

Exploitation of Land and Farmers (31:38-40)
38. If my land has cried out against me,
    and its furrows have wept together,
39. If I have eaten of its yield without payment,
    and I have extinguished the life of its owners,
40. Let thorns grow in the place of wheat,
    and stink weeds instead of barley.

Laws protecting the land from exploitation included: sacred times (the sabbath and Jubilee year; Exod. 23:10-11; Lev. 25:1-22), prohibitions against seed mixing (Lev. 19:19; Deut. 22:9) and not picking the fruit of newly planted trees for three years (Lev. 19:23-25). Social legislation involving the land included the requirement that harvesters leave some of the crops for the poor and the law of familial land ownership (Lev. 19:9-10; 23:22; 25:23-28). Exploitation of land and farmers resulted in legal punishment and divine retribution, often leading to famine (Deut. 28:22; Amos 4:6). In P, the pollution of the earth by murder was the cause of the cosmic flood. Abel's blood, having polluted the land, cries out to God for justice (Gen. 4:10), a text echoed by Job in 16:18.

Job also denies that he has either eaten crops "without payment" or has "extinguished the life of its owners." The first denial pertains either to thievery or to the withholding of wages from day laborers (see Lev. 19:13; Deut. 24:14-15; Job 7; Jer. 22:13; Mal. 3:5). The second denial refers either to the murder of landowners or to participating in business dealings that lead to their impoverishment and possibly death by starvation (cf. the murder of Naboth by Ahab and Jezebel, 1 Kings 21).

The punishment for this crime echoes Genesis 3:17-18 and 4:12, the curse God placed on the soil because of human disobedience in the first instance and fratricide in the second. Thorns and stink weed will grow instead of wheat and barley. Sterility will replace productivity of the soil. Following traditional wisdom teaching, Job's defense is based on the view that righteous actions will lead to well-being for human communities, who will reap nature's bounty, while sin exploits creation, destroys life, and leads to destruction.

Job's oath of innocence performs two functions. First, as a conventional legal procedure, he has demonstrated his innocence. Questions about his moral integrity are answered and put to rest. Second, Job challenges God to present his indictment in a court setting. Should God meet him in court, Job is convinced he could not only prove his own innocence, but also demonstrate

167

that the divine king is guilty of malevolent misrule and should be removed from his throne. Job's Promethean defiance is undergirded by his use of royal imagery to redescribe his role and function. Job is demanding to meet God, not as a submissive slave, but as a royal prince.

Even more interesting is the fact that the shift in anthropological paradigm from slave to king carries with it a use of rather conventional legal language, based on the ideal of justice as that which permeates reality. After all, the desperate resorting to self-cursing carries weight, only if the norms of justice, undergirding this legal procedure, are allowed to operate. For Job, God has perverted these standards and thus must be brought to trial and removed from his throne. The demand to meet God in court is not simply an issue of affirming Job's integrity, but also is a radical call for a return to justice as the moral order of the world. In terms of metaphorical theology, Job strives to redescribe reality as a just order ruled, not by a corrupt deity, but by human beings who embody the highest ideals of righteousness, exemplified in the ethical structure and character of the oath of innocence.

THE SPEECHES FROM THE WHIRLWIND (JOB 38:1–42:6)

Introduction

The book of Job reaches its dramatic climax in the appearance of Yahweh, who speaks as the "voice from the whirlwind." Metaphors of word and combat dominate these exchanges between God and Job. Job's encounter with the creator of heaven and earth, who has come to engage in combat both the mortal revolutionary and the immortal monsters of chaos, destabilizes the newly emerging paradigm of the first man, symbolic of all human creatures, who is to rule over creation. The poet replaces it with a redescription of reality in which the creator of heaven and earth engages in battle with chaos to sustain the continuation of creation. Job and the audience who may have identified with his newly emerging mythos reexperience the collapse of meaning (in mythical terms the fall), but at the same time the components for redescribing reality are present and allow for restabilization and a new paradigm of meaning. Both the experience of theophanic event and the metaphorical content of the speeches present a new and dramatic vision of faith.

Literary Unity

The debate about the literary integrity of the final section continues, with one position attempting to present only one Yahweh speech and one Joban response.[101] However, the arguments used in support of this literary analysis are not particularly convincing.[102] The removal of key passages, for example those that portray Leviathan and Behemoth, does violence, in my judgment, to the meaning of the entire book. The metaphor cluster of combat is critical to the interpretation of the book, at least in the reading offered here. Furthermore, the two responses of Job make for a very important movement in the hero's thinking—from silence (40:3-5) to doxology (42:1-6). While there may well have been some minor literary reshaping of these speeches, the texts will be interpreted in their present form.

THE FIRST SPEECH OF GOD AND JOB'S RESPONSE
(JOB 38:1–40:5)

Restabilization of Metaphors of Cosmology

Opening with questions of challenge and imperative, Yahweh's introduction uses the two metaphors that provide the controlling images for the disputation with Job: word and struggle. The form of the speeches is that of disputation, appropriate both for these two metaphors and for the continuation of the earlier debate between Job and his human opponents. The first speech opens in the following way (38:1-3):

> 1. Then Yahweh answered Job out of the whirlwind and said:
> 2. Who is this who darkens counsel
>   with words lacking in knowledge?
> 3. Gird up your loins like a warrior,[103]
>   I will question you and you reveal to me.

Typical for theophanies in the Old Testament, Yahweh comes as the Storm God to do battle, now with a human rebel who has dared to oppose divine rule.[104] The opening question challenges the opponent to a battle of words and expresses disdain or contempt (Exod. 5:2; Judg. 9:28, 38; 1 Sam. 17:26; 25:10; Job 26:4; Isa. 28:9). "Counsel" refers to Yahweh's providential plan in creating and ruling the world (cf. Job 12:13; Ps. 33:11; Prov. 8:14). This divine counsel is contrasted with Job's word (curse, challenge, disputation, and indictment), which "darkens" Yahweh's life-giving plan—that is, returns the world to primordial chaos by subverting the structures of social life and creation (cf. chap. 3). By use of the imagery of battle, Yahweh challenges Job to a war of words (Ps. 45:4; Isa. 5:27; 8:9; Jer. 1:17).

Moving directly into the first major section of his speech, Yahweh combines a hymnic description of creation with questions of disputation (38:4-18):

> Strophe I: The Earth (38:4-7)
> 4. Where were you when I founded the earth?
>   Tell me, if you have insight.

169

5. Who established its measurements? Surely you know!
   Or who stretched out the measuring line upon it?
6. Upon what were the earth's pillars sunk,
   or who laid its cornerstone,
7. When the morning stars cried in exultation,
   and all the sons of the gods shouted in praise?

Strophe II: Sea (38:8-11)

8. Who shut in Yam with doors,
   when he burst forth, issuing from the womb,
9. When I made a cloud his garment,
   and a dark cloud his swaddling band,
10. When I restrained him with my statute,
    and I set up a bolt and doors,
11. And I said, "Thus far you may come, but no farther,
    and here must your arrogant waves be stayed?"

Strophe III: The Heavens (38:12-15)

12. Have you in your lifetime commanded Morning,
    or have you made the Dawn know his place,
13. In order to seize the corners of the earth
    and shake out the wicked,
14. When it[105] changes like clay pressed by a seal,
    or like a garment that is dyed?[106]
15. Their light is withheld from the wicked,
    whose uplifted arm is broken.

Strophe IV: The Underworld (38:16-18)

16. Have you entered into the sources of the sea,
    and have you walked in the recesses of the Deep?
17. Have Death's gates been revealed unto you,
    and have you seen the gates of the Netherworld?
18. Have you comprehended the broad expanses of the cosmos?
    Tell me, if you know all of it.

These rhetorical questions, here and throughout the two divine speeches, are designed to evoke from Job the recognition that only Yahweh, not an ordinary mortal like Job, has the knowledge and power to rule the cosmos.[107] Their purpose is to humble Job into words of contrite doxology—that is, to praise the justice of the creator of heaven and earth and to admit his own guilt.

In describing the cosmos, which is divided into the four spheres of earth, sea, heavens, and underworld, this section uses the three traditional wisdom metaphors of artistry, birth, and word. In the first strophe, Yahweh is the divine architect whose masterful construction of the earth evokes the praise of the heavenly choir of the divine council and morning stars.

In the second strophe, the birth of Yam is depicted with Yahweh being either the divine parent or, more likely, the midwife who wraps the newborn in swaddling clothes. What is especially shocking is that it is infant chaos, not human mortals, whom Yahweh nurtures. The conflict metaphor appears in the incarceration of Yam in a prison with doors with a crossbar. Then in the metaphor of word Yahweh issues an edict that restrains the ruler of chaos from flooding creation.

In the third strophe (38:12-15), the light of Morning and Dawn not only ferrets out evil, but also is denied to those who defy the rule of God. Each day God commands into existence a new creation, operating according to the norms of justice. And in the final strophe, the mystery of the abyss and the city of death (Pss. 9:14; 107:18) remain hidden to human understanding.

The second section of Yahweh's initial speech consists of some six strophes that direct questions to Job concerning the heavenly region: light and darkness, weather, precipitation, the constellations, and the clouds (38:19-38).

Strophe I: Light and Darkness (38:19-21)
19. Where is the path to the dwelling of light,
    and as for darkness, where is its place,
20. That you may take to its border,
    and perceive the pathways to its house?
21. You know, for you were born then,
    and the number of your days are many!

Strophe II: Snow, Hail, Light, East Wind (38:22-24)
22. Have you entered the reservoirs of the snow,
    and have you seen the storehouses of the hail,
23. Which I have reserved for a time of trouble,
    for the day of battle and war?
24. What is the manner by which light is distributed,
    or the east wind travels over the earth?

Strophe III: Rain (38:25-27)
25. Who has cleft a channel for the flood,
    and a path for the thunderbolt,
26. To bring rain upon the earth when there was no human,
    upon the desert when there was no person upon it?
27. To satisfy the desolate land,
    and to make the grass to sprout forth?

Strophe IV: Rain, Dew, Hoarfrost, Ice (38:28-30)
28. Does the rain have a father,
    or who fathered the dewdrops?
29. From whose womb did the ice come forth,
    and who gave birth to the hoarfrost of heaven?
30. The waters become hard like stone,
    and the face of the deep is frozen.

Strophe V: Constellations (38:31-33)

31. Can you bind the bonds[108] of the Pleiades,
    or loose the cords of Orion?
32. Can you bring forth the Mazzaroth in its season,
    and can you guide the Bear and her cubs?
33. Do you know the statutes of heaven,
    or can you establish heaven's rule on the earth?

Strophe VI: Clouds (38:34-38)

34. Can you lift your voice to the clouds,
    so that the flood of waters will cover you?
35. Can you send forth lightnings so that they may go,
    and will they say to you, "Here we are?"
36. Who placed wisdom in the ibis,
    or who gave insight to the cock?
37. Who counts the clouds by wisdom,
    and who can tilt the waterskins of heaven,
38. When dust compacts into a mass,
    and clods cleave together?

Once more the cosmological metaphors for God as artisan, giver of fertility, judge, king, sage, and warrior shape these strophes. God constructs a cosmic irrigation canal to water a wasteland uninhabited by humans (vv. 25-27; see Gen. 2:4b-7). God is both the father and the mother of moisture, necessary for life (vv. 28-30), while God's voice of thunder commands the waters of the clouds and the gift of divine wisdom enables the ibis and the cock to announce that a storm is drawing nigh.[109] God's wisdom and decree tilt the waterskins of the heavens to water creation (v. 37). As divine warrior, Yahweh stores up snow and hail to use as weapons during "a time of trouble" and "the day of battle and war" (see Judg. 5:20-21; Pss. 18:3-4; 29:1-9; Isa. 30:30; Amos 5:8-9; 9:6) and binds the Pleiades and Orion, ancient Titans challenging divine rule (cf. 9:9; 25:2-3).

The Anthropological Tradition: The Deconstruction of the King Metaphor

The fourth major section of this first speech from the whirlwind sets forth the providential care of animals, especially wild beasts untamed by human creatures (38:39–39:30; see Psalm 104).

Strophe I: Lion and Raven (38:39-41)

39. Can you hunt prey for the lion,
    can you satisfy the appetite of young lions?
40. When they crouch in the dens,
    and lie in wait in the thicket?
41. Who provides the raven its prey,
    when its offspring cry out to God,
    and wander about without food?

Strophe II: Ibex and Hind (39:1-4)

1. Do you know the time when mountain goats are born,
    Do you observe the travail of hinds.
2. Can you number the months they must fulfill,
    Do you know the time when they bring forth,
3. When they crouch down to give birth to their young,
    when they bring forth their offspring?
4. Their young ones grow strong,
     they grow up in the open,
     they go forth and do not return to them.

Strophe III: Wild Ass and Wild Ox (39:5-12)

5. Who sends forth the wild ass to freedom,
     and who looses the bonds of the onager,
6. Whose home I have made the steppe,
     and whose habitat is the salt plain?
7. He laughs at the noise of the city,
     the shouts of the driver he does not hear.
8. He ranges over the mountains as his pasture,
     and he searches after all that is green.
9. Is the wild ox willing to serve you,
     or to spend the night at your feeding trough?
10. Can you bind him in the furrow with ropes,
     or will he harrow the valleys behind you?
11. Can you trust him when his strength increases,
     or can you leave your produce to him?
12. Do you trust him to return,
     and gather your seed to your threshing floor?

Strophe IV: Ostrich and Horse (39:13-25)

13. The wing of the ostrich flaps joyously;
     is it a kindly pinion and plumage?
14. For she leaves her eggs on the ground,
     and lets them be warmed on the soil.
15. For she forgets that a foot may crush them,
     or a wild beast may trample them.
16. Her offspring are treated roughly without her;
     while her labor may be in vain,
     she remains without fear.
17. Because God has made her forget wisdom,
     and has not imparted insight to her!
18. When she flaps proudly,
     she scoffs at the horse and its rider.
19. Did you give the horse its strength,
     did you clothe his neck with a quivering mane?
20. Do you make him leap like the locust?
     His snorting is majestic and dreadful.
21. He paws in the valley and rejoices in his strength,
     he goes out to meet the weapons.
22. He laughs at fear and is not dismayed,
     he does not retreat from the sword.

23. The quiver rattles upon him,
   the flashing lance and javelin.
24. He stamps the ground and shakes with excitement,
   not able to believe that the trumpet sounds.
25. At the trumpet's blast he says, "Aha,"
   and sniffs out the battle from afar,
   the shouts of officers and the cry of war.

Strophe V: Hawk and Vulture (39:26-30)
26. Does the hawk soar by means of your wisdom,
   when he spreads his wings toward the south?
27. Does the vulture mount up at your command,
   and make his nest on high?
28. He makes his home on the rock,
   upon the pointed crag and towering cliff.
29. He searches for food from there,
   his eyes gazing from afar.
30. His brood drink blood,
   for where the slain are, there he is.

Yahweh is the "Lord of the Creatures" who providentially cares for five pairs of animals, providing them with various things necessary for survival, from instinct to food to the capacity to reproduce. Important to notice is the fact that each of these creatures, with the exception of the horse, is a wild beast that dwells in regions uninhabited by human beings and is uncontrolled by human efforts. Unlike Genesis 9:1-17, these creatures do not fear humans, ordained in this Priestly text to reign as God's surrogate in the world. It is also important to notice that many of these beasts are hunted by ancient Near Eastern kings in ritual acts designed to secure order in society and the cosmos.[110] In a striking repudiation of an anthropology in which humans are kings in God's creation (see Psalm 8), Yahweh speaks of sustaining a world hostile to human life (see Isa. 13:9-22; 32:12-14; 34:8-15; Jer. 50:39-40). The anthropological tradition grounded in the metaphor of humanity as king is shattered. Dwelling in a reality that is not anthropocentric, Job receives no divine commission to go forth and subdue the cosmos.

The first speech ends with an inclusio that resumes the challenge to the one who has revolted against divine rule (40:1-2). Should he answer these questions, thereby acknowledging not only his own weakness and ignorance but also the power and justice of God, Job would be forced to confess that he is unable to rule God's creation.

The First Response of Job (40:3-5)

Job's response to Yahweh's overwhelming challenge is silence:

174

3. Then Job answered the Lord.
4. Since I am despised (by you), how shall I answer you?
   I place my hand on my mouth.
5. Seeing I have spoken once, I will not answer,
   I will not continue a second time. (40:3-5)

The NRSV translates the initial line: "See, I am of small account," suggesting that Job may be acknowledging his own insignificance. More likely, Job is shocked to discover how little he (and humanity, for that matter) counts in Yahweh's world. The Hebrew particle *hēn* usually means "since" or "seeing that this is so," while *qallōtî* (a *qal* verb) clearly means "to be held in contempt" by another (Gen. 16:4-5). Holding the rebel in contempt, God demands from Job doxology, not indictment.

Instead, Job is struck dumb (cf. 2:13). His emerging world of justice administered by human kings in place of a dethroned deity has collapsed. In the world of divine making, humans are not at the center of the universe and retributive justice is a false teaching. God even cares for a part of the world that is hostile to human life. Incapable of doxology or defiance, Job has become inarticulate. Meaning has once again fragmented.

THE SECOND SPEECH OF GOD AND JOB'S RESPONSE (40:6–42:6)

The Anthropological Tradition:
The Deconstruction of the Metaphor of Ruler

Yahweh's second disputation constructs a hermeneutic that allows silent lips to speak. Developing the earlier theme that humans are not royal creatures at the center of creation and nurtured by divine providence, Yahweh offers the upstart mortal the divine throne under one condition: He must rid the world of evil and defeat the dreaded monsters of chaos, Behemoth ("mighty creature") and Leviathan (dragon of the seas). In this second speech, beginning in 40:6, the controlling metaphor is battle. After repeating the challenge (cf. 38:3), Yahweh asks:

8. Will you negate my justice,
   Will you pronounce me guilty that you might be declared innocent?
9. Do you have an arm like El,
   And can you thunder with a voice like his?
10. Deck yourself with greatness and exaltation,
    clothe yourself with majesty and splendor.
11. Scatter forth your fury,
    look upon every arrogant one and humble him.
12. Look upon every proud person and subdue him,

and tread down the wicked in their place.
13. Hide them in the grave together,
    bind their faces in the darkness.
14. Then I will also praise you,
    Because your right hand will have brought you victory.

Yahweh begins by defending his own justice, arguing that Job's innocence is not necessarily predicated on divine guilt. Job's attack of divine rule is more than simply denying God's justice. He is attempting "to negate" (*parar*) the righteous rule of God, which undergirds the structures of life. This same verb is used to describe the "splitting" of the chaos monster in the battle preceding creation (Ps. 74:13). The "strong arm" and "thunder" are images associated with the storm god who comes to do battle with chaos.[111]

Yahweh then taunts Job to put on the royal vestments of "greatness," "exaltation," "majesty," and "splendor." These are traditionally used to describe the royal sovereignty of God in ruling the cosmos and directing history (Ps. 21:6; 45:4; 104:1; 111:3). In the traditional mythical pattern, following the defeat of chaos the wicked and the revolutionaries are sentenced. "Humbling," "subduing," and "treading" on the backs of the enemy reflect language of the defeat of enemies by victorious kings and gods. If Job succeeds in destroying the wicked, then Yahweh will "praise" him as ruler of heaven and earth (see Pss. 18:50; 30:13; 35:18; 43:4; 44:9; 54:8; 99:3). Yahweh does not directly state that he is the one who maintains justice by the defeat of the wicked and the proud, but it is nevertheless implied.

The Cosmological Metaphor of Struggle

Yahweh now turns to praise the two monsters of mythical lore: Behemoth and Leviathan.[112] Yahweh is the divine warrior who, preceding the onslaught of battle, praises his opponents. If indeed Job wishes to rule the cosmos, he must defend it against these awesome opponents. The first is Behemoth (40:15-24).

Strophe I: Behemoth's Power (40:15-19)
15. Behold now, Behemoth, whom I made as I made you,
    he eats grass like an ox.
16. Behold, his strength is in his loins,
    and his rigor is in the muscles of his belly.
17. He stiffens his tail like a cedar,
    the sinews of his thighs are knit together.
18. His bones are bronze tubes,
    his limbs are like iron bars.
19. He is the first of the works of God,
    let the one who created him bring near his sword.

Strophe I: Behemoth's Domain (40:20-24)

20. For the mountains bring him their tribute,
    where every beast of the field cavorts.
21. Under the lotus plants he lies,
    in the covert of reeds and swamp.
22. The lotus trees cover him with shade,
    the willows of the brook surround him.
23. If the river swells with turbulence, he is not alarmed,
    he is confident though Jordan burst forth against his mouth.
24. One takes him by his eyes,
    and pierces his nose with lures.

Behemoth is a plural of *majesty* in Hebrew and means "great beast," probably a large animal (hippopotamus[113] or water buffalo[114]) that symbolizes chaos.[115] A creature made by God, Behemoth is the "first of God's works," an honor reserved for Woman Wisdom in Proverbs 8:22 and for the first man in Genesis 2:4b-7. Here chaos is the first and presumably the most important element of creation. Now it is Behemoth, not wisdom or humanity, who reigns as a king over a domain of wild beasts, accepting tribute from the mountains, the supporting pillars of the earth. This "king of the beasts" dwells in marshes and streams and knows no fear.

Behemoth is one primordial monster with whom the ruler of creation must contend for sovereignty over the cosmos. In Egyptian religion as early as the First Dynasty, the king, in the role of the god Horus, hunted the red hippopotamus who symbolized Seth, the god of chaos, who killed Osiris, the father of Horus.[116] After winning the mythological battle, Horus assumed the throne of Egypt and order was established in creation and society. This mythic battle was reenacted during the enthronement of new kings. Yahweh now has come to do battle with Behemoth, the embodiment of chaos, who opposes divine rule. If Job wishes to rule the universe, he must defeat and then attempt to control Behemoth (see 40:8-14). The point of all this seems not to be that Yahweh is indicting himself for originating evil, but that the powers of chaos are mighty and must be defeated on a regular basis for life to continue.

The last section of Yahweh's second speech turns to the praise of the ruler of the seas, Leviathan (40:25–41:26).

Strophe I: Fighting Leviathan (40:25-32)

25. Can you draw out Leviathan with a hook,
    and press down his tongue with a cord?
26. Can you place a rope in his nose,
    or pierce his jaw with a hook?
27. Will he multiply his supplications to you,
    or speak to you soft words?
28. Will he cut a covenant with you,
    will you take him as a servant forever?

177

29. Will you make sport with him as though he were afraid,
     or bind him for your girls?
30. Will partners barter for him,
     will they divide him up among merchants?
31. Can you fill his skin with spears,
     and his head with a fishing harpoon?
32. Lay your hand upon him and think of the battle,
     you will not do so again!

Strophe II: Opposing Yahweh (41:1-3)

1. Behold one's hope is shown to be false,
     is one not overwhelmed at the mere sight of him?
2. There is no one so fierce that he should awaken him,
     and who is he who would dare to stand before me?
3. Who has confronted me that I should make him payment?
     All under the heavens is mine.

Strophe III: Leviathan's Frame (41:4-9)

4. I will not keep silent about his limbs,
     or his strength and the grace of his proportions.
5. Who can strip his outer garment,
     who can penetrate his double coat of mail?
6. Who dares to open the doors of his face?
     Terror surrounds his teeth.
7. His back consists of rows of shields,
     shut up tightly like a seal.
8. They are so close to each other,
     no air comes between them.
9. They join one to another,
     each clasps the other and cannot be separated.

Strophe IV: Breath of Fire (41:10-13)

10. His sneezings flash forth light,
     and his eyes are like the eyelids of the dawn.
11. Torches go forth from his mouth,
     they escape like sparks of fire.
12. Smoke comes forth from his nostrils,
     as from a boiling pot set upon dry rushes.
13. His breath ignites coals,
     and a flame burns from his mouth.

Strophe V: Intimidation of Gods (41:14-17)

14. Strength resides in his neck,
     and terror dances before his eyes.
15. The folds of his flesh cleave together,
     cast like metal, immovable upon him.
16. His heart is hard as a rock,
     as hard as a lower millstone.
17. At his rising gods stand back in fear,
     at his crashings they are awestruck.

Strophe VI: Repelling Weapons (41:18-21)

18. Though the sword may reach him, it has no avail,
    neither does the spear, the dart, and the lance.
19. He considers iron as straw,
    and bronze as rotting wood.
20. An arrow cannot put him to flight,
    slingstones become as stubble to him.
21. Clubs are accounted as straw,
    and he laughs at the casting of javelins.

Strophe VII: Home in the Deep (41:22-24)

22. His underparts are sharpened potsherds,
    he spreads out like a threshing sledge on the mire.
23. He makes the deep boil like a cooking pot,
    he makes the sea like an ointment pan.
24. He leaves a shining wake behind him,
    one would think the Deep has a hoary head.

Strophe VIII: The Rule of Leviathan (41:25-26)

25. No one upon the earth can rule over him,
    a creature without fear.
26. He beholds everyone who is haughty,
    he is king over all the proud beasts.

Even more fearful than Behemoth is Leviathan. This monster of the seas, representing chaos, must be defeated for the cosmos to endure. Any pretender to Yahweh's throne must face in mortal combat this awesome foe. Can Job use hooks and ropes to capture this terrible monster and make him beg for his life? Can Job force Leviathan into a covenant (Gen. 9:1-17) that would make him Job's slave forever? If mortals quake in fear at even the thought of "arousing" the powerful Leviathan (see Job 3:8), would they dare "to stand before" (i.e., oppose) Yahweh (see 2 Sam. 22:6, 19 [= Ps. 18:6, 19]; Ps. 17:13)? Does Job truly contemplate doing battle with Yahweh for kingship? This lengthy hymnlike text in praise of Leviathan concludes with the statement that "no one upon earth can rule over him." He "is king over all the proud beasts," most probably those fierce animals in the first speech who are untamed by human creatures (see Job 28:8).[117] Unlike the animals who are in fear of humans in the Priestly narrative (Gen. 9:2), Leviathan is without fear.

In this speech, Yahweh has come to do battle with the two great incarnations of chaos that oppose his rule: Behemoth and Leviathan. His victory would result in the recreation of heaven and earth, allowing life to continue. If Job truly wishes to dethrone Yahweh, then Job is challenged first to defeat these two fierce monsters.

Creation and Reality in the Yahweh Speeches

In these two speeches, the reality described by Yahweh is an orderly cosmos ruled over by the divine warrior. The various metaphors of reality include a beautiful building or a kingdom of dikes and canals built by a divine architect; a household in which the divine parent nurtures Yam, his darling infant; and fertile, well-watered fields that formerly were a wasteland. However, what dominates the imagery of these two speeches is reality as a kingdom ruled over by the head of the divine council, who has fought and continues to battle chaos for supremacy. This is an ever-recurring battle, for even when Behemoth and Leviathan are defeated, they continue to wait their chance for insurrection, threatening all life. When they are subdued, at least for a time, Yahweh's edicts order the world in justice by providing the necessities of life for all creatures. Even wild beasts hostile to human life are providentially sustained.

What is shocking, of course, is the rejection of the anthropological tradition of humanity as the center of the universe, ruling as God's surrogate over the created order. Indeed, human creation and sustenance are almost ignored, save for the incidental reference to Behemoth as a creature God made even as he created Job (40:15). If Job wishes to rule the divine kingdom, he must not only possess the power and wisdom to order and sustain creation, he must also face the prospect of a life-and-death struggle with Behemoth and Leviathan, the powers of chaos, who continually threaten existence.

The Second Response of Job

Job's second response contains at least features of the doxology in which he acknowledges that Yahweh has the power and wisdom to create and sustain the world. Whether this is praise or tongue-in-cheek satire depends on the translation and meaning of 42:6.

> 1. Then Job answered the Lord:
> 2. I know that you are capable of all things,
>   and that no plan you propose will be impossible for you.
> 3. "Who is this who conceals counsel without knowledge?"
>   Therefore I have acknowledged I do not understand,
>   there are divine acts too wonderful for me which I do not know.
> 4. "Listen now, and I will speak,
>   I will question you and you inform me."
> 5. I have heard you with my own ears,
>   even now my eye beholds you.
> 6. I reject[118] and am comforted over dust and ashes (42:1-6).

In this response, Job ceases his attack on God and ends his speech making with a desire to praise Yahweh.[119] In 42:2 ("I know you are capable of all things, and that no plan you propose will be impossible for you"), Job's words echo Yahweh's judgment in Genesis 11:6, bringing to mind the story of the Tower of Babel (Gen. 11:1-9). In this story of rebellion, humans filled with hubris reject God's sovereignty by building a tower that would allow them to scale the heavens and rule over their own destiny. Yahweh's word of judgment confuses their language, resulting in their scattering over the earth. Job's echo (almost a quotation) of this famous text serves to emphasize that only Yahweh is the sovereign ruler of the divine kingdom, whose word of judgment determines the destiny of the world.

In verse 3, quoting Yahweh's earlier words introducing his first speech (38:2), Job acknowledges that he does not possess the knowledge to understand divine acts in creation and history, "wondrous things" that redeem and bring life. What Job needs now is instruction in a new language to praise God for such deeds. Yahweh's description of his power, knowledge, and justice is designed to evoke from Job a doxology. Having "heard and seen Yahweh" in this theophany, Job moves to hymnic praise. But what Job rejects in v. 6 is penitential lamentation and words of rebellion designed to subvert the order of creation (cf. chap. 3). Job abandons lament ("I reject [ema'as][120] and am comforted over [nihamtî][121] dust and ashes [aphar wā 'eper]"[122]) and begins the attempt to sing words of praise, which his earlier experience of pain and dumbness has not allowed. The time for lament and accusation is at an end.[123]

THE FINAL JUDGMENT (JOB 42)

The Restoration of Job and the Redemption of God

The reappearance of the didactic tale offers the opportunity to enter once again into the naive world of a wisdom unchastened by the crisis of holocaust. The return to this world, however, is no a longer first, but rather a second, naiveté, for with the retelling of the tale by the insertion of the poetic dialogues and speeches from the whirlwind, it is impossible simply to reaffirm the notions of retribution, the discipline of undeserved suffering, and divine caprice. In the retelling of the tale, there is not only the restoration of Job, but also the redemption of God.

The epilogue has two scenes: judgment (42:7-9) and restoration (42:10-17). The original formulation of the narrative most likely told of the vindication of Job's refusal to curse God, in spite of his wife's counsel. It may be that the original advice of the friends in the narrative encouraged Job to abandon God; in any case, this earlier dialogue is replaced by the poetic speeches of Job and his opponents. In the original tale, Job did "fear God for naught," for he expected no reward for even perfect piety and morality. His intercession for faithless friends presented the highest ideals of the righteous sage whose mediation brought the possibility of redemption to the wicked. Job's restoration, which included a double portion of possessions and the birth of ten new children even though he apparently has the same wife, demonstrates that God does finally reward those who suffer patiently and quietly. As a wisdom narrative, the old tale presented the heroic embodiment of the virtue of unquestioned faith in spite of even horrible suffering.

Metaphorical Theology and Cosmology

The rewriting of the tale by the poet, accomplished by the replacement of Job's exchanges with the friends with new dialogues and the whirlwind speeches, presents a new and rather shocking rendition of the classic story. Job, not the friends who defended with unflagging loyalty the justice of God, has his integrity upheld by the ruler of the divine assembly, who now renders judgment. The friends have spoken "incorrectly" about God, while Job's depiction of God as a malevolent deity corrupting the norms of justice are said to be "correct." Correctly speaking about God takes precedence over the matter of Job's integrity and just suffering. The false theology of retribution and the uncontested sovereignty of God are the twin features of the "incorrect" views of the opponents of Job. The questioning of divine justice and the demand that God be attentive to the pleas of victims in ruling the universe are affirmed as the right theological posture.

Furthermore, not only is Job's integrity upheld by the divine verdict of the cosmic judge, but in addition God is also vindicated. God's allowing "the satan" to create suspicion about Job's real intentions in pious obedience and faithful living led to the unjust and terribly brutal affliction of Job, not only in losing his own possessions and health, but also in the lives of his ten children. Such a theological portrait of a divine tyrant willing to destroy even those who are rumored to be disloyal cannot stand in the face of overwhelming crisis. God must act to set things right, which, after all, is the job of the šōpheṭ—the judge. Subsequently, Job's restoration leads to the redemption of God.

Metaphorical Anthropology and the Narrative Conclusion

In the retelling of the tale, Job once again is declared to be a "slave" (ʿebed). However, even a slave may and should question unjust and inhumane treatment received from the hand of a master turned cruel. Job may not be a royal figure who is commissioned by God to rule over creation, but, as a representative of the righteous sage and perhaps just humans, he is to strive with God when divine support of justice seems to have been per-

182

verted into cosmic misrule. Job must confront evil face to face. As God comes once again to contest Behemoth and Leviathan for rulership of the cosmos, so Job and all those concerned with justice must confront evil. After all, the continuation of creation and the possibilities of life depend on the victory of God and the human creature concerned with righteousness. Justice continues to be the ground of existence for God's creation.

Metaphors and Reality in the Epilogue

At the end, the readers return with Job to the narrative world of kingdom and assembly ruled over by Yahweh. It is New Year's, and God again sits on heaven's throne to determine destinies. Only now, God is no longer suspicious of human motive and susceptible to satanic deceit leading to destruction. God affirms the integrity of Job, including his assault on the divine miscarriage of justice, and not the incredulous piety of unquestioned obedience. Divine edict does sustain the world, but only when used to "set things right."

The Metaphorical Process: Transformation and Restabilization

The reclaiming of traditional metaphors has been accomplished in this retelling of the tale. However, these metaphors of creation of the world, human nature, and redescription of reality have been imbued with new meaning. Humans may still be slaves, not kings in the world of God's own making, but they are not subject to divine abuse occasioned by satanic whim. Then, too, they are to strive in their own dealings for justice, for this struggle undergirds the structures of life. God once more is the royal king who has won and continues to defend his rule over the divine assembly against the assaults of the chaos monsters who ever wait their opportunity to return the world to the darkness of eternal night. And there is always the possibility that in the next battle they may win. The world is God's kingdom, subject to his royal decree. However, it is not a nightmare world of injustice ruled over by a capricious tyrant, but a domain of life made possible by righteous existence that requires active confrontation with evil. The new language of faith, made possible by the activation of imagination that envisions the world anew, is now open to revitalization by the reclaiming of metaphors of belief and action.

THE SEARCH FOR WISDOM (JOB 28) AND THE SPEECHES OF ELIHU (JOB 32–37)

Two later insertions derive from traditional sages who were not comfortable with the retelling of the Joban tale by the poet: the hymn on the inaccessibility of wisdom (chap. 28) and the speeches of the interloper, Elihu (32–37). Each

183

attempts to take the traditional metaphors of faith and reclaim an earlier naiveté, untroubled by the horrors of holocaust. The first, the poem on wisdom, derives most likely from the piety, though still upper class and aristocratic, of post-exilic Judaism centering on Torah, Temple, and wisdom. The second, the speeches of Elihu, are the outpourings most likely of a populist wisdom that derives from religious piety and social concerns in the country-side, outside the centers of localized political power.

THE HYMN ON THE DISCOVERY OF WISDOM (JOB 28)

Introduction

A beautiful poem speaks of the inability of humans to discover and understand divine wisdom. Divided into four strophes (vv. 1-6, vv. 7-12, vv. 13-20, and vv. 21-28), the refrain asks the question that embodies the theme: "Where shall wisdom be found, and where is the place of insight?" (vv. 12, 20).

Strophe I (vv. 1-6)

1. For there is a mine for silver,
    and a place where gold is refined.
2. Iron is taken from the earth,
    and copper is smelted from ore.
3. Humanity puts an end to darkness,
    and searches every hidden recess
    for ore in dark and gloomy places.
4. They open shafts where there are no inhabitants,
    places untrod by the foot of humans,
    bereft of the presence of people who wander about.
5. The earth—from it comes bread,
    but below it is transformed by fire.
6. It is a place for lapis lazuli embedded in its stones,
    while its particles of dust contain gold.

Strophe II (vv. 7-12)

7. That path is unknown by the bird of prey,
    and unseen by the falcon's eye.
8. The proud beasts have not trodden it,
    nor has the lion passed over it.
9. Humans put their hands to the flint,
    they overturn mountains at their base.
10. They cut channels in the rocks,
    and everything precious their eyes have seen.
11. They probe the sources of rivers,
    and each secret they bring to light.
12. But where shall Wisdom be found,
    and where is the place of Insight?

Strophe III (vv. 13-20)

13. Humans do not know her value,
     and she cannot be found in the land of the living.
14. The Abyss says, "She is not in me,"
     and Yam says, "She is not with me."
15. Gold cannot buy her,
     nor can silver be weighed out for her price.
16. Her value cannot be measured in the gold of Ophir,
     in precious onyx or lapis lazuli.
17. Gold and glass do not equal her value,
     nor can vessels of fine gold be exchanged for her.
18. Corals and crystal need not be mentioned,
     Wisdom's price is above that of pearls.
19. Topaz from Ethiopia does not equal her value,
     she cannot be valued in pure gold.
20. Yet from where does Wisdom come,
     and where is the place of Insight?

Strophe IV (vv. 21-28)

21. She is hidden from the eyes of all living,
     and concealed from the birds of heaven.
22. Abaddon and Death say:
     "We have heard a rumor of her."
23. God perceives her way,
     and knows her place.
24. For he looks to the ends of the earth,
     he observes all things under the heavens.
25. When he allotted weight to the wind,
     and meted out water by measure.
26. When he made an ordinance for the rain,
     and a way for the thunderbolt.
27. Then he saw her and described her,
     he established her, and searched her out.
28. Then he said to Adam,
     "Behold the fear of the Lord is wisdom,
     and to turn from evil is insight."

Metaphor and Cosmology

In this hymn, God is both craftsman and judge who shapes a reality of beautiful proportions and then issues decrees that regulate the order of creation. A world of beauty and delight and a kingdom ruled by a mysterious, but benign creator are the images of reality in this poem. God alone knows the location of cosmic wisdom, a knowledge denied to human beings. Indeed, revelation of ultimate matters is denied them. Instead of seeking out answers to questions that deal with the nature of reality and divine character, they are to "fear God and turn from evil," as did the unreflecting and naive Job of the prologue.

Only God knows the location of wisdom, that revealer of divine reality and activity and the meaning of the cosmos. God is the divine architect who weighed the wind and measured the water and the divine judge who gives rain and lightning their destiny. Thus reality is beautifully proportioned and guided by the justice of the edicts of God.

More to the point, wisdom originated in the imagination of God, who saw her in his mind and then spoke her into existence. He then "established" her much as he secured the foundations of the world (Jer. 10:12), the mountains (Ps. 65:7), and the heavens (Prov. 8:27). In this image, wisdom serves as the foundation of the cosmos. Yet the same verb, "established," also refers to the securing of a ruler's throne (2 Sam. 5:12; 1 Kings 2:24), thus pointing to wisdom's reign as the Queen of Heaven (cf. Proverbs 8). Finally, God "searched her out," indicating his intimate knowledge of her very being (Job 5:27; Ps. 139:1; Prov. 25:2). God alone knows her location and her being.

Creation and Human Destiny

Finally, the divine judge and sage, following creation, instructed the first human and all who followed him:

> Behold the fear of the Lord is wisdom,
> and to turn from evil is insight.

Human destiny, in compliance with divine teaching, is to live as an unquestioning, pious, and righteous slave to God. The rebel of the prologue is, in the view of this later sage-poet, engaged in acts of hubris, both in desiring to know the secrets of divine rule and the nature of the cosmos and in the assault on God's rule.

THE SOVEREIGNTY OF GOD AND HUMAN SLAVERY: THE SPEECHES OF ELIHU (JOB 32–37)

Introduction

The four disputations of Elihu represent a second rejection of the earlier poet's rewriting of the Joban narrative: 32:6–33:33; 34:1-37; 35:1-16; and 36:1–37:24. The youth intrudes because the friends had declared God (not Job!) to be in the wrong.[124] Creation language figures prominently in the first, second, and especially fourth disputations. The first two draw on the anthropological tradition, while the cosmological tradition is at the center of the last speech.

Metaphors of Creation and Human Nature

One of the more interesting developments in the speeches of Elihu is his view of inspiration, which gives authority to teaching based on human insight. For example, he argues

> But it is the spirit (*rûaḥ*) in a person,
>   the breath *(neš̆amâ)* of the Almighty that makes him understand (32:8).

It is the "breath" (*neš̆amâ*) of life (Gen 2:7; 7:22; Job 27:3; 33:4; 34:14) or the divine "spirit" (*rûaḥ*) animating the human person (Gen. 6:17; 7:15, 22; Qoh. 3:19; Isa. 42:5; Ezek. 37:5, 6, 8, 10, 14; Zech. 12:1) that is the source of inspiration (cf. Num. 11:26-30).[125] He takes this general "vital principle," this "breath of Shaddai," and makes it a prophetic charisma. Job and he both are created as mortals, made of clay and given the gift of the divine breath, so that even Job's age and experience provide him with no advantage. Elihu proposes this view of inspiration in opposition to the traditional sapiential teaching that wisdom is especially associated with old age and experience. Most likely, the sage behind the Elihu speeches sees the inability of Job and his friends to find convincing answers and to present persuasive arguments to be the failure of both traditional and radical wisdom. Instead, Elihu offers, not unlike the Papyrus Insinger and Onchsheshonq in Late Dynastic Egypt,[126] popular wisdom obtainable by the common folk as the source of true understanding. The wranglings of scholars lead nowhere.

In 32:21-22, Elihu elaborates a doctrine of retribution that is grounded in this understanding of inspired talk. Rejecting flattery and respect of persons as vices, Elihu indicates that his creator would bring him to destruction for such improper speech and behavior. God not only breathes into a person the inspired and animating breath, but he also destroys those who misuse language in corrupt ways to distort. Likewise, this same inspiration is at work in God's warning humans of their iniquity by means of visions in the night so that they may turn from evil and save their lives from death (33:12-18).

In the second speech, Elihu makes use of a more traditional image associated with creation when he refers to the breath of God as the animating principle of all life (34:14-15):

> 14. Should he (God) put his mind to it,
>   to gather to himself his spirit and his breath,
> 15. all flesh would expire together,
>   and humanity would return to the dust.

The text echoes others in the Bible that speak of God's animating breath, including especially Psalm 104 (see Gen. 3:19; 7:21-23). For Elihu, the divine breath that animates creation dwells within human nature, giving insight and understanding to those who would listen to God's instruction.

Human Destiny and the Royal Metaphor

Elihu emphasizes that the mighty and the wealthy enjoy no special favor with God, for their origins are the same as the poor (34:17-20):

> 17. Shall one who hates justice govern,
>   or would you condemn one who is just and mighty?
> 18. Who says to a king, "Worthless one,"
>   and to princes, "Guilty."
> 19. Who does not show deference to princes,
>   and does not favor nobles over the poor,
>   because they are the work of his hands.
> 20. In a moment they die, at midnight,
>   people are convulsed and they pass away,
>   the mighty are taken away, but not by a human hand.

Elihu rejects Job's attack on divine justice by arguing that God, the divine artisan who shapes both rich and poor, lowly and mighty in the womb, is no respecter of persons, for they all are the work of his hands. God brings quick and unexpected destruction upon sinful human beings, regardless of their social status. Even so, Elihu especially dwells on divine retribution against the mighty aristocracy (34:17-30).

Elihu is no romantic who depicts the poor as innately noble, pious, and long-suffering people who always exemplify a humble and quiet piety. In his third speech, he notes that even the victims are not heard, if they question divine justice, as has Job, or ask where God is in the midst of their trials. Such faithless questioning leads God not to respond, asserts Elihu, although here he stands not only against Job but also against the tradition of laments in the Psalter.

In 36:5-12 Elihu presents one of the most striking examples of the exaltation of the righteous, using royal language in the process.

> 5. Behold God is powerful, but does not despise,
>   he is strong and mighty in heart.
> 6. He does not sustain the life of the wicked,
>   but justice he gives to the oppressed.
> 7. He does not withdraw his eyes from the righteous,
>   but enthrones them with kings,
>   and he seats them there forever and exalts them.
> 8. And if they are imprisoned in fetters,
>   captured by cords of affliction,
> 9. Then he will reveal to them their work,
>   and their transgressions,

that they have become arrogant.
10. He opens their ear to discipline,
   and tells them they should turn from evil.
11. If they are obedient and subservient,
   they will complete their days in well-being,
   and their years in delight.
. 12. And if they are not obedient,
   they will perish by the sword,
   and they will expire without knowledge.

Drawing heavily on images associated with the enthronement of kings (cf. Genesis 1; 1 Kgs 1:32-40; Job 40:10-14; Psalms 2; 8; 110), Elihu speaks of God's exaltation of the oppressed righteous to sit on royal thrones forever. Contrasting images of slavery are used to describe those chained up by sin, particularly by hubris (cf. Isaiah 14; Ezekiel 28). Rebels, according to Elihu, and these include Job, may hope for deliverance only through obedient service to God.

Missing in these four speeches are images of divine struggle with chaos. Elihu does describe God in terms of a storm theophany, but he does so to speak of the fearful and terrible deity who frightens reality into submission. This absence of combat is most likely explained by the radical sovereignty of God in the theology of Elihu. In addition, God, for Elihu, is a mysterious tyrant who carries out his work within the cloud of secrecy. What is disappointing is that Elihu has advanced the thought of the friends or of Job or of Yahweh very little, save in his more populist views of the exaltation of the righteous and the punishment of the mighty and the rich.

In the concluding section of the last speech (37:14-24), following a doxology in praise of Yahweh, Elihu asks Job questions no mortal can answer; like those of Yahweh, they deal with the "wonderful works of God." Unlike the interrogation of Job by Yahweh in the speeches from the whirlwind, Elihu's questions are not designed to move Job from silence to praise. Rather, Elihu's interrogation is designed to humiliate Job, to emphasize the power, justice, and mystery of the Almighty in contrast to the weakness and dark ignorance of his mortal antagonist. The desire is not to evoke praise, but to induce feelings of terror and intimidation before the awesomeness of God.

Conclusion

Neither Job 28 nor the rhetoric of Elihu speaks of reality as a battle between the Divine Warrior and the forces of chaos. Instead, more traditional metaphors are used. Thus in Job 28, God is the artisan who created the world to be a beautiful and elegant place, and yet has hidden cosmological wisdom from human view. Humans are kings, filled with hubris, seeking to possess what they are not given. Yet they fail, for cosmological wisdom alone belongs to God. Humans, then, are to fear God and turn from evil, the same posture exemplified by the naive Job in the prologue. God, for Elihu, is the radical sovereign whose decrees shape reality. In both cases, these metaphors do not succeed in redescribing reality or in transforming human understanding and purpose in the world. These worn expressions of theological language lead to sterile faith, not to lively engagement.

SAPIENTIAL IMAGINATION AND CREATION THEOLOGY IN THE BOOK OF JOB

The Joban poet has taken earlier renderings of God in Israelite and ancient Near Eastern traditions of creation of the world and humanity in the effort to construe a transformed understanding of God, of humanity, and of the world. Perhaps the poet lived in a world of holocaust in which previous theological representations were inadequate. These previous understandings were not sufficient to explain the horrors of innocent suffering.

The poet critically examined these metaphorical portrayals of God, humanity, and the world in earlier wisdom by moving in two directions in the poetic dialogues, before the Voice from the Whirlwind offers a new discourse and thus a transformed vision of reality. The first direction is taken by the friends of Job, who demanded of their cosmology more than even earlier sages deemed possible. For them, the activities of God are portrayed as those of a divine tyrant who rules the world according to retributive justice. God presides over a kingdom world as a stern, just judge whose edicts bring the wicked to destruction. Suffering may be a test of the faithfulness of the righteous and wise servants of God, who should continue in their loyal obedience and through this process emerge chastened and more disciplined. Even so, this God rules the world with compassion, making it possible even for the wicked to repent and then to experience divine salvation.

Humans, according to the friends, are corrupt by nature. Indeed, Bildad even calls them maggots. They are predisposed to evil and should expect divine retribution. Their only hope is to turn to God, utter a doxology that both praises the just creator and expresses human culpability, and plead for mercy. These are images associated with the metaphor of slave. For the friends, humans are not the royal surrogates of God, whose just and wise actions shape cosmic and social reality in ways that enhance the structures of life. The friends argue for the radical sovereignty of God and the depravity of the human creature.

The second direction is taken by Job in the dialogues. Reflecting on his own justice and wisdom, embodied in his life, and on the torment that he is experiencing, Job cannot find satisfying answers in earlier traditions of faith. Indeed, he remains convinced that justice ought to be the order of reality. Since this is not the case, Job concludes that God, for whatever reason, has become a cruel sadist who misrules the universe. In his own imaginative vision of reality, Job draws on images of the divine warrior and chaos mythology to render God as a destructive monster who has turned against his own creation and its creatures. Indeed, God has created the world through a power and wisdom that far exceed those of human mortals. But justice does not permeate the world, and God does not lovingly sustain creation and its creatures through a compassionate application of justice. This divine sadist directs human history so as to bring destruction against people and nations. Humans are not the beloved children of God, created in the womb and nurtured through life, but the victims of divine abuse. God is their creator, but he has made them into objects for torture and death. Human existence is couched in terms of slaves and day laborers whose lives are those of misery eased only by the finality of death. Job and humans may have been kings in God's good creation, but now they have become helpless slaves. But even slaves may cry out against their oppressor. As the dialogues reach their climax, Job becomes the rebel who seeks to remove God from the throne. Job uses the legal language of oath and indictment to absolve himself of guilt and to bring charges against the Almighty. Humans, ruling the world in compassionate justice, should replace God as sovereign over creation and history. Job has assaulted the metaphorical renderings of God in earlier tradition and seeks to set forth a new mythos in which humans, not God, rule the world. If left unchallenged, this transformation of reality and its meaning system would present a new and radically altered way of envisioning human existence in the world.

However, the silence of God is broken by the voice from the whirlwind, who comes with questions, if not answers. In these two divine speeches, Yahweh reclaims the earlier metaphorical portrayals of reality, but imbues them with new and, at least for Job, disorienting meaning. God is, indeed, a parent who engenders and sustains, but it is not humanity but Prince Yam who is the creator's child. God is the compassionate provider who rules over and cares for animals that humans often cannot restrain and certainly do not understand, but there is no mention of the divine parent who gives birth to and then nurtures the human creature. Indeed, God sustained a cosmos even before humans were present, a view that shatters an anthropocentric understanding that places humanity at the center of creation. The one mention of the creation of humanity, or more specifically of Job, is in the context of the description of Behemoth, one of the embodiments of chaos. In a shocking statement, God has created the chaos monster even as he has created Job. Indeed, Behemoth, and not Job or humanity, is the first of God's creation. The comforting renderings of the creation of humanity and of individuals in earlier traditions are shattered in these speeches.

But the imagery of the Storm God who comes to do battle with chaos, embodied in Behemoth and the even more fearful monster Leviathan, dominates this linguistic portrayal of reality, humanity's role and function, and the nature and activity of God. Job is offered Yahweh's throne, if he can destroy these monsters, remove evil from the face of the earth, and then rule the world in justice and compassion. These are the tasks of Yahweh. Once again, the Divine Warrior has come to assert sovereignty over the earth and to keep back the forces of chaos. Job, offered the throne, cowers in submission before the sovereignty of God.

The retelling of the folk tale that had portrayed God as a suspicious tyrant destroying even innocent children renders a new world view. The theological discourse of the friends is rejected, while Job's language about God is presented as "true." Once more as the divine judge whose task it is to issue a judgment that determines destiny and recreates the world, Yahweh formulates an edict that leads not only to the restoration of Job but also to the redemption of God. Job and humanity may continue to be presented in the images of "slave," but even Yahweh's slave has the task of calling the creator to a just accounting of divine misdeeds. The retelling of the Joban tale leaves many unanswered questions about God, reality, and human existence. The poet does not, indeed cannot, eliminate entirely the mysteries of God and creation, but some answers are provided. The later additions, the poem on wisdom's inaccessibility and the speeches of Elihu, are not content with this ambiguity, but they offer less insightful understandings. The former seeks comfort in a more mysterious rendering of God and humanity in the world, while the latter prefers a return to a rigid system of retribution that has already been negated by the earlier poet.

CHAPTER FIVE

"I Will Make a Test of Pleasure"

THE TYRANNY OF GOD AND QOHELETH'S
QUEST FOR THE GOOD

INTRODUCTION

The Identity and Social World of Qoheleth

The book of Qoheleth was written in Hebrew by a Jewish sage living in Jerusalem, probably near the end of the fourth or beginning of the third century B.C.E.[1] The specific meaning of the word *Qoheleth,* a feminine participle of the verb *qahal,* "to gather," "to assemble," is unclear. It is not a personal name, but it may refer to the role or office of the teacher, who gathers or assembles students in a school setting or to an editor who gathers and puts together wisdom materials to comprise a collection or book. Either would fit the description of Qoheleth in the epilogue (12:9-10), which indicates that he was "wise," "taught the people knowledge," and "weighed, studied, and arranged many sayings."

Cosmology and the Crisis of Imagination

For Qoheleth, the cosmology of traditional wisdom, conveyed through important root metaphors, did not provide suitable answers to the questions he raised about discovering the good in human existence. This sage was unable to move from perceptions of the world and the extension of what is perceived in creation to shape vital images into compelling articulations of faith and the moral life. Tradition no longer provided a reservoir for cosmological images of faith, due to both the failure of collective memory and the inability of sapiential teachings, especially those concerning retribution, to withstand the critical engagement of Qoheleth's experience and observation. Further, Qoheleth could not envision a world of sacred dwelling in which justice and well-being prevailed.

The crisis for Qoheleth was both an ethical and a theological one, since he came to assert, because of his own critical reflection on and experience of present existence, that the observable connection between the moral life and cosmology had broken down.[2] Order for this sage assumes the dimensions of rigidity and tyranny, because of the rule and character of a hidden God. The ethical life was no longer one of living in conformity with cosmic order and seeking to establish a sphere of beneficence in which well-being would result. The cosmological rendering of a world of goodness in which moral action led to desirable consequences could no longer sustain itself in an enigmatic and frightening reality unresponsive to human behavior.[3] When the prevailing cosmology lost its power to convict, the moral system dependent on that world view was replaced by one no longer upheld by divine sanctions and a pervasive justice present in the world, society, and human nature. Thus a very different way of looking at human existence in the world needed to emerge. What was called for was a new world view shaped by Qoheleth's own imagination. To find the resources for this human-centered reality, Qoheleth turns to the anthropological tradition. This tradition is reconceived in this sage's imagination, and central to this reconception is his metaphor of *hebel* ("breath").

THE GENRE OF QOHELETH

Introduction

The question of genre is important for understanding the book of Qoheleth and its imaginative construction of creation theology.[4] Scholars usually place Qoheleth in two different form-critical categories: sayings collections and first-person narratives.[5] In comparing Qoheleth to Proverbs, Ben Sira, and Pirke Aboth, the book takes on the appearance, in some important ways, of a sayings collection.[6] Sayings collections and their subunits may possess a general overarching rhetorical structure that combines the individual forms of poems, sayings, and instructions with content. Even so, collections lack a tight rhetorical structure, thematic coherence, and logical progression of thought. Their purpose is not to inform and persuade through reasoned argument, but to shape a world of esthesis—that is, a moral order of beauty and delight that is shaped by metaphors and rhetorical structures of individual forms and smaller collections. Understood in this way, the book of Qoheleth is a collection of sayings of a wise teacher on a variety of topics that assume the individual forms of sayings, instructions, poems, and first-person observations (cf. 12:9-12). The loose overarching rhetorical structure of the entire collection would derive from the general repetition of themes, images, and expressions.

While the book of Qoheleth contains many similarities to sayings collections, it also contains important features of first-person narratives, common in ancient Near Eastern wisdom literature. Indeed, the first-person narration of the book is its most important distinguishing characteristic among the books in the Israelite and Jewish wisdom corpus.[7] First-person narratives from the wisdom literatures of the ancient Near East provide important insights into the genre and meaning of Qoheleth.

Righteous Sufferer Poems[8]

One group of wisdom texts that offers formal comparison to Qoheleth is "righteous sufferer poems." Modeled on the style of the individual lament, a righteous sufferer narrates his various trials and calamities, including his questioning of traditional wisdom teaching and cultic piety. Continuing to plead his case, he finally is redeemed by his personal god. Two texts illustrate this type of poem: the Sumerian "Man and His God" (*ANET*, 589-91) and the Akkadian "I Will Praise the Lord of Wisdom" (*ANET*, 596-600). In the first, a young aristocratic sage endures great suffering, including the displeasure of his ruler. Speaking in the first-person voice, the youth protests his innocence and even accuses his personal god of afflicting him with evil. Yet he continues to lament and to ask his god to deliver him, and in the concluding episode the voice of a third-person narrator intrudes to describe the young man's deliverance.

Dating from the early twelfth century B.C.E., "I Will Praise the Lord of Wisdom" is a lengthy poem in which a feudal lord and ruler of a city (possibly Babylon) describes in the first person the anger of his lord (a Cassite king), his descent to the social position of a slave, treachery by his former courtiers, the disloyalty of relatives and friends, the attack of demonic forces that rob him of health, and the inexplicable desertion of his personal god. This autobiographical narrative chronicles the lord's fall from grace, suffering, continuing lamentation to Marduk, final restoration, and appearance in the temple of Esagil, where he performs sacrifices of thanksgiving before Marduk and his consort.

These poems have some affinities with Qoheleth. They are first-person narratives told by members of the aristocracy. Their reflections on suffering, the justice of the gods, and the condition of human nature place them within what some scholars characterize as the critical wisdom traditions of Israel and the ancient Near East. However, unlike Qoheleth, the first-person narrators continue to lament to their gods in the hope of divine deliverance. And they are eventually rewarded and restored for their persistent faith. Qoheleth, by contrast, experiences a radical gulf between God and the human world. For Qoheleth, "God is in heaven and you [i.e., humans] are upon the earth" (5:1). Human words, including those of the lament, do not affect divine action.[9] The comparison with Qoheleth is mainly in the form of the first-person narrative and the raising of the questions of justice and human suffering.

"The Dialogue of Pessimism"

"The Dialogue of Pessimism" (*ANET,* 600-601), also dating perhaps from the twelfth century B.C.E.,[10] bears some similarity to Qoheleth, though the format of a dialogue finds closer parallels in Job and the "Babylonian Theodicy" (*ANET,* 601-4). In the dialogue, a noble, speaking in the first person, announces a course of action that he intends to pursue. This is followed in turn by the first-person response of his wise slave, who supports the decision with a proverbial reply. Then the noble abruptly changes his mind, whereupon the slave once again supports the decision, this time using sapiential observations about possible disastrous consequences the action would have produced. This disputation continues through nine sections that involve the following values: prestige, dining, leisure time, family, power, love, religion, business, and patriotism. In the conclusion, the master asks the slave, "What, then, is good?" To this query the slave responds: "To have my neck and your neck broken and to be thrown into the river is good." The slave supports this action with two impossible questions:

> Who is so tall as to ascend to the heavens?
> Who is so broad as to compass the underworld?

Underscoring the severe limits placed on human knowledge and the inability to determine both the general "good" in human existence and the specific result that may follow socially and religiously sanctioned activities normally deemed wise and good, the wise slave concludes that reality is without meaning. The only proper response to this sad state of affairs is suicide. Testing the sincerity of this counsel, the noble suggests that he will put the slave to death first. To this the slave responds that the master would become so despondent over life that he would not wait three days before he followed in death.

Of particular importance for establishing the formal character of Qoheleth are two features of this text: the first-person voices of the two characters and the structure that supports opposite decisions by sapiential counsel. While the book of Qoheleth does not have two characters in conversation, the sage does engage in interior dialogue: "I said in my heart" (1:16; 2:1; 3:18). And bipolar opposition also plays an integral role in the structure of the book. Qoheleth will affirm a particular action, value, or belief as true, and then immediately negate it (cf. 3:16-22). The normal intent of bipolar opposition was to weigh the value of an action by examining various possible results or to get at the

196

truth of a matter by the critical examination of two opposing hypotheses.[11] Possessing wisdom and knowledge, the sage was to know the times and circumstances well enough to control successful outcomes for various activities. Yet the "Dialogue of Pessimism" places such severe limits on human knowledge that suicide is the only action where the results are sure. While Qoheleth also underscores similar epistemological limits, any thoughts of suicide (4:1-3) quickly pass in favor of the life-affirming counsel of the celebration of life (*carpe diem*—"seize the day").

These examples from Mesopotamian wisdom point to several features in common with the form and content of the book of Qoheleth: the first-person narrative voice, the voice's persona as a sage and/or king, the criticism of traditional wisdom by means of personal experience, and the technique of bipolar opposition. These combine with a questioning perspective in providing sapiential prototypes for Qoheleth. However, it is from Egyptian wisdom that the best form-critical parallels are found.

"The Songs of the Harper" [12]

H. Wheeler Robinson's remark that the book of Qoheleth has "the smell of the tomb about it" may reflect not only the document's preoccupation with death, but also its literary genre.[13] First-person narratives from Egypt that have their "life setting" in situations involving death include the "Songs of the Harper," grave biographies, and royal instructions. These three related categories of wisdom literature provide the closest form-critical parallels to the book of Qoheleth.

"Make Merry Songs" are a genre of secular songs in Egypt that occasionally entered funerary contexts. Here they were accompanied by tomb reliefs depicting a harper entertaining guests at a feast. In their original setting of secular banquets, they tended to question the belief in the future life, emphasizing instead the celebration of life in the present. In their adaptation to funerary contexts, they were altered in order to reassure the deceased that the proper mortuary rituals have been performed and that the gods were pleased with their devotees' religious service during life.

One rather striking song, found in the Papyrus Harris 500, does not undergo the normal adaptation to a funeral context, although it is found in this setting (*ANET*, 467). Originating during the First Intermediate period (2160–2040 B.C.E.), the song was later placed in the tomb of one of the Intef Kings. This period witnessed the political and social disintegration of the Old Kingdom and its confidence in the eternal order of *ma'at* ("truth, harmony, and justice") that permeated and undergirded creation and the Egyptian state. Also brought into serious question was the doctrine of the afterlife, especially as it was associated with funerary religion. This questioning spirit is reflected by the harper, for he is quite skeptical about the future life (Strophe I). By contrast he emphasizes the celebration of life in the present (Strophe II) and exhorts the living to "make holiday, and weary not therein!"

The parallels in form and content with Qoheleth are significant: the first-person narrative, skepticism about the future life (cf. Qoh. 3:16-22), the inevitability of death for every person, and the vanishing of the dead from human memory (cf. Qoh. 9:5). The harper also parallels Qoheleth in the emphasis placed on the celebration of life. For the harper, the living should "follow their desire" (cf. Qoh. 2:24-26, etc.), "place myrrh upon their head" (cf. Qoh. 9:8), wear "clothing of fine linen" (cf. Qoh. 9:8), enjoy the god's favor (cf. Qoh. 2:24-26), and fulfill their physical needs (cf. Qoh. 2:24, etc.). The harper affirms that the dead do not hear lamentation and that weeping does not save people from their descent into the underworld. Indeed, from death there is no return, and what people have accumulated cannot accompany them (cf. Qoh 5:12-16). The festive setting of the harper's song suggests a parallel with Qoheleth's repeated emphasis on eating and drinking. Similar to Qoheleth, the harper's song also combines first-person reflections with teachings based on personal experience.

Grave Biographies[14]

Even closer formal parallels to Qoheleth are provided by grave biographies. From the Old Kingdom through the Hellenistic period, these texts were placed on the walls of Egyptian tombs, inscribed on funerary stelae, and, beginning in the eighteenth dynasty, written on temple statues.[15] Placed in the mouth of the deceased and spoken in the first person, these biographies were presented as posthumous speeches addressed to visitors to the tomb. These life stories normally contained three literary features: an autobiographical narrative, maxims of an ethical import, and instructions and exhortations to visitors to the tomb. The autobiography proper included the titles and accomplishments of the deceased, while the maxims offered were the same that guided the dead speaker through life. Important themes were faithful performance of duties to the gods and to rulers, responsibilities to the family and other members of Egyptian society, including particularly the poor, and the expectation that the gods rewarded the "god-fearers" with health, goods, long life, children, a proper burial, and life beyond the grave. Often found in grave inscriptions are affirmations of the importance of joy in living: "follow the heart" (*sms ib*)[16] points to the fulfillment of one's desires, while "happiness" (*ndm ib*)[17] connotes satisfaction with life, a type of contemplative joy in which one finds contentment in what one has. In addition, the deceased often exhorted visitors to the tomb to reflect on their own death and requested them to offer grave offerings and sacrifices while remembering the name of the occupant of the tomb. The intent of these biographies is twofold: to demonstrate that the deceased have lived in accordance with the principles of *ma'at* and to make a bold case for admission into the afterlife.

In form and content, grave biographies bear the markings of traditional Egyptian wisdom literature, especially the instructions.[18] This probably results from the fact that the authors of the inscriptions were scribes of lower ranks who studied in the wisdom schools. Indeed, the "Instruction of Ptahhotep" even has features of a tomb biography at its conclusion.[19]

However, from the time of the New Kingdom onward, a darker, more pessimistic strand began to appear in some of the biographies. For instance, there is an increasing emphasis placed on the sovereignty of the gods, to the point that the gods act freely, without the constraint of retributive justice.[20] The more carefree and harmonious existence in the Old Kingdom was replaced with increasing doubts about the efficacy of official mortuary religion. This was due no doubt to the turmoil of the First Intermediate period, which witnessed the disruption of political and social stability. Some of the tomb biographies even pointed to death as both a time of great sorrow and loss and an entrance into the dark unknown. Thus the hope for the continuance of a good name, the remembrance of virtuous deeds, and survival by means of numerous progeny became increasingly important in the later periods.[21]

These later Egyptian grave inscriptions exhibit remarkable parallels to Qoheleth. The fictional persona of the narrator's voice in the book is that of a wise ruler who has experienced life to the full and is facing his own demise. Indeed, the intrusive, third-person voice in the epilogue provides a type of obituary for Qoheleth, summarizing his life in terms of the activities of a sage who taught people wisdom, wrote words of truth, and collected and arranged sayings (12:9-10).[22] Furthermore, the three features of autobiography, sayings, and instructions characterize the individual forms present in the book of Qoheleth. In 1:12–2:26, the narrator tells of his position as king over Israel in Jerusalem and outlines the major accomplishments of his reign. This autobiographical style continues throughout the book. Sayings are also present throughout the book (esp. 4:5-6, 9, 13; 5:7; 7:1-13; 10:1-20), while there are several instructions and exhortations to the audience on a variety of topics, including warnings to reflect on the end of life (e.g., 7:2).

Parallels in content to Qoheleth are especially noticeable in grave inscriptions of the later periods of Egyptian history. The growing doubt about the efficacy of mortuary religion, anxiety about death, and the dreadful state of the dead in this later literature find an even darker, more pessimistic expression in Qoheleth, who regards the grave as an eternal home where there is neither light nor knowledge nor passion nor activity (9:1-6). The stress on the total dependence of humans on the will of the sovereign deity in the later periods is also paralleled in Qoheleth.

The emphasis on the celebration of life in these later grave inscriptions[23] also has an important place in Qoheleth. Included in both are eating, drinking, lovemaking, a faithful companion, and children. Indeed, the celebration of life in these later Egyptian texts forms the major positive counsel that Qoheleth issues to his students (2:24-26; 5:18-20; etc.).

Royal Instructions

Grave biographies find their closest parallels in the classical instructions of wisdom literature, the primary genre of Egyptian wisdom. Present in each of the major historical periods, from the Old Kingdom well into the Hellenistic age, the genre assumed two major forms.[24] The first form usually included a title that provided the name of the type of writing (an instruction) and the titular and personal name of the teacher. The formal title was followed by a series of admonitions and exhortations in the second person, occasionally bolstered by third-person sayings. At times the first-person speech of the teacher enters into the text. On occasion the teaching concludes with an epilogue or an exordium in which the scribe who wrote the instruction or made the copy speaks both of the work he has transmitted and of himself. Two examples are "The Instruction of Hordedef" (*ANET*, 419-20) and "The Instruction for King Merikare" (*ANET*, 414-18). The second form inserts a prologue, or introductory narrative, between the title and the series of admonitions and exhortations in order to provide the occasion for the teaching. Examples of this more extended type are "The Instruction of Ptah-hotep" (*ANET*, 412-14), "The Instruction of Amenemhet," and "The Instruction of Amenemopet" (*ANET*, 421-25). The biography provides the occasion for the instruction. For example, Ptah-hotep, because of old age and approaching death, issues his instruction to his successor, who is soon to enter into the service of the king.

Royal instructions began to appear during the First Intermediate period and continued into the New Kingdom. They may have been part of the literary efforts designed to bring to struggling or very new dynasties legitimation and authority.[25] Two of the best examples of royal instructions are "The Instruction for King Merikare," and "The Instruction of Amenemhet." Placed on the lips of dead rulers by their successors, these instructions were probably read during the New Year's enthronement festival, which inaugurated the rule of the kings.[26]

Originating during the First Intermediate period (2160–2040 B.C.E.), "The Instruction for King Merikare" sets forth his platform of government. Merikare's father, speaking in the first person, instructs his son in matters of royal responsibility for the actualization of cosmic order in nature and society and in the details of how to govern wisely and successfully.[27] In addition, the dead king listed his own achievements and candidly admitted the failures of his own reign. "The Instruction of Amenemhet" was attributed to the founder of the twelfth dynasty, the dynasty that began the Middle Kingdom (2040–1558 B.C.E.). In first-person style, this king recounts both the circumstances leading to his assassination and the significant achievements he produced during his reign. The theme of loyalty integrates this instruction, with the dead king warning his successor to trust no one.

Two examples of royal instructions are found, at least in a partial form, in the Hebrew Bible: the Testament of David (1 Kings 2:1-12) and "The Words of Lemuel, King of Massa, which were taught him by his mother" (Prov. 31:1-9). In the first case, David, approaching death, instructs young Solomon on how to rule the empire. The setting is quite similar to that of the Egyptian royal instructions: the time of transition of royal rule. In the second text, the mother of Lemuel warns her son against the dangers of women and strong drink and exhorts him to maintain justice, especially for the weak members of society. While the setting is not given for this instruction, it would fit very well the time of the transition to the inauguration of a young king's rule. Royal instructions are similar to later Jewish testament literature, represented by such texts as "The Testament of the Twelve Patriarchs" and "The Testament of Job."[28] The fictional setting given for each of these is the approaching death of the patriarch, who wishes to instruct his descendants in the moral life.

There are important similarities among royal instructions, Jewish testaments, and the book of Qoheleth.[29] These include the royal voice of the narrator (Solomon), the listing of royal achievements (2:1-11), and the giving of counsel on a variety of topics. The difficulty in identifying the meaning of the name Qoheleth, whether an office or a personal name,[30] should not obscure the fact that the voice of the narrator is identified as Qoheleth, a king over Israel in Jerusalem (1:12) and a son of David (1:1). The clear intimation is that the narrator is Solomon. His is the voice that the author, a wise teacher, adopted for the narrator. While not explicitly named Solomon, the implication is that the narrator is this king, who in tradition was the royal patron of wisdom (see 1 Kings 3–10). Indeed, the royal accomplishments listed in 2:1-11 suggest some of those for which Solomon traditionally was renowned.

The fiction of Solomon as speaker is a literary device assumed by a sage who speaks in the guise of this dead king. The association of the book with a famous person (i.e., Solomon) follows the pattern of pseudonymity in which sapiential writings were attributed to well-known people from the past (e.g., the Testament of the Twelve Patriarchs, the Testament of Job, Pirke Aboth, the "Instruction of Ptah-hotep," the "Instruction of Amenemhet," and the "Instruction of Ahiqar").[31] However, the concluding postscript by a second narrator's voice in the third person ignores the literary fiction of Solomon as narrator and identifies Qoheleth with the author of the book: a sage who taught, collected, and wrote wisdom.[32] Nevertheless, we should not ignore the introduction's direction to think of Solomon as the primary voice who speaks. The author's desired effect for the original audience (probably students in a school in Jerusalem who are mainly preparing for civil and religious scribal careers) is to imagine an aged Solomon, long since dead, as the one addressing them from the tomb on the meaning of life.

Conclusion

The two types of sapiential literature that provide the closest form-critical parallels to the book of Qoheleth are grave biographies and royal testaments. Both create the literary fiction of a dead person who, speaking from the tomb, undertakes to instruct the living in the wisdom of life. The purpose is to ground the life of the person in the just order of the cosmos, to indicate that he or she lived in harmony with creation. On the basis of these parallels, the book of Qoheleth is best seen as the fictional testament of Israel's most famous king, who is presented as speaking to his audience either in his old age, shortly before death, or perhaps from the tomb.[33] This fiction of the royal voice plays an important role in the understanding of creation theology in Qoheleth, particularly in regard to the intersection of cosmology and anthropology and the role of the king in establishing and maintaining cosmic and social order.[34]

NARRATORS AND NARRATIVE STRUCTURE IN THE BOOK OF QOHELETH

Narrators in Qoheleth

In line with much ancient literature, the author chooses a fictional narrator, in this case Solomon, to serve as the primary voice that tells the story and instructs the audience.[35] This means that a second voice was responsible for at least the titulary in 1:1, the opening statement of the narrative following the poem (1:12), the occasional intrusions (7:27, "says the Qoheleth"; 11:9c) and the epilogue (12:9-14). This second voice in 12:9-10 leads through the fictional voice to the implied author,[36] who is understood to be a sage who taught people, presumably in a wisdom school, searched out and ordered proverbs, was concerned with the beauty of the language that he crafted, and had a passion for the truth.[37]

In the writing of this testament, or first-person narrative, the implied author enables the narrator to instruct future generations by selecting a variety of experiences and teachings that are primarily impressionistic and thematic, not chronological, and placing them within the literary structure of the composition. Far from a chronological, historical reconstruction of life, this fictional first-person narrative seeks to impose coherence and meaning on selected events and experiences by transforming them into a teaching about life.

First-person narratives, real or fictional, represent an attempt at self-justification—that is, to find something redeeming in the storyteller's life and experiences and to declare its meaning. It is a way of reconciling the self of the narrator to the world and to affirm that one has not lived in vain. If we move back through the narrative voice to the implied author of the book of Qoheleth, the quest of the sage to find the good in life through critical reflection on reality and testing by human experience issues forth from his own desire to justify his life, to provide the values that he has embodied, and to transmit something of lasting value to others. The fictional testament may even represent the efforts of the sage to live beyond his own finite boundaries, to speak to future generations through the mouth of Solomon. Indeed, the mind of the sage—the implied author—and the voice of the narrator often merge.[38] The discovery and articulation of the good through the voice of the royal narrator justifies the life of the wise author who has discovered and then lived his life in accordance with this central value.[39] By means of the fictional royal testament, the implied author bequeathed this value, this "good," to others, thereby achieving self-justification and, perhaps ironically, some measure of life after death. The authenticating of the "good" in human existence gains in stature and authority, because it is articulated by Solomon, the great king and paragon of Jewish wisdom.[40]

Literary Structure

The question of the presence or absence of a discernible literary structure in Qoheleth continues to be debated. Many have argued that Qoheleth lacks any real structure, and instead is only loosely held together by the frequent repetition of themes, words, phrases, and images.[41] Others have attempted to uncover a rhetorical structure for Qoheleth.[42] It is the case that the second voice indicates that Qoheleth did order sayings with great care to express an esthesis of beauty and truth (12:9), suggesting that more than a haphazard collection of sayings is present in the work. The following structure draws in significant ways upon the work of Addison Wright[43] and François Rousseau.[44]

Frame 1:1-11 and 11:9–12:14

Introduction	Conclusion
1:1 Title	12:9-14 Epilogue
1:2 Theme: "Breath of breaths," says Q.	12:8 Theme: "Breath of
"Breath of breaths. All is breath."	breaths," says Q. "All is breath."

1:3 Central Question: "What remains to a person from all the labor at which he/she toils under the sun?"

1:4-11 Two Stanza Poem	11:9–12:7 Two Stanza Poem
Cosmology (vv. 4-7)	Anthropology: Carpe Diem
Anthropology (toil; vv. 8-11)	(11:9-10)
	Cosmology and Death
	(12:1-8)

Internal Structure: 1:12–11:8

I. 1:12–5:19. Cosmology, Anthropology, and the Moral Order:
        Human Action
     Key refrain: "Breath (and a striving after the vital spirit)."
     1:12-18. Two-fold Introduction to Sections I and II

A. 2:1–2:26	Solomon's Accomplishments
	Carpe Diem: Conclusion (2:24-26)
B. 3:1-13	Time: Human Toil and Divine Action
	Carpe Diem: Interlude (3:12-13)
C. 3:14-22	Judgment and Human Nature
	Carpe Diem: Conclusion (3:22)
D. 4:1–5:19	Royal Rule and the Cult
	Carpe Diem: Conclusion (5:17-19)

     6:1-9. Interlude: Joy, Appetite, and Desire

II. 6:10–11:8. The Sovereignty of God and the Moral Order:
        Human Knowing
     Key refrain: "Cannot find out / who can find out?" chaps. 7–8
     "Do not know / no knowledge." chaps. 9–11

E. 6:10–8:15	Divine Sovereignty and Human Wisdom (A)
	Carpe Diem: Conclusion (8:14-15)
F. 8:16–9:10	Divine Sovereignty and Human Wisdom (B)
	Carpe Diem: Conclusion (9:7-10)
G. 9:11–11:8	Divine Sovereignty and Human Wisdom (C)

As Wright has demonstrated, the two poems on cosmology and anthropology (1:4-11; 11:9–12:7) and the repetition of the major *leitmotif* ("breath of breath," says Qoheleth, "all is breath") at the opening and conclusion of the testament proper (1:2; 12:8) provide the literary frame for the book. And the internal structure (the "moral life") has been properly divided by Wright into two major parts ("doing" and "knowing"), marked off by the occurrence of

204

two sets of key words: "breath [and a desire for the vital spirit]" in part I; and "cannot find out [who can find out]" and "do not know [no knowledge]" in part II. However, Rousseau also appears correct in arguing that the internal structure of the book is divided into seven major sections, marked off by the repetition of the *carpe diem:* 2:24-26; 3:12-13; 3:22; 5:17-19; 8:14-15; 9:7-10; 11:9-10.[45] These repeated exhortations focus on the central, organizing virtue, which the implied author has discovered. Separating the two internal sections is an interlude (6:1-9), which notes the abject misery of a life devoid of joy.

The genre and rhetorical structure are key to understanding the book. In Qoheleth we have the fiction of Israel's greatest and wisest king, presumably the one best able to master life and to know by wisdom the meaning of existence, undertaking the quest to determine the "good" in human living. This "good" is the organizing virtue for all other human values and the basis for the moral life. Thus there is something of a progression of the voice, action, and observations of the narrator in moving through the two sections, from "doing" to "knowing," the twin poles of the historicality of human existence. And the thematic verse in 1:3 emphasizes that the "good" issues from human life and action. Then, on the basis of what the king has learned from his experiences during his lifelong quest, he instructs his audience from the grave.

The opening and closing poems provide an inclusio that establishes the parameters for the quest and the subsequent instruction. Both deal with cosmology and anthropology, setting up these two elements as the twin frames for contexting, yet limiting, historical reality. The life of the narrator, as well as the existence of all human beings, takes place within the dynamics and limits of these two poles, cosmos and anthropos, or creation and death. Within the frame of the two poems, the internal structure features the historical quest of the wise king to master life and to determine the "good" in human existence. In this quest, Solomon, the fictive voice, engages in the two major activities of humans in seeking to live and understand the ethical life: doing and knowing.[46] And as we shall see what Solomon—i.e., Qoheleth the sage—discovers as the "good" in human existence is a highly valued, albeit relative, one. The "good" that he discovers is the *carpe diem.* But it is a relative good, because it, like life itself, does not endure. It, like everything else save for creation and the tomb, is *hebel* ("breath"), the major metaphor that construes the notion of impermanence. "All is breath"—that is, nothing endures, save for the cosmos and the tomb. Conceived in terms of literary structure, the historicality and linguisticality of human existence (life, action, and thought) are framed within the two constants of creation: cosmology and human nature. Philosophically conceived, human history is both shaped and limited by creation and death.[47]

THE OPENING FRAME OF THE TESTAMENT OF QOHELETH (1:1-11)

Title, Theme, and Central Question (1:1-3)

The thematic sentence that sets the tone and establishes the course for the entire work is issued in 1:2 and repeated in 12:8, thus framing the entire book:

> *hăbēl hăbālîm*, says Qoheleth,
> *hăbēl hăbālîm*, all is *hăbel*.

This organizing theme is formed with the superlative *hăbēl hăbālîm*, followed by the categorical, seemingly all inclusive, statement of the second line: "all is *hăbel*." The word *hebel* occurs thirty-eight times in Qoheleth and plays the central role in the key refrain for the first half of the internal structure of the book (cf. Wright). The interpretation of the book hinges on the meaning or semantic range of this word.[48] Generally, most interpreters have looked for one basic meaning of the term, though a variety of other connotations generally come into play at different points in the book. The most common definitions or "root" meanings given to *hebel* include:

1. "Vanity," in the sense of meaninglessness, emptiness;[49]
2. "Absurdity," i.e., a disparity between what is reasonably expected and what occurs and the irrational, which deprives "human actions of significance and undermines morality";[50]
3. "Absurdity," in the sense of what is inconsistent, unpredictable, and mysterious;[51]
4. "Ephemerality," implying that which quickly passes.[52]

While the semantic field of *hebel* in Qoheleth includes each of these elements, we should return to the original metaphorical character of *hebel*, consider its meaning in relationship to the ambiguous expression that is attached to *hebel* some seven times: *rĕʿût (raʿôn) rûaḥ* (1:14; 2:11, 17, 26; 4:4, 16; 6:9), and examine the implications of its meaning for Qoheleth's quest to discover the "good" in human existence.

The literal meaning of *hebel* is "breath." For example, in Job 7:16, Job wishes his pain would end, that God would cease tormenting him and allow him to die in peace, for his days are a "breath" (*hebel*). Here *hebel* metaphorically connotes the idea of evanescence and ephemerality (cf. Pss. 39:6, 12; 62:10). This appears to be the major connotation of the term in Qoheleth (3:19; 6:12; 7:15; 9:9; 11:8). For example, in 6:12 Qoheleth writes, "For who knows what is good for one while living the few days of one's brief [*hebel*] life, for he [God] has made them like a shadow?" "Shadow" is another metaphor for the brevity of life in the Hebrew Bible. Thus everything in human existence for Qoheleth is to be seen through the metaphor of breath: life, experience, activities, events, and human thought. This does not mean that other connotations do not often come into play in Qoheleth (absurdity, futility, and vanity),[53] but the root meaning that underlies the term, and thus human existence, is ephemerality.[54]

The root meaning of *hebel* as "ephemerality" also may be supported from the key statement occurring in 1:14; 2:11, 17, 26; 4:4, 16; 6:9—*hakkōl hebel ûrĕ 'ût rûah*. While this sentence is subject to a wide variety of possible translations, I propose the following: "all is ephemeral and a desire for (life's) vital spirit." Human existence and the accomplishments of mortals are ephemeral—that is, they are quickly passing. Yet humans still have the innate desire for life's vital spirit, the life-giving breath that comes from the creator (Ps. 104:30; Qoh. 12:7).[55] *Rûah* is the vital power originating with God that activates and sustains both human life (Job 27:3; Isa. 42:5; Zech. 12:1) and creation (Ps. 104:29-30). *Rĕ 'ût* derives from one of two words: Hebrew *rā 'â*, "to pasture," or Aramaic *rĕ 'ā'*, meaning "to take pleasure in," "to desire" (cf. the noun *rĕ 'ût* in Ezra 5:17; 7:18). The latter term is also frequent in late Hebrew.[56] Both meanings are possible. If one takes *rûah* to mean "wind" in this phase in Qoheleth, then "pasturing the wind" would suggest an act of futility and thus would provide a comparable image to that of *hebel* as meaning "vanity," "futility," or "absurdity." Hence life is as futile as attempting to shepherd (control, direct, harness) the wind. However, if *rĕ 'ût* means "desire"[57] and *rûah* is understood to include the God-given breath or spirit that activates and sustains life, we have the fundamental, yet tragic, paradox that resides at the heart of human existence and experience: the ephemeral nature of human existence, contrasted with the innate desire to retain the vital spirit that animates human life. If we paraphrase Qoheleth's larger expression, it would be: "all is breath quickly passing and a desire to retain life's animating spirit." Placed within the narrative experience of time in the text of Qoheleth, this theme emphasizes the unhappy fate of humans who strive for immortality either through accomplishments or through retaining the divine spirit that animates their lives. Neither is possible; they, along with their accomplishments, do not endure.

If the translations of *hebel* and the fuller statement "all is breath [*hebel*] quickly passing and a desire to retain life's animating spirit [*rûah*]" are plausible for many of the occurrences of the thematic statement, then we have a very important key to understanding the book of Qoheleth. Instead of essentially regarding all of life and its activities as meaningless and absurd, Qoheleth primarily laments the fact that life so quickly passes. This seems to be the emphasis in the concluding poem: Celebrate life during the heights of your powers, when you are young, for youth quickly passes, and old age robs existence of its vitality and joy. And then death comes to bring life to its final conclusion. Yet even in this context the metaphors for life convey its value: "the silver cord," "the golden bowl," "the pitcher at the fountain," and the water-wheel. This does not mean that Qoheleth does not recognize the ultimate tragedy of life; while there is the innate desire for life and its continuance, it is impossible to grasp and retain the life-giving spirit (8:8). Death is the irrevocable destiny of each human being.

The thematic statement is followed by the programmatic question for the first section:

> What is the *yitrôn* to a person in all his labor,
> at which he labors under the sun? (1:3)

In translating *yitrôn* as "profit," this question is sometimes understood to be a rhetorical one. Thus it is another way of saying that life's actions are without profit. Yet, this would suggest more the interpretation that Qoheleth regards all of life as ultimately meaningless. Another interpretation for this key expression is more likely. *Yitrôn* occurs only in Qoheleth (1:3; 2:11, 13; 3:9; 5:8, 15; 7:12; 10:10-11) and is usually translated to mean "profit" or "advantage." However, the term occurs in a family of Hebrew words that include the verb *ytr,* "to remain."[58] For example, in 1 Samuel 25:34 the verb means "to survive" or "to remain," in reference to those who would have survived a battle. Qoheleth is obsessed with discovering something that endures, that would enable one to live beyond the grave at least in human memory. It may well be that *yitrôn* in Qoheleth suggests not so much the idea of "profit" or "advantage" as it does "continuation" or "endurance." Thus he may be asking, "What continues to endure from the labor at which one toils during life?" This question serves as a programmatic inquiry that prompts Qoheleth to launch his quest to find an answer, a quest that is set forth in the internal structure of his testament narrative.

Introductory Poem:
Cosmology and Anthropology (1:4-11)

Following the introduction is a poem on cosmology and anthropology.

Strophe I (1:4-7)
4. A generation goes and a generation comes,
  but the earth stands throughout eternity.
5. The sun rises[59] and the sun sets,

and it labors towards its place.
There it rises.
6. (The wind) goes to the south and around to the north,
round and round it goes,
and on its circuits the wind (*rûaḥ*) returns.
7. All streams go to the sea,
but the sea is not full.
To the place where the streams are going,
there they return.

Strophe II (1:8-11)
8. All words become wearisome,
a person is unable to continue speaking.
The eye is not satisfied with seeing.
nor is the ear filled with hearing.
9. Whatever was is that which shall be,
and whatever was done is that which shall be done.
And there is nothing new under the sun.
10. Is there a matter of which someone has said,
"See this, it is new!"
It has already been in the ages that were before us.
11. There is no remembrance of former ones,
nor of those who shall come after.
They shall have no memorial,
with those who are later.

The introductory poem establishes the theological parameters for the entire narrative: cosmology and anthropology.[60] The two traditions of creation are introduced, yet radically altered from their usual character. Strophe I sets forth the nature of the cosmos. Unlike human generations, which are characterized by an endless succession of birth and death, the cosmos (*hā 'āreṣ*) is eternal (*'ôlām*).[61] With a more sophisticated view of time (cf. 3:1-15), Qoheleth may well move beyond his predecessors to understand that *'ôlām* conveys the notion of eternity. For Qoheleth, the one thing that endures throughout perpetuity is the cosmos. All else, save the grave (12:5—humanity's "eternal home"), is ephemeral. It is within these two frames of eternity (the cosmos, 1:4; and death, 12:5) that historical time, the temporal framework for human acting and knowing, occurs (1:12–11:8). Indeed, the temporal framework for Qoheleth is the movement from cosmos to history to death.[62]

The contrast in the initial poem between the eternal cosmos and the "generations" is significant, because human generations, like individual humans, are also ephemeral. They go and they come in steady succession, reflecting both linear (historical) and cyclical time (repetitive). Furthermore, the nature of the cosmos is characterized by the three active and moving physical agents of reality: the sun, which rises and sets; the wind, which blows on its circuitous rounds; and the streams, which run in an unending course into the sea. Light, wind, and water are the three active agents of the physical universe for Qoheleth. Yet, what characterizes them is their constant, laborious, and cyclical motion, which has no end. Since time for the endurance of the cosmos is eternal, the poem constructs an endless and cyclical time for the physical agents of motion. Some might take comfort in the stability and predictability of the cosmic order. But for Qoheleth the cyclical movement of the cosmos is wearisome motion that knows no end, leads to no change, and has no meaning.[63]

When examining this brief description of the cosmos, it becomes immediately clear that traditional creation theology is absent. Indeed, Qoheleth later speaks of God as creator, but in this introductory poem, there is a cosmology, but no cosmogony and theology—that is, there is no description of God creating or even sustaining the world. There is activity in the universe, but it is devoid of any observable divine providence or purpose. Indeed, God is absent from both the strophe and the cosmos.[64] God's causing the sun to rise and to set, signaling a new creation with each new dawn; the divine "wind" or "breath" (Ps. 104:29-30) that revitalizes the earth; and the providential sending of life-giving waters (rain, streams; cf. Job 38–41 and Psalm 104) are not even intimated by this strophe. These traditional features of Israel's creation theology are transformed into a more modern understanding of nature's seemingly operating according to its own inflexible laws, devoid of any divine involvement. This orderly movement evokes no human praise, but only wearies the human spirit.[65]

The second strophe centers on anthropology, especially the two major features of human nature: knowing and doing. For traditional wisdom, the three major senses (speech, sight, and hearing) are the divinely given gifts for empirical observation, rational analysis, and reflective synthesis. Through the proper use of these means, which parallel in number the three active agents of the cosmos in the first strophe, the traditional sages taught that God enabled them to observe the world around them, and through their experience to come to an understanding of themselves and reality. Indeed, reality could be shaped, life could be mastered, and well-being could be secured. Through these senses and the images they perceived, the sages came to imagine how to live and act so as to create a sphere of well-being in which they could exist. And at least to a limited extent, the sages believed that through their observation of the world they could imagine the nature and character of God. Indeed, the personified voice of God, Woman Wisdom, spoke to them and revealed to them not only the secrets of the universe, but also the will and actions of God.

In this introductory poem, God is not seemingly present in the workings of nature. At least God cannot be observed by the human senses to be active in the processes of nature. Indeed, through the activation of perception, humans search not only for God but also for insight into the nature of the world, an understanding of human existence and the world in which they exist, and ultimately for their own proper place in reality. Yet, the very process of shaping sapiential knowledge, which was deemed to be life-giving in its capacity to direct human lives, is now for Qoheleth a wearisome and fruitless activity.[66] Like the constant, unending movement of the three natural forces, humans continue to search for meaning and insight, but to no avail. They are no longer able to claim that the cosmos is made for the well-being of the human creature.[67] Qoheleth hears no divine voice in creation, revealing the meaning of existence and instructing him in the ways of life.

The second element of human nature, the capacity to act, is developed in verses 9-10. For Qoheleth, humans are driven to accomplish something that is new, unique in human history. Motivating this ambition is the quest for some type of immortality; in Qoheleth's way of putting it, the desire to establish a name that will last beyond their lifetime. This would allow people not only to achieve an honored and enduring place in human memory, but also to escape at least in a way the oblivion for which all are destined. Yet even the claim that something is new is false, for it has already been discovered or accomplished in the preceding ages. Due to the weakness of human memory, people have simply forgotten that the "new" thing has already been known or done. Entrance into the world of forgetfulness is the inevitable fate of all humans, even those who may falsely think they have accomplished something new and lasting. Ultimately, for Qoheleth, history has no value. Not only are even notable deeds forgotten due to increasing attenuation of collective memory, but also history, like the movements of the physical forces in the cosmos, is a cyclical and wearisome repetition of acts that do not cohere into a meaningful construct.[68]

The occurrence of one of the repeated expressions, "under the sun" (1:3, 9, 14; 2:3, 11, 17-20, 22; 3:1, 16; 4:1, 3, 7, 15; 5:12, 17; 6:1, 12; 8:9, 15, 17; 9:3, 6, 9, 11, 13; 10:5) serves in this poem, as well as in the entire book, to distance humanity from God. Indeed, the cosmology (heaven, earth, and Sheol) present in the book of Qoheleth almost omits any reference to heaven (1:13; 5:1).[69] The key text is 5:1: "God is in heaven and you are upon the earth." For Qoheleth, the divine world is impervious to human perception. Like God, this world is mysterious and remote. A radical gulf separates the human and divine worlds. Even Jerusalem, which is the setting for the Temple (4:17 and 8:10 = the "holy place"), appears to be desacralized in Qoheleth, for God dwells in heaven, not upon the earth. Jerusalem is not the *axis mundi,* the center of creation, securing order against the threat of chaos. Neither is it the sacred mount where God dwells and rules the cosmos (see Psalms 46; 48; 76). Rather, the city is the place of power where the royal voice once ruled as king (1:12), and where now the wicked practice their evil deeds and yet are praised for what they do (8:10). It is not the seat of the divinely chosen king, the son of David, who rules by means of God's eternal covenant (cf. Psalm 89).

For Qoheleth, the two spheres for human dwelling are earth, the place where humans live and act (the spatial context for 1:12–11:8), and Sheol, the end point of human destiny. While humans live on the earth, God is the tyrannical ruler who determines in secret the course of history. Sheol is humanity's "eternal home" (12:5), the one place to which all creatures go (3:20; 6:6), the abode of darkness where humans dwell without any conscious awareness (9:5-6, 10). It is the cosmic womb to which one returns naked (5:14). Humans are made from the dust (ʿāpār), and to dust they return (3:20; 12:7; cf. Job 10:9); and the memory of them eventually is lost. ʿApār is a term usually associated with the lifeless earth from which humans are made and signifies mortality and weakness (Gen. 3:19; Job 4:19; Ps. 103:14-16). Only the breath of God, the divine life-giving breath, animates creatures (cf. Gen. 2:7; Ps. 104:29). Indeed, ʿāpār is often associated with death and is a synonym for Sheol (Job 7:21; 20:11; 21:26; Ps. 22:30). Rûaḥ is the divine, animating breath that returns to God at death (12:7). Qoheleth is skeptical that one can knowingly distinguish between the life-giving spirit of humans and that of animals (3:21).

Finally, in a closure for the poem, Qoheleth returns to the succession of the generations, noting that there is no lasting "memorial" (cf. Exod. 17:14; Mal. 3:16) that humans may achieve, whether that of a great deed, a new discovery, or even a grave that is remembered and its inhabitant honored. If the fiction of a dead king, Solomon, is recalled, his royal tomb by this time may well have been obliterated and forgotten. Even the great achievements of Solomon will eventually lose, like his grave, their place in human memory. In the "Song of the Harper," the minstrel asks rhetorically where the graves of two of the greatest sages in Egyptian tradition, Ii-em-hotep and Hor-dedef, are. Ironically, the surviving fragment of Hor-dedef's instruction places special emphasis on making preparations for death by securing a tomb and having children to make burial preparations. Indeed, their graves are despoiled, laments the harpist. It is as though these savants had never existed. Qoheleth would agree.

The implications of an unchanging world and the inability of humans to affect in any important way reality in its cosmic and historical dimensions for understanding society are dramatic.[70] Social oppression is a datum of reality; the world does not operate according to the dictates of divine justice; and humans are not able to engage in acts that will confront and defeat oppression. Indeed, whether this is intended in Qoheleth's agenda, his teaching will essentially support the status quo of what even he recognizes as an inherently corrupt social world.[71]

212

COSMOLOGY, ANTHROPOLOGY, AND THE ETHICAL
ORDER: HUMAN ACTION (1:12–5:19)

Twofold Introduction to Sections I and II (1:12-18)

In the introduction to both sections, Qoheleth sets forth his titulary ("king over Israel in Jerusalem") and then announces his intention to use wisdom to investigate "all which is done under heaven"—that is, all divine and human actions. In anticipating his conclusion, Qoheleth observes that it is "an evil task that God has given humans with which to busy themselves." This ambiguous remark is immediately clarified by the observation that "all which is done under the sun" is *hebel* (ephemeral?), and yet is tragically motivated by the desire for *rûah* (life-giving breath). This means that all human actions are guided by two objectives: the creation of something that lasts and endures and the sustaining and lengthening of life. Certainly, these two objectives were at the center of the motivations that shaped the actions of the traditional sages. Yet, both are denied to human beings by the divine tyrant who determines success and failure, sets the life spans of humans, and sentences them all to the oblivion of forgetfulness. Tragically humans pursue what God denies them. This assertion of divine tyranny is supported by a two-line, parallel saying:

> What is crooked cannot be straightened,
> and what is missing cannot be counted (1:15).

The voice of King Solomon then becomes even more pronounced, emphasizing the superiority of his wisdom above all who came to Jerusalem and presented themselves before him (cf. 1 Kings 4:29-34 = MT 5:9-14; 10:1-13, 23-25). And his quest for the totality of knowledge ("to know wisdom and folly"; cf. the "tree of knowledge of good and evil" in Genesis 2–3) was also characterized by the "desire for *rûah*" (the life-giving and sustaining breath). The quest for wisdom in sapiential literature was often motivated by the desire for the abundance of life (both longevity and well-being). In Proverbs wisdom is personified as a goddess who holds long life in her right hand and riches and honor in her left (3:16). Also in Proverbs wisdom is presented as a "tree of life" (cf. the "tree of life" in Genesis 2–3) to those who grasp her insights (3:18). In Genesis 2–3 the Yahwist separates wisdom and life, depicting the primeval pair as those who foolishly sacrifice their immortality in their illicit desire for divine wisdom. The royal voice in Qoheleth follows the more typical association of wisdom and life in the sapiential tradition by noting that the pursuit of wisdom was motivated by the desire for life. But the result is similar

213

to that in the J narrative. The gaining of wisdom not only fails to secure life, but it also increases anger and pain.

Solomon's Accomplishments (2:1-26)

In Part A (2:1-26) of section I, the king describes his marvelous feats. Borrowing from the legendary accomplishments and wisdom of Solomon in tradition and lore (cf. 1 Kings 3–11), the royal voice mentions the constructing of houses (palace and Temple, 1 Kings 5–9); vineyards (Cant. 6:2; 8:11; Jer. 52:7); gardens, parks, and every kind of fruit tree (Gen. 2:8-9, 15-17; 2 Kings 25:4; Neh. 3:15; Jer. 39:4; 52:7); and pools (Neh. 2:14; 3:15). These most probably refer to Solomon's building activities on the sacred mount: the palace-Temple complex, replete with private and sacred landscaping, groves of trees, and pools of waters (cf. 1 Kings 5–9). Then Qoheleth outlines the fabulous wealth that he acquired, counted in the form of slaves, flocks, silver and gold, provinces, and singers and concubines for the esthetic and more physical enjoyment of kings (cf. 1 Kings 5:2-8; 10:1–11:3). He then claims his wealth and accomplishments, obtained by wisdom (cf. 1 Kings 3:28; 5:14; 10:7-9), surpassed that of all who presented themselves before him in Jerusalem (see, for example, the Queen of Sheba, mentioned in 1 Kings 10).

This laudatory passing in review of noble accomplishments and tangible signs of divine blessing echoes the grave biographies and royal instructions of Egypt. Prudent and righteous actions in traditional wisdom were thought to secure the stability and well-being of the cosmos and society, and they demonstrated that the deceased had lived in accordance with the dictates of world order. Part of the descriptions of royal accomplishments in Qoheleth and 1 Kings 3–11 reflects the mythological tradition of the wise and wealthy king, the primal man who lived in the garden, located on the mountain of God (Ezekiel 28). In the more positive formulation of the tradition, this primeval ruler experienced the fullness and abundance of life and well-being, though rebellion and death became another construal present in Ezekiel 28 and Genesis 2–3. Hertzberg is on the mark when he notes the similarity to the paradise tradition in Genesis: "The delights that Solomon creates are those of paradise."[72]

It is also significant to note that "the great works" that Solomon accomplishes break down naturally into seven sections, perhaps suggesting to the audience the seven days of creation in Genesis 1:1–2:4a. Each of the seven sections consists of a poetic line of two parts (i.e., a couplet):

1. I built houses and planted vineyards for myself;
2. I made gardens and parks for myself, and planted every type of fruit tree in them;

3. I made pools of water for myself to water the forest of growing trees;
4. I purchased slaves and maid-servants, including household slaves;
5. Also I had herds of cattle and sheep, more than anyone before me in Jerusalem;
6. I also amassed for myself silver and gold, the treasures of kings and provinces;
7. I obtained for myself male and female singers, and the pleasures of men—a great number of women.

In Genesis 1:31– 2:4*a,* at the end of creation, God judged "everything that he had made" to be "very good" (or pleasing). God then rested on the seventh day "from all his work that he had done." However, when the royal voice assesses what his "hands had done and the labor expended in accomplishing these things, behold all was ephemeral [*hebel*] and a desire for life-giving breath [*rûaḥ*], for there is nothing that remains under the sun." The one benefit he derived from his toil was the pleasure *(śimḥâ)* he experienced in his work. By the time of the writing of the book of Qoheleth (late fourth to early third centuries B.C.E.), Solomon's magnificent palace and Temple had been destroyed, his possessions and wealth were gone, and his lands and descendants had fallen under the rule of several successive foreign empires (Assyrian, Egyptian, Babylonian, Persian, and now Greek). He himself was buried in a tomb, most likely forgotten. Neither he nor anything for which he had labored remained. The king's sole benefit for all of his labors was the joy *(śimḥâ)* he had experienced while alive. And even this was ephemeral.

The king then turns to a comprehensive evaluation of human labor in general. He begins with a rhetorical question that might be paraphrased and expanded in the following words: "If even I, Solomon, have failed to accomplish something that endures and have experienced the tragic anguish resulting from the failure to retain the life-giving spirit, what could those who follow me possibly hope to do?" While wisdom has an advantage over folly, both the fool and the sage eventually experience a common fate: death. Both have the same desire to retain the breath of life, but are unable to keep it within their grasp. Both desire to reside in human memory, even after death, but each ultimately passes into the darkness of human forgetfulness. Wisdom's greatest promises—lasting fame ("name") and enduring life (Prov. 10:7; Sir. 41:11-13)—were seductive lies. Recognizing that both he and his deeds were ephemeral, the king came to hate life.

Also distressing to Solomon was the recognition that what he accomplished must be left behind to his successor. And who knows if that person will be wise or foolish? Having not labored for what he inherits, he nevertheless will rule *(šālaṭ)* over the world the king has built and own the possessions that the king has acquired. If the intention is to continue the fiction of Solomon's voice, then the audience would surely recall the folly of Rehoboam and the resultant loss of the empire during his disastrous reign (1 Kings 12).

Time: Human Toil and Divine Action (3:1-13)

The sages were concerned to come to a knowledge of the temporal order of cosmology and history, for this comprehensive structure provided the context in which individual actions could be guided to successful outcomes (Wis. 7:15-22). Distinctive in biblical understanding is the sapiential teaching of the "correct" or "appropriate" time for the acts of individuals (Prov. 27:23-27; Qoh. 3:12; Sir. 4:20).[73] In the wisdom tradition, event and time were inseparable. Actions were meaningful and successful, only if a judicious, moral event occurred at the proper time.[74] To be wise entailed not only righteous behavior, but also knowing the appropriate time for prudent action. Knowing when to undertake a particular course of action was the key to its successful outcome. Within the larger temporal order of cosmology and history governed by the rule of God, there are episodic times for every event associated with individual life.[75] While cosmic and historical times, as well as certain episodic events, are not under human control (e.g., the day of birth), others involving everyday activities are. Individuals possessed the capacity of freedom to shape at least in limited ways their own existence.

Qoheleth's initial poem (1:4-11) depicts two understandings of cosmic time: the unending endurance of the cosmos and the cyclical repetition of physical forces—the sun, the wind, and streams. As regards human beings, the same poem speaks of the steady succession of the generations of human beings, one following after another. Their labors merely reproduce what earlier generations had accomplished. However, due to self-deception they falsely believe they accomplish or discover something new. This view of time may not state precisely a cyclical view of history—say in the platonic sense, where the same individuals are destined to relive repeatedly the same events of their own past. However, for Qoheleth humans do simply repeat what earlier generations had accomplished. And he rejects any optimistic view of history where human civilization represents a steady and progressive march forward.

Qoheleth's well-known poem in 3:1-8 places episodic times for specific events within the larger context of cosmic and historical time: "there is a temporal order [zĕmān] for all reality [hakkōl], and an occasion ['ēt] for every event [ḥēpeṣ] under the heavens" (3:1).[76] In speaking of episodic times, Qoheleth lists fourteen pairs of opposites that comprise the major events of human life, ranging from birth and death to war and peace. Avowing a strong determinism in which God was ultimately responsible for all significant events within the larger structure of cosmological and historical time, Qoheleth's poem reflects the sapiential doctrine of the appropriate time for individual human actions. While the times for birth and death are determined by God, the other activities of life still reside within the domain of individual choice.[77]

The king then gives his own commentary on this traditional wisdom poem. His repetition in verse 9 of the programmatic question of 1:3 ("What remains to the laborer from his toil?") by now has become for the implied audience a rhetorical question. Human activities negate each other, and nothing remains. Qoheleth then examines individual actions within the larger structure of time. He affirms the sapiential doctrine of the esthetic, if not moral, goodness of creation by noting that everything God has created has an appropriate (*yāpâ*; literally, "beautiful") time for existing. This may echo the divine evaluation of creation in Genesis 1:31 ("everything which he had made . . . was very good"), though the word is *ṭôb,* "good." However, the problem for Qoheleth is that God denies even to sages any comprehension of the larger temporal order of the cosmos: God "has put eternity [*'lm*[78]] into humanity's mind; yet they cannot discover what God does from the beginning to the end" (3:11-12). Not only are humans unable to influence the course of cosmic and historical events directed by God, they also are denied comprehension of the larger structure of time (the *'ôlām*) within which these events occur (cf. 8:17; 11:5). God governs the world in mystery and power. Consequently, the correlation of episodic, human action with divinely determined times is impossible. One may only ponder, but cannot clearly know, what has gone before and what is yet to come. Denied the comprehensive knowledge of the cosmic and historical components of time and the course of divine events—in the past, present, and future—humanity is trapped in an opaque, mysterious, and ambiguous present, unaware of what may or may not happen. Control over events and their outcome passes from human hands either to God or to mere chance. One may only rejoice in the "day of prosperity" and learn from the "day of adversity" that God is the one who structures time and determines the course of significant events (7:14). It is impossible even for sages to know the appropriate time for episodic events.[79] Thus all actions are accompanied by risk.[80]

The inability to discern divine activity undercuts both the theologies of salvation history and cultic ritual, which represented and reactualized in sacred drama deeds of divine redemption. And the failure to perceive a coherent pattern for historical time, so evident in prophetic and historical texts in Israel, results in the fragmentation of experience and the loss of collective and individual identity. The human quest for identity and self-understanding within a common tradition requires the integration of temporal phases (past, present, and future) as a unity. Memory enables both the community and the individual to recall and sequence significant events from the past in order to explain the present. Memory allows humans to tap the reservoirs of tradition to find root metaphors to convey meaning. And the anticipation of the future course of history allows both the individual and the community to give informed direction to their actions. Memory and anticipation are creative acts of the imagination that organize and interpret experience. The individual and the community come to self-understanding through the narratives they construct. The incorporation of individual life within the larger tradition provides a meaning structure in which self-understanding reaches culmination and produces coherence (cf. Ben Sira's "In Praise of Honored Heroes," Sirach 44–50). Thus individual life becomes a part of the community's past experience, present existence, and anticipated future. The crisis for Qoheleth is the inevitable loss of collective (1:8-11) and individual (5:21) memory. With the loss of memory, experience does not achieve unity through time. Rather, experience fragments into disconnected pieces of isolated perceptions. All that remains is the immediacy of the present moment.[81]

Judgment and Human Nature (3:14-22)

Now Qoheleth contrasts the disconnected actions of humans that in no case endure with divine actions that are characterized by sovereign power and unending continuation. Indeed, this is the basis for the fear of God: the eternity and enormous power of "the God" contrasted with the impotence and ephemerality of the human. Furthermore, only God has the ability to "seek out what has been driven away"—the past, which humans forget, and the future, which they cannot anticipate—and to transform time and experience (past, present, and future) into a coherent whole. The tragedy for humans is that God does not reveal to them the direction of cosmos and history. Nevertheless, the mystery and power of God to shape the course of events within a temporal framework form the basis for human piety. Humans especially fear what they cannot understand, yet has the power to control their lives.

Qoheleth observes the injustice that characterizes human actions in the "place of judgment" (the court), a remark made all the more striking when one remembers the responsibility of kings for justice (Psalm 73) and their role in the courts as supreme judges (cf. 1 Kings 3). Qoheleth appears to reverse himself by affirming the doctrine of a time for judgment (3:16-17). This time for judgment of human affairs and deeds may be either the prophetic "Day of the Lord," an event within historical time, or the apocalyptic judgment at the end of historical time (at least the end of the present age), when the wicked would be destroyed and the righteous would be vindicated (Daniel 7), or even the priestly understanding of divine judgment within the context of the New Year's festival, when fates are sealed for the coming year. Whatever the precise meaning of judgment, Qoheleth quickly negates what he has affirmed.[82] God's judgment is no more than a divine examination whereby he demonstrates to humans that they share the same nature and subsequently the same fate as animals: mortality and death. Alluding to Genesis 2–3, Qoheleth argues that humans and animals have the same vital spirit (*rûaḥ*; see Job 27:3; Ps. 104:29-30; Isa. 42:5) and at death return to the same place: the dust (*ʿāphār*) of the ground (Gen. 3:19; Job 10:9; 34:15; Pss. 104:29; 146:4).[83] The term *ʿāpār* is often used for "death" and "Sheol" (Job 7:21; 20:11; Ps. 22:30). The belief that at death only the breath (*rûaḥ*) of humans returns to God, while that of animals goes down to the earth (*ʿereṣ*),[84] thus suggesting some sort of heavenly afterlife, is for Qoheleth idle speculation. Indeed, he often affirms that death is oblivion (e.g., 9:5-6). He does indicate in 12:7 that at death "the dust returns to the earth and the spirit [*rûaḥ*] returns to God who gave it," but this is in the context of the grave as the eternal home of humankind. In this latter setting, Qoheleth is simply noting that the divine breath, which animates human life, now returns to its source at death. Qoheleth's view negates the more optimistic tradition of human creation in the Hebrew Bible, including especially the exaltation of human beings over the creatures to rule as God's surrogate (Gen. 1:26-28; Psalm 8). Indeed, Qoheleth comes much closer to the more pessimistic understanding of a corrupt humanity in the Yahwist's primeval narrative (Genesis 2–11).

What is surprising in Qoheleth's views of time is the absence of or even any allusion to sacred time (contrast Ben Sira). With the negation of times that are holy, humans are denied the opportunity to enter and participate in sacred seasons and thus to reactualize salvific events of divine creation and redemption. Qoheleth notes that people do participate in cultic activity, presumably when they come to the Temple during pilgrimage festivals and perhaps the sabbath. But there is no mention of sacred time. Thus the reexperiencing of the sacred past through story and ritual and the proleptic realization of future salvation through priestly oracle are foreign to Qoheleth's teaching. Indeed, the loss of memory and the inability to envision the future would seem to enervate sacred seasons, not to mention the salvific acts these times celebrate and actualize.

Royal Rule and the Cult (4:1–5:19)

Now Qoheleth, continuing to speak as Solomon, directs his attention to royal rule and the cult, two spheres intimately connected in the Israelite understanding of kingship. Typically Qoheleth draws from his personal observations general insights into human existence. His often critical remarks about kingship are paralleled by Egyptian royal instructions and subsequently do not suggest that the author has now abandoned the fiction of the Solomonic voice. Certainly the criticism of the tyranny of Solomon's rule is present even in the largely pro-Solomonic narrative (1 Kings 3–11, especially chap. 11), and it is quite appropriate for a king to point out the failures and excesses of his own rule (cf. "The Instruction for King Merikare").

Kingship is a common topos in the wisdom tradition. While the sages respected and even feared the enormous power of kings and taught prudence and discretion in the presence of their royal patrons (Prov. 16:14-15), they ideally conceived of kingship as the institution that, being grounded in the cosmic order, sustained a just and prosperous society. The best example of this is the image of the throne being *yikkôn biṣdāqâ:* "established in/by means of righteousness" (Prov. 16:12).[85] "Established" (*kûn*) is a common term for the divine act of the creative securing of the cosmic order (Prov. 3:19-20; 8:27). If the preposition *be* is taken to be a locative ("in"), the saying indicates that the institution of monarchy is grounded "in" the cosmic order. If *be* is given an instrumental function, then the saying emphasizes that the stability of the throne (and subsequently the entire social order) is secured "by means of" the king's righteous rule (cf. Prov. 20:28 [LXX]; 25:5). Both meanings are probably suggested by this saying. Thus kingship, having its origins in the eternal order of the cosmos as an institution created by God for social order and well-being, is responsible for securing and maintaining justice and the consequent good fortune of the nation. Furthermore, the sages believed that God chose kings to rule, endowed them with wisdom and righteousness, and required from them justice (Prov. 8:15-16). The gifts of God offered to kings through Woman Wisdom are riches, honor, and most coveted of all, life (Prov. 8:17-21, 32-36). Being clients of rulers, the sages did not engage in critical reviews of kings and kingship.

In Qoheleth, however, the royal voice of Solomon makes itself heard in new and startling fashion. The greatest patron of the sages and wisest of all of the Israelite and Jewish kings engages in a rather stunning critique of royal rule, undermining the theological basis for the legitimation of the monarchy. What this royal voice observes is "oppression" (ʿsq), a term usually associated with the abuse of society's underprivileged and vulnerable groups: slaves, corvée workers, day laborers, the poor, widows, and orphans (Jer. 22:13-19; Ezek. 22:6-12, 29).[86] The prophets attacked the ruling elite for two reasons: They denied the poor and often defenseless members of society the justice guaranteed to them by torah, and they certainly extended to them no mercy or compassion in going beyond the protection of the law (Amos 2:6-8; 4:1-3).

220

God was often depicted in the prophetic traditions as the special protector of the poor, and would see to it that their rights, including access to food and other essentials necessary for life, were maintained (Jer. 22:2-5). Indeed, God was the one who would wipe away the "tears of the oppressed" (Isa. 25:8). Some of the sages were part of the power elite, while others were the clientele of the nobility. Hence, there is a less confrontational and judgmental character in their presentations of royal rule and social justice. Even so, an important dimension of sapiential ethics was to provide for the needs of the poor (Prov. 14:31; 22:16; 28:27).[87]

The theological undergirding for the social support of the impoverished was the affirmation that both rich and poor had the same origins: the mother's womb, where God was active in the birth process to conceive life and to protect each individual (Job 31:13-15; Prov. 17:5; 22:2). Indeed, sages were to speak out on behalf of the poor at court, while wise judges were to see that they were protected from abuse, for the divine judge is also their advocate (Prov. 22:22-23). Kings who oppressed their subjects could not expect a lengthy rule (Prov. 28:16). Behind the legal system were kings, and behind the kings was the righteous God who grounded the monarchy and its legal system in the just order of the cosmos. And not simply justice, but also kindness and compassion were to be extended to the poor (Job 6:14; Prov. 11:17; 14:21; 20:28; 21:21).

But when Solomon speaks in chapters 4–5, it is to articulate his observation of the oppression (ʿsq) of victims (literally, "the oppressed") by the power elite. And even more startling is his observation of the "tears of the oppressed," who cried out for mercy, but had no "one to comfort them"—that is, "show them compassion" (nḥm). Those negligent of social duty would include both the ruling aristocracy and God. Indeed, royal actions not only subverted justice, but faced no retributive response from God as well. Solomon's dedicatory prayer for the Temple emphasized the importance of justice and God's righteous response to the afflicted (1 Kings 8:22-61). The monarchy for Qoheleth, however, is grounded in an order of tyranny (kōaḥ, "power"), which includes oppressive rule. And standing behind the oppressive rule of kings is God. It is at this point that Qoheleth shatters the creation of humanity tradition by declaring not only that the dead are better off than the living, but also that more fortunate than the living or the dead is the "one who has not been, and has not experienced the evil deeds that are done under the sun" (4:3). This compares to Job's (chap. 3) and Jeremiah's (20:14-18) cursing of their conception and birth and their desire never to have seen the light of life.[88]

The king then articulates a series of general observations about human activity in 4:4-12. All human activity and skill, he affirms, derive from envy. A fool's indigence leads to starvation, yet contentment is better than incessant work. And a series of proverbial affirmations are made about activity and a

221

"second one." One may only pity the fool who works without ceasing in order to acquire wealth, yet is without someone (son or brother) with whom to share it. The support and comfort derived from human relationships are highly valued over loneliness.

In 4:13-16 the royal voice returns to his teaching about kingship. Here he speaks about the tragedy of a poor, but wise, youth who rises from a "house of prisoners" (prison) or a "house of revolutionaries" to the throne, replacing a king who had grown old and foolish.[89] Wisdom was an important asset of kings (cf. the charismatic endowment of the ideal king in Isa. 11:1-9). Ideally, this gift enabled them to rule in justice and to establish well-being for the nation. Age, of course, was seen as an important attribute in traditional wisdom texts, for one's wisdom and insight were thought to increase with the years. Youth was normally seen in a negative light, for it was the time of frivolity and foolishness. Yet, in Qoheleth's parable, old age led to the king's becoming foolish, and the youth was able to use his wisdom to gain the throne. This "Horatio Alger" story, however, does not have the expected happy ending. Instead, Qoheleth observes that the crowd who originally had greeted the youth's kingship with favor later found no pleasure in his reign. And there is, of course, the successor, "the second youth," and often the son of the foolish ruler, who waits in the wings, ambitiously ready to replace the new king on the throne.

If the audience does have in mind Solomon as the voice who speaks to them, David (a poor shepherd youth who supplants Saul and Saul's house to gain the throne) could illustrate the youth, and Saul could easily fit the example of the old and foolish king who would not take counsel. Solomon, of course, was chosen as David's successor, ruling as a youthful coregent prior to David's death (1 Kings 1–2). Thus the successor (literally, the "second one would stand in his place," v. 15) would be an indirect reference of the royal narrator to himself. But whether the royal narrator speaks generally about kingship (cf. "The Instruction of Amenemhet" and the theme of sedition and succession) or is alluding to his own situation, the point is still the same: Even a highly successful and popular king eventually loses favor with the populace and faces the inevitability of his successor one day taking his place. Success and power eventually wane. They, too, are "ephemeral," even though rooted in the desire for enduring existence.

In a royal testament from Solomon, it would be appropriate to have a section on the temple cult (4:17–5:6). The Solomonic tradition, shaped by Deuteronomic editors, gives significant attention to the building of the Temple and the inauguration of the royal cult (1 Kings 5:15–8:65). In his lengthy prayer in 1 Kings 8, Solomon emphasizes that God's all-encompassing presence could not be contained even by heaven and earth, much less the Temple (1 Kings 8:27-30). Here as elsewhere, the Deuteronomic school solves the problem of divine transcendence and immanence by stressing that God made "his name" to dwell in the Temple. He then sets forth the various situations in which prayers, especially laments and oaths, will be offered, asking God to hear these prayers and respond in justice and mercy. After the royal blessing upon God and Israel (8:54-61), peace offerings (22,000 oxen and 120,000 sheep), a burnt offering, a cereal offering, and a great feast ensue. In the Deuteronomic formulation of Solomon's speech, the Temple and its cultic activities are necessary for maintaining the covenant relationship with God, especially when Israel has sinned. Sin violates the integrity of the covenant, causes a breach in the relationship with God, and leads to punishment. However, by means of the cultic activities of prayer, blessing, and sacrifice the breach may be repaired and the well-being of both nation and repentant sinners restored.

In Qoheleth, however, a strikingly different instruction is given concerning cultic activity in the Temple. The king issues five admonitions dealing with sacrifice, prayer, vows, willful sin, and piety. In the first admonition, the king sets the tone for the entire instruction: "Be on your guard when you approach the house of God." Caution, understood as fearful foreboding, should characterize one's activity in the cultic realm, for it is the place where destruction, not life-sustaining blessing, may occur. This admonition is undergirded by a better saying: "to draw near to listen is better than the sacrifice of fools, who do not know that they are practicing evil." Now the wise Solomon characterizes foolish behavior to include the offering of sacrifices, and he counsels silence over the variety of cultic prayers (which would have included hymns, thanksgivings, and laments).

The second admonition more specifically mentions prayer. One should guard one's mouth so as not to speak to God in a hasty fashion, for "God is in heaven and you are upon the earth, therefore let your words be few." This may well draw from Solomon's emphasis in 1 Kings 8:27-30 that God's presence could not be contained by the sacred precincts of the Temple. However, the king in this instruction emphasizes the radical distance between the transcendent and unknown God and the world of human habitation. For Qoheleth, even cultic action could have no positive influence in leading to divine blessing, thereby directly contradicting priestly theology and the central emphasis on prayer in 1 Kings 8. And to return to the theme of this section, quiet discretion in the context of the holy, Qoheleth emphasizes that "a dream comes on account of much activity, and the voice of a fool with many words." Dreams were often taken as divine signs, especially if given their proper interpretation by cultic officials or apocalyptic seers. For Qoheleth, they are the result of too much work. Hence only fools (priestly interpreters and worshipers) speak often and long in the Temple.

The third and fourth admonitions deal with vows and willful sins of the tongue (lying, false oaths) respectively, two further examples of foolish talk. If foolish enough to make a vow to God, one is obligated to pay it, and in good time. It is better, counsels Qoheleth, in line with traditional priestly teaching at this point (Numbers 30; Deut. 23:22-24), not to vow than to vow and then fail to pay. And one should be careful to avoid sins of the tongue. Telling the messenger sent by the court (or by God) that the lie was only an "unconscious or inadvertent sin" only compounds one's guilt, leading to God's destroying the "labors of one's hands." Here Qoheleth returns to his theme of human activity in general.

The king's final admonition is to "fear God." However, for Qoheleth, the "fear of God" is not the humble recognition that the deity is the creator and sustainer of the cosmos who rules the world in justice, as it is confessed elsewhere in the wisdom corpus. Rather, the "fear of God" is terror before the powerful, divine tyrant who is able to destroy one's work and to take one's life at his discretion, even caprice.[90] Qoheleth's God is no compassionate and just creator who blesses his human creatures who worship him in the sacred sphere of the Temple. Thus careful speech, not sacrifices and repeated prayers, is indeed the proper decorum in the Temple.

What one now has from the mouth of Solomon, the builder of the Temple and the high priest who dedicates it with a great festival, is the repudiation of much of the value of cultic religion. Cultic acts do not order the cosmos, do not procure divine blessing, and do not bring society into harmony with God and world. Indeed, they are primarily acts of folly that may bring destruction, if the worshiper is not careful. God is far removed from the world of human dwelling, and it is best not to draw attention to oneself by a misdeed or foolish act within the sacred precincts. True piety consists of fearing the mysterious God who has ultimate power over each and every life.

In 5:7-16, Qoheleth returns to his theme of social injustice. In verse 7 he depicts a hierarchy of officials who oppress the poor, with each level of officials as corrupt and oppressive as the one immediately below. Thus there is no sense in making an appeal to a higher official in the hopes of just redress of grievances. Verse 8 is notoriously difficult to translate and understand. It could be that Qoheleth is observing the corrupt process by which the king comes into possession of a cultivated field. In other words, the king is the ultimate and final beneficiary of the corruption of his officials. Yet Qoheleth at this juncture does become the moralist (vv. 9-15), warning corrupt officials and rulers that the love of money does not bring satisfaction; that the only gain one has from wealth is not in its actual use, but only in seeing one's possessions with the eyes; and that wealth is easily lost so that leaving nothing to his son, one dies in old age a penniless man. How foolish it is, then, to have labored so hard for wealth, experiencing only anger, sickness, and resentment instead of joy (see 5:17-19).

Summary of Section I (1:12–5:19)

In this first major section, Solomon speaks about human labor, at times alluding to his own impressive accomplishments: the building of great and beautiful structures, the accumulation of wealth, physical pleasures, royal rule, legal decisions, the typical human activities that have their opposites, the success story of coming to the throne, and cultic activities. In every case the king concludes that each human activity and its results are ephemeral. Every action is grounded in the desire to master and perpetuate life, but this desire cannot be fulfilled. Actions guided by wisdom cannot guarantee success, and success without joy lacks value. Even Solomon, Israel's greatest king, could not master life, could not truly extend it through his labors, and could not expect to endure forever in human memory. Even the memory of his glory will eventually fade into the oblivion of human forgetfulness, a fate to which all are eventually doomed. The desire for the life-giving spirit, residing at the basis of all human activity, is not fulfilled. Nothing remains. All is breath.

Interlude: Joy, Appetite, and Desire (6:1-9)

Qoheleth now presents something of an interlude, situated between his two major sections on human doing and knowing. His initial topic (6:1-6), appropriate for this juncture, is joy—or more precisely, its absence. As noted earlier, his major observation to this point has been that the primary good in human existence is the divine gift of joy, which one may experience from what one does. What one accomplishes in life is ephemeral, even as one's own existence is likened to breath that quickly vanishes. Subsequently, the experience of joy, while also fleeting, is the single value that one may or, for that matter, may not experience. Qoheleth continues to remind his audience that even this ephemeral value is a gift, completely dependent on divine will.

At this transitional point in the testament, Qoheleth, speaking as Solomon, issues his reflection on the tragedy of the absence of joy. In doing so, he provides two examples of this tragedy. The first tragic example (6:2) is that of humans, to whom God gives great wealth, possessions, and honor—indeed, all that they desire—and yet does not grant them the capacity to enjoy them (cf. 2:24-26).[91] Instead, a stranger (*nokrî*), not even a family member or descendant, enjoys them (cf. 5:12-14). The second tragic example is that of the person who begets a hundred children and lives many years. Long life and many children are intrinsic values in wisdom literature. However, for Qoheleth, if the person does not enjoy or find satisfaction in the good things of life, then a stillborn child, who does not enjoy even a burial but goes immediately into the darkness, is better off. The stillborn is better off, because it experiences rest, than the person who, while having many children and long life, does not find contentment or joy. Using hyperbole, Qoheleth emphasizes that even if this person who does not experience the good should live two thousand years, the stillborn child who has never lived nor seen the sun is still better off. But, all in all, the same ultimate fate awaits them both: the land of darkness, Sheol.

The second part of the interlude has to do with insatiable appetite, the lack of advantage of possessing wisdom, the lack of advantage of the poor person who knows how to conduct himself according to wisdom, and the folly of limitless desire (6:7-9). The juxtaposition of this section with 6:1-6 is to emphasize that joy is not to be identified with the satiation of appetites and the fulfillment of desires. Neither appetites nor desires is capable of being met in satisfying ways. Even wisdom and an ethic grounded in poverty do not provide access to joy, the one satisfying experience in human existence. God alone provides this gift, which resides beyond human striving.

THE SOVEREIGNTY OF GOD AND THE MORAL ORDER: HUMAN KNOWING (6:10–11:8)

Introduction

Having investigated the major elements of human activity, Qoheleth now examines human knowing. He seeks to determine the scope, limits, and nature of sapiential epistemology, keeping in mind his essential question: "What is good to humanity in living?" But other elements enter into the evaluation: the possibilities and limits of wisdom, the advantages of wisdom over folly, and the use of wisdom in mastering life. However, all of these are subsumed under the acknowledged sovereignty of the unknown God.[92] As Wright has demonstrated, the key refrains for this section are "cannot find out / who can find out?" and "do not know / no knowledge." Obviously, this anticipates the major conclusions reached by Qoheleth in his investigation of human knowing. While there is no allusion to the royal stature of the voice in this section, it seems plausible to suggest that the fiction of Solomon as the narrator continues.

Divine Sovereignty and Human Wisdom (A): 6:10–8:15

In the introduction to this section (6:10-12), Qoheleth begins with a programmatic statement about the creation of humans: What exists is that which has been named. "Naming" is a common expression for the act of creation in the Bible and the ancient Near East (e.g., Isa. 40:26). Involved in this act is the notion that the name embodies the character and nature of what is created. God has named humanity (ʾādām), says Qoheleth—that is, God has created them and determined their nature, subjecting them to critical scrutiny and understanding by the wise (cf. Gen. 1:5, 8, 10, etc.). Human nature and function are open to the assessment and understanding of the wise. The characteristic features that Qoheleth chooses to emphasize is weakness vis-à-vis God; humans (ʾādām) cannot argue with one who is stronger than they—God. While it is possible that there is an allusion to the struggle of Job with God (cf. 9:13-19),[93] it is more probable that Qoheleth is emphasizing the radical sovereignty of God, who rules the world and determines the destinies of human beings. Thus Isaiah of Babylon (Isa. 45:9-13) points to the futility of the earthen vessel's (a human being) attempting to strive with and resist the potter (the creator). However, for Qoheleth the sovereignty of God is grounded in power alone, and not justice. Hence, striving with God in the form of disputation (cf. Job and the opponents in Second Isaiah) is doomed to defeat.

This description of human nature, emphasizing the weakness of humanity and the inability to defeat God with sapiential disputation, decisively shapes Qoheleth's examination of human knowing. Unlike Job, Qoheleth will not engage in disputation in the attempt to challenge divine governance of the world. Rather, the quest to find the good in human existence and to come to an understanding of the nature of reality will proceed with the acknowledgment of the radical sovereignty of God and the required subordination of weak humanity. Whatever conclusions Qoheleth reaches, he will not attempt to change this fundamental reality. He then asks two questions that, in similar fashion to the single question in 1:3, set the tone and determine the content of the entire section: "Who knows what is good for humans in living the few days of their ephemeral life?" "Who can tell humans what will follow them under the sun?" Thus Qoheleth begins his quest to study wisdom in order to determine the good in life and to discover the course of future events.

As one would expect from a sage, especially Solomon to whom are attributed proverbial collections (the book of Proverbs) and the ability to construct proverbs (1 Kings 5:9-14 = Eng. 4:29-34), this section begins with a collection of mĕšālîm (7:1-14): proverbs, better sayings, and admonitions. The key emphasis in this section is placed on the term *good,* sometimes used in the construction of "better" sayings—this is, "better" than or has an advantage over something else. Hence, Qoheleth seeks to set forth in the form of sayings what the "good" in human life is.

Yet, the first four sayings unexpectedly value death over life, the "house of mourning" (tomb) over visiting the "house of feasting," and sorrow over laughter. These sayings appear to be subversive aphorisms, sayings that have as their purpose the overturning of the conventional world view and its undergirding by the social knowledge of the wisdom tradition.[94] These aphorisms serve to remind people that the world is in disarray, and that it is not a just order where well-being is achieved by righteous actions and wise insight. With this destabilizing of the collection, the other sayings that follow, being more in line with traditional wisdom, lose their legitimation and authority— the rebuke of the wise is preferable to the laughter of fools; the sage should avoid oppression that corrupts his wisdom. Wisdom is deemed to be "good" when it is accompanied by an inheritance, when it protects its owner like money, and when it gives life to those who possess it (vv. 11-12).

In the final two sayings (vv. 13-14), Qoheleth's subversive theme of divine tyranny reappears; the proverbial affirmation that divine works cannot be changed by human beings is followed by the statement that God creates both the good day and the bad day. Hence one should rejoice during the good day and recall on the bad day that God is the creator of both; God alone determines the course of events and their times in order to prevent humans from finding out anything that will occur after them. Similar to the conclusion reached in 3:1-13, Qoheleth attributes to divine action once again both the structure of cosmic and historical time and the episodic events associated with particular moments. The theme of the sovereignty of God and the inability of human beings to effect change reemerges in a powerful testimony. With these sayings providing closure for the collection, Qoheleth successfully seals off and delegitimates the traditional sayings encompassed by two groupings of subversive wisdom.

Beginning in 7:15, Qoheleth returns to his more typical first-person narration once again to undercut further the traditional sayings about the advantage of wisdom in verses 5-12. Indeed, Qoheleth has observed a righteous person who, nonetheless, perishes in his righteousness, and a wicked person who continues to lengthen his life by evil deeds. Obviously wise and righteous deeds do not establish a sphere of well-being and protection for the sage. So, with a heavy degree of satire, Qoheleth warns just as much against excessive righteousness and knowledge as he does excessive wickedness and folly. It seems both can destroy! Thus perhaps it is only moderation between the extremes that is the way to achieve success and longevity of life! But best of all, Qoheleth mocks, the "god-fearer" succeeds above all others.[95] This is, of course, obvious satire.

Qoheleth then lists several traditional sayings (7:19-22), with the first emphasizing wisdom's value over many rulers. Yet, once again Qoheleth returns to his first-person stance to engage in a devaluation of traditional wisdom. Qoheleth tells of his own failed efforts to come to a comprehensive understanding of reality (both good and evil) through experience and knowledge. He laments that the effort to become wise was for him futile. Reality ("that which is") is enigmatic, incapable of being understood. No one can discover its meaning. His experience with the seductress probably is explained in terms of the general Near Eastern metaphorical model for folly. Dame folly leads to destruction and premature death (cf. Prov. 9:13-18).[96] Only the one whom God has favored escapes the destruction she brings, while the one not favored by God she ensnares. Only the capricious decision of divine favor saves one from the destruction of folly, not one's wisdom, which helps to make life-giving decisions. Returning to the assessment of human nature, Qoheleth notes that he has found only one righteous man in a thousand, but he has never found among these a righteous woman.[97] This number may allude to Solomon's 700 wives and 300 concubines. In any case, this is hardly a case of extreme sexist talk in which males are valued over females. The men in Qoheleth's audience could take little comfort in the superiority of their sex. In essence, the voice is saying that all are wicked, both male and female. In any case, Qoheleth did find as true the observation that "God made humans upright, but they have sought out various devices."[98] This means that God did not create humans by nature to be corrupt, and thus is not culpable for their wicked deeds.

Qoheleth once again quotes traditional wisdom sayings, this time concerning the importance of the knowledge and interpretative skill of the sage and proper obedience to the king, who reigns in unchallenged supremacy (8:1-5). Emphasized is the traditional wisdom teaching that the sage knows how and when to act in the presence of the sovereign so as to avoid his wrath and cultivate his favor. Qoheleth counters this teaching by contending that human evil burdens the mind so that one is not capable of knowing how to act so as to secure the royal blessing and thereby avoid the king's destruction. Indeed, no one is able to predict the outcome of a future course of action. And no one (not even kings, appears to be the suggestion) is able to control the life-giving spirit or to rule over the day of one's death. God alone has the power to give and take life, and to this power all people must yield. Qoheleth does not contradict the sovereignty of the king, though his power over human beings is to their detriment. But even kings must recognize God's sovereignty over them.

Qoheleth then turns to examine the perplexing issue of the delay of the punishment of the wicked, an oft-discussed problem in regard to divine governance of the world. He observes the burial of the wicked, who repeatedly entered the holy place (the Temple?) and were praised in the city (Jerusalem?) for their piety. While punishment delays in coming, leading to the increase in evil, and sinners prolong their life by wickedness, one day their day of retribution will come. They eventually die and are buried. By contrast, contends Qoheleth, the god-fearer will experience well-being, while the

229

wicked, lacking in true piety, will not continue to lengthen their days. Is this a traditional affirmation by Qoheleth, who refuses at this point to deny that retributive justice is operative in the world? More likely it is a traditional belief that he casts aside in the next verse (v. 14): Just retribution does not bring punishment to the wicked and reward to the righteous. Indeed, often the very opposite occurs. Divine sovereignty obviously does not include governing the world by retributive justice.

Divine Sovereignty and Human Wisdom (B): 8:16–9:10

Qoheleth begins this second, though brief, examination of divine sovereignty and human wisdom by attempting once again, with great effort, to understand the divine governance of the world. In spite of his best efforts, however, Qoheleth admits he has failed. And once more he anticipates his later conclusion. From his own failure, he concludes that no one may find out the principles of divine governance, not even a sage who may pretend to know.

He then branches out into a larger analysis of providence, affirming that the righteous and the wise are in the "hand" of God. "Hand" in Hebrew may suggest the idea of protective care, an image often associated with divine providence. More likely, "hand" in this context has the more threatening meaning of "power." This is a point Qoheleth has already made. In elaborating on this fact, Qoheleth remarks that one cannot be sure that coming under the power of God is a result of divine hatred or divine love. In any case, all humans share the same fate: death. Qoheleth places humanity within a series of bipolar oppositions, concluding that the people within completely opposite categories still share the same and final end (cf. the opposites in the poem on time, chap. 3). These oppositions include the righteous and the wicked, the good and the evil, the clean and the unclean, the one who sacrifices and the one who does not, the good person and the sinner, and the one who swears and the one who avoids oaths. Of course, the ultimate classification of oppositions is the living and the dead. Humans also share the same general state of wickedness, for "the hearts of humans are full of evil" (cf. Gen. 6:5). Restating the integrative theme of the lack of knowledge, Qoheleth contends that the dead know absolutely nothing at all. At least the living, by contrast, know they will die. This is the one inevitable outcome to life that humans "know." But knowledge of the manner and time of death's occurrence is denied them.

Divine Sovereignty and Human Wisdom (C): 9:11–11:8

Acknowledging that God rules the world in uncontested power, Qoheleth still allows for random chance. Indeed, wisdom is of little use to combat contingencies that may dramatically affect one's life. Once again Qoheleth denies that humans have the capacity to know "their time"—that is, the temporal structure within which events occur and more specifically the occasion of their demise. Thus humans, like the fish and the birds, are subject to entrapment at an evil time. Turning to a parable, Qoheleth examines another feature that severely restricts the value of human knowing: the caprice of human fame. Under assault by a mighty king, a city is saved from conquest by a poor sage, but no one remembers his name. Nevertheless, Qoheleth affirms the value of wisdom over might, even when the words of the sage are rejected.

In 9:17–11:8, Qoheleth incorporates a collection of sayings, many of them reflecting the tenets of traditional wisdom, most of them contrasting the sage and the fool, especially their different language and actions. There are also several sayings pertaining to kingship. Within this semantic field of traditional wisdom, Qoheleth's voice twice enters to destabilize this world of reason and moral causality:

> There is an evil I have seen under the sun. It is like an error which proceeds from the ruler. The fools are placed in many exalted positions, while the wealthy sit in a humble place. I have seen slaves upon horses, and princes walking like slaves upon the ground. (10:5-7)

This classic depiction of a "world upside down," in which the normal social order has become topsy-turvy, subverts the structured world of the sages, where the wise succeed and prosper and the fools fail because of their own stupidity. The absurdity of the present social order demonstrates the impotency of wisdom to steer a rational course toward certainty and well-being.

The second intrusion of Qoheleth's voice is in the concluding section, which weaves together sayings and admonitions (11:1-8). Four times the theme of "not knowing" emerges. The first occurs within the context of an admonition, exhorting the distribution of charity to many, thereby establishing a social network that may protect one from future contingencies ("you do not know what evil may happen on the earth"). The fourth occurrence also deals with contingencies and the inability to know what will succeed. This should not lead to paralysis; rather, the sage should proceed with a life based on wisdom.[99]

More significantly, in the second and third examples, Qoheleth subverts the tradition of the creation of the individual, which affirmed that God shapes and forms individuals in the womb, breathes into them the breath of life, and protects them in daily living (Job 10:8-12; Ps. 139:13-16). By contrast, Qoheleth depersonalizes the tradition with the remark:

231

Even as you do not know what is the way of the breath in[100] the bones in a womb that is with child, so you do not know the work of God who does everything. (11:5)

Obviously, the repetition of "do not know" points to Qoheleth's emphasis on human ignorance and divine mystery. Yet, by omitting any reference to divine activity in the shaping of life in the womb, the initial part of the comparison goes beyond the simple acknowledgment of the mystery of conception and birth. Indeed, the statement disassembles one of the central traditions of creation in the Hebrew Bible. The second part of the comparison underlines once more Qoheleth's conclusion that God determines the events of reality, yet such action cannot be understood, predicted, or known by even the wisest of analysts.

CONCLUDING FRAME OF THE TESTAMENT OF QOHELETH (11:9–12:14)

Poem on Anthropology, Cosmology, and Death (11:9–12:7)

The concluding poem provides the Royal Testament of Qoheleth its closure, balancing the anthropology and cosmology of the two strophes of the introductory poem.[101] The two themes of the poem are joy (*smḥ*) in strophe I and "remember" (*zkr*) in strophe II. In the first strophe (11:9-10) there is the seventh and final occurrence of the *carpe diem*, which, exploiting the creation image of light and darkness, admonishes the audience of students to rejoice in the sweetness of youth, for "childhood and youth are *hebel*" (i.e., quickly pass). In spite of the caution of a second voice in 11:9c, that of the redactor, who intrudes to warn the young against consummating their joy in unlicensed frivolity ("but know that God will bring you into judgment for all these things"), Qoheleth's counsel remains clear: Enjoy life while the physical capacities for celebration are at their height.

The translation and interpretation of the second strophe have followed two lines: an allegory of old age and increasing decrepitude, or the metaphorical description of physical decline and death in terms of a large estate or city.[102] The allegorical interpretation is often strained, leaving much to the imagination. The interpretation of the decline of a large estate or city follows a more literal and obvious translation. This decline becomes a metaphor for the decline and death of human beings.[103] I would suggest a variation on the second interpretation by proposing that this description represents the end of the world of human dwelling and nature, occasioned by the death of the human creature. Death returns history and the cosmos (civilization and nature) to chaos in a depiction that is quite similar to that found in Jeremiah 4:23-26.

The second strophe, found in 12:1-7, begins with a continuation of the *carpe diem,* but quickly changes in mood and substance: "Remember your creator [or is it "tomb"?] in the days of your youth," the sage instructs, adding the somber note: "before the evil days come, and the years draw near in which you say, 'I have no pleasure in them.' " The opening line contains a crux interpretatum (*bôre'ekā*), most normally translated as "your creator." However, this translation is questionable due to the plural noun ("creators"). In the oldest surviving interpretation of this text, preserved in the tractate Abot 3:1 in the Mishnah and attributed to Rabbi Akabia ben Mahalalel, one reads:

> Reflect upon three things and thou wilt not come within the power of transgression: know whence thou art come, and whither thou art going, and before Whom thou wilt in future render account and reckoning. "Whence thou art come"—from a fetid drop; "and whither thou art going"—to a place of dust, worms and maggots; "and before Whom thou wilt in future render account and reckoning"—before the Supreme King of kings, the Holy One, Blessed be He.

According to the Y. Soṭa [II, 18a], Rabbi Akabia is reflecting on Qoheleth 12:1a in this teaching and has in mind three similar terms: your well (*bě'erkā*), your pit (*bôrekā*), and your creator (*bôrě 'ekā*). "Well" and "pit" are metaphors respectively for the mother's womb and the grave.

The author of Qoheleth has carefully chosen a term that, through similarity in sound and spelling, would stimulate the imagination to think of all three. This is the understanding of the Mishnaic and Talmudic interpretations and is not an uncommon procedure in Hebrew rhetoric. If so, the resultant meaning for the poem would be as follows. First, in regard to "well" (womb), conventional wisdom and the creation of humanity tradition present God as both the father who produces the child and the mother who conceives and bears the fetus in her womb. At birth God serves as the midwife and then the caring parent who nurtures the child through life. This parent is the one upon whom to call for redemption from distress. However, for Qoheleth, God is not the divine parent who redeems his children from distress. In recalling the remark in 11:5, which mentions the breath of life entering into the embryo of a pregnant woman, there is no mention of the tradition of divine creation of the individual. Even the idea of divine nurture of the new life is alien to Qoheleth's theology. To "remember" one's origins in the womb, for Qoheleth, would be simply to remember one's mortality.

The second term, "pit" (grave), picks up a major theme in Qoheleth. For the sage, death is the final end of the human creature. To remember one's grave reflects a traditional wisdom teaching: One is to provide for parents and oneself a proper burial (2 Kings 9:33-37; Job 21:32; Isa. 14:19; 22:16). In traditional Egyptian wisdom this process was necessary for continuance into the afterlife. In Israel, it is a moral and customary responsibility to provide for the family tomb. Yet Qoheleth's use of the traditional teaching is unsettling. For this sage the visit to the ancestral tomb should give one pause, for it is here that one sees the eternal home to which one is called.

The third term, "creator," is also given a different and subversive context. In the traditional creation theology of wisdom and especially the psalms of lament, "remember your creator" involves the human and divine response to suffering. The congregation is to recall the mighty deeds and salvific acts of God, including the slaying of the chaos monster and the creation of the world, in order to establish the basis for hope in present redemption and to remind God to act to redeem his people (cf. Psalms 74; 77). For God to "remember" his people means to deliver them (Ps. 74:3). For Qoheleth, God is indeed the powerful tyrant whose power directs the world and determines the fates of human beings, but he is not the redeemer who enters into life to save the human creature. Thus, while the students are instructed to remember God, they should not expect God to remember them.

Following this opening exhortation, Qoheleth crafts a second strophe that divides into four subdivisions, all introduced by temporal adverbs or adverbial phrases common to creation texts: *'ad 'ăšer lō'* (v. 1*b*), *'ad 'ăšer lō'* (v. 2*a*), *bayyôm* (v. 3*a*), and *'ad 'ăšer lō'* (v. 6). In creation contexts these temporal phrases normally provide a prolegomenon to divine creation by describing primordial chaos in terms of what did not exist previously (cf. Gen. 1:1-2; 2:4*b*-5; Prov. 8:22-26; and the *Enuma elish*).

These and similar temporal phrases introduce the four divisions of Qoheleth's second strophe: the approach of old age when joy is negated (v. 1*b-c*); the cataclysmic end of the cosmos, signified by the darkening of light and the return of the primeval deep (v. 2); the end of civilization and the fertility of nature (vv. 3-5); and the final end of human life (vv. 6-7). Thus the poem captures the same movement of the testament: from cosmos to history to death. However, these temporal phrases do not introduce descriptions of chaos prior to creation, but the state of nonexistence following the end of creation. Here one finds the inextricable entwining of anthropology and cosmology in Qoheleth: The decline of human vitality and death eventuates in the decline and death of the cosmos. Indeed, creation is reversed; the movement is from life to death, from cosmos to chaos.

The inevitable approach of death (v. 1*b-c*) is the context for the meaning of the final three divisions. Thus the students are exhorted to remember their creator (or grave) when they are young:

"I WILL MAKE A TEST OF PLEASURE"

Before [ʿad ʾăšer lōʾ] the evil days come,
and the years draw near in which you say:
I find no joy in them.

For Qoheleth joy is the one gift of God to humans, an experience that derives from the celebration of life. Yet death ("the evil days") negates the capacity for joy.

With this introduction, the second subdivision (v. 2) moves into the obliteration of the cosmos:

Before [ʿad ʾăšer lōʾ] the sun darkens, the light, the moon and the stars,
and the clouds return after the rain.

This initial position of the darkening of light, the first act that negates the cosmos, echoes the creation of light by its separation from darkness on the first day (Gen. 1:3-5), though the creation of the stars of the heaven and "the greater and lesser lights"—the sun and the moon—occurs later on the fourth day (vv. 14-19). The darkening of light, signaling the end of the world, is a common motif in cosmological myths of reversal, prophetic eschatology, and apocalyptic (e.g., Job 9:7; Jer. 4:23; Amos 5:8; Hab. 3:11). Even the reference to the "clouds returning after the rain [gešem]" may suggest the flood tradition in which God lets loose the waters of the deep to inundate the inhabited world, bringing all life to an end (e.g., Genesis 6–9; Amos 5:8).[104]

The third division (12:3-5), introduced by the temporal phrase bayyôm (cf. Gen. 2:4b), points to the end of civilization and the decline of nature:

3. On the day the watchmen of the palace quake,
    and the men of strength prostrate themselves;
  When the women grinding the grain become diminished
    and cease their labor,
  and the women who look through the windows are
    in darkness;
4. When the doors of the marketplace are shut,
    and the sound of the mill becomes faint;
  When the fowl take to flight at the sound [of the trumpet?],
    and all the songbirds cease their singing;
5. They take their gaze from on exalted heights,
    beholding frightful destruction in the street;
  When the almond tree blossoms, the locusts take their fill,
    and the berry of the caper bush fails;
  For humanity goes to their eternal home,
    and mourners go about in the street.

The end of civilization and the failure of nature are graphically depicted in this section (vv. 3-5). The devastation is total and complete. The watchmen

235

who guard the city against surprise assault quake in awestruck terror, and even virile warriors bow their backs in submission before the unnamed foe. Several images point to the end of fertility: women cease grinding grain, and those who "look through the windows" (an image for fertility priestesses or prostitutes) are encased in darkness.[105] The birds of heaven are frightened away by noise (the trumpet's blast?), and the city no longer enjoys the sweet melodies of songbirds. The vegetation of the land is devoured by grasshoppers (cf. Joel 2), who fatten themselves on the blossoms of almond trees, the first tree to bloom in spring, while the berries of the caperbush, gathered in the fall harvest and thought to be an aphrodisiac, fail to produce.[106] This decline and end of civilization and nature is occasioned by humanity's (*hā'ādām*) marching toward their "eternal home," a common expression in Egyptian and post-biblical Hebrew for the grave.[107] And mourners who survive the holocaust perform their rituals of lamentations in the streets (cf. Jer. 22:18-19).

The final section (vv. 6-7) concludes the second strophe and the poem. Introduced by the temporal phrase *'ad 'ăšer lō'* ("before"), four striking and grand images are used to express the end of life:

> 6. Before the silver cord is taken,
>   and the golden bowl is broken,
>   And the pitcher is shattered against the fountain,
>   and the wheel is broken at the cistern.

These four images for life and its end are followed by a concluding line, which is taken from the creation of humanity tradition (see Gen. 2:7; 3:19; Job 10:9; Ps. 104:29-30).

> 7. And the dust returns unto the earth from which it came,
>   and the breath returns to the God who gave it.

With this climactic conclusion, Qoheleth portrays a dramatic reversal of cosmic creation that is occasioned by the death of the human creature. The end of civilization, of light and life, and the onset of eternal oblivion is occasioned by the death of human beings. Death issues a resounding no to all traditional theologies of cosmic creation, providential guidance, and divine redemption.

Theme (12:8) and Epilogue (12:9-14)

In verse 8, Qoheleth returns to the theme of the book. "Breath of breath," says Qoheleth, "all is breath," thereby fashioning his final closure (cf. 1:2). For Qoheleth, speaking as Solomon, human life, its experiences and accomplishments, are ephemeral. Nothing human endures, including even the memory of who has existed and what he or she has accomplished.

The concluding epilogue (12:9-14), consisting of three parts, was attached by an editor, who speaks in a third-person voice. This third-person voice begins by listing the major activities of Qoheleth: "teaching the people knowledge," reflecting on the meaning and value of proverbs, and editing them into a collection, "the sayings of the sages."

The narrator then turns to his or her own understanding of the nature and purpose of collections of wisdom sayings by using two metaphors: "goads," which prod one to action, and "firmly fixed nails," which provide stability and structure in life. The narrator then warns against speculative teachings that move beyond the guidance and stability of sayings collections. Indeed, while there is no end to the writing of books, the narrator concludes that too much study is without profit, producing not enlightened understanding and proper behavior, but weariness.

The narrator concludes with his admonition that summarizes his or her own understanding of wisdom: piety ("fear God") and obedience to the law ("commandments"). These two elements combine to form the whole duty of the faithful sage. The motivation for piety and obedience is divine judgment: God will bring every action to judgment, including even what is done in secret, both good and evil (cf. 11:9).

CONCLUSION: COSMOLOGY AND ANTHROPOLOGY IN THE TESTAMENT OF QOHELETH

Carpe Diem *as the "Good" in Human Existence*

All is not "gloom and doom" in Qoheleth. The literary structure of Qoheleth is organized around the sevenfold occurrence of the *carpe diem*: 2:24-26; 3:12-13; 3:22; 5:17-19; 8:15; 9:7-10; 11:9-10. In the first five occurrences, the form is that of declaration based on personal experience. However, in the last two formulations the change is to second- and third-person admonitions, indicating that the voice of the wise king moves from personal testimony and experience to the admonitory style of teaching. Admonitions are rare in Qoheleth, occurring only in the instruction concerning the cult in 4:17–5:6, the collection of sayings in 7:1-12 and Qoheleth's instruction that follows in 7:13-18, the warning in 7:21, and the instruction in 11:1-6. This counsel to experience joy and celebrate life represents what Qoheleth has discovered to be the single value in human living and, therefore, wishes to transmit to his audience. The interlude in 6:1-9 describes the utter worthlessness of life without joy. Negating once more the creation of humanity tradition, Qoheleth affirms that it is better to be an aborted fetus than a person who has wealth, possessions, honor, one hundred children, and long life, but all without joy. Indeed, these various items represent what the sages most coveted. However, for Qoheleth, even living 1,000 years times two is of no value, if these years are unaccompanied by joy.

In the analysis of these seven occurrences, one finds four themes. Most important is the joy one has in labor, living, eating and drinking, the lover, and youth. The second theme is that God determines whether one will experience joy. The third theme is eating and drinking, which probably includes more than the simple activities that sustain life. Rather, eating and drinking may well refer to the occasions of celebration, meals, and festivals, when human relationships are experienced in intimate ways. The fourth theme represents a series of caveats that impinge on the experience of joy: No one can enable a person to see what happens on earth after death (3:22); joy anesthetizes one to many of the experiences of life and makes one forget the past (5:19); excess may lead to a loss of joy or the inability to experience it; and the days of darkness (death) are many in contrast to the brief time one is alive.[108] Of course, the *carpe diem* is not itself lasting. Yet, if joy comes, it is the one experience that makes life worth living. If it is passed by and not fully savored, then life is indeed without meaning and value. While joy is a limited good, it is the only good in human living.[109]

Creation and the Quest for the Good in Qoheleth

In the book of Qoheleth a voice from the distant past, Solomon, patron of the sages and the wise king renowned for establishing and ruling a great empire, speaks to students engaged in the pursuit of wisdom. Issuing a royal testament, Solomon teaches a somber and sobering lesson from the tomb: All is breath that quickly vanishes. This is the dominating metaphor for Qoheleth's rendering of human life. The ephemerality of human existence and human accomplishments is made worse by the innate desire to retain the life-giving spirit that comes from God, but only for a passing moment.

Through the act of imagination, the teacher, commonly referred to as Qoheleth, enters into the persona of Solomon to give a rendering of God, the world, and human existence. The teacher focuses his attention on determining the "good" in human existence. In Solomon's quest to determine this good, the teacher composes a narrative testament embodying moral instruction that constructs a world offered for human habitation. It is not a comforting world, but it nevertheless is a new world view that calls for the transformation of the way that sages had conceived of God, reality, and the place and role of humanity. By entering into the boundaries of this world, the students of the teacher were offered another way of existing.

Assuming the role of a person renowned for wisdom, power, and wealth, Qoheleth engages in his quest to find the good in human existence. He shapes his testament in the major categories of doing and knowing—the historicality and linguisticality of human nature. These two aspects of human reality are couched within the rhetorical structure of the creation of the world and the creation of humanity. Within the rhetorical structure of his testament, the teacher brings under critical scrutiny the Solomonic legacy of traditional wisdom teachings in Proverbs and in particular their representations of creation. And within this same rhetorical structure, he assaults and fragments traditional metaphorical renderings of the world. But the teacher's efforts are not entirely nihilistic, for he seeks a transformed view of human existence within a new meaning system actualized by the shape and contours of royal testament.

Depicting cosmic order with the characteristics of rigidity and tyranny, Qoheleth separates goodness or beauty from righteousness. The cosmos, while beautiful, is not a just order deriving from the righteousness of God. Nature's daily occurrences of sunrise and sunset, the blowing of the wind, and the flowing of streams did not reveal a moral order or a divine purpose, eliciting the response of wonder, awe, and praise. Instead, the movement in nature is monotonous, unending repetition. Qoheleth affirms that all human activities have an appropriate time to take place. And he even allows for the possibility of a comprehensive structure of cosmic time that provides a temporal arrangement for the specific moments of various human activities. Yet the tragedy for humans is their inability to know both this larger temporal structure and the specific times in which certain actions are to occur. Stripped of the understanding of time, humans cannot possibly master life—that is, know when an activity is to be pursued in order to achieve success and to enter into harmony with the cosmic order. And there is a greater tragedy. God has placed the idea of this cosmic, temporal structure, this 'ōlām, in the human mind without giving humans the ability to understand it. Hence, the ethical life, the "good" in human existence, is not grounded in cosmology or in the attempt to live in harmony with a just and moral universe.

Qoheleth also rejects another traditional theological grounding for ethics. There was for Qoheleth a deep-seated erosion of confidence in the providence of God. One problem is the retreat of the creator into the impenetrable darkness of the heavenly regions. This *deus absconditus* remains in heaven, far removed from human observation, while humanity is on the earth where "the God" is absent but still rules with unalterable decrees. Even wisdom cannot mediate between the two cosmological spheres. This creator is not revealed to humanity in nature, history, divine commandments, or sapiential instruction. There is no divine voice in creation or in wisdom to provide human beings with the guidelines for moral existence. The other problem, in Qoheleth's view, is the creator's unchallenged use of power and even capricious disregard for justice. What order prevails in heaven and on earth rests only on the power, not the justice, of the divine tyrant.

Even social ethics fall under the weight of Qoheleth's indictment. Kingship is also based on power and caprice, not on justice. It certainly has no grounding in a righteous, social order or in the justice of God. The victims of social oppression have no one to hear their plea, no just legal system to redress their grievances and to sustain their lives. The kings themselves participate in acts of injustice and may fall victim to their own folly. Age does not necessarily bring to rulers wisdom. The government over which they preside is a hierarchical one subject to corruption. The power of kings is to be feared and respected, and the sage is to avoid the king's wrath and the possible destruction that it brings. But there is no call for social justice or prophetic condemnation of royal abuses.

Subsequently, Qoheleth seeks to ground his ethics, and the value of the "good" that is at the center, in anthropology—in human doing and knowing. Moral reasoning in Qoheleth is grounded in the desire for "the good [ṭôb] in human existence." The question for this sage turns on defining the good and then determining how this desire is to be realized. Thus he undergoes an intensive examination of human doing and knowing, both of which are assessed within his rather stark view of human nature. Qoheleth speaks of the mystery of conception, but does not present this mystery in the images of the divine parent or artisan who shapes the fetus in the womb and receives the newborn at birth. Using the metaphor of king, specifically the royal voice of a long-dead Solomon, the author subverts wisdom's traditional anthropology of humanity's going forth to master life and to rule over creation and other creatures. Even Solomon, the greatest and wisest of Israel's kings, could not shape and sustain a beneficent social reality through his actions and knowledge. Human efforts to achieve a lasting memorial were doomed to failure. Although Qoheleth does not explicitly use the metaphor of slave to describe the human condition, he develops an anthropology that is indebted to the "slave" tradition, which identifies evil with the limits placed on human knowledge and life and immorality with actions antithetical to righteous conduct. This sage draws on the tradition of the creation of humanity, particularly as it is set forth in the Yahwist source in Genesis 3 and Psalm 104. Twice Qoheleth alludes to this tradition to emphasize that the inevitable fate of all human beings is death. At death they return to dust (ʾāpār), while the animating spirit (rûaḥ) perhaps "ascends upward"—that is, returns to God

(3:16-22). At the end of his testament, Qoheleth does conclude that the "spirit" returns to the creator (12:7). However, he does not suggest anything more than the return of the life-giving spirit to the God who gave it. Humans are weak, sinful, and mortal creatures whose one certainty resides in the recognition that they are destined for the grave. Not the living world, but the tomb is humanity's eternal home. Death for Qoheleth is oblivion, the complete cessation of all life, when there is no memory of the past or awareness of the present. From this fate there is no escape and no return.

In a section that points to the wickedness of human behavior (7:23-29), Qoheleth affirms that "God created humanity upright [yāšār]), but they follow their own contrivances." Unlike Job's friends, Qoheleth does not associate evil with the substance of human nature, but with human actions. Humans are responsible for their own evil deeds and thoughts.

For Qoheleth sages have the capacity for a wisdom that provides at least limited guidance in decisions and actions, though few come into its possession. The possession of wisdom does not mean that humans will be righteous, for in the teacher's experience it is rare to find a just and honest person. The pragmatic value of obtaining wisdom and acting righteously is greatly diminished, seeing that no righteous, enduring, cosmic order is discernible to human perception. Even sages suffer the unalterable decree of death and the contingencies of life. While God has placed "eternity" (ʿōlām) in the human mind, it remained impossible to understand the activities and schemes of providence. Ironically, the increase of wisdom brings with it the liability of recognizing the absence of a righteous order and the utter futility of attempting to establish one in human society and even in individual life.

Nor does the search for wisdom lead to life in its various dimensions. Qoheleth undercuts the basic sapiential affirmation that the obtaining of wisdom results in life—longevity, happiness, well-being, and security, offered in Proverbs by Woman Wisdom. The metaphor of Woman Wisdom as the goddess who holds long life in one hand and riches and honor in the other has no place in Qoheleth. Indeed, for Qoheleth wisdom is unable to provide insight into the structure of time or the plans and actions of God or to discern any purpose to the nature of the cosmos. Denied the memory of the past and insight into the future, even the sage is unable to know the appropriate time for successful actions. The effort to obtain wisdom ends only in the increase of pain and frustration. While not abandoning wisdom, Qoheleth recognizes that it is severely limited in a world of divine fate. Qoheleth's crisis is one of the imagination. Access to the past through memory and entrance into the future by vision are denied even to the sage.

Even so, Qoheleth does not end his quest for "the good" in resignation. He counsels his students to "fear God," emphasizing that they should submit to the reality of divine sovereignty. Humanity is not the center of reality, nor are humans the measure of all things.[110] God, not humanity, rules over creation and directs history, though in utter secrecy. The temporal character of human existence is contrasted to the eternity of God and the cosmos. It is futile to attempt to use the meager abilities of individual power and knowledge to transcend human mortality and insignificance. These strivings result in wasted effort and are doomed to fail, for one cannot escape one's own finitude. Nothing associated with human being and doing endures. All is breath, quickly passing. Indeed, failure to accept God's unlimited rule of the earth and to acknowledge human limitations in wisdom and power could lead to the forfeiture of the one divine gift that is awarded to those who please God and make life worthwhile. This gift is joy. Qoheleth associates well-being with the human capacity to experience "joy" that comes from three sources: eating and drinking, the intimate associations of family and friends, and human labor.[111] Eating and drinking, human relationships, and work provide the only sources of joy that Qoheleth concludes are accessible to people. Yet even joy is ultimately contingent on the caprice of divine favor and destiny's unalterable decree. Joy may come to those who please God, but Qoheleth can find no way of existing that curries divine favor. Joy is a divine gift that may or may not come. Like life and its accomplishments, even joy quickly passes. Nevertheless, *carpe diem*; "seize the day."

CHAPTER SIX

"I Covered the Earth Like a Mist"

COSMOS AND HISTORY IN BEN SIRA

INTRODUCTION TO THE TEACHINGS OF JESUS BEN SIRA

Authorship and Historical Setting

The collection of wisdom teachings in the book known as Ben Sira (Hebrew), Sirach (Greek), or Ecclesiasticus (Latin) is attributed in the prologue to a scholar of the Jewish Law, Prophets, and other ancestral books who bore the name of Yeshua ben Eleazar ben Sira. The author of this prologue is Ben Sira's grandson who writes that in the thirty-eighth year of the reign of Euergetes (most probably Ptolemy VII Physkon Euergetes II, 170–117 B.C.E.) he came to Egypt to study. The thirty-eighth year of Ptolemy VII's reign is 132 B.C.E. During his stay, the grandson states that he translated his grandfather's book from Hebrew into Greek. Toward the end of the book, a concluding colophon in 50:27-29 (obscured somewhat by the addition of an appendix in chap. 51) is written in the first person. The author of the "book" identifies himself as Jesus, the son of Eleazar, the son of Sira, of Jerusalem. Finally, in the subscription at the end of 51:30 of Cairo Geniza MS B, the name in 50:27 reappears.

Ben Sira's collection and the testimony of his grandson indicate he was a widely read man of letters with an impressive breadth of knowledge. He was well versed in both biblical and Hellenistic literature.[1] It is likely that he was a wise teacher, a scholar sage, who taught and wrote in a wisdom school in Jerusalem during the early part of the second century B.C.E. This is suggested in his invitation in 51:23:

> Turn to me, O unlearned ones,
>> and take up residence in my house of study (*bēt midrāš*).

Ben Sira most likely taught in and ran a residential school in the sacred city that educated youths, particularly males, for a variety of careers open to affluent Jews of some means and considerable education (see the portrait of

243

the ideal sage in 38:24–39:11).[2] Indeed, in the description of the ideal sage, which may even be autobiographical, Ben Sira exalts the scribal profession above all others and then indicates that features of sapiential life and activities include the study of scripture (law, wisdom, and prophecies) and wisdom texts and language (proverbs and parables as well as thanksgiving), participation in public councils and assemblies, serving as judges, engagement in prayer and supplication, the transmission of the speeches of famous persons, attendance to great people, appearance before rulers, and diplomatic service in foreign countries.[3]

Based on the prologue, the mature activity of Ben Sira as a teacher most likely took place in the first quarter of the second century B.C.E.[4] The panegyric to Simeon II (the son of Jochanan and high priest from 219 to 196 B.C.E.) in chapter 50 suggests that this important Jewish leader had only recently died. And while Ben Sira appears to urge support for Simeon's successor (Onias III) during a period in which the high priesthood was the object of political struggle, the collection does not reflect either the rise to power of Antiochus IV Epiphanes (175–163 B.C.E.) or his persecution of practicing Jews.[5]

The grandson notes that Ben Sira devoted his life to the study of scripture (the threefold division of Law, Prophets, and other books) and the writing of instruction and wisdom so that those who "love learning" should be better able to follow the Law. Indeed, the language and literary style of scripture imbue the writings of Ben Sira in a remarkable way.[6] Martin Hengel suggests that Ben Sira may have held an important position as a judge or political counselor and perhaps was even a member of the gerousia, a legal body of Jewish lay leaders or elders given some authority in local civil and religious affairs.[7] Ben Sira may even have belonged to the Temple scribes mentioned in one of the royal decrees of Antiochus III (Josephus, *Ant. XII,* 138-39).[8] He certainly supported very strongly the institution of high priest, those who held this office, and the temple.

Ben Sira's work as a sage also points in the direction of the activity of a learned scribe who studies, transmits, and interprets sacred teachings from the past. One finds in Ben Sira two streams of interpretation of sacred literature that eventually coursed their way into two different reservoirs of hermeneutical activity: "inspired" prophecy centered in the Law and the Prophets (see the Essenes, Zealots, and early Christians) and a more scribal approach with particular exegetical methods and principles taking shape within what became Rabbinic Judaism.[9]

The references to Ben Sira, however, should not lead to the disputable conclusion that everything in the book is written by or reflective of only the individual thoughts and values of this one sage. Wisdom literature in general, including the materials put together in Ben Sira, is largely traditional and often expressive of the values and beliefs of a sapiential school and perhaps even a larger Jewish community.

The period in which Ben Sira lived was an uneasy time that served as a prelude to Syrian persecution and Jewish revolution. Hellenization was a program of cultural synthesis, originating with Alexander the Great (336–323 B.C.E.) and designed to unify the polyglot of nations and cultures brought under Greek hegemony through wars of conquest. After struggles among Alexander's successors for control of different parts of his far-flung empire, Palestine finally fell in 301 B.C.E. under the sway of the Ptolemies, whose rule, centered in Alexandria, Egypt, continued over the Jews for a century. Their policy toward Palestinian Jews seemed to be largely one of benign rule, as long as they were dutiful citizens, and not contentious troublemakers. An aristocratic priesthood in Jerusalem practiced a good deal of local religious and social control, though a military governor supported by armed forces administered the country and had supreme military and civil power. The times were prosperous and peaceful.

The situation began to change when the Seleucid kingdom, centered in Antioch, came into control of Palestine during the reign of Antiochus III (223–187 B.C.E.) when he defeated the Egyptians in 198 B.C.E. at Panium (Caesarea Phillippi in northern Galilee). The Jews even supported the efforts of Antiochus III, who expressed his gratitude by granting certain permanent tax exemptions to Temple personnel, offering a three-year tax exemption to all Jews and reducing their tribute. Religious tolerance was practiced, thus allowing Jews to follow freely their own laws. Following the assassination of Antiochus III, his son Seleucus IV Philopator (187–175 B.C.E.) came to the throne. While he continued the same policies of his father toward the Jews, he did pillage the Temple treasury in Jerusalem (2 Macc. 3:4-40). The Ptolemies and Seleucids both pursued a policy of Hellenization. But it was not until the Seleucid ruler Antiochus IV Epiphanes (175–164 B.C.E.) assumed the throne following the assassination of his brother, Seleucus IV, that active and militant force was used to coerce people within his kingdom to abandon native religions and customs in favor of Hellenistic culture. The fact that some tensions with Greek (particularly Seleucid) rule were developing, however, may be surmised from the prayer of Ben Sira in 36:1-22, which calls upon God to bring judgment and retribution against the foreign people. Furthermore, the nationalistic epic in chapters 44–50, which traces Jewish history from the ancestors to Simeon II, contends that Second Temple Judaism is the divinely directed culmination of creation and human history.

The office of high priest was contested during the period immediately following the death of Simeon II in 196 B.C.E. Onias III succeeded to the position, though his brother Jason, promising to carry out a program of

Hellenization among the Jews, bribed Antiochus IV with 360 talents of silver to give the post to him (2 Macc. 4:7-16). However, after holding the office only three years, Jason was removed when Menelaus purchased it with a larger bribe (2 Macc. 4:23-26). Several passages in Ben Sira suggest some growing concern with the disputes developing over the high priestly office, though there is no indication that matters had yet deteriorated to the point of the forced abdication of Onias III (7:4-7; 45:26f.; and 50:1-21).

This selling of the high priesthood to the highest bidder was only a prelude to a wholesale persecution of religious Jews who, in the effort to practice their traditional religion and customs, rejected many features of Hellenization. Angered and determined to end the practice of Judaism, Antiochus IV forbade the observance of Jewish festivals and the sabbath, the offering of sacrifices, circumcision, and dietary laws. The "abomination of abominations" (Dan. 8:13; 9:27; 11:31; 12:11) was the setting up of an idol of the Olympian Zeus over the altar of holocausts in the Jerusalem Temple in 167 B.C.E. These acts of persecution precipitated the Maccabean revolt, which led to the establishment of an independent Jewish state, ruled by the Maccabees.

These dark times of persecution and rebellion are not reflected in traditions of Ben Sira, though there are tensions with political powers (4:26-27; 8:1). In addition, Ben Sira's teachings, whether his own or those of the larger sapiential community to which he belonged, reflect some of the tension between openness to Hellenism and a conservative affirmation of more traditional Judaism.[10] On the one hand, there are in Ben Sira traditional emphases on the Torah as the authoritative basis for Jewish life, Israel's sacred history, and the theocratic character of postexilic Judaism most clearly expressed in the Temple and its worship along with the important religious and political role of the high priest. On the other hand, Hellenistic culture, including the ideals of *paideia* ("learning"), Greek values, and the social organization of the Hellenistic city, are also present in Ben Sira. This tension is not so much an external one between a conservative Ben Sira and a liberal Hellenistic Jewish aristocracy. Rather, the tension is more internal to the tradition Ben Sira helps to shape. What he attempts is the forging of a somewhat uneasy synthesis between older Israelite and Jewish wisdom and Hellenistic *paideia*.[11] Indeed, the universal character and liberal spirit of Israelite and Jewish wisdom especially enabled traditional Judaism to engage constructively Hellenism. This engagement is at work in Ben Sira's collection that seeks to bring Judaism and Hellenism into a constructive, if not always compatible, relationship.

The Text of Ben Sira

While we know that Ben Sira originally wrote in Hebrew, the textual history of this book of fifty-one chapters is extremely complicated.[12] The Greek translation (Septuagint) has two major recensions: a short text (GI) and a longer expanded one (GII). The Hebrew text is preserved in part (a little over two-thirds) in five or six different Cairo Genizah[13] manuscripts (A, B, C, D, E, and possibly F), fragments from Qumran (2Q18; 11QPsa), and a lengthy section (39:27–44:71) found at Masada (M). These Hebrew texts also point to two different recensions: a short text (HTI) and a longer, expanded text (HTII). The translations of texts that follow will necessarily be based on an eclectic, textual critical approach, while chapter and verse designations follow the system of the critical Greek text of the Göttingen Septuagint, established by J. Ziegler.[14]

Literary Character

The final form of the book of Ben Sira consists of three major sections: 1–24, 25–43, and 44–51. Each of these sections concludes with a poem or psalm: 24 (a hymn of wisdom's self-praise), 42:15–43:33 (a hymn on creation), and 51:13-30 (a poem describing Ben Sira's search for wisdom). The concluding chapter (51) also encompasses and unites the three sections: Ben Sira's prayer of thanksgiving for Yahweh's deliverance (vv. 1-12); the call to his audience to give thanks to Yahweh for his salvific deeds, issuing forth from his mercy, which "endures forever" (present in the Hebrew); and a description of his own successful quest to find wisdom, which becomes the basis for his invitation to enter his school (vv. 13-30).

In addition to the larger rhetorical structure, one finds a wide assortment of traditional wisdom forms common to earlier wisdom texts, especially proverbs, broaching a large number of topics.[15] There are sections of sayings and instructions that focus on a single topic at greater length than is normally the case in Proverbs (e.g., Sir. 13:1–14:2 handles the topic of "rich and poor"). The epic poem on the "praise of famous men," modeled on the Greek *enconium,* is found in 44–50.[16] Finally, a variety of other forms makes its way into the literary expression of Ben Sira's teachings, including those more common to the prophets and the psalms.[17] One would expect a variety of literary forms to make its way into a text composed by a sage who, along with other scribes of the period, saw himself as both interpreter and tradent of scripture.

CREATION AND WISDOM IN BEN SIRA

The Origin and Gift of Wisdom (Sir. 1:1-10)

This poem on wisdom and creation, preserved in Greek and not Hebrew, introduces the book by focusing on its most important theme (cf. the poems on personified wisdom: 4:11-19; 6:18-31; 14:20–15:10; 24). Indeed, this poem's emphasis on wisdom and creation matches well the one on wisdom, which concluded the first section (chap. 24), and the one on creation in 42:15–43:33, which concludes the second part of the book. These two poems provide a striking inclusio that underscores wisdom and creation as the major subject and integrating theological theme of the first two sections of the book.

This initial poem makes several important, related assertions about wisdom and creation that will reverberate throughout the entire writing and provide its most important thematic coherence: Wisdom originates with God, who created her before all other things; cosmic Wisdom is identified with both the revelatory word of God and the divine commandments of the Torah; only God comprehends the mystery and expanse of Wisdom; and the Wisdom that shapes and then permeates all creation is a divine gift to those who love God.

Wisdom and Creation (1:1-10)

1. All wisdom is from the Lord
    and is with him for ever.
2. Who can count the sand of the sea,
    the rain drops, or the days of eternity?
3. Who can measure heaven's height,
    earth's broad expanse, the underworld, and wisdom?
4. Wisdom was created before all things,
    and prudent understanding has existed from of old.
5. Wisdom's source is God's word in the heights,
    and her ways are the eternal commandments.
6. To whom has Wisdom's root been revealed?
    And who has known her clever deeds?
7. To whom has the knowledge about Wisdom been made manifest?
    And who has realized her wealth of experience?
8. There is one who is wise, exceedingly terrible,
    sitting upon his throne.
9. The Lord is he who created her,
    he beheld and apportioned her,
    he poured her out upon all his works.
10. She resides with all flesh according to his gift,
    and he generously has given her to those who love him.
    The love of the Lord is Wisdom that makes noble,
    he gives her to those to whom he appears, enabling
    them to see him.[18]

Counting the additions from the expanded Greek text, the literary structure of this poem is built upon four questions, found in verses 2, 3, 6, and 7, the first two asking about the incomprehensible and vast nature of creation and the last two about the knowledge of Wisdom, in particular her origins and activities. The answers are given in verses 8-10: Wisdom, the key to understanding the cosmos, is known in her totality only by God. He is the one who is "exceedingly wise" sitting on the divine throne. This cosmic ruler is the creator and designer of Wisdom and pours her out over all creation. Yet, this divine, cosmic Wisdom is imparted only to those who love God, making known at least some of the secrets of creation and divine activity to the sages. The larger framework of the poem is constructed on the foundation of this question-and-answer form. Assuming the character of a hymn of praise, the poem consists of two strophes: Wisdom's origins and presence with God (vv. 1-4); and the gift of Wisdom to the lovers of God (vv. 6, 8-10*ab*). The first strophe was expanded in GII by the addition of verse 5, while the second grew with the addition of verses 7 and 10*cd*. The dominant theme of the poem, and indeed of the entire book, is Wisdom, an attribute of God here personified as a woman.[19]

This poem on wisdom and creation borrows significantly from two earlier sapiential poems: Proverbs 8:22-31 and Job 28. In Proverbs 8:22-31, God created Wisdom before all other things; Wisdom was present at creation, and perhaps was even the divine instrument that shaped all things. The inability of humans to find Wisdom and her presence with the God who created her are central themes to Job 28.[20] These two poems are combined by Ben Sira to form a new and compelling statement on wisdom and creation.

God permeates all creation with Wisdom. This pouring out of preexistent Wisdom over all creation points to the understanding that life-giving, divine Wisdom supports and sustains an orderly cosmos that is open to the imagination and perception. Through meditation and studied reflection on creation, the sages come to an understanding of the nature and character of God. Divine Wisdom's sustaining of life is grounded in the beneficence of God toward creation. The same Wisdom that infuses all of God's works of creation and providence is offered to those who love God.

Ben Sira identifies Wisdom with the word of God, in this case primarily understood as the spoken word that brought creation into existence (Gen. 1:1–2:4*a*; Psalm 33). The metaphor of word in creation texts points to the power of divine language that actualizes the contours of forms taking shape in God's imagination. The classical texts that speak of creation by the word point to an orderly structure, a cosmos originating through divine imagination, which is open to human comprehension. The power of language brings into existence what the creator has envisioned in his mind. Yet, the imagery of the word also bears the connotation of life creating and life giving. The life-giving spirit (*rûaḥ*) comes forth from God's mouth and gives existence to all creation (Psalm 104), while the breath (*nešāmâ*) of the creator animates the living creature (*nepeš ḥayyâ*; Gen. 2:7). Finally, the word of God also points to the formulation of law and the rendering of judgment that order and maintain creation and direct human history. In Ben Sira's poem, then, personified Wisdom is the creative language that brings reality into existence, the life-giving word that gives vitality and being to creation and creatures, and the legal decree that orders and regulates creation and human history.

This poem identifies Wisdom with the "eternal commandments" that for Ben Sira undoubtedly comprise the Torah or at least the legal statutes in the Books of Moses.[21] There are, of course, wisdom texts that speak of God as the divine judge sitting upon his throne and issuing statutes and commandments both at creation and during the course of human history to regulate the cosmos and to keep chaos at bay (e.g., Job 38:8-15). But Ben Sira identifies Wisdom with the law of Moses, which had already achieved the status of authoritative scripture in Second Temple Judaism (see 24:23). Sages over the centuries had been involved in the formulations of law codes and their applications and interpretations in Israelite and Jewish jurisprudence, and it is likely that one group of wise scribes was involved in the compilation of Deuteronomy and the Deuteronomic redaction of a large number of books.[22] In Second Temple Judaism, the Torah achieved normative status for regulating religious and social status so far as the foreign rulers would allow (see the book of Ezra). Scribes were trained especially for the interpretation and application of the law to Jewish life through religious instruction, education in the schools, and the religious and civil courts. Wisdom's close relationship with the growing compendia of laws and statutes that became a part of the Torah is also seen in sapiential piety that focuses on the Law as the objective of meditation and reflection (see Psalms 19B and 119). For Ben Sira, Wisdom's identification with the Torah not only gives the teachings of the sages greater authority, but also suggests that the Law itself, as well as sapiential teaching, are grounded in the order of creation and are the instruments for bringing the individual, society, and creation into a harmonious relationship. Wisdom and Torah, identified with the order of creation, enable humans to live in concert with God, society, and the cosmos through study and application to life.

Finally, Wisdom is the gift of God. In verses 1, 4, and 8, God is the source of Wisdom, a point that underscores the sages' teaching that Wisdom is neither a human invention nor accessible to human beings through their own striving. The catechistic questions in verses 2-3 and 6-7 expect the answer to be that only God, not humans, can comprehend Wisdom in its totality.[23] This Wisdom, divine in origin and known comprehensively only by the creator, comes to human beings only as a divine gift. For the earlier sages, no one is born truly wise, and even the human quest to obtain Wisdom by any means, including diligent study grounded in pious devotion, falls far short. Unlike Job 28, which speaks of the mystery and inaccessibility of Wisdom, Ben Sira asserts that God has poured out Wisdom upon all creation (see Joel 3:1f.; Acts 2:17; 3) and every creature, and has generously given her to those who love him. Wisdom is a gift, not the object of striving, and she is freely imparted to those who love God.

In this text and later ones, as was the case with earlier wisdom literature, Ben Sira's esthetic, metaphorical presentation stimulates and engages the imagination of the audience who reads and listens. In 1:1-10, the dominant metaphor is word theology, especially in terms of Wisdom as the life-giving and ordering principle of creation and as the commandments that give direction to life. Divine love, in this case, is not so clearly represented in the images of a fertility goddess as is the case in Proverbs 1–9, though Wisdom is personified as the one who dwells with God, is poured out on all divine works, and, as the result of a divine gift, resides with those who love God. This gift of Woman Wisdom evokes certain metaphorical images of love. Love for God is mediated through love for Woman Wisdom, who dwells eternally with God, an image that is suggestive of the presentation of Woman Wisdom as the consort and lover of God, made more explicit in the Wisdom of Solomon (especially chap. 7). Divine Wisdom, the lover of God, becomes, through God's charity, the lover of the wise, making God and God's creation and providence open at least to limited understanding. However, for Ben Sira, the complete comprehension of creation and even Wisdom herself is available only to God.

The Fear of the Lord and Human Wisdom (1:11-21)

The next poem consists of five strophes bound together by the theme of "fear of the Lord" and its corollary, wisdom: the benefits of piety (vv. 11-13), wisdom's origins and guidance (vv. 14-15), the fruits of wisdom (vv. 16-17), the blessings of wisdom (vv. 18-19), and wisdom's and piety's benefits (vv. 20-21).

Strophe I (vv. 11-13)
11. The fear of the Lord is glory and exultation
    and gladness and a crown of rejoicing.
12. The fear of the Lord shall delight the heart
    and will give gladness and joy and length of days.
    The fear of the Lord is a gift from the Lord,
    for it places (people) upon the paths of love.

13. It will be well at the end for those who fear the Lord,
    and in the day of his death, he shall be blessed.

Strophe II (vv. 14-15)
14. The beginning of Wisdom is the fear of the Lord,
    and she was created with the faithful in their mother's womb.
15. She has built[24] among humanity an everlasting foundation,
    and with their descendants she shall be trusted.

Strophe III (vv. 16-17)
16. The fullness of Wisdom is to fear the Lord,
    and she satisfies them from her fruits.
17. She fills all their house with desirable things,
    and (their) storehouses with her produce.

Strophe IV (vv. 18-19)
18. The crown of Wisdom is the fear of the Lord,
    causing peace and health to flourish.
    And both are gifts of God for peace,
    and he increases boasting to those who love him.
19. And he beheld and apportioned her,[25]
    She pours out understanding and insightful knowledge,
    and exalts the glory of them who hold her fast.

Strophe V (vv. 20-21)
20. The root of Wisdom is the fear of the Lord,
    and her branches are length in days.
21. The fear of the Lord drives away sins,
    and abiding, it dispels all anger.[26]

In this engaging poem on the "fear of the Lord" and Woman Wisdom, Ben Sira shapes the contours of the relationship of two major themes in his collection. The affirmation that the "fear of the Lord is the beginning of wisdom" is an important theme in early wisdom literature (Job 28:28; Prov. 1:7; 9:10). "Fear of the Lord" intimates not only personal piety and reverence for God, but also faith's expression that the creator of heaven and earth is the one who through Wisdom guides and directs the cosmos, human history, and indeed the life of the sage.[27] In this poem, and elsewhere in the collection, the "fear of the Lord" is identified with Wisdom, that primeval, divine attribute of God that existed before all else and was the instrument of creation. Yet Wisdom comes only to those who fear God and keep the commandments.[28]

Of significance for creation theology is the poem's portrayal of Wisdom as a fertility goddess who bestows upon those who possess her blessings of life (vv. 16-20; see Proverbs 8). The gifts of fertility she offers are listed in verses 16-17: "She satisfies them with her fruits, fills their house with desirable things, and [their] storehouses with her produce." The image of Wisdom as a tree in verse 20 is one often associated with fertility goddesses (cf. Asherah; Prov. 3:18; Sir. 24:13-17). Other gifts from Goddess Wisdom, whose "crown" is the fear of the Lord, include peace, health, knowledge, glory, and length of days (vv. 18-20). The metaphor of fertility in this poem points to Wisdom's providential role in guiding the god-fearers to success and well-being.

Verses 14-15 combine the tradition of the creation of humanity with that of Wisdom's role in guiding the godly throughout the generations. The providential leading of the generations of the faithful, of course, is a theme developed in detail in the panegyric to the ancestors in chapters 44–50 (cf. Wisdom of Solomon 10–19). The verses begin with a traditional affirmation: "the beginning [or "starting point" or "best"] of wisdom is the fear of the Lord" (see Job 28:28; Prov. 1:7; Qoh. 8:12). However, Ben Sira's emphasis on the formation of wisdom with the faithful in their mother's womb suggests something strikingly new in sapiential reflection on the creation of humanity. Traditionally, the sages regarded wisdom as both a gift of God to the pious and faithful who took up the call to study and learn and as an object of human striving, possessed by those who pursued the teachings of the wise with all of their hearts. "Gift" and "object of human striving," while in some degree of tension, were the usual ways of describing the reception of wisdom.

Now the sage asserts that wisdom and its corollary, fear of God, are "created with the faithful in their mother's womb." Two points bear consideration. First, the faithful are predestined to godly lives, not an uncommon idea in biblical theology. For instance, Jeremiah's call indicates that he was predestined from the womb to be a "prophet to the nations" (1:4-10). The psalmist in the lament in Psalm 139, in speaking of his wondrous formation by the creator in the womb, asserts that God wrote down the number of days he would live even before his birth (v. 16). And Qoheleth moves close to a broader doctrine of divine determination when he asserts that God decrees what happens, even though humans, including the sages, cannot know what he does (3:10-11; 8:16-17). Second, the "faithful" from the point of their formation in the womb are given the gift of wisdom. This is a new thought for the sages. Ben Sira argues that the wise are indeed wise from birth, are filled with the fear of God from their time of creation in the womb.[29] One may infer from Ben Sira's initial statement that all wisdom comes from the Lord (1:1) that he is saying here that the creator, who forms people in their mothers' wombs, endows the faithful with wisdom and the fear of God.

Following the description of the creation of the godly and their endowment with wisdom, Ben Sira then speaks of Wisdom's taking up residence (literally, "nesting") among humans whose descendants will trust her. This declaration of Wisdom's universal dwelling among humans is limited specifically to Israel in chapter 24, as is the heroes' guidance of the generations in the epic poem in chapters 44–50. This metaphor of Woman Wisdom, nesting or building an eternal foundation and taking up her dwelling among humans, is one way the sages express their understanding of divine providence. Reality is a household in which Wisdom, residing in their midst, nurtures humans from the womb and continues to guide them to well-being and life.

Duties to the Poor (4:1-10)

Ben Sira's teaching about charity includes an instruction on duties to the poor. In the midst of this instruction, he admonishes his son not to turn aside or ignore the poor, lest they utter a curse against him for ignoring their plea:

> Do not despise the requests of the poor man,
>   and do not give to him an occasion to curse you.
> The one who cries out in the bitterness of spirit and in
>   the agony of his being,
>   his creator will hear the sound of his plea. (vv. 4-6)[30]

The widening gap between rich and poor during the Hellenistic period, prior to the Maccabean revolt, may have given special occasion for Ben Sira's urging that the downtrodden of society be supported through charity.[31] The attention given to caring for the impoverished in Israelite and Jewish society by the sages has already been treated in chapter 3. But particular notice should be given to Ben Sira's warning about the curse of the poor against the neglectful sage.

Curses, as noted in the chapter on Job, contain an inherent power to bring destruction. In particular, curses uttered in the name of God associated divine power with the language of maledictions and invoked divine responsibility for bringing destruction to the object under verbal assault (see Job 31). The curse of the righteous person was thought to be especially powerful (see Job 5:3-7; 31:30). Here, Ben Sira speaks of the danger of the curse of the poor and the possibility that their prayer will be "heard" or answered by God. In the Hebrew Bible, of course, God was especially the defender of the poor.

The designation for God in the motivating sentence (v. 6) is Hebrew ṣûrô: "his rock," a frequent metaphor for God in the Hebrew Bible (Deut. 32:15; Pss. 31:3; 62:8; 71:3 Isa. 17:10). More likely is the Greek reading of the Hebrew as "the one who made him." This reading takes the Hebrew to be either from yāṣar or ṣûr, both meaning "to form" or "to fashion." These two verbs evoke the metaphor of Yahweh as the craftsman who fashions the fetus in the womb. If this is the more correct rendering, then the tradition of the creation of humanity is drawn upon by Ben Sira to bolster the importance of charity extended to the poor. God hears their prayer, because God is their creator. They, too, are the valued objects of God's artistic crafting, the works of his hands, those in whom he takes delight.

Providence and Human Nature (5:14; 7:15)

In numerous places in Ben Sira, providence is described in terms of divine determination and oversight of both the components and the actions of reality. Providence is seen by the sage as God's direct continuation and sustaining of creation. Two examples that point to providence as the continuation of originating acts of creation are 5:14 and 7:15:

> Do not be called a deceiver,
>   and do not speak evil slander with your tongue.
> Because shame has been created for the thief,
>   and an evil reproach for the deceiver. (5:14)[32]
> Do not feel loathing[33] for the hard service of labor,
>   which is assigned by[34] God. (7:15)

The first prohibition is a part of a larger instruction that addresses the topic of the destructive misuse of language (5:9-15). This is the initial section in the book that addresses the use of speech. As has been noted in previous discussions in this volume, the sages regarded language as both a divine and a human activity that contained within its features the capacities both to create life, order, and well-being, and to destroy the cosmic, social, and individual components of reality. The power of the divine word to create and sustain reality (Gen. 1:1–2:4a; Psalm 33) was a common metaphor of the wise for divine activity, but this same power to create reality was also at the core of sapiential imagination. Through the forms of wise speech, reality was conveyed, but also shaped and sustained. Yet, the sages also recognized the destructive power of language, from curses, to gossip, to libel and slander, to silly and loquacious talk. Language could be misused to destroy creation (see Job 3), to subvert the social order, and to harm individual existence.

In Ben Sira's first admonition (5:14), he warns against deceptive and slanderous talk, presumably because it undermines social relationships and abuses those who are misled. Yet, common to Ben Sira's thinking is the idea that divine providence has established at the time of creation a continuing order of retributive justice that punishes in various ways those who pervert the structures of justice that undergird reality.[35] "Shame" for the thief and "evil reproach" for the deceiver is a mode of undesirable and painful existence in which people are held in contempt by others in their social networks. Shame and evil reproach are "created" (*nibrā 'â*) by God and are intrinsic to the way social reality operates.[36] God has created a system of retribution through which divine justice is administered.

The second admonition indicates that "hard service" (or "laborious toil") has been "assigned"[37] by God. Human labor has a positive note in Genesis 2, for humans were to be active in the shaping of the orders of creation and in overseeing its continuation. However, for the Yahwist the sin of the first human pair led to a series of divine cursings, one of which was that difficult manual labor would be required to make the earth yield its produce (Genesis 3). It is quite possible that Ben Sira has this understanding in mind when he admonishes his audience not to despise the human condition, which may require hard manual work to sustain existence.[38] Indeed, he may be countering Job's lament, which depicts metaphorically the human condition as that of a slave or day laborer divinely ordained to a dreadful existence (see Job 7). This does not mean that Ben Sira harbored a romanticized view of manual labor, since occupations requiring hard work denied to people the time and opportunity to study and to become sages (see 38:24–39:11). But it does mean that Ben Sira stresses that people whose divinely ordained lot it is to serve in these physically demanding occupations should be content with their place in life. Socially conservative, Ben Sira wished to preserve the order of Jewish communal existence that had developed at the beginning of the second century B.C.E.

Creation and Cultic Service (7:29-32)

Located within the context of an instruction on a variety of topics dealing with family, piety, and charity (7:18-36) is a brief section of three admonitions that exhort one to fear God and to honor and support the priests (7:29-31). One of the theological titles given to God in this section is "maker" (or "creator"):

> Love your maker with all your strength,
> do not neglect his ministers. (7:30)[39]

The theological basis for the maintenance of the priesthood through the "portion" that is their due (Exod. 29:26-28; Lev. 2:1-10; 7:31-36; Num. 18:9-20; Deut. 14:28-29) and for honoring them is "loving the creator with all one's strength." Ben Sira's language in this instruction reflects the Shema in Deuteronomy 6:4-9, which commands Israel to love "the Lord your God with all your heart, and with all your soul, and with all your strength" (v. 5).[40] The Shema in Deuteronomy emphasizes that the worship of the one Yahweh is actualized through love of God and faithful obedience to the divine commandments. The love of God in the Shema is expressed in the loyalty and devotion of one's entire being ("heart," "soul," and "strength") to Yahweh.

Ben Sira uses this traditional, well-known language to speak of fearing, loving, and honoring God. But his subtle shifts in emphasis provide different theological nuances. To love with all one's strength the creator who has made the worshiper and given him or her life entails, at least in part, obedience to the commandment to honor and provide for God's representatives, the priests. In addition, through the giving of the priests their "portion," the worshiper acknowledges that God is the creator and sustainer of all life. Ben Sira's strong allegiance to and support of the priesthood as well as the entire sacrificial system is obvious (see esp. 45:6-22, 26; 50). This suggests that his own probable profession is that of teacher and scribe of sacred texts whose work enjoys the patronage of the Temple hierarchy.

The Sovereignty of God and Human Arrogance (10:1-18)

This collection of various types of sayings addresses, at least implicitly, rulers on the matter of just governance. The teaching reminds rulers of the sovereignty of God in the hierarchy of power and lordship, the activity of divine providence in selecting kings and nations to exercise dominion over the earth and in shaping the structures of justice, and the corruption of human nature, limiting the efforts of mortals to govern wisely and well. Rulers are warned in particular about the folly of arrogance, the most destructive of mortal sins when it is allowed to take root.

This collection of sayings may be broken down thematically into three sections: human rule and divine sovereignty (vv. 1-5), the folly of arrogance (vv. 6-11), and God's judgment against insolent rulers (vv. 12-18).

    1. A wise judge establishes his people,
        and the government of a perceptive person is well ordered.
    2. As the people's judge, so are his ministers;
        as the chief of a city, so are its inhabitants.
    3. A disorderly king will destroy a city,
        but a city will continue by means of its officials' wisdom.
    4. Sovereignty over the inhabited world is in the hand of God,
        and at the proper time he will establish a person over it.
    5. Sovereignty over everyone is in the hand of God,
        who sets his glory before the ruler.
    6. Do not repay your neighbor with evil for every transgression,
        and do not walk in the path of arrogance.
    7. Pride is hateful to both the Lord and humans,
        and oppression is treacherous to them both.
    8. Sovereignty passes from one nation to another,
        because of the violence of the proud.
    9. How can one who is dust and ashes be full of pride?
        Even while he lives, his body is full of worms.
   10. A whisper of an illness, the physician mocks,

He is king today, and tomorrow he is dead.

11. When a person dies, he inherits worms,
    maggots, and crawlers.

12. The beginning of pride is human insolence,
    for he turns his heart away from his creator.

13. For the gathering of insolence is sin,
    and its fountain bubbles forth an evil plan.

14. The throne of rulers God overturns,
    and he sets the humble in their place.

15. The Lord uproots the roots of the nations,
    and plants the humble in their place.[41]

16. The remnant of the nations God buries,
    and he exterminates their root in the soil.

17. He removes them from the land and roots them up,
    and exterminates their memory from the land.

18. Insolence is not fitting for a human,
    nor presumptuousness for one born of woman.

Numerous instructions and sayings collections in Israel and the ancient Near East broach the subject of divine and human kingship by presenting teachings about beneficent and just rule.[42] The wise king who establishes justice and rules beneficently is a common topos in biblical texts (2 Sam. 14:17, 20; 1 Kings 3–11; Prov. 8:15-16; 16:12; 20:8, 28; 25–29; 31:1-9; Isa. 9:5; 11:1-9).[43] In the Hellenistic period, the ideal ruler was the philosopher king who would suppress self-interest in order to rule wisely and well.[44] In this collection, arrogance, one of the more dangerous sins condemned in sapiential literature (Prov. 14:3; 29:23), is especially destructive when distorting the character and reign of human rulers. The Yahwist in Genesis 2–11 regards the first and primary sin that alienates humanity from both God and the environment, the sexes, and the nations to be hubris, the desire of the creature to become like the creator in giving and taking life and in establishing and controlling human destiny. Ezekiel argues that the arrogance of the King of Tyre, expressed especially in his desire to sit on God's throne and rule the earth, has corrupted his wisdom. Divine judgment will lead to his being cast down into the pit (chap. 28).

In Ben Sira's teaching, pride turns the creature's heart away from the creator, leading to a fundamental breach that results, if not corrected, in divine judgment and human ruin, both for the ruler and for those governed. God is the judge who removes the arrogant from their thrones and replaces them with those who are humble of heart. Indeed, the very memory of arrogant rulers is erased from the land. God also takes away dominion from arrogant nations whose violence leads to destruction.

This section in Ben Sira contrasts the life-giving justice of royal wisdom with the arrogance of human rulers, which brings destruction to both nation and king. Especially important is the emphasis placed on divine sovereignty: God is the one who rules the earth, chooses rulers to reign over nations, and removes the proud from their throne.

The teaching also turns to creation anthropology to emphasize that the mortality of humans, including kings, should mitigate against the folly of arrogance. "Dust and ashes" (v. 9) is an expression of deprecation that points both to the insignificant worth of human beings and the lowly place of humanity in contrast to the exalted position of God (Gen. 18:27; Job 30:19; 42:6). Even rulers, whose hint of an illness is laughed away by the reassurance of their physicians, die quickly, and, like all mortals, their corpses decay and become food for worms (cf. Job 3:11-19).

Cosmos, Humanity, and Divine Judgment (16:24–18:14)

This lengthy section on creation and providence, one of several extended compositions on this subject (see 39:12-35 and 42:15–43:33), consists of five poems: the creation of the cosmos (16:24-30), the creation of humanity (17:1-10), law and judgment (17:11-24), a call to repentance (17:25-32), and divine mercy (18:1-14). This composition, along with the two others mentioned above, are what one might best regard as "poetic commentaries" on creation and providence in the Hebrew Bible and particularly Genesis 1–2.[45]

Following a general introduction to the larger section that affirms Ben Sira's wisdom as inspired (16:24-25), the first poem consists of two strophes (vv. 26-28 and vv. 29-30) that use different images to present God as creator. First, by means of the spoken word God assigns every natural element of creation to its place and enables each of his works to accomplish its particular task or function forever (vv. 26-28). The "works" most likely are the heavens and the earth, along with the natural elements that comprise each sphere: the heavenly bodies of sun, moon, and stars, as well as the wind, rivers, plants, and trees. Elaborating on the first creation account in Genesis 1:1–2:4a (the power and ordering of the divine word), this continuous regularity and order in the operations of the heavens and the earth is achieved because the works of creation are obedient to the divine imperative (see Isa. 40:26). The works of creation are personified, not as divine powers possessing their own will, but as obedient forces following the directives of the sovereign God for their own operations. All things are created to exist in harmony and are obedient to the divine will in following what God has determined for them to do and to be.

26. When God created his works from the beginning,
    and making them, he assigned their tasks,
27. He ordered their works forever,
    and their domains for their generations.

> They have neither hungered nor grown weary,
>   and they have not abandoned their assigned works.
> 28. Each has not crowded out its neighbor,
>   and they have never disobeyed his word.

This is the critical point for the entire section (16:24–18:14): Obedience to God's commandments, whether by the spheres and elements of creation or by the human creature, leads to harmony, order, and well-being.

The second strophe (vv. 29-30) elaborates on the creation of living beings in Genesis 1:20-25, 2:19, and Psalm 104 (esp. vv. 24-30) by presenting God as the beneficent Lord who, having looked upon the earth, fills it with good things, covering its surface with every kind of living being. The poem suggests that "every living creature" is taken from the earth and at death returns to it (see Gen. 2:19; 3:19; Ps. 104:24-30; Qoh. 12:7).

> 29. And after this the Lord looked upon the earth,
>   and he filled it with his good things.
> 30. He covered its surface with every manner of living creature,
>   and to it (i.e., the earth) they return.

The world is filled with "good" things, echoing Genesis 1:1–2:4a, which describes each element of reality as "good" and the entire creation as "very good." This poem continues the general Israelite view that creation is "good"—that is, orderly, beautiful, and life enhancing and sustaining.

The creation of the cosmos is followed, then, by the creation of humanity (17:1-10; cf. esp. Gen. 1:26-28; 2:7; 3:19; Job 10; Psalms 8; 139).[46]

> 1. The Lord created humanity from the earth,
>   and he returns each one to the earth again.
> 2. He numbered their days and gave them a set time,
>   and gave them authority over the things upon the earth.
> 3. He clothed them with strength that is appropriate for them,
>   and he made them in his image.
> 4. He placed the fear of them in all flesh,
>   and gave them rule over both beasts and fowl.[47]
> 6. Deliberation and tongue and eyes,
>   ears and heart he gave to enable them to reason.
> 7. He filled them with the knowledge of insight,
>   and he showed them good and evil.
> 8. He placed the fear of him in their hearts,
>   to demonstrate to them the majesty of his works.
> 9. That they might forever glory in his marvels,
> 10.   and praise his holy name.

This poem also consists of two parts: the creation and function of humanity in the cosmos (vv. 1-4); and the gifts of wisdom and piety (vv. 6-10). The first strophe, then, emphasizes that humans, even though they are made in "God's image," also, like all other living creatures, are created from the same earth to which they also must return (Gen. 3:19; Ps. 146:4; Qoh. 3:20-21; 12:7).[48] God as creator of humanity is the divine craftsman who shapes humanity from the soil, but also the ruler who gives human creatures sovereignty over the earth. They, like the other "works" of God, are assigned a function (dominion over the earth; cf. Gen. 1:26-28; Psalm 8), a place to inhabit (or space; i.e., the earth; cf. Gen. 1:28; Prov. 8:30-31), and a set time for existence (i.e., the human life span; cf. Job 14:1-2; Ps. 90:10; Isa. 65:20). This poem acknowledges that the divine image, possessed by all humans, has primarily to do with function, not nature—that is, as is the case in Genesis 1 and Psalm 8, God gives to humanity the role of ruling over all other things on the earth (but not the heavens, for they are under the direct control of God). To facilitate this human rule, God "clothes them with strength that is appropriate for them" and places in all other "flesh" the fear of humanity (see Gen. 9:2). The "strength" with which they are clothed most likely refers to the appropriate power humans possess to carry out the divine imperative of ruling over the earth (contrast Job 10:4-9, which describes the frailty of human existence).[49] The terror that animals have of humanity aids human control over the earth. As the cosmos is obedient to divine rule, so the animal kingdom is to be obedient to human sovereignty.

The second strophe of the poem takes on a decidedly sapiential character, for it now describes human nature as possessing two important features: wisdom (here the ability to deliberate and reason by means of the organs of perception; cf. 1 Kings 3:9; Prov. 20:12) and piety (i.e., "the fear of the Lord"; cf. Prov. 1:7). The divine wisdom operative in the cosmos becomes the pattern for human understanding and moral behavior.[50] Wisdom does not receive the negative implications of "knowledge of good and evil" in the J story of creation (Genesis 2–3). There "knowledge of good and evil" was denied to the first human pair (cf. esp. 2:17; 3:5, 22). In J the "knowledge of good and evil" was the primary boundary between divine and human existence, separating creator from human creature, and its acquisition by the first pair is not simply an act of disobedience but a crossing of the line between divinity and humanity. In Ben Sira's poem, however, wisdom enables humanity to know and then to choose between "good and evil" (see Gen. 2:9, 16-17). Humans, described by the metaphor of king, are endowed with wisdom, enabling them to rule beneficently and well God's good creation. The gift of wisdom to kings is a common topos in ancient Near Eastern royal ideology.[51] Humans, through God's gift of wisdom, have the capacity to reason and to choose the "good" that will enhance and extend life and well-being.

In addition, God places in the human heart the "fear of him" (i.e., piety) so that they may praise the creator for his marvelous deeds (cf. 1:11-20). The "fear of God" is the acknowledgment of the sovereignty of God, which leads to faithful praise. It, too, is seen in royal ideology as a charismatic endowment (e.g., Solomon's prayer for wisdom in 1 Kings 3 and the gifts of the spirit given to the ideal king in Isa. 11:1-9). And as is made clear in the following poem (vv. 11-24), wisdom and piety are the foundations of obedience to law and faithfulness to the covenant.

Ben Sira's next poem (17:11-24) moves from the creation and ordering of the world and from the creation and dominion of humanity over the earth to specific features of Jewish election (the first strophe, vv. 11-17) and divine judgment (the second strophe, vv. 18-24). Ben Sira is the first sage to bring sapiential teaching about creation into the normative traditions of Israelite faith that focused on salvation history. In this poem, the election traditions of covenant and law are grounded in the theological formulations of the creation of the world (16:24-30) and the creation of humanity (17:1-10).

> 11. He set before them (Israel) knowledge,
>   and he gave them a law of life as their inheritance.[52]
> 12. He established an eternal covenant with them,
>   and his commandments he has shown them.
> 13. Their eyes beheld the majesty of his glory,
>   and their ear heard the glory of his voice.
> 14. And he said to them, "Avoid all unrighteousness,"
>   and he commanded each of them concerning his neighbor.
> 15. Their ways are before him forever,
>   they will not be hidden from his eyes.[53]
> 17. Over every nation he has established a ruler,
>   but the portion of the Lord is Israel.[54]

Ben Sira now identifies the knowledge of wisdom with the Law, reflecting most likely his role as a scribe of Torah. This legal instruction, which encompasses the teachings of wisdom, is a "law of life." This presentation of the Torah's relationship to life (cf. 45:5) is borrowed from Deuteronomy (30:11-20; 32:46-47), though the connection of wisdom (= Law for Ben Sira) with life is a frequent concept in sapiential teachings (e.g., Prov. 1:32-33; 8:32-36). In Deuteronomy, obedience to the law brings life, whereas disobedience leads to death.

For Ben Sira the Law also is an "inheritance" for Israel, a special revelation that only the chosen have received from God. The Law is set within an "eternal covenant" that God has established with Israel. In the Hebrew Bible, the expression "eternal covenant" may refer to several covenants: the covenant between God and all living creatures in which God promises not to destroy again the creation (Gen. 9:16); the covenant between God and Abraham and his descendants (Gen. 17:7, 13, 19); and the covenant between God and Moses (Exod. 31:16; Lev. 24:8; Num. 18:19). From the language of Israel's seeing the glory of God and hearing his voice (v. 13), it is clear that the "eternal covenant" in Ben Sira is the Mosaic covenant, established at Mount Sinai (Exod. 19:16-19; 24:15-17; see Sirach 24).

For this poem, God's revelation at Sinai is summarized in two parts: "avoiding all unrighteousness" and commandments concerning the neighbor. The avoidance of evil is most likely a summary of the Law's and wisdom's comprehensive teaching about moral conduct (see the various legal codes in the Pentateuch as well as the expression "turn from evil" in Job 1:1, 8; 2:3; 28:28), while the commandments concerning the neighbor emphasize the Law's and wisdom's concern to establish a social environment that regulates human relationships that are just and that enhance life and well-being (cf. Exod. 20:16-17; Lev. 19:18; Prov. 14:21, 31).

God's universal providence is evidenced in his appointment of a "ruler" over every nation: either a king chosen to rule justly (cf. Prov. 8:15-16) or an angel, common to mythical (Psalm 82) and apocalyptic thought, who oversees the welfare of a nation (Dan. 10:13-21). But God has chosen Israel to be his special "portion" to nurture and sustain (Exod. 19:5; Deut. 7:6; 14:2).

In the remainder of the poem (vv. 19-24), the emphasis then shifts to divine judgment, in which God, who is aware of human behavior, requites the wicked and the righteous with their just deserts. Retribution is based on obedience or disobedience to the revelation of Torah to Israel, a deuteronomic teaching. Thus it is not the nations, but the elect who are the subject of the poem's emphasis on divine judgment. With election comes more responsibility.

The fourth poem in this section (17:25-32) is a call to repentance that echoes prophetic and sapiential texts (see Prov. 1:20-33; Jer. 3:11–4:4). In speaking of repentance and the mercy of God, the poem moves back to creation. God's mercy is directed to humans, for they are but "dust and ashes." Here, the poem's understanding of divine mercy is grounded in Ben Sira's anthropology: The limitations of human existence (mortality and weakness) are recognized by a merciful God who is sure to forgive those who repent and turn to him.

Finally, the last poem (18:1-14) consists of three parts (vv. 1-6, 7-10, 11-14) that pick up three of the main themes of the earlier poems: the creation of the cosmos, the creation and function of humanity, and the compassionate mercy of God. The first strophe speaks of God's wondrous deeds, mighty power, and inexhaustible mercies, which defy description and understanding. God is portrayed as the eternal and just judge who rules in majestic glory and great power over his creation. As a contrast, the insignificance of humanity is

263

expressed in the second strophe. This strophe in verse 8*a* echoes Psalm 8:4 with the question "What is a human being, and what worth is he?" (cf. Job 7:17).

The strophe underlines humanity's brief life span, little worth, small accomplishments, and inability to comprehend the wonders and glory of God and his works. In view of the greatness of God and the insignificance of humanity, even human good and evil are worth little consideration.[55] This contrast between the sovereignty and greatness of God and the insignificance of human beings is the poem's basis for the forbearance and mercy of Yahweh toward humans, depicted in the third strophe (vv. 11-14). The divine judge is patient with mortals for their weaknesses and is forgiving of their sins. Indeed, like the wise teacher, God reproves, admonishes, teaches, and shepherds human creatures. Subsequently, those who are obedient to the teachings of God are especially the beneficiaries of divine forgiveness.

In this lengthy composition (16:24–18:14) on creation, providence, and election, what unites the five poems is the theme of order and obedience. For Ben Sira the order and regularity of the cosmos result not only from the wisdom and governance of the creator but also from the obedience of the world to the rules governing its existence, established by God at creation. Humans, too, made in the divine image and given dominion over the other creatures, are endowed by the creator with wisdom and the "fear of God," which form the basis and potentiality for obedience. Thus obedience to God, the basis for order and regularity in nature and human society, is grounded in creation theology.

This is not to say that the special revelation of Torah to Israel does not receive an important consideration in this discussion. On the contrary, Ben Sira integrates into his general understanding of creation theology the particularity of election. Jews, as the chosen people with an eternal covenant, have the special gift of the Law, which guides them in their moral existence and sustains their common life. Even so, the weaknesses common to all humanity which Jews share is acknowledged by God and becomes the basis for his forgiveness of those who repent and turn to a patient and merciful Lord.

Sirach 24: Cosmic Wisdom Takes Up Residence in Israel

In this chapter, Wisdom is personified as a heavenly goddess who engages in a hymn of self-praise (see Proverbs 8).[56] Hymns of praise uttered by worshiping communities in praise of deities are a common literary form in Israel and the ancient Near East, and there are some examples of hymns in which gods and goddesses of the ancient Near East sang hymns of praise (or aretalogies[57]) in honor of themselves.[58]

Ben Sira borrows from this rich tradition in the Hebrew Bible and the eastern Mediterranean world in composing his literary hymn in which personified Woman Wisdom praises herself in the midst of two audiences: her own people (the Jews) and the divine council. This hymn describes the origins and cosmic rule of Wisdom, her taking up residence in Israel and Jerusalem, her identification with the Temple cult and the Law, her description as the tree and waters of life, and her invitation to participate in a banquet of life that offers her fruit to her followers.[59] She becomes identified with both the transcendent realm of divine dwelling and the immanent presence of God on the earth and particularly among the chosen people.

Introit (vv. 1-2)[60]
1. Wisdom praises herself,
   and boasts in the midst of her people.
2. In the assembly of the Most High, she opens her mouth,
   and before his host she will boast.

Strophe I (vv. 3-6)
3. I came forth from the mouth of the Most High:
   and I covered the earth like a mist.
4. I dwelt in the heights,
   and my throne was in the pillar of the cloud.
5. I alone have encircled the vault of heaven,
   and walked in the depth of the abyss.
6. I ruled over the waves of the sea and over all the earth,
   and over every people and nation.

Strophe II (vv. 7-11)
7. I sought rest among all of these:
   in whose inheritance should I dwell?
8. Then the creator of all commanded me,
   and he who fashioned me brought my tent to a place of rest.
   And he said, "Set up your tent in Jacob,
   and make Israel your inheritance."
9. Before the ages, from the beginning, he created me,
   and I shall not cease forever.
10. I ministered before him in the holy tabernacle,
   for thus in Zion I was firmly established.
11. Likewise in the beloved city he gave me rest,
   and my authority was in Jerusalem.

Strophe III (vv. 12-17)
12. So I took root among an honored people,
   in the portion of the Lord was my inheritance.
13. Like a cedar in Lebanon I was exalted,
   like a cypress in the mountains of Hermon.
14. Like a date palm I was lifted up in Ein Geddi,
   like rose bushes in Jericho.

265

Like a beautiful olive tree in the plain,
  like a plane tree I became lofty.
15. Like cassia and camel-thorn I gave forth aromas,
  like myrrh I gave forth a pleasing fragrance.
Like galbanum and onycha and mastic,
  like the smoke of incense in the tabernacle.
16. Like a terebinth, I stretched forth my branches,
  and my branches are branches of glory and grace.
17. Like a vine, I produced graciousness,
  and my blooms gave forth fruit of honor and wealth.[61]

Strophe IV (vv. 19-22)

19. Come to me, all who desire me,
  and eat your fill of my produce.
20. For the remembrance of me is sweeter than honey,
  and my inheritance is sweeter than a honeycomb.
21. Those who eat me will still hunger for me,
  and those who drink me will yet thirst for me.
22. He who obeys me will never be ashamed,
  and those who work with me will not transgress.

Strophe V (vv. 23-29)

23. All these things are the Book of the Covenant of God Most High,
  the Law which Moses commanded us as an inheritance
  for the congregations of Jacob.[62]
25. It makes wisdom abundant like the Pishon,
  and like the Tigris during the days of first fruits.
26. It makes understanding full like the Euphrates,
  and like the Jordan in days of harvest.
27. It overflows like the Nile with instruction,[63]
  like the Gihon in days of vintage.
28. The first man did not come to know her (Wisdom) fully,
  nor will the last trace her out.
29. For her thoughts are more vast than the sea,
  and her counsels deeper than the abyss.

Strophe VI (vv. 30-34)

30. And I came forth like a canal from a river,
  and like an aqueduct into a garden.
31. I said, I shall water my garden,
  and I shall water abundantly my flower bed.
And behold, my canal became a river,
  and my river became a sea.
32. I will again make discipline shine like the dawn,
  and I will make these things glow from afar.
33. I shall pour out teaching like prophecy,
  and I shall leave it to future generations.
34. See that I have not labored for myself alone,
  but for all those who seek her.

This poem on cosmic Wisdom assumes the following literary structure: a third-person introit (vv. 1-2), the origins and rule of cosmic Wisdom (Strophe I: vv. 3-6), cosmic Wisdom's residence in Israel and Jerusalem (Strophe II: vv. 7-11), cosmic Wisdom and the tree of life (vv. 12-17), cosmic Wisdom's invitation to the banquet of life (vv. 19-22), cosmic Wisdom's identification with the Law and comparison to the rivers of life (vv. 23-29), and the life-giving waters of cosmic Wisdom's teaching (30–34). The thematic movement of the poem points to the actualization of heavenly Wisdom in the socioreligious reality of Second Temple Judaism.

The introduction (vv. 1-2) positions Woman Wisdom within the "assembly of the Most High" and indicates that she opens her mouth to praise herself. The title for God, "Most High," is one of exaltation, originating in Canaanite religion, in which the creator god, El, was the ruler of the council of the gods. The "assembly of the Most High" is the divine council (see Job 1–2; Psalm 83; Isaiah 6), which by Ben Sira's time had become a heavenly court consisting of God and the "host" of heaven, the latter being demythologized deities who now are heavenly creatures given a variety of functions.[64] Among them is Wisdom, a divine attribute used in creating a beneficent order of life and well-being in both cosmos and history, personified as a goddess. This personification of Wisdom is an additional example of the poet's using the language of myth to narrate divine creation and providential rule (see 1:1-10; Prov. 8:22-31; Wis. 7-9).[65]

In the first strophe (vv. 3-6), cosmic Wisdom describes her origins as emanating from the mouth of the Most High, evoking the metaphor of God's creation of the world by means of speaking reality into existence (see Gen. 1:1–2:4a; Psalm 33). Wisdom, then, is compared to a "mist" that covers the earth, poetically identifying this ordering principle of creation with the "mist that arises from earth that waters the entire face of the ground" (Gen. 2:6). In Genesis 2:6 (part of the J narrative), the first act of creation was the watering of the land. Ben Sira borrows this fertility metaphor in imagining Wisdom as the water that permeates and brings life to the land (see vv. 23-29, 30-31).

Ben Sira goes on to describe Wisdom's dwelling place in the heights or mountains, a typical location in ancient Near Eastern and Israelite mythology for the dwelling of deities, most likely because their peaks extended into the heavens and were covered with clouds (e.g., Mt. Sinai/Horeb, Exodus 3; 19; 24; and Mt. Zion, Pss. 48:2; 68:16). The "pillar of the cloud," another dwelling place of Wisdom, may reflect this mountain or heavenly imagery, but it should be noted that the "pillar of the cloud" was also, like the pillar of fire by night, the sign of divine presence and guidance in leading Israel through the Sinai wilderness during the day (Exod. 13:21-22). The "pillar of cloud" also represented a theophany associated with the tent of meeting in Exodus

33:7-11, the place where Moses received the oracle of God. In the poetic imagination of Ben Sira, Wisdom's dwellings express both the transcendence and immanence of God and their association with creation, redemption, and revelation.

The latter part of the first strophe (vv. 5-6) emphasizes that Wisdom has explored and now rules over the three spheres of the cosmos: heaven, the abyss, and the earth (cf. Yahweh in Job 38–41). The "vault of the heaven" refers to the firmament that in Genesis 1 separates the waters into two regions: the waters above and the waters below (see Job 22:14; Prov. 8:27; Sir. 43:12). In the Priestly creation story, this vault is called heaven and contains the lights that separate night from day and determine the festivals, seasons, and years (see Gen. 1:6-8, 14-19). The "depth of the abyss" refers to the lower regions, especially the cosmic ocean or chaos that existed in P prior to creation (Gen. 1:1-2). In mythological texts the habitation of chaos monsters, particularly Leviathan, is the Deep. In Ugaritic mythology, Prince Yam, the nemesis of Baal, the god of fertility, ruled over this region and contended with his rival for sovereignty over the earth. Yahweh also fought with monsters of the Deep and Prince Yam in gaining and maintaining sovereignty over the earth (see Job 38:8-11; Ps. 74:12-17). In Ben Sira, however, it is Wisdom who claims to "rule over the waves of the sea and over all the earth." Wisdom now assumes the role of surrogate of divine sovereignty as she rules the cosmos (heavens, earth, and sea) on behalf of God.

An important contrast to Wisdom's presence in, knowledge of, and rule over the three spheres of the cosmos is found in the initial half of the first speech from the whirlwind (Job 38), when Yahweh asks Job if he has been in the various regions of the cosmos, including the deep and the underworld, and therefore come to understand the nature of reality. Has Job visited the upper regions, the heavens, so that he may understand the fundamental operations of wind, rain, and snow? Does he rule over Yam, whose surging waves threaten world order? Of course, Job's answer to each question, while unexpressed, is nevertheless no. By contrast, the implication is that Yahweh is present in, understands, and rules over these three cosmic regions. In Ben Sira, however, Wisdom is the manifestation of divine presence and rule over heaven, earth, and sea, and Wisdom knows or understands each sphere.

Additionally, Wisdom's rule is not simply over the cosmic regions, but also over nations and peoples (v. 6; cf. Wisdom of Solomon 10–19). This expression of Wisdom's sovereignty over the nations has been encountered in wisdom literature before, in Proverbs 8 where she reigns as the Queen of Heaven. Elsewhere in wisdom literature, God rules the nations, a point clearly articulated in Job 12. For Ben Sira, Wisdom is mistress over nature and history.

The second strophe (vv. 7-11) entwines creation and sovereignty with the election of Israel and the study and embodiment of wisdom. Cosmic Wisdom, fashioned by God, goes in search of a people among whom to take up residence ("rest") and is commanded by her creator to "set up her tent" in Jacob and to "make her inheritance" Israel.[66] Language of election fills the imagery of this strophe. "Inheritance" is a common election term that denotes Israel as the special property of God (Deut. 4:20; 1 Sam. 10:1; 1 Kings 8:53; etc.). Wisdom's seeking of "rest" (*anapausis*) in verse 7, echoing Israel's own experience in the Sinai wilderness after the exodus and prior to settlement in Canaan, uses the same Greek word for resting from labors on the seventh day in the Septuagint's translation of Exodus 23:12. It is the same invigorating, renewing, life-giving rest promised to those who respond to the sage's invitation (*protrepsis*) to take up the study of wisdom (Gr. Sir. 6:28; Gr. Sir. 51:27). Taking up lodging (*aulizomai*) in Ben Sira's "house of learning" (Gr. Sir. 51:23) to pursue his course of study reflects Wisdom's dwelling (*aulizomai*) and flourishing in Israel.

In Greek Exodus 23:12, the rest on the sabbath not only reinvigorates the weary, but also liberates from the oppression of hard labor, a common theme in exodus theology. The twofold reference to the tent or tabernacle echoes the wilderness tradition and its celebration in the pilgrimage festival of Tabernacles. In this tradition and its reactualization in worship and sacred memory, God's providential guidance through the Sinai, symbolized by the dwelling in tents of pilgrims who come to Jerusalem for the festival, is celebrated. Israel's transient existence in the wilderness time is reflected in her living in tents or tabernacles. Yet Ben Sira also has in mind the sacred tent or tabernacle. According to the Priestly tradition (Exodus 26; 40), Yahweh's presence was revealed in the sacred tabernacle. To relate his reign to the older traditions of exodus and wilderness wandering, David set up Yahweh's tabernacle in Jerusalem and transferred to it the ark, which signified divine presence (see 2 Samuel 6). Later, in royal tradition, Solomon's Temple, housing the ark, replaces the tabernacle as the dwelling place of Yahweh. In Psalm 132, a royal psalm probably used to celebrate the finding of the ark and its relocation in Jerusalem, David swears that he will not rest until he finds a dwelling place for Yahweh. In verse 8 of this psalm, Yahweh is asked to enter into the sanctuary and to come to his "place of rest," an action symbolized in the procession of the ark into the Temple. Now it is Wisdom who finds her resting place in the Temple.

The election of Zion (Jerusalem) is another significant sacred tradition used by Ben Sira in this second strophe (vv. 10-11). Wisdom is present in and ministers before God in the Temple in Jerusalem, the "beloved city." Now Wisdom is identified with the priesthood, which "ministers to" or "serves"

269

(*leitourgeo*) the creator first in the tabernacle in the wilderness and later in the Temple (Exodus 28–29; Leviticus 6–9) in the "beloved city" of Jerusalem (cf. Pss. 87:2; 132:14). The election of Jerusalem as God's place of dwelling enters into Israelite theology at the time of David, when the city becomes both the political capital and the religious center of the empire. Jerusalem did not lose its prominence in the Persian and Hellenistic periods, for it became the center of developing Judaism. In the biblical and postbiblical traditions of Jerusalem, the city and especially the Temple take on cosmic significance as the center of the earth where God as creator and lord of history dwells and defeats the forces of chaos (both mythical and historical) that threaten his sovereignty and the order of creation and history (e.g., Psalms 46; 48; 76).

Ben Sira entwines this election tradition with creation theology in the second strophe in several ways: God, the "creator of all," "fashioned" eternal Wisdom and "commanded" her to dwell among the Israelites. Ben Sira's use of the term for "rest" (*anapausis*) not only echoes the sacred traditions of wilderness and settlement, but also suggests the priestly understanding of the sabbath and creation: God "rested" (*katapauo*) on the seventh day, following creation (Gr. Gen. 2:1-4*a*) and commanded the Israelites to sanctify the sabbath by resting (*katapauo*) from their labors (Gr. Exod. 20:8-11). Subsequently, Wisdom's "resting" among the Israelites suggests their election as the people of God, the wilderness and conquest traditions important in Israelite faith, the creation and renewal of the earth through sabbath rest and worship, and the invigorating renewal of life that comes through sapiential discipline (piety and study; *mûsār*).

Thus, for Ben Sira, in this second strophe it is cosmic Wisdom, created by God, whose sacred tent is pitched in Israel following a time of wandering and searching for a resting place; it is Wisdom who, taking up residence in her tabernacle, represents the divine presence among Jacob. And it is Wisdom who engages in sacred service in the tent, identifying the liturgical rituals of the priestly service with the study and devotion of the sage. Through the worship of God and the pursuit of wisdom, life in all of its abundance is experienced and renewed.

The third strophe (vv. 12-17) develops two images: paradise and cultic service. Wisdom speaks of her "taking root among an honored people," presenting herself now as a flourishing tree that takes root and sends out its branches in arable soil for nourishment. Israel now nourishes Wisdom, enabling her to grow. Wisdom is compared to six different types of luxuriant, graceful, and mighty trees (cedar, cypress, date palm, olive, plane, and terebinth), to rose bushes in Jericho, and to a fruitful vine. Ben Sira may have in mind a comparison of wisdom with the garden in Eden, where trees pleasant to the sight included fruit-producing ones that were good for food (Gen. 2:8-9,

15-17). Among these trees was the "tree of life" (v. 9) with whom Wisdom was identified in sapiential imagination (cf. Prov. 3:18).

In verse 15, Ben Sira mentions the fragrances and aromas identified with cultic service, including incense used in tabernacle worship. The perfumes in 15a were mixed with olive oil to produce a holy oil used to anoint the tent, the ark, other sacred equipment, and the priests (Exod. 30:23-30), while various resins (galbanum and mastic) and the oil of mollusks (onycha) were blended with frankincense to produce incense for sacred service in the holy tabernacle (Exod. 30:34-38). For Ben Sira wisdom's identification with the cultus points to the important relationship of these two avenues to God, blessing, and life. Wisdom, like the priesthood and the cultus, functions as an intermediary between God and the world. Through her, like the cult, God is approached and life is attained.

Ben Sira concludes this strophe with the depiction of wisdom as a luxuriant tree (here a terebinth) whose branches are characterized by "glory and grace" and as a vine that produces "graciousness" or "grace" (*charis*)—that is, divine mercy or favor that saves from destruction and leads to life (Gen. 6:8; Exod. 33:12; Qoh. 10:12) and offers the "fruit of honor and wealth." Honor and wealth are the gifts that wisdom offers her followers (Prov. 3:16).

Now Wisdom issues in the fourth strophe (vv. 19-22) the invitation (*protrepsis*; cf. Prov. 8:32-36; Isa. 55:1-3; Matt. 11:28-30) to eat and drink of her. Eating and drinking are associated with the banquet to which Wisdom invites the "unlearned" after having built her spacious manse to celebrate the inauguration of her reign of life (Prov. 9:1-6). These images reflect those of a sacred meal of communion with God and humans (e.g., Exodus 24), only now it is the eating and drinking of wisdom that bring life and well-being. It is important to note that the appetite and thirst for wisdom are never satiated and quenched. This suggests that the pursuit and study of wisdom are lifelong tasks.

The fifth strophe (vv. 23-29) makes the clear identification of wisdom with the Torah (cf. the language of Deut. 33:4) and returns to the images of paradise and election to stress Wisdom's life-giving powers and sovereignty over the nations. Paradise is suggested by the four rivers (Pishon, Gihon, Tigris, and Euphrates) that, once the cosmic life-giving river watering the Garden of Eden left the garden, became the tributaries flowing throughout the earth (Gen. 2:10-14). Ben Sira also identifies Wisdom's instruction with fertility of the land made possible by two rivers: the Nile and the Gihon. The inundation of the Nile valley by the Nile River enriches the soil and makes agriculture in Egypt possible, while in Israel the Gihon's waters brought life to nearby vineyards.[67] The point is that the abundant waters of all six rivers that bring fertility to the land illustrate the life-giving powers of Wisdom.

Ben Sira goes on to state that the first man (Adam) did not come to a full knowledge of Wisdom, even as the last will not. Here he appears to pick up, not the negative view of the "tree of the knowledge of good and evil" in the J narrative (Genesis 2–3), but the association of wisdom with the first man, often in mythological settings a king (see Ezekiel 27–28). Ben Sira's emphasis on the inability to comprehend the vastness of wisdom does not mean that he endorses the skepticism of the poem on the inaccessibility of wisdom (Job 28), denying knowledge of cosmic wisdom. But Ben Sira does stress that the totality of wisdom cannot be grasped by any human being, a point common to most wisdom literature.

The final strophe (vv. 30-34) returns to the images of Wisdom as life-giving waters, only now she is compared to a canal or aqueduct that brings water from a river to nourish a garden. It is from the abundance of the water coursing through the canal and aqueduct that a river and then a sea are formed. The comparison of wisdom to life-giving water is common in wisdom (see Psalm 1, where the righteous person who studies Torah is like a tree planted by a stream).

In the latter part of the strophe (vv. 32-34; cf. 16:24-25), Ben Sira speaks again as an inspired teacher whose instruction is compared to the light of the dawn and whose teaching is "poured out like prophecy" (cf. Joel 2:28).[68] His inspired teachings, he claims, are to benefit future generations of those who seek wisdom.

The Creation of Opposites (33:7-15)[69]

This poem of three strophes addresses the general theme of the providence of God by focusing on the theme of contrasting opposites (see a similar description in 39:12-35). The poem serves well as a theodicy, for it provides the essential structure of Ben Sira's formulation of a response to the questioning of the justice of God.[70] Here and elsewhere (see esp. 39:12-35) Ben Sira proclaims that God has separated the components of reality into contrasting opposites. In this poem, the two categories of opposites are time (sacred and profane) and humans (the good and the bad).

The initial strophe of the poem on the bipolar order of creation begins with a question in verse 7:

> 7. Why is one day superior to another day,
> when all daylight in the year is from the sun?

The opening question asks why one day is separated from and then regarded as superior to another day, when the sun produces the same light for each day. Verses 8-9 answer this temporal question about creation.

272

> 8. By the Lord's knowledge, they were distinguished,
>   for he designated some of them as seasons and feasts.
> 9. Some of them he exalted and sanctified,
>   and some of them he established as profane days.

The answer given to the question in verse 7 is grounded in divine sovereignty; while in one sense all days are the same (the sun provides daylight for them all), nevertheless, God through means of his knowledge (an alternative term for wisdom in Ben Sira) providentially designated certain days as set apart (i.e., "sanctified or made holy") to be sacred seasons or festival times. These "seasons and feasts" that were made distinct from other times would have included the sabbath (the seventh day); the major pilgrimage festivals of Passover and Unleavened Bread (a festival in the first month, occurring on the eve of Nisan 14 and concluding on Nisan 21), Weeks (a one-day festival early in the third month, on the fiftieth day after the offering of the barley sheaf during the Festival of Unleavened Bread), and Tabernacles (a seven-day festival beginning on the fifteenth day of the seventh month); the feast of the New Moon; the Day of Atonement (a communal fast on the tenth day of the seventh month); and perhaps the seventh (sabbatical) year and the year of Jubilee (the fiftieth year).

Ben Sira contends that the separation of time into profane and sacred periods leads then to a consideration of a second differentiation in reality: humans who are separated into the two categories of the righteous and the wicked. Thus he moves from cosmology, in particular the bipolar structure of time, to anthropology, where he posits the same dualistic system of opposites.

Strophe II (vv. 10-13)

> 10. All humans are from the soil,
>   and from the earth, Adam was created.
> 11. With the fullness of knowledge, the Lord made distinctions
>   among people,
>   and he altered their paths.
> 12. He blessed and exalted some of them,
>   and some of them he sanctified and brought near to himself.
>   Some of them he cursed and brought low,
>   and he turned them from their place.
> 13. Like potter's clay in his hand,
>   to form it according to his desire.
>   Thus people are in the hand of the one who made them,
>   to distribute to them according to his judgment.

Ben Sira argues that all humans have the same origins as their primordial ancestor Adam: They are created by God from the soil (cf. Gen. 2:7; 3:19; Qoh. 12:7). Even so, God, following the privilege of divine sovereignty, elected some to be blessed, exalted, sanctified, and brought near to himself.

Ben Sira uses cultic language to speak, at least implicitly, of two entities: Israel and its ancestors, elected to be a holy nation, set apart for divine service to mediate between God and the world (Gen. 9:1, 26; 12:3; Lev. 19:2); and the priesthood, sanctified and set apart for divine service to mediate between God and the rest of Israel (Num. 16:5; Ezek. 40:46; 42:13; 45:4). "Blessed" refers to the enhancement of life, while "exalted" points to election or the selection of its object for a special role and stature, in this case divine service. To be sanctified refers to the act of God's separating out someone or something for divine service. "To draw near" refers to the approaching of the holy in sacred worship. Here, Ben Sira uses the language of Israel's election to enlarge the boundaries of the chosen to include all those who are righteous. But they belong to the category of the elect by reason of divine determination, not human choice.

By contrast, God has determined others among humanity to be "cursed" (afflicted with destruction), "brought low or degraded" (probably a social designation for those who are subservient to others; e.g., Gen. 9:25), and "turned from their place" (i.e., people removed from a high or favored position and put in an inferior one; cf. Isa. 22:19). In addition, the sage may have in mind the election of Israel with its exaltation among the nations and the disfavor shown toward other groups, especially the Canaanites of old.

Ben Sira then uses the common metaphor of humans as clay molded by the potter into the desired shape (see Gen. 2:7; Job 10:8-9; Isa. 29:16; Jer. 18:1-6). The point is clear: God destines some humans to be blessed and others to be cursed. The image of the clay in the potter's hand underscores Ben Sira's contention that the radical sovereignty of God extends to the divine determination of human destiny. Thus humans are placed by God into one of two groups: the blessed and the cursed. Ben Sira more than likely has in mind the election of Israel from among the nations, a status that is based on the action of God, not Israel's own merit.

Finally, the third strophe (vv. 14-15) sets forth the general principle of the bipolar division of reality.

Strophe III (vv. 14-15)

14. Good is the opposite of evil and life the opposite of death;
    thus the sinner is the opposite of the pious.
15. Therefore look upon all the works of the Most High,
    they are two by two, one opposite the other.

The three contrasting opposites in reality are evil and good, death and life, and sinners and the pious. This "doctrine of opposites" may point to Ben Sira's attempt to address the problem of theodicy—the justice of God. God is responsible for all opposites that, together, comprise the fundamental structure of reality, including good and evil. It is the radical sovereignty of God that Ben Sira articulates. God shaped reality into contrasting opposites.

A Creation Hymn (39:12-35)

In 39:12-35, Ben Sira crafts an elegant wisdom hymn that praises God as creator and sustainer of reality, and at the same time gives voice to a stirring defense of divine justice.

Double Introduction (vv. 12-15)

12. Now having reflected I shall speak
for I have become full like the moon.
13. Listen to me, O pious sons, and sprout forth,
like a rose planted by streams of water;
14. Emit fragrance like frankincense,
and send forth blossoms like a lily.
Raise your voice and together sing praise,
and bless the Lord for all his works.
15. Ascribe greatness to his name,
and praise him with a hymn of praise,[71]
In songs accompanied by the lyre and other stringed instruments,
thus you shall say in thanksgiving:

Strophe I: Concerning Creation and Providence (vv. 16-20)

16. All the works created by God are good,
for he will provide for every need at the appropriate time.
17. By his word, he placed in orderly arrangement the heap of waters,
And at the utterance of his mouth the reservoirs.
18. By his command, all is good,
and nothing limits his salvation.
19. The activity of everyone is before him,
and nothing is hidden from his eyes.
20. From age to age he observes,
and there is no counting of his acts of salvation.
There is nothing too small and insignificant for him,
and nothing is too marvelous and strong for him.

Strophe II: The Creation of Good (vv. 21-27)

21. Let no one say, "What is the purpose of this?"
because everything is selected to meet a need.
Let no one say, "This is worse than that,"
because everything will come to fruition in its time.
22. His blessing overflows like the Nile,
even as the Euphrates drenches the inhabited world.
23. The nations inherit his rage,
even as he turns fresh water into salt water.
24. The paths of the pure are straight,
but for the lawless they become crooked.
25. Good things were apportioned to the good from the beginning,
but both good and evil were to the wicked.

26. Chief among the essentials for human existence are
    water and fire, iron and salt,
    wheat flour, milk, and honey,
    wine, oil, and clothing.
27. All of these are good for the good,
    yet they are turned into evil for the wicked.

Strophe III: The Creation of Evil (vv. 28-31)

28. There are winds that have been formed for judgment,
    and in their wrath they move mountains.
  And at the time of consummation, they will hurl forth their power,
    even while they soothe the spirit of their creator.
29. Fire and hail, famine and pestilence,
    these also have been created for judgment.
30. The teeth of the wild beast, the scorpion, the venomous serpent,
    and the sword of vengeance to destroy the wicked.
  All these things have been created for their function;
    they are mustered in the storehouse and at the proper time
31. They will leap forth when he commands them,
    and in their tasks they will not rebel against his word.

Double Conclusion (vv. 32-35)

32. Therefore, from the beginning I have taken my stand,
    and I have reflected and put it down in writing.
33. All the works created by God are good,
    for he will provide for every need at the appropriate time.
34. Let no one say, "This is worse than that,"
    because everything will come to fruition in its time.
35. Now with all your heart give forth praise,
    and bless the name of the Holy One.

The sage awakens the imagination to consider the just nature of divine rule and then to break forth in unrestrained praise of the creator by shaping a poem of three strophes around the form and content of three wisdom sayings. The first two sayings are disputations (diatribes) found in verse 21:

> Let no one say, "What is the purpose of this?"
> because everything is selected to meet a need.
> Let no one say, "This is worse than that,"
> because everything will come to fruition in its time.

The second disputation is repeated in verse 34:

> 34. Let no one say, "This is worse than that,"
> because everything will come to fruition in its time.

Disputations, or diatribes, set forth the arguments or questions of opponents and then answer them with a reasoned response. The questions in verse 21 bring to conclusion the first strophe, which addresses the goodness of both creation and providence. The repetition of the second question in verse 34 emphasizes at the conclusion of the hymn that even things that may appear evil are indeed good, if one recognizes their function: the punishment of the wicked. Ben Sira makes frequent use of the disputation in his polemics with his opponents who questioned the goodness of God due to the existence of evil.

The second wisdom form is a proverb that occurs first in verse 16 and then again in verse 33:

> All the works created by God are good,
> for he will provide for every need at the appropriate time.

This saying also occurs in two strategic places within the rhetorical structure of the hymn. Its first occurrence, verse 16, initiates the first strophe (vv. 16-21) that praises the works of God in both creation and history as good. The saying recurs at the end of the poem (v. 33), summarizing what Ben Sira has learned through his reflection on reality, which takes new shape in the form of artistically crafted praise. The saying becomes a confession of faith, expressed in the form of hymnic praise.

The wisdom poem begins with a double introduction: the typical call to listen, addressed in this case to the "pious ones," that occurs in the wisdom instruction (vv. 12-14a; cf. Prov. 4:1); and the call to praise, common to hymns used in worship (vv. 14b-15; cf. Pss. 47:1; 66:1-2). The double introduction is paralleled by the twofold conclusion: the proverb in verse 33 and the disputatious question in verse 34, followed by the reissuing of the call to praise in verse 35.

In speaking of creation and providence in the first strophe, Ben Sira affirms the goodness of divine creation and action in ruling the earth (v. 16) and then describes God's omnipotence ("nothing limits his salvation") and omniscience ("nothing is hidden from his eyes," v. 19). Even the waters of chaos are ordered by the power of the word of the creator. All things are subject to the will of God. This emphasis on the sovereignty of God is developed by the affirmation that he is able to see and know all that happens throughout the ages of the earth.

The sage in the second strophe quickly moves to the issue of theodicy in the second and third strophes. Opposing hypothetical arguments of opponents who question the purpose or usefulness of a divine action or an object of creation or who question why some things seem worse than others—that is, inherently evil—Ben Sira uses the "science of opposites" (cf. 33:7-15) to argue that good things in creation (see the list in v. 26) are created for the well-being of the righteous, while the same things are harmful to the wicked. Even things that are evil (see the list in vv. 29-30) are good in terms of their function: the destruction of the wicked. Ben Sira also makes use of the sapiential understanding of time to reinforce his case for theodicy by submitting that the worth of an object of divine creation is proven at the appropriate time. That is, even something considered evil in itself (e.g., a viper) is good when at the appropriate time of divine judgment retribution comes to the wicked.

Ben Sira is not so bold or audacious as to suggest that there is some mechanical system of reward and punishment that is a part of the structure of reality. And he does not claim that the mysteries of reality, including divine actions, may be penetrated by acts of human knowing. God is still the one who makes judgments and issues decrees that bless the righteous and punish the wicked. And there are things and occurrences that are beyond the ken of human perception. Even so, the affirmation of God as a just Lord of creation and history breaks forth in spontaneous praise from the lips of the pious sage.

In his reflection on the nature of divine creation and providence, Ben Sira approaches the problem of theodicy that threatens the fear of God: the affirmation of God as the creator of the world who rules over the earth in justice. Particularly disturbing is the presence of things that have the appearance of evil. Ben Sira does not deny that God created these things, but he argues that they are good in terms of their purpose: the punishment of the wicked at the appropriate time. This solution to the problem of theodicy is shaped into a hymn of praise to the creator and sustainer of the world, who rules over the earth in justice. Critical reflection, an essential part of sapiential imagination, leads then to the faithful affirmation of the justice of God, shaped in the form of elegant praise.

A Hymn to the God of Creation (42:15–43:33)[72]

Ben Sira's last major text devoted to creation is a cosmological hymn that engages the imagination by the presentation of God as the sage whose wisdom shapes a reality of beauty, coherence, justice, and life.[73] The rhetorical structure of this hymn includes the announcement of the intent to praise (42:15-17), the unfathomable wisdom of God (42:18-21), the beauty and purpose of divine works (42:22-25), the wonder of sky and moisture (43:1-22), the teeming life of the expansive Deep (43:23-25), and the concluding call to praise (43:26-33). At the center of this hymn is the metaphor of divine wisdom, which orders and sustains a world of elegance and wonderment.

In the first strophe ("The Intent to Praise," 42:15-17), the reality shaped by sapiential imagination is grounded in collective memory. Yet the memory of sacred tradition, transmitted by sapiential communities, receives the critical assessment of sages in the present who correlate the teachings of the past with the results of present experience and critical reflection. In this hymn, there is both memory and critical evaluation, leading eventually to the praise of the creator for his mighty works of beauty and life.

> 15. I shall bring to mind now the deeds of God,
>   for what I have seen I shall declare.
>   God's works occur through the utterance of his word,
>   and he works out his will according to his decree.
> 16. As the shining sun is revealed unto all,
>   so the glory of the Lord is over all his works.
> 17. The holy ones of God are not sufficient
>   to recount the marvelous deeds of the Lord.
>   God has strengthened his hosts,
>   to be able to stand firm before his glory.

In the opening strophe of this poem, Ben Sira remembers ("brings to mind") divine deeds that he has witnessed and experienced, deeds that provide the basis for the praise of God. These deeds of God include, not world origins, but providence—the continuing governance of reality. And yet those who are to praise God by recounting in song his great deeds extend beyond the sage himself to the "holy ones of God," those members of the divine council who dwell in the presence of the Lord (see Job 15:15), and the divine "hosts," in this context the personified heavenly bodies of the cosmos who respond obediently by carrying out the commands of the sovereign Lord.

The dominant metaphor for divine providence throughout this poem is the word of the creator, which sustains life and establishes justice by means of divine decree (42:15; 43:26). The imagery, then, is that of the divine sovereign whose edicts create and rule his kingdom.

In this introductory strophe, Ben Sira appropriates an important image from priestly language and connects it to the metaphor of word: the "glory" of the Lord. The "glory" (kābôd) of the Lord refers especially to the "manifestation" of divine presence for the purpose of revelation. In Priestly tradition, the "glory" of the Lord is described either as a cloud or in a cloud that guides Israel through the wilderness (Exod. 16:10), covers Mt. Sinai at the giving of the Law (Exod. 24:15-18b), and fills the tabernacle and the Temple (Exod. 40:34; Num. 20:6; Pss. 24:7-10; 78:60-61). While this way of speaking about divine manifestation connotes mystery and otherness, it also indicates that the purpose of theophany is revelation: God manifests himself in order to issue divine teaching. Ben Sira takes up this imagery to speak of the revelation of the works of creation that point to the power, majesty, and benevolence of God. Thus God's glory, like the rays of the sun, is present in all of his works, and they in turn reveal his greatness (see Psalm 19). For Ben Sira, then, the glory of the Lord points to revelation: Creation testifies to the majesty and sovereignty of the creator. Yet at the same time, this creation that manifests the Lord is the avenue of divine instruction. Creation not only reveals the creator, but also becomes the instrument of his teaching given to those who seek wisdom.

The second strophe of this poem ("The Unfathomable Wisdom of God," 42:18-21) moves to the praise of God and focuses especially on divine wisdom. Through wisdom, the ruler of heaven and earth knows the hidden secrets even of the Deep (*tĕhôm*), that region of chaos that defies divine order and rule (see Job 26:12-13; Pss. 33:7; 89:10-11), and of the human heart (or "mind"), that part of human nature where decisions are made and secret thoughts are harbored (see Prov. 15:11). Even the hidden plottings of chaos and the wicked do not escape the notice of the cosmic sovereign, for his wisdom finds them out.

> 18. He searches out both the Deep and the heart,
>   and he perceives all their cunning devices.
>   For the Most High knows all,
>   and he sees the signs of the age.
> 19. He declares changes that occur,
>   and reveals the searching out of hidden things.
> 20. He does not lack insight,
>   and nothing escapes him.
> 21. The might of his wisdom he measures out,
>   He is the same from eternity.
>   Nothing is added and nothing is withdrawn,
>   and there is no need for any one to instruct him.

As the possessor of wisdom, the Lord is omniscient, knowing all that happens, whether in the past, the present, or even the future. Indeed, the Lord declares what will be, and in the declaration brings the future into reality. In other words, God who does not himself change has been and continues to be in charge of the course of human events.[74] The security and sameness of reality are guaranteed by the God who does not change. Unlike human kings, who need counselors to advise them in the setting of royal policy and its implementation (see 2 Sam. 16:15–17:23), the Lord requires instruction by no teacher or adviser. It is his wisdom that enables him to rule the earth, discover evil, bring its perpetrators to justice, and direct the course of world events.

Ben Sira then sings of the beauty of the works of God, noting that the divine language of judgment and wisdom also possesses within itself both beauty and the capacity to shape like a skilled poet works of wonderment and elegance ("The Beauty and Purpose of Divine Works," 42:22-25).

> 22. Are not all of his works desirable,
>   how dazzling they are to behold.

23. Everything is vital and endures forever,
    all is preserved for every need.
24. All of them are different, one from another,
    and he has not made any of them in vain.
25. One thing may surpass the excellence of another,
    yet who shall ever be satisfied with beholding their radiance?

Ben Sira notes that there are things within creation that may be more beautiful than others, and yet all of them have a degree of elegance that evokes human appreciation. Even so, the works of God are "beautiful" or "good," not simply in regard to their appearance, but also in terms of their function. Ben Sira articulates, then, a view of the world as an esthesis—that is, an order that is both beautiful and filled with purpose. It is in both of these senses that God's works (both the activities and the objects of divine creation) are "beautiful" and "good" (both terms are proper translations of the Hebrew word *ṭôb*). Nothing is created "in vain," without purpose. Each object of divine creation meets a specified need. All things taken together, within the totality or synthesis of reality, point to an order that is both beautiful and good and continues the same from the beginning of the world throughout all eternity.

Continuing the cosmology of esthesis of the earlier poem, the fourth and longest strophe (43:1-22) praises the creator for the wonders of sky and moisture that are objects of both beauty and purpose.

1. The appearance of the heights and the shining firmament,
    the heavens themselves behold their own splendor.
2. The sun gives forth heat, when it goes forth,
    how awesome are the works of the Lord.
3. At noontime it scorches the inhabited world,
    who can endure before its heat?
4. A stoked furnace produces cast works by heat,
    so the rays of the sun ignite the mountains.
   The tongue of the sun consumes the inhabited land,
    and its light burns the eye.
5. Because great is the Lord who made it,
    and his words make brilliant his mighty ones.
6. So also the moon marks the seasons,
    holding dominion over the times as an eternal sign.
7. Among them are the sacred seasons and festival times,
    a light which wanes after its fullness.
8. The moon in its newness renews itself,
    how awe-inspiring it is in its phases.
   An instrument of the host of the clouds on high,
    hammering the firmament with its rays.
9. The beauty of the heavens and the glory of the stars,
    a shining light in the heights of God.
10. By the word of God, the decree will stand,
    they will not sleep during their watches.

281

11. See the rainbow and bless its creator,
     because exceedingly majestic is its glory.
12. It encircles the vault of heavens in its glory,
     and the hand of God stretches it out in power.
13. His might sends forth the lightning,
     and makes the fire-brands of justice flash.
14. For his own purpose he has unleashed the storehouse,
     and the clouds fly forth like birds of prey.
15. His might supports the clouds,
     and he hews out the hailstones.
16. By his strength he shakes the mountains,
     his word urges on the south wind.
17. The voice of his thunder makes the land writhe,
     the scorching north wind, tempest, and whirlwind.
   Like a bird he makes his snow to fly,
     its descent is like the settling of locusts.
18. The beauty of its whiteness enlarges the eyes,
     and the heart quickens at the fall of the rain.
19. Like salt he pours out the hoarfrost,
     and it causes flowers to bloom like sapphires.
20. He causes the cold of the north wind to return,
     that hardens the springs like solid ground.
   He freezes over every pool of water,
     and the water wears the ice like a coat of mail.
21. The vegetation of the mountains burns with heat,
     and the dwelling of plants go up like a flame.
22. Then the cloud distills the dew bringing relief to them all,
     making the parched soil to sprout and grow.

Ben Sira praises the beauty and order of the heavens and the radiance and life-giving vitality of the various forms of moisture (see Job 38:4-38). The sage begins with a poetic commentary on Genesis 1:14-19 that describes in particular the creation of sun and moon, and also the heavenly host.

The sun gives forth light and heat that not only are necessary for existence, but also may desiccate the inhabited earth. Yet, its radiance reveals the power of the Lord who made it. The beauty of the moon, which evokes the wonderment of the observer, is complemented by its purpose of marking and distinguishing among the times and the seasons. The Jewish calendar, to which Ben Sira here refers, is a lunar one that designates sacred times among the days and months of the year by reference to the phases of the moon. These sacred times would have included the sabbath, festivals, and times of fasting.

These two great lights (see Genesis 1) are among the stars and other heavenly phenomena that possess a glory that originates in the majesty of God and carry out the decrees of the creator. These include the rainbow, lightning, thunder, winds, and clouds. Even the variety of the forms of moisture (rain, snow, hail, and dew) bring both life and destruction as instruments of divine judgment. Similar to theophanic hymns (see Judges 5; Psalms 18, 68, 104; Habakkuk 3) that describe the coming of Yahweh to do battle against chaos in order to establish justice and continue life, these cosmic forces are the instruments of God's power in ruling over the earth to punish the wicked and to establish order and life in cosmos.

While the preceding strophe speaks of the heavens and the earth, this one (43:23-35) describes God's rule over the third part of reality: the Deep (*tēhôm*), or the waters of chaos that oppose divine sovereignty.

> 23. His thought causes Rahab to abate,
>   and he spreads out the islands in the Deep.
> 24. Those who go down to the sea tell of its extent,
>   when we hear with our ears we are astounded.
> 25. There are wonders, the signs of his work,
>   the variety of life and the mighty ones of the Great Deep.

Once again, divine wisdom, or "thought," controls the chaos monster, Rahab, while God places the islands in the Deep and fills its cosmic waters with a great variety of life, including the "mighty ones," most likely a reference to the great sea monsters of Genesis 1:20-23. For Ben Sira, the Deep does not pose a threat to divine rule, for God's wisdom keeps both the chaos monster and the mighty waters in check.

In his conclusion (43:26-33), Ben Sira draws his hymn of praise to an end with the summary statement (v. 26) that each element of creation functions according to its purpose, even as the creator's words bring about what he desires. Each element of creation serves as the messenger of God, carrying out with purpose and success the divine decree.

> 26. For his purpose each messenger will succeed,
>   and by his words he works his desire.
> 27. Yet we will not add more things than these,
>   the end of the matter: "He is the all."
> 28. Let us exult even more for he is unsearchable,
>   and he is greater than all his works.
> 29. Fearful is the Lord and exceedingly great,
>   and wondrous are his deeds.
> 30. Lift up your voice and praise the Lord,
>   with all you are able for there is yet more.
>   Renew your strength and praise him,
>   and do not grow weary though you cannot search him out.
> 31. For who has seen him to be able to describe him,
>   and who can praise him just as he is?
> 32. Many things greater than these are hidden,
>   for I have seen just a few of his works.
> 33. For the Lord has made all things,
>   and to the pious he has given wisdom.

Ben Sira notes that the creator's wondrous mystery and majesty extend beyond the greatness and awesomeness of his works. True, Ben Sira affirms that God "is the all"—the one whose nature and glory are revealed in his works. Yet even those few works the sage can observe and then describe are but an indication of greater, more magnificent things that remain hidden to human perception, even as the majesty of the creator is far greater than these divine works reveal. Yet while the sage has glimpsed only a small part of the esthesis of order and delight, it is enough to provide the basis for grateful praise. Finally, he affirms in a concluding saying (v. 33) that God has given to those "pious ones" who praise him the same divine wisdom that orders and sustains the world. These "pious ones" (*anšê ḥesed*) are the heroes of the faith praised in 44–50. They are the ones who, by means of wisdom, embody Israel's salvific history and experience the redemption intended for cosmos and history.

PROVIDENCE AND SALVATION HISTORY (44:1–50:24)

In the last of the three major sections of his book, Ben Sira moves from the theme of Wisdom and creation to God's role in Israel's salvation history. Ben Sira's is the first wisdom book to embrace the traditional theological themes of salvation history (exodus, wilderness wandering, entrance into the land) and covenant and to relate them to the sapiential theology of creation. While other sages through their wisdom texts on occasion interpret the law of Moses, Ben Sira explicitly identifies wisdom with Torah. Of course, the earlier sages affirm providence in the sense of God's guidance of history (Job 12) and direction of an individual's life (Job 10). But now faith in providence is expressed in the traditional language of God's mighty acts in history, the covenant at Sinai (and other covenants), and the giving of the Torah.

As noted above, the correlations of providence and history, creation and covenant, and wisdom and Torah occur in dramatic form in the poem in chapter 24. However, the second place where these correlations occur is the panegyric to famous men in chapters 44–50, an epic poem on Jewish history that follows immediately one of the hymns on creation in 42:15–43:33. According to Burton Mack, this epic poem focuses on the heroes of Jewish history and provides a "mythic etiology" of Second Temple Judaism. In other words, the purpose of creation and the goal of history are the actualization of Second Temple Judaism with its components of Torah, wisdom, priesthood, and Temple.[75]

Ben Sira's epic history is shaped by the Greek encomium that intends to praise the virtues of human beings and the social institutions that were to incorporate cultural values. The culture heroes who embodied the highest ideals and virtues of Greek life included kings, military commanders, athletes, rhetors, and philosophers. In addition, the corporate entities of cities and civic institutions were praised as paradigms of these ideals.[76]

These men, the *ḥăsîdîm* ("pious ones") who are the recipients of divine wisdom (43:33), are a roll call of famous heroes of Israelite and Jewish history: Enoch, Noah, Abraham, Isaac, Jacob, Moses, Aaron, Phinehas, Joshua, Caleb, the judges, Samuel, David, Solomon, Solomon's successors (Rehoboam and Jeroboam—one foolish, the other sinful), Elijah, Elisha, Hezekiah, Isaiah, Josiah, Josiah, the kings of Judah, Jeremiah, Ezekiel, the twelve prophets, Zerubbabel, Jeshua, Nehemiah, Enoch, Joseph, Shem, Seth, Adam, and Simon.[77] Each holds one or more of the critically important social and religious offices of ancient Israel and early Judaism: primeval ancestor, patriarch, priest, prophet, king, and judge. The characterization of each combines seven features: a description of the office, the person's divine election, a reference to a covenant, the individual's piety, an account of the person's deeds, the historical situation, and the blessings accruing to both the person and the community.[78] The climax of this impressive list is Simon II, the high priest who apparently has recently died when the poem is written (chap. 50). These are those who, in Jewish history, were led by providence and achieved great and noble things that led to their remembrance by later generations.

The literary structure of this text, according to Mack, comprises some five parts: the establishment of covenants (seven heroes); the taking of or entrance into the land (three heroes); the interaction of the history of the prophets (seven mentioned, plus one general reference) and the history of the kings (also seven, plus one), which underscores the tension between vision (prophets) and action (kings); the restoration to the land (three heroes); and the climax in the priesthood of Simon, who actualizes the sacred order of the first seven heroes.[79]

But more is at stake here than a Greco-Roman concern to praise the lives of noble heroes who were paradigms of virtue. Rather, these Jewish heroes, through their obedience to wisdom and guidance by divine providence, became the embodiments and conveyors of Jewish history that climaxed in the sacral theocracy envisioned by Ben Sira: the priest who presides over the sacred people in the holy city and the sacral ruler whose office made God present in the Temple and in the midst of the chosen. Indeed, what takes precedence over personal virtue is the sacral office for which these men were divinely chosen and the accompanying divine glory that came to them by holding these offices. Through divine promise, now realized, Israelite and Jewish history is shaped into the form of the deeds and offices of past heroes, culminating in the most important person holding the most important office, that of high priest. The new Jerusalem of Ben Sira's time represents the crescendo and culmination of creation and history.

COSMOS AND HISTORY IN BEN SIRA

Ben Sira and Sapiential Imagination

In the early second century B.C.E., a Jewish sage living in the Temple community of Jerusalem and teaching in a wisdom school sets forth a theological synthesis that unites the twin poles of creation and redemption into a compelling vision. This sage stands within a long and continuous stream of wisdom teachers and scribes whose literary heritage he uses to shape his own imaginative rendering of God, the world, humanity, and Israel's election. Yet, Ben Sira is not simply a tradent of the wisdom tradition, but also is an interpreter of a growing canon that includes the Prophets and is expanding to include other writings. Indeed, if Ben Sira is a representative of the larger scribal community in Jerusalem at the time, there is little doubt that the role of the sages in shaping authoritative tradition and the paradigms for existing in the world is quite significant.

Through the activation of memory, Ben Sira draws on much literature from his culture. The personification of wisdom and its characteristic features borrow from earlier wisdom (Job 28; Prov. 1:20-33; 8–9). His identification of wisdom with the "fear of God" certainly has precedence in earlier wisdom, from Proverbs to Job to Qoheleth. Perhaps the best example of the activation of memory to recall the past to inform the present is his recounting of Jewish history through the offices and lives of important heroes of the faith. Ben Sira is the first sage of whom we have knowledge who clearly situates the Jewish community of his own day squarely within a continuous stream of history that, to his mind, goes back to Adam at the dawn of creation. The varied sources of collective memory from which he drew at least included the literature of the emerging canon, though oral performances of Jewish history in the context of cultic celebration and perhaps libraries and archives in Jerusalem, especially the Temple, may have been used.

Ben Sira did not simply represent the sapiential traditions of the past. They, along with the teachings of Torah and prophets, are merged into a new theological expression in which scribal interpretation has obviously broadened its literary base. His combination of creation theology with redemptive history is an impressive accomplishment, though others, especially Second Isaiah, paved the way for him. At the same time, the presence of Hellenistic culture was neither ignored nor assaulted. Reflecting a period that had not yet experienced open hostilities between a resurgent Jewish nationalism and an inflexible foreign political system that used Hellenization to impose a wide sweeping social conformity, Ben Sira selectively drew on Greek forms and thought that would merge with elements of Judaism to comprise his own imaginative articulation of cosmos and history. The use of the Greek enco-mium is the best example of how Ben Sira took a Hellenistic form and imbued it with the spirit and substance of Jewish history, religion, and wisdom. The articulation of history, even contemporary, is an imaginative act that tries on the basis of fragmentary data to recreate the past within a literary mode.[80] Ben Sira's narrative presentation of Jewish history uses the Greek encomium as a strategy of discourse.

Ben Sira's narrative rendering, described above, moves forward by means of his understanding of Jewish history, grounded in a larger universal history going back to Adam. History reaches its culmination in the office and virtuous life of Simeon II.[81] If one chooses to designate Ben Sira's move into historical recounting in terms of a literary mode, it becomes more like a romance where, through the guidance of divine providence, Jewish heroes in a world that is at times oppressive were able to triumph over the evil forces of nature and history by faithfulness to God and virtuous performance of the duties associated with their offices and roles. Ben Sira's accounting of the lives of famous men sees history under the impress of providence moving forward to its final goal, the Temple community in Jerusalem in his own time, ruled over by the high priest Simeon II. His construal of Jewish history is largely conservative in that he sees the present as a static embodiment of the ideal society. He does not look back to a Golden Age of Jewish life that has been lost or that must be recovered. Rather, his is a progressive view of history that reaches its climax in his own time.

Ben Sira's imaginative rendering of reality also envisions the future in an important way, though his is a largely realized eschatology. In his vision, creation and history have been providentially guided toward the establishment of the Jewish community in Jerusalem during his own day. To borrow an image from apocalyptic, the New Jerusalem is now present in the Temple commu-nity, ruled by the high priest. Wisdom is identified with Jewish piety, the Torah and emerging canon, the covenant of Moses, Temple worship, and scribal education; and she guides the actions of the high priest in his religious and political responsibilities. These are the major features and social institutions of Judaism of the early second century B.C.E. Together they comprise the ideal form of the elect community existing in harmony with God and creation.

By means of the personification of Wisdom, God takes up residence in the world of Ben Sira's making, but at the same time exists outside of its restricting boundaries to bring it into judgment. The immanence of God, rendered especially through the figure of Wisdom, is actualized in Wisdom's covering of creation like a mist and in her taking up residence in the Temple, the wisdom school, and the Torah. Ben Sira is suggesting that through the performance of sacred liturgy and the teaching of Torah and the wisdom tradition divine presence is realized in the life of the Temple community. Yet Ben Sira does not compromise divine transcendence, for he points to Wisdom's coming forth from the heavenly world, being the imaginative incarnation of the words that came from the mouth of God. While active in creation and history, God is still the judge of history and creation, bringing punishment and pronouncing blessing. Wisdom, then, represents both the transcendence and the immanence of God.

For Ben Sira, the historical and linguistic character of human being and action is presented in numerous ways. The teaching of wisdom and Torah presents a literary mode of existence that is to be embodied in faithful living and moral discourse. Ben Sira's teachings cover a wide variety of responsibilities in the areas of thought, speech, and behavior. Through this embodiment of *mûsār,* one becomes wise. Like his sapiential predecessors, Ben Sira regards wisdom as more than an intellectual activity. Through reflection and meditation on the teachings of the ancestors, filtered through the engagement of contemporary life, the sage attempts to embody the moral life. Wisdom combines faith and action with piety and ethics in a tradition that is to be taught, transmitted, and lived. Through this embodiment of cosmic wisdom, the sages both realize and constitute world order.[82]

In spite of the voice of Wisdom, which reveals the nature and character of God, Ben Sira recognizes the mystery of God. Even in his praise of divine creation, he realizes that he has caught but a glimpse of God's majesty and works. However, he is far more secure in his teaching that God may be known through the traditions and institutions of Judaism in his own day as well as observation of the mighty acts of God in creation. Certainly Ben Sira's attempts to understand a part of the mystery of God are less reserved and cautious than Proverbs.

The Activation of Imagination Through Rhetoric and Metaphor

Ben Sira's literary actualization of the world constructed by his imagination contains three major sections, each of which has a poem that forms the conclusion. The theme of the first section is wisdom's role in creation, identification with piety, and presence in the sapiential tradition (chaps. 1–24). The magnificent hymn on cosmic Wisdom's taking up residence among the chosen brings this section to an end (chap. 24). The theme of the second section is providence, with the concluding hymn praising God's powerful and wondrous governance of the operations of the cosmos. The third section focuses on the theme of divine providence in guiding the history of Israel's ancestors, with the concluding chapter describing Ben Sira's giving thanks to God for redeeming him from distress, issuing a call to his audience to give thanks to the divine redeemer of Jewish history who has established the institutions of Jewish life that convey divine blessing, and inviting would-be students to undertake the quest to find Wisdom even as he has done. This rhetorical structure moves forward at times in a linear fashion, but at other times in concentric circles by going back to an earlier topic to restate and develop it in other ways. But the ultimate direction of the thematic movement is clear: from creation to history to realization in the new Jerusalem.

The concluding chapter (51) brings to an end not only the third part of the composition (i.e., the praise of the ancestors in 44–50), but also evidences the sage's own movement within the rhetorical boundaries of the imaginative reality he has shaped. Thus, in his thanksgiving to God, he points to his own distress from which he was redeemed. His prayer to God moved him to act to save, and for this the sage gives thanks. On the basis of his own experience of redemption, Ben Sira then calls upon his community to give thanks to the Lord of Israel's salvation history. He then speaks of his own search for Wisdom, beginning with his prayer for her in the Temple. His quest to find and then embody Wisdom through learning and its implementation in a life of piety, moral behavior and discourse, and praise begins with his youth and will continue through his life. Finally, he invites students to enter into his house of study to engage in the pursuit of wisdom. The school is more than likely a circle of students and perhaps a building. But it may also be, like Wisdom's house in Proverbs 9:1-6, a symbolic universe in which those who seek wisdom take up residence and live.

Important for the reality constructed by Ben Sira is the presence of metaphors. Like the earlier sages, Ben Sira prefers to describe divine activities but not specifically attribute to God human titles. The major metaphor cluster for the activity of God in creation centers on the divine word (including wisdom, commandment, and mouth). Through his word, God creates and orders the cosmos. From his mouth, Wisdom comes forth to cover the earth like a mist. Yahweh's wisdom is the life-giving power that creates and sustains life. God's word establishes and directs the bipolar character of reality, which divides into things that are good for the righteous and things that are bad for the wicked. His thought controls the chaos monster Rahab, causing its waters to recede. As king he issues divine edicts that govern the operations of the creation and are embodied in the Torah, which regulates the life of the chosen. Thus obedience to the Torah and the following of wisdom enable one to experience the life-giving power of the cosmic order in which law and sapiential teaching have their grounding.

When Ben Sira speaks of the creation of humanity, he does so especially in terms of images of artistry. God is the divine potter who shapes the nature and destiny of human beings. God created Adam from the earth, and all humans

289

are made from the soil. When Ben Sira speaks of conception, he points to God's forming humans in the womb and giving at least the faithful the gifts of wisdom and piety. The poor enjoy the protection of the artisan God, who "formed" them. Humanity's place in the cosmos is described in royal images. Not only does God select human kings to rule over their nations, but he also gives to humanity the august place of ruling over creation. They are created in the divine image, rule over the beasts of the earth and the birds of the air, and are feared by the other creatures. God gives humans wisdom that they may rule the world in justice.

The fertility metaphor appears primarily in association with Woman Wisdom, portrayed in images of a fertility goddess who offers her blessing to those who love her. Wisdom is also the "tree of life" or luxuriant vine who offers those who seek her the fruits of honor, peace, health, knowledge, wealth, glory, and long life. She is also identified with the life-giving waters that come from the garden of paradise to bring life to the earth.

These metaphors for divine creation suggest that Ben Sira imagines God primarily as a king sitting on his heavenly throne, ruling over creation and directing providence through the divine word. The royal images are also used in the description of Woman Wisdom, who sits on her throne and rules over creation and nations. Ben Sira stresses the radical sovereignty of God over creation and human creatures. While humans are chosen to rule over creation, their lowliness is contrasted to the majesty and power of their creator. It is on the basis of divine sovereignty that God predestines some humans to be righteous and others to be evil. Divine sovereignty is expressed in the election of Israel and the providential direction of its history.

The world for Ben Sira is an object of great beauty whose operations and glory lead to wonderment and praise. Its marvelous nature is but a small indication of God's own greatness and glory. The world is also a garden or paradise made fertile and alive by the presence of Wisdom as a tree of life and a canal or aqueduct of waters.

These metaphors provide the means by which Ben Sira conveys his understanding of creation. Placed within the rhetorical structures of language, they provoke the imagination to shape a world of beauty and justice in which God rules as creator and sustainer.

"Wisdom, the Artificer of All, Instructed Me"

CREATION AND REDEMPTION IN THE WISDOM OF SOLOMON

INTRODUCTION TO THE WISDOM OF SOLOMON

Historical Setting in the Hellenistic World

The Wisdom of Solomon is composed in Greek by an unknown Jewish wisdom teacher who likely lived in Alexandria, Egypt, perhaps as early as the first century B.C.E.[1] During this period, Alexandria had become the major center of Hellenistic culture and philosophy in the Near East.[2] Three important stimuli led to the composition of the Wisdom of Solomon.

One stimulus was nascent anti-Judaism, evidenced by the sometimes virulent polemics of certain Hellenistic philosophers. The primary center of anti-Judaism was Alexandria. These antagonists aimed their attacks at the religious and social teachings of Judaism that were especially opposed to the syncretistic character of Hellenism. They charged orthodox Jews with atheism, since they rejected idolatry and polytheism in favor of an iconoclastic deity whose teachings denied the existence of other gods. Charges of cultic murder, philosophical irrationality, and barbarism were also leveled. Jewish scholars responded to these attacks in a variety of ways, including the composition of a body of mission (or apologetic) literature that sought not only to defend Judaism, but also to convert its opponents at least to an appreciation of Jewish religion and culture. At the same time, mission literature sought to steady those Jews harassed by the sharp attacks of Hellenistic critics and to bring back into the fold Jewish apostates.[3]

In addition to overt attacks, the lure of Hellenistic culture proved especially appealing to Diaspora Jews living within those areas that came under the sway of the empire built by Alexander the Great. Greek culture, including religion, philosophy, and language, became the common basis for linking together the configuration of diverse nations and traditions. The lure of Hellenism was especially powerful in those areas of the East where Hellenization sank deep roots. The author of the Wisdom of Solomon sought to represent the teachings of Judaism in a fashion that would maintain the integrity of Jewish faith, but in a decidedly Hellenistic guise that would allow for adaptation to the dominant cultural and intellectual forms common to the period.[4] The bringing together of two different worlds, Jewish and Greek, is one task he seeks to accomplish.

A final stimulus for the composition of the Wisdom of Solomon and other mission literature was what may best be described as an internal crisis of the religious spirit in Hellenism, leading to a growing disenchantment with Greek state religion and the Olympian gods. Thus the wisdom of the East (including Judaism), mystery religions, and the rise of philosophical schools that taught their adherents how to conduct their lives were important, though often competing alternatives for those living in the Hellenistic world.

As a result, Jewish writers, including the sage who wrote the Wisdom of Solomon, set forth a Judaism that was more attuned to Greek cultural ideals. These writers stressed three major emphases: monotheism and the evils of idolatry, the spiritual nature of true revelation, and the election of Israel.[5] The Wisdom of Solomon shares these three emphases and brings them to bear on its specific formulation of creation theology. The teacher seeks to convince Jews and their cultured despisers that monotheistic Judaism is of a higher moral order than the pagan polytheistic religions of their neighbors.[6]

Literary Form

In terms of its genre, the Wisdom of Solomon is an exhortatory speech or homily of persuasion (*logos protreptikos*; protreptic[7]) that seeks to convince an audience to pursue a particular course of study, way of life, or course of action (e.g., Wis. 6:12).[8] Thus the function of protreptic is persuasion or conversion. Several different groups comprised the audience addressed. One group consisted of non-Jews who might lend a sympathetic ear to a careful exposition of Judaism, if coupled with compelling argument. In this case, protreptic acts to persuade or convert. Another group were faithful Jews who stood in need of reaffirmation of their commitment to the ancestral faith in order to keep from wavering from their course. Exhortatory speech in this case serves as confirmation. Finally, a third group were apostate Jews who strayed from their path and needed to be exhorted to return. For this group, protreptic was a call to return to a former way of life presently abandoned.[9] Whether Jews, apostates, or pagans, the path to wisdom, both divine and immortal, was the goal to which they were exhorted to strive, for in the obtaining of wisdom, revealed to and possessed most fully by faithful Jews, there is the gift of immortality.[10]

The author was more than likely a Jewish teacher living in Alexandria, though it is difficult to say much more than this. One could imagine that he taught in a Jewish school in this city of Hellenistic culture and possibly had access to the royal court, as did a variety of philosophers and teachers in the Hellenistic world.[11] While not calling himself a "son of David, king in Jerusalem," as did Qoheleth, the author of the Wisdom of Solomon clearly presents himself as the long-dead king (chaps. 7–9). Communications from the dead, which include instructions and exhortations on how to conduct one's affairs and live one's life, were common to the various literatures of the Eastern Mediterranean world, including Jewish and Egyptian writings.[12] In the case of the Wisdom of Solomon, the speaker addresses kings (6:1) and "judges of the earth" (1:1) and seeks to instruct them in matters of proper rule centered in justice. This audience of kings could reflect a teacher who had access to the royal court, though this identity of the audience may have been as fictional as the narrator's portrayal as Solomon. This fiction of a royal author provokes the imagination of Jews and potential converts to listen to the teaching of Israel's most famous sage, who speaks from the grave to defend a Judaism growing on pagan soil and to convince pagans of the truth and integrity of Jewish faith.

Literary Structure

The unity of the Wisdom of Solomon is not at issue, although different proposals have been made regarding its specific structure. Addison Wright has argued that the book is arranged into two major sections, each consisting of 251 verses of poetry: 1:1–11:1 (560 stichoi), and 11:2–19:22 (561 stichoi).[13] His outline of the book, which we shall largely follow, includes the following sections and subsections:[14]

I. The praises of Wisdom (1:1–11:1)
   A. Immortality is the reward of Wisdom (1:1–6:21)
      1. Exhortation to justice (1:1-15)
      2. The wicked invite death (1:16–2:24)
      3. The hidden counsels of God (3:1–4:20)
      2′. The final judgment (5:1-23)
      1′. Exhortation to seek wisdom (6:1-21)
   B. The nature of Wisdom and Solomon's quest for her (6:22–11:1)
      1. Introduction (6:22-25)
      2. Solomon's speech (7:1–8:21)
      3. Solomon's prayer for Wisdom (9:1-18)
      4. Transitional section: Wisdom saves her own (10:1–11:1)
II. God's fidelity to his people in the exodus (11:2–19:22)

A. Introductory narrative (11:2-4)

B. Theme: Israel is benefited by the very things that punish Egypt (11:5)

C. Illustration of the theme in five antithetical diptychs (11:6–19:22)

    1. Water from the rock instead of the plague of the Nile (11:6-14)

    2. Quail instead of the plague of little animals (11:15–16:15)

    3. A rain of manna instead of the plague of storms (16:16-29)

    4. The pillar of fire instead of the plague of darkness (17:1–18:4)

    5. The tenth plague and the exodus by which God punished the Egyptians and glorified Israel (18:5–19:22)

THE PRAISES OF WISDOM (1:1–11:1)[15]

Immortality Is The Reward Of Wisdom (1:1–6:21)

The book begins with an instruction, a royal testament addressed to the rulers of the earth.[16] The rhetorical structure and content of the instruction is shaped in part by the word *righteousness,* occurring in the first (v. 1) and last lines (v. 15). Righteousness is the moral order of the cosmos and of human behavior that kings are to incorporate in their rule and people are to embody in their behavior and speech. Indeed, righteousness is the fundamental characteristic of both the Lord, presented primarily as the divine judge in this instruction, and Wisdom, who in this text permeates the cosmos, dwells in pure and honest souls, and indicts the wicked for their evil thoughts and wicked speech. Finally, righteousness is immortal, and through its embodiment humans come to possess eternal life.

The poetic instruction breaks down into three interwoven parts: the address of the kings of the earth (1:1-3), Wisdom and evil speech (1:4-11), and the origins of death and the immortality of justice (1:12-15):

> Strophe I: Address of the Rulers of the Earth (1:1-3)
> 1. Love righteousness, O rulers of the earth,
>> Set your mind on the Lord in goodness,
>> and in single-mindedness search him out.
> 2. For he is found by those who do not test him,
>> but he appears to those who trust him.
> 3. Dishonest thoughts separate people from God,
>> And divine power, when put to the test, convicts the foolish.

Strophe II: Wisdom and Evil Speech (1:4-11)

4. Wisdom will not enter an evil soul,
    and sin does not dwell in a body that is indebted to sin.
5. For the holy spirit of discipline flees from guile,
    will turn away from foolish thoughts,
    and will be ashamed at the approach of injustice.
6. Wisdom is a benevolent spirit,
    and she will not hold guiltless one who utters blasphemy with his lips,
    for God is a witness of his thoughts,
    a true observer of his mind,
    and a hearer of what his tongue says.
7. The spirit of the Lord fills the inhabited earth,
    and that which holds together all things knows what is said.
8. Therefore no one who utters unrighteousness will escape attention,
    and justice, who convicts, will not pass him by.
9. The schemings of the impious will be examined,
    and a report of his words will come before the Lord,
    in order to convict him for his lawless acts.
10. Because a jealous ear hears all,
    and the noise of murmurings does not go unheeded.
11. Beware then of unprofitable murmurings, and avoid all slander,
    because secret sounds will not go unnoticed,
    and a lying mouth brings destruction to the soul.

Strophe III: The Origins of Death and the Immortality of Justice (1:12-15)

12. Do not seek Death by means of your deceitful life,
    and do not attract destruction by the works of your hands.
13. Because God did not create Death,
    nor does he enjoy the destruction of the living.
14. For he created all things that they might exist,
    and the generative powers of the earth for preservation;
    there is no deadly poison in them,
    and Hades does not rule upon the earth.
15. For righteousness is immortal.

In the initial strophe, the authorial voice, a teacher engaged in moral discourse who speaks through the lips of the long-dead Solomon addresses the "rulers of the earth" and calls upon them to love righteousness (cf. 1 Kings 3:9; Pss. 45:8; 72). For the teacher, the object of contemplation for the possession and understanding of righteousness is the Lord, who, being sought, may be found only by those who trust him. As in earlier wisdom texts that proclaim that the beginning of the quest for wisdom was piety ("fear of God"), this teacher points to trust in the Lord as the proper orientation to come to an understanding of God.

In this exhortation, the teacher indicates that the knowledge of God, which leads to the understanding and practice of justice, is made possible by trusting God and avoiding "dishonest thoughts" (cf. LXX Prov. 6:18), a motif that is developed in detail in the second strophe. Wisdom (*sophia*), the divine power or holy spirit (*pneuma*)—which embodies righteousness, teaches *paideia* or moral learning, loves humanity (*philanthropon*),[17] and convicts the wicked—enters only a righteous, pure-thinking soul (*psyche*) and a body (*soma*) not "indebted to sin" (1:4).[18] The anthropology of the teacher indicates, then, that humans are composed of body and soul[19] and that Wisdom, that righteous power that is an attribute of God, may dwell only within those who are pure in mind and in body. For this teacher's anthropology, humans are not evil by nature (see 8:20), but may become so by wicked deeds and thoughts. In addition, Wisdom is connected to, though not equated with, the rational capacity of humanity. While the rational capacity is indigenous to human nature, the enlightenment or illumination of Wisdom—which reveals God, teaches righteousness, and leads to immortality—is not. As the teacher indicates later, Wisdom must be the object of human desire, longed for, sought, and finally embraced. Although she is a lover of humans, being a holy spirit, Wisdom is driven away by sinfulness, deceit, all kinds of wicked language, and illogical reasoning. Only those who embody righteousness and think pure thoughts are the repositories for the indwelling of divine Wisdom. The teacher may be addressing "rulers," but in a metaphorical sense he is addressing all human beings, for the purpose of God's creation of humans is that they were to share in his kingship.[20] With the metaphor of ruler, the teacher indicates that all humans, who trust in God and are pure in soul and body, may find God and, as the end of the poem indicates, embody immortal righteousness, enabling them to participate in God's rule over creation.

In this second strophe, Wisdom is not only a holy spirit who takes up her dwelling within the righteous of body and soul in order to reveal God to them, but she is also the "spirit of the Lord" who has "filled the inhabited earth" (1:7-11) and "holds together all things." Here Wisdom is like the Stoic soul (spirit, reason, providence, destiny, universal law).[21] While the teacher moves in this second part from anthropology (Wisdom's indwelling) to cosmology (Wisdom as pervasive presence and unifying power in the cosmos), the purpose is to address the moral virtue of proper speech.

Wisdom "holds together all things," indicating that she is the force that keeps creation from returning to chaos or fragmenting into unformed matter. Yet the pertinent point for the teacher is that this omnipresent cosmic Wisdom has knowledge of every sound, including human language and even secret machinations, and, as the prosecuting attorney of the divine judge, brings a report of what humans think and say to the Lord for the distribution of divine judgment. Wisdom literature's emphasis on proper speech and correct thoughts is reflected in this teacher's exhortation. Wisdom, the one who knows all that is spoken and even thought, brings to justice the wicked who misuse their speech and thoughts to cause evil that brings destruction.

296

The teacher then issues a theodicy in the final strophe that explains, in part, the origins of Death's incursion into the world of God's making (1:12-15). The teacher personifies Death as a ruler opposed to life. Warning his audience to avoid seeking Death through deceitful behavior, he explains that God "did not make Death," an absolving of the charge of divine complicity in the creating of human life's greatest tragedy. Instead, he argues, God "created all things to exist" (v. 14)—that is, all living things were made to continue to live their life, not die. He adds that God takes no pleasure in the destruction of living things; rather, God created "generative powers"[22] to preserve and sustain life. Indeed, Death is not inherent to existing things (i.e., they do not contain within themselves "deadly poison"). Death (Hades) holds no royal sway over God's creation; rather, it is the God of life who rules over the kingdom of the living world.[23] For the teacher, Death's rulership is limited to his own kingdom of the underworld and does not include the kingdom of the earth.

Using mythical images, the teacher implies that Death existed prior to creation and continues to hold dominion over his own kingdom. God did not create Death, but instead shaped a world of life in which creatures were made to live. Death's incursion into the creation is made possible only by humans who invite him into the world of the living by their own sinfulness (cf. Prov. 8:32-36; Qoh. 7:29; 1 Enoch 98:4). As the teacher explains in the following section, the wicked are those who by their evil "summoned Death" (1:16–2:24). This is the origin of Death: He entered the world as a result of human sin (cf. Genesis 2–3). Death was not a part of God's original design for creation.

By contrast, righteousness, the attribute of God and Wisdom that may be embodied in human life, is immortal. The teacher argues that through the possession of righteousness, Wisdom dwells within the human soul and body, bringing immortality.[24]

The Wicked Invite Death (1:16–2:24)

The second part (1:16–2:24) of the subsection dealing with immortality addresses the tradition of creation and anthropology from two contrasting perspectives: the wicked's view of human life and destiny and the teacher's presentation of God's purposes in the making of human life. The images for human existence as seen by the friends are associated with what we have called the "slave" metaphor, while images of the royal metaphor are at the heart of the teacher's understanding. This second part also continues to develop the theme of theodicy addressed in 1:12-15 by explaining in more detail how Death entered into the world.

This subsection contains an introduction, "The Covenant with Death" (1:16), followed by four strophes: "The Wicked's Assessment of Human Existence" (2:1-5), "The Commitment to Sensuality" (2:6-9), "The Oppression of the Righteous Man" (2:10-20), and "The Purposes of God" (2:21-24).

Introduction: The Covenant with Death (1:16)

16. But the ungodly through deeds and words summoned Death,
    they pined away, considering him to be a friend,
    and they established a covenant with him,
    because they are worthy to belong to his party.

Strophe II: The Wicked's Assessment of Human Existence (2:1-5)

1. For they said to themselves, having reasoned unsoundly,
    Our life is both of short duration and sorrowful,
    and there is no healing for the final end of a person,
    and no one has been known to return from Hades.
2. For we were brought forth by mere chance,
    and afterwards we shall be as if we did not exist,
  because the breath in our nostrils is but smoke,
    and reason is but a spark within the movement of our heart.
3. When it is quenched, the body will turn to ashes,
    and the spirit shall vanish like empty air.
4. And our name will be forgotten in time,
    and no one will remember our works.
  And our life shall pass away like the traces of a cloud,
    and like a mist it shall be scattered,
  being driven away by the rays of the sun,
    and being overcome by its heat.
5. For our time is the passing of a shadow,
    and there is no return from our final end,
    for it is sealed and no one overturns it.

Continuing the use of mythical images in personifying Death, the teacher blames the wicked for calling him forth and then entering into a covenant with him (Isa. 28:15). In a manner common to the diatribe, the teacher constructs the speeches of the wicked, who, in this imaginary representation, speak for themselves. Drawing on the text in Isaiah 28, the teacher suggests that the wicked enter into covenant with Death in order to preserve their lives, at least for a time. They hope this covenant will stay their demise, though their anthropology denies that there is any final escape from death. Thus a covenant with Death, whom they consider their friend and for whom they pine, offers, they hope, a temporary reprieve from the final, unalterable fate that awaits them (cf. the sexual liaison with Woman Folly, which leads to death, in Prov. 9:13-18).

The wicked are presented as viewing human existence in pessimistic, materialistic terms. For them, the duration of life is brief and the mode of human existence is sorrowful. And even then, it ends in a final nonexistence (see Job 7:1-10; 10:20; 14:1-2; Ps. 144:4; Qoh. 2:23; 3:2, 19, 21; 5:17; 12:5). There is neither a final reprieve from death nor, once entered, any hope for a return from the underworld (see Job 7:7-10). Death is but nonexistence, likened to the nothingness prior to birth. And having died, the wicked believe even their name and memory will be forgotten (cf. Job 18:17; Qoh. 2:16; 9:5). According to the wicked, even the hope for existence beyond death by means of human memory is an illusion (see Qoh. 1:11; 2:16; 4:16; 9:5, 15; cf. Prov. 10:7; Isa. 56:5; Sir. 37:26; 41:13; 44:8; Wis. 8:13).

In contrast to the tradition of the creation of humanity (e.g., Genesis 2; Psalm 139), the wicked also deny the purposeful creation of human life. Their origins they trace, not to the design and activity of the creator, but to mere chance. Life is a fortuitous occurrence, a chance happening that represents no plan or thought-out scheme. Instead of God's breathing into their nostrils the breath of life (Gen. 2:7; 7:22; Job 27:3; Isa. 2:22), the wicked liken their breath to smoke. And reason, the human faculty that for the teacher partakes of cosmic wisdom, is attributed, not to the divine shaping of organs of perception and thought (Prov. 20:12), but to a spark generated by the beating of the heart. The heart as the organ responsible for the origination of thought was common in Hebrew and Greek thought. For the wicked, the beating heart generates fire that becomes thoughts and smoke that becomes breath. Once the spark is extinguished, the body turns to ashes and the breath of life or spirit, equated with smoke, simply evaporates into the empty air.[25] For the wicked, there is no immortal spirit inhabiting the human body and that is liberated at death. Humans do not even contain a divine breath that, for Qoheleth, returns to the creator at death (12:7).

Seeing no purpose to their creation and recognizing that death is the final end of human life, the wicked decide on a course of action that combines both the pursuit of pleasure, considered by them to be their allotted fate, and the oppression of the righteous person whose life and teachings are a reproach to their own way of life (2:6-20). They wish to prove that the faithful, moral existence of the righteous is an illusion.

The identity of the wicked in this section has been the subject of considerable debate.[26] The wicked have been identified as followers of Qoheleth or Epicurus who misuse their teachings to legitimate hedonism and the persecution of the righteous.[27] More likely, they are a literary mosaic of the wicked in general, including apostate Jews, that is shaped by the teacher.[28]

Strophe IV: The Purposes of God (2:21-24)
21. These things they reasoned, but they were deceived,
    for their wickedness blinded them.
22. For they neither knew the mystery of God,

299

> nor hoped for the wages of holiness,
> nor considered the honored prize of blameless souls.
> 23. For God created humanity for incorruption,
>   and he made him in the image of his own being.
> 24. But through the envy of the devil, Death entered into the world,
>   and those belonging to his party experience him.

In the concluding strophe, the teacher argues that faulty reasoning and the lack of knowledge of God's purposes for the creation of humanity have led them astray. They are unaware of the divine mystery concerning the afterlife and the destiny for which God has created humans (cf. 1 Enoch 103:2). They are unaware that God has created humanity in the image (see Gen. 1:26-28; 5:1) of his very own being, meaning for the teacher that divine immortality is not so much a feature of human nature, but what God originally intended for humans to receive. However, immortality is the reward of the righteous, who, in regard to moral virtue, are like athletes striving to obtain the "honored prize" of immortality. By contrast, immortality, through the corruption of the human spirit by wickedness, may be lost.

Now the teacher attributes Death's entrance into the world of creation to the devil's envy (cf. Life of Adam 12–17; 2 Enoch 31:3-6), the precursor to human sin. The reference may be to the description of the fall in Genesis 3 when the serpent tempts the woman and the man to eat of the tree of knowledge of good and evil.[29] Their disobedience to the prohibition against partaking of the fruit led to expulsion from the garden, the denial of access to the tree of life, and the sentence of death. This would be then an early identification of the devil with the serpent in the garden.[30] The teacher argues that the devil is envious of humanity, for they were created incorruptible, given dominion over the earth to rule as God's surrogates, and were worthy of adoration. Thus, through the devil's (serpent's?) envy of humanity's role as rulers in God's creation (cf. Genesis 1; Psalm 8), Death eventually entered into the world of God's creation. The teacher thus alludes to the apocalyptic notion of a devil, opposed to humanity and to divine rule, who is in control of death and is responsible for corrupting the design of God's creation of life. Only they who belong to the devil's party—the wicked who are aligned with him—experience death.

The Hidden Counsels of God (3:1–4:20) and the Final Judgment (5:1-23)

The next two parts of the larger section dealing with wisdom's leading to immortality describe the fate of the righteous in the hand of God (3:1–4:20) and the final judgment when the immortal righteous render judgment against the wicked (5:1-23).

In 3:1–4:20 and 5:1-23, the teacher asserts that the souls of the righteous dead are at peace in God's hand and are full of the hope of immortality (cf. 4:1; 5:15). Then at judgment time ("the time of their visitation") they will receive the gift of eternal life and hold judgment over all the earth, even as the Lord will be their king forever (3:8). While on earth, they have suffered, been tested, and died a sacrificial death for their embodiment of virtue and faith. But after their death, they will begin a new, immortal life. While judgment, in some fashion, may immediately follow death, the teacher seems to be thinking especially of an eschatological reckoning for which the dead wait.[31]

> 3:7. In the time of their visitation they will shine forth,
>   like sparks in stubble, they will run quickly.
> They shall judge nations and rule over peoples,
>   and the Lord shall reign over them for ever.

Continuing with the royal metaphor, the teacher speaks of the eternal life that comes to the righteous, who will one day receive from God a "beautiful crown" (5:15-16).

> 15. But the righteous live for ever,
>   for their reward is in the Lord,
>   and the Most High has them in mind.
> 16. Therefore, they will receive a glorious royalty,
>   and a beautiful crown from the hand of the Lord,
>   because he shall cover them with his right hand,
>   and with his arm he shall shield them.

It is the righteous who during the final reckoning will judge peoples and nations, not the wicked who have persecuted them. Indeed, when they perish, God's taking the righteous from the presence of the wicked is a blessing, for they are safe in the care and mind of God until the final judgment. The metaphor of royalty, important for construing traditional wisdom's understanding of the role and function of humanity in the world, is taken by this teacher and transferred to the future life when the righteous dead "will receive a glorious royalty, and a beautiful crown." This affirmation of the righteous dead's receiving a crown and reigning as kings after the eschatological judgment is an important theme in Jewish and early Christian apocalyptic.[32]

Even so, God has not abandoned creation to the misrule of the wicked. In shaping a theodicy for defending divine providence, the teacher asserts that the divine warrior, dressed in battle gear, will be joined by creation to defeat the wicked (5:17-23). This hymnic description of divine and cosmic battle is divided into two parts, as signified by the introductory verse: the Lord's armor (vv. 18-20*a*) and the weapons of creation (vv. 20*b*-23).

> 17. He (the Lord) shall take his zeal as his full armor,
>   and will arm creation to retaliate against his enemies.
> 18. He shall put on righteousness as his breastplate,
>   and he shall wear impartial justice as his helmet.
> 19. He shall have holiness as his invincible shield,
> 20. And he shall sharpen stern wrath to be his sword,
>   and the cosmos will join him in battle against madmen.
> 21. Javelins of lightning will fly with accurate aim,
>   and as from an arched bow made of clouds, they will leap upon the target.
> 22. And hailstones full of wrath will be cast as from a catapult,
>   the waters of the sea shall rage against them,
>   and rivers will wash relentlessly over them.
> 23. And a mighty wind shall rise against them,
>   and like a tempest it will winnow them.
>   And lawlessness will lay waste to all the earth,
>   and evil activity will overthrow the thrones of rulers.

God's zeal, righteousness, justice, and holiness comprise his armor, while the forces of creation (lightning, hailstones, the waters of the sea and rivers, and wind) turn into weapons to defeat the wicked (see 18:14-16; 19:13-17). The metaphor of the Divine Warrior, armed with the weapons of natural forces, is a common one in the Hebrew Bible (see esp. Isa. 59:16-18). But here the teacher wishes to emphasize that creation joins the Lord in battle to defeat the wicked. Because of the eschatological thrust of chapters 11–19, it could be that this defeat of the wicked is an apocalyptic event still residing in the future, but this is not necessary for a future vision. The language of 11–19 indicates that the elements of creation are able to transform themselves to redeem the righteous and punish the wicked.[33] In any case, the teacher wishes to assure his audience that this eventual defeat of the wicked is certain. The wicked will not only experience divine retribution in this life, but they will die without the hope of immortality as well. In the judgment time, the righteous will stand up to condemn the wicked, who will recognize too late the folly of their false reasoning and their persecution of the righteous. Indeed, their hope of immortality is "dispersed before the wind like smoke" (5:14).

The Exhortation to Seek Wisdom (6:1-21)

On the basis of this view of the immortality of the righteous and the annihilation of the wicked, the teacher, speaking through the lips of Solomon, now warns the kings and judges of the earth of the righteous judgment of God, who, having given them sovereignty over the earth, will punish them when they are unjust (6:1-20). It is only in the learning of wisdom that the teacher offers both escape from punishment and the gift of life. Indeed, those who observe the teacher's (Solomon's) word will learn wisdom and become holy through their observance of holy things in holiness (6:9-11). It is through *paideia*—the discipline that is shaped by the desire of wisdom, piety, study, and obedience—that there is both the assurance of immortality and the gift of sovereignty (6:17-21). Kings who desire to continue to reign may do so forever by pursuing wisdom. Their reign is not limited to earthly rule, but through wisdom's gift of immortality continues in God's eternal kingdom.

THE NATURE OF WISDOM AND SOLOMON'S QUEST TO OBTAIN HER (6:22–11:1)

Introduction (6:22-25)

In the second major subsection of the first half of the book, the teacher, continuing to speak through the voice of Solomon, sets out to describe the nature of Woman Wisdom, beginning with her origins at the time of creation (cf. Job 28:23-28; Prov. 8:22-31; Sir. 1:4; 24:9), and how he possessed her (cf. 1 Kings 3:1-15).

Solomon's Speech (7:1–8:21)

Solomon, the narrator, begins with a description of his origins (7:1-6), describing his conception, formation in the womb, gestation period, and birth.[34] There are important references to the tradition of God's creation of humanity, especially the one that speaks of the formation of "the first formed child of the earth" (7:1; 10:1) and the other that describes Solomon's being "fashioned into flesh" in his mother's womb, a passive verb that is one grammatical way of referring obliquely to divine activity (see Job 10:8-12; Ps. 139:13-16; Qoh. 11:5). The metaphor for the creation of Solomon is that of the divine artisan who creates humanity as a work of art. Solomon descends from Adam, who was formed by God from the earth, imagery alluding to the activity of a potter who shapes the clay into a vessel (Gen. 2:7; cf. Sir. 17:1). "Fashioned" in the womb points to God as a sculptor who sculpts humanity into a beautiful work of art.[35]

Solomon especially emphasizes the common origins that he shares with all human beings (see Prov. 22:2; 29:13). Even he, a great monarch, had no special birth. He, like all people, is a mortal, a descendant of Adam, and not a divine king who is the offspring of gods, as was claimed by some kings in the Eastern Mediterranean world.[36] For Solomon, all people share the same beginning and the same departure (7:6; see Job 1:21; Qoh. 3:19-20; 9:3; Sir. 40:1-2). Wisdom, therefore, may be possessed by anyone, regardless of status.

Solomon asserts that wisdom comes through prayer, and not because of the claims of divine nature or royal status.

Telling of his prayer for Wisdom (cf. 1 Kings 3:5-15) and the good things that accompanied God's gift of her, Solomon describes her inestimable worth and then indicates that his own renowned wisdom was due to God's endowment (7:7-14; cf. Job 28:15-19; Psalm 19B; Prov. 3:13-18; 8:15-21). Through this gift, Solomon says that he came to know the structure of the cosmos (cosmology) and what exists on earth (7:17-22a).

> 17. He (God) gave to me unerring knowledge of the things that are,
>   to know the structure of the cosmos and the activity of the elements;
> 18. the beginning and end and middle of times,
>   the changes of the solstices and the vicissitudes of the seasons;
> 19. the cycles of the year and the constellations of the
>   stars;
> 20. the nature of living creatures and the tempers of wild beasts;
>   the strength of spirits and the reasonings of humans;
>   the varieties of plants and the virtues of roots;
> 21. I came to know what is hidden and what is revealed;
> 22a. For wisdom, the artificer of all, instructed me.

Solomon attributes his astute knowledge of the physical world and all that it contains to the instruction of Wisdom, given to him by God (cf. 1 Kings 5:9-14). Through Wisdom he received a comprehensive, unerring knowledge of all that exists as well as the structure of the cosmos (cosmology) and the activity of its elements (physics),[37] the temporal order (calendar) and its association with the heavens (astronomy), animals (zoology), the powers of spirits (either demonology or the impulses associated with human passions),[38] humans (anthropology, philosophy, and psychology), and plants (botany and pharmacy). Solomon becomes the scientist and philosopher who knows the whole of reality and all that exists within it.

In verse 22 Wisdom is described as the *technitis,* or artificer, who fashioned all things (cf. 8:6; Prov. 8:30). This role of Wisdom in creation, shaping and forming what exists (8:6), provides her with an intimate knowledge of reality. Wisdom is the artisan who is at work in the shaping of the cosmos. Subsequently, she is able to teach her knowledge of the cosmos to Solomon (see 14:2). In 9:1-2, God created all that exists through his word, and by his wisdom he formed humanity to have dominion over the earth. Here Wisdom is active in the creating of human beings, who are created to rule as God's surrogates over the world. Subsequently, Wisdom as artisan is linked to both traditions of creation, cosmology and anthropology.

Solomon then proceeds to describe the character and nature of Wisdom (7:22b–8:1).

7:22b. For there is in her an intelligent spirit, holy,
    unique in kind, manifold, subtle,
    movable, lucid, unstained,
    clear, invulnerable, lover of the good, sharp,
23. unhindered, beneficent, philanthropic,
    mobile, lucid, free from care,
    all powerful, watching over all,
    and penetrating through all spirits
    that are intelligent, pure, and subtle.
24. For Wisdom is more mobile than any motion;
    and because of her purity she pervades and permeates all things.
25. For she is a breath of the power of God,
    and a pure emanation of the glory of the Almighty;
    therefore, nothing defiled gains entrance to her.
26. For she is an effulgence of eternal light,
    and a spotless mirror of the activity of God,
    and an image of his goodness.
27. Though being one, she is able to do all,
    and remaining in herself she renews all things;
    entering in each generation into holy souls,
    and making them friends of God and prophets;
28. For nothing pleases God except that which cohabits with wisdom.
29. For she is more beautiful than the sun,
    and excels all the constellations;
    and compared to the light she is found to be superior;
30. For it is succeeded by the night,
    but evil does not prevail against wisdom.
8:1. But with strength she stretches from one end to another,
    and she orders all things well.

In his description of the nature and activity of Wisdom (7:22b–8:1), Solomon points to some twenty-one qualities she possesses, a number produced by multiples of three and seven. Both are sacred numbers that point to completion and perfection.[39] Solomon presents Wisdom as an attribute of God, who, partaking of God's essence, becomes almost a divine being.[40] Thus cosmic Wisdom is transcendent and participates in the divine nature and activity of God. Yet, Wisdom's ability to "permeate all things" is the sage's way of speaking also of divine immanence while avoiding the sticky problem of pantheism.

Of particular interest are Wisdom's presentation as the breath of God, her ability to renew all things (v. 27), and her entrance into holy souls in each generation. Wisdom's origins as the "breath of the power of God" (v. 25; cf. Sir. 24:3) picks up an image from Ben Sira (Sir. 24:3). She is identified with the creative breath or spirit of God active in creation (Gen. 1:2; Ps. 104:29-30).

Solomon describes the nature, character, and activity of Wisdom primarily in relationship to those features of God. She is a "pure emanation" of divine glory as well as an "effulgence of eternal light," images that point to Wisdom's

305

reflection of the light that radiates from God's being. She reflects not only the holiness and glory of God's presence, but also his character, being in the "image of his goodness." Finally, Wisdom reflects the activity of God in creation and history.

Her creative power enables the generations of the cosmos to be renewed and to continue (cf. Ps. 104:30). Wisdom also renews the human generations, enabling them to endure. And her dwelling among holy souls enables them to become "friends of God" (a designation of Abraham in 2 Chron. 20:7; Isa. 41:8) and prophets. "Friends" are those who are loved by God, while "prophets" are those who are inspired by Wisdom to know the will of God. The "holy souls" are sages who through *paideia* seek instruction and embody it in their character and actions. Indeed, in a graphic metaphor of fertility, Solomon asserts that God especially loves those who cohabit with Wisdom. Fertility imagery is used by the teacher to describe both the well-being experienced by those who pursue wisdom and the bonds of love between the wise and Woman Wisdom, who is depicted as a goddess and lover (cf. Prov. 3:13-18; 9:1-6).

Finally, Wisdom extends over all creation and "orders [*diakei*] all things well," giving all that exists a structure, a pattern of activity, a time, and a place to exist, and providentially directing reality in the fashion of one who administers and governs an ideal house or city.[41] Here the cosmos is a well-ordered house or city under the direction of Woman Wisdom (cf. Prov. 31:10-31).

Solomon then speaks of his passion for Wisdom and his desire to take her as his bride (8:2-21; cf. Prov. 8:12-21). Solomon, the passionate lover of many women (cf. Canticles), now seeks to embrace the most desirable woman of all: Woman Wisdom. The quest for Wisdom assumes the images of sexual passion (cf. Proverbs 8–9). Once again, he describes nature and activities, including Wisdom's role in creation and providence.

> 2. This one I loved and searched for from my youth,
>   I sought to take her for my bride,
>   and I became enamored of her beauty.
> 3. She glorifies her noble birth by living intimately with God,
>   and the Ruler of all loved her.
> 4. For she is an initiate in the knowledge of God,
>   and a chooser of his works.
> 5. And if wealth is a desirable possession in life,
>   what is richer than Wisdom who effectuates all things?
> 6. And if understanding is effective,
>   who more than she is the artificer of all that exists?

Wisdom, desired by Solomon to be his bride (cf. Prov. 7:4; Sir. 15:2), is already God's lover.[42] Images of royal passion for fertility goddesses are used to describe Solomon's desire for Woman Wisdom, God's lover. As God's intimate companion, Wisdom "glorifies her noble birth," reflecting her hymn of self-praise in Proverbs 8:22-31—Yahweh fathers her, gives her birth, and takes delight in his child. Now the child has become the intimate lover of God.[43] These images of the birth point to the sage's use of the fertility metaphor to speak of the origins of Wisdom.

Intimacy with God also becomes the source of Wisdom's divine knowledge and the basis for her role in creation. She chooses the things that are to be created and becomes both the instrument of his activity and the artisan of what is formed. The possession of her is more valuable than wealth and the objects of wealth (cf. Psalm 19B; Prov. 3:13-18; 8:10-11, 18-19). Possessed by those who seek her, she becomes their teacher and instructs them in the knowledge of what exists in every temporal mode, from past to present to future. And most important of all, her possession, made possible only by God's gift, leads to immortality (8:13, 17).

Solomon's Prayer for Wisdom (9:1-18)

Solomon's desire for Wisdom leads, then, to his prayer to have her, since she may come only as God's gift (7:7-10). The prayer exhibits the following structure: address of God and request for wisdom (vv. 1-4), the basis for the request (5-8), the advantage of having Wisdom (9-12), and the inability to understand God's will without Wisdom (13-18). In the opening of the prayer, God is addressed as the creator of both reality and human beings:

1. O God of the fathers and Lord of mercy,
   the One who made all things by your word,
2. And by your Wisdom you have constructed humanity,
   in order that they may have dominion over the creatures who
   exist because of you,
3. And that they may manage the cosmos in holiness and righteousness,
   and that they may execute justice in uprightness of soul,
4. Give me Wisdom who is besides your throne,
   and do not reject me from among your children.

Traditions of cosmology and humanity figure prominently in shaping the theology of this prayer. The prayer begins with the metaphor of word to depict God's creation of all things (cf. Gen. 1:1–2:4a; Psalm 33; Sir. 24; 42:15). Building on Solomon's petition for wisdom in 1 Kings 3:3-15,[44] the prayer combines a royal petition for Wisdom to enable the king to rule and judge a people with the general human need for her in order to be successful in executing humanity's commission to have dominion over the creatures and to "manage the cosmos with holiness and righteousness." Wisdom, located

307

besides the throne of God (cf. Prov. 8:12-21), is portrayed as the skill and knowledge of the divine builder in the construction (*kataskeuasas*) of human beings (v. 2; cf. Gen. 2:7; Job 10; Psalm 139).[45] Drawing from the tradition of humanity as king over the earth (Genesis 1; Psalm 8), humans are created to reign over God's creatures and to rule the cosmos in "holiness" and "righteousness"—they are to recognize divine sovereignty and rule according to the dictates of divine teaching, embodied in Torah and wisdom.[46] God has given to humans the responsibility to be the surrogates of divine rule and the stewards of creation. The prayer acknowledges that, due to human weakness, mortals are unable to carry out this commission of ruling and managing the cosmos without the gift of Wisdom.

Later in the same prayer, Solomon speaks of Wisdom's presence at the beginning of creation (cf. Prov. 8:22-31):

> 9:9. With you is Wisdom, the knower of your works,
> who was present when you were making the cosmos,
> And knows what is pleasing in your sight,
> and what is right according to your commandments.

Solomon asks that God send him Wisdom, since she was present with God at the time of creation and thus knows his work (Prov. 8:22-31). Wisdom, also, knows the will of God expressed in the Torah and thus is able to guide one in behavior that will be acceptable to God. The commandments embody the order and life-giving power of creation. Without this gift of Wisdom, no mortal has the ability to know God's will and to act in ways that are pleasing to him, for the rational capacity is limited by a mortal body that restricts the mind's ability to think and to learn.[47] Here, Wisdom is the revelation of the will of God (9:13-18; cf. Prov. 30:1-4).

Wisdom Saves Her Own (10:1–11:1)[48]

This poem is transitional, marking the movement from Solomon as the wise king to God's deliverance of his people. The poem is divided into seven sections, each of which speaks of Wisdom's redemption of a person. Following the form and nature of a Greek encomium (cf. Sirach 44–50) the focus now is on individuals, from Adam to Moses, who, because of their righteousness were saved by Wisdom (cf. Sirach 44–50). The two individuals who are not specifically called a "righteous man" are Adam and Moses. Wisdom delivers Adam from his transgression (cf. Genesis 3), while, in the last example, Wisdom enters into the soul of Moses and saves the Israelites, who are designated as "the righteous" (v. 20), from the Egyptians. Adam's transgression, narrated in the fall in Genesis 3, more than likely precludes his being listed as a "righteous man," in spite of the fact that a later tradition ("The Life of Adam and Eve") speaks of his repentance and restoration. However, entering into the soul of Moses is another way of expressing the righteousness of Moses (see 1:4). Human examples (*paradeigmata*) of moral behavior are common in Greek literature.[49] Their character and actions embody the virtues of moral instruction and thus are noble examples not only to remember but to emulate as well. The teacher also refers to the wicked who were embodiments of vices and thus examples of what not to be.

Now Wisdom, a personified attribute of God who was involved in the creation of the cosmos and humanity, becomes the redeemer engaged in acts of deliverance of righteous individuals, who, though not named, are easily identifiable through the teacher's descriptions.[50] This salvific role of Woman Wisdom in redeeming the righteous underscores the teacher's affirmation that those who are faithful and righteous may hope for their own deliverance and salvation now and in the eschaton (19:22).[51] Wisdom's redemptive activity is not limited to the past, but continues through the present into the future. Important is the change in emphasis from God's performing mighty acts of redemption on Israel's behalf (i.e., the exodus, wilderness wandering, gift of Canaan; see Psalms 78; 105; 106; 135; 136) to Wisdom's redemption of Israel's ancestors: Adam, Noah, Abraham, Lot, Jacob, Joseph, and Moses, who number seven (see Enoch in 4:10 = Gen. 5:21-24, and the apocalyptic literature associated with him). This parallels Ben Sira's litany of ancestors ("pious men") in the epic poem in Sirach 44–50. In Wisdom of Solomon 10, the ancestors are saved because of their righteousness and following of Wisdom, while others who were wicked and spurned Wisdom perished: Cain; the foreign nations in Abraham's time (Gen. 11:1-9); the inhabitants of the Five Cities in the Lot narrative (Genesis 19); Lot's wife; the oppressors of Jacob, including Esau; the false accusers of Joseph; and the Egyptians in conflict with Moses and Israel.

The chapter begins with a description of Wisdom's salvation of Adam, the "first formed father of the world."

> 10:1. She (Wisdom) protected the first formed father of the world,
>   when he alone had been created,
>   And she delivered him from his own transgression.
> 2. She gave to him the strength to have mastery over all things.

Referring to the Yahwist tradition in Genesis 2–3, the teacher speaks of the creation and fall. The "first formed father of the world" is Adam (7:1; Gen. 2:7),[52] who "alone had been created," since Eve was formed from his rib and all other humans were born. His transgression is mentioned in general, though not specified. It is interesting that only his sin, and not Eve's complicity, is touched on. The repentance and restoration of Adam are found in postbiblical literature (cf. "The Life of Adam and Eve"), and this may be the tradition that allows the teacher to begin with him in listing the ancestors who were saved. Also mentioned is the commission to rule over creation, a continuation of the creation tradition that picks up the royal metaphor to describe humanity's role in the world (9:2; Gen. 1:26-28; 9:2; Psalm 8).

GOD'S FIDELITY TO HIS PEOPLE IN THE EXODUS AND WILDERNESS (11:2–19:22)

Introduction and Theme (11:2-5)

This extensive narrative on the exodus and wilderness (11:2–19:22) points to the continuing providence of God, who acts to redeem his own people in the past. But the narrative looks not simply to the past, but also to the present and future, as the redemptive acts of God continue to save the chosen (19:22).[53] Now the emphasis is no longer on Wisdom as redeemer who saves righteous ancestors of the past, but rather on God and the chosen. The introduction, describing Israel's wilderness experience, expresses in verse 5 the theme that unites the entire narrative: "For the things by which their enemies were punished, they themselves, being in need, were benefited."[54] This is itself a double-edged theme or contrast: That which punishes the enemies of Israel becomes for her a blessing. A variation of the theme is the point that one is punished by "the very things by which one sins" (11:16).[55]

This theme is central to the narrative structure of 11:2–19:22, comprised of five major sections (11:6-14; 11:15–16:15; 16:16-29; 17:1–18:4; 18:5–19:22) with each dividing into two contrasting parts (antitheses).[56] This linkage of multiple parts is called a syncrisis, or "comparison," a literary-philosophical technique in shaping a piece of literature and/or argument by uniting a series of contrasts by a common theme. The objective is to determine what is "equal, better, or worse."[57] In each contrast, the elements of creation that God uses to punish Israel's opponents (here typified by the Egyptians during the time of the Exodus) become at the same time the means of blessing for the Israelites. The five contrasts are Israel's receiving water from the rock and the plague of the Nile that afflicts the Egyptians; the Israelites' receiving the gift of quail while the Egyptians suffer the plague of little animals; the Israelites' receiving the rain of manna while the Egyptians are punished by the plague of storms; the Israelites' being led by the pillar of fire while the Egyptians are forced to endure the plague of darkness; and the death of the firstborn, leading to the exodus, punishing Egypt but glorying Israel.[58] What is important to note is that the teacher combines a theology of redemption history with a theology

310

of creation: Creation is not a dormant or static entity, but is an order of blessing and punishment through which God works to bring deliverance. At the same time, this uniting of creation and redemption presents a compelling theodicy, demonstrating that divine justice is operative in the cosmos. God uses the very same things in creation to punish the wicked and to bless the righteous. Yet, the afflictions of the Egyptians, who typify all those who oppress righteous Jews, are not simply designed to be punitive, but to help them come to a conscious understanding of the reality and power of the Lord. Through their reflections on this narrative of salvation history, the wicked not only come to attribute their own punishment to the Lord, but also to recognize that it was he who afflicted them with the very same instruments that he used to bless the righteous. Subsequently, they should learn that the Lord is both the creator of the cosmos and the ruler of history. And the wicked should also learn that they are punished by the very things by which they sin. At the same time, the wicked should learn of the love of God, who does not create anything that he would loathe, but seeks at all times to bring redemption to all. Even so, God's patience is not unending, and after a time of testing and waiting, he will bring destruction to the wicked. Here, the teacher speaks of an imminent eschatology in which divine justice will soon be meted out.[59]

The Gift of Quail and the Plague of Little Animals (11:15–16:15)

The second contrast is a lengthy one, interrupted by a diversion that addresses the origin and folly of idolatry (13:1–15:17). Once more the theme of being punished by means of the sins committed is articulated as the unifying theme for this contrast (11:15-16). In the opening (11:15-20) of this larger section, the teacher addresses God and speaks of his divine mercy in not afflicting the Egyptians with newly created, even more ferocious beasts, seeing that God's "all-powerful hand created the cosmos out of formless matter." For the teacher, creation is not *ex nihilo,* but rather a process of shaping preexistent matter. The eternal existence of matter was a common Greek idea. In the Hebrew Bible, creation also is not *ex nihilo*; rather, God shapes chaos (*tōhû wābōhû,* "formless waste"; Gen. 1:2) into things that exist and have form and purpose. The teacher emphasizes that while God as creator had the power to create new categories of fearsome beasts to destroy the Egyptians, he did not do so because his mercy extends to all who repent (v. 23; cf. 12:10; Ps. 145:8-9). So it is that God will not unnecessarily or often intrude into the natural order, though he has the power to do so. Rather, the universe is arranged by God according to certain laws of measure and number (see Job 28:25; Isa. 40:12, 26) that govern its existence, so that divine activity

311

does not arbitrarily interfere in the workings of the cosmos (vv. 20-22). In other words, God works through the natural processes.

The teacher then praises God for loving all that he has created, a love that is both the ground of the Lord's act of creation and the basis for his providential care, which sustains all that exists. Nothing exists or endures except by the love of God. Indeed, because of this divine love, God's imperishable spirit resides within all life, making the beginning and continuation of existence possible.

> 11:24. For you love all things that exist,
>   and you do not detest anything that you have made,
>   for you would not have constructed anything you hate.
>   25. And how would anything endure, unless you had willed it,
>   or how would something not called forth by you have been preserved?
>   26. For you spare all things, for they are yours, O Sovereign,
>   who loves the living.
> 12:1. For your imperishable spirit is in all things.

Two specific metaphors of creation and providence are used by the teacher at this juncture. The first is that of God who constructs (9:2) like an architect or builder that which he creates (11:24). The metaphor of word occurs in speaking of God "calling forth" things that exist and in the statement that the divine, "imperishable spirit" resides within all life (Psalm 104). This divine spirit, equated elsewhere with Wisdom (1:4-7) is "imperishable," providing life that continues. Only sin causes death, not God (1:12-15).

Later, in a section that speaks of God's patience and compassion extended to the Canaanites in order to give them the time to repent, the teacher speaks in more general terms of divine providence. God is pictured in the metaphor of a powerful king ruling over history and judging with justice, tempered with mercy, the world (12:12-18):

> 12. For who will say, "What have you done?"
>   Or who will oppose your judgment?
>   Who will accuse you for the destruction of nations which you have made?
>   Or who will come and stand before you as an advocate for the unrighteous?
> 13. For there is no God except you, whose care is for all;
>   there is not need for you to demonstrate that you have not judged unjustly.
> 14. Nor can any king or tyrant defy you in regard to those you have punished.
> 15. But being righteous, you manage all things righteously;
>   to condemn the one who does not deserve to be punished
>   you deem to be alien to your power.
> 16. For your strength is the source of righteousness,
>   and your sovereignty over all things enables you to spare all.
> 17. You do show forth your strength when there is doubt
>   concerning the perfection of your power,
>   and you do rebuke the insolence among those who are aware of your power.

18. For being sovereign in strength, you judge fairly,
    and with great mildness you exercise authority over us.
    for it is in your power to act whenever you will.

While the sovereignty of God cannot be successfully opposed by any other power, God's justice is unquestioned, and his mercy is considerable. It is extended even to the Canaanites, who were evil by nature (12:10-11), an idea traced back, not to creation, but to Noah's curse (Gen. 9:18-27). God punishes only those who deserve it and cannot, by his very nature, do otherwise. Yet the overriding emphasis is placed on divine mercy, for God extends his compassion to all. God, then, is the sovereign ruling the world in justice, "managing" (9:3) it as an orderly household or a well-administered city or nation.

The Folly of Pagan Religions (13:1–15:17)

Leaving aside for the moment his discourse about the opposites in creation, the teacher digresses from his syncrisis of contrasts to engage in a polemic against pagan religion. Four different pagan religions are criticized: nature religion, the worship of animals, fertility cults (especially the Dionysian mystery), and idolatry. This digression contains the following literary structure:

    The Religion of Nature (13:1-9)
    The Idolatrous Wood-Cutter (13:10-19)
    The Idolatrous Sea-Farer (14:1-10)
    The Invention of Idols and the Origin of Immorality (14:11-31)
    The Faithfulness of Israel (15:1-6)
    The Idolatrous Potter (15:7-13)
    The Religion of Egypt (15:14-17).[60]

In this section, the teacher draws on creation theology in important ways to speak of the superiority of Jewish religion and the true God it reveals.

In the polemic against nature worship (13:1-9), the teacher argues against the deification of nature, which results from the failure of humans, even philosophers, to differentiate between the creator and the works by which he should be known. Indeed, the creator should be recognized as superior to the works he has shaped.

1. For all humans are foolish by nature, having no knowledge of God;
    they are not able to know the one who is by reason
    of the good things which are seen.
Nor did they recognize the artificer by giving consideration to his works.

2. But rather they supposed that fire, or wind, or swift air,
    or the circle of stars or turbulent water,
    or the lights of heaven were gods ruling the world.
3. If they, delighting in beautiful things, took them to be gods,
        then they should have known how superior is the Lord of these things;
    for the creator of beauty has made them.
4. And if they were amazed at power and activity,
        let them perceive from these things how much more
    powerful is the one who shaped them.
5. For from the greatness and beauty of created things
        is the one who generated them analogously perceived.
6. But little blame comes upon these people,
        for they are deceived,
    while seeking and wishing to discover God.
7. For dwelling among his works, they continue to search,
        and they are persuaded by what they see, because the
    things seen are beautiful.
8. But again, they are not to be excused,
9. For if they had the ability to know so much
        that they might be able to infer the world,
    how is it they did not quickly find the sovereign of all things?

The teacher begins by returning to his view that humans are not born with a knowledge of God; rather, this knowledge must be learned. Humans by nature are "foolish" (*mataioi*), a word used to refer to idols (e.g., Jer. 2:5; 8:19; 10:15) as well as to idol makers in the LXX (Ps. 62:10; Isa. 44:9). God is "the one who is" (*tov onta*; cf. the LXX's translation of the meaning of the name *Yahweh*: "I am the one who is" [*ego eimi ho on*]).[61] The issue for the teacher is coming to a knowledge of the "one who is" apart from special revelation (i.e., scripture). Is it possible to come to this knowledge through a revelation of nature? For the teacher, the answer is yes.[62]

The teacher uses the metaphor of God as artisan or artificer (*technites*)[63] to argue that, since artisans are to be known by and yet differentiated from and superior to what they make, those who worship nature or elements of nature have failed to use their reason to conclude that God is known through his works (cf. Job 38–41; Ps. 19:1; Sir. 43:9-12). Indeed, they should have realized that the divine craftsman is not to be identified with his works, but exists in distinction from them. He, too, is greater than what he has created. It may be that the teacher is criticizing the tendency of some philosophers to identify the cosmos with the creator himself. Others have simply identified various cosmic forces (fire, wind, air, constellations, and heavenly lights—i.e., sun, moon, and stars) as gods who "rule the world"—in Greek religion, Hepaestus (fire), Hera (air), Demeter (earth), Poseidon (sea), Apollo (sun), and Artemis (moon). Parallels to the deification of nature are found in other religions of the eastern Mediterranean world. Even the philosophers associated creative

314

power with certain elements: fire (Heraclitus), water (Thales), air (Anaximenes), and heat (Pythagoras).[64]

A second argument, one based on analogy, is used by the teacher to suggest that philosophers should have made the correlation between the "goodness" and "greatness and beauty of created things" and the one who created them. This act of correlation would have enabled them to know the nature and character of the creator and his superiority even to the wondrous things he has made. While the teacher argues that humans are ignorant by nature, including lacking knowledge of God, they should be able to use their powers of reason to deduce the existence and, to some extent, the nature and character of God from the existence and character of creation. Even so, nature worshipers are "little to be blamed," especially in comparison to those who practice other pagan religions, like idolatry, animal worship, and fertility cults, for those who worship nature continue to search for God.

In this section on pagan religions, the teacher directs considerable criticism toward idolatry,[65] and in so doing draws upon idol satires found in Jeremiah and especially Second Isaiah (Jer. 10:1-16; Isa. 40:18-20; 41:1-7; 44:9-20; cf. Pss. 115:3-8; 135:15-18). Indeed, idolatry, argues the teacher, is responsible for the origins of immorality and the deification and worship of humans, especially kings (14:12-21). Important is the teacher's argument that idolatry is both an aberration of creation theology and a failure to understand and recognize the power and knowledge of God in matters of providence.[66] However, he especially emphasizes the folly of idolatry.

In the teacher's discussion of the idolatry of the sailor (14:1-10), he contrasts divine providence with the inability of idols attached to ships to provide guidance through the perils of sea voyages.

> 1. And again, someone making preparations for a voyage and
>   about to sail through raging waves,
>   calls upon wood that is more unsound than the ship that carries him.
> 2. For it was the desire for gain that conceived the vessel,
>   and wisdom was the builder that constructed it.
> 3. But it is your providence, O Father, that pilots it,
>   because you have provided a way in the sea,
>   and a safe path through the waves,
> 4. Showing that you are able to rescue from all dangers,
>   so that even one without skill may set sail.

The teacher develops his argument against this practice of idolatry in several ways. First, the sailor prays to a piece of wood that is more fragile than the ship that carries him. Second, the teacher contrasts the wisdom (*sophia*) of the shipbuilder (the *technites,* "artisan," "artificer")[67] who constructs the vessel with the folly of the person who makes idols. The idol maker is not an

315

"artisan" who uses wisdom to create images made with human hands. Third, the teacher contrasts divine providence (*pronoia*; 14:3; cf. 17:2), which pilots the ship and shapes creation to provide "safe pathways" through the sea, with idols that do not have the knowledge of nature and the power to guide a ship safely to port (cf. Ps. 77:19; Isa. 43:16).[68]

Elsewhere in the teacher's discussion of idolatry, he draws on the tradition of the creation of the cosmos in arguing that idol makers pervert creation by taking some of its natural elements (wood, stone, metals, etc.) and turning them into abominations (14:11). Elements of creation that are in themselves good, though perishable in contrast to the immortal creator, are perverted by their use in the making of abominable idols.

Idolatry is also an aberration of the creation of humanity, because human idol makers attempt to give life and traits of existence to lifeless objects like stone and wood. Humans, in the constructing of an idol, are not only attempting to play God, but ironically are trying to create a god in a human image and to name something made of perishable material a deity as well. Here, the teacher contrasts the folly and hubris of the human idol maker with God's work in making humanity in the divine image (cf. Gen. 1:26-28). In another sense, idolatry is an aberration, because it denigrates the creation of humanity tradition. This line of argument winds along several paths. One path leads to the conclusion that idolatry is an act of irrationality. Idol makers and worshipers fail to use their reason, the capacity for which is a part of their created nature, to understand the foolishness of creating and holding in reverence objects that do not possess even the limited abilities of their makers.

Another path points to the supreme irony of using the same clay from which humans, including the idol maker, are made to fashion a worthless god (9:2; Gen. 2:7; Job 10:9). This is the argument in 15:7-11:

> 7. For a potter, laboriously kneads soft clay,
>   forms each one for our use;
>   he fashions out of the same clay
>   both vessels that are for a clean use
>   and vessels of the opposite kind, all alike;
>   but what shall be the use of each of these
>   the worker in clay decides.
> 8. And with misspent toil he fashions a vain god out of the very same clay,
>   he who but a short time before was made of earth
>   and after a little while goes to the earth from which he was taken.
> 9. But he has no concern that he is destined for disaster, or that his life is short,
>   for he competes with workers in gold and silver,
>   and imitates coppersmiths,
>   and considers it glorious that he fashions spurious things.
> 10. His heart is ashes, his hope is cheaper than dirt,
>   and his life is worth less than clay,

11. because he did not know the one who fashioned him,
    infused in him an active soul,
    and breathed into him a vital spirit.

The teacher observes that the clay from which the idol maker gathers his materials to construct his image is the same clay to which he will one day return when his soul at death must return to the God who gave it (Gen. 3:19; Qoh. 12:7). The foolish idol maker is unable to observe the features of his own existence and to come to a knowledge of the one who made him and breathed into him the breath of life (Gen. 2:7).

A Rain of Manna Instead of the Plague of Storms (16:16-29)

The third contrast in the syncrisis opposes the plague of storms that brought destruction to the Egyptians with the manna from heaven. The burning fire and lightning consumed the ungodly, continuing to burn in spite of the water. By contrast, manna, metaphorically described as snow and ice and called the "food of angels," is not destroyed by the fire (sunlight). Once again, in the world of retributive justice, fire "forgets its own power" in order that the righteous might eat (v. 23). The teacher then moves to his key argument in speaking about the constitution of creation and God's ability to transform its elements to serve divine purposes (16:24-25):

24. For the creation, serving you, the one who made it,
    tenses in order to punish the wicked,
    but relaxes in kindness on behalf of those who trust in you.
25. Therefore, also, at that time, being transformed into all things,
    it (creation) served your all-nourishing bounty,
    according to the desire of those who make petition.

The Tenth Plague and the Exodus (18:5–19:22)

The final contrast is that of the death of the firstborn of Egypt, which leads to the liberation of Israel. In continuing his unifying theme, the teacher argues that the very events by which the Egyptians are punished bring blessing upon the Israelites. In describing God's judgment against Egypt at the Red Sea and Israel's deliverance, the teacher explains:

19:6 For the entire creation in its nature was refashioned,
    serving your commands,
    in order that your children might be preserved unharmed.

According to the teacher, the transformation of nature occurs by means of the principle of the interchangeability of the basic physical elements in order

317

that the righteous might be saved.[69] The creator possesses this power of transformation in reshaping nature, but it is a transformation in line with the nature of the physical constitution of creation.

In his conclusion to the plagues and the Red Sea (19:18-21), the teacher explains that the elements that comprise the forces and creatures of nature exchanged with one another, in the same fashion as notes on a musical score may be changed to alter the rhythm (cf. 16:24-25). Thus land animals became water creatures and vice versa. Fire was not quenched by water, and its flames failed to consume or melt. This argument allows the teacher to avoid the notion of divine miracles interrupting natural processes or going against natural law.[70] It is at this point that the teacher abruptly concludes his homily of persuasion by praising the Lord of creation and history, who continues to redeem his people.

CREATION AND REDEMPTION IN WISDOM

Living among a Jewish community in the Hellenistic world of Alexandria, Egypt, a wisdom teacher composes an exhortatory speech designed to encourage faithful and wavering Jews to maintain their loyalty to their ancestral faith, to persuade apostate Jews to return to their religious traditions, and to convince pagans of both the integrity and superiority of Jewish religion. Through his speech of artful persuasion informed by Hellenistic literary and philosophical conventions, the teacher shapes a world of imagination that through the activation of memory lays claim to the theological traditions of the past in the effort to address at least one community of the Jewish Diaspora. He skillfully combines Jewish traditions of salvation history and creation with familiar Hellenistic form and thought to construct a new theological synthesis.[71]

Drawing on earlier formulations of a personified wisdom (Job 28; Prov. 1:20-33; 8; 9; Sirach 24), the teacher gives divine-like characteristics to Woman Wisdom, who dwells beside the divine throne and reflects the glory and attributes of God's nature and embodies the divine activities of creation and redemption in history. She is the artificer through whom God worked in creating the structure of the cosmos (cf. Prov. 3:19-20; 8:22-31), the divine spirit that dwells within and orders creation (cf. Sirach 24), the vital force that renews all things (cf. Psalm 104), and the indwelling spirit that enters into righteous human souls in each generation and blesses them with the bounty of her gifts (cf. Prov. 3:13-18). Indeed, those who pray to God for her, earnestly seeking to possess her, may expect her to come and take up her dwelling within them (cf. 1 Kings 3). The teacher also draws on the traditions of redemptive history in reciting first a litany of those saved by Wisdom (cf. Sirach 44–50)

318

and then retelling God's deliverance of the Israelites from the Egyptians (cf. Sir. 45:1-5).

Even so, the teacher is not content simply to recite the past, but, by an act of the imagination, he reshapes it in part with a new literary form, a *logos protreptikos* (speech of exhortation), which follows Hellenistic literary conventions (for example the syncrisis), and with new understandings. His thesis in the second part of the book, for example, articulates the theme that those things in creation that blessed the Israelites became the means by which God punished the Egyptians. A variation of this idea is the Stoic concept that the elements of nature were reconfigured in order to act in new and different ways. This both preserved the integrity of the laws guiding the physical world and allowed for God's redemption of the Israelites and punishment of the Egyptians. Instead of rejecting Hellenistic thought and literary expression, the teacher makes use of both to communicate his restatement of Jewish faith and to lessen the allure of Greek culture.

The imaginative world of instruction and narrative also moves toward a new vision of reality that is yet to exist fully. The teacher's exhortatory speech contains an eschatological character, for he promises that God's acts of redemption in the past will continue in the future. Because of God's love for creation and all his creatures, he offers even to pagans and apostates the opportunity to pursue righteousness and to come to a knowledge of their creator. Kings of the earth, along with all mortals everywhere, may shape within themselves a righteous character that allows them to receive wisdom and through wisdom obtain the gift of immortality. Righteous Jews, even those who perish because of loyalty to their faith and the witness of their character, have the hope of immortality. Indeed they will be the ones who in judgment will stand and condemn the wicked. Only the righteous have the gift of immortality made possible through Wisdom. There will be a reckoning in which the wicked will be punished, while the righteous will reign over the new world.

The teacher's speech of exhortation, through its rhetorical structure, enacts a world that allows for the active presence of God and the participation of those who become wise. The first major section speaks of Wisdom's indwelling in creation and entrance into the souls of the righteous. Wisdom is the artificer of creation who renews all life, while she also dwells within the righteous in reconciling them to God and leading them to immortality. The wicked deny divine creation, attributing their existence to mere chance. Through their evil, death entered into the world, and in their efforts to deny divine purpose to life they persecute and seek to destroy the righteous. Solomon, the narrator through whose voice the teacher speaks, becomes the example of the righteous person whose prayer for Wisdom leads to her possession. At the end of the first major section, Wisdom takes on the role of the redeemer who saves the righteous from destruction.

The second part of this speech of persuasion narrates God's redemption of Israel and punishment of Egyptians as paradigmatic for divine action in the world and the purpose toward which God directs cosmos and history. The focus is on the deliverance of Israel from Egyptian slavery and the wilderness time that follows thereafter. Through the use of a Greek literary convention— the syncrisis, which in this case consists of five parts—the teacher stresses that the wicked (exemplified by the Egyptians of old) are punished by means of the very things that bless Israel. Creation's elements are reshaped to redeem the righteous and to punish the wicked. The teacher ends his exhortatory address with affirmation: God has always exalted and glorified Israel and does not neglect his people in any and all circumstances.

There is an extensive digression in the second major unit that deals with the folly of pagan religions. Within the structure of the entire speech there is a movement that, while returning to earlier intonations, goes from creation to the dwelling within the righteous, to redemptive history, to the eschatological glimpse of a future time of divine salvation. The rhetorical structure of the speech aids the stimulation and activation of the imagination.

Metaphors of creation play an important role in the structure and content of the sage's theology. In Solomon's prayer, God is addressed as the one who created all things through his word and formed humankind to have dominion over the creatures (9:1-2). God created the world out of "formless matter" (11:17), meaning that the creation is not *ex nihilo* ("out of nothing"), but rather a process of shaping and forming matter into the forms of things that are created.[72] However, it is especially Woman Wisdom who serves as both the instrument of divine activity in creation and the artificer (7:22; 8:6; God is the artificer in 13:1) of what is formed. Divine Wisdom is now more than a literary device or a personification of a divine attribute. She has become an existing being, mediating between heaven and earth. Woman Wisdom permeates creation, holds it together, and provides it with a structure and order, while as the divine spirit she renews all life. Cosmic Wisdom enters into and dwells in pure and honest souls in each generation, making them friends of God, while indicting the wicked, who face destruction. Through the indwelling of Wisdom comes the greatest gift of God: the possession of immortality. Yet Woman Wisdom is also a lover, serving as the consort of God and becoming the object of human passion. Through their love for Wisdom, humans come into her possession and through her experience the gift of immortality. Indeed, in history she leads the righteous to salvation. She is the embodiment of providence, identified with God's mind, which controls and directs the operations of the cosmos. The figure of Wisdom allowed the sage to speak of both the transcendence and the immanence of God.

In addition to metaphors of word and wisdom, creation theology is shaped by images of God as the Divine warrior, who, armed with righteousness, justice, and holiness, will enlist the powers of creation to defeat the wicked. Indeed, God uses the natural order to bless the Israelites and to afflict the wicked Egyptians during the time of the exodus.

God is the artisan who shapes the firstborn of the earth, the divine sculptor who forms humanity in the womb, and the builder or architect of human beings. The greatest folly of idolatry is that it is an aberration of the theology of God as the creator of humanity. Humans try to fashion a god who is greatly inferior to themselves and are unwilling or unable by faulty reasoning to recognize that God is their creator, who fashioned them, gave them a soul, and breathed into them a vital spirit.

The most important metaphor for humanity is that of king. In his prayer, Solomon addresses God as the one who formed humanity to rule over the creatures and to actualize justice in reigning over the world (9:1-2). The teacher emphasizes the common origins of all people, including even the renowned Solomon. This king describes his origins by drawing on the creation of humanity tradition, describing in normal ways his conception, formation in the womb, gestation, and birth. A descendant of Adam who was shaped from the earth by the artisan God, Solomon, like all other humans, had a normal human birth. In the fiction of the speech, those addressed are rulers of the earth, while the narrator's voice is King Solomon, the paragon of wisdom in Jewish tradition. Solomon embodies the attributes not only of the ideal king, but also of humans who seek wisdom, actualize righteousness in word and deed, and obtain the gift of immortality. The audience is also a larger one, consisting of Jews, apostates, and pagans. The suffering of the righteous in the present may involve even death for the sake of faith and virtue. Nevertheless, the righteous will inherit immortality and reign over a future life.

In the speeches of the wicked, the implicit metaphor is that of slave. The wicked deny that there is any escape from death. Chance, not purposeful creation, is the reason for their existence. For them, human thought is not an extension of the cosmic principle of wisdom permeating the cosmos. Rather, in their view, thought derives from the physical beating of the heart. The beating heart generates fire that becomes thought and smoke that becomes breath. Once the fire is extinguished, the body turns to ashes and breath evaporates into the vapors of air. For the wicked, there is no divine reason (wisdom) or breath that is a part of human nature and character. There is no understanding that humanity is created in the divine image for immortality. There is no continuing memory of who humans are and what they do. At death their memory disappears, together with their bodies and their breath. The wicked enter into a pact with Death, not in the hope of escaping their ultimate end, but because they desire to continue their lives for a little longer.

Finally, for this teacher the world is a kingdom ruled over by God through wisdom. Death rules over its own kingdom of the underworld, and its incursion into the world of the living is because of human sin and the devil's envy of humanity's divinely ordained place of sovereignty over the creatures. God has appointed humans to rule the earth in justice, to reign in his place over the cosmos. A similar metaphor depicts the cosmos in terms of Wisdom's administering and governing a well-ordered house or city.

For the teacher, God is in control of creation and human history. Although a kindly providence waits patiently for the wicked to repent, there is and will be divine judgment. The righteous, possessing and being led by Wisdom, may wait in confident hope for justice. Because of faithful living, they may rest assured that they will receive the gift of immortality.

PART III

Wisdom Theology, Sapiential Imagination, and Metaphor

CHAPTER EIGHT

"Wisdom Has Built Her House, She Has Hewn Her Seven Pillars"

SUMMARY AND CONCLUSIONS

INTRODUCTION

How does one speak of the mystery of God? How does one attempt the impossible? In Western Christian theology, linguistic renderings largely have been discursive and denotative, seeking to define in creedal and systematic form what the church has believed about God, humanity, and the world. Israelite and Jewish sages chose another type of language to present and convey these cherished beliefs. They expressed their faith in story, poem, instruction, and saying. They articulated their theology through imagination, rhetorical structure, and metaphors. The sages could live with contrast, difference, ambiguity, and even contradiction in the formulations of their most sacred affirmations. Contemporary theologians call systematic renderings of the faith second-order theology, while they regard the theological language of the Bible to be first-order theology. When Old Testament theologians present Israelite and Jewish faith in discursive and systematic form, they begin by examining the views of God, humanity, and the world in narratives and poems. They then move into a rational, discursive, even systematic mode. However, these moves into the second order of theological language may have been made at the expense of the presentation, meaning, and diversity of texts.

Narrative theologians in contemporary theology have reminded us of the importance of how stories actualize meaning. The same may be said of poetry. When the content of the narratives and poems is taken out of these forms and shaped into a systematic presentation, a different rendering of faith and its meaning occurs. I would not deny the importance of second-order language for expressing the Old Testament witness. But I also think that to give an account of Old Testament faith we need to begin by paying careful attention to the language of the narratives and poems themselves.[1] James Muilenburg and Phyllis Trible, among others, have stressed that the formal and rhetorical features of language cannot be discarded in the effort to distill the content.[2] Form, rhetoric, and content belong together, for they are the constituent parts of language. To separate them is to alter the meaning of the text. Elsewhere I have taken a first step into the second order of theological language by presenting the theology of the sages in systematic form.[3] To do so here would have required another type of approach, indeed another book.

In presenting the theology of the sages, I have gone beyond what the sages often did with their language. I have even explicitly named the metaphors for God, to which the sages alluded but usually did not directly state. They preferred to describe the activity of God in metaphorical terms, but not to name God with specifically human titles. Naming God in anthropomorphic terms, at least for many sages, would have penetrated too far beyond the veil of divine mystery. They might even have regarded human titles as idolatrous. Calling God names would also place limitations and restrictions on one whose greatness and majesty cannot be expressed, but only imagined. However, I have taken this step in the effort to have a closer look at their understandings of God. While these metaphorical pictures of God were imaginatively present in depicting divine activity, the sages did not attempt to translate these renderings into literal objects of faith and inflexible representations.

METAPHORICAL THEOLOGY IN SAPIENTIAL TRADITIONS

In the sapiential corpus of literature, God's wisdom is the divine capacity to design, form, and order creation and to rule providentially over what has been brought into being. Divine wisdom is closely associated with the power to create and sustain the cosmos and guide providentially both individual lives and human history (Job 9:4; 12:12-16; 38:36-37; Ps. 104:24; Prov. 3:19; Isa. 33:5-6; 40:12-31; Jer. 10:12; 51:15). God alone is the one who truly knows and understands wisdom (Job 28:23), and he dispenses it to human beings (1 Kings 5:9, 26; Job 11:6; 28; Pss. 51:8; 90:12; Prov. 2:6). Human wisdom is the ability to imagine a righteous and beneficent order in the world,[4] to shape and sustain just institutions, to enable the social order to exist in concert with creation, to engage in the moral life that is in harmony with the cosmos and the larger society, and to experience well-being and success.[5]

Thematically expressed, wisdom theology centers in creation. This theology has a universal character, for God is the God of the world and all its inhabitants and not simply a national deity. While the sages understood God to be the creator and sustainer of the world, human beings, and social reality from the early formation of their tradition, they embraced the particularistic, election traditions of Israel very late. It is only with the writings of Ben Sira that the sages brought into their theological imagination the witness of many

326

other Old Testament texts to redemptive history—that is, Yahweh is the one who brought Israel into existence through mighty acts of salvation history and sustained the nation in order to move it toward an envisioned future for the world. The important themes of salvation history (exodus, wilderness wandering, covenant and law at Sinai, the gift of the land of Canaan, the covenant with David, and Jerusalem as the City of God) do not make their appearance in wisdom literature until the writings of Jesus ben Sira. Rather, for the sages, God is the universal deity who created and providentially guides the world and its inhabitants. This does not mean that the God of the sages does not direct human history, but it does indicate that the particularity of God's choosing of Israel, accompanied by salvific traditions that articulate in various ways the meaning of election, is absent from their theological expressions until the early second century B.C.E. Israel's election theology plays no role in sapiential reflection for many centuries. Thus it is not astonishing to find non-Israelite wisdom, acknowledged to be so, in the Bible (e.g., Prov. 31:1-9). It is also not astonishing to discover that the hero Job is likely a foreigner, possibly even an Edomite!

Theologically, then, this absence of salvation history does not mean that the traditional sages were secular thinkers and teachers interested only in the everyday life of ordinary human existence and not in religious matters. Rather, sapiential teaching, even from its inception, is grounded in religious piety ("the fear of God"), specifically a piety that trusts in the God who creates and sustains both a cosmos that is beautiful and good and human creatures who are the object of special care. Indeed, creation theology speaks not simply of origins, but also of the continuation of the world and providential nurturing of human beings (including their history and their social institutions). For the traditional sages, God is both absolutely just and transcendent, and humanely compassionate and immanent. As the object of devotion and contemplation, both the righteousness and the humaneness of God are significant. This tension between justice and love in the nature of God is found throughout sapiential literature.

In speaking of the transcendence and absolutely just nature of God, the sages acknowledged their own limitations and mortality, recognizing that God alone is the one who creates, sustains, exists forever, and provides hope for salvation. At the same time, God's immanence and compassionate humaneness are portrayed in expressions of divine care for the good creation and its mortal creatures. The God of the sages acts in justice and love to create, sustain, and bless all life.[6] This is the great dialectic, that of love and justice, continuing through the wisdom corpus. This world, in which God is the center and focus for human devotion and orientation, is the place in which the wise by means of both birth and imagination take up residence and dwell.

In wisdom literature, divine governance of the world, human history, and individual life at times conflict with human freedom and individual responsibility. Ben Sira indicates that God creates wisdom and piety for the faithful in the womb, while Qoheleth depicts the deity as determining the times and events of larger reality and perhaps even individual destiny. According to the prologue of Job, God determines the fate of the hero, at least to a degree. However, humans also are represented as having the freedom to decide to pursue wisdom, to make individual decisions that make an impact on their own lives as well as the lives of their communities, and even to ignore the voice of God in creation and the wisdom tradition. In many texts, God does not predestine human beings to particular fates that have no relationship to their own moral behavior. There was the expectation that wise, righteous behavior of people led to well-being, both for individuals and their larger social networks, and that wicked-foolish behavior led to disastrous consequences, for this expectation was grounded in a firm belief in justice.

While the sages believed that an order of justice permeated reality and that the creator was a righteous God who judged the wicked and rescued the perishing, with the exception perhaps of Job's three opponents, they did not posit the notion that there was an inflexible order of retributive justice in which each word or deed produced an inevitable result. While God was primarily one who administered justice, divine freedom was not compromised.[7] God was not only just, but also merciful and patient. There was the expectation that good works and wise thoughts led to well-being (understood in a wide variety of ways, from concrete rewards to less tangible blessings), and there was the expectation that evil and foolishness led to destruction (understood in specific as well as more general terms). However, these expectations are more an affirmation of trust than a dogmatic assertion, more an expression of faith in justice and a righteous God than a blind, incredulous, and naive asseveration, and more an optimistic affirmation of the goodness of God and his creation than a stern avowal that wickedness and evildoers inevitably reap the harvest of the seed they sow.[8] The freedom of God transcended any falsely conceived, impenetrable order unreceptive to divine intrusions. Not only did God choose if and when to bring judgment but also divine grace that transcended law and human distinctions between good and evil guided providence. God's power and justice transcend a legalistic understanding of retribution, while divine grace softens their force. This does not mean that there will not be a final reckoning or disposition that God brings to a situation of good or evil, but it does mean that God's grace does allow, at least for a time, forgiveness and reconciliation.

As did other religious literature in the ancient Near East (priests, prophets, and sages), Israel's sages spoke of God as creator and sustainer in two separate traditions: cosmology and anthropology. Texts that belong to the cosmological tradition portray in a variety of ways the origins of the cosmos and providential guidance of creation. When humans and social institutions are mentioned, they are regarded as a part of this larger cosmic order. The anthropological tradition depicts the origins of humanity, comments on human nature, and speaks of the divine guidance of history and communities. However, at times, this tradition also describes the creation of individuals and their specific destiny. Sometimes the two traditions of cosmos and anthropology are integrated, but most often they are separate. A familiar example outside the wisdom corpus is the cosmological tradition in the Priestly source (Gen. 1:1–2:4a), which immediately precedes the Yahwist's anthropological depiction of creation (Gen. 2:4b-25). Qoheleth presents both of these in his initial poem in 1:4-11.

The sapiential portrayals of origins result, not from speculative curiosity, but from existential concern; the intent is to legitimate the teachings of the wise by grounding them in the order of the cosmos, human nature, and an authoritative world view. Also important to the theological intentionality behind wisdom teachings is the belief that wise behavior and speech extend and preserve both the order of creation and the social order that organizes in just and humane ways the interactions of people residing in human communities. The sages are not primarily interested in the hoary past of primeval origins to answer questions provoked by human curiosity. They are decidedly interested in ensuring the continuation of creation and the well-being of human life.

Creation theology in Israel and the ancient Near East is not rendered by discursive prose and systematic formulation. The literary embodiments of creation theology include poems, narratives, instructions, and sayings. In addition, the rhetoric of each piece of literature participates with the content and form in shaping a minute esthesis, a world of beauty and substance, that gives coherence and meaning to life. When speaking of creation, the sages usually filled these texts with the content and images of organizing metaphors and metaphor clusters. These metaphors and metaphor clusters may be inferred from the linguistic construals of sapiential literature, for they are not always directly stated. At least this is often true in naming God. The attention is placed on the activity of creation, rather than on the naming of the creator in other than rather generic terms (God, "the God," "maker," Yahweh) or by indirect reference (pronouns, Voice from the Whirlwind). Nevertheless, the identification of the metaphorical referents of the languaging of God, the world, and humanity is an important task for seeing how the sages actualize theological meaning. The metaphors for construing the acts of creation and providence in the wisdom tradition include fertility, artistry, word, and battle. These infer, then, that God as creator and sustainer is king, judge, artist, warrior, parent, lover, husband, and sage. Metaphors for human beings include children of God, lovers of wisdom, objects of art, kings, and slaves, while the world humans inhabit is most often depicted as a fertile field or garden, kingdom, city, household, or building.

METAPHORS IN THE COSMOLOGICAL TRADITION

Fertility

In the ancient Near East, an important cluster of metaphors used to speak of world origins and maintenance is fertility.[9] Through sexual prowess and fecundity of deities, reality was created and sustained. Through intercourse, gods were conceived and born (theogonies) and the alternating seasonal rhythm of fertility and sterility was maintained.[10] Even fertility goddesses like Ishtar and Isis were considered deities of wisdom who dispensed life and fecundity to devoted followers. Gods were represented metaphorically, then, as consorts, lovers, and spouses.

Popular religion in Israel gave Yahweh a fertility goddess, most often Asherah, to be his consort. The prophets adapted this metaphor to speak of Israel as the consort or bride of Yahweh, her lover and husband (see Isa. 54:5-8; Jer. 3:1–4:4; Ezekiel 18; Hosea 2). As husband and lover of Israel, Yahweh provided life-giving rain and enriched the fertility of soil and crops, which made existence possible. In the face of barrenness of people and flocks, Yahweh as Lord of the Womb ensured that reproduction would give life to present and future generations. Through the love of wisdom and its incorporation in life, humans participated in the creative, generative power of reality.

The sages appropriated the fertility metaphor to speak of Woman Wisdom as the lover and consort of God (cf. Wisdom of Solomon 6–9). Wisdom is rendered as, if not actually named, a lover, a hierodule, and a fertility goddess who seeks to attract young students to her embrace (Prov. 7; 9:1-6).[11] In contrast to Folly, who is portrayed as a seductive harlot leading to death (7:6-27; 9:13-18), Wisdom is depicted in the roles of the Queen of Heaven and divine consort of Yahweh who brings life, fertility, and blessing to those who love her and follow her instruction. In the portrayal of divine activities, Yahweh is seen in the roles of the lover and consort of Woman Wisdom, as well as her father and mother. She in turn becomes the instrument of creation and mediator between God and humanity (Prov. 8:2-31). Through God's love of Wisdom, life in the cosmos originated and continues. Through their love of Wisdom, the wise participated in the generative power of reality and helped to sustain and continue life.

Artistry

A second important metaphor cluster that construes the origins of the creation of the world in the ancient Near East is artistry. For example, the activities of creator deities are described at times in terms of an architect or builder who constructs the cosmos into a well-formed house, elegant palace, or a city for human habitation. The storytellers and poets of Israel borrowed this mythic metaphor to describe the world as a house secured on firm foundations (Pss. 18:8; 82:5), with a roof (the firmament or sky; see Gen. 1:6-8; Job 37:18) supported by cosmic pillars (normally the mountains; see Job 9:6; Ps. 7:54; cf. Isa. 40:12; 48:13).

One way the sages understood wisdom was in terms of the design and skill of the artisan God, who created and continues to maintain the well-ordered world:

> The Lord by means of wisdom established the earth;
> the heavens were secured through understanding.
> By means of his knowledge the primeval deep was divided,
> and the skies continue to drip their dew.
>> (Prov. 3:19-20; see Ps. 104:24)

While God is rarely called "wise," it is clear that wisdom is a divine attribute. As an attribute of God, Wisdom sometimes assumes this role of builder or artificer of all things (Prov. 9:1-6; Wis. 7:22; 8:6).[12] In the first strophe of an elegant poem (Prov. 9:1-6), Woman Wisdom constructs her spacious house (or temple), supported by seven pillars, pointing to its beauty, strength, and perfection. She then invites students to enter into her house and dwell—that is, to take up the study of the wisdom tradition and to live.

Word

The third major metaphor cluster in Israel and the ancient Near East that portrays the origins and maintenance of the cosmos is word.[13] The creator speaks creation into existence and sustains it by the power of language.[14] Metaphorical variations of creation through language include the spoken word, spirit or breath, wisdom, edict, and thought. God in this metaphor cluster is portrayed as acting like a king who issues a royal decree, or a sage whose wisdom imagines and then brings into being creatures and world, or a poet whose elegant language shapes an esthesis of coherence, beauty, and justice. The power of the divine breath animates existence, while its withdrawal leads to sterility and death. The sages speak of creation by word (Sir. 39:17), point to the ordinances that govern the heavenly bodies and meteorological phenomena (Job 28:26; 38:33), and tell of God's royal edict that establishes the boundaries for a threatening Sea to keep his floods from overwhelming creation (Job 38:8-11; Prov. 8:29; cf. Jer. 5:22). The origins and maintenance of the cosmos, then, depend on the power of divine language.

Wisdom is not only the imagination, skill, and talent of the artist and poet to create beauty, but it is also analytical and constructive reason that both observes and posits coherence and order, whether in reference to elements of nature or in the persuasive arguments of moral discourse. For the sages, divine wisdom creates and orders the world, originates and sustains all life, and, embodied in sapiential language, teaches those who take up the path to sagehood (see Job 28; Prov. 8:22-31; Sirach 24). The sapiential tradition contained, then, this same creative, divine wisdom that brings and nurtures life and well-being. As the voice of God, Wisdom is present in every work of creation, goes in search of those who desire life, reveals the divine will, and points the way to blessing (Prov. 1:20-33; 8:1-36; Wis. 1:7; 8:1-4; 9:17-18). For the sages, language contained the power both to create and to destroy. Each teaching contained the potency to bring about well-being, success, and vital existence, while each foolish word, thoughtlessly spoken, could result in failure, misery, even death (Prov. 10:1, 20-21; 12:6; 18:21). Language could create and sustain a beneficent order of life, or subvert this same order and lead to destruction. Through wise and prudent language, the sages engaged in the creative activities of shaping and sustaining the cosmos, human community, and individual life.

In Israel and other cultures of the ancient Near East, the creative and destructive power of language was at times associated with breath, considered to be the life force of creaturely existence and thus the vital, life-giving power that permeates all of the cosmos.[15] In the Hebrew Bible, God's breath or spirit gives life and sustenance to all creatures (Psalm 104; also see Gen. 2:7; Isa. 42:5). Elihu uses this tradition in speaking of the sovereignty of God and the utter dependency of creation upon God's vital breath (Job 34:14-15). Ben Sira speaks of Wisdom's coming forth from the mouth of God and then permeating creation like a mist (Sirach 24). The author of the Wisdom of Solomon equates wisdom with this life-giving and sustaining spirit of God, which is present in all of creation (1:6-7).[16]

The power of divine edict is also associated with the creative and destructive potency of language. Justice is the divine force that permeates all of reality and keeps it from returning to chaos. Reality is construed as a kingdom regulated by divine laws that, combined together, comprise cosmic justice. Through obedience to laws and wisdom teachings, humans participate in the ordering of this reality. At least during the monarchy, kingship was legitimated by this tradition, for the king is responsible for laws that reflect the justice that permeates the cosmos (cf. Prov. 16:12). Other institutions, including those of scribes and teachers, had a similar responsibility, even though less influential.

The metaphor cluster of divine word was very significant in the wisdom tradition. The frequent emphasis on proper speech points to the importance of this image. Eventually, the sapiential tradition and its cluster of word metaphors were identified with the written Torah (Psalms 19B; 119; Sirach 24). Torah and wisdom teaching became the embodiment of the divine life-giving and sustaining power of creation.

Battle

A fourth metaphor for the origins and maintenance of world creation is battle.[17] Creation issues from the contest between the divine warrior and primeval chaos, often personified as a dragon or serpent residing in the cosmic waters. Through the defeat of chaos, the creator ascends the throne as a cosmic ruler who then creates the world and issues decrees that determine human destiny, sustain creation, and order human society. Yet, this rule is not uncontested, but continues to be opposed by the forces of chaos that seek to destroy the cosmic government of the creator and to bring to an end the order of life. In this cluster of metaphors involving struggle, the creator is both the divine warrior who battles chaos for supremacy over the cosmos and the victorious king who assumes rule over the divine assembly and the entire cosmos.

METAPHORS AND THE ANTHROPOLOGICAL TRADITION

Introduction

Israelite and Jewish sages not only alluded to metaphors that construed their imaginative envisioning of the creation and maintenance of the cosmos, but also spoke of human origins, sustenance, and nature. Humanity and human individuals are created and sustained by God's acts of fertility and nurturing, creative artistry, and inbreathing of the divine spirit. To portray human nature and destiny, the sages spoke of humanity both in terms of the actions and roles associated with children, king, and slave, and objects of beauty and art. At times humanity was named or specifically described by these images. At other times, their activities and roles are indirectly imagined in these terms.

Birth and Nurture

The sages of Israel and later Judaism drew from the literary cache of metaphors of fertility for speaking about God as creator and sustainer of humans.[18] Before the creation of the world, God engendered and gave birth to Woman Wisdom, who dances before her divine parent and rejoices in the inhabited world (Prov. 8:22-31). In Job 10, God is the one who formed Job in the womb, bestowed steadfast love upon him, and cared for him. Job is now bewildered that his creator has turned against him, since God in an earlier time had given him life and nurtured him as a parent would a child. In Proverbs, the voice of Woman Wisdom calls her children to follow her path in order to find success, peace, honor, and life. In the anthropological tradition, then, humans are described as the children of God, conceived in the womb, given birth, and nurtured throughout life by the divine parent.

Artistry

The metaphor of artistry is also prominent in sapiential imaginings of human beings. Divine activities are portrayed as those of the weaver who knits together human bones and sinews and the potter who creates the first man from the soil. Job complains that Yahweh's own hands fashioned him, like a weaver knitting him together in the womb and like a potter shaping him out of clay. Later, after birth, God turned against him to destroy him (chap. 10; cf. Job 33:6; 34:19). The Wisdom of Solomon (chaps. 13–15) uses the metaphor of artistry to attack the making of idols, because God is the skillful artist who shapes human beings in the divine image. Humans were wondrous creations of beauty, elegance, and delight with intelligence, life, and vitality, while idols were inert objects without life, power, or sense. How ironic and tragic that humans, made of the earth, try to render their creator in images of clay. Israelite and later Jewish sages may not have glorified the human body to the extent that the Greeks came to do. But the Israelite sages valued and honored the human form, thought, and life as objects of beauty and goodness.

The Breath of God

Even as the breath or spirit of God animates all creation (see Job 34:14-15; Psalm 104), so humanity (Gen. 2:7; Job 34:14-15; Qoh. 11:5; 12:7) and individuals receive this vital life-giving power from God (Job 33:4). Elihu indicates that all "flesh," including all humans, is totally dependent upon the "breath" or "spirit" of God for existence (34:14-15). Qoheleth observes that it is at death that this vital power, given at birth (11:5), returns to God (12:7). Humans, then, are vital beings, animated by the breath of God; yet they are also mortals, dependent on the divine breath, which returns to God at death.

King

The literary traditions of the ancient Near East use metaphors not only to describe human origins, but also to depict human functions and destiny. Two of the most common are drawn from society: king and slave. In Israel, humans, both male and female, were created in the image of God and received the divine commission to rule as God's royal surrogates over all creation (Gen. 1:26-28; cf. Psalm 8). Chosen by Woman Wisdom, kings and princes ruled over the earth and sustained its life-giving order through righteous rule (see Proverbs 8). Elihu goes a step further than Proverbs 8 to argue that God not only shows no partiality to kings and nobles over the poor (34:18-20), but also exalts the righteous, even those who are oppressed, to rule as kings (36:7). Job parodies the tradition of humanity's royal place in the cosmos, most elegantly articulated in Psalm 8, when he speaks of God's attack on the human creature (7:17-21). Qoheleth's narrator is King Solomon, whose voice from the past speaks to tell a new generation of students that even he could not master life; thus how could they? Drawing on the tradition of human sovereignty in Genesis 1 and 9 as well as Psalm 8, Ben Sira speaks of God's giving humans dominion over creation, though the sage will still emphasize the dramatic difference between the majesty and power of God and the insignificance and weakness of humanity (16:24–18:14). The sages took elements of the royal tradition and applied them to all those who sought wisdom's instruction. The word *masal,* after all, means not only the form in which the teachings of the wise were placed, but also the ability to "rule" or "master" life. The metaphor of humans ruling as kings over God's good creation affirmed that human nature was not corrupt, but rather intrinsically good. Having at least a measure of freedom, God gave humans the responsibility to go forth and rule over the good creation and to bring the social order into conformity not only with that of the cosmos but also with the divine will.

Job speaks metaphorically of humans as kings, only to discover in his own experience that slavery, not kingship, is the role and destiny of humanity. Job's revolt against the creator, though finally abandoned, is a contest of sovereignty over the earth. Qoheleth also uses the royal metaphor in fashioning for Solomon a royal testament that speaks of his search, typical of every sage, to find the "good in life," even though he concludes that the mysterious creator, not humans, rules over the cosmos. Qoheleth assumes the voice of the long-dead paragon of wisdom, King Solomon, who takes his audience with him on his journey to discover what is the good in living.

335

Slave

The second prominent metaphor for human destiny in the ancient Near East was slavery. In Mesopotamia especially, the gods decreed the fate of humanity and determined individual destinies. The lot assigned to human creatures was not an especially appealing one, for humanity's primary duty is to serve the gods. In Israel, the metaphor of slave was used on occasion to describe the relationship of humanity to God.[19] The first man in the J creation story is created to "work" (*ābad*) the garden, a role that becomes one of drudgery after the fall, when humanity must till the soil by the "sweat of their brow" until they return to the dust from which they were taken (Genesis 2–3).

However, as a metaphor for human existence it was Job and Qoheleth who came to describe human existence in terms of slavery, an assertion that opposes the royal anthropology emerging in the exile (cf. P and Psalm 8). Although Qoheleth never seems to entertain the possibility, Job engages in a wholesale revolt against the rule of God (see Isa. 14:14b-21; Ezek. 28). Having experienced the drudgery and oppression of life, Job has had quite enough.

In speaking of humanity in images and activities associated with slaves, this common metaphor denies to humans significant human freedom, making predestination and divine rule the dominant theological affirmation. In addition, the metaphor suggests that a largely corrupt human nature inclines people to evil and denies them the ability to engage in actions that create and sustain a just order in the cosmos and human society. This metaphor renders the theological view of the radical sovereignty of God and the depravity of human nature.

METAPHORS OF REALITY

Introduction

In both traditions of cosmology and anthropology, sapiential imagination conceived of reality in language associated with kingdom, household, city, building, and garden. The descriptions of social reality and the literary metaphors of imagination entwine in the sapiential tradition. Social and political institutions common to the life of Israel and Judah are taken by the sages to construe the totality of reality. Israel, and later on Judah, existed within sociopolitical configurations of a nation (monarchy and then colony of empires), while the family was the central unit of society. In their imaginative construal, the sages did two things. First, they traced these social realities to originating and sustaining acts of divine creation in primeval times. In other words, Israel's and Judah's institutions, grounded in the order of creation, were the divinely legitimated organizations for social life. Second, they considered these institutions, particularly kingdom and family, to reflect the larger order of divine reality. That is to say, these institutions functioned at times as metaphorical renderings to construe all of reality. Divine activities and relationships were conceived in images associated with a monarch, who, together with a consort—the Queen of Heaven, Woman Wisdom—ruled over the cosmos and nations. Their domain was a universal one. In addition, the divine reality included a familial dimension in that the activities and relationships of God were associated with images suggesting a divine parent, husband, and lover of Wisdom. Through the voice of the teacher, all people, but especially the wise, were the children of God and Woman Wisdom, who resided behind the tradition. These images of kingdom and family, then, were used to construe the world.

Kingdom

We have already seen that one of the traditional metaphors for the creator in Israel and the ancient Near East is king. In combat mythology, the deity struggles with chaos, wins the victory, ascends to the throne as king, creates the world, and rules over creation. Creation, then, is envisioned as a kingdom over which the deity reigns by issuing decrees to order and sustain both nature and social life.

One of the acts of the creator in ordering reality is to establish civilization among humanity: culture, science, agriculture and husbandry, and sociopolitical organizations. Kingship is founded as the institution for governing human beings, and individual kings as well as dynasties are chosen to rule. Kings in general are the surrogates of the divine ruler who typically heads an assembly of gods.

In wisdom, the metaphor of reality as a monarchic state is intimated by many texts. In the didactic narrative of Job (1–2; 42:7-17), Yahweh functions as the king of the divine assembly whose decrees determine the fates of nations and individuals. In one speech of Bildad (Job 25), Yahweh is depicted as a powerful and stern ruler, commanding heavenly armies. In primeval times, Yahweh established peace by defeating his enemies, and now he watches over his world empire. No part of this empire is hidden from the watchful eye of God. Qoheleth's view of reality suggests that he conceived of it as a kingdom ruled over by an enigmatic, powerful, and capricious divine king. In Proverbs 8, Woman Wisdom is depicted in images of the Queen of Heaven, who rules over an earthly kingdom and chooses princes to rule as her surrogates. Ben Sira also presents God as a ruler and reality as his kingdom.

Household

A second social institution in Israel and Judah that became an important metaphorical lens for conceiving reality is the household (Prov. 9:1-6). The world was not simply an impersonal monarchic state, but also a home where both social roles and intimacy informed and sustained relationships. Like kingship, the institution of the household is traced to an originating act of the creator, often in primeval times.

In this household-reality, Yahweh is depicted in images of parent and husband, while Wisdom is construed as child and lover (cf. Prov. 8:22-36). Humans are the children of God and Wisdom and Wisdom's lovers. Even the wisdom schools use familial language; students are children and siblings, while teachers are parents. These are borrowed social images to speak not only of the relationship between students and teachers, but also between God, Wisdom, and those in search of divine teaching.

City

The sages did not separate wisdom from everyday life. Rather, the activities of life were the context for the presence and actualization of wisdom. This is intimated by the presentation of reality in images of a city. In Proverbs 1, 8, and 9, Woman Wisdom goes to the city to invite students to take up her course of study. She walks along its walls, teaches in its gates, stands on its street corners, and takes up residence on its acropolis, exhorting the simple to learn of her. Ben Sira takes a step further in speaking of Wisdom's residence in the holy city and especially its temple. This language not only suggests the social location of wisdom teaching, but also construes reality.

Garden

The world was also a fertile, life-filled environment in which humans and other creatures dwell, and thus at times was depicted as a verdant garden. The metaphor of garden, used by the Yahwist to depict the original state of the world before the fall (Genesis 2–3), on occasion is appropriated by the sages to describe the reality envisioned by their imagination. Wisdom is the tree of life, planted within a fertile garden, who offers her fruits to those who would partake of her nourishment (Prov. 3:13-20; Sirach 24). The use of this metaphor did not mean that there were no deserts or barren fields or salt water, or that chaos did not threaten to overwhelm the created order. But it did mean that the world was an environment teeming with life, made possible and nurtured by divine providence.

THE RHETORIC OF SAPIENTIAL LANGUAGE

Metaphors played a central role in the rhetorical composition of sapiential language. Through artistic expression, the sages shaped an esthesis of beauty and order to express their views of God, humanity, and the world. Through reasoned arguments, the sages attempted to persuade their hearers to follow their teachings. In addition, they also depended on the power of language to create a world view that stimulated the imagination of those they addressed. The poems about Woman Wisdom, the sayings about the responsibility of the wealthy to care for the poor, the speeches of Job and the voice from the whirlwind, the royal testament of Qoheleth, the tripartite structure of Ben Sira's collection, and the literary shaping of the exhortative speech of the Wisdom of Solomon are well-crafted texts designed to create a world of imagination that expressed different sapiential understandings of God, humanity, and the world. I have only touched on some of the major features of this rhetorical casting of sapiential language. Perhaps these examples have demonstrated how important rhetoric was for the sages in construing their teachings.

METAPHOR AND METAPHORICAL PROCESS
IN WISDOM THEOLOGY

As often noted in the preceding discussions, the metaphors of creation present directly or inferentially in the sapiential literature were not simply poetic enhancements of unencumbered, declarative speech; rather, they became linguistic construals of God, human nature, and the world. They helped to present the most cherished beliefs and values of Israel's sages. Metaphors provoked the imagination to conceive of and experience reality in compelling ways that required commitment and devotion. Indeed, they became the organizing centers for ethical life and moral discourse. Through the content and rhetoric of language and the activation of their imagination, the more traditional sages constructed a world of beauty, justice, and life, offered to those who would seek and find wisdom. Through knowledge and its embodiment in life, the sage dwelt within this reality and experienced its gifts.

Even the poetic Job, shown the power of God, the wonders of creation, and the awesome powers of chaos, finally opens his mouth to praise. The vision of the world seen through the eyes of the Job of the dialogues is transformed. A new way of existing in the world is formed through the power of the metaphor of cosmic battle and human struggle. Qoheleth, passing through the collapsing worlds of old meaning no longer able to convict and persuade, is tormented by thoughts of death and oblivion and finds no comfort in a nightmare reality ruled by a capricious tyrant. Life is breath, and all human accomplishments are quickly passing. However, even he is able to affirm that the experience of joy in life, regardless of how fleeting, is good.

SAPIENTIAL IMAGINATION AND CREATION THEOLOGY

Each of the wisdom texts finds its theological center in creation. By the activation of memory that draws on the metaphors contained in past traditions, the sages who composed and compiled this literature engaged the past to inform their own views of reality. Yet, they did not rest content with mere affirmation. They tested the authenticity of past teachings in the arena of their own experience. They also envisioned a reality that was not always entirely present, but could be lived into being through moral discourse and righteous behavior. This was possible, because God was the Lord of creation and of history and providentially guided the course of the world and human events. They imagined the God of wisdom as residing within the world they created through their language, but also as standing outside it to bring it into judgment. Even Qoheleth, who denied the potency of human memory and the ability to envision the future, could still posit a world that was ruled by the cosmic tyrant who dwelt outside its boundaries. The realities created by the imagination of less skeptical sages also did not penetrate entirely the mystery of God. Still, they believed that in listening to the voice of wisdom in creation they possessed the means to come to at least a limited knowledge of God, the world, and humanity and thus to live an existence that ultimately was good. Through sapiential discourse and righteous behavior, they believed they could live in harmony with God, the world, and humanity and that they could realize and even constitute a moral and beneficent order that undergirded the structures of life.

WISDOM AND OLD TESTAMENT THEOLOGY

We conclude by returning to the beginning. We began with the comment that wisdom has been either ignored or given little place in Old Testament theologies written since the Second World War. This has been due to the prominence given to salvation history and the events of Sinai in these theological presentations. Ben Sira is the first sage to incorporate these elements into his writings, but even his collection is often dismissed by Protestant Old Testament theologians due to its inclusion in the deutero-canonical literature and not the Jewish Bible. But what of the distinctive themes of creation and providence running through the wisdom corpus? For wisdom to contribute to the larger renderings of Old Testament and biblical theologies, several streams of theological reflection need to converge.

First, renderings of the theology of wisdom literature need to be written and refined. Regardless of the interpretative paradigm, articulations of the faith of the sages are necessary. Otherwise, the literature will not be taken seriously in formulations of comprehensive Old Testament and biblical theologies.

Second, it should be recognized that the category of salvation history, including covenant and law at Sinai, cannot subsume the entire Old Testament under its confines. Many Old Testament texts, from Esther to the Song of Songs to numerous psalms, set forth a faith and a piety that are not grounded in a theology of election. A one-sided emphasis on salvation history and Sinai excludes the theological understandings of a substantial part of the Old Testament and not simply the wisdom literature. Historically speaking, Israelite religion and piety were diverse enough to include expressions and practices that were based on theological understandings that were not limited to salvation history and covenant.

Third, we need to remind ourselves that creation and providence are not secondary or unimportant theological affirmations in texts outside the wisdom literature. The universal thrust of the J narrative, the priestly grounding of the sabbath law in the creation and order of the cosmos, Jeremiah's depiction of the destruction of Judah by the enemy from the North in images of a return to chaos, Second Isaiah's theology that integrates a New Exodus with a New Creation, and Psalm 104's hymnic praise of God's majestic creation and rule over the cosmos are significant examples of the role that creation and providence play even in nonsapiential biblical texts.

Fourth, it should be obvious that even renderings of salvation history and covenant are misconstrued without taking into serious account the biblical portraits of cosmology and anthropology. Israel's place in the cosmos and the relationship of the chosen people to the other nations are properly understood only by reference to the larger questions of the nature and character of the cosmos and humanity. It is also true that divine activity and providence are not limited to Israel's election and history. Election may be properly understood only within the larger theological parameters of divine creation and providential rule over cosmos and history.

Finally, without a careful delineation of biblical cosmology and anthropology, much of what the Old Testament and indeed the larger Christian canon have to contribute to contemporary theology will be ignored. The modern interest in cosmology and anthropology has been stimulated in part by the existential crises of our age: the threat of nuclear holocaust, the deterioration of the biosphere, ethnic cleansings, racism, and patriarchy. There is much in the Bible on creation and humanity that addresses these issues. Only the clear articulation of the contours and content of the biblical witness will enable the Bible to have a role to play in shaping a compelling theological response.

Wisdom theology, with its emphasis on creation and providence, should be a valued resource, not only for reconstructing ancient Israelite and early Jewish faith, but also for contributing to the contemporary articulations of believing communities seeking to describe their faith in coherent and meaningful ways. The sapiential vision of justice and of living in harmony with God, the world, and other humans, if carefully articulated, will be an important witness for contemporary theologians.

N O T E S

1. Where Shall Wisdom Be Found?

1. For a recent overview of Old Testament theology since World War II, see Leo G. Perdue, *The Collapse of History: The Reconstruction of Old Testament Theology,* Overtures to Biblical Theology (Minneapolis: Fortress, 1994). An excellent summary of the treatment of wisdom in Old Testament theology is found in Henning Graf Reventlow's *Problems of Old Testament Theology in the Twentieth Century* (Philadelphia: Fortress, 1985) 168-86. Also see Roland Murphy, "Proverbs and Theological Exegesis," *The Hermeneutical Quest,* ed. D. G. Miller (Allison Park: Pickwick, 1986) 87-95.

2. See George Ernest Wright, *God Who Acts: Biblical Theology as Recital,* SBT 8 (London: SCM, 1952); *The Old Testament Against Its Environment,* SBT 2 (London: SCM, 1950); *Biblical Archaeology* (Philadelphia: Westminster, 1957); and *The Old Testament and Theology* (New York: Harper & Row, 1969).

3. See Brevard S. Childs, *Biblical Theology in Crisis* (Philadelphia: Westminster, 1970).

4. Edgar Krentz, *Historical Criticism,* Guides to Biblical Scholarship (Philadelphia: Fortress, 1975).

5. Wright, *The Old Testament and Theology,* 70-96.

6. Wright, *The Old Testament Against Its Environment,* 71.

7. Wright, *Biblical Archaeology,* 17.

8. Wright noted that, while Proverbs borrows much from a pagan environment, the book nevertheless includes the Old Testament understanding of prophetic justice and a revealed law *(The Old Testament Against Its Environment,* 44-45 n. 2). See also *God Who Acts,* 102-5.

9. Wright, *The Old Testament Against Its Environment,* 16.

10. Wright, *The Old Testament and Theology,* 72.

11. Gerhard von Rad, *Old Testament Theology,* 2 vols. (New York: Harper & Row, 1962, 1965); and *Wisdom in Israel* (Nashville: Abingdon Press, 1972). The second work, which

sets forth the major features of wisdom thought, will be dealt with in the following section on approaches to wisdom theology.

12. Von Rad, *Old Testament Theology,* 2:357. On tradition history, see Walter Rast, *Tradition History and the Old Testament,* Guides to Biblical Scholarship (Philadelphia: Fortress, 1972).

13. Von Rad, *Old Testament Theology,* 1:417.

14. Ibid., 1:418-41.

15. Ibid., 1:418.

16. Ibid., 1:421.

17. Ibid., 1:427.

18. Ibid., 1:432.

19. Ibid., 1:441-53.

20. Ibid., 1:449.

21. Ibid., 1:453-59.

22. Ibid., 1:455. For von Rad, the only distinctive element of Qoheleth's cyclical thought was its secular, not sacral, expression.

23. See Claus Westermann, *Theologie des Alten Testaments in Grundzügen,* ATD Ergänzungsheft 6 (Göttingen: Vandenhoeck & Ruprecht, 1978); *Creation* (Philadelphia: Fortress, 1974); *Blessing in the Bible and the Life of the Church* (Philadelphia: Westminster, 1978); *Genesis 1–11* (Minneapolis: Augsburg, 1984); and *Wurzeln der Weisheit. Die ältesten Sprüche Israels und anderer Völker* (Göttingen: Vandenhoeck & Ruprecht, 1990).

24. "We can say then of Israel's worship that at its center was God's action of deliverance for his people, his mighty acts on their behalf and his covenant with them. But God's activity in blessing his people had an essential place in that worship" (Westermann, *Blessing in the Bible and the Life of the Church,* 37).

25. See ibid., 37-39.

26. See Westermann, *Wurzeln der Weisheit,* 93-99.

27. See Brevard Childs, *Introduction to the Old Testament as Scripture* (Philadelphia: Fortress, 1979); *Old Testament Theology in a Canonical Context* (Philadelphia: Fortress, 1985); and *Biblical Theology of the Old and New Testaments: Theological Reflection on the Christian Bible* (Minneapolis: Fortress, 1993).

28. Childs, *Introduction to the Old Testament as Scripture,* 526-44.

29. Ibid., 537.

30. Ibid., 545-59.

31. Ibid., 580-89.

32. Childs, *Old Testament Theology in a Canonical Context,* 34.

33. Ibid., 35.

34. See the chapter "The Shape of the Obedient Life," in ibid., 204-221.

35. For an important treatment of wisdom by means of the canonical approach, see the work of G. T. Shepherd, *Wisdom as a Hermeneutical Construct. A Study in the Sapientializing of the Old Testament,* BZAW 151 (Berlin: de Gruyter, 1980). Childs devotes significant attention to prophets, priests, and agents of God's rule (Moses, judges, and kings), but ignores scribes and sages. See John G. Gammie and Leo G. Perdue, eds., *The Sage in Israel and the Ancient Near East* (Winona Lake: Eisenbrauns, 1990).

36. Brevard Childs, *Biblical Theology of the Old and New Testaments.*

37. Ibid., 91.

38. Ibid., 97.

39. Ibid., 107-18.

40. Ibid., 187-90.

41. Ibid., 191.

42. "Five Loaves and Two Fishes: Feminist Hermeneutics and Biblical Theology," *TS* 50 (1989) 279-95.

43. *God and the Rhetoric of Sexuality,* Overtures to Biblical Theology (Philadelphia: Fortress, 1977); and *Texts of Terror,* Overtures to Biblical Theology (Philadelphia: Fortress, 1985). For a discussion of rhetorical criticism, see Toni Craven, *Artistry and Faith in the Book of Judith,* SBLDS 70 (Chico, Calif.: Scholars Press, 1983), 11-46.

44. See especially Trible, *God and the Rhetoric of Sexuality,* 36-38.

45. See, for example, Claudia Camp, *Wisdom and the Feminine in the Book of Proverbs,* Bible and Literature Series 11 (Sheffield: JSOT/Almond, 1985).

46. For an overview of creation theology in Old Testament studies, see Perdue *The Collapse of History,* chap. 5.

47. The major treatments are von Rad's *Wisdom in Israel*; and Ronald Clements's Didsbury lectures in 1989, *Wisdom in Theology* (Grand Rapids: Eerdmans, 1992).

48. Walther Zimmerli, "The Place and Limit of the Wisdom in the Framework of the Old Testament Theology," *SJTH* 17 (1964): 146-58.

49. See Leo G. Perdue, *Wisdom in Revolt: Creation Theology in the Book of Job,* JSOT 121 (Sheffield: JSOT Press and Almond Press, 1991) 12-21.

50. These include Walter Brueggemann, *In Man We Trust* (Atlanta: John Knox, 1972); John Priest, "Where Is Wisdom to Be Placed?" *Studies in Ancient Israelite Wisdom (SAIW),* ed. James L. Crenshaw (New York: Ktav, 1976) 281-88; "Humanism, Skepticism, and Pessimism," *JAAR* 36 (1968) 311-26; O. S. Rankin, *Israel's Wisdom Literature* (Edinburgh: T. & T. Clark, 1936); and Walther Zimmerli, "The Place and Limit of the Wisdom," 314-26.

51. Walther Zimmerli, "Zur Struktur der alttestamentlichen Weisheit," *ZAW* 51 (1933) 177-204.

52. Zimmerli, "The Place and Limit of the Wisdom," 149.

53. Ibid., 151.

54. Elsewhere Zimmerli notes: "The Old Testament is concerned with this creature, man, at the same time ennobled and endangered by his own freedom, yet destined to full involvement in the world" (*The Old Testament and the World* [Atlanta: John Knox, 1976] 26).

55. Rankin, *Israel's Wisdom Literature,* 1-3.

56. Ibid., 38.

57. Priest, "Humanism, Skepticism, and Pessimism," 312-13.

58. Alfred Dünner, *Die Gerechtigkeit nach dem Alten Testament,* Schriften zur Rechtslehre und Politik 42 (Bonn: H. Bouvier u. Co. Verlag, 1963); Hartmut Gese, *Lehre und Wirklichkeit in der alten Weisheit* (Tübingen: J. C. B. Mohr [Paul Siebeck], 1958); Hans-Jürgen Hermisson, "Observations on the Creation Theology in Wisdom," *Israelite Wisdom,* eds. John G. Gammie et al. (Missoula, Mont.: Scholars Press, 1978) 43-57; H. D. Preuss, "Das Gottesbild der älteren Weisheit Israels," *SVT* 23 (1972) 117-45; "Erwägungen zum theologischen Ort alttestamentlicher Weisheitsliteratur," *EvTh* 30 (1970) 393-417; H. H. Schmid, *Gerechtigkeit als Weltordnung,* BHT 40 (Tübingen: J. C. B. Mohr [Paul Siebeck], 1968); *Altorientalische Welt in der alttestamentlichen Theologie* (Zürich: Theologischer Verlag, 1974); "Creation, Righteousness, and Salvation," *Creation in the Old Testament,* ed. B. W. Anderson (Philadelphia: Fortress, 1984) 102-17; and James Williams, *Those Who Ponder Proverbs,* Bible and Literature Series (Sheffield: Almond, 1981).

59. Gese, *Lehre und Wirklichkeit in der alten Weisheit,* 5-32.

60. Schmid, *Gerechtigkeit als Weltordnung,* 67.

61. For a detailed discussion of the historical nature of wisdom, see Schmid's *Wesen und Geschichte der Weisheit,* BZAW 101 (Berlin: Walter de Gruyter, 1966).

62. "Erwägungen zum theologischen Ort alttestamentlicher Weisheitsliteratur"; and *Einführung in die alttestamentliche Weisheitsliteratur,* Urban-Taschenbücher 383 (Stuttgart: Kohlhammer, 1987).

63. Preuss denies to wisdom any legitimate place in either normative Old Testament theology or Christian faith. This is based on his conclusion that wisdom thought is essentially pagan. Indeed, the "fear of God," a theme absent in older wisdom, becomes a constitutive feature of the later tradition only due to the impress of Yahwistic faith. Pointing to salvation history as the normative theological tradition for both Old Testament theology and Christian faith, creation, retribution, and sapiential empiricism are devalued as natural theology. See Horst Dietrich Preuss, "Alttestamentliche Weisheit in christlicher Theologie?" *Questions disputées d'Ancien Testament,* ed. C. Brekelmans, BETL 33 (Leuven: University Press, 1974), 165-82.

64. Hans Jürgen Hermisson, *Studien zur Israelitischen Spruchweisheit,* WMANT 28 (Neukirchen-Vluyn: Neukirchener, 1968).

65. Hermisson, "Observations on the Creation Theology in Wisdom," 43-57.

66. See James L. Crenshaw, "Popular Questioning of the Justice of God," *ZAW* 82 (1970) 380-95; "Prolegomenon," *SIAW,* 1-45 ; "In Search of Divine Presence," *RevExp* 74 (1977) 353-69; and Burton L. Mack, "Wisdom Myth and Mytho-Logy," *Int* 24 (1970) 46-60.

67. See James L. Crenshaw, "Introduction: The Shift from Theodicy to Anthropodicy," *Theodicy in the Old Testament,* ed. James L. Crenshaw (London: SCM, 1983) 1-16; "The Human Dilemma and Literature of Dissent," *Tradition and Theology in the Old Testament,* ed. Douglas A. Knight (Philadelphia: Fortress, 1974) 235-58; and *Whirlpool of Torment,* Overtures to Biblical Theology (Philadelphia: Fortress, 1985).

68. Crenshaw, "In Search of Divine Presence," 364. He later appears to give more emphasis to anthropology as the key to understanding wisdom's cosmology. See his *Old Testament Wisdom* (Atlanta: John Knox, 1981) 17-21.

69. Crenshaw, "Prolegomenon," 27.

70. Ibid., 28.

71. Ibid., 34.

72. Mack, "Wisdom Myth and Mytho-Logy."

73. Gerhard von Rad, "Die ältere Weisheit Israels," *KD* 2 (1956) 54-72 (= *Old Testament Theology,* 1:418-41).

74. Von Rad, *Old Testament Theology,* 1:441-53.

75. Von Rad, *Wisdom in Israel,* 61.

76. Ibid., 138.

77. Ibid., 80.

78. Ibid., 97-113.

79. Westermann, *Genesis 1–11,* 19-47; and *Creation* (Philadelphia: Fortress, 1974).

80. Rainer Albertz, *Weltschöpfung und Menschenschöpfung,* Calwer Theologische Monographien, Reihe A: Bibelwissenschaft 3 (Stuttgart: Calwer, 1974); and Peter Doll, *Menschenschöpfung und Weltschöpfung in der alttestamentlichen Weisheit,* SBS 117 (Stuttgart: Katholisches Bibelwerk, 1985).

81. Albertz, *Weltschöpfung und Menschenschöpfung,* 132-50.

82. Roland E. Murphy, "Wisdom and Creation," *JBL* 104 (1985) 3-11; and *The Tree of Life: An Exploration of Biblical Wisdom Literature,* ABRL (New York: Doubleday, 1990) 111-31.

83. Murphy, "Wisdom and Creation," 5.

84. Ibid., 7.

85. Clements, *Wisdom in Theology.*

86. Ibid., 44.

87. Ibid., 45.
88. Ibid., 47-58.
89. Ibid., 56.
90. Ibid., 157.
91. Ibid., 159-70.
92. See A. De Buck, "Het Religieus Karakter der oudste egyptische Wijsheid," *NTT* 21 (1932) 322-39; Berend Gemser, "The Spiritual Structure of Biblical Aphoristic Wisdom," *SAIW* 208-19; Hellmut Brunner, "Der freie Wille Gottes in der ägyptischen Weisheit," *SPOA*, 203; and Alan W. Jenks, "Theological Presuppositions of Israel's Wisdom Literature," *HBT* 7 (1985) 43-75.
93. Leo G. Perdue, "The Social Character of Paraenesis and Paraenetic Literature," *Semeia* 50 (1990) 5-39.
94. Murphy, "Wisdom and Creation."
95. Crenshaw, "Popular Questioning of the Justice of God."
96. Schmid, *Wesen und Geschichte der Weisheit*.
97. Perdue, *Wisdom in Revolt*, 21-22.

2. "Come to Me, Those Who Are Unlearned, and Lodge in My School"

1. See Perdue *The Collapse of History*, chap. 9. Among the important studies on imagination and religion, see Stephen Crites, "Unfinished Figure: On Theology and Imagination," *Unfinished . . . : Essays in Honor of Ray Hart*, ed. Mark C. Taylor, *JAAR* Thematic Studies (Chico, Calif.: Scholars Press, 1981) 155-84; Garrett Green, *Imagining God: Theology and the Religious Imagination* (San Francisco: Harper & Row, 1989); Gordan Kaufman, *An Essay on Theological Method*, 2nd ed. (Missoula, Mont.: Scholars Press, 1979); *The Theological Imagination: Constructing the Concept of God* (Philadelphia: Westminster, 1981); Paul Ricoeur, "The Narrative Function," *Semeia* 13 (1978) 177-202; David Tracy, *Analogical Imagination* (New York: Crossroad, 1981); Mary Warnock, *Imagination* (Berkeley: University of California Press, 1976); and Amos Wilder, *Theopoetic: Theology and the Religious Imagination* (Philadelphia: Fortress, 1976).
2. See Crites, "Unfinished Figure: On Theology and Imagination," 172; and Warnock, *Imagination*, 10.
3. Kaufman reasons: "Unlike other animals, human beings have the power of imagination, the ability to envision possibilities which do not actually exist. This power to entertain the merely possible, the not-now-actual, and then to work to make these possibilities into actualities has enabled creation of the whole distinctively human world of culture and history; it has freed humanity from being bound to the actual, the given, in the way all other animals are bound" (*Theological Imagination*, 60-61).
4. See Williams, *Those Who Ponder Proverbs*, 24-26.
5. See Othmar Keel, *The Symbolism of the Biblical World* (New York: Seabury, 1978) 186-87.
6. See James L. Crenshaw, *Prophetic Conflict*, BZAW 124 (Berlin: Walter de Gruyter, 1971) 116-23.
7. See Eckart Otto, "Schöpfung als Kategorie der Vermittlung von Gott und Welt in Biblischer Theologie," *"Wenn nicht jetzt, wann dann?"* ed. Hans-Georg Geger (Neukirchen-Vluyn: Neukirchener, 1983) 53f.
8. For a discussion of metaphors in the book of Job, see Perdue, *Wisdom in Revolt*.
9. There are many fine studies on metaphor, including Ian Barbour, *Myths, Models and Paradigms* (New York: Harper & Row, 1974); Max Black, *Models and Metaphors* (Ithaca, N.Y.: Cornell, 1962); Frederick Ferré, "Metaphors, Models, and Religion," *Soundings* 51

(1968) 327-45; George Lakoff and Mark Johnson, *Metaphors We Live By* (Chicago: University of Chicago Press, 1980); I. A. Richards, *The Philosophy of Rhetoric* (New York: Oxford University Press, 1936); Paul Ricoeur, "The Metaphorical Process," *Semeia* 4 (1975) 75-106; *Interpretation Theory: Discourse and the Surplus of Meaning* (Fort Worth: Texas Christian University Press, 1976); *The Rule of Metaphor* (Toronto: University of Toronto Press, 1977); Sheldon Sacks, ed. *On Metaphor* (Chicago: University of Chicago Press, 1979); and Phillip Wheelwright, *Metaphor and Reality* (Bloomington: Indiana University Press, 1962).

10. John Middleton Murry, *Countries of the Mind* (London: Oxford University Press, 1931) 1-2.

11. Wheelwright, *Metaphor and Reality,* 19.

12. "Metaphorical use of language differs in significant ways from literal use but is no less comprehensible, no more recondite, no less practical, and no more independent of truth and falsity than is literal use. Far from being a mere matter of ornament, it participates fully in the progress of knowledge: in replacing some stale 'natural' kinds with novel and illuminating categories, in contriving facts, in revising theory, and in bringing us new worlds" (Goodman, in Sacks, "Metaphor as Moonlighting," *On Metaphor,* 175).

13. See Tracy's remarks about the importance of root metaphors in conveying the ideas of human culture, in "Metaphor and Religion: The Test Case of Christian Texts," in Sacks, *On Metaphor,* 80.

14. See Richards, *The Philosophy of Rhetoric,* 96. He proposes an interactional model for metaphors in which the tenor and vehicle interact to develop meaning.

15. Wayne Booth, *A Rhetoric of Irony* (Chicago: University of Chicago Press, 1974) 22.

16. See Thorkild Jacobsen, *The Treasures of Darkness* (New Haven: Yale University Press, 1976) 3-5.

17. See Ferré, "Metaphors, Models, and Religion," 330; Ricoeur, "The Metaphorical Process," 78-79; and *The Rule of Metaphor,* 199.

18. Goodman, "Metaphor as Moonlighting," 175.

19. Ricoeur, "The Metaphorical Process," 77-78.

20. Goodman, "Metaphor as Moonlighting," 175.

21. Wheelwright, *Metaphor and Reality,* 45f.

22. See Ferré, "Metaphors, Models, and Religion," 331; Ricoeur, "The Metaphorical Process," 75.

23. See Ferré, "Metaphors, Models, and Religion," 331.

24. See Ricoeur, "The Metaphorical Process," 75.

25. See Sallie McFague, *Metaphorical Theology* (Philadelphia: Fortress, 1982) 37; and Wheelwright, *Metaphor and Reality,* 45-69.

26. See Karsten Harries, "Metaphor and Transcendence," in Sacks, *On Metaphor,* 71f.

27. See Wheelwright, *Metaphor and Reality,* 45-69.

28. See Goodman, "Metaphor as Moonlighting," 176.

29. See Wheelwright, *Metaphor and Reality,* 33.

30. See McFague, *Metaphorical Theology,* 41.

31. See James G. Williams, "The Power of Form: A Study of Biblical Proverbs," *Semeia* 17 (1980) 35-58.

32. See James L. Crenshaw, "Wisdom," in *Old Testament Form Criticism,* ed. John H. Hayes (San Antonio: Trinity University Press, 1974) 225-64; and Roland Murphy, *Wisdom Literature: Job, Proverbs, Ruth, Canticles, Ecclesiastes, Esther,* FOTL 13 (Grand Rapids: Eerdmans, 1981).

33. See J. R. Porter, "Samson's Riddle: Judges XIV. 14, 18," *JTS* (1962) 106-9. Also see Leo G. Perdue, "The Riddles of Psalm 49," *JBL* 93 (1974) 533-42.

34. Bernhard Lang, *Die weisheitliche Lehrrede,* SBS 54 (Stuttgart: KBW, 1972).

35. See Philip Johannes Nel, *The Structure and Ethos of the Wisdom Admonitions in Proverbs,* BZAW 158 (Berlin: Walter de Gruyter, 1982).

36. For an introduction to rhetorical criticism, see James Muilenburg, "Form Criticism and Beyond," *JBL* 88 (1969) 1-18; Norman Gottwald, "Poetry, Hebrew," *IDB* 3 (1962) 829-38; Jared J. Jackson and Martin Kessler, eds. *Rhetorical Criticism: Essays in Honor of James Muilenburg,* PTMS 1 (Pittsburgh: Pickwick, 1974); and Craven, *Artistry and Faith in the Book of Judith,* 11-46. Trible's forthcoming study of rhetorical criticism for Guides to Biblical Scholarship should be an important statement as well.

37. See James Kugel, *The Idea of Biblical Poetry* (New Haven: Yale University Press, 1981).

38. See David L. Petersen and Kent Harold Richards, *Interpreting Hebrew Poetry,* Guides to Biblical Scholarship (Minneapolis: Fortress, 1992).

39. See Eberhard Gerstenberger, *Wesen und Herkunft des sogenannten 'apodiktischen Rechts' im Alten Testament,* WMANT 20 (Neukirchen-Vluyn: Neukirchener, 1965); Claus Westermann, "Weisheit im Sprichwort," in *Schalom: Studien zu Glaube und Geschichte Israels,* ed. K.-H. Bernhardt (Stuttgart: Calwer, 1971) 73-84; Carole R. Fontaine, "The Sage in Family and Tribe," in Gammie and Perdue, *The Sage in Israel and the Ancient Near East,* 155-81; *Traditional Sayings in the Old Testament: A Contextual Study,* Bible and Literature 5 (Sheffield: Almond, 1982); and Claudia Camp, *Wisdom and the Feminine in the Book of Proverbs.*

40. For early Israel (1250–1050 B.C.E.), see Norman Gottwald, *The Tribes of Yahweh* (Maryknoll: Orbis, 1979) 237-386. A comprehensive study of the family in ancient Israel is currently under preparation. Contributors are Leo G. Perdue, Carol Meyers, John Collins, and Joseph Blenkinsopp. The volume is scheduled to appear in 1996.

41. See Lawrence Stager, "The Archaeology of the Family in Ancient Israel," *BASOR* 206 (1985) 1-35.

42. Fontaine, "The Sage in Family and Tribe," 161.

43. See R. N. Whybray, "Wisdom Literature in the Reigns of David and Solomon," in *Studies in the Period of David and Solomon and Other Essays,* ed. T. Ishida (Winona Lake: Eisenbrauns, 1982) 13-26; and "The Sage in the Israelite Royal Court," in Gammie and Perdue, *The Sage in Israel and the Ancient Near East,* 133-39. For the cultivation of wisdom in the courts, see the following in Gammie and Perdue, *The Sage in Israel and the Ancient Near East:* Ronald J. Williams, "The Sage in Egyptian Literature," 19-30; "The Functions of the Sage in the Egyptian Royal Court," 95-98; Samuel Kramer, "The Sage in Sumerian Literature: A Composite Portrait," 31-44; Ronald F. G. Sweet, "The Sage in Akkadian Literature: A Philological Study," 45-65; "The Sage in Mesopotamian Palaces and Royal Courts," 99-107; Loren R. Mack-Fisher, "The Scribe (and Sage) in the Royal Court at Ugarit," 109-15; and John G. Gammie, "The Sage in Hellenistic Royal Courts," 147-53.

44. See Albrecht Alt, "Solomonic Wisdom," *SAIW,* 102-12; and Walter Brueggemann, "The Social Significance of Solomon as a Patron of Wisdom," in Gammie and Perdue, *The Sage in Israel and the Ancient Near East,* 117-32. Brueggemann argues that Solomon's royal rule was a "sociocultural mutation" in Israel that introduced significant changes in politics and social organization, together with their accompanying ideology and technology. R. B. Y. Scott, "Solomon and the Beginnings of Wisdom in Israel," in *Wisdom in Israel and in the Ancient Near East,* eds. Martin Noth and D. Winton Thomas, VTSup 3 (Leiden: Brill, 1955) 262-79, and James L. Crenshaw, *Old Testament Wisdom* (Atlanta: John Knox, 1981) 42-54, argue against the position that 1 Kings 3–11 represents a historical foundation for Solomon's association with the wisdom tradition.

45. Proverbs 1:1 attributes the entire book (or possibly the first collection in chaps. 1–9) to Solomon, while 10:1 associates the second collection (10:1–22:16) with him. Proverbs 25:1 regards the third collection in 25–29 as originally the work of Solomon transmitted by "the men of Hezekiah, King of Judah."

46. For important discussions of the social character of the Israelite state, see F. Crüzemann, *Der Widerstand gegen das Königtum,* WMANT 49 (Neukirchen-Vluyn: Neukirchener, 1978); F. S. Frick, *The Formation of the State of Ancient Israel* (Sheffield: Almond, 1985); and Edward Neufeld, "The Emergence of a Royal-Urban Society in Ancient Israel," *HUCA* 31 (1960) 31-52.

47. For a study of the religious legitimation of the monarchy and royal state, see Moshe Weinfeld, "Zion and Jerusalem as Religious and Political Capital: Ideology and Utopia," in *The Poet and the Historian,* ed. R. E. Friedman (Chico, Calif.: Scholars Press, 1983) 75-115.

48. For a discussion of the royal administration and officials in the Solomonic state, see G. W. Ahlström, *Royal Administration and National Religion in Ancient Palestine,* Studies in the History of the Ancient Near East 1 (Leiden: Brill, 1982); J. Begrich, *"Sofer* und *mazkir*: Ein Beitrag zur inneren Geschichte des davidisch-salomonischen Grossreiches und des Königreiches Judah," *ZAW* 58 (1940–41) 1-29; P. A. H. de Boer, "The Counselor," *Wisdom in Israel and the Ancient Near East,* 2-71; A. Malamat, "Organs of Statecraft in the Israelite Monarchy," *BA* 28 (1965) 34-65; and T. N. G. Mettinger, *Solomonic State Officials* (Lund: Gleerup, 1971). Also see Robert Gordis, "The Social Background of Wisdom Literature," *HUCA* 18 (1944) 77-118; E. W. Heaton, *Solomon's New Men* (New York: Pica, 1975); and Brian W. Kovacs, "Is There a Class-Ethic in Proverbs?" in *Essays in Old Testament Ethics,* eds. James L. Crenshaw and John T. Willis (New York: Ktav, 1974) 171-89. Whybray preferred to speak of intellectuals rather than sages as a social class with specific social roles. See Whybray, *The Intellectual Tradition in the Old Testament,* BZAW 115 (Berlin: Walter de Gruyter, 1974).

49. See Leo G. Perdue, "The Social Character of Paraenesis," *Semeia* 50 (1990) 5-39.

50. Ernest W. Nicholson, *God and His People* (Oxford: Clarendon, 1986) 193-210.

51. Brueggemann notes that in the hands of ideologues interested only in supporting the state, creation theology can become a dangerous legitimation for an unjust social order ("The Social Significance of Solomon as a Patron of Wisdom," 117-32).

52. For Israelite schools, see James L. Crenshaw, "Education in Ancient Israel," *JBL* 104 (1985) 601-15; Lorenz Dürr, *Das Erziehungswesen im Alten Testament und in Antiken Orient,* MVAG 36 (Leipzig: Hinrich, 1932); Menahem Haran, "On the Diffusion of Literacy and Schools in Ancient Israel," in *Congress Volume: Jerusalem 1986,* ed. J. A. Emerton, VTSup 40 (Leiden: Brill, 1988) 81-95; *Temples and Temple-Service in Ancient Israel: An Inquiry into Biblical Cult Phenomena and the Historical Setting of the Priestly School* (Oxford: Clarendon, 1978); Hermisson, *Studien zur israelitischen Spruchweisheit,* 97-136; David Jamieson-Drake, *Scribes and Schools in Monarchic Judah: A Socio-Archaeological Approach,* JSOT 109 (Sheffield: JSOT Press, 1991); August Klostermann, "Schulwesen im alten Israel," *Theologische Studien: Theodor Zahn,* eds. Nathanael Bonwetsch et al. (Leipzig: Deichert [Büehme], 1908) 193-232; Bernhard Lang, "Schule und Unterricht im alten Israel," in *La Sagesse de l'Ancien Testament,* ed. Maurice Gilbert (BETL 51 (Gembloux: Duculot; Louvain: Leuven University Press, 1979) 186-201; André Lemaire, "The Sage in School and Temple," in Gammie and Perdue, *The Sage in Israel and the Ancient Near East,* 165-81; *Les écoles et la formation de la Bible dans l'ancien Israël,* OBO 39 (Göttingen: Vandenhoeck & Ruprecht; Freiburg: Universitätsverlag, 1981); Emile Puech, "Les écoles dans l'Israël préexilique: données epigraphiques," in *Congress Volume: Jerusalem 1986,* 189-203; Hans H. Schaeder, *Esra der Schreiber,* BHT 5 (Tübingen: Mohr, 1940); and N. Shupak, "The 'Sitz im Leben' of the Book of Proverbs

in the Light of a Comparison of Biblical and Egyptian Wisdom Literature," *RB* 94 (1987) 98-119. Whybray concluded in his study in 1974 that the evidence for schools in ancient Israel, before the late postexilic period, is very minimal (*The Intellectual Tradition in the Old Testament,* 43). Friedemann W. Golka has argued vigorously against the existence of royal wisdom and schools. See "Die israelitische Weisheitsschule oder 'des Kaiser neue Kleider,' " *VT* 33 (1983) 257-70; and "Die Königs—und Hofsprüche und der Ursprung der israelitischen Weisheit," *VT* 36 (1986) 13-36. Schools and scribal education in ancient Egypt have been studied by Hellmut Brunner, *Altägyptische Erziehung* (Wiesbaden: Harrassowitz, 1957); and R. J. Williams, "Scribal Training in Ancient Egypt," *JAOS* 92 (1972) 214-21. For Mesopotamian schools, see Miguel Civil, "Sur les 'livres d'ecolier' a l'epoque paleo-babylonienne," in *Miscellanea Babylonica: Melanges offerts a Maurice Birot,* eds. Jean-Marie Durand and Jean-Robert Kupper (Paris: ERC, 1985) 67-78; Adam Falkenstein, "Die babylonische Schule," *Saeculum* 4 (1953) 125-37; Åke W. Sjöberg, "The Old Babylonian Edubba," in *Sumerological Studies in Honor of Thorkild Jacobsen,* Assyriological Studies 20 (Chicago: The Oriental Institute of the University of Chicago Press, 1975) 159-79; "Der Vater und sein Missratener Sohn," *JCS* 25 (1973) 105-69; and H. L. J. Vanstiphout, "How Did They Learn Sumerian?" *JCS* 31 (1979) 118-26. For Ugarit, see W. J. Horwitz, "The Ugaritic Scribe," *UF* 11 (1979) 389-94; J. P. J. Olivier, "Schools and Wisdom Literature," *JNSL* 4 (1975) 49-60; and Anson F. Rainey, "The Scribe at Ugarit: His Position and Influence," *Proceedings of the Israel Academy of Sciences and Humanities* 3 (1969) 126-47.

53. See Lemaire, "The Sage in School and Temple," 167-68.

54. See ibid., "The Sage in School and Temple," 170-71. Also see A. R. Millard, "An Assessment of the Evidence of Writing in Ancient Israel," in *Biblical Archaeology Today: Proceedings of the International Congress on Biblical Archaeology, Jerusalem, April 1984* (Jerusalem: Israel Exploration Society, 1985) 308.

55. See Shupak, "The 'Sitz im Leben' of the Book of Proverbs," 98-119.

56. See Lemaire, "The Sage in School and Temple," 176-80; and "Ecritures et langues du Moyen-Orient ancien," *Ecrits de l'Orient ancien et sources bibliques,* Petite Bibliothèque des Sciences Bibliques: Ancien Testament 2 (Paris: Desclée, 1986) 9-57.

57. See Moshe Weinfeld, *Deuteronomy and the Deuteronomic School* (Oxford: Clarendon, 1972). He suggests that the family of Shaphan, prominently mentioned in Jeremiah (see esp. Jer. 36), included leading deuteronomic scribes (p. 160).

58. Such schools were likely the predecessors of later rabbinic schools that were at times associated with synagogues in Second Temple Judaism. The origins of the synagogue are unclear, but by the first century of the common era synagogues were becoming a major institution in Judaism. See F. Hüttenmeister and G. Reeg, *Die antiken Synagogen in Israel 1: Die jüdischen Synagogen, Lehrhaüser und Gerichtshöfe* (Wiesbaden: Reichert, 1977) 205-14. The Temple precincts also provided a place for teaching (see Luke 2:46-52; 19:47; 20:1; etc.).

59. See Leo G. Perdue, "Wisdom in the Book of Job," in *In Search of Wisdom: Essays in Memory of John G. Gammie,* eds. Leo G. Perdue et al. (Louisville: Westminister/John Knox, 1993).

3. "The Lord Created Me at the Beginning of His Work"

1. The sages' emphasis on proper speaking points to both the content and the literary beauty of sapiential language to shape reality. See Walter Bühlmann, *Vom Rechten Reden und Schweigen. Studien zu Proverbien 10–31,* OBO 12 (Göttingen: Vandenhoeck & Ruprecht, 1976).

2. See Christa Bauer Kayatz, *Studien zu Proverbien 1–9*, WMANT 22 (Neukirchen-Vluyn: Neukirchener Verlag, 1966); Jean Noel Aletti, "Seduction et parole en Proverbes I–IX," *VT* 27 (1977) 129-44; and Carol A. Newsom, "Woman and the Discourse of Patriarchal Wisdom: A Study of Proverbs 1–9," in *Gender and Difference in Ancient Israel,* ed. Peggy L. Day (Minneapolis: Fortress, 1989) 142-60.

3. See Kayatz, *Studien zu Proverbien 1–9.*

4. See Lang, *Die weisheitliche Lehrrede,* 29. Also see R. N. Whybray, *Wisdom in Proverbs,* SBT 45 (London: SCM Press, 1965). Those who date Proverbs 1–9 in the post-exilic period include Roland Murphy, "The Kerygma of the Book of Proverbs," *Int* 20 [1966] 4; and Georg Fohrer, *Introduction to the Old Testament* (Nashville: Abingdon, 1968) 219

5. For a study of Woman Wisdom's role as metaphor, see Claudia V. Camp, "Woman Wisdom as Root Metaphor: A Theological Consideration," *The Listening Heart,* eds. Kenneth G. Hoglund et al., JSOT 58 (Sheffield: Sheffield Academic Press, 1987) 45-76.

6. See Newsom, "Woman and the Discourse of Patriarchal Wisdom."

7. See Otto Plöger, *Sprüche Salomos,* BKAT 17 (Neukirchen-Vluyn: Neukirchener, 1981) 8-10.

8. In Greek rhetoric, the invitation is a protrepsis, or exhortation, to youths to study under a teacher who will teach them philosophy as a way of life. See Perdue "The Social Character of Paraenesis."

9. Rudolf Otto, *The Idea of the Holy* (Oxford: Oxford University Press, 1950).

10. For comprehensive treatments of "fear of the Lord," see J. Becker, *Gottesfurcht im Alten Testament,* AnBib 25 (Rome: Pontifical Biblical Institute, 1965); J. Marböck, "Im Horizont der Gottesfurcht: Stellungnahme zu Welt und Leben in der alttestamentlichen Weisheit," *BN* 26 (1985) 47-70; Nel, *The Structure and Ethos of the Wisdom Admonitions in Proverbs,* 101; and S. Plath, *Furcht Gottes* (Stuttgart: Calwer 1962).

11. Against William McKane, *Proverbs,* OTL (Philadelphia: Westminster, 1970); and *Prophets and Wise Men,* SBT 44 (Naperville, Ill.: A. R. Allenson, 1965). I have argued elsewhere that wisdom is grounded in religious piety from its earliest inception; see Perdue, *Wisdom and Cult,* 229-30 n. 29.

12. See Albertz, *Weltschöpfung und Menschenschöpfung*; Doll, *Menschenschöpfung und Weltschöpfung in der alttestamentlichen Weisheit;* and Hermisson, "Observations on the Creation Theology in Wisdom," 43-57.

13. For discussions of Woman Wisdom, see P.-E. Bonnard, "De la sagesse personnifiée dans l'Ancien Testament à la sagesse en personne dans le Nouveau," in *La Sagesse de l'Ancien Testament,* 117-49; Bernard Lang, *Wisdom and the Book of Proverbs: An Israelite Goddess Redefined* (New York: Pilgrim Press, 1986); Ralph Marcus, "On Biblical Hypostases of Wisdom," *HUCA* 23 (1950–51) 57-171; Murphy, *The Tree of Life,* 133-49; Helmer Ringgren, *Word and Wisdom: Studies in the Hypostatization of Divine Qualities and Functions in the Ancient Near East* (Lund: H. Ohlssons, 1947); and A. Robert, "Les attaches litteraires bibliques de Prov. I-IX," *RB* 43 (1934) 172-204. Dennis McCarthy points to the sexual overtones of *qānâ* in his essay, "Creation Motifs in Ancient Hebrew Poetry," *CBQ* 29 (1967) 398.

14. Roland Murphy, "The Kerygma of the Book of Proverbs," 3-14, notes that life in Proverbs is characterized by length of days (3:16; 28:16), a good name (10:7; 22:1); and abundant resources (22:4).

15. See Perdue, *Wisdom and Cult,* 299-312; and Plöger, *Sprüche Salomos,* 36. Also see Arndt Meinhold, "Gott und Mensch in Proverbien 3," *VT* 37 (1987) 468-77. According to Meinhold, Proverbs 3 argues that those who possess the proper attitude toward God and their fellow humans live in harmony with creation.

16. See James L. Crenshaw, "Wisdom," 225-64; Erhard S. Gerstenberger, *Psalms 1*, FOTL 14, eds. Rolf Knierim and Gene M. Tucker (Grand Rapids: Eerdmans, 1988) 16-19; Hans-Joachim Kraus, *Psalms 1–59: A Commentary* (Minneapolis: Augsburg, 1988); and Claus Westermann, *The Praise of God in the Psalms* (Richmond: John Knox, 1965).

17. Among others, see Kayatz, *Studien zu Proverbien 1–9*.

18. Kayatz notes a large number of examples of the goddess Ma'at holding a symbol of life in one hand and a scepter symbolizing wealth and honor in the other. See ibid., 105. Also see W. F. Albright, "The Goddess of Life and Wisdom," *AJSL* 36 (1919–1920) 258-94.

19. See Berend Gemser, *Sprüche Salomos,* 2nd ed., HAT 10 (Tübingen: J. C. B. Mohr [Paul Siebeck], 1963) 29.

20. See Ralph Marcus, "The Tree of Life in Proverbs," *JBL* 62 (1942) 118-20; Ivan Engnell, in *Wisdom in Israel and in the Ancient Near East,* 103-19; and G. Widengren, *Sakrales Königtum im Alten Testament und im Judentum* (Stuttgart: Kohlhammer, 1955). The image of the tree of life in Proverbs is associated with wisdom, the "fruit" of the righteous, "fulfilled desire," and a "gentle tongue."

21. See Norman Habel, "The Symbolism of Wisdom in Proverbs 1–9," *Int* 26 (1972) 131-57. The terms in this text that often parallel "wisdom" (*hokmâ*) are "understanding" (*tĕbûnâ*; cf. Job 28:2, 7, 11; Prov. 4:5) and "knowledge" (*da'at*; cf. Prov. 21:11; Qoh. 12:9).

22. Proverbs 3:19 closely compares to Jer. 10:12 (= 51:15): "It is he who creates the earth with his strength, who establishes the inhabited earth with his wisdom, and by means of his understanding stretches out the heavens." The Jeremiah passages likely originate with scribal redaction.

23. Keel, *The Symbolism of the Biblical World,* 16-26; Luis I. Stadelmann, *The Hebrew Conception of the World,* AB 39 (Rome: Pontifical Biblical Institute, 1970); and Gemser, *Sprüche Salomos,* 30.

24. See Mary K. Wakemann, *God's Battle with the Monster* (Leiden: Brill, 1973); McCurley, *Ancient Myths and Biblical Faith,* 11-71; and John Levenson, *Creation and the Persistence of Evil* (San Francisco: Harper, 1988) 3-50. See Gen. 7:11, which speaks of the "fountains of the great deep being split open" during the great flood. This text has only distant echoes of a cosmic struggle, as is the case with the proverbial poem under consideration.

25. For a discussion of mythic images of the chaos monster's defeat in creation, see H. Gunkel, *Schöpfung und Chaos in Urzeit und Endzeit,* 2nd ed. (Göttingen: Vandenhoeck & Ruprecht, 1921).

26. See Gemser, *Sprüche Salomos,* 30.

27. See James G. Williams, "Proverbs and Ecclesiastes," *The Literary Guide to the Bible,* eds. Robert Alter and Frank Kermode (Cambridge: Harvard University Press, 1987) 263-76.

28. See M. Gilbert, "Le discours de la sagesse en Proverbes 8," in *La Sagesse de l'Ancien Testament,* 202-18; and Patrick Skehan, "Structures in Poems on Wisdom: Proverbs 8 and Sirach 24," *CBQ* 41 (1979) 365-79. Another well-crafted poem on Woman Wisdom is found in 1:20-33; see Phyllis Trible, "Wisdom Builds a Poem: the Architecture of Proverbs 1:20-33," *JBL* 94 (1975) 509-18; and Roland Murphy, "Wisdom's Song: Proverbs 1:20-33," *CBQ* 48 (1986) 456-60.

29. Wisdom is personified as a goddess initiating her cult in 9:1-6 and as an Israelite wife in 31:10-31. For the latter, see especially Thomas P. McCreesh, "Wisdom as Wife: Proverbs 31:10-31," *RB* 92 (1985) 25-46.

30. See Lang, *Wisdom and the Book of Proverbs.*

31. "On the street" ("or along the way") is not present in the LXX. The LXX reads: "On the lofty summits she is, amid the ways she stands."

32. *Bēt netîbôt* literally means "house of paths." It has been translated in various ways, including "cross-roads" (see NEB). I suggest that *bēt* (literally "house") may refer to the Temple, since the immediate context speaks of wisdom standing like a goddess or cultic functionary at the top of the acropolis or high place (see similar imagery in Prov. 9:1-6). Also see the same imagery used to describe Dame Folly in 7:6-27 and 9:13-18. Depicted as a prostitute, her house is also located on the heights.

33. *Qrt* is a rare word for "city" (see Job 29:7; Prov 9:3, 14; 11:11), occurring here instead of the more common word *îr*.

34. "Heights" (*merōmîm*) also may be the mountains or hills (Judg. 5:18; 2 Kings 19:23; Jer. 49:16) or the heavenly region (Ps. 18:17; Isa. 24:21; 33:5).

35. See Keel, *The Symbolism of the Biblical World*, 16-26.

36. See Yigal Shiloh, *Excavations at the City of David* (Jerusalem: Institute of Archaeology, Hebrew University Press, 1984).

37. For the sages, justice and its embodiment in law were not static. Rather, justice, given expression in institutions of jurisprudence, is a divine act that is continually produced. Subsequently, human actions that are just are to actualize this dynamic power of divine justice in communal life. See Jacques Ellul, *Die theologische Begründung des Rechtes*, Beiträge zur Evangelischen Theologie 10 (München: Chr. Kaiser Verlag, 1948) 56-89.

38. One location mentioned in 1:20-33, but not repeated here, is the "square" (*rehôb*). While open to a variety of uses, the square or plaza is the place where business dealings were pursued, especially the buying and selling of goods (see Neh. 8:1, 3, 16) and where people gathered for various types of public assembly (2 Chron. 29:4; 32:6; Ezra 10:9).

39. See Norman Habel's study of the "way," "The Symbolism of Wisdom in Proverbs 1–9," *Interp* 26 (1972) 131-57 Habel, using Ricoeur's understanding of "symbol," argues that *derek* ("way") points to three "symbolic zones": personal experience (chaps. 4–6), Yahwistic religion and covenant (chaps. 1–3), and cosmological reflection (chaps. 7–9).

40. Creation also was the "voice" of God speaking words that revealed the glory and handiwork of the creator (Ps. 19:4).

41. Reading *hākînû* for *hăbînû* (see the LXX).

42. The MT has "princes," though *BHS* suggests either different vowel points to read "upright" or a different word, *nekōhim*, which means "upright things."

43. Verse 11 is almost a repeat of 3:15.

44. BHS suggests reading *šekentî* ("my neighbor") for *šakantî* ("I dwell"). This would lead to the translation of the first line: "I, Wisdom, prudence is my neighbor."

45. Following the LXX and V, BHS suggests reading *yišpetû* ("they will judge") for *kol-šopetê* ("all judges").

46. See the discussion by Alfred Jepsen, "צדק und צדקה im Alten Testament," in *Gottes Wort und Gottes Land*, ed. H. Graf Reventlow, FS Hans-Wilhelm Hertzberg (Göttingen: Vandenhoeck & Ruprecht, 1965) 79f.

47. See P. A. H. de Boer, "The Counselor," in *Wisdom in Israel and in the Ancient Near East*, 42-71.

48. See Roland Murphy, "Wisdom and Eros in Prov. 1–9," *CBQ* 50 (1988) 600-603.

49. See Jean Noel Aletti, "Proverbes 8:22-31: étude et structure," *Bib* 57 (1976) 25-37; Mitchell Dahood, "Proverbs 8, 22-31. Translation and Commentary," *CBQ* 30 (1968) 512-21; George M. Landes, "Creation Tradition in Proverbs 8:22-31 and Genesis 1," *A Light Unto My Path*, Gettysburg Theological Studies 4 (Philadelphia: Temple University Press, 1974) 279-93; R. B. Y. Scott, "Wisdom in Creation: The *Amon* of Proverbs VIII 30," *VT* 10 (1960) 213-23; Bruce Vawter, "Prov. 8:22: Wisdom and Creation," *JBL* 99 (1980) 205-16; R. N. Whybray, "Proverbs VIII, 22-31 and Its Supposed Prototypes," *VT*

15 (1965) 504-14; and Gale A. Yee, "An Analysis of Prov. 8:22-31 According to Style and Structure," *ZAW* 94 (1982) 58-66.

50. While the MT reads the plural noun *s̆aʿăs̆ûʿîm* ("delights"), the reading of the LXX and S is preferred.

51. See H. Donner, "Die religionsgeschictlichen Ursprünge von Prov. Sal. 8, 22-31," *ZÄS* 82 (1957) 8-18; Kayatz, *Studien zu Proverbien 1-9*; Eichrodt, *Theology of the Old Testament* 2, 80f.; Othmar Keel, *Die Weisheit Spielt vor Gott* (Göttingen: Vandenhoeck & Ruprecht, 1974); Mack, "Wisdom Myth and Mytho-Logy," 44-60; and Ringgren, *Word and Wisdom*. For a discussion of the birth of gods and goddesses (theogonies) in Egyptian mythology, see Viktor Notter, *Biblischer Schöpfungsbericht und Ägyptische Schöpfungsmythen,* SBS 68 (Stuttgart: KBW Verlag, 1974) 21f.

52. The verb *qnh* may mean "to acquire or obtain," as in the sense of acquiring wisdom (Prov. 1:5; 4:5, 7), or "to purchase," as in buying a male Hebrew slave (Exod. 21:2). This is the meaning given by Vawter, "Prov. 8:22: Wisdom and Creation." In several texts, the verb means "to create," as in God's creating heaven and earth (Gen. 14:19, 22) or human beings (Ps. 139:13). In the case of creating, the specific nuance is that of procreating, as in Deut. 32:6 where God created—i.e., fathered—Israel. "Create" fits the sense of the entire text, especially since the verb *ḥûl* is used in vv. 24-25 ("to writhe in birth pains"). See Paul Humbert, " *'Qana* en hebreu biblique," in *Festschrift Alfred Bertholet,* eds. W. Baumgartner et al. (Tübingen: J. C. B. Mohr [Paul Siebeck], 1950) 259-66. For *qnh* as an epithet of God as creator, also see the inscription *qn ʾarṣ* ("creator of the earth"), found on the Western Hill in Jerusalem, and the Phoenician inscription of Karatepe, *el qoneh aretz* ("El, creator of the earth").

53. See Prov. 8:24-25. The verb (*ḥûl*) reflects the activity of writhing in birth pains (Deut. 32:18; Job 39:1; Pss. 29:9; 51:7; 90:2). The verb in 8:24-25 is passive, "I was brought forth" or "I was given birth," with the one who bears not specifically named. However, it would seem from the context that wisdom as the child (*ʾamôn*) of God is created—i.e., fathered—and given birth by Yahweh.

54. An alternative possibility is the notion of "chief " or "choice" (see Jer. 49:35; Amos 6:1).

55. See the struggle for this birthright between Jacob and Esau in Gen. 25:24-26; (cf. 38:27-30). For a full discussion of the privileges of the firstborn, see Roland de Vaux, *Ancient Israel,* vol. 1, *Social Institutions* (New York: McGraw Hill, 1965) 40-41.

56. See Job 40:19, where Behemoth, a chaos monster, is the "first (or best) of El's works" of creation. *Drk* is placed in parallel to *pĕ ʿālāv* ("his acts"), a term referring to various types of works or actions, including creation and God's activities as creator (Job 36:3; Prov. 16:4; Isa. 45:9, 11).

57. The Masoretic pointing makes *layyām* read "to the sea." However, repointing the consonants allows one to read *lĕyām,* "to Yam."

58. The word *ʾamôn* occurs elsewhere only in Jer.52:15, where it perhaps refers to a group of artisans. A related term, *ʾammān,* appears in Cant 7:2, possibly meaning "master workman."

59. See Yahweh's "rejoicing" (*s̆aʿăs̆ûʿîm*) over his dear son, Ephraim, who, though worthy of condemnation for iniquity, will receive his parent's mercy (Jer. 31:20; cf. Isa. 66:12).

60. See Keel, *Die Weisheit Spielt vor Gott.* Compare the wise psalmist's "rejoicing" over the Torah (Pss. 119:24, 77, 92, 143, 174).

61. See H.-J. Kraus, *Die Verkündigung der Weisheit,* BS 2 (Buchhandlung des Erziehungsvereins Neukirchen Kreis Moers, 1951).

62. Eliade notes that traditional societies seek through mythic celebration to return to those formative acts of creation in the beginning of time in order to secure and empower

the present. The sages sought through their moral discourse and righteous behavior to participate in that life-giving power of creation in the beginning that continues to form and sustain life in the present. See Mircea Eliade, *Cosmos and History: The Myth of the Eternal Return* (New York: Harper & Row/Harper Torchbooks, 1954).

63. For a discussion of death in the Old Testament, see Ludwig Wächter, *Der Tod im Alten Testament,* Arbeiten zur Theologie 8 (Stuttgart: Calwer, 1964).

64. See Norbert Lohfink, "Der Mensch vor dem Tod," in *Das Siegeslied am Schilfmeer,* 2nd ed. (Frankfurt: Josef Knecht, 1966) 198-243.

65. Wisdom's house has been interpreted as the inhabited world (cosmos), a patrician's house, a palace, a house, and a school. Albright's argument that the house is a temple with free-standing columns while the meal is a cultic one is followed in his discussion in "Some Canaanite-Phoenician Sources of Hebrew Wisdom," in *Wisdom in Israel and in the Ancient Near East,* 1-15. "Building a house" refers on occasion to the construction of a temple: 2 Sam. 7:5, 7, 16; 1 Kgs. 5:17, 19, 32; 6:1, 2, 5, 9, 12, 14; Isa. 66:1; Hag. 1:8; and Zech. 5:11.

66. Jonas Greenfield has argued that v. 1 originally read: "Wisdom has built her house, The Seven have set its foundations." He argues that "Seven" refers to the seven *apkallus* or primeval sages in Mesopotamian mythology who were endowed with wisdom by Ea and became the ancestors of civilization. See Greenfield, "The Seven Pillars of Wisdom (Prov. 9:1): a Mistranslation," *JQR* 76 (1985) 13-20.

67. See J. Daniélou, *Le signe du temple ou de la présence de dieu* (Paris: Gallimard, 1942); "Le symbolisme cosmique du temple de Jerusalem," *Symbolisme cosmique et monuments religieux* 1 (Paris: Musée Guimet, 1953) 61-64. Also see *Temples and High Places in Biblical Times,* ed. Avraham Biran (Jerusalem: Hebrew Union College, 1981); and Menahem Haran, *Temples and Temple Service in Ancient Israel* (Oxford: Clarendon, 1978).

68. Compare Baal's construction of his temple to inaugurate his reign and Luke's parable of the Great Banquet that inaugurates the kingdom of God (Luke 14).

69. See Richard J. Clifford, "Woman Wisdom in the Book of Proverbs," in *Biblische Theologie und gesellschaftlicher Wandel,* eds. Georg Braulik et al. (Freiburg: Herder, 1993) 61-72. Clifford makes the intriguing argument that Provs. 1–9 borrows from the "epic type-scene" (cf., e.g., Gilgamesh and Ishtar, Aqhat and Anat) in exhorting Israelite youth to yoke themselves to Woman Wisdom and not Woman Folly.

70. McKane, *Proverbs,* 360. McKane notes that the maidens of Wisdom "invite young men not to bed, but to school."

71. See Bernhard Lang, "Die sieben Säulen der Weisheit (Sprüche IX 1)im Licht israelitischer Architektur," *VT* 33 (1983) 488-91.

72. A variation of this argument is presented by Skehan, who argues that the seven pillars of Wisdom's house are seven poems of uniform length in chapters 2–7. See "The Seven Columns of Wisdom's House in Proverbs 1-9," in *Studies in Israelite Poetry and Wisdom,* CBQMS 1 (Washington, D.C.: The Catholic Biblical Association, 1971) 9-14.

73. Whether Canticles is a part of the wisdom corpus is a matter of debate, but this collection of love songs with explicit sexual images speaks of actual human sexuality, and not the metaphorical depiction of Yahweh and Israel or of Woman Wisdom and Woman Folly.

74. See Perdue, *Wisdom and Cult,* 146-55. Also see G. Boström, *Proverbiastudien: Die Weisheit und das fremde Weib in Spr 1-9,* Lunds Universitet Arsskrift N.F. Avd. 1, Bd 30 Nr. 3 (Lund: Gleerup, 1935); and J.-N. Aletti, "Séduction et parole en Proverbes I-IX," 129-44. The "strange woman" is a frequent topos in Proverbs: 2:1, 9, 16-19; 5:1-8, 21; 6:20-25, 32; 7:1-17; and 9:13-18.

75. Some scholars argue that this section is an intrusion between the two strophes of the poem on Wisdom and Folly in 9:1-6, 13-18. See, e.g., Helmer Ringgren, *Sprüche,* ATD 16 (Göttingen: Vandenhoeck & Ruprecht, 1962) 43.

76. A graphic metaphor for entrance into the underworld is that of Death's (Mot's) swallowing of the dead (Prov. 1:12).

77. See Gale A. Yee, " 'I Have Perfumed My Bed with Myrrh': The Foreign Woman (*'issa zara*) in Proverbs 1-9," *JSOT* 43 (1989) 53-68.

78. See Richard J. Clifford, "Prov IX: A Suggested Ugaritic Parallel," *VT* 25 (1975) 298-306. Clifford argues here also that the strange woman parallels Anat, who offers Aqht the false promise of immortality. Also see S. Amsler, "La sagesse de la femme," in *La Sagesse de l'Ancien Testament,* 112-16. Amsler notes that the emphasis is placed on her seductive language; see Aletti, "Séduction et parole en Proverbes I-IX," 129-44.

79. See Boström, *Proverbiastudien.*

80. The rephaim are usually the dead, portrayed as shadowy inhabitants of the underworld (see Ps. 88:11; Prov. 1:18; 21:16; Isa. 26:14). See Conrad L'Heureux, *Rank Among the Canaanite Gods,* HSM 21 (Missoula, Mont.: Scholars Press, 1979) 201-27.

81. McKane, *Proverbs,* 341.

82. See Gemser, *Sprüche Salomos,* 55. Gemser notes repetitions of key words, associations of literary features of sayings, and clusters of topics (e.g., a series on kingship occurs in chap. 16), but even so the connections of these materials are rather loose, indicating that each saying is largely independent. For a detailing of themes in this collection, see U. Skladny, *Die ältesten Spruchsammlungen in Israel* (Berlin: Vandenhoeck & Ruprecht, 1961).

83. Bühlmann, *Vom Rechten Reden und Schweigen.*

84. The topic of rich and poor is a common one in this collection (10:15; 11:28; 13:7, 18, 23; 14:20-21, 31; 17:5; 18:23; 19:4, 7, 17, 22; 21:13; 22:2, 7, 16 ; cf. 3:27f.; 23:4f.; 28:6, 11; 30:7-9). For an overview of this topic in the Old Testament, see A. Kuschke, "Arm und Reich im Alten Testament," *ZAW* 57 (1939) 31-57. For the book of Proverbs, see Norman Habel, "Wisdom, Wealth and Poverty Paradigms in the Book of Proverbs," *Bible Bhashyam* 14 (1988) 26-49; Raymond van Leeuwen, "Wealth and Poverty: System and Contradiction in Proverbs," *Hebrew Studies* 33 (1992) 25-36; Harold C. Washington, "Wealth and Poverty in the Instruction of Amenemope and the Hebrew Proverbs." Ph.D. dissertation, Princeton Theological Seminary, 1992; R. N. Whybray, *Wealth and Poverty in the Book of Proverbs,* JSOTSup 99 (Sheffield: JSOT Press, 1990); and J. David Pleins, "Poverty in the Social World of the Wise," *JSOT* 37 (1987) 61-78. Pleins argues that the perspectives on poverty in wisdom texts tend to reflect the ethos of a ruling elite in which wisdom was cultivated.

85. De Vaux, *Ancient Israel* 1:21-22.

86. Ibid., 1:21-22, 37-38.

87. Ibid., 1:72-74.

88. See Washington, "Wealth and Poverty in the Instruction of Amenemope and the Hebrew Proverbs." He argues that the contrasting views of wealth and poverty may be explained largely by sayings originating within two social groups. The sayings that defend and support the poor, he argues, most likely originated in scribal circles in Jerusalem as early as the United Monarchy. Indeed, this group of scribes was influenced by the Egyptian "Instruction of Amenemope," who regards the poor in a similar way. By contrast, the sayings that emphasize the virtues of hard work and communal interdependence while criticizing the poor originate, in his estimation, within the folk wisdom of Judean village society. This is a novel and provocative thesis, but his effort to trace different sayings to particular social locations is extremely difficult.

89. See Van Leeuwen, "Wealth and Poverty," 33. A righteous order exists before its embodiment in communal law, going back to the origins of creation. Providing for the poor, a duty encapsulated in law and social mores, is an enactment of divine justice that is identified with the order of creation. What is more, God is present in each act of justice or injustice seeing to it that righteousness prevails. See Ellul, *Die theologische Begründung des Rechtes*, 79f.

90. See Dünner, *Die Gerechtigkeit nach dem Alten Testament*, 63f.

91. Skladny notes: "The responsibility of humans to both their fellow human beings and to Yahweh and his order result from the recognition of their creaturely status" (*Die Ältesten Spruchsammlungen*, 27).

92. Another common term for poor is *'anî* (Deut. 15:11; 24:11, 15; Job 24:12; Prov. 31:20; Isa. 3:14, 15).

93. For a detailed discussion of this theme in the Hebrew Bible, see Levenson, *Creation and the Persistence of Evil*. Also see Crenshaw, "Introduction: The Shift from Theodicy to Anthropodicy," in *Theodicy in the Old Testament*, 1-16; "The Human Dilemma and Literature of Dissent," in *Tradition and Theology in the Old Testament*, 235-58; and *Whirlpool of Torment*.

94. See von Rad, *Wisdom in Israel*, 138-43.

95. See chapter 6 of this book.

96. See Schmid, *Gerechtigkeit als Weltordnung*.

97. See "Gerechtigkeit als Fundament des Thrones," *VT* 8 (1958) 426-28.

98. See de Vaux, *Ancient Israel* 2, 195-209.

99. See R. B. Y. Scott, *Proverbs. Ecclesiastes*, AB 18 (Garden City, N.Y.: Doubleday, 1965) 110.

100. See the charismatic endowments of the ideal ruler in Isa. 11:1-9.

101. McKane offers another understanding of "meet together." He suggests that the expression "can indicate no more than that rich and poor are found side by side in every community, that social structures everywhere have this polarity of wealth and poverty" (*Proverbs*, 569-70). Scott offers three possibilities of the meaning of "meet together": "This may mean (a) that they share a common humanity, (b) that God has willed their station in life, and may reverse it, or (c) that personal worth is more important than wealth" (*Proverbs. Ecclesiastes*, 128).

102. Contrast this with a saying of Amenemopet, the Egyptian sage: "Man is clay and straw, and the god is his builder. . . . He makes a thousand poor men as he wishes [or] he makes a thousand men [as overseers]" (*ANET*, 424).

103. See Crawford H. Toy, *A Critical and Exegetical Commentary on the Book of Proverbs*, ICC (Edinburgh: T. & T. Clark, 1899) 414.

104. Based on a comparison with Sehetepibre (see *ANET*, 431) and the "Kemyt," the Egyptian schoolbook of the Middle Kingdom that deals with the education of a court scribe, Glendon Bryce has argued that 25:2-27 is a sayings collection that deals with the relationship of the ruler (vv. 6-15) and the wicked (vv. 16-26). See Bryce, "Another Wisdom 'Book' in Proverbs," *JBL* 91 (1972) 145-57.

105. Van Leeuwen argues that chapters 25–27 consist of the following: a proverb poem addressed to courtiers (25:2-27); a proverb poem dealing with the fool (26:1-12); a proverb poem focusing on the sluggard (26:13-16); a proverb poem that develops the themes of chapter 25 (26:17-18); a collection of miscellaneous proverbs (27:1-22); and an admonitory poem addressed to a shepherd, possibly meaning the king (27:23-27). See Raymond van Leeuwen, *Context and Meaning in Proverbs 25–27*, SBLDS 96 (Atlanta: Scholars Press, 1988).

106. See James L. Crenshaw, *Ecclesiastes*, OTL (Philadelphia: Westminster, 1987) 149.

107. A less likely interpretation would be that "enlighten" refers to the giving of understanding (Pss. 19:9; 119:130) to both the poor and their oppressors so that a ready and just adjudication of the grievance might be obtained. Another possibility would be that "giving light" would allow each grieving party to treat the other with graciousness (Qoh. 8:1).

108. See G. Sauer, *Die Sprüche Agurs*, BWANT 4 (Stuttgart: Kohlhammer, 1963); Paul Franklyn, "The Sayings of *Agur* in Prov 30: Piety or Scepticism?" *ZAW* 95 (1983) 238-51.

109. "Words" (*dĕbārîm*) are used in several wisdom texts to refer to the content and various forms of language present in sapiential collections (Prov. 4:20; 31:1, Qoh. 1:1).

110. Wisdom and prophecy are usually contrasting traditions, with very different understandings of theology, revelation, and epistemology. However, it is interesting that the wisdom text the "Admonitions of Ipuwer" in Egypt of the First Intermediate Period (2160–2040 B.C.E.), is associated with prophecy, particularly in terms of judgment and eschatology.

111. See Hans-Peter Müller, "Mantische Weisheit und Apokalyptik," *Congress Volume: Uppsala 1971*, VTSup 22 (Leiden: Brill, 1972) 268-93.

112. This meaning of *nĕ'ūm* is supported also by the possible rendering of *maśśā'* in the heading, not as a geographical location, but as an "oracle" (Isa. 14:28; Jer. 23:33-40).

113. The middle part of verse 1 is notoriously difficult to translate, leading to many different proposals. Other translations include: "I am not God, I am not God"; "God is not with me, God is not with me"; "Surely God is with me, surely God is with me"; "To Ithiel, to Ithiel and Ucal" (two addressees of the collection?); "there is no God, there is no God."

114. *Qĕdōšîm* is plural and probably refers to the members of the divine council (Job 5:1; 15:15; Ps. 89:6, 8).

115. Compare Job 38–41 (Yahweh's many questions to Job, which are similarly directed toward creation). See Perdue, *Wisdom in Revolt*.

116. This is true of Yahweh's rhetorical questions to his human antagonist, Job; they have obvious answers. Yahweh, not Job, is the one who has the wisdom and power to create and sustain the universe.

117. Arrogance is a dominant theme in this collection: 30:13, 21-23, 29-31, 33..

118. See *BWL*, 139-49; Jean Bottero, "Le 'Dialogue Pessimiste' et la transcendance," *RThPh* 16 (1966) 7-24; G. Buccellati, "Tre saggi sulla sapienza mesopotamica, II. Il Dialogo del Pessimismo: la scienza delgi oppositi come ideale sapienziale," *OrAnt* 11 (1972) 81-100; and E. A. Speiser, "The Case of the Obliging Servant," *JCS* 8 (1954) 98-105.

119. See *ANET*, 79.

120. For a detailed discussion of the divine, life-giving spirit or breath, see Walther Eichrodt, *Theology of the Old Testament* OTL (Philadelphia: Westminster, 1967) 2:46-66.

121. See Raymond van Leeuwen, "Proverbs 30:21-23 and the Biblical World Upside Down," *JBL* 105 (1986) 599-610.

122. While *nbl* usually refers to the fool (Job 30:8; Prov. 17:7, 21), it may also mean a person of low social rank (2 Sam. 3:33). See Toy, *The Book of Proverbs*, 533.

123. See Ringgren, *Sprüche*, 116; Toy, *The Book of Proverbs*, 352.

124. Scott (*Proverbs.Ecclesiastes*, 181) makes the intriguing argument that the term for "spurned" (*śĕnū'â*) is a "technical term for one of two wives who is rejected by her husband" (Gen. 29:30-31; Deut. 20:15-17).

4. "You Have Not Spoken Rightly About Me"

1. For a more detailed treatment of creation theology in Job, see Perdue *Wisdom in Revolt*.

2. See Samuel Terrien, "Job," *IB* 3 (New York: Abingdon, 1954) 884-92.

3. See Fohrer, *Introduction to the Old Testament,* 330; A. de Wilde, *Das Buch Hiob, OTS* 22 (Leiden: E. J. Brill, 1981) 52.

4. Daniel is probably Dan'el, a Canaanite king of Ugarit. See *ANET,* 149-55.

5. See Murphy, *Wisdom Literature,* for the literary forms in Job.

6. See Claus Westermann, *The Structure of the Book of Job* (Philadelphia: Fortress, 1981).

7. See Gese, *Lehre und Wirklichkeit in der alten Weisheit.*

8. See Heinz Richter, *Studien zu Hiob,* Theologische Arbeiten 11 (Berlin: Evangelische Verlaganstalt, 1955) 131; and B. Gemser, "The Rib—or Controversy Pattern—in Hebrew Mentality," in *Wisdom in Israel and in the Ancient Near East,* 120-37.

9. Georg Fohrer, *Das Buch Hiob,* KAT 16 (Gütersloh: Gerd Mohn, 1963).

10. J. W. Whedbee, "The Comedy of Job," *Semeia* 7 (1970) 182-200. Also see the literary interpretations of Norman Habel, *The Book of Job,* OTL (Philadelphia: Westminster, 1985); and J. Gerald Janzen, *Job,* Interpretation (Atlanta: John Knox, 1985).

11. Marvin Pope, *Job,* AB 15 (Garden City: Doubleday, 1965) xxxi.

12. See Hans Peter Müller, "Die weisheitliche Lehrerzählung im Alten Testament und seiner Umwelt," *WO* 9 (1977) 77-98.

13. See Eberhard Gerstenberger, "The Psalms," in *Old Testament Form Criticism,* ed. John Hayes (San Antonio: Trinity, 1977) 179-223.

14. *ANET,* 601-4; see Perdue, *Wisdom and Cult,* 105f.

15. *ANET,* 405-7; see Perdue, *Wisdom and Cult,* 31f.

16. *ANET* 475-79.

17. See E. Gordon, "A New Look at the Wisdom of Sumer and Akkad," *BO* 17 (1960) 122-52. The Edubba was the center for learning and culture in ancient Sumer.

18. See the disputations in *BWL.*

19. See Gemser, "The Rib—or Controversy Pattern—in Hebrew Mentality," 120-37.

20. See Fohrer, *Introduction to the Old Testament,* 326-27.

21. See Habel, *Job,* 37.

22. See ibid.; and Janzen, *Job.* See my response to their arguments in *Wisdom in Revolt,* 80-82.

23. See Fohrer, *Introduction to the Old Testament,* 327-29.

24. See Fohrer, "Überlieferung und Wandlung der Hioblegende," *Studien zum Buche Hiob,* 2nd ed. (Gütersloh: Gerd Mohn, 1982); and Nahum Sarna, "Epic Substratum in the Prose of Job," *JBL* 76 (1957) 13-25.

25. See Janzen, *Job,* 22-24; Habel, *Job,* 35-39.

26. See Plath's discussion of the "fear of God" in *Furcht Gottes.*

27. "The satan" refers to either an opponent in a law court or a prosecutor (Ps. 109:6), not a personal name, as in 1 Chron. 21:1 and Zech. 3:1. See Rivkah S. Kluger, *Satan in the Old Testament* (Evanston, Ill.: Northwestern University Press, 1967).

28. Yom Kippur in late Judaism is the time for determining destinies. See H. H. Rowley, *Job* (Don Mills, Ontario: Thomas Nelson & Sons, 1970) 36.

29. See Theodor E. Mullen, *The Assembly of the Gods,* HSS 24 (Missoula, Mont.: Scholars Press, 1980).

30. See Leo G. Perdue "Job's Assault on Creation," *HAR* 10 (1987) 295-315.

31. Reading *ga'al* as "defile," not "redeem" (Zeph. 3:1; Mal. 1:7).

32. Reading *kmry,* "priests of," for *kmryry,* "darkness" (dittography?). The *kmr* is the pagan priest (2 Kings 23:5; Hos. 10:5; Zeph. 1:4).

33. Reading *yām* for *yôm* ("day").

34. Reading once again *yām* for *yôm* (cf. v. 5).

35. The origination of light and its separation from darkness was the first divine act of creation in the Priestly narrative (Gen. 1:3-5). Light is more than a natural element; it is a fundamental power that brings life, the manifestation of the presence and power of God, illumination of insight, and the force that overcomes darkness and keeps it at bay. Darkness is one of the features of chaos existing before the creation and is associated with Sheol and death, the absence of divine presence, the blindness of ignorance and folly, and the opponent of life and well-being. See O. Piper, "Light, Light and Darkness," *IDB* 3 (1962) 130-31.

36. See Dermont Cox, "The Desire for Oblivion in Job 3," *Studi Biblici Franciscani* 23 (1973) 37-49; *The Triumph of Impotence,* Analecta Gregoriana 212 (Rome: U. Gregoriana) 1978.

37. See Eichrodt, *Theology of the Old Testament* 2, 69f.

38. See Michael Fishbane, "Jeremiah IV 23-26 and Job III 3-13. A Recovered Use of the Creation Pattern," *VT* 21 (1971) 151-62.

39. Day and night are an important word pair in creation texts; see Gen. 1:5-18; 8:22; Pss. 74:16; 136:7-9; Jer. 31:35.

40. Yam in Canaanite mythology is the ruler of the primeval ocean who contested Baal for the rulership of the earth. For the adaptation of this mythology by biblical texts, see Exod. 15; Job 7:12; 38:8-11; Ps. 46; Hab. 3:15.

41. Compare Yahweh's battle against Leviathan in Isa. 27:1; Job 40:25–41:26; Pss. 74:12-17; 104:25-26.

42. *ANET,* 64.

43. See Judg. 5:20-21, which speaks of the "stars from the heavens" fighting against Sisera.

44. See Yahweh's curse of the soil in Gen. 3:17.

45. The final lament of Jeremiah (20:14-18) strongly resembles this first strophe, though the power of Jeremiah's curse is grounded in the tradition of the destruction of Sodom and Gomorrah (Gen. 19:12-29).

46. See Albertz, "Der sozialgeschichtliche Hintergrund des Hiobbuches und der 'Babylonischen Theodizee,' " in *Die Botschaft und die Boten,* eds. J. Jeremias and L. Perlitt, FS H. W. Wolff (Neukirchen-Vluyn: Neukirchener, 1981) 349-72.

47. See the reference to the authority of tradition in 15:18-19 (cf. Bildad in 8:8-10).

48. See F. Horst, *Hiob,* BKAT 16 (Neukirchen-Vluyn: Neukirchener 1969) 64. See also Josh. 7:19; 1 Sam. 6:5; Ps. 118:17-21; Jer. 13:15f.; Amos 4:13; 5:8). For detailed discussions, see James L. Crenshaw's *Hymnic Affirmation of Divine Justice,* SBLDS 24 (Missoula, Mont.: Scholars Press, 1975); and "The Doxologies of Amos and Job 5:9-16 and 9:5-10," *ZAW* 79 (1967) 42-51.

49. These are acts of creation in Job (9:10; 37:5), not acts of salvation history (Pss. 71:19; 106:21).

50. Reading *moḥorab* ("desolated") for *meḥereb* ("from the sword"). See E. Dhorme, *A Commentary on the Book of Job* (London: Nelson, 1967) 67.

51. See William McKane, *Prophets and Wise Men,* SBT 44 (Naperville: Alec R. Allenson, 1965).

52. See Artur Weiser, *Hiob,* 7th ed. (Göttingen: Vandenhoeck & Ruprecht, 1980) 52.

53. Reading *šēm* ("name") for MT's *mēśîm* ("to place").

54. Reading *ṣemē 'îm* ("thirsty ones") for MT's *ṣammîm.*

55. Reading *lū* ' ("surely") for MT's *lō* ' ("no").

56. See D. Conrad, "Der Gott Reschef," *ZAW* 83 (1971) 157-83; and W. J. Fulco, *The Canaanite God Resep* (New Haven: American Oriental Society, 1976).

57. Reading *zhmh* ("loathes") for MT's *hmmh* (cf. Job 33:20).

58. See J. Jeremias, *Theophanie,* WMANT 10 (Neukirchen-Vluyn: Neukirchener, 1965).

59. See Pss. 74:13; 148:7; Isa. 27:1; 51:9; Ezek. 28:3; 32:2). *Yam* and *dragon* are a word pair in Ps. 74:13.

60. Following the correction of the Massoretic scribes and the LXX's "to you" in place of MT's "to me."

61. See de Vaux, *Ancient Israel* 1, 80-90; Walther Zimmerli and Joachim Jeremias, *The Servant of God,* SBT 20 (Naperville, Ill.: Alec R. Allenson, 1965).

62. See Hans Walter Wolff, *Anthropology of the Old Testament* (Philadelphia: Fortress, 1974) 10f.

63. For a discussion of humanity's place in creation as seen through the lens of royal imagery, see Eichrodt, *Theology of the Old Testament,* 118f.; and Wolff, *Anthropology of the Old Testament,* 159f.

64. See K. Budde, *Das Buch Hiob,* 2nd ed., Göttinger Handkommentar zum Alten Testament (Göttingen: Vandenhoeck & Ruprecht, 1913) 42; and R. Gordis, *The Book of Job* (New York: Jewish Theological Seminary of America, 1978) 522.

65. See Jeremias, *Theophanie,* 151.

66. Reading *lū'* ("would") for MT's *lō"* ("not"). *See William Irwin, "Job's Redeemer,"* JBL 81 (1962) 217-29. M. B. Dick, "The Legal Metaphor in Job 31," *CBQ* 41 (1979) 37-50, and Habel, *Job,* 196-97, argue that Job wishes for an arbiter to settle the dispute before coming to trial.

67. See F. Hesse, *Hiob* (Zürich: Theologischer Verlag, 1978) 85.

68. Following the LXX for MT's "made me together all around."

69. See Wolff, *Anthropology of the Old Testament,* 26-27.

70. See Mot's swallowing of Baal, *ANET,* 138, 140.

71. See Katherine Doob-Sakenfeld, *The Meaning of hesed in the Hebrew Bible,* HSM 17 (Missoula, Mont.: Scholars Press, 1977).

72. Othmar Keel, *Jahwes Entgegnung an Ijob,* FRLANT 121 (Göttingen: Vandenhoeck & Ruprecht, 1978) 62f.

73. A vision of death often concludes Job's speeches (7:21; 14:20-22; 17:13-16; 21:32-33).

74. See A. De Guglielmo, "Job 12:7-9 and the Knowability of God," *CBQ* 6 (1944) 476-82.

75. Reading "him" with the LXX for MT's "me."

76. For a detailed discussion of the divine word in creation, see Lorenz Dürr, *Die Wertung des Göttlichen Wortes im Alten Testament und im Antiken Orient,* MVAG 42 (Leipzig: J. C. Hinrichs Verlag, 1938); and Werner H. Schmidt, *Die Schöpfungsgeschichte,* 2nd ed., WMANT 17 (Neukirchen-Vluyn: Neukirchener, 1967) 173-74.

77. See Keel, *The Symbolism of the Biblical World,* figs. 46-48, 479-480.

78. See Jacobsen, *The Treasures of Darkness,* 22-74; and McCurley, *Ancient Myths and Biblical Faith,* 75-78.

79. *Yālad* means "to father" or "to give birth," while *hûl* means "to give birth" or "to have offspring" (Job 39:1; Isa. 51:2). In Hebrew poetry, God is metaphorically described as a mother who "gives birth" to the earth (Ps. 90:2), to Israel (Deut. 32:18), and to wisdom (Prov. 8:24).

80. Wisdom also claims to be the "first" of God's "ways," i.e., first in origins and rank, a similar claim being made for the primal man. In 40:19 Yahweh says that Behemoth is "the first" of the divine acts of creation. Thus wisdom, humanity, and chaos vie to be first and primary in the order of creation.

81. For myths of primordial sages who possessed great wisdom and knew some of the secrets of the universe and were the creators of culture, see Erica Reiner, "The Etiological

Myth of the 'Seven Sages,' " *Orientalia* 30 (1961) 1-11; Benjamin Foster, "Wisdom and the Gods in Ancient Mesopotamia," *Orientalia* 13 (1974) 344-54; and W. H. Shea, "Adam in Ancient Mesopotamian Tradition," *Andrews University Semitic Studies* 15 (1977) 27-41.

82. See Henri Frankfort, *Kingship and the Gods* (Chicago: University of Chicago Press, 1948) 215-333.

83. Reading *śîm yām* ("place Sea") for MT's *šāmayim* ("heavens").

84. *Śiphrâ* is a *hapax legomenon*. The word may reflect Marduk's ensnaring of Tiamat in a "net" (*saparu*) before dispatching her (*ANET*, 67). See N. H. Tur-Sinai, *The Book of Job* (Jerusalem: Kiryath Sepher, 1957) 383; and Pope, *Job*, 185-86.

85. See Fohrer, *Hiob*, 375; Gordis, *Job*, 276; Pope, *Job*, 181.

86. See L'Heureux, *Rank Among the Canaanite Gods*, 201-27.

87. Abaddon, "place of destruction," is a synonym for Sheol (Job 28:22; 31:12; Prov. 15:11; 27:20). See Nicholas J. Tromp, *Primitive Conceptions of Death and the Netherworld in the Old Testament*, Biblica et Orientalia 21 (Rome: Pontifical Biblical Institute, 1969) 80.

88. See Norman Habel, "He Who Stretches Out the Heavens," *CBQ* 34 (1972) 417-30. Habel notes that in the Old Testament the stretching out of the tent points to the preparations for the advent of God, who comes to exercise his rule as creator and judge of the world. Habel notes that this image anchors the belief in divine revelation within the larger theology of the continuation of creation.

89. See Georg Fohrer, "The Righteous Man in Job 31," in *Old Testament Ethics*, eds. James L. Crenshaw and John Willis (New York: Ktav, 1974) 1-22.

90. Reading with the LXX and a few Hebrew manuscripts *hem'â* ("curds," "curdled milk").

91. See Albertz, "Der sozialgeschichtliche Hintergrund des Hiobbuches."

92. Compare the glorious bow of Aqhat (*ANET*, 151).

93. See Fohrer, "The Righteous Man in Job 31."

94. See Habel, *Job*, 438-39.

95. See Dick, "The Legal Metaphor in Job," 37-50.

96. Habel suggests the *spr* was perhaps a "deed of renunciation" that would have formally exonerated Job (*Job*, 439).

97. See Sheldon H. Blank, "The Curse, Blasphemy, the Spell, and the Oath," *HUCA* 23 (1950–51) 73-95; and J. Scharbert, " 'Fluchen' und 'Segnen' im Alten Testament," *Bib* 39 (1958) 1-26.

98. The apodosis was often omitted in Old Testament curses, perhaps because of the destructive power associated with them.

99. Reading "us" in place of MT's "him."

100. See Exod. 20:10; 21:1-11, 20f., 26f.; Lev. 25:39-55; Deut. 5:14f.; 12:18; 15:12-18; 16:11; 23:16f.; Jer. 34:8-22.

101. For example, see Rowley, *Job*, 254f.; and Westermann, *The Structure of the Book of Job*, 122, 125.

102. See Veronika Kubina, *Die Gottesreden im Buche Hiob*, Freiburger Theologische Studien 115 (Freiburg: Herder, 1979) 115-23; Gordis, *Job*, 556-63, 567; and Keel, *Jahwes Entgegnung an Ijob*, 38f.

103. An alternative reading is "warrior" (*gibbōr*).

104. See Preuss, "Jahwes Antwort an Hiob und die sogenannte Hiobliteratur des alten Vorderen Orients," in *Beiträge zur alttestamentlichen Theologie*, eds. Herbert Donner et al., FS W. Zimmerli (Göttingen: Vandenhoeck & Ruprecht, 1977) 338.

105. The image points to the changing of the color of the earth as light appears and extends over the land.

106. Reading *tiṣṣāba* ("dyed") for MT's *yityaṣṣebû* ("to set or station oneself," "to take one's stand").

107. See Kubina, *Die Gottesreden im Buche Hiob,* 131-42. She notes that rhetorical questions belong to the repertoire of legal interrogation and in divine lawsuits are designed to prove Yahweh is the one true God (40:12-26).

108. Reading *ma'anaddôt* ("bonds") for *ma'adannôt.*

109. See Gordis, *Job,* 453.

110. See Keel, *Jahwes Entgegnung an Ijob,* 65, 71f.

111. See Weiser, *Hiob,* 258.

112. The pairing of these two mythical myths is comparable to the five pairs of wild animals in the first Yahweh speech. Gunkel rightly notes that these two creatures are more than simply ferocious animals. They are mythic monsters who oppose Yahweh's rule over creation (*Schöpfung und Chaos in Urzeit und Endzeit,* 48f.).

113. See Fohrer, *Hiob,* 523; Gordis, *Job,* 571.

114. See B. Couroyer, "Qui est Behemoth?" *RB* 82 (1975) 418-43.

115. See Keel, *Jahwes Entgegnung an Ijob,* 127f.; Kubina, *Die Gottesreden im Buche Hiob,* 44.

116. See G. J. Botterweck, *ThDOT* 2 (1975) 6-20; Keel, *Jahwes Entgegnung an Ijob,* 127f.; E. Ruprecht, "Das Nilpferd im Hiobbuch. Beobachtungen zu der sogennanten zweiten Gottesrede," *VT* 21 (1971) 209-31; and T. Säve-Söderbergh, *On Egyptian Representations of Hippopotamus Hunting as a Religious Motive,* Horae Soederblomianae 3 (Uppsala, N.Y.: C. W. K. Gleerup, 1953).

117. See the list of the pieces of glyptic art that portray the theme of the "Lord of the animals" in Keel, *Jahwes Entgegnung an Ijob,* 86-87.

118. Some scholars follow the LXX and Qumran Targum and read *māsas* ("to melt," "to be poured out") for MT *mā'as* ("to despise," "to reject," "to protest"). See S. R. Driver and G. B. Gray, *Job,* ICC (Edinburgh: T. & T. Clark, 1921) 348; and Terrien, "Job," 1191. However, *mā'as* ("to reject") is retained as a transitive verb with "dust and ashes" as its direct object.

119. See Kubina, *Die Gottesreden im Buche Hiob,* 152; Dale Patrick, "Job's Address of God," *ZAW* 91 (1979) 268-82; and Westermann, *The Structure of the Book of Job,* 105-29.

120. *'em'as* is an active verb and cannot mean "I despise *myself.*" As an intransitive verb, it means "to protest" (Job 7:16; 34:33; 36:5). With a direct object, as is the case here ("dust and ashes"), the verb means "to despise" (Job 19:18; Prov. 15:32; Amos 5:21) or "to reject" (1 Sam. 15:23, 26; Jer. 7:29; Hos. 4:6; 9:17).

121. The Niphal of *nhm* followed by *'al* means "comforted over" (2 Sam. 13:39; Jer. 16:7; Ezek. 14:22), and "have compassion for" (Ps. 90:13). This construction means "to repent of" only when followed by the word for "evil" (Jer. 8:6; 18:8; Joel 2:13). Job is not "repenting in" dust and ashes, but is "comforted" by the vision and words of Yahweh. It is time for Job to stop grieving and move on to praise God.

122. Both Gen. 18:27 and Job 30:19 indicate that the expression "dust and ashes" points to that which is insignificant or worthless.

123. Habel (*Job,* 578) argues that Job is retracting his lawsuit.

124. A scribe has changed "they declared God guilty" in 32:3 to "they declared Job guilty."

125. See Habel, *Job,* 450-51.

126. See S. R. K. Glanville, *Catalogue of Demotic Papyri in the British Museum,* vol. 2 (London: The British Museum, 1955); Berend Gemser, "The Instructions of 'Onchsheshonqy and Biblical Wisdom Literature," *VTSup* 7 (Leiden: Brill, 1960) 102-45; and B. H. Stricker, "De Wijsheid van Anchsjesjonqy," *JEOL* 15 (1933) 11-33. The Papyrus

Insinger from Ptolemaic Egypt may also reflect a more populist tradition. See P. A. A. Boeser, *Transkription und Übersetzung des Papyrus Insinger,* Oudheidkundige Medeelingen 3 (Uit 'Srijksmuseum van Oudheden Te Leiden, 1922); and Aksel Volten, *Das Demotische Weisheitsbuch* (Kopenhagen: Einar Munksgaard, 1941).

5. "I Will Make a Test of Pleasure"

1. See Murphy, *The Tree of Life,* 49.

2. See Frank Crüsemann, "The Unchangeable World: The 'Crisis of Wisdom' in Koheleth," in *God of the Lowly,* eds. Willy Schottroff and Wolfgang Stegemann (Maryknoll, N.Y.: Orbis, 1984) 57-77; Aarre Lauha, "Die Krise des Religiösen Glaubens bei Kohelet," in *Wisdom in Israel and in the Ancient Near East,* eds. Martin Noth and D. Winton Ronas, VTSup 3 (Leiden: Brill, 1955), 183-91; Hans-Peter Müller, "Neige der althebräischen 'Weisheit.' Zum Denken Qohäläts," *ZAW* 90 (1978) 238-64; Roland Murphy, "The Faith of Qoheleth," *Word & World* 7 (1987) 253-60.

3. See H. Gese, "Die Krisis der Weisheit bei Koheleth," *Les Sagesses du Proche-Orient Ancien* (Paris: Presses Universitaires de France, 1961) 139-51.

4. See Diethelm Michel, *Untersuchungen zur Eigenart des Buches Qohelet. Mit einem Anhang: Reinhard Lehmann, Bibliographie zu Qohelet,* BZAW 183 (Berlin: Walter de Gruyter, 1989); Michael V. Fox, *Qohelet and His Contradictions,* JSOTSup 18 (Sheffield: Almond, 1989).

5. Walther Zimmerli, "Das Buch Kohelet—Traktat oder Sentenzensammlung," *VT* 24 (1974) 221-30. Zimmerli thinks that while the book does not have a recognizable structure it is more than simply a loose collection of different sayings, as is the case with Proverbs.

6. See Aarre Lauha, *Kohelet,* BKAT 19 (Neukirchen-Vluyn: Neukirchener, 1978) 5.

7. There are several examples of first-person narratives in Israelite and Jewish wisdom texts: Ps. 73; Prov. 24:30-34; Sir. 33:16-19. For an overview of these texts, see Crenshaw's essay "Wisdom," 256-58.

8. See Gordon, "A New Look at the Wisdom of Sumer and Akkad," 49.

9. See Perdue, *Wisdom and Cult,* 178-88.

10. See Bottero, "Le 'Dialogue Pessimiste' et la transcendance," 7-24.

11. See Buccellati, "Tre saggi sulla sapienza mesopotamica," 2:81-100.

12. See Miriam Lichtheim, "The Songs of the Harpers," *JNES* 4 (1945) 178-212; Pierre Gilbert, "Les chants du harpiste," *Chronique d'Egypte* 15 (1940) 38-44; and Edward Went, "Egyptian 'Make Merry' Songs Reconsidered," *JNES* 21 (1962) 118-28.

13. See H. Wheeler Robinson, *Inspiration and Revelation in the Old Testament* (Oxford: Clarendon, 1946) 258.

14. See Eberhard Otto, *Die Biographischen Inschriften der Ägyptischen Spätzeit,* Probleme der Ägyptologie 2 (Leiden: Brill, 1954); and Schmid, *Wesen und Geschichte der Weisheit,* 44-46, 206-9.

15. See Eberhard Otto, "Biographien," *Ägyptologie,* HdO 1 (Leiden: Brill, 1952) 148-57.

16. See Otto, *Die Biographischen Inschriften,* 70f. See inscriptions 46, 58b, 58c, 127, etc..

17. See ibid., inscriptions 10c, 10h, 19, 46, 58, etc.

18. See Jan Bergman, "Gedanken zum Thema 'Lehre-Testament-Grab-Name,' " in *Studien zu Altägyptischen Lebenslehren,* eds. Erik Hornung and Othmar Keel, OBO 28 (Göttingen: Vandenhoeck & Ruprecht, 1979) 73-104.

19. *ANET,* 412-14.

20. See Otto, *Die Biographischen Inschriften.*

21. Ibid., 61.

22. Fox argues that Qoheleth is the composer of the epilogue and the author of the book. The persona—i.e., the one who tells the story and is active in it—is Qoheleth himself. See Fox, *Qohelet and His Contradictions*, 311-21. Harold Fisch argues that the epilogue (12:9-14) derives from the same person who put together the rest of the book. See his "Qohelet: A Hebrew Ironist," *Poetry with a Purpose: Biblical Poetics and Interpretation* (Bloomington: Indiana University Press, 1988) 158-78.

23. Otto includes the following inscription from the statue of Neb-neteru: "The exit from life is sorrow, signifying want from what was yours formerly and emptiness of possessions. It means sitting in the hall of unconsciousness awaiting the announcement of a morning which never comes. It offers as compensation an eye that weeps—take care, for it comes! It means knowing nothing and sleep, when the sun is in the East. It means thirst for beer! Therefore, the West itself answers: 'Give . . . to the one who follows his heart! The heart is a god. Desire is its shrine. It rejoices when the body's members are in a festive mood' " (*Die Biographischen Inscriptionen*, Inscription 5; cf. Inscription 57).

24. See Hellmut Brunner, "Die Weisheitsliteratur," *Ägyptologie*, HdO 1 (Leiden: Brill, 1952) 90-110; and Kenneth A. Kitchen, "The Basic Literary Forms and Formulations of Ancient Instructional Writings in Egypt and Western Asia," *Studien zu altägyptischen Lebenslehren*, OBO 28 (Göttingen: Vandenhoeck & Ruprecht, 1979) 235-82.

25. See G. Posener, *Littérature et politique dans l'Égypte de la XIIe dynastie* (Paris: Librairie Ancienne Honoré Champion, 1956); Aksel Volten, *Zwei altägyptische politische schriften*, Analecta Aegyptiaca 4 (Copenhagen: Einar Munksgaard, 1945); and R. J. Williams, "Literature as a Medium of Political Propaganda in Ancient Egypt," *The Seed of Wisdom* (Toronto: University of Toronto Press, 1964) 14-30.

26. See Leo G. Perdue, "The Testament of David and Egyptian Royal Instructions," in *Scripture in Context*, vol. 2; eds. William W. Hallo, James Moyer, and Leo G. Perdue (Winona Lake: Eisenbrauns, 1983) 79-96.

27. According to S. Herrmann, royal testaments grounded divine rule in the order of the cosmos established by the creator in the beginning of time. See "Die Naturlehre des Schöpfungsberichtes," *TLZ* 86 (1961) 413-23.

28. See Eckhard von Nordheim, *Die Lehre der Alten*, vol. 1, Arbeiten zum Literatur und Geschichte des Hellenistischen Judentum 13 (Leiden: Brill, 1980).

29. Both Oswald Loretz (*Qoheleth und der Alte Orient* [Freiburg: Herder, 1964] 148, 161, 212-13) and von Rad (*Wisdom in Israel*, 226) have argued that the royal testament was the literary form for the entire book of Qoheleth. Others limit the form to 1:12–2:26.

30. For a summary of different positions on the meaning, see James Crenshaw, *Ecclesiastes*, OTL (Philadelphia: Westminster, 1987) 32-34. Much of the ambiguity results from the different ways the term *Qoheleth* is used in the book. On occasion Qoheleth appears to be a personal name, or a name for one who performed the act of assembling (1:1-2, 12; 12:9-10). Elsewhere the word bears the definite article, pointing to it as an office or function (12:8 and probably 7:27; "the one who assembles"). Feminine participles are used elsewhere for offices: the scribe and the one who binds gazelles (Ezra 2:55-57; Neh. 7:59).

31. For a list of Egyptian sapiential texts ascribed to famous sages in the past, see "In Praise of Learned Scribes," *ANET*, 431-32.

32. Gerald T. Shepherd argues that the composer of the epilogue is a commentator who, like Ben Sira, seeks to establish a relationship between wisdom and the Torah. See his "The Epilogue to Qoheleth as Theological Commentary," *CBQ* 39 (1977) 182-89.

33. The setting of death for instructions is a common one. See Perdue, "Paraenesis and the Death of the Sage," 81-109.

34. See Karl-Heinz Bernhardt, *Das Problem der altorientalischen Königs Ideologie im Alten Testament*, VTSup 8 (Leiden: Brill, 1961); Ivan Engnell, *Studies in Divine Kingship*

in the Ancient Near East (Oxford: Blackwell, 1967); Leonidas Kalugila, *The Wise King,* CB 15 (Uppsala, N.Y.: CWK Gleerup, 1980); and Schmid, *Gerechtigkeit als Weltordnung.*

35. See Rüdiger Lux, " 'Ich, Kohelet, bin König . . . ' Die Fiktion als Schlüssel zur Wirklichkeit in Kohelet 1:12-2:26," *EvT* 50 (1990) 331-42.

36. The implied author is the one whose thoughts, values, and feelings are conveyed in the text. See Wayne Booth, *The Rhetoric of Fiction* (Chicago: University of Chicago Press, 1961) 70-77.

37. For a discussion of narrators and the implied author in Qoheleth, see Michael V. Fox, "Frame-Narrative and Composition in the Book of Qohelet," *HUCA* 48 (1977) 83-106.

38. This is often true of modern fiction. See, e.g., Charles Dickens's *David Copperfield.*

39. See Herrmann, "Die Naturlehre des Schöpfungsberichtes," 413-23.

40. Oswald Loretz agrees that the form of Qoheleth is a first-person narrative, but he denies that one may discern anything of the thoughts and feelings of Qoheleth himself. See his "Zur Darbietungsform der 'Ich-Erzählung im Buche Qoheleth," *CBQ* 25 (1963) 46-59.

41. See, e.g., James G. Williams, "Proverbs and Ecclesiastes," in *The Literary Guide to the Bible,* eds. Robert Alter and Frank Kermode (Cambridge, Mass.: Harvard, 1987) 277.

42. For a survey of many different proposals for the literary structure of Qoheleth, see James L. Crenshaw, "Qoheleth in Current Research," *HAR* 7 (1983) 41-56; *Ecclesiasties,* 34-49; and Diethelm Michel, *Qohelet,* EF 258 (Darmstadt: Wissenschaftliche Buchgesell-schaft, 1988) 9-45.

43. Especially see Addison Wright, "The Riddle of the Sphinx: The Structure of the Book of Qoheleth," *CBQ* 30 (1968) 313-34. Also see "The Riddle of the Sphinx Revisited: Numerical Patterns in the Book of Qoheleth," *CBQ* 42 (1980) 33-51; and "Additional Numerical Patterns in Qoheleth," *CBQ* 45 (1983) 32-43.

44. See François Rousseau, "Structure de Qohelet I 4-11 et plan du livre," *VT* 31 (1981) 200-217.

45. Those who argue that joy and the enjoyment of life are at the heart of Qoheleth's teaching include Gordis, *Koheleth—The Man and His World,* 3rd. ed, (New York: Schocken Books, 1968) 129-31; R. Johnston, " 'Confessions of a Workaholic': A Reappraisal of Qoheleth," *CBQ* 38 (1976) 14-28; and R. N. Whybray, "Qoheleth, Preacher of Joy," *JSOT* 23 (1982) 87-98.

46. See Rüdiger Bartelmus, "Haben oder Sein—Anmerkungen zur Anthropologie des Buches Kohelet," *Biblische Notizen* 53 (1990) 38-67.

47. Mathias Schubert has argued that creation is central to the theology of Qoheleth. See his *Schöpfungstheologie bei Kohelet,* Beiträge zur Erforschung des Alten Testaments und des Antiken Judentums 15 (Frankfurt: Peter Lang, 1989).

48. See K. Seybold, *"Hebel," TWAT* 3, eds. G. Johannes Botterweck and Helmer Ringgren (Stuttgart: W. Kohlhammer, 1974) 313-20. Seybold gives *hebel* a rather wide semantic range. He argues that the terms often paralleled to *hebel* in the Bible are *rîq* ("empty"), *tohû* ("emptiness," "nothingness"), *šeqer* ("lie"), *'awen* ("delusion," "illusion," "fraud"), *šāv* ("emptiness"), *lō' hô'îl* ("worthless," "good for nothing"), and especially *rûah ("wind," "breath," "spirit").* Of the semantic field for *rûah, hebel* shares the meanings of "wind," "breath," "storm" and "breath of life." Rousseau concludes that the term means in six places "brevity of life," in two contexts "uselessness of speech," and in twenty-nine occurrences "deception" ("Structure de Qohelet I 4-11 et Plan du Livre," 208). Michael Fox has argued that *hebel* in Qoheleth has one overriding meaning: "absurd/absurdity" ("The Meaning of *Hebel* for Qohelet," *JBL* 105 [1986] 409-27). Michel also translates *hebel* this same way (*Qohelet,* 86). Graham Ogden thinks that *hebel* means "enigmatic." Thus life has much that is incomprehensible and mysterious, and there are

many questions that cannot be answered (*Qoheleth* [Sheffield: Almond Press, 1987] 22; " 'Vanity' It Certainly Is Not," *BT* 38 [1987] 307). Murphy prefers the meaning "incomprehensible" ("On translating Ecclesiastes," *CBQ* 53 [1991] 573).

49. Crenshaw, *Ecclesiastes*, 23; Rudi Kroeber, *Der Prediger*, Schriften und Quellen der Alten Welt 13 (Berlin: Akademie, 1963) 122; Lauha, *Kohelet*, 18.

50. Michael V. Fox, "The Meaning of *Hebel* for Qohelet," *JBL* 105 (1986) 409-27. Drawing from Camus, Fox explains: "The absurd is an affront to reason, in the broad sense of the human faculty that looks for order in the world about us. The quality of absurdity does not inhere in a being, act, or event in and of itself (though these may be called 'absurd'), but rather in the tension between a certain reality and a framework of expectations" (p. 409)." Fox adds other connotations, including "alienation, frustration, resentment, ephemeral, and inequitable."

51. See W. E. Staples, "Vanity of Vanities," *CJTh* 1 (1955) 141-56.

52. See Kurt Galling, *Der Prediger*, 2nd ed., HAT 18 (Tübingen: J. C. B. Mohr [Paul Siebeck], 1969) 79; Gordis, *Koheleth*, 20; Scott, *Proverbs. Ecclesiastes*, 202; Oswald Loretz, *Qohelet und der alte Orient* (Freiburg: Herder, 1964) 223. Loretz suggests other meanings, including "Gewichtlos-Leichten, Wertlos, Leer, Macht-und Hilflos."

53. See John Gammie, "Stoicism and Anti-Stoicism in Qoheleth," *HAR* 9 (1985) 169-87.

54. See Williams, "Proverbs and Ecclesiastes," 280.

55. Another term for "breath" is *nešamâ*, the breath that God breathes into human beings at creation, making them a "living being" (i.e., *nepeš*; cf. Gen. 2:7).

56. See Marcus Jastrow, *A Dictionary of the Targumim, The Talmud Babli and Yerushalmi, and the Midrashic Literature* (New York: The Judaica Press, 1985) 1486.

57. See Gordis, *Koheleth*, 210; and Walther Zimmerli, *Das Buch des Predigers Salomo*, ATD 16 (Göttingen: Vandenhoeck & Ruprecht, 1962) 48.

58. See Hans Wilhelm Hertzberg, *Der Prediger*, KAT 17 (Gütersloh: Gerd Mohn, 1963) 69.

59. Reading the perfect verb as a participle.

60. See Edwin Good, "The Unfilled Sea: Style and Meaning in Ecclesiastes 1:2-11," in Gammie et al., *Israelite Wisdom*, 59-73; and R. N. Whybray, "Ecclesiastes 1:5-7 and the Wonders of Nature," *JSOT* 41 (1988) 105-12.

61. E. Jenni sees *'ôlam* as meaning "an extensive expanse of time" ("Das Wort *olam* im Alten Testament," *ZAW* 64 [1952] 197-248; 65 [1953] 1-35).

62. See Perdue, "Cosmology and the Social Order in the Wisdom Tradition," in Gammie and Perdue, *The Sage in Israel and the Ancient Near East*, 457-78.

63. See Young-Jin Min, "How Do the Rivers Flow? (Ecclesiastes 1:7)," *BT* 42 (1991) 229.

64. Crüsemann notes that God in Qoheleth has become an impersonal power that cannot be known or influenced ("The Unchangeable World: The 'Crisis of Wisdom' in Koheleth," 59).

65. See Kroeber, *Der Prediger*, 124; O. S. Rankin, "The Book of Ecclesiastes," *IB* 5 (1956) 17.

66. Ogden notes that this unceasing activity of human senses parallels the cosmic movements of nature and points to the lack of completion's or fulfillment's ever being obtained. See his "The Interpretation of הוה in Ecclesiastes 1.4," *JSOT* 34 (1986) 92. Fox argues that wisdom is a body of knowledge to be transmitted by sages, whose job it was to convince their students to accept the teaching without much argumentation or persuasion. By contrast, Qoheleth emphasized much more critical reflection on wisdom and an effort to correlate its affirmations with individual experience. See his "Qohelet's Epistemology," *HUCA* 58 (1987) 137-55.

67. See J. Pedersen, "Scepticisme israélite," *RHPhR* 10 (1939–40) 345.

68. Aarre Lauha, "Kohelets Verhältnis zur Geschichte," in Jeremias and Perlitt, *Die Botschaft und die Boten,* 393-401.

69. See 3:21, which expresses some skepticism about the human breath (*rûaḥ*) "going upward" (presumably to the abode of God in heaven).

70. See Lauha, "Kohelets Verhältnis zur Geschichte," 393-401. Zimmerli argues that Qoheleth points, not to an unchangeable world, but to the limits of human existence and knowledge (" 'Unveränderbare Welt' oder 'Gott ist Gott'? Ein Plädoyer für die Unaufgebbarkeit der Predigerbuches," in *"Wenn nicht jetzt wann dann?"* eds. Hans-Georg Geger et al. [Neukirchener-Vluyn: Neukirchener, 1983] 103-14).

71. See Crüsemann, "The Unchangeable World: The Crisis of Wisdom in Koheleth," 57-77.

72. Hertzberg, *Der Prediger,* 87.

73. See von Rad, *Wisdom in Israel,* 139.

74. Ibid., 138-43.

75. See Hans Walter Wolff, *Anthropology of the Old Testament* (Philadelphia: Fortress, 1974) 89-92.

76. For Qoheleth, "the all" (*hakkōl*) refers on occasion to cosmic reality or "all things" ("heaven and earth," humans and creatures, society and nature; cf. 1:2, 14, 2:11, 17; 3:19), while *ḥēpeṣ* periodically refers to individual events or matters (3:17; 5:7; 8:6). Similarly, *zĕman* in Qoheleth appears to suggest the larger structure of cosmic time, while *ʿēt* designates episodic time.

77. See the argument by Bernhard Lang that there are still choices humans can make, in "Ist der Mensch hilflos?" *TQ* 159 (1979) 109-24.

78. Reading the root as "eternity." Other suggestions are "darkness," the "desire for eternity," and the "world."

79. See James Crenshaw, "The Eternal Gospel," in *Essays in Old Testament Ethics,* eds. James L. Crenshaw and John T. Willis (New York: Ktav, 1974) 25-55; and Kurt Galling, "Das Rätsel der Zeit," *ZThK* 58 (1961) 1-15.

80. See Daniel Lys, "L'être et le temps," in *La Sagesse de l'Ancien Testament,* 249-58.

81. See Stephen Crites, "The Narrative Quality of Experience," *JAAR* 39 (1971) 291-311.

82. This literary strategy is common to Qoheleth and compares with "The Dialogue of Pessimism" from Babylonian wisdom literature. See J. A. Loader, *Polar Structures in the Book of Qoheleth,* BZAW 152 (Berlin: de Gruyter, 1979).

83. Hertzberg sees 3:20 as an approximate citation of Gen. 3:19. Indeed, Gordis and he both argue that Qoheleth knew the Genesis creation tradition in its final form. See Hertzberg, *Der Prediger,* 46, 227-30; Gordis, *Koheleth,* 43. See also C. C. Forman, "Koheleth's Use of Genesis," *JSS* 5 (1960) 256-63.

84. The word *ʾereṣ* also occasionally refers to the underworld (Job 10:21-22).

85. See H. Brunner, "Gerechtigkeit als Fundament des Thrones," *VT* 8 (1958) 426-28.

86. See the discussion of Prov. 14:31 in chapter 3 of this book.

87. See chapter 3 of this book.

88. For a discussion of Qoheleth's debate with sapiential tradition, see Roland Murphy, "Qohelet's 'Quarrel' with the Fathers," in *From Faith to Faith,* ed. D. Y. Hadidian, PTMS 31 (Pittsburgh: Pickwick, 1979) 235-45.

89. The MT points the word as *hā ʾăsûrîm* ("the prisoners"), thus "house of the prisoners" (prison). However, *sûrîm* as "rebels" also makes good sense in the context (cf. Jer. 6:28; 17:13).

90. For a discussion, see E. Pfeiffer, "Die Gottesfurcht im Buche Kohelet," in *Gottes Wort und Gottes Land,* ed. H. G. Reventlow (Göttingen: Vandenhoeck & Ruprecht, 1965) 133-58.

91. See 2 Chron. 1:11, which speaks of the divine gifts of possessions, wealth, and honor bestowed on Solomon. Crenshaw notes that the verb *le̒ ̌ekōl* ("to eat") most likely means "to enjoy," since what is "eaten" includes riches, possessions, and honor (*Ecclesiastes,* 126).

92. For discussions of Qoheleth's views of God, see H.-P. Müller, "Wie sprach Qohälät von Gott?" *VT* 128 (1968) 507-21; and L. Gorssen, "La cohérence de la conception de dieu dans l'Ecclesiaste," *ETL* 46 (1970) 282-324.

93. See Kroeber, *Der Prediger,* 29.

94. Loader notes that Qoheleth engages in polemics against traditional wisdom by turning its own topoi and forms against it (*Polar Structures*).

95. Whybray sees this as a warning against self-righteousness. See his "Qoheleth the Immoralist?" (Qoh 7:16-17) *Israelite Wisdom,* 191-204.

96. The topos of the "foreign woman" is a common one in wisdom texts (Prov. 2:16-19; 5:1-6; 6:24-35; 7:6-27; Ani, III, 13f., Ptah-hotep 275f., and Papyrus Insinger 8:5f.).

97. This appears to be a proverb quoted by Qoheleth that by hyperbole affirms that human beings are universally wicked. See Galling, *Prediger Salomo,* 109; Kroeber, *Der Prediger,* 148. See also 7:20; 1 Kings 8:46.

98. The word translated "devices" occurs only here and in 2 Chron. 26:15, where it refers to war machines. Qoheleth may be using the term as a metaphor for evil, destruction, or even death.

99. See Graham Ogden, "Qoheleth XI 1-6," *VT* 33 (1983) 222-30.

100. Reading "in" (*b*) with many Hebrew mss. and the Targum in the place of MT's "like" (*c*).

101. See Graham S. Ogden, "Qoheleth XI 7-XII 8: Qoheleth's Summons to Enjoyment and Reflection," *VT* 34 (1984) 27-38.

102. See Denis Buzy, "Le portrait de la vieillesse (Ecclesiaste xii, 1-7)," *RB* 41 (1932) 329-40; James L. Crenshaw, "Youth and Old Age in Qoheleth, " *HAR* 10 (1986) 1-13; Michael V. Fox, "Aging and Death in Qohelet 12," *JSOT* 42 (1988) 55-77; Maurice Gilbert, "La Description de la vieillesse en Qohelet XII 1-7, est-elle allegorique?" in *Congress Volume Vienna,* ed. J. A. Emerton, VTSup 32 (Leiden: Brill, 1981) 96-109; John F. A. Sawyer, "The Ruined House in Ecclesiastes 12: A Reconstruction of the Original Parable," *JBL* 94 (1975) 519-31; and Hagia Wizenrath, *Süss ist das Licht* (St. Ottilien: EOS, 1979).

103. Crüsemann notes that "the deterioration of old age and the picture of its obnoxiousness that is given in 12:1-8 represent a typical reversal of segmentary thinking, according to which the elderly embody the human ideal" ("The Unchangeable World: The 'Crisis of Wisdom' in Koheleth," 69).

104. *Gesem* is used in Gen. 7:11-12 and 8:2-3 to refer to the rains that inundated the earth during the primeval flood (cf. Ezek 38:22).

105. See Prov. 7:6. An alternative interpretation is aristocratic ladies awaiting the return of their heroic warriors with spoils of war (Judg. 5:28).

106. See H. B. Tristram, *The Natural History of the Bible,* 2nd ed. (London: SPCK, 1868) 332-33; 457-58.

107. See Galling, *Der Prediger,* 122-23.

108. See Denis Buzy, "La notion du bonheur dans l'Ecclésiaste," *RB* 43 (1934) 494-516.

109. See R. N. Whybray, "Qoheleth, Preacher of Joy," *JSOT* 23 (1982) 87-98. He notes: "These seven texts are clearly more than mere marginal comments or asides. They punctuate the whole book, forming a kind of Leitmotiv; they increase steadily in emphasis

as the book proceeds" (p. 88). See also Norbert Lohfink, "Qoheleth 5:17-19—Revelation by Joy, "*CBQ* 52 (1990) 625-35. Lohfink argues that in this text joy is a divine gift, a "revelation" (*m'nh*) when for a passing moment humans are able to see things that normally God alone sees. God is revealed in the joy of the heart. Gordis notes that Qoheleth is no social reformer or revolutionary seeking to build a better world. Yet he does argue that each person has the right to experience "joy," if and when God gives it to him (Koheleth, *The Man and His World*, 122-32).

110. See Scott, *Proverbs. Ecclesiastes*, 205; and Walther Zimmerli " 'Unveränderbare Welt' oder 'Gott ist Gott'?" *Wenn nicht jezt wann dann?*, 103-14.

111. See Robert Gordis, "The Wisdom of Qoheleth," *Poets, Prophets, and Sages* (Bloomington: Indiana University Press, 1971) 337-38.

6. "I Covered the Earth Like a Mist"

1. See T. Middendorf, *Die Stellung Jesus ben Siras zwischen Judentum und Hellenismus* (Leiden: Brill, 1973). For the contention that Ben Sira read and borrowed from Egyptian wisdom literature, especially Papyrus Insinger, see Jack T. Sanders, *Ben Sira and Demotic Wisdom*, SBLMS 28 (Chico, Calif.: Scholars Press, 1985).

2. See John G. Gammie, "The Sage in Sirach," in Gammie and Perdue, *The Sage in Israel and the Ancient Near East*, 355-72. Cf. the Egyptian "Satire on the Trades," *ANET*, 432-34.

3. See Johannes Marböck, "Sir. 38, 24-39, 11: Der schriftgelehrte Weise," in *La Sagesse de l'Ancien Testament*, 293-316.

4. See Othmar Schilling, *Das Buch Jesus Sirach*, Herders Bibelkommentar: Die Heilige Schrift (Freiburg: Herder, 1956) 1.

5. Martin Hengel, *Judaism and Hellenism* (Philadelphia: Fortress, 1974) 1:131; and R. A. F. MacKenzie, *Sirach*, Old Testament Message (Wilmington, Del.: Michael Glazier, 1983) 13. For a detailed discussion of dating the book, see A. H. Forster, "The Date of Ecclesiasticus," *ATR* 41 (1959) 1-9.

6. See H. Duesberg and I. Fransen, *Ecclesiastico*, La Sacra Bibbia (Turin: Marietti, 1966) 69f.; J. G. Snaith, "Biblical Quotations in the Hebrew of Ecclesiasticus," *JTS* 18 (1967) 1-12; and J. L. Koole,"Die Bibel des Ben-Sira," *OTS* 14 (1965) 374-96.

7. Hengel, *Judaism and Hellenism* 1:131-62.

8. Ibid., 247. See J. Marböck, *Weisheit im Wandel*, BBB 37 (Bonn: Peter Hanstein, 1971) 83.

9. Hengel, *Judaism and Hellenism* 1:135-36.

10. Ibid., 1:134-53. Also see Alexander Di Lella,"Conservative and Progressive Theology: Sirach and Wisdom," *CBQ* 28 (1966) 139-54; and Rudolf Smend, *Die Weisheit des Jesus Sirachs erklärt* (Berlin: Reimer, 1906) xxxiiif. These scholars stress more the antagonism between Ben Sira and Hellenism, though they recognize that the Jewish teacher was influenced by Greek philosophy and culture.

11. See Burton Mack, *Wisdom and the Hebrew Epic: Ben Sira's Hymn in Praise of the Fathers* (Chicago: University of Chicago Press, 1985). Also see R. Pautrel,"Ben Sira et le Stoïcisme," *RSR* 51 (1963) 535-49; and Middendorf, *Die Stellung Jesus ben Siras zwischen Judentum und Hellenismus*. These scholars find in Ben Sira a far more positive adaptation of Hellenism to Jewish thought and culture than those listed in the preceding note.

12. Important discussions of the textual history of Ben Sira include those of Patrick Skehan and Alexander Di Lella, *The Wisdom of Ben Sira*, AB 39 (Garden City, N.Y.: Doubleday, 1987) 51-82; Maurice Gilbert, "L'Ecclésiastique: Quel texte? Quelle autorité?" *RB* (1987) 233-50; and C. Kearns, "Ecclesiasticus, or the Wisdom of Jesus the Son of Sirach," in *A New Catholic Commentary on Holy Scripture*, eds. R. C. Fuller et al. (London:

Nelson, 1969) 541-62; and Hans Peter Rüger, *Text und Textform im hebräischen Sirach,* BZAW 112 (Berlin: Walter de Gruyter, 1970). I am particularly indebted to the textual work in the commentary by Skehan and Di Lella.

13. *Genizah* means "storeroom," for the storing of manuscripts.

14. J. Ziegler, *Sapientia Iesu Filii Sirach,* Septuaginta 12/2 (Göttingen: Vandenhoeck & Ruprecht, 1965).

15. See Sanders, *Ben Sira and Demotic Wisdom.*

16. For a discussion of the enconium, see T. R. Lee, *Studies in the Form of Sirach 44–50,* SBLDS 75 (Atlanta: Scholars Press, 1986); and Mack, *Wisdom and the Hebrew Epic.*

17. See Walther Baumgartner, "Die literarischen Gattungen in der Weisheit des Jesus Sirach," *ZAW* 34 (1914) 161-98.

18. This text has not been preserved in Hebrew. GII, the expanded Greek text, has added to GI vv. 5, 7, and the second half of 10.

19. Among those who consider wisdom the dominant theme of Ben Sira, see von Rad, *Wisdom in Israel,* 242, and Marböck, *Weisheit im Wandel.*

20. Verse 9 especially borrows the thought and the language of Job 28:26-27.

21. See Koole, "Die Bibel des Ben-Sira," 376-77.

22. See Moshe Weinfeld, *Deuteronomy and the Deuteronomic School* (Oxford: Clarendon, 1972).

23. See MacKenzie, *Sirach,* 24.

24. Literally, "nested."

25. 19*a* is a repetition of 1:9*b* and appears to be a later insertion into this text.

26. This poem on the fear of the Lord is not preserved in Hebrew. The translation is based on the Greek text. Two expansions are added in GII (12*cd* and 18*cd*).

27. For a detailed discussion, see J. Haspecker, *Gottesfurcht bei Jesus Sirach: Ihre religiöse Struktur und ihre literarische doctrinäre Bedeutung,* AnBib 30 (Rome: Pontifical Biblical Institute, 1967).

28. See Skehan and Di Lella, *The Wisdom of Ben Sira,* 76.

29. Compare Ps. 53:2 and Wis. 12:10, which speak of the wicked as inherently corrupt from birth.

30. Reading Hebrew MS A. Verses 4*b*-5*a* are absent in MS A.

31. See John G. Snaith, *Ecclesiasticus, CBC* (Cambridge: Cambridge University Press, 1974) 15-26.

32. Translating Hebrew MS A.

33. Reading *tāqûs* ("to feel loathing") for *tā 'îs* ("to be pressed"). See *The Book of Ben Sira: Text, Concordance and an Analysis of the Vocabulary,* The Historical Dictionary of the Hebrew Language (Jerusalem: The Academy of the Hebrew Language and the Shrine of the Book, 1973) 314; and G ("do not hate").

34. Reading Hebrew *b* for *k.*

35. See James L. Crenshaw, "The Problem of Theodicy in Sirach: On Human Bondage," *JBL* 94 (1975) 47-64.

36. See Claudia Camp, "Understanding a Patriarchy: Women in Second Century Jerusalem Through the Eyes of Ben Sira," in *"Women Like This": New Perspectives on Jewish Women in the Greco-Roman World,* ed. Amy-Jill Levine, Early Judaism and Its Literature 1 (Atlanta: Scholars Press, 1991) 1-39.

37. Hebrew *hlq* refers here to divine determination.

38. See Di Lella, *The Wisdom of Ben Sira,* 201; and Snaith, *Ecclesiasticus,* 43.

39. This is the reading of the Hebrew MS A.

40. The Greek text reads "with your whole heart" (v. 27); "with all your soul" (v. 29), and "with all your strength" (v. 30). Hebrew MS A does not include v. 27. It also reads "heart" instead of "soul" in v. 29.

41. Reading G's version of v. 15, which is missing in MS A.

42. See Perdue, "The Testament of David and Egyptian Royal Instructions," 79-96.

43. See Kalugila, *The Wise King*; and Schmid, *Gerechtigkeit als Weltordnung*.

44. See MacKenzie, *Sirach*, 54-55.

45. See ibid., 77. This text of five related poems (16:26–18:14) is taken entirely from G.

46. See L. Alonso Schökel, "The Vision of Man in Sirach 16:24–17:14," in Gammie et al., *Israelite Wisdom*, 235-45.

47. Verse 5 comes from the expanded Greek text. See Skehan and Di Lella, *The Wisdom of Ben Sira*, 276.

48. See Schökel, "The Vision of Man in Sirach 16:24–17:14," 235-45.

49. See Skehan and Di Lella, *The Wisdom of Ben Sira*, 282.

50. See W. O. E. Oesterley, *The Wisdom of Jesus the Son of Sirach, or Ecclesiasticus*, Cambridge Bible for Schools and Colleges (Cambridge: Cambridge University Press, 1912) 113.

51. See 1 Kings 3:1-14 and Isa. 11:1-9. For a full discussion, see Kalugila, *The Wise King*.

52. The expanded Greek text (GII) adds: "In order that they may perceive that they, now alive, are mortal."

53. Verse 16 is from the expanded Greek text (GII).

54. Verse 18 is from the expanded Greek text (GII).

55. See Skehan and Di Lella, *The Wisdom of Ben Sira*, 285.

56. See Lang, *Wisdom and the Book of Proverbs*; Mack, "Wisdom Myth and Mythology," 46-60; Marböck, *Weisheit im Wandel*; and Ringgren, *Word and Wisdom*.

57. MacKenzie, *Sirach*, 101, notes concerning this hymn in Sir. 24: "It is a hymn of self-praise by a divine being, a goddess who describes her own beauty, virtues, and readiness to bless and help humanity."

58. For hymns in general, see Gerstenberger's introduction in *Psalms* 1; Kraus's introduction in *Psalms 1–59*; Patrick Miller, *Interpreting the Biblical Psalms* (Philadelphia: Fortress, 1986) chap. 5; and Westermann, *The Praise of God in the Psalms*.

59. Ben Sira is the first sage to teach that wisdom is the active principle in both creation and history. See Edmond Jacob, "Wisdom and Religion in Sirach," in *Israelite Wisdom*, 247-60.

60. The translation is based on G. The chapter did not survive in any of the Hebrew manuscripts.

61. Verse 18 is a later addition from GII: "I am the mother of beautiful love, reverence, knowledge, and holy hope. And to all my children who are called by him, I give everlasting life."

62. Verse 24 is an expansion from GII: "Do not weary being strong in the Lord, and cleave to him in order that he may strengthen you. The Lord Almighty is the only God, and there is no other savior besides him."

63. The reading is based on Syr. G and reads: "It makes instruction shine like the light."

64. See Mullen, *The Assembly of the Gods*.

65. See Mack, "Wisdom Myth and Mythology."

66. Cf. Enoch 42:1-2 where Wisdom, failing to find an earthly abode, is given a home in heaven.

67. The Gihon was also the spring flowing near Jerusalem and during the monarchy was the sacred stream where the royal ritual of the anointing of new kings occurred (1 Kings 1:33-45).

68. See G. L. Prato, "La lumière interprète de la sagesse dans la tradition textuelle de Ben Sira," in *La Sagesse de l'Ancien Testament*, 317-46. Prato traces the theme of light

throughout Ben Sira to point to the connection between the cosmos and ethics. Ethical conduct and the teaching that encompasses morality are compared to illumination from on high.

69. This text is not well preserved in the Hebrew. Ms. E is the only witness, and it is corrupt, with words and letters on the left edge of the manuscript missing. The translation follows Ms. E, with some dependence on GI in difficult places. While the Old Latin has preserved the proper sequence of chapters, two sections in the Greek manuscripts have exchanged places: 30:25-13*a* and 33:13*b*–36:16*a*.

70. See G. L. Prato, *Il problema della teodicea in Ben Sira,* AnBib 65 (Rome: Pontifical Biblical Institute, 1975); and Crenshaw, "The Problem of Theodicy in Sirach: On Human Bondage," 47-64.

71. Verses 12-15*b* are absent in Ms B; thus G is followed. Elsewhere G and Hebrew B, the major Hebrew witness to the poem, are in essential agreement, though G places the second disputation of v. 21*b* before v. 17. The Peshitta has both disputations coming before v. 17.

72. The translation largely follows Heb. Ms. B, with evidence from other witnesses (BMarg, M, and G) in textually problematic areas.

73. Compare the essay on God in the book of Job by Norman C. Habel, "In Defense of God the Sage," *The Voice from the Whirlwind,* eds. Leo G. Perdue and W. Clark Gilpin (Nashville: Abingdon Press 1992) 21-38.

74. See Smend, *Die Weisheit des Jesus Sirachs erklärt,* 396.

75. Mack, *Wisdom and the Hebrew Epic.* Also see Enno Janssen, *Das Gottesvolk und seine Geschichte* (Neukirchen-Vluyn: Neukirchener Verlag, 1971); Edmond Jacob, "L'histoire d'Israël vue par Ben Sira," *Mélanges bibliques André Robert* (Paris: Bloud & Gay, 1957) 288-94; and Robert T. Siebeneck, "May Their Bones Return to Life! Sirach's Praise of the Fathers," *CBQ* 21 (1959) 411-28. Siebeneck argues that Ben Sira uses the heroes of the Jewish past to illustrate the superiority of Hebrew wisdom to that of Hellenism.

76. Mack, *Wisdom and the Hebrew Epic.*

77. Because of his importance in Jewish history and particularly his emphasis on the law, it is surprising that Ezra is omitted from this lengthy panegyric to famous men.

78. See Mack, *Wisdom and the Hebrew Epic.*

79. Ibid., 37-65.

80. See Hayden White, *Metahistory: The Historical Imagination in Nineteenth-Century Europe* (Baltimore: Johns Hopkins, 1973). Also see his essay "The Value of Narrativity in the Representation of Reality," *Critical Inquiry* 7 (1980) 5-27.

81. See George F. Moore, "Simon the Righteous," *Jewish Studies in Memory of Israel Abrahams* (New York: Jewish Institute of Religion, 1927) 348-64.

82. See Marböck, *Weisheit im Wandel.*

7. "Wisdom, the Artificer of All, Instructed Me"

1. For discussions of possible dates of composition, ranging from the second century B.C.E. to the first century C.E., and the probable location of Alexandria, see P. Dalbert, *Die Theologie der hellenistisch-jüdischen Missionsliteratur unter Ausschluss von Philo und Josephus* (Hamburg-Volksdorf: Herbert Reich, 1954) 71f.; Johannes Fichtner, *Weisheit Salomos,* HAT 6 (Tübingen: J. C. B. Mohr, 1938) 5; A. Goodrick, *The Book of Wisdom* (New York: Macmillan, 1913) 5; Joseph Reider, *The Book of Wisdom* (New York: Harper and Bros., 1957) 14f.; and David Winston, *The Wisdom of Solomon,* AB (Garden City, N.Y.: Doubleday, 1979) 12-25.

2. For a discussion of Hellenism's impact on Judaism, see Martin Hengel, *Judaism and Hellenism,* vols. 1 and 2. For the impact on the Wisdom of Solomon, see J. M. Reese,

Hellenistic Influence on the Book of Wisdom and Its Consequences, AnBib 41 (Rome: Pontifical Biblical Institute, 1970).

3. See Dalbert, *Die Theologie der hellenistisch-jüdischen Missionsliteratur,* 14f. Jewish writers included Pseudo-Aristeas, Aristobulus, The Wise Menander, Pseudo-Phocylides, Artapanus, the authors of the Sibylline Oracles and IV Maccabees, Josephus, and Philo. The philosophical critics of Judaism included Hecataeus of Abdera, Mnaseas, Posidonius, Apion, Democritus, and Apollonius Molo.

4. Hellenistic elements included the original composition of the piece in Greek, the four cardinal virtues of Stoicism (8:7), the harmony of the elements (chap. 19), the argument from design (13:1-5), the stoic ideal of a world soul, and the immortality of the soul. See especially C. Larcher, *Études sur le Livre de la Sagesse,* Etudes Bibliques (Paris: J. Gabalda et Cie, 1969) 201f.; and Reese, *Hellenistic Influence on the Book of Wisdom and Its Consequences.*

5. See W. D. Davies, "The Jewish State in the Hellenistic World," in *Peake's Commentary on the Bible,* ed. Matthew Black (New York: Nelson, 1962) 686-92.

6. See Robert T. Siebeneck, "The Midrash of Wisdom 10-19," *CBQ* 22 (1960) 176f.

7. See Winston, *The Wisdom of Solomon,* 18-20; and Reese, *Hellenistic Influence on the Book of Wisdom,* 117f. Reece notes: "The protreptic, then, is not a formal treatise on the abstract aspects of philosophy, but an appeal to follow a meaningful philosophy as a way of life."

8. See Theodore Burgess, "Epideictic Literature," *Studies in Classical Philology* (Chicago: University of Chicago Press, 1902) 3:229-30; and Stanley K. Stowers, *Letter Writing in Greco-Roman Antiquity,* Library of Early Christianity (Philadelphia: Westminster, 1986) 92.

9. See John G. Gammie, "Toward the Morphology of a Secondary Genre," *Semeia* 50 (1990) 52.

10. See J. Pedersen, "Wisdom and Immortality," in *Wisdom in Israel and in the Ancient Near East,* 238-46.

11. See John G. Gammie, "The Sage in Hellenistic Royal Courts," in Gammie and Perdue, *The Sage in Israel and the Ancient Near East,* 147-53.

12. See the literature from the dead, discussed in chapter 5 (Qoheleth).

13. Addison Wright, "The Structure of the Book of Wisdom," *Bib* 48 (1967) 165-84; and "The Structure of Wisdom 11–19," *CBQ* 27 (1965) 28-34. For another analysis of the structure, see James M. Reese, "Plan and Structure in the Book of Wisdom" *CBQ* 27 (1965) 391-99.

14. Wright, "The Structure of the Book of Wisdom," 168-69.

15. The critical Greek text used is Joseph Ziegler, *Sapientia Salomonis,* Göttingen Septuagint 12/1 (Göttingen: Vandenhoeck & Ruprecht, 1962).

16. For examples of royal testaments, see "The Instruction of Amenemhet" and "The Instruction for King Merikare" from Egypt, "The Counsel of a Prince" from Mesopotamia, and the instruction of Solomon by David in 1 Kings 2:1-9. See Leo G. Perdue, "The Testament of David and Egyptian Royal Instructions," 2:79-96.

17. See Wisdom's love of humanity in Prov. 8:17f.

18. For a detailed discussion, see Ringgren, *Word and Wisdom.*

19. The teacher does not distinguish among "soul" (*psychē*), "mind" (*nous*), or "spirit" (*pneuma*). See Goodrick, *The Book of Wisdom,* 87.

20. See Winston, *The Wisdom of Solomon,* 101. See Wis. 5:16; 6:21; and 9:3.

21. See Reider, *The Book of Wisdom,* 54.

22. Or "creatures."

23. Cf. the battle between Baal and Mot (death) in Ugaritic literature, a battle that is taken up in the Old Testament (e.g., Isa. 25:7). In Greek mythology, Pluto is the god of the underworld.

24. See M. Delcor, "L'immortalité de l'âme dans le livre de la Sagesse et dans les documents de Qumran," *Nouvelle Revue Théologique* 77 (1955) 614-30; and Roland E. Murphy, " 'To Know Your Might Is the Root of Immortality,' " *CBQ* 25 (1963) 88-93.

25. See C. Larcher, *Études sur le Livre de la Sagesse* (Paris: Gabalda, 1969), 217. He notes that, unlike the Stoics, who identify the soul as a fire that gives life to nature and is identical to reason that permeates the cosmos, the wicked give a materialistic explanation to thought and breath as a kind of combustion process caused by the beating of the heart (pp. 218-19).

26. See John P. Weisengoff, "The Impious of Wisdom 2," *CBQ* 11 (1949) 40-65.

27. See Goodrick, *The Book of Wisdom,* 100.

28. See Larcher, *Études sur le Livre de la Sagesse,* 227; Winston, *The Wisdom of Solomon,* 114.

29. Another possibility is Cain's jealousy, which leads him to murder his brother Abel (Gen. 4:1-16).

30. Also see Josephus, *Ant.* i.I.4.; and 3 Baruch 4:8.

31. See Goodrick, *The Wisdom of Solomon,* 126.

32. Elihu had argued that the righteous are exalted to the position of rulers (36:7), but he does not envision a final, eschatological judgment.

33. See Ernest G. Clarke, *The Wisdom of Solomon,* CBC (Cambridge: Cambridge University Press, 1973) 42.

34. For a gestation period of ten (lunar) months, see 4 Macc. 16:17; Philo, *Legis. Allegor.,* i.iv; Plutarch, *Num.* 12; Virgil, *Ecl.,* 14.61; Pliny, *his. nat.,* vii.5. The teacher reflects the idea that conception occurs by the coagulation of menstrual blood, mixed with male sperm. See Larcher, *Études sur le Livre de la Sagesse,* 445f., and Clark, *The Wisdom of Solomon,* 50.

35. Larcher, *Études sur le Livre de la Sagesse,* 444.

36. See ibid. *Études sur le Livre de la Saggesse,* 443f.

37. See Wis. 13:2; 19:18. The four major elements that comprise reality and are active agents in the cosmos, according to Greek thought, were earth, air, fire, water. See Clark, *The Wisdom of Solomon,* 52).

38. Goodrick, *The Book of Wisdom,* 191, suggests that this may refer to the tradition of Solomon's power over demons. See Josephus, *Ant.,* viii.ii.5). Larcher thinks the reference may be to psychological impulses considered to be an area within the human passions (*Études sur le Livre de la Sagesse,* 445).

39. See Burton L. Mack, *Logos und Sophia. Untersuchungen zur Weisheitstheologie im hellenistischen Judentum,* SUNT 10 (Göttingen: Vandenhoeck & Ruprecht; 1973); Reider, *The Book of Wisdom,* 115.

40. See Ringgren, *Word and Wisdom.*

41. See Larcher, *Études sur le Livre de la Sagesse,* 516-17.

42. Cf. the metaphor of Israel as the wife and lover of God in Hos. 1–3 and Jer. 2.

43. Cf. the allegory of Ezek. 16, where Jerusalem was an abandoned female child raised to maturity and then married by Yahweh.

44. Cf. the royal prayers of David in 1 Chron. 29:10-19 and Solomon in 1 Kings 8:22-53 (= 2 Chron. 6:12-42).

45. A primary use of the verb *kataskeuasas* is to refer to the "construction" of ships (14:2) and buildings. Another meaning is "to organize," "to equip." See William F. Arndt and F. Wilbur Gingrich, *A Greek-English Lexicon of the New Testament and Other Early Christian Literature* (Chicago: University of Chicago Press, 1957) 419

46. See Goodrick, *The Book of Wisdom,* 215-16.

47. Some have seen v. 15 as referring to something comparable to the Platonic duality of mortal body and immortal soul. See Plato, *Phaedo,* 81c Cf. Philo, *Gig.,* 31. See the

discussions in Goodrick, *The Book of Wisdom,* 221; Larcher, *Études sur le Livre de la Sagesse,* 595f.; and Winston, *The Book of Wisdom,* 207.

48. See Mack's discussion of the relationship of Wisdom and soteriology (*Logos und Sophia,* 72f.).

49. See Perdue, "The Social Character of Paraenesis," 16-17.

50. See Armin Schmitt, "Struktur, Herkunft und Bedeutung der Beispielreihe in Weish 10," *BZ* 21 (1977) 1-22. He argues that this list of redeemed follows, not summaries of salvation history in the Old Testament, but Hellenistic literature.

51. John Collins argues that the book of Wisdom shares with apocalyptic a "cosmological conviction"—i.e., the path to salvation resides in understanding the structure of the universe and living life accordingly. Apocalyptic, however, rejected Wisdom's claim that there is order in the present creation. Apocalyptic looked forward to a new order formed by the transformation of the old. See his "Cosmos and Salvation: Jewish Wisdom and Apocalyptic in the Hellenistic Age," *HR* 17 (1977) 121-42.

52. See A. Dupont-Sommer, "Adam 'Père du Monde' dans la Sagesse de Salomon (10, 1-21)," *RHR* 119 (1939) 182-203.

53. See Siebeneck, "The Midrash of Wisdom 10-19," 178f.

54. Fichtner, *Weisheit Salomos,* 42-43.

55. See Edmund Stein, "Ein jüdisch-hellenistischer Midrasch über den Auszug aus Ägypten," *MGWJ* 78 (1934) 559f.

56. For an alternative literary analysis of chaps. 11–19 that sees the narrative using the literary technique of syncresis to shape a grand "pedagogical drama," see Peter T. Van Rooden, "Die Antike Elementarlehre und der Aufbau von Sap. Sal. 11-19," in *Tradition and Re-Interpretation in Jewish and Early Christian Literature,* eds. J. W. Van Henten et al., Studia Post-Biblica 36 (Leiden: E. J. Brill, 1986) 81-96.

57. Winston, *The Book of Wisdom,* 227.

58. See Addison Wright, "The Structure of the Book of Wisdom."

59. See M.-J. Lagrange, "Le Livre de la Sagesse," *RB* 16 (1907) 85-104.

60. See Maurice Gilbert, *La critique des dieux dans le Livre de la Sagesse,* AnBib 13 (Rome: Pontifical Biblical Institute, 1973); Friedo Ricken, "Gab es eine hellenistische Vorlage für Weish 13-15?" *Bib* 49 (1968) 54-86.

60. See Goodrick, *The Book of Wisdom,* 275.

62. See Georg Ziener, *Die theologische Begriffssprache im Buche der Weisheit,* BBB 11 (Bonn: Peter Hanstein, 1966) 128f.

63. The feminine form of the noun was applied to Wisdom (8:6).

64. See Reider, *The Book of Wisdom,* 160.

65. See H. Eising, "Der Weisheitslehrer und die Göttesbilder," *Bib* 40 (1959) 393-408.

66. See Horst Dietrich Preuss, *Verspottung fremder Religionen im Alten Testament,* BWANT 92 (Stuttgart: W. Kohlhammer, 1971) 265.

67. This is probably human wisdom, which involves the knowledge and skill of a craftsperson (cf. Exod. 28:3; 31:3, 6; 35:26, 31, 35), not the cosmic Wisdom of God, which shapes the world and human beings (8:6). However, see Winston, *The Book of Wisdom,* 264-65.

68. The texts in Isaiah and Psalms point to God's making a path in the Red Sea to deliver Israel from the Egyptians (cf. Exod. 14–15).

69. Winston notes that this principle was articulated by the Stoics, allowing the gods to act so as not to violate nature's laws (*The Wisdom of Solomon,* 325).

70. See Clarke, *The Wisdom of Solomon,* 126; and Ziener, *Die theologische Begriffssprache im Buche der Weisheit,* 148f.

71. See Walter Vogels, "The God Who Creates Is the God Who Saves: The Book of Wisdom's Reversal of the Biblical Pattern," *Église et Théologie* 22 (1991) 315-35.

72. See David Winston, "The Book of Wisdom's Theory of Cosmogony," *HR* 11 (1971) 185-202.

8. "Wisdom Has Built Her House, She Has Hewn Her Seven Pillars"

1. Sallie McFague argues that contemporary theology should examine the metaphors and images of faith in serious ways, before moving into systematic presentation. See her *Metaphorical Theology.* Also see her *Models of God: Theology for an Ecological, Nuclear Age* (Philadelphia: Fortress, 1987).

2. James Muilenburg, "Form Criticism and Beyond," 1-18; Phyllis Trible, *God and the Rhetoric of Sexuality.* For a discussion of narrative theology and metaphorical theology, see Perdue *Collapse of History,* chaps. 7–8.

3. See Perdue, "Cosmology and the Social Order in the Wisdom Tradition," 457-78.

4. See D. J. McCarthy, "Be Sober and Watch," *The Way* 14 (1974) 167.

5. Human wisdom involves a number of features. These include administrative skill and knowledge to govern beneficently and justly the social order or one of its institutions (Gen. 41:33, 39; Deut. 1:13, 15; 16:19; 34:9; 2 Sam. 14:20; 1 Kings 2:6; 3:28; 5:9-10, 14, 26; 10:4, 6-8, 23-24 [= 2 Chron. 9:3, 5-7, 22-23]; 1 Kings 11:41; 2 Chron. 1:10-12; Prov. 20:26; Isa. 29:14; Jer. 49:7); counsel given by advisers to kings (Isa. 19:11-12; 29:14; Jer. 18:18); the knowledge of teachers transmitted to students (Prov. 1:2-7; Qoh. 12:9); the skill and ability to conduct war (Isa. 10:13); the skill and knowledge of artisans (Exod. 28:3; 31:3, 6; 35:10, 26, 31, 35; 36:1-2, 4, 8; 1 Kings 7:14; 1 Chron. 28:1; Jer. 10:9); the skill and knowledge of sailors (Ps. 107:27; Ezek. 27:8); the esoteric knowledge of magicians and prophets (Isa. 47:10; Dan. 1:4, 17, 20); the knowledge and learning of scribes (Jer. 8:8-9); and religious piety and obedient faithfulness to divine instruction (Deut. 4:6; Job 28:28; Pss. 51:8; 111:10; Prov. 1:7; 15:33) .

6. Gordan Kaufman summarizes by saying: "The Christian image/concept of God, as I have presented it here, is an imaginative construct which orients selves and communities so as to facilitate development toward loving and caring selfhood, and toward communities of openness, love, and freedom" (*The Theological Imagination,* 48).

7. For detailed discussions, see Klaus Koch, "Gibt es ein Vergeltungsdogma im Alten Testament?," *ZTK* 52 (1955) 1-42; translated in Crenshaw, *Theodicy in the Old Testament,* 57-87; and J. Barton, "Natural Law and Poetic Justice," *JTS* 30 (1979) 1-14.

8. See U. Luck, *Welterfahrung und Glaube als Grundproblem biblischer Theologie,* TEH 191 (Munich: Kaiser, 1976).

9. See the *Enuma elish* (Mesopotamia); the Baal Cycle (Canaan); and the Osiris-Horus myth (Egypt).

10. See McCurley, *Ancient Myths and Biblical Faith,* 73-124; and Keel, *The Symbolism of the Biblical World*; 201f.

11. See Bernhard Lang, *Frau Weisheit* (Düsseldorf: Patmos, 1975). A revised version in English is *Wisdom and the Book of Proverbs.*

12. Cf. the discussion of Prov. 8:30 in chap. 3.

13. See Dürr, *Die Wertung des Göttlichen Wortes im Alten Testament und im Antiken Orient.*

14. For example, Jacobsen notes: "The creative power of the word underlies all Mesopotamian religious literature" (*Treasure of Darkness,* 15).

15. See the "Instruction for King Meri-ka-Re," *ANET,* 417. For other Egyptian examples, see Notter, *Biblischer Schöpfungsbericht und Ägyptische Schöpfungsmythen,* 145-49.

16. God's breath brings destruction against the wicked (see Exod. 15:8; Ps. 18:15).

17. See McCurley, *Ancient Myths and Biblical Faith,* 12-57.

18. See Job 32:22; 35:10; 36:3. Qoheleth may refer to God as "your creator" (12:1).

19. The word *'ebed* means both "slave" and "servant."

SELECT BIBLIOGRAPHY

Texts and Translation

Biblia Hebraica Stuttgartensia. Stuttgart: Deutsche Bibelgesellschaft, 1984.

The Book of Ben Sira: Text, Concordance and an Anaylsis of the Vocabulary. The Historical Dictionary of the Hebrew Language and the Shrine of the Book. Jerusalem: The Academy of the Hebrew Language and the Shrine of the Book, 1973.

Lambert, W. G., ed. *Babylonian Wisdom Literature*. Oxford: Clarendon, 1960.

Lichtheim, Miriam, ed. *Ancient Egyptian Literature*. 3 vols. Berkeley: University of California Press, 1973–80.

Pritchard, James B., ed. *Ancient Near Eastern Texts*. 3rd ed. Princeton: Princeton University Press, 1969.

Septuaginta: Vetus Testamentum Graecum. Göttingen: Vandenhoeck & Ruprecht, 1931–.

Scholarly Literature

Albertz, Rainer. *Weltschöpfung und Menschenschöpfung*. Calwer Theologische Monographien. Reihe A: Bibelwissenschaft 3. Stuttgart: Calwer, 1974.

Albright, W. F. "The Goddess of Life and Wisdom." *AJSL* 36 (1919–1920) 258-94.

Aletti, J. N. "Seduction et parole en Proverbes I-IX," *VT* 27 (1977) 129-44.

Barbour, Ian. *Myths, Models and Paradigms*. New York: Harper & Row, 1974.

Baumgartner, Walter. "Die literarischen Gattungen in der Weisheit des Jesus Sirach." *ZAW* 34 (1914) 161-98.

———. *Israelitische und Altorientalische Weisheit*. Tübingen: J. C. B. Mohr (Paul Siebeck), 1933.

Becker, Joachim. *Gottesfurcht im Alten Testament*. AB 25. Rome: Pontifical Biblical Institute, 1965.

Begrich, J. "*Sofer* und *Mazkir*: Ein Beitrag zur inneren Geschichte des davidisch-salomonischen Grossreiches und des Königreiches Judah." *ZAW* 58 (1940–41) 1-29.

379

SELECT BIBLIOGRAPHY

Bergman, Jan. "Gedanken zum Thema 'Lehre-Testament-Grab-Name.' " Pages 73-104 in *Studien zu Altägyptischen Lebenslehren.* Edited by Erik Hornung and Othmar Keel. OBO 28. Göttingen: Vandenhoeck & Ruprecht, 1979.

Boer, P. A. H. de. "The Counselor." Pages 42-71 in *Wisdom in Israel and the Ancient Near East.* Edited by Martin Noth and D. Winton Thomas. VTSup 3. Leiden: Brill, 1955.

Böstrom, G. *Proverbiastudien: Die Weisheit und das fremde Weib in Spr 1-9.* Lunds Universitet Årsskrift N. F. Avd. 1, Bd 30 Nr. 3. Lund: Gleerup, 1935.

Booth, Wayne. *The Rhetoric of Fiction.* Chicago: University of Chicago Press, 1961.

————. *A Rhetoric of Irony.* Chicago: University of Chicago, 1974.

Brueggemann, Walter. *In Man We Trust.* Atlanta: John Knox, 1972.

Bryce, Glendon. "Another Wisdom 'Book' in Proverbs." *JBL* 91 (1972): 145-57.

Bühlmann, Walter. *Vom Rechten Reden und Schweigen. Studien zu Proverbien 10-31.* OBO 12. Göttingen: Vandenhoeck & Ruprecht, 1976.

Burgess, Theodore. "Epideictic Literature." Pages 89-261 in *Studies in Classical Philology* 3. Chicago: University of Chicago Press, 1902.

Camp, Claudia. "Understanding a Patriarchy: Women in Second Century Jerusalem Through the Eyes of Ben Sira." Pages 1-39 in *"Women Like This": New Perspectives on Jewish Women in the Greco-Roman World.* Edited by Amy-Jill Levine. Early Judaism and Its Literature 1. Atlanta: Scholars Press, 1991.

————. *Wisdom and the Feminine in the Book of Proverbs.* Bible and Literature Series 11. Sheffield: JSOT/Almond, 1985.

————. "Woman Wisdom as Root Metaphor: A Theological Consideration." Pages 45-76 in *The Listening Heart.* Edited by Kenneth G. Hoglund et al. JSOT 58. Sheffield: Sheffield Academic Press, 1987.

Childs, Brevard. *Biblical Theology in Crisis.* Philadelphia: Westminster, 1970.

————. *Biblical Theology of the Old and New Testaments.* Minneapolis: Fortress, 1993.

————. *Introduction to the Old Testament as Scripture.* Philadelphia: Fortress, 1979.

Clarke, Ernest G. *The Wisdom of Solomon.* CBC. Cambridge: Cambridge University Press, 1973.

Clements, Ronald. *Wisdom in Theology.* Grand Rapids: Eerdmans, 1992.

Clifford, Richard J. "Prov IX: A Suggested Ugaritic Parallel." *VT* 25 (1975) 298-306.

Collins, John J. "Cosmos and Salvation: Jewish Wisdom and Apocalyptic in the Hellenistic Age." *HR* 17 (1977): 121-42.

Cox, D. *The Triumph of Impotence: Job and the Tradition of the Absurd.* Analecta Gregoriana 212. Rome: U. Gregoriana, 1978.

Crenshaw, James L. *Ecclesiastes.* OTL. Philadelphia: Westminster, 1987.

————. "Education in Ancient Israel." *JBL* 104 (1985): 601-15.

————. "In Search of Divine Presence." *REx* 74 (1977): 353-69.

————. "Introduction: The Shift from Theodicy to Anthropodicy." Pages 1-16 in *Theodicy in the Old Testament.* Edited by James L. Crenshaw. London: SCM Press, 1983.

————. *Old Testament Wisdom.* Atlanta: John Knox, 1981.

————. "Wisdom." Pages 225-64 in *Old Testament Form Criticism.* Edited by John H. Hayes. San Antonio: Trinity University Press, 1974.

————. "Youth and Old Age in Qohelet 12." *JSOT* 42 (1988): 1-13.

Crites, Stephen. "The Narrative Quality of Experience." *JAAR* 39 (1971): 291-311.

————. "Unfinished Figure: On Theology and Imagination." Pages 155-84 in *Unfinished . . . . : Essays in Honor of Ray Hart.* Edited by Mark C. Taylor. JAAR Thematic Studies. Chico, Calif.: Scholars Press, 1981.

Crook, M. B. *The Cruel God.* Boston: Beacon, 1959.

SELECT BIBLIOGRAPHY

Crüsemann, F. "Hiob und Kohelet." Pages 373-93 in *Werden und Wirken des Alten Testaments*. Edited by Rainer Albertz et al. FS Claus Westermann. Göttingen: Vandenhoeck & Ruprecht, 1980.

———. "The Unchangeable World: The 'Crisis of Wisdom' in Koheleth." Pages 55-77 in *God of the Lowly*. Edited by Willy Schottroff and Wolfgang Stegemann. Maryknoll, N.Y.: Orbis, 1984.

Dalbert, P. *Die Theologie der hellenistisch-jüdischen Missionsliteratur unter Ausschluss von Philo und Josephus*. Hamburg-Volksdorf: Herbert Reich, 1954.

Delcor, M. "L'immortalité de l'ame dans le livre de la Sagesse et dans les documents de Qumran." *Nouvelle Revue Theologique* 77 (1955): 614-30.

Dhorme, E. *A Commentary on the Book of Job*. London: Nelson, 1967.

Dick, M. B. "The Legal Metaphor in Job 31." *CBQ* 41 (1979) 37-50.

Di Lella, Alexander. "Conservative and Progressive Theology: Sirach and Wisdom." *CBQ* 28 (1966) 139-54.

Doll, Peter. *Menschenschöpfung und Weltschöpfung in der alttestamentlichen Weisheit*. SBS 117. Stuttgart: Katholisches Bibelwerk, 1985.

Donner, H. "Die religionsgeschichtlichen Ursprünge von Prov. Sal. 8, 22-31." *ZÄS* 82 (1957) 8-18.

Doob-Sakenfeld, Katherine. *The Meaning of ḥesed in the Hebrew Bible*. HSM 17. Missoula: Scholars Press, 1977.

Driver, S. R., and G. B. Gray. *Job*. ICC. Edinburgh: T. & T. Clark, 1921.

Dünner, Alfred. *Die Gerechtigkeit nach dem Alten Testament*. Schriften zur Rechtslehre und Politik 42. Bonn: H. Bouvier, 1963.

Dürr, Lorenz. *Das Erziehungswesen im Alten Testament und im Alten Orient*. MVAG 36. Leipzig: J. C. Hinrichs, 1932.

———. *Die Wertung des Göttlichen Wortes im Alten Testament und in Antiken Orient*. MVAG 42. Leipzig: J. C. Hinrichs, 1938.

Duesberg, H., and I. Fransen. *Les scribes inspires*. Rev. ed. Marsedsous: Marsedsous, 1966.

Duhm, B. *Das Buch Hiob*. Freiburg: J. C. B. Mohr (Paul Siebeck), 1897.

Eichrodt, Walther. *Theology of the Old Testament* 1 & 2. OTL. Philadelphia: Westminster, 1961.

Eliade, Mircea. *Cosmos and History: The Myth of the Eternal Return*. New York: Harper and Bros., 1954.

Ferré, Frederick. "Metaphors, Models, and Religion." *Soundings* 51 (1968) 327-45.

Fichtner, Johannes. *Die altorientalische Weisheit in ihrer israelitisch-jüdischen Ausprägung*. BZAW 62. Giessen: Alfred Töpelmann, 1933.

———. *Weisheit Salomos*. HAT 6. Tübingen: J. C. B. Mohr, 1938.

———. "Zum Problem Glaube und Geschichte in der israelitisch-jüdischen Weisheitsliteratur." *ThLZ* 76 (1951) 146-50.

Fisch, Harold. "Qohelet: A Hebrew Ironist." Pages 158-78 in *Poetry with a Purpose: Biblical Poetics and Interpretation*. Bloomington: Indiana University Press, 1988.

Fishbane, Michael. "Jer. 4 and Job 3: A Recovered Use of the Creation Pattern." *VT* 21 (1971) 151-62.

Fohrer, Georg. *Das Buch Hiob*. KAT 16. Gütersloh: Gerd Mohn, 1963.

———. *Introduction to the Old Testament*. Nashville: Abingdon, 1968.

———. "The Righteous Man in Job 31." Pages 1-22 in *Essays in Old Testament Ethics*. Edited by James L. Crenshaw and John T. Willis. New York: Ktav, 1974.

———. *Studien zum Buche Hiob*. 2nd ed. Gütersloh: Gerd Mohn, 1982.

Fontaine, Carole R. *Traditional Sayings in the Old Testament*. Bible and Literature 5. Sheffield: Almond, 1982.

————. "The Sage in Family and Tribe." Pages 155-64 in *The Sage in Israel and the Ancient Near East*. Edited by John G. Gammie and Leo G. Perdue. Winona Lake: Eisenbrauns, 1990.

Fox, Michael V. "Frame-Narrative and Composition in the Book of Qohelet." *HUCA* 48 (1977) 83-106.

————. "The Meaning of *Hebel* for Qohelet." *JBL* 105 (1986) 409-27.

————. *Qohelet and His Contradictions*. JSOTSup 18. Sheffield: Almond, 1989.

————. "Qohelet's Epistemology." *HUCA* 58 (1987) 137-55.

Franklyn, Paul. "The Sayings of *Agur* in Prov 30: Piety or Skepticism?" *ZAW* 95 (1983) 238-51.

Galling, Kurt. "Das Rätsel der Zeit." *ZThK* 58 (1961) 1-15.

————. *Der Prediger*. 2nd ed. HAT 18. Tübingen: J. C. B. Mohr (Paul Siebeck), 1969.

Gammie, John. "Behemoth and Leviathan: On the Didactic and Theological Significance of Job 40:15–41:26." Pages 217-31 in *Israelite Wisdom*. Edited by John G. Gammie et al. FS Samuel Terrien. Missoula: Scholars Press, 1978.

————. "Paraenetic Literature: Toward the Morphology of a Secondary Genre." *Semeia* 50 (1990) 41-77.

————. "The Sage in Sirach." Pages 355-72 in *The Sage in Israel and the Ancient Near East*. Edited by John G. Gammie and Leo G. Perdue. Winona Lake: Eisenbrauns, 1990.

————. "The Spiritual Structure of Biblical Aphoristic Wisdom." Pages 138-49 in *Adhuc Loquitur*. Pretoria Oriental Series 7. Leiden: Brill, 1968.

Gammie, John G., and Leo G. Perdue, eds. *The Sage in Israel and the Ancient Near East*. Winona Lake: Eisenbrauns, 1990.

Gemser, B. *Sprüche Salomos*. 2nd ed. HAT 10. Tübingen: J. C. B. Mohr (Paul Siebeck), 1963.

Gerstenberger, Eberhard. *Psalms 1*. FOTL 14. Edited by Rolf Knierim and Gene M. Tucker. Grand Rapids: Eerdmans, 1988.

————. *Wesen und Herkunft des sogenannten 'apodiktischen Rechts' im Alten Testament*. WMANT 20. Neukirchen-Vluyn: Neukirchener, 1965.

Gese, H. "Die Krisis der Weisheit bei Koheleth." Pages 139-51 in *Les Sagesses du Proche-Orient Ancien*. Paris: Presses Universitaires de France, 1961.

————. *Lehre und Wirklichkeit in der alten Weisheit*. Tübingen: J. C. B. Mohr (Paul Siebeck), 1958.

Gilbert, M. *La critique des dieux dans le Livre de la Sagesse*. AnBib 13. Rome: Pontifical Biblical Institute, 1973.

————. "La description de la vieillesse en Qohelet XII 1-7, est-elle allegorique?" Pages 96-109 in *Congress Volume Vienna*. Edited by J. A. Emerton. VTSup 32. Leiden: Brill, 1981.

————. "Le discours de la sagesse en Proverbes 8." Pages 202-18 in *La Sagesse de l'Ancien Testament*. Edited by M. Gilbert. BETL 51. Gembloux: Leuven, 1979.

————. "L'Ecclesiastique: Quel texte? Quelle autorité?" *RB* (1987) 233-50.

Good, Edwin M. *In Turns of Tempest: A Reading of Job with a Translation*. Stanford: Stanford University Press, 1990.

Golka, Friedemann W. "Die israelitische Weisheitsschule oder 'des Kaiser neue Kleider.' " *VT* 33 (1983) 257-70.

————. "Die Königs- und Hofsprüche und der Ursprung der israelitischen Weisheit." *VT* 36 (1986) 13-36.

Goodrick, A. *The Book of Wisdom*. New York: Macmillan, 1913.

Gordis, Robert. *Koheleth—The Man and His World*. 3rd ed. New York: Schocken Books, 1968.

————. *The Book of Job*. New York: Jewish Theological Seminary of America, 1978.

————. "The Social Background of Wisdom Literature." *HUCA* 18 (1944): 77-118.

Green, Garrett. *Imagining God: Theology and the Religious Imagination.* San Francisco: Harper & Row, 1989.

Guillaume, A. *Studies in the Book of Job.* Leiden: Brill, 1968.

Gunkel, H. *Schöpfung und Chaos in Urzeit und Endzeit.* 2nd ed. Göttingen: Vandenhoeck & Ruprecht, 1921.

Habel, Norman. "In Defense of God the Sage." Pages 21-38 in *The Voice from the Whirlwind.* Edited by Leo G. Perdue and W. Clark Gilpin. Nashville: Abingdon, 1992.

————. *Job.* OTL. Philadephia: Westminster, 1985.

————. "The Symbolism of Wisdom in Proverbs 1-9." *Int* 26 (1972) 131-57.

————. "Wisdom, Wealth and Poverty Paradigms in the Book of Proverbs." *Bible Bhashyam* 14 (1988) 26-49.

Haspecker, J. *Gottesfurcht bei Jesus Sirach. Ihre religiöse Struktur und ihre literarische doctrinäre Bedeutung.* AnBib 30. Rome: Pontifical Biblical Institute, 1967.

Heaton, E. W. *Solomon's New Men.* New York: Pica, 1975.

Hengel, Martin. *Judaism and Hellenism.* 1 & 2. Philadelphia: Fortress, 1974.

Hermisson, Hans-Jürgen. "Observations on the Creation Theology in Wisdom." Pages 43-57 in *Israelite Wisdom.* Edited by John G. Gammie et al. Missoula: Scholars Press, 1978.

————. *Studien zur Israelitischen Spruchweisheit.* WMANT 28. Neukirchen-Vluyn: Neukirchener Verlag, 1968.

Hertzberg, Hans Wilhelm. *Der Prediger.* KAT 17. Gütersloh: Gerd Mohn, 1963.

Hesse, F. *Hiob.* Zürich: Theologischer Verlag, 1978.

Hölscher, G. *Das Buch Hiob.* 2nd ed. HAT 17. Tübingen: J. C. B. Mohr (Paul Siebeck), 1952.

Horst, F. *Hiob.* BKAT 16. Neukirchener Verlag, 1969.

Irwin, William A. "Job and Prometheus." *JR* 30 (1950) 90-108.

————. "Job's Redeemer." *JBL* 81 (1962) 217-29.

Jacob, Edmond. "L'histoire de'Israël vue par Ben Sira." Pages 288-94 in *Melanges bibliques André Robert.* Paris: Bloud & Gay, 1957.

————. "Wisdom and Religion in Sirach." Pages 247-60 in *Israelite Wisdom.* Edited by John G. Gammie et al. FS Samuel Terrien. Missoula: Scholars Press, 1978.

Jamieson-Drake, David. *Scribes and Schools in Monarchic Judah: A Socio-Archaeological Approach.* JSOT 109. Sheffield: JSOT Press, 1991.

Janzen, J. Gerald. *Job. Interpretation.* Atlanta: John Knox, 1985.

Jenks, Alan W. "Theological Presuppositions of Israel's Wisdom Literture." *HBT* 7 (1985) 43-75.

Jeremias, J. *Theophanie.* WMANT 10. Neukirchen-Vluyn: Neukirchener Verlag, 1965.

Johnston, R. " 'Confessions of a Workaholic.' A Reappraisal of Qoheleth." *CBQ* 38 (1976) 14-28.

Kaiser, Walter C. "Wisdom Theology and the Centre of Old Testament Theology." *Evangelical Quarterly* 50 (1978) 132-46.

Kaufman, Gordon. *The Theological Imagination: Constructing the Concept of God.* Philadelphia: Westminster, 1981.

Kayatz, Christa Bauer. *Einführung in die alttestamentliche Weisheit.* Biblische Studien 55. Neukirchener Verlag, 1969.

————. *Studien zu Proverbien 1-9.* WMANT 22. Neukirchen-Vluyn: Neukirchener Verlag, 1966.

Kearns, C. "Ecclesiasticus, or the Wisdom of Jesus the Son of Sirach." Pages 541-62 in *A New Catholic Commentary on Holy Scripture.* Edited by R. C. Fuller et al. London: Nelson, 1969.

SELECT BIBLIOGRAPHY

Keel, O. *Jahwes Entgegnung an Ijob*. FRLANT 121. Göttingen: Vandenhoeck & Ruprecht, 1978.

———. *The Symbolism of the Biblical World*. New York: Seabury, 1978.

———. *Die Weisheit Spielt vor Gott* (Göttingen: Vandenhoeck & Ruprecht, 1974).

Kluger, Rivkah S. *Satan in the Old Testament*. Evanston, Ill.: Northwestern University Press, 1967.

Knierim, Rolf. "Cosmos and History in Israel's Theology." Pages 59-123 in *Werden und Wirken der Alten Testaments*. Göttingen: Vandenhoeck & Ruprecht, 1980.

———. "The Task of Old Testament Theology," *Horizons in Biblical Theology* 6 (1984) 25-57.

Koch, Klaus. "Gibt es ein Vergeltungsdogma im Alten Testament?" *ZTK* 52 (1955) 1-42. English trans. in James L. Crenshaw, *Theodicy in the Old Testament*, 57-87.

Koole, J. L. "Die Bibel des Ben-Sira." *OTS* 14 (1965) 374-96.

Kraus, Hans-Joachim. *Die Verkündigung der Weisheit*. BS 2. Buchhandlung des Erziehungsvereins Neukirchen Kreis Moers, 1951.

———. *Psalms 1–59: A Commentary*. Minneapolis: Augsburg, 1988.

Kroeber, Rudi. *Der Prediger*. Schriften und Quellen der Alten Welt 13. Berlin: Akademie, 1963.

Kubina, Veronika. *Die Gottesreden im Buche Hiob*. Frieburger Theologische Studien 115. Freiburg: Herder, 1979.

Kugel, James. *The Idea of Biblical Poetry*. New Haven: Yale University Press, 1981.

Lakoff, George, and Mark Johnson. *Metaphors We Live By*. Chicago: University of Chicago Press, 1980.

Landes, George M. "Creation and Liberation." Pages 135-51 in *Creation in the Old Testament*. Edited by B. W. Anderson. Issues in Religion and Theology 6. Philadelphia: Fortress Press, 1984.

———. "Creation Tradition in Proverbs 8:22-31." Pages 279-93 in *A Light unto My Path*. Gettysburg Theological Studies 4. Philadelphia: Temple University Press, 1974.

Lang, Bernhard. *Die weisheitliche Lehrrede*. Stuttgarter Bibelstudien 54. Stuttgart: KBW, 1971.

———. *Frau Weisheit*. Düsseldorf: Patmos, 1975.

———. *Wisdom and the Book of Proverbs: An Israelite Goddess Redefined*. New York: Pilgrim, 1986.

Larcher, C. *Études sur le Livre de la Sagesse*. Études Bibliques. Paris: J. Gabalda et Cie, 1969.

———. *Le Livre de la Sagesse; ou, La Sagesse de Salomon*. 1 and 2. Études Bibliques. Paris: J. Gabalda et Cie, 1983–84.

Lauha, Aarre. "Die Krise des Religiösen Glaubens bei Kohelet." In *Wisdom in Israel and in the Ancient Near East*. Edited by Martin Noth and D. Winton Thomas. VTSup 3. Leiden: Brill, 1955, 183-91.

———. *Kohelet*. BKAT 19. Neukirchen-Vluyn: Neukirchener Verlag, 1978.

———. "Kohelets Verhältnis zur Geschichte." Pages 393-401 in *Die Botschaft und die Boten*. Edited by Jörg Jeremiah and Lothar Perlitt. FS H. W. Wolff. Neukirchen-Vluyn: Neukirchener Verlag, 1981.

Lee, T. R. *Studies in the Form of Sirach 44-50*. SBLDS 75. Atlanta: Scholars Press, 1986.

Lemaire, André. *Les écoles et la formation de la Bible dans l'ancien Israël*. OBO 39. Göttingen: Vandenhoeck & Ruprecht, 1981.

Leeuwen, Raymond Van. *Context and Meaning in Proverbs 25–27*. SBLDS 96. Atlanta: Scholars Press, 1988.

———. "Proverbs 30:21-23 and the Biblical World Upside Down." *JBL* 105 (1986) 599-610.

———. "Wealth and Poverty: System and Contradiction in Proverbs." *Hebrew Studies* 33 (1992) 25-36.

Levenson, Jon. *Creation and the Persistence of Evil*. San Francisco: Harper & Row, 1988.

Lévêque, J. *Job et son dieu*. 2 vols. Paris: Librairie Lecoffre, 1970.

Loader, J. A. *Polar Structures in the Book of Qoheleth*. BZAW 152. Berlin: Walter de Gruyter, 1979.

Lohfink, Norbert. "Der Mensch vor dem Tod." Pages 198-243 in *Das Siegeslied am Schilfmeer*. 2nd ed. Frankfurt: Josef Knecht, 1966.

———. "Qoheleth 5:17-19—Revelation by Joy." *CBQ* 52 (1990) 625-35.

Loretz, Oswald. *Qohelet und der alte Orient*. Freiburg: Herder, 1964.

———. "Zur Darbietungsform der Ich-Erzählung im Buche Qoheleth." *CBQ* 25 (1963) 46-59.

Lux, Rüdiger. " 'Ich, Kohelet, bin König' . . . Die Fiktion als Schlüssel zur Wirklichkeit in Kohelet 1:12-2:26." *EvT* 50 (1990) 331-42.

Maag, V. *Hiob: Wandlung und Verarbeitung des Problems in Novelle, Dialogdichtung und Spätfassungen*. Göttingen: Vandenhoeck & Ruprecht, 1982.

McCreesh, Thomas P. "Wisdom as Wife: Proverbs 31:10-31." *RB* 92 (1985) 25-46.

McCurley, Foster. *Ancient Myths and Biblical Faith*. Philadelphia: Fortress, 1983.

McFague, Sallie. *Metaphorical Theology: Models of God in Religious Language*. Philadelphia: Fortress, 1982.

———. *Models of God: Theology for an Ecological, Nuclear Age*. Philadelphia: Fortress, 1987.

Mack, Burton. *Logos und Sophia. Untersuchungen zur Weisheitstheologie im hellenistischen Judentum*. SUNT 10. Göttingen: Vandenhoeck & Ruprecht, 1973.

———. *Wisdom and the Hebrew Epic: Ben Sira's Hymn in Praise of the Fathers*. Chicago: University of Chicago Press, 1985.

———. "Wisdom Myth and Mytho-Logy." *Interp* 24 (1970) 46-60.

McKane, William. *Prophets and Wise Men*. SBT 44. Naperville, Ill.: Alec R. Allenson, 1965.

———. *Proverbs*. OTL. Philadelphia: Westminster, 1970.

Mackenzie, R. A. F. *Sirach*. Old Testament Message. Wilmington, Del.: Michael Glazier, 1983.

Marböck, J. "Im Horizont der Gottesfurcht: Stellungnahme zu Welt und Leben in der alttestamentlichen Weisheit." *BN* 26 (1985) 47-70.

———. "Sir. 38, 24-39, 11: Der schriftgelehrte Weise." Pages 293-316 in *La Sagesse de l'Ancien Testament*. Edited by M. Gilbert. BETL 51. Gembloux: Leuven, 1979.

———. *Weisheit im Wandel*. BBB 37. Bonn: Peter Hanstein, 1971.

Michel, Diethelm. *Qohelet*. EF 258. Darmstadt: Wissenschaftliche Buchgesellschaft, 1988.

———. *Untersuchungen zur Eigenart des Buches Qohelet. Mit einem Anhang: Reinhard Lehmann, Bibliographie zu Qohelet*. BZAW 183. Berlin: Walter de Gruyter, 1989.

Middendorf, T. *Die Stellung Jesus ben Siras zwischen Judentum und Hellenismus*. Leiden: Brill, 1973.

Müller, H.-P. *Das Hiobproblem*. Erträge der Forschung 84. Darmstadt: Wissenschaftliche Buchgesellschaft, 1978.

———. "Die weisheitliche Lehrerzählung im Alten Testament und seiner Umwelt." *WO* 9 (1977) 77-98.

———. *Hiob und seine Freunde*. Theologische Studien 105. Zürich: EVZ-Verlag, 1970.

———. "Neige der althebräischen 'Weisheit.' Zum Denken Qohäläts." *ZAW* 90 (1978) 238-68.

————. "Welt als 'Wiederholung.' " Pages 355-72 in *Werden und Wirken des Alten Testaments*. Edited by Rainer Albertz et. al. F. S. Claus Westermann. Göttingen: Vandenhoeck & Ruprecht, 1980.

————. "Wie sprach Qohälät von Gott?" *VT* 128 (1968) 507-21.

Muilenburg, James. "Form Criticism and Beyond." *JBL* 88 (1969) 1-18.

Murphy, Roland. "The Kerygma of the Book of Proverbs." *Int* 20 (1966) 3-14.

————. "Proverbs and Theological Exegesis." Pages 87-95 in *The Hermeneutical Quest*. Edited by D. G. Miller. Allison Park: Pickwick, 1986.

————. "Qohelet's 'Quarrel' with the Fathers." Pages 235-45 in *From Faith to Faith*. Edited by D. Y. Hadidian. PTMS 31. Pittsburgh: Pickwick, 1979.

————. *The Tree of Life: An Exploration of Biblical Wisdom Literature*. ABRL. New York: Doubleday, 1990.

————. "Wisdom and Creation." *JBL* 104 (1985) 3-11.

————. "Wisdom and Eros." *CBQ* 50 (1988) 600-603.

————. *Wisdom Literature*. FOTL 13. Grand Rapids: Eerdmans, 1981.

————. "Wisdom's Song: Proverbs 1:20-33." *CBQ* 48 (1986) 456-60.

Nel, Philip Johannes. *The Structure and Ethos of the Wisdom Admonitions in Proverbs*. BZAW 158. Berlin: Walter de Gruyter, 1982.

Newsom, Carol A. "Woman and the Discourse of Patriarchal Wisdom: A Study of Proverbs 1–9." Pages 142-60 in *Gender and Difference in Ancient Israel*. Edited by Peggy L. Day. Minneapolis: Fortress, 1989.

Nordheim, Eckhard von. *Die Lehre der Alten* 1. Arbeiten zum Literatur und Geschichte des Hellenistischen Judentum 13. Leiden: Brill, 1980.

Oesterley, W. O. E. *The Wisdom of Jesus the Son of Sirach, or Ecclesiasticus*. Cambridge Bible for Schools and Colleges. Cambridge: Cambridge University Press, 1912.

Ogden, Graham. *Qoheleth*. Sheffield: Almond Press, 1987.

Patrick, Dale. "Job's Address of God." *ZAW* 91 (1979) 268-82.

Pautrel, R. "Ben Sira et le Stoïcisme." *RSR* 51 (1963) 535-49.

Pedersen, J. "Scepticisme israelite." *RHPR* 10 (1930) 317-70.

Perdue, Leo G. *The Collapse of History: The Reconstruction of Old Testament Theology*. Overtures to Biblical Theology. Minneapolis: Fortress, 1994.

————. "Cosmology and the Social Order in the Wisdom Literature." Pages 457-78 in *The Sage in Israel and the Ancient Near East*. Edited by John G. Gammie and Leo G. Perdue. Winona Lake: Eisenbrauns, 1990.

————, ed. *The Family in Ancient Israel and Early Judaism*. Louisville: Westminster/John Knox, forthcoming.

————. "Job's Assault on Creation." *HAR* 10 (1987) 295-315.

————. "Paraenesis and the Death of the Sage." *Semeia* 50 (1990) 81-109.

————. "The Social Character of Paraenesis and Paraenetic Literature." *Semeia* 50 (1990) 5-39.

————. *Wisdom and Cult*. SBLDS 30. Missoula, Mont.: Scholars Press, 1977.

————. *Wisdom in Revolt: Creation Theology in the Book of Job*. JSOT 121. Sheffield: JSOT/Almond, 1991.

————. "Wisdom in the Book of Job." In *In Search of Wisdom: Essays in Memory of John G. Gammie*. Edited by Leo G. Perdue et al. Louisville: Westminster/John Knox, 1993.

Petersen, David L., and Kent Harold Richards. *Interpreting Hebrew Poetry*. Guides to Biblical Scholarship. Minneapolis: Fortress, 1992.

Plath, Siegfried. *Furcht Gottes*. Arbeiten zur Theologie 2. Stuttgart: Calwer, 1962.

Pleins, J. David. "Poverty in the Social World of the Wise." *JSOT* 37 (1987) 61-78.

Plöger, Otto. *Sprüche Salomos*. BKAT 17. Neukirchen-Vluyn: Neukirchener Verlag, 1981.

Pope, Marvin. *Job*. AB 15. Garden City, N.Y.: Doubleday, 1965.

Prato, G. L. "La lumière interprète de la sagesse dans la tradition textuelle de Ben Sira." Pages 317-46 in *La Sagesse de l'Ancien Testament.* Edited by M. Gilbert. BETL 51. Gembloux: Leuven, 1979.

Preuss, H. D. "Alttestamentliche Weisheit in christlicher Theologie?" Pages 165-82 in *Questions disputées d'Ancien Testament.* Edited by C. Brekelmans. BETL 33. Leuven: Leuven University Press, 1974.

———. "Das Gottesbild der äteren Weisheit Israels." Pages 117-45 in *Studies in the Religion of Ancient Israel.* SVT 23. Leiden: Brill, 1972.

———. *Einführung in die alttestamentliche Weisheitsliteratur.* Urban-Taschenbücher 383. Stuttgart: Kohlhammer, 1987.

———. "Erwägungen zum theologischen Ort alttestamentlicher Weisheitsliteratur." *EvTh* 30 (1970), 393-417.

———. "Jahwes Antwort an Hiob und die sogenannte Hiobliteratur des alten Vorderen Orients." Pages 323-45 in *Beiträge zur alttestamentlichen Theologie.* Edited by Herbert Donner et al. FS W. Zimmerli. Göttingen: Vandenhoeck & Ruprecht, 1977.

Rad, Gerhard von. *Old Testament Theology* 1 & 2. New York: Harper & Row, 1962, 1965.

———. *Wisdom in Israel.* Nashville: Abingdon, 1972.

Rankin, O. S. *Israel's Wisdom Literature.* Edinburgh: T. & T. Clark, 1936.

———. "The Book of Ecclesiastes." Pages 3-88 in *IB* 5. New York: Abingdon, 1956.

Reese, J. M. *Hellenistic Influence on the Book of Wisdom and its Consequences.* AnBib 41. Rome: Pontifical Biblical Institute, 1970.

———. "Plan and Structure in the Book of Wisdom." *CBQ* 27 (1965) 391-99.

Reider, Joseph. *The Book of Wisdom.* New York: Harper and Bros., 1957.

Reventlow, H. Graf. *Problems of Old Testament Theology in the Twentieth Century.* Philadelphia: Fortress, 1985.

Ricoeur, Paul. "The Metaphorical Process." *Semeia* 4 (1975) 75-106.

———. "The Narrative Function." *Semeia* 13 (1978) 177-202.

———. *The Rule of Metaphor.* Toronto: The University of Toronto Press, 1977.

Richards, I. A. *The Philsophy of Rhetoric.* New York: Oxford University Press, 1936.

Richter, H. "Die Naturweisheit des Alten Testament im Buche Hiob." *ZAW* 70 (1958) 1-19.

———. *Studien zu Hiob.* Theologische Arbeiten 11. Berlin: Evangelische Verlagsanstalt, 1955.

Ringgren, Helmer. *Sprüche.* ATD 16. Göttingen: Vandenhoeck & Ruprecht, 1962.

———. *Word and Wisdom: Studies in the Hypostatization of Divine Qualities and Functions in the Ancient Near East.* Lund: H. Ohlssons, 1947.

Robertson, David. *The Old Testament and the Literary Critic.* Philadelphia: Fortress, 1977.

Rooden, Peter T. Van. "Die Antike Elementarlehre und der Aufbau von Sap. Sal. 11-19." Pages 81-96 in *Tradition and Re-Interpretation in Jewish and Early Christian Literature.* Edited by J. W. Van Henten et al. Studia Post-Biblica 36. Leiden: Brill, 1986.

Rousseau, François. "Structure de Qohelet I 4-11 et plan du livre." *VT* 31 (1981) 200-17.

Rowley, H. H. *Job.* The Century Bible. Don Mills, Ontario: Thomas Nelson and Sons, 1970.

Rüger, Hans Peter. *Text und Textform im hebräischen Sirach.* BZAW 112. Berlin: Walter de Gruyter, 1970.

Rylaarsdam, J. Coert. *Revelation in Jewish Wisdom Literature.* Chicago: University of Chicago Press, 1946.

Sacks, Sheldon, ed. *On Metaphor.* Chicago: University of Chicago Press, 1979.

Säve-Söderbergh, T. *On Egyptian Representations of Hippopotomus Hunting as a Religious Motive.* Horae Soderblomianae 3. Lund: C. W. K. Gleerup, 1953.

Sauer, G. *Die Sprüche Agurs.* BWANT 4. Stuttgart: Kohlhammer, 1963.

Sawyer, John F. A. "The Ruined House in Ecclesiastes 12: A Reconstruction of the Original Parable." *JBL* 94 (1975) 519-31.

Schilling, Othmar. *Das Buch Jesus Sirach*. Herders Bibelkommentar: Die Heilige Schrift. Freiburg: Herder, 1956.

Schmid, H. H. *Altorientalische Welt in der alttestamentlichen Theologie*. Zürich: Theologischer Verlag, 1974.

———. "Creation, Righteousness, and Salvation." Pages 102-17 in *Creation in the Old Testament*. Edited by B. W. Anderson. Issues in Religion & Theology 6. Philadelphia: Fortress, 1984.

———. *Gerechtigkeit als Weltordnung*. BHT 40. Tübingen: J. C. B. Mohr (Paul Siebeck), 1968.

———. *Wesen und Geschichte der Weisheit*. BZAW 101. Berlin: Walter de Gruyter, 1966.

Schmidt, P. "Sinnfrage und Glaubenskrise. Ansätze zu einer kritischen Theologie der Schöpfung im Buche Hiob." *Geist und Leben* 45 (1972) 348-61.

Schmitt, Armin. "Struktur, Herkunft und Bedeutung der Beispielreihe in Weish 10." *BZ* 21 (1977) 1-22.

Schökel, A. "Towards a Dramatic Reading of the Book of Job." *Semeia* 7 (1977) 45-61.

———. "The Vision of Man in Sirach 16:24–17:14." Pages 235-45 in *Israelite Wisdom*. Edited by John G. Gammie et al. FS Samuel Terrien. Missoula, Mont.: Scholars Press, 1978.

Schottroff, W. *Der altisraelitische Fluchspruch*. WMANT 30. Neukirchen-Vluyn: Neukirchener Verlag, 1969.

Schubert, Mathias. *Schöpfungstheologie bei Kohelet*. Beiträge zur Erforschung des Alten Testaments und des Antiken Judentums 15. Frankfurt: Peter Lang, 1989.

Scott, R. B. Y. *Proverbs. Ecclesiastes*. AB. Englewood Cliffs, N.J.: Doubleday, 1965.

———. "Solomon and the Beginnings of Wisdom in Israel." Pages 262-79 in *Wisdom in Israel and in the Ancient Near East*. Edited by Martin Noth and D. Winton Thomas. VTSup 3. Leiden: Brill, 1955.

———. *The Way of Wisdom*. New York: Macmillan, 1971.

———. "Wisdom in Creation. The '*Amon* of Proverbs VIII 30." *VT* 10 (1960) 213-23.

Sekine, Masao. "Schöpfung und Erlösung im Buche Hiob." Pages 213-23 in *Von Ugarit nach Qumran*. BZAW 77. Berlin: Töpelmann, 1961.

Shepherd, G. T. "The Epilogue to Qoheleth as Theological Commentary." *CBQ* 39 (1977) 182-89.

———. *Wisdom as a Hermeneutical Construct*. BZAW 151. Berlin: Walter de Gruyter, 1980.

Shupak, N. "The 'Sitz im Leben' of the Book of Proverbs in the Light of a Comparison of Biblical and Egyptian Wisdom Literature." *RB* 94 (1987) 98-119.

Siebeneck, Robert T. "May Their Bones Return to Life! Sirach's Praise of the Fathers." *CBQ* 21 (1959) 411-28.

———. "The Midrash of Wisdom 10–19." *CBQ* 22 (1960) 176-82.

Skehan, P. W. "Job's Final Plea (Job 29–31) and the Lord's Reply." *Biblica* 45 (1964) 51-62.

———. "The Seven Columns of Wisdom's House in Proverbs 1–9." Pages 9-14 in *Studies in Israelite Poetry and Wisdom*. CBQMS 1. Washington: Catholic Biblical Association, 1971.

———. "Structures in Poems on Wisdom: Proverbs 8 and Sirach 24." *CBQ* 41 (1979) 365-79.

Skehan, Patrick, and Alexander Di Lella. *The Wisdom of Ben Sira*. AB 39. Garden City, N.Y.: Doubleday, 1987.

Skladny, U. *Die ältesten Spruchsammlungen in Israel*. Berlin: Vandenhoeck & Ruprecht, 1961.

Smend, Rudolf. *Die Weisheit des Jesus Sirachs erklärt*. Berlin: Reimer, 1906.

Snaith, John G. *Ecclesiasticus*. CBC. Cambridge: Cambridge University Press, 1974.

Snaith, Norman H. *The Book of Job*. SBT 11. Naperville, Ill.: Alec R. Allenson, 1968.

Stowers, Stanley K. *Letter Writing in Greco-Roman Antiquity*. Library of Early Christianity. Philadelphia: Westminster, 1986.

Terrien, S. "The Book of Job." Pages 877-1198 in *IB* 3. Nashville: Abingdon, 1955.

———. "The Jahve Speeches and Job's Responses." *REx* 68 (1971) 497-509.

Toy, C. H. *A Critical and Exegetical Commentary on the Book of Proverbs*. ICC. Edinburgh: T. & T. Clark, 1899.

Tracy, David. *Analogical Imagination*. New York: Crossroad, 1981.

Trible, Phyllis. "Five Loaves and Two Fishes: Feminist Hermeneutics and Biblical Theology," *TS* 50 (1989) 279-95.

———. *God and the Rhetoric of Sexuality*. Overtures to Biblical Theology. Philadelphia: Fortress, 1985.

———. *Texts of Terror*. Overtures to Biblical Theology. Philadelphia: Fortress, 1985.

———. "Wisdom Builds a Poem: The Architecture of Proverbs 1:20-33." *JBL* 94 (1975) 509-18.

Tsevat, Matitiahu. "The Meaning of the Book of Job." *HUCA* 37 (1966) 73-106.

Tur-Sinai, N. H. *The Book of Job*. Jerusalem: Kiryath Sepher, 1957.

Vogels, Walter. "The God Who Creates Is the God Who Saves: The Book of Wisdom's Reversal of the Biblical Pattern." *Eglise et Théologie* 22 (1991) 315-35.

Volz, Paul. *Weisheit*. SAT 2. Göttingen: Vandenhoeck & Ruprecht, 1911.

Warnock, Mary. *Imagination*. Berkeley: University of California Press, 1976.

Washington, Harold C. "Wealth and Poverty in the Instruction of Amenemope and the Hebrew Proverbs." Ph.D. dissertation. Princeton Theological Seminary, 1992.

Weiser, Artur. *Das Buch Hiob*. 7th ed. ATD 13. Göttingen: Vandenhoeck & Ruprecht, 1980.

———. "Das Problem der sittlichen Weltordnung im Buche Hiob." *ThBl* 2 (1923) 158-64.

Weinfeld, Moshe. *Deuteronomy and the Deuteronomic School*. Oxford: Clarendon Press, 1972.

Westermann, Claus. "Biblical Reflections on Creator-Creation." Pages 90-101 in *Creation in the Old Testament*. Edited by B. W. Anderson. Issues in Religion and Theology 6. Philadelphia: Fortress, 1984.

———. *Blessing in the Bible and the Life of the Church*. Philadelphia: Westminster, 1978.

———. *Creation*. Philadelphia: Fortress, 1974.

———. *Genesis 1–11*. Minneapolis: Augsburg, 1984.

———. *The Structure of the Book of Job*. Philadelphia: Fortress, 1981.

———. *Theologie des Alten Testaments in Grundzügen*. ATD Ergänzungsheft 6. Göttingen: Vandenhoeck & Ruprecht, 1978.

———. "Weisheit im Sprichwort." Pages 73-84 in *Schalom: Studien zu Glaube und Geschichte Israels*. Edited by K.-H. Bernhardt. Stuttgart: Calwer, 1971.

———. *Wurzeln der Weisheit. Die ältesten Sprüche Israels und anderer Völker*. Göttingen: Vandenhoeck & Ruprecht, 1990.

Whedbee, J. W. "The Comedy of Job." *Semeia* 7 (1970) 182-200.

Wheelwright, Phillip. *Metaphor and Reality*. Bloomington: Indiana University Press, 1962.

White, Hayden. *Metahistory: The Historical Imagination in Nineteenth-Century Europe*. Baltimore: Johns Hopkins, 1973.

Whybray, R. N. *The Intellectual Tradition in the Old Testament*. BZAW 135. Berlin: Walter de Gruyter, 1974.

————. "Proverbs VIII, 22-31 and Its Supposed Prototypes." *VT* 15 (1965) 504-14.

————. "Qoheleth, Preacher of Joy." *JSOT* 23 (1982) 87-98.

————. "Qoheleth the Immoralist? (Qoh. 7:16-17)." Pages 191-204 in *Israelite Wisdom*. Edited by John G. Gammie et al. FS Samuel Terrien. Missoula, Mont.: Scholars Press, 1978.

————. *Wealth and Poverty in the Book of Proverbs*. JSOTSup 99. Sheffield: JSOT, 1990.

————. *Wisdom in Proverbs*. SBT 45. London: SCM Press, 1965.

Wilde, A. de. *Das Buch Hiob*. OTS 22. Leiden: E. J. Brill, 1981.

Wilder, Amos. *Theopoetic: Theology and the Religious Imagination*. Philadelphia: Fortress, 1976.

Williams, James G. "Deciphering the Unspoken: The Theophany of Job." *HUCA* 49 (1978) 59-72.

————. "The Power of Form: A Study of Biblical Proverbs." *Semeia* 17 (1980) 35-58.

————. "Proverbs and Ecclesiastes." Pages 263-76 in *The Literary Guide to the Bible*. Edited by Robert Alter and Frank Kermode. Cambridge, Mass.: Harvard University Press, 1987.

————. *Those Who Ponder Proverbs*. Bible and Literature Series 2. Sheffield: Almond, 1981.

————. " 'You Have Not Spoken Truth of Me.' Mystery and Irony in Job." *ZAW* 83 (1971) 231-55.

Winston, David. "The Book of Wisdom's Theory of Cosmogony." *HR* 11 (1971) 185-202.

————. *The Wisdom of Solomon*. AB. Garden City, N.Y.: Doubleday, 1979.

Wolff, Hans Walter. *Anthropology of the Old Testament*. Philadelphia: Fortress, 1974.

Wright, Addison. "Additional Numerical Patterns in Qoheleth." *CBQ* 45 (1983) 32-43.

————. "The Riddle of the Sphinx: The Structure of the Book of Qoheleth." *CBQ* 30 (1968) 313-34.

————. "The Riddle of the Sphinx Revisited: Numerical Patterns in the Book of Qoheleth." *CBQ* 42 (1980) 33-51.

————. "The Structure of the Book of Wisdom." *Bib* 48 (1967) 165-184.

Wright, George E. *God Who Acts*. SBT 8. London: SCM, 1952.

————. *The Old Testament Against Its Environment*. SBT 2. London: SCM, 1950.

————. *The Old Testament and Theology*. New York: Harper & Row, 1969.

Yee, Gale A. " 'I Have Perfumed My Bed with Myrrh': The Foreign Woman (*'issa zara*) in Proverbs 1–9." *JSOT* 43 (1989) 53-68.

Ziener, Georg. *Die theologische Begriffssprache im Buche der Weisheit*. BBB 11. Bonn: Peter Hanstein, 1966.

Zimmerli, Walther. *Das Buch des Predigers Salomo*. ATD 16. Göttingen: Vandenhoeck & Ruprecht, 1962.

————. "The Place and Limit of the Wisdom in the Framework of the Old Testament Theology." *SJT* 17 (1964) 146-58.

————. " 'Unveränderbare Welt' oder 'Gott ist Gott'? Ein Plädoyer für die Unaufgebbarkeit der Predigerbuches." Pages 103-14 in *"Wenn nicht jetz wann dann?"* Edited by Hans-Georg Geger et al. Neukirchen-Vluyn: Neukirchener Verlag, 1983.

————. "Zur Struktur der alttestamentlichen Weisheit." *ZAW* 51 (1933) 177-204.

INDEX OF
MODERN AUTHORS

INDEX OF SCRIPTURAL AND DEUTEROCANONICAL REFERENCES

INDEX OF SCRIPTURAL AND DEUTEROCANONICAL REFERENCES

INDEX OF SCRIPTURAL AND DEUTEROCANONICAL REFERENCES